PERSONNEL
The Management of Human Resources

Second Edition

R. Wayne Mondy, SPHR
Northeast Louisiana University

Robert M. Noe III, SPHR
East Texas State University

in collaboration with

Harry N. Mills, Jr., SPHR
East Texas State University

Arthur Sharplin
Northeast Louisiana University

Allyn and Bacon, Inc.
Boston   London   Sydney   Toronto

To Judy Bandy Mondy
whose love and support I will always cherish
R.W.M.

To Sis
and our remarkable aunts
R.M.N.

Library of Congress Cataloging in Publication Data

Mondy, R. Wayne, 1940–
    Personnel, the management of human resources.

    Bibliography: p.
    Includes index.
    1. Personnel management—United States.   2. Personnel
management.   I. Noe, Robert M.   II. Mills, Harry N.
III. Sharplin, Arthur.   IV. Title.
HF5549.2.U5M66 1983   658.3   83-22388
ISBN 0-205-08058-8

Printed in the United States of America.
10 9 8 7 6 5 4 3   87 86 85

Contents

Preface

The second edition of *Personnel: The Management of Human Resources* offers a practical and realistic approach to the study of personnel management. While the book is essentially pragmatic, it is balanced throughout by current human resources management concepts. A common theme — the interrelationships of the various personnel functions — runs throughout the book. Each of the functions is described from the standpoint of its relation to the total needs of human resources management. The book is written primarily for students who are being exposed to personnel management for the first time. It puts the student in touch with the real world through the use of numerous illustrations, quotations from personnel professionals, and company material showing how personnel management is practiced in today's organizations. Some of the highlights of the book are described below.

Chapter 2–The Environment of Human Resources Management This chapter develops a comprehensive model which is used throughout the book to show the many interrelationships that exist in human resources management. Both external and internal environmental factors are examined.

Appendix to Chapter 2: The Legal Environment Significant laws, Executive Orders, and Supreme Court decisions are highlighted in this section. The manner in which they affect each personnel function will be described in the appropriate section.

Part II: Planning, Recruitment, and Selection Topics included within the staffing function are job analysis, human resources planning, recruitment, and selection. A separate chapter covering job analysis has been added and the entire staffing section includes considerable company material.

Chapters 7 and 8: Training and Development Here we illustrate that change can occur on both macro and micro organizational levels. We believe that this approach assists students in understanding the training and development process. Chapter 7 is devoted to macro-level approaches, while Chapter 8 focuses on micro-level methods.

Chapter 9: Career Planning and Development This chapter is totally new. It stresses the importance of career planning and development in today's organizations. Meaningful information about careers in personnel management is also provided.

Chapter 10: Performance Appraisal This chapter describes both traditional methods of appraisal and management by objectives (MBO). A comprehensive example of an MBO system is also illustrated.

Chapters 11 and 12: Compensation A unique model is developed in this chapter to describe the factors which must be considered in determining an employee's compensation. Both financial and nonfinancial compensation factors are described. These chapters are essentially pragmatic and should provide stimulating reading.

Chapter 13: Safety and Health We believe this section will be quite interesting to students. This expanded chapter includes the topics of stress management and burnout.

Chapters 14 and 15: Labor Unions and Collective Bargaining The labor movement is described in a manner that should appeal to students. We are especially pleased with the sections depicting the development of the collective bargaining relationship and the bargaining process.

Chapter 16: Discipline and the Grievance Process Both grievance handling under a collective bargaining agreement and grievance handling for nonunion employees are explained in this chapter.

Chapter 17: Nonunion Organizations This chapter is not typically found in personnel management books. However, we believe that students of personnel management need exposure to the topic. The chapter takes a middle-of-the-road approach to the discussion and describes the conditions that typically exist in nonunion firms.

Chapter 18: Personnel Research The rapidly growing field of human resources management is described from the viewpoint of its impact on each of the other personnel functions. An example of the use of personnel research is provided.

FEATURES OF THE BOOK

We have included the following features to promote the readability and understanding of important human resources management concepts:

- A model (see Figure 2-1) is developed which provides a vehicle for relating all personnel management topics. We believe that the overview provided will serve as an excellent teaching device.
- Objectives are listed at the beginning of each chapter to provide the general purpose and key concepts of the chapter.
- Each chapter begins with brief incidents which introduce pertinent personnel concepts and problems.
- Career profiles of personnel professionals are included in each chapter to demonstrate the work that personnel people do and to convey their philosophical comments regarding human resources management.
- Responses from personnel professionals to the question, "What words of advice would you give to students who desire a career in personnel management?" are included in every chapter. We believe that these insights will provide students with a feeling for the real business world.
- Actual company material is used throughout the book to illustrate how a concept is actually used in organizations. For instance, when discussing management by objectives, a Monsanto Company example is provided.
- Illustrations help to make specific points about selected topics.

- Review questions appear at the end of each chapter to test the student's understanding of the material.
- Key terms are listed at the end of each chapter. In addition, a key term is presented in bold print the first time it is defined or described in the chapter.
- Two new cases are provided at the end of each chapter. These highlight material covered in the chapter.
- A comprehensive long case is developed which ties all of the sections together.
- A list of references by chapter is provided at the end of the book to permit additional in-depth study of selected topics.
- Finally, a glossary of all key terms appears at the end of the book.

IMPROVEMENTS TO THE SECOND EDITION

The first edition of *Personnel: The Management of Human Resources* enjoyed considerable success. Many of our users provided us with suggestions for improving the second edition. Topics which have been added or have been given additional coverage are provided below.

- Two entirely new chapters have been added. First, a chapter entitled *Job Analysis* has been included because of its basic significance to all personnel functions. Second, the chapter *Career Planning and Development* has been added because of its importance in today's human resources management environment.
- An appendix has been added to Chapter 2 highlighting significant legislation, Executive Orders, and court decisions affecting human resources management.
- Cost/Benefit Analyses have been added to the major chapters which are affected.
- Demand forecasting techniques (Chapter 4).
- Honeywell's human resources planning system is described in Chapter 4.
- Uniform Guidelines and Adverse Impact (Chapter 5).
- Affirmative action (Chapter 5).
- Reliability, validity, objectivity, and standardization (Chapter 6).
- Realistic job previews (Chapter 6).
- Employee orientation (Chapter 6).
- Monsanto Company MBO example (Chapter 7).
- Quality circles (Chapter 7).
- IBM management development program example (Chapter 8).
- Legal implications for job evaluation (Chapter 11).
- Telecommuting (Chapter 12).
- Stress management and burnout (Chapter 13).
- Public sector collective bargaining (Chapter 14).
- Exclusive bargaining shop (Chapter 15).
- Trends in collective bargaining (Chapter 15).

All of these features were designed to promote and stimulate student interest. The numerous company examples and quotations from professionals were used to demonstrate how "textbook" concepts are actually being used in the real world. We sincerely hope that students of personnel management derive as much pleasure from reading the book as we did in writing it.

Acknowledgments

Many people's assistance and encouragement is normally required in the writing of any book. It is especially true in the writing of *Personnel: The Management of Human Resources*. Although it would be virtually impossible to list each person who assisted in this project, we feel that certain people must be credited because of the magnitude of their contribution.

Our sincere thanks go to many members of the faculty and staff at Northeast Louisiana University and East Texas State University. Dean Van McGraw; David L. Loudon, Head, Department of Management and Marketing; and Professors Art Bethke, David Robertson, all of Northeast Louisiana University, provided encouragement throughout the project. Professor Mike Dolecheck deserves a special note of appreciation for putting up with the many phone calls of one of the authors. Trezzie A. Pressley, Head of the Department of Marketing and Management; Jerry M. DeHay; and Suzanne H. McCall, all encouraged us to see the project through to completion. For their positive influence on our early careers, we thank Frank N. Edens of Louisiana Tech University, C. L. Littlefield of North Texas State University, and James R. Young of East Texas State University. Barbara Kener provided great assistance in typing and editing the manuscript. Judy Noe deserves special thanks for her thorough library research.

Our wives also deserve a special note of appreciation for their constant patience, understanding, and encouragement. They kept us of sane mind during the arduous process of reviews and rewrites.

Special thanks are due to the following individuals for their in-depth review and critique of the manuscript.

Professor Matt M. Amano—Oregon State University
Professor Charlotte M. Erb—California State University
Professor David Estenson—University of California at Berkeley
Professor Roger W. T. Gill—State Univ. of New York at Binghamton
Professor James Klingler—Villanova University
Professor Ray Montagno—Ball State University
Professor Peter Richardson—Southwest Missouri State University
Professor George E. Stevens—Arizona State University
Professor R. A. Whitehorne—University of S. Carolina
Professor Michael N. Wolfe—Arizona State University

Because we stressed the use of real-life examples in the book, it was necessary to secure the assistance of many personnel executives. The encouragement and advice of Drew M. Young, Vice President, Employee Relations, ARCO Oil and Gas Company (Retired); Robert E. Edwards, Vice President, Personnel, Southwestern Life Insurance

Company; and John Quigley, Vice President—Human Resources for Dr. Pepper Company, during the initial planning for the book were especially helpful. John H. Strandquist, Vice President of Administration for the American Society for Personnel Administration, provided us with valuable material for the preparation of the instructor's manual which accompanies this book.

In addition, we are grateful to personnel executives from the following firms for providing us with valuable inputs which brought realism to this human resources management book. (The firms are listed in alphabetical order.)

A. B. Dick Company
Alumax, Inc.
American Coil Spring Company
American Express Company
American General Life Insurance Company
American Greetings Corporation
American Society for Personnel Administration
Ampex Corporation
ARCO Oil and Gas Company
Ashland Oil, Incorporated
Atlantic Richfield Company
The Bendix Corporation
Bristol-Myers Company
Bristol-Myers Products
Bryan Memorial Hospital
Campbell Soup Company
Cessna Aircraft Company
Champion International Corporation
Chevron U.S.A., Inc.
Conoco, Inc.
Control Data Corporation
Crown Central Petroleum Company
Delta Airlines, Inc.
Denny's Incorporated
Detroit Edison Company
Drake-Beam Morin, Inc.
The Dr Pepper Company
The Dun & Bradstreet Corporation
E-Systems, Inc.
Fairchild Instrument & Camera Corporation
First Interstate Bancorp
Fleming Companies, Inc.
Ford Motor Company
Fotomat Corporation
GAF Corporation
Gates Learjet
General Cable Corporation
General Electric Company
General Mills, Incorporated
Georgia-Pacific Corporation
Gerber Products Company
Grumman Aerospace Corporation
Hart Schaffner and Marx
Honeywell, Inc.
Information Science Incorporated
Inland Container Corporation

International Business Machines Corporation
International Multifoods
International Paper Company
International Telephone and Telegraph
Johns-Manville Corporation
Kemper Corporation
Kemper Insurance Companies
Kimberly-Clark Corporation
Korn/Ferry International
Kraft, Inc.
Lone Star Industries, Inc.
Merck and Company, Inc.
Monsanto Company
Motorola, Incorporated
Nabisco, Incorporated
New York Times Company
Ohio Bell Telephone Company
Owens-Illinois, Inc.
Pacific Gamble Robinson Company Incorporated
Pennzoil Company
PPG Industries, Incorporated
Presbyterian Hospital of Dallas
Quest Personnel and Temporary Agency
Rockwell International Corporation
St. Paul Property and Liability Insurance
Schering-Plough Corporation
Schlumberger-Doll Research Center
Sea-Land Service, Inc.
Shell Oil Company
The Singer Company
Southeast Banking Corporation
Southwestern Life Insurance Company
Squibb Corporation
Standard Oil Company (Indiana)
Standard Oil Company of California
Stokely-Van Camp Incorporated
TRW Systems Group
Teledyne, Inc.
Texas Instruments Incorporated
3M
Trans World Airlines
The Upjohn Company
U.S. Steel Corporation
Walt Disney Productions
Western Airlines
Xerox Corporation

Part I

Introduction

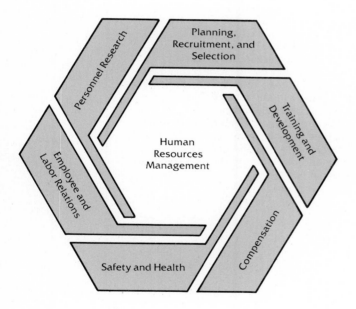

Chapter Objectives

1. Define management and state its basic tasks.
2. Explain the relationship of management, human resources management, and the personnel manager.
3. Define the functions of human resources management.
4. Describe changes that have taken place in the personnel field during relatively recent years.
5. Define a personnel executive, specialist, and generalist.
6. Describe the changes that occur in the personnel function as a firm grows in size and complexity.
7. Express the nature and direction professionalization in the field of Personnel has taken.

Chapter 1 _____

Personnel:
An Overview

David Curtis, personnel director for Nelson Enterprises in New York City, has just learned that his firm intends to open a new plant in Mobile, Alabama. When the plant is completed, one thousand new employees will be hired in addition to the two hundred personnel who will be transferred from New York to Mobile. David's job is to ensure that the best qualified people are hired and trained by the time the plant opens.

Carl Vargas is the supervisor of fifteen convenience stores for a grocery chain in Houston, Texas. He is in charge of all employment activities for these stores. If one of his store managers fails to show up for the assigned shift and Carl cannot find a replacement, he must work the shift. It is Friday afternoon and Carl is hurriedly attempting to locate a replacement as one store manager has just resigned after giving five minutes notice.

Judy Lynley is vice president for industrial relations of Axton Manufacturing Company, a unionized firm that employs fifteen thousand workers nationwide. She has been negotiating with union leaders for five weeks under the threat of a strike. The union members have threatened to walk off the job, if it is not resolved by midnight. However, if Judy's firm agrees to all the union's demands, it will no longer be in a competitive position in the industry because of a higher wage level.

David, Carl, and Judy all have one thing in common: they are deeply involved with some of the challenges and problems related to personnel and human resources management. Managers must constantly deal with the often volatile and unpredictable human element. Managing people in organizations is more important than ever in our rapidly growing, changing, and complex work environment.

WHAT IS MANAGEMENT?

The title of this book, *Personnel: The Management of Human Resources*, implies that an understanding of management is required in the study of Personnel. This being the case, what do we mean by management? While many definitions exist, most have a common theme. **Management** is concerned with the accomplishment of objectives through the efforts of people. An **objective,** or goal, is an end result we are striving to achieve. The goals of business firms are directed toward economic success. However, goals may be social, as with a sorority or fraternity. The Red Cross and YWCA have service oriented objectives. Organizations are created for the sole purpose of achieving objectives.

To achieve organizational objectives, managers must perform the following basic tasks:

- *Planning:* Determining how the goals of the organization are to be achieved.
- *Organizing:* Determining and allocating resources needed to accomplish the established objectives.
- *Staffing:* Determining and obtaining the type of workers that are needed to accomplish the established objectives.
- *Directing:* Encouraging workers to accomplish the goals of the organization.
- *Controlling:* Comparing results achieved to planned goals and taking necessary corrective action.

Management may then be defined as the process of planning, organizing, staffing, directing, and controlling to accomplish organizational goals through the coordinated use of the firm's resources. This definition applies whether the person is a manager of marketing, production, finance, or personnel.

THE PRACTICE OF HUMAN RESOURCES MANAGEMENT AND THE PERSONNEL MANAGER

Before we progress further, a major distinction should be made between two terms—human resources management and the personnel manager. By definition, all managers in the organization are vitally concerned with **human resources management.** (HRM, also referred to as personnel management). They must achieve organizational goals through other people's efforts. The production manager ensures that products are manufactured in sufficient numbers and quality; the marketing manager works through sales representatives to sell the firm's products; and the finance manager obtains capital to ensure that the business has sufficient operating funds. In all of these instances, managers have certain specialized functions as their primary responsibility. They are "line managers" because they are responsible for achieving their firm's primary objectives. These individuals must also be concerned with human resources management. Carl Vargas, the convenience store supervisor from Houston, Texas, fully understands the problems a line manager has with personnel management. As a line manager, if he cannot find a replacement, Carl will have to work the Friday night shift. William B. Pardue, senior vice president for American General Life Insurance Company says, "The real personnel manager's game is played by the line manager. The personnel manager's role is to develop policies and programs—the rules of the game—and to function as a catalyst and energizer to the relationship between line management and employees."

Personnel managers, as Pardue suggests, normally act in an advisory (staff) capacity when working with other managers. They have the primary responsibility of coordinating the firm's human resources management activities. M. Jane Kay, vice president of employee relations for Detroit Edison Company, states, "The personnel manager acts more in an advisory capacity, but should be a catalyst in proposing human relations policies to be implemented by line managers." The distinction between human resources management and the personnel manager becomes clearer when the following situation is considered:

> Bill Brown, the production supervisor for Ajax Manufacturing, has just learned that one of his machine operators quit. He immediately calls Sandra Williams, the personnel manager, and says, "Sandra, I just had a Class A machine operator quit down here. Can you find some qualified people for me to interview?" "Sure, Bill," Sandra replies, "I'll send two or three down to you within the week and you can select the one that best fits your needs."

In the above instance, both Bill and Sandra are concerned with accomplishing organizational goals but from different perspectives. Sandra, as a personnel manager, identifies applicants who meet the criteria specified by Bill. Yet Bill will make the final decision as to who is hired because he is responsible for the machine operator's performance. His primary responsibility is production, whereas Sandra's is personnel. As personnel manager, Sandra must constantly deal with the many personnel related problems faced by Bill and other managers. She must view the human resources needs of the entire organization. In this book, we will refer to her function as personnel, human resources management, employee relations, or industrial relations.

HUMAN RESOURCES MANAGEMENT FUNCTION

As previously mentioned, all managers are concerned with human resources management (HRM). The personnel, or human resources, manager is at the

W. T. (Tom) Beebe
Chairman of the Board, Delta Airlines, Inc.

Today, W. T. (Tom) Beebe is chairman of the board of one of the most successful airlines in the free world. From 1954 to 1966, Mr. Beebe was vice president of personnel at Delta. He says, "My background in Personnel has affected my performance as president and chairman of the board in enforcing the conviction of all of us that our Delta folks are our most important assets. The role of personnel

at Delta has always been extremely important. It is considered a major division of the company and carries very heavy responsibilities in the operation of the airlines."

Tom graduated from the University of Minnesota with a major in business and a minor in personnel and psychology. He went directly from college to General Electric as a business trainee. Their training program at that time consisted of three years of indoctrination in numerous job functions during the day and mostly financial courses at night. Upon leaving General Electric, Mr. Beebe became personnel director at the Hamilton Standard Division of United Aircraft Corporation. In 1947, he joined Chicago and Southern Airlines as personnel director.

When asked if there were any particularly critical moments in his career, he replied, "There were two. One was leaving United Aircraft in 1947 to join a brand new management team at Chicago and Southern Air Lines. I had progressed rapidly in responsibilities at United and thought that there was an excellent future there. However, when the former vice president and general manager of

heart of a human resources management system. Today's personnel problems are enormous. The personnel manager is suddenly "grappling with discontented and restless employees and unions, myriad government regulations dealing with everything from safety standards to minority hiring, new trends in executive recruitment and compensation, and much more."[1] These areas are now receiving top priority by management. The personnel executive who is able to cope effectively with these problems is often recognized as one of the firm's top managers. As Frederick W. Bahl, director of personnel administration for Alumax, Inc., states, "Actions taken by personnel executives nearly always affect every stratum of the organization."

Personnel managers work with the firm's human element so the organization's goals can be achieved. The firm must attract, select, train, motivate, and retain qualified people. At the same time, employees must be permitted to satisfy personal needs.

The personnel manager must perform tasks in six functional areas (see Figure 1–1). The sound management practices required for successful performance in each of the six functional specialties will be discussed next.

[1]"It's Hell in Personnel," *Dun's Review* 97 (March 1971): 40–43.

the Hamilton Standard Propeller Division decided to go to C&S as president, I decided to join him. This was a very risky move because C&S was suffering consistent losses and the new management was brought in to try to turn C&S around and make it profitable. The appeal of this new challenge was so strong that I decided to join the other two members of the new team.

"The second critical moment of my career was approximately a year after the merger of Chicago and Southern Air Lines into Delta Air Lines. My two associates from C&S who with me had formed the new management team at C&S resigned to go with other companies. At that time there were many management consultant firms who were looking for management personnel for a large number of clients. I received a great many extremely attractive offers and was hard pressed to make a decision whether to leave Delta for a much larger job at considerably more money. However, Delta appeared to have such a bright growth future that I decided to cast my lot permanently with them."

Mr. Beebe was also asked what critical decisions he has made regarding human resources management. To this he replied, "There have been a great many critical decisions made regarding human resources management. The company is overwhelmingly people oriented, and this orientation is by design, not happenstance. Over the years we have indoctrinated our management personnel to being personnel managers first and specialists in their fields second. We have group meetings systemwide in all divisions every year. All personnel are invited to at least one of these meetings. The meetings cover where Delta is at the present time, its future plans, and its problems. There are always senior officers at the meetings to answer questions and to listen to and respond to a great variety of suggestions for improving the company. Questions which cannot be answered on the spot are always answered in writing after the information needed for the response is obtained."

The role of Personnel at Delta Airlines is an important one. Mr. Beebe's leadership has been an important guiding force in developing an attitude that Delta's employees are truly their most important assets.

Figure 1–1.   **The human resources management system.**

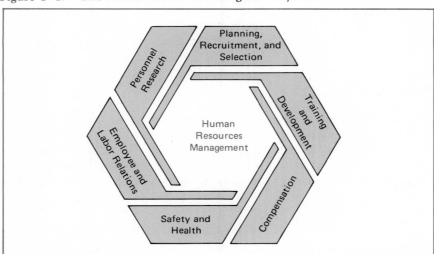

Human Resources Planning, Recruitment, and Selection

A firm must ensure that it has qualified workers available at all levels in the organization if company objectives are to be achieved. The means by which this goal is accomplished is referred to as staffing. Some of the primary tasks included in the staffing process include personnel planning, recruitment, and selection. The analysis of future personnel requirements is referred to as **human resources planning**. **Recruitment** involves encouraging individuals with the needed skills to apply for employment with the firm. **Selection** is the process of identifying those recruited individuals who will best be able to assist the firm in achieving organizational goals. David Curtis, personnel director for Nelson Enterprises, will be required to become deeply involved in planning, recruitment, and selection. These three tasks must be carefully coordinated if his firm is to satisfy its workforce requirements.

Training and Development

Training and development (T&D) programs are designed to assist individuals, groups, and the entire organization to become more effective. Training is needed because people, jobs, and organizations are always changing.[2] T&D should begin when individuals join the firm and continue throughout their careers. Large scale T&D programs are referred to as **organization development** (OD). The purpose of OD is to alter the environment within the firm to assist people in performing more productively.[3]

Other aspects of T&D include career planning and development and performance appraisal. **Individual career planning** is a process whereby personal goals are set and the means to achieve them are established. Individual and organizational careers are not separate and distinct. Organizations should assist employees in career planning so that the needs of both can be satisfied.

Through **performance appraisal,** employees are evaluated to determine how well they are performing their assigned tasks. Any deficiencies identified can often be overcome through effective training and development programs.

Compensation

The question of what constitutes a fair day's pay has plagued managers for decades. Employees must be provided with adequate and equitable rewards for their contributions to organizational goals. In this book, **compensation** includes all rewards individuals receive as a result of their employment. As such, it is more than monetary income. The reward may be one or a combination of

[2]Thomas A. DeCotiis and Richard A. Morano, "Applying Job Analysis to Training," *Training and Development Journal* 31 (July 1977): 20.
[3]Lester A. Digman, "Let's Keep the OD People Honest," *Personnel* 56 (January–February 1979): 23.

"Career opportunities in Personnel are varied and many because of the rapidly growing recognition that the personnel function is making, and must make, a vital contribution to the bottom line of an organization. Top management is aware that as much as 70 to 80 percent of a company's expense dollars could be tied up in its human resources, and so management is beginning to focus on the effectiveness of the personnel function with the same intensity that it traditionally devoted to finance, marketing, and production."

**Gerrit Starke, Director of Corporate Personnel
Kemper Corporation**

the following:

- *Pay:* The money that a person receives for performing jobs. It is the cash that you can jingle in your pockets.
- *Benefits:* Additional financial rewards other than base pay such as paid holidays and medical insurance.
- *Nonfinancial:* Nonmonetary rewards that an employee may receive such as enjoyment of the work performed and a pleasant working environment.

Safety and Health

Safety involves protecting employees from injuries due to work-related accidents. **Health** refers to the employees' freedom from illness and their general physical and mental well-being. These topics are important because employees who enjoy good health and work in a safe environment are more likely to be efficient. For this reason, forward thinking managers have long advocated advanced safety and health programs. Today, because of federal legislation, all organizations have become concerned with their employees' safety and health.[4]

Employee and Labor Relations

Over twenty-two million employees currently belong to labor unions and employee associations.[5] Business firms are required by law to recognize unions and bargain with them in good faith, and this relationship has become an accepted way of life for many employers. But, as Judy Lynley, vice president for Axton

[4]The key law in the area of health and safety is the Occupational Safety and Health Act of 1970. The effect of this act will be discussed later in this book.
[5]Dale Yoder and Paul D. Standohar, "Assessing the Decline of Unions in the U.S." *Personnel Administrator* 27 (October 1982): 12–16.

Manufacturing Company, has discovered, there are often difficult problems to solve when dealing with the union. If the workers walk off the job, the firm's products cannot be manufactured. On the other hand, agreeing to all the union's demands may mean that the firm's products cannot be competitively priced. She must be a skilled negotiator to solve these problems. When a labor union is present, the personnel activity is often referred to as industrial relations. As in Judy's case, this department typically serves as a coordinator between union and management.

The vast majority of workers in the United States are not union members. In 1980, only 20.9 percent of the labor force was unionized, a drop of 3.8 percent since 1970.[6] However, nonunion organizations are often knowledgeable about union goals and activities. These firms typically strive to satisfy their employees' needs in every reasonable manner. They attempt to make it clear that a union is not necessary for individuals to achieve their personal goals.

Personnel Research

The personnel manager's research laboratory is the work environment. The need for effective research permeates every personnel function. For instance, research may be conducted to determine the type of workers who will prove to be most successful in the firm.[7] Or, it may be directed toward determining the causes of certain work-related accidents.[8] Because of the growing need for personnel research, personnel professionals are beginning to develop greater quantitative skills and are becoming much more adept in using the computer. As will be seen in chapter 18, there are numerous quantitative methods that are appropriate for use in personnel research. This function is expected to be increasingly important to all forms of organizations in the future.

The Interrelationships of HRM Functions

The previously mentioned functional areas of HRM should not be considered separate and distinct. They are highly interrelated. Decisions in one area must be made in light of the impact they will have on the others. For instance, it will do little good to emphasize the recruiting and training of the firm's sales force while neglecting to provide adequate compensation. In addition, if a firm's goal is to remain nonunion, management must certainly ensure that a safe and healthy work environment exists. Throughout the book we will emphasize the high degree of interrelationships that exist among the six HRM functional areas.

[6]*Ibid.*, p. 12.
[7]R. Wayne Mondy and Frank N. Edens, "An Empirical Test of the Decision to Participate Model," *Journal of Management* 2 (Fall 1976): 11–16.
[8]Dan Cordtz, "Safety On the Job Becomes a Major Job for Management," *Fortune* 86 (November 1972): 114.

THE REVOLUTION OF THE PERSONNEL FUNCTION

One of the major changes on the business scene in recent years has been the increase in the amount of time and effort that managers must spend in dealing with personnel problems and challenges. Every manager has been affected by this trend. The personnel department has had to respond in a positive manner. Line management increasingly needs and expects greater support from Personnel.

Not many decades ago, individuals engaged in personnel work had titles such as "welfare secretary" and "employment clerk." Their duties were rather restrictive and often dealt only with such items as workers' wages, minor medical affairs, recreation, and housing.[9] Personnel was generally held in low esteem and its organizational position was typically near the bottom of the hierarchy. "In the past," says John L. Quigley, vice president of human resources, Dr Pepper Company, "the personnel executive was the 'glad hander' or 'back slapper' who kept morale up in a company by running the company picnic, handling the United Fund drive, and making sure the recreation program went off well." These days are over in many organizations. The personnel director's position is no longer a "retirement" position given managers who cannot perform adequately anywhere else in the organization.[10] The overall increase in the personnel function's value is emphasized in the following article.

> **Business**
> **Personnel Jobs Gain Ground**
> Once upon a time, the personnel department was the graveyard of the business world. Workers were expected to process application forms and cherish few hopes for advancement. No longer. The rapid increase in job discrimination suits, pension laws, federal regulations, and labor disputes has made the personnel worker's job more demanding and more important to the company than ever before.
>
> Big corporations often have a sizable staff of personnel specialists who handle recruiting, employee counseling, psychological testing, wage and salary administration, training, affirmative action, fringe benefits, and compliance with government regulations. Training in business or personnel administration can be good preparation for entry-level jobs—but the personnel field is still open to ambitious graduates with liberal arts degrees.
>
> Advancement often requires more education, however. Highly paid negotiators who handle collective bargaining contracts often hold either a law degree or a master's in industrial relations.
>
> One thing seems clear, though: the personnel department is no longer a corporate backwater. In fact, some companies have decorated their top personnel staffer with the lofty title of Vice President for Human Resources.[11]

[9]Henry Eibirt, "The Development of Personnel Management in the United States," *Business History Review* 33 (Autumn 1969): 348–349.
[10]Lawrence A. Wangler, "The Intensification of the Personnel Role," *Personnel Journal* 58 (February 1979): 111–19.
[11]Gina Pera, "Business: Personnel Jobs Gain Ground," *Ford's Insider: A Continuing Series of College Newspaper Supplements* (February 1979). Published by 13–30 Corporation.

M. Jane Kay, AEP
Vice President of Employee Relations
The Detroit Edison Company

Jane Kay's professional life began on a disappointing note. After high school, she dreamed of becoming a secretary. However, she flunked her typing and shorthand tests and had to settle for a clerk's job. This early setback provided the impetus for a brilliant career. Work-

ing as an auditing clerk convinced her that if she were ever going to progress in business, additional education would be needed. After attending school and working part-time, she received a B.S. in industrial management from the University of Detroit in 1948.

After graduation, Ms. Kay returned to Detroit Edison as an employment interviewer. Two years later she was promoted to senior personnel interviewer. Realizing a need for further education, she worked toward her M.A. in personnel psychology and graduated from Wayne State University in 1952. In 1960 another promotion placed Ms. Kay in the position of personnel coordinator for women. During this period she continued her search for knowledge and received an M.B.A. from the University of Michigan in 1963. From this time, Detroit Edison continued to recognize her professionalism by giving her a series of promotions. In addition to developing an impressive business background, Jane has extensive teaching experience and numerous publications to her credit. She is a member of

Perhaps going one step further, Lester B. Korn, president of the consulting firm Korn/Ferry International, has stated:

> Personnel is now one of the most exciting functions in the entire business world. It has become the focus of the highest level thinking and policy making, and the best thing about it for the personnel chief is that more and more he or she is the one doing the best thinking and making the most important policies.[12]

In addition to becoming more significant, the field of Personnel is experiencing rapid growth. In 1976 there were approximately 335,000 individuals working directly in Personnel. It is estimated that there will be 21,000 job openings in this field each year through 1985. The projected growth for established professionals in the field prompted *Money* magazine to include personnel administrators in the ten future career fields that appear most promising.[13]

Salaries for practitioners range from $11,000 to $180,000 depending on company size and the responsibility level associated with the job. As reported in a salary survey of top personnel executives in firms with over $2 billion in

[12]"Personnel—Fast Track to the Top," *Dun's Review* 105 (April 1975): 74–77.
[13]Jerry Main, "Careers for the 1980's: '10 of the Best and 10 of the Worst'," *Money* 6 (November 1977): 62–69.

ASPA, ASTD, and many other professional and civic organizations.

Today, Jane is vice president of employee relations in an organization with over eleven thousand employees. She has overall responsibility for employee relations policies and practices as well as for the functional areas of personnel services, union relations, and organizational planning and development. Her position also requires interaction with federal, state, and local government agencies. She is a member of the Senior Management Committee. Jane may well occupy the highest ranking personnel position held by a women in the utility industry. "Let's face it," she says. "One element of my success is that I've been around here forever. My Mom worked for Edison and I feel like I was just dropped on its doorstep." It is obvious that Jane Kay has bounced very high.

When Jane was asked to describe some of the typical business she encounters, she replied, "As chairman of the Appeal Board, which is the final recourse in the employee complaint procedure for nonrepresented employees, I am frequently in the position of reviewing actions by my associates. In some cases it is necessary to reverse their decisions. My objective is to assure that the Appeal Board judges these matters in conformance to policies and procedures rather than trying to second guess the judgement of other individuals." Ms. Kay went on to say, "The personnel executive is sometimes in the position of having to exercise a control function. For instance, there is a tendency for managers to seek the highest possible grades for positions in their area. We have organized rating committees with representatives from each of the line areas to make joint decisions on job evaluation matters."

Jane's career in Personnel was not accidental. She planned it that way. "I had thought about where a woman would have the best chance of getting ahead," she says, "and concluded that it would be in Personnel."

gross sales, the median (middle) salary was $110,500. For companies with over $250 million in gross sales, the median salary was $49,520.[14] As impressive as these figures may appear, the salaries of individuals engaged in personnel work typically continue to lag behind those in other major functional areas. However, their relative compensation position is rapidly improving.

Numerous individuals have progressed from Personnel to other top executive positions. For instance, Ernest F. Boyce, a former vice president for personnel, is now chairman of the board and chief executive officer for Colonial Stores, Inc., the billion dollar southwestern supermarket chain. William L. Mobraaten, formerly personnel vice president at Pacific Telephone and Telegraph Company, is now president and director of Bell Telephone Company of Pennsylvania.[15] W. T. Beebe, chairman of the board of Delta Airlines was vice president of personnel for Delta from 1954 to 1966.

The increased status of the personnel field is not limited to the United States. In his research on Japanese industry, William Ouchi found that, "ordinarily, the most senior and the most respected managing director is in charge of Personnel."[16] Another study showed that in Germany, Scandinavia, Switz-

[14]"Salary Survey," *Action* 14, no. 4 (August 1978): 1.
[15]"Personnel—Fast Track to the Top," p. 74.
[16]William G. Ouchi, *Theory Z* (Reading, MA: Addison-Wesley Publishing Company, 1981): 30.

erland, and the United Kingdom, over half of the top personnel executives were also directors in their companies.[17] This trend is expected to continue as personnel management grows in importance.

PERSONNEL EXECUTIVES, GENERALISTS, AND SPECIALISTS

Within Personnel, there are various classifications that should be understood. Throughout this book, we will refer to personnel executives, generalists, and specialists. **Executives** are top level managers. They report directly to the corporation's chief executive officer (CEO) or the head of a major division. A **generalist** (who is often an executive) is a person who performs tasks in a wide variety of personnel related activities. This individual is often involved with several or all of the six personnel functions previously described. On the other hand, a **specialist** is typically concerned with only one of the six functional areas. A specialist may be either a top executive, a middle manager, or a nonmanager.

Figure 1-2 helps clarify the nature of executives, generalists, and specialists. The vice president of industrial relations, in this example, specializes

Figure 1–2.   Personnel executives, generalists, and specialists.

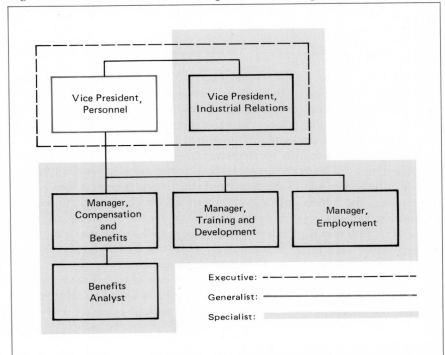

17Sandra Salman, "Personnel: A New Route to the Top," *International Management* 32 (May 1977): 25.

Starting Assignment	
Specialist	*Generalist*
Work for a supervisor in an area like labor relations, employment, training benefits. This would be at a larger location, where the function is broken down into areas of specialty.	Work for a supervisor or superintendent in several areas. You might be responsible for training, communications, employment, benefits, safety. This would be at a smaller location with two or three personnel professionals on the staff.

Later Assignments	
Specialist	*Generalist*
Manage one or two areas of responsibility, such as labor relations, training and development, a combination of employment and benefits. Again, this would be at a larger location.	Manage the total personnel function * For a sub-unit within the location (such as for the maintenance department, or for a geographic area within the location), * For a smaller Monsanto location, * For a larger location.

Operating Company/Staff Department	
Specialist	*Generalist*
Manage one or two functions such as personnel planning, compensation, recruiting, or an entire company or staff department.	Manage the total personnel function for a sub-unit within a company (e.g., a division) or for the entire company or staff department.

Corporate	
Specialist	
Work in or manage an entire area of expertise for the corporation, such as labor relations, equal employment opportunity, development, benefits.	

Two bits of advice:
  • Don't get hung up on whether you begin your career as a specialist or generalist. The lines between generalist and specialist are not as neat as the chart would indicate. For example, as an employment "specialist," you would daily become involved with questions of labor relations, compensation, personnel planning and equal employment policy—and much more! Or as a small-plant "generalist," you would have to learn the basics of several specialties. Also, the overwhelming odds are that you will get both types of exposure—specialist and generalist—in your career.
  • Career development will not always be "up." It's to the professional's advantage to get as much experience and exposure as possible—and many times, this will mean lateral moves into different areas of specialty.

Figure 1–3. **Career Development at Monsanto**

primarily in union related matters. He or she is both an executive and a specialist. The personnel vice president is both a generalist and an executive because he or she is responsible for a wide variety of functions. The manager of compensation and benefits is a specialist, as is the benefits analyst. An executive may be identified by his or her position level in the organization. Generalists and specialists are distinguished by their position's breadth of responsibility.

The distinction made between generalists and specialists may become even clearer by referring to the Monsanto example in Figure 1–3, which lists the type of general work assignments at various levels in the organization for both generalists and specialists. Notice the "two bits of advice" which Monsanto gives to personnel professionals with regard to career development.

THE PERSONNEL FUNCTION IN DIFFERENT SIZE ORGANIZATIONS

All firms from the small corner grocery store to General Motors Corporation are concerned with human resources management. However, the personnel function's structure tends to change as firms grow in size and complexity and as the function gains importance. The basic purpose of Personnel remains the same, but the approach followed in accomplishing its mission is often altered.

In small businesses, there is usually no formal personnel unit. Rather, executives in the company bear the entire burden of handling their own personnel activities. These activities include insuring that capable people are hired and retained (see Figure 1–3). Some aspects of the personnel function may actually be more significant in the smaller firm than in larger organizations. For instance, if a small business hires its first and only full-time salesperson, and this individual alienates the firm's customers, the company might actually go out of business. In a larger firm, such an error would be less devastating.

A separate personnel staff function may be required to coordinate human resources activities as the firm grows in size. The individual chosen will be expected to handle most of the personnel activities (see Figure 1–4). For this size

Figure 1–4. **The personnel function of a small business.**

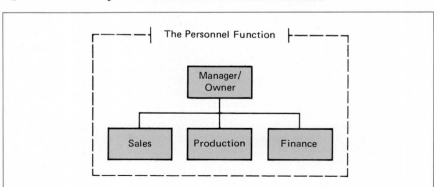

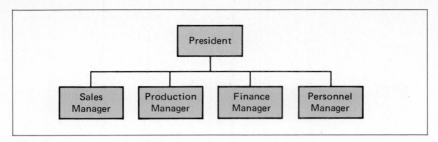

Figure 1–5. **The personnel function of a medium-sized firm.**

firm there is little specialization. A secretary may be available to handle correspondence, but the personnel manager is essentially the entire department.

When the personnel function in an organization cannot be adequately performed by one person, separate sections are created and often placed under the direction of a personnel manager. These sections will typically handle tasks involving such areas as training and development, compensation and benefits, employment, safety and health, and labor relations (see Figure 1–5).

In large firms, the personnel function becomes a unit using even greater specialization (see Figure 1–6 for the organization chart for Champion International Corporation). For instance, the unit responsible for compensation will most likely include specialists who concentrate on hourly wages and others who devote their time to salary administration. The employee relations vice president works closely with top management in formulating corporate policies. The scope of the duties of the employee relations executive is provided in Table 1–1. As you can see, the scope of the position is quite broad, ranging from the coordination, recommendation, and implementation of plans to auditing performance.

Figure 1–6. **The personnel functions of a medium-large-sized firm.**

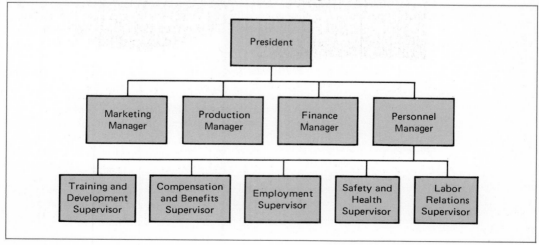

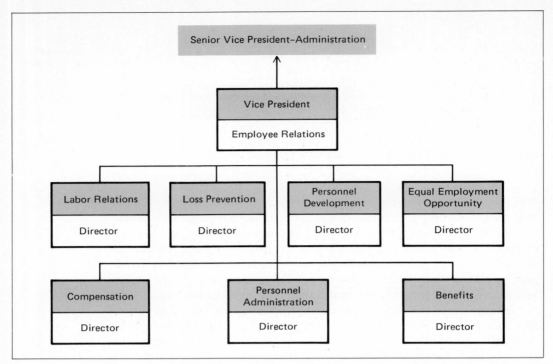

Figure 1–7. **The employee relations organization—Champion International Corporation. (Source: Champion International Corporation.)**

Table 1–1. Champion International Corporation Corporate Employee Relations

Charter:	To provide operating and staff management with professional centralized services that will assure the competence and continuity of the company's human resources
Scope:	• To provide expertise and centralized services • To coordinate plans, recommendations, implementation, and review of corporate projects • To recommend general policies • To establish functional procedures for designated activities • To audit performance and compliance with general policies and procedures for designated activities
Objectives:	• To provide direction and support to each functional director and his department • To require quality and excellence in total performance of function • To assure that professional positions are occupied by competent people who can and do respond to the company's needs and requirements

Source: Champion International Corporation

A **profession** is characterized by the existence of a common body of knowledge and a procedure for certifying members of the profession. Performance standards are established by members of the profession (self-regulation) as opposed to outsiders. It must also have an effective representative organization which permits its members to exchange ideas of mutual concern. In Personnel, there are several well-known organizations. Among the more prominent are the American Society for Training and Development, the American Compensation Association, the American Society for Personnel Administration, the International Association for Personnel Women, and the Personnel Accreditation Institute.

American Society for Training and Development

Founded in 1944, the American Society for Training and Development (ASTD) has grown to become the largest specialized personnel organization. The membership exceeds 20,000 and has over 120 local groups.[18] The membership is comprised of individuals who are concerned specifically with the training and development of personnel.

American Compensation Association

The American Compensation Association (ACA) was founded in 1954. The membership exceeds six thousand.[19] The ACA is comprised of managerial and personnel professionals who are responsible for the establishment, execution, administration, or application of compensation practices and policies in their organizations.

American Society for Personnel Administration

The largest national professional organization for individuals interested in personnel and human resources management is the American Society for Personnel Administration (ASPA). The basic goals of ASPA include defining, maintaining, and improving standards of excellence in the practice of personnel. ASPA membership consists of thirty-six thousand individuals.[20] There are currently more than three hundred and thirty-three local chapters. Titles of ASPA members range from corporate vice president to division personnel manager to compensation specialist. There are also numerous student chapters of ASPA on university campuses across the country.

[18]*Encyclopedia of Associations*, Denise S. Akey, editor, 16th Edition, Volume 1 (Detroit, MI: Gale Research Co., 1982): 194.
[19]*Ibid.*
[20]*Ibid.*

International Association for Personnel Women

Founded in 1950, the International Association for Personnel Women (IAPW) was established to expand and improve the professionalism of women in personnel management. Its membership consists of personnel executives in business, industry, education, and government. As of 1982, there were approximately 2000 members.[21]

Personnel Accreditation Institute

One of the more significant undertakings in the field of Personnel has been accomplished by the Personnel Accreditation Institute (PAI). PAI's goal is to recognize personnel professionals through an accreditation program.[22] This program encourages personnel professionals to continuously update their knowledge in the field. Accreditation indicates that they have mastered a validated common body of knowledge. The advantages of personnel accreditation were outlined a number of years ago by a former national president of ASPA, Wiley Beavers, who wrote:

> First, we would benefit at the college and university level. The development of the body of knowledge required for successful practice in the various areas of personnel would provide invaluable assistance in curricula design. The breakdown of the field into its specialties would also allow students to focus on career directions earlier in their educations.
>
> Second, young practitioners would have sound guidelines and information covering areas in which they should be boning up and could avoid the mistakes many of us older types make.
>
> Third, senior practitioners would be encouraged to update their knowledge. (Don't know how many of them will be interested in accreditation. There will be an appreciable reaction along the lines of: "I don't need to take tests to prove I know what I'm doing. I have already proven it by the job I'm doing." And they will be right in about 50 percent of the cases.)[23]

DESIGN OF THIS BOOK

Effective personnel and human resources management is critical for every firm's success. In order to be successful, managers must understand and practice effective personnel management. This personnel and human resources management book is designed to provide you with:

- Greater knowledge and insight into the role of personnel and human resources management in today's organizations

[21]*Ibid.*
[22]Details of the PAI are shown in the appendix to this chapter.
[23]Wiley Beavers, "Accreditation: What Do We Need That For?" *The Personnel Administrator* 18 (November 1975): 39–41.

- Increased knowledge about human resources planning, recruitment, and selection
- Perception of the importance of training and development in modern organizations
- An appreciation of how compensation and benefits programs are determined and administered
- An understanding of safety and health factors as they impact a firm's profitability
- An opportunity to view employee and labor relations from both union and nonunion standpoints
- Greater understanding of the role of personnel research in today's organizations

Students often question whether the content of a book corresponds with the realities of the business world. In our research efforts, we have drawn heavily upon the comments, observations, and experiences of personnel practitioners. Personnel practices followed by leading business organizations are cited to illustrate that theory can be applied. Our intent is to enable students to visualize actual business experience in action.

This book is organized into seven sections as shown in Figure 1–8. We believe that this approach will provide you with an appreciation of the importance of personnel and human resources management. As you read this book, we hope you will be stimulated to continue your search for knowledge in this rapidly changing and expanding field.

SUMMARY

All managers in the organization are vitally concerned with personnel management. They must achieve organizational goals through other people's efforts. Personnel managers normally act in an advisory (staff) capacity when working with other managers. They have the primary responsibility of coordinating the firm's human resources management activities. The personnel, or human resources, manager is at the heart of a human resources management system.

In order to fulfill the firm's personnel and human resources needs, the personnel manager must perform tasks in a wide variety of functions. These include: (1) personnel planning, recruitment, and selection, (2) training and development, (3) compensation, (4) safety and health, (5) employee and labor relations, and (6) personnel research. The personnel department has had to respond in a positive manner to the many major changes on the business scene in recent years. Line management increasingly needs and expects greater support from Personnel.

Within Personnel there are various classifications which should be understood. An executive is a top level manager. Generalists are people who per-

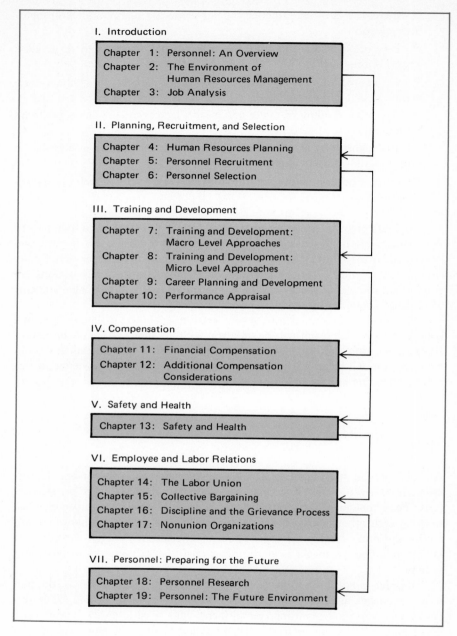

Figure 1–8. **The organization of this book.**

form tasks in a wide variety of personnel-related activities. Specialists are concerned with but one of six functional areas. Many of these personnel people have progressed to their firm's top level managerial position.

A profession exists when there is a common body of knowledge and there is a procedure for certifying members of the profession. In Personnel, there are several well known organizations. Among the more prominent are the American Society for Training and Development, the American Compensation Association, the American Society for Personnel Administration, the International Association of Personnel Women, and the Personnel Accreditation Institute.

Questions for Review

1. Justify the statement, "All managers are involved in human resources management."
2. Distinguish between personnel management and the personnel manager.
3. What personnel functions must be performed regardless of the size of the organization?
4. Distinguish by definition and example between personnel executives, personnel generalists, and personnel specialists.
5. How does the personnel function change as a firm grows in size? Briefly describe each stage of development.
6. Do you believe the field of personnel management should be professionalized? Explain your answer.

Terms for Review

Management
Objective
Human resources management
Personnel planning
Recruitment
Selection
Training and development
Organization development
Individual career planning

Performance appraisal
Compensation
Safety
Health
Executive
Generalist
Specialist
Profession

The day was one of the happiest in Ed Beaver's life. He was told that morning that he was being promoted to corporate vice president for personnel from his present position as personnel manager for his firm's large New York plant. As he leaned back in his office chair, he felt a deep sense of accomplishment. He thought back to the day fifteen years earlier when, fresh out of college, he joined Duncan Foods as an assistant compensation specialist. He had always wanted to be in personnel, but he got his degree in business management because the university did not have a personnel curriculum. Ed remembered how tense he was when he arrived at work that first day. College graduates were rarely given the opportunity to start work directly in personnel and he was the youngest employee in the department.

Ed learned his job well and the older workers quickly accepted him. Three years later he was promoted to compensation manager. Immediately after the promotion he was given the task of designing a new pay system for operative employees. As he remembers, "Designing the system wasn't difficult. Convincing the employees that the new system was better than the old one was the real chore." But he overcame that obstacle.

A few years later Ed moved up again. He was chosen to become the new personnel manager for a small Duncan plant outside Chicago. The move required a major readjustment for his family. Ed's wife remarked, "I sure hate to move in the middle of the school year. And we've just begun to enjoy our new house." Ed was able to find another home the family liked just as well, and the children adjusted quickly. The job was certainly no bed of roses. Six months after Ed arrived he led negotiations for a new union contract. He worked night and day for months to develop a contract that would be acceptable to both the company and the union. Successful signing of the new agreement was one of his most satisfying experiences.

Four years later, Ed was asked if he would accept the position of personnel manager for the large New York plant. This plant employed five times as many workers as the Chicago plant and had many different types of problems. After a family discussion the Beavers were off to new adventures in the Big Apple.

At that moment, Ed's nostalgia came to a halt. The challenge of the new job suddenly came home to him. As vice president of personnel for Duncan Foods he would be responsible for personnel management for fifty plants and warehouses employing 13,000 people. What an overwhelming responsibility he was facing! Personnel management had changed greatly during the previous fifteen years and the rate of change seemed to be increasing. Ed wondered about the problems he would face and what role he would play in solving them as the new vice president for personnel.

Questions

1. Trace Ed's progression to vice president of personnel. Do you feel that this progression qualifies him well for the job?
2. What problems do you imagine Ed will face in his new role compared to his problems as plant personnel manager?
3. What new challenges do you feel Ed will confront in the changing field of personnel in the future?

It was a nervous Jerry Fox who was ushered into the company president's office by the secretary. In the office he encountered Allen Anderson, the vice president of personnel, and Vince Gorman, the president. Jerry was flattered when the president stood to shake his hand. "I'll make this short and sweet," Mr. Gorman said. "You probably have heard that Mr. Anderson has arranged his retirement at the end of next year. We would like to move you in as his assistant to learn the job. If things work out the position will be yours when he retires." Flabbergasted, Jerry responded, "Why me? I'm a purchasing manager, I've never even worked in a personnel office." "Well," continued Mr. Gorman, "we've been watching you carefully. I have personally reviewed your qualifications. From the company's standpoint, we know you can do the job. You have to decide now whether this is the direction you want to go. I have a meeting in a few minutes so I'll have to leave. Spend a few hours with Allen today and we can talk tomorrow."

At age thirty-three Jerry had been with Levitt Manufacturing Company for seven years.

His business administration degree had included a heavy concentration in behavioral science courses. But he had worked only in purchasing. After three successful years as a buyer, he had been promoted to purchasing manager, with responsibility for supervising eight buyers and a small clerical staff.

He knew that he had attained an excellent reputation throughout the company. This was especially true in the production department, which had a great deal of interaction with purchasing. The production manager made no secret of his high regard for Jerry. Jerry also had taken time to get to know members of the finance and research departments. His purpose in pursuing all of these relationships was to help him do his purchasing manager job better, though. He had no idea at all that he would be considered for a job in Personnel.

As Jerry left the president's office with Mr. Anderson he thought about what he might be getting into. Not only was he unsure about his qualifications for the personnel job, but he wondered how the experience might prepare him for future promotion opportunities.

Questions

1. What *is* Jerry getting into? What are likely to be his responsibilities?

2. How has Jerry's background prepared him for each of the six functional areas of personnel?

___ Appendix to Chapter One ___

The Personnel Accreditation Institute's program provides for two levels of accreditation:

Basic: Professional in Human Resources (PHR)
Senior: Senior Professional in Human Resources (SPHR)

Qualification levels depend upon an individual's educational attainment, work experience and responsibility level. One of two possible routes may be followed for senior level accreditation—specialist or generalist.

Accreditation for senior specialist requires knowledge, experience and successful completion of an examination which focuses upon one of the following areas:

- Employment, placement and personnel planning
- Training and Development
- Compensation and Benefits
- Health, safety and security
- Employee and labor relations
- Personnel research

Senior generalist accreditation requires knowledge, experience and successful completion of an examination covering the specialty areas previously described in addition to general management practices. Senior generalists must be personnel management practitioners.

Basic generalist accreditation is also available to those individuals who do not meet the advanced level experience or job scope requirements. Although college students may not initially meet experience requirements, experience

Figure A1–1. An advertisement for accredited personnel specialists. (Source: Dr Pepper Company.)

PERSONNEL ADMINISTRATOR

The Dr Pepper Company is seeking an individual who would like to join the most aggressive soft drink company in the beverage industry.

The Personnel Administrator candidate should have 1–2 years of personnel experience, degree typing skills, and **PHR** preferred. Will be responsible for the following areas: benefits; ERISA and EEO administration; employment background investigations; technical skills testing; monthly company newsletter publishing; some employee interviewing; preparation of required EEO1 and other federal reports. This position has excellent opportunity for growth based on performance. We offer excellent salary and benefits. Send detailed resume and salary history to:

DR PEPPER COMPANY
P.O. Box 226083
Personnel Department – PA
Dallas, TX 75222

EQUAL OPPORTUNITY EMPLOYER

credit is given for a bachelors degree and for a masters. Accreditation is granted as soon as experience requirements are met. For instance, a college senior could pass the examination and be eligible for accreditation after receiving two years experience. Students with majors in personnel, industrial relations, and other related areas may take the basic level accreditation examination on any regular test date.

Accreditation may prove helpful for both students and practitioners who are seeking jobs. A growing number of employers view accreditation as an important factor in identifying qualified personnel professionals (see Figure A1–1). Since its inception in 1976, the PAI has granted accreditation to more than 4,000 specialists and generalists. The number of accredited individuals will likely increase substantially as the benefits of accreditation become more apparent.

For additional information about personnel accreditation, contact:
   Personnel Accreditation Institute
   P. O. Box 19648
   Alexandria, VA 22320
   (703) 684-8327

Chapter Objectives

1. Explain the factors which influence human resources management.
2. Relate how the size and characteristics of the labor force are expected to change by 1990.
3. Describe the environmental factors that affect a firm's human resources from outside the organizational boundaries.
4. Explain factors in the internal environment and state how they exert pressure upon the human resources management functions.
5. Identify and describe the factors which influence a firm's organizational climate.
6. Explain the concept referred to as quality of work life.

Chapter 2 _____

The Environment of Human Resources Management

Alice Baker, director of personnel for Superite Products, Inc., had just returned from an executive staff meeting. A critical decision regarding the firm's future had been made. Over the next three years, the firm's mission would change from that of producing relatively low quality products to one of manufacturing higher quality products. Conditions had changed in the industry, thus making the higher quality product more marketable. As Alice sat in her office she began to think how this change would affect her work. She thought, "This will require a drastic change in technology. Some of our current employees can be cross-trained, but many can't because of the higher skills level required. We will virtually have to obtain a new work force. I don't know if there are enough people in the area work force to support this change."

Because customers now desire a higher quality product (a change in the external environment), Superite's internal environment must be altered. The firm's mission has changed, and it may prove difficult to obtain qualified workers from the area work force to support the new mission.

In this chapter we will first identify the numerous factors comprising Personnel's environment. Then we will describe how specific external environmental factors can influence the personnel manager's work and discuss some of the major internal environmental factors which can affect the personnel manager's job. Finally, we will discuss quality of work life programs (QWL) as they relate to human resources management.

ENVIRONMENTAL FACTORS AFFECTING HUMAN RESOURCES MANAGEMENT

Notice in Figure 2–1 that there are many interrelating factors affecting human resources management. They can be subdivided into the external and internal environment. The **external environment** consists of those factors which affect a firm's human resources from outside the organizational boundaries. Major external factors include: legal considerations, the labor force, the public, unions, stockholders/owners, competition, customers, and technology: the state of the art. The primary internal factors include company objectives, company policies, and organizational climate. In addition, personnel professionals constantly work with people from other functional areas such as marketing, production, and finance. They must understand the different perspectives of people from various disciplines in order to perform their tasks.

Understanding the many interrelationships implied in the model is quite important as the personnel professional works with other managers to assist them in resolving their daily problems. For instance, a production manager may want to give a substantial pay raise to a particular employee. The personnel manager may know that this individual does an exceptional job, but should also know that if this raise is granted, it will not only affect the department where the individual works but may also set a precedent for the entire firm. The personnel manager may have to explain to this manager that such action is not an isolated decision and that alternatives may need to be considered as a means of rewarding superior performance. Perhaps the personnel manager knows of a higher paying position that this employee would be qualified to fill. The manager may also be able to move the deserving worker into a supervisory position. Whatever the case, the effect of a particular act must be considered in light of its impact upon the entire organization. The model provides personnel managers with a framework which emphasizes viewing the big picture rather than concentrating upon a narrow phase of the company's operation.

The basic tasks assigned the personnel manager remain essentially the same no matter what impact is exerted from either the external or internal

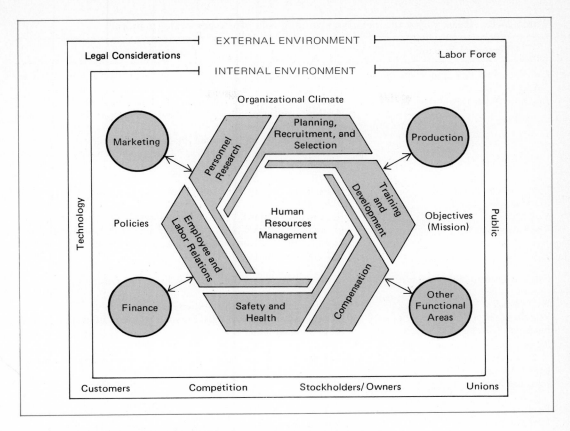

Figure 2–1. **The environment of human resources management.**

environments. However, the manner in which they are accomplished may be altered substantially. The remainder of this chapter is devoted to consideration of the external and internal factors which affect human resources management.

THE EXTERNAL ENVIRONMENT

The external environment is comprised of those factors which affect a firm's human resources from outside the organizational boundaries. As Figure 2–1 illustrates, they include legal considerations, the labor force, the public, unions, stockholders/owners, competition, customers, and technology. Each of these, separately or in combination, can result in constraints upon the personnel manager's job.

Legal Considerations

One of the most significant external forces a manager must face relates to federal, state, and local legislation. The comments of selected personnel professionals when responding to the question, "What are the reasons for the rapidly

Table 2–1. Reasons for the rapidly expanding role of the personnel manager

Personnel Executive	Comments
Crown Central Petroleum Corporation Jerome L. Valentine Employee Relations Manager	• Federal legislation (EEO; OSHA; ERISA; Privacy Act; Age Discrimination in Employment Act, as amended April 6, 1978). • Social awareness of individual rights under the above. • Attitudes and demands of the NOW Generation (but not in the negative sense). • Need for more sophisticated management programs and techniques in training, development of meaningful employee relations programs.
Detroit Edison Company M. Jane Kay, AEP Vice President Employee Relations	• Legislation directly affecting personnel field (EEO, OSHA, ERISA, ADEA). • Increased importance of the human resource—considering need for increased productivity, cost, development of future managers. • Need for input in corporate decisions from someone with expertise in human relations.

Fairchild Camera and Instrument
  Corporation
W. J. Bowles
Vice President of
Industrial Relations
Pacific Gamble Robinson
  Company, Incorporated
Jerry F. Scroggs, AEP
Personnel Manager
	• Government regulation of actions previously optional to management.
	• Broad social change in values, attitudes, etc.
	• Growing awareness that "good human relations are good business" (after all these years!).
	• Federal and state legislation.
	• Complexity of business activities including more diverse operations.

Pennzoil Company John Kajander Vice President Employee Relations	• New laws making personnel actions much more subject to regulations of all sorts.

PPG Industries, Incorporated
Donald E. Van Cleef
Director of Employee, Public and
  Government Relations Chemicals
Control Data Corporation
Eugene L. Baker, AEP
Vice President
Human Resource Management
  Services
	• Proliferation of government regulations impacting on personnel considerations.
	• Increased recognition by line management of the importance of the human factor in reaching business goals.
	• Change in employee expectations—employees are demanding a higher level of satisfaction from their job, the work place, and life itself.
	• Change in the law—legislation and regulations regarding the treatment, selection, and handling of employees has been strengthened and has become much more complicated.
	• Change in managerial attitudes—management has continually increased its awareness of the importance of effective management of the human resource asset.

Honeywell, Inc. Charles E. Brown Vice President Employee Relations	• I believe the primary reasons stem from changing social expectations. The private sector is more and more expected to provide enlarged social services, as well as products and commercial services. Examples are expectations in the areas of equal employment opportunity, clean air and water, safety, health, and industrial hygiene.

expanding role of the personnel manager?" attest to the impact that government laws and regulations are having upon their jobs (see Table 2–1). As you can see, personnel practitioners view government legislation as affecting the entire spectrum of personnel policies. Significant legislation affecting the manager's job performance will be highlighted in the appendix to this chapter. The manner in which these laws affect each of the personnel functions will be described in the particular chapter in which that function is discussed.

33

Chapter 2
The
Environment of
Human
Resources
Management

The Labor Force

The number and characteristics of individuals in the labor force is another major external factor. The nature of this group may be quite different in the future.[1] By 1990, there will be approximately 119 million people in the civilian labor force. This estimate represents an 18.5 percent increase over the 1978 figure of 100 million. As may be seen in Figure 2–2, although the population has grown more slowly in recent years the figures do not tell the entire story. The labor force composition is also changing. While the participation rate for men continues to decline, the participation rate for women is rising (see Figure 2–3). Women are moving into traditionally male-dominated jobs in ever increasing numbers.

Figure 2–2. **Civilian labor force growth and projected growth.**

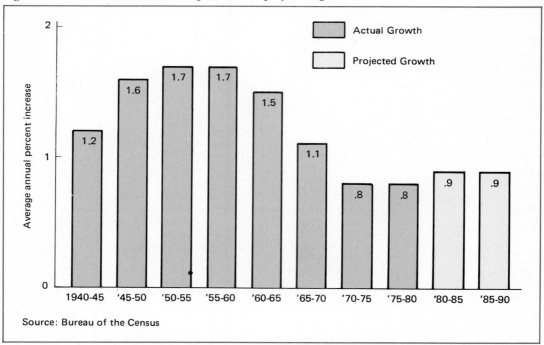

Source: Bureau of the Census

[1]For a more detailed discussion of future labor force characteristics see *Occupational Outlook Handbook*, 1980–81 ed., U.S. Government Bulletin, Number 2075.

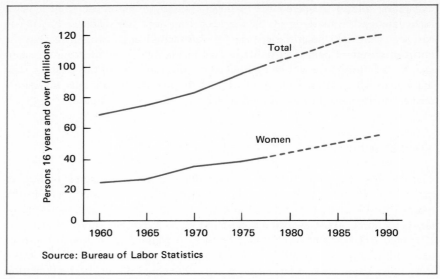

Figure 2–3.   **Participation rate in the labor force for women and men.**

Figure 2–4.   **Number of workers in service industries versus good industries.**

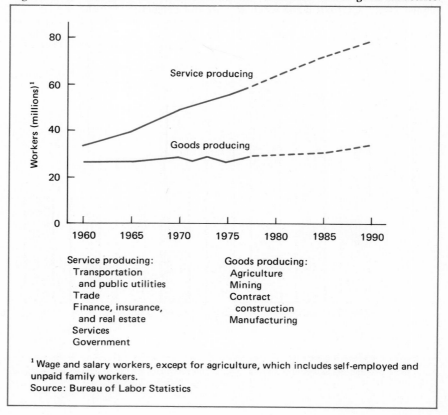

The industries that will be capable of absorbing these additional employees will also likely be different from those of today. This change has already begun as job opportunities increase in service-producing industries such as transportation, public utilities, finance, insurance, real estate, and government (see Figure 2–4). The goods-producing industries such as agriculture, construction, mining, and manufacturing are expected to remain relatively stable in terms of employment. By 1990, employment in service industries is expected to have expanded by 30 percent over 1978 figures. In goods-producing industries, employment is projected to increase by 13 percent. A projection of employment growth by industry is presented in Figure 2–5.

Once a small proportion of the total labor force, white-collar workers now represent about half of the total. The number of service workers has also risen rapidly, while the blue-collar work force has grown only slowly and the number of farm workers has declined. Projected distribution of employment by occupation in 1990 may be seen in Figure 2–6.

The job openings that will be available by 1990 are determined by the growth of a particular industry and the number of replacement personnel needed. As you can see in Figure 2–7, a large number of industries are projecting growth in employment by 1990. The challenge in filling these job openings will be enormous. Personnel managers must not only adapt to the

35

Chapter 2
The
Environment of
Human
Resources
Management

Figure 2–5. **Employment growth by industry through the 1980s.**

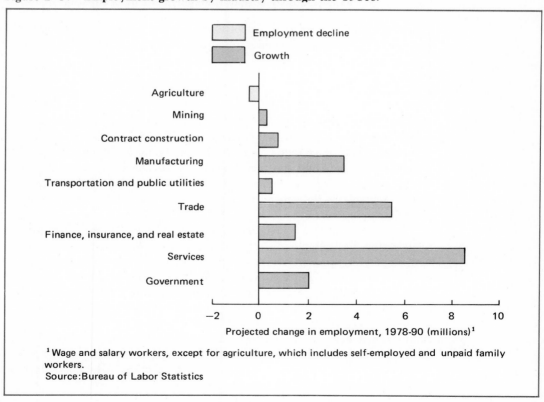

[1] Wage and salary workers, except for agriculture, which includes self-employed and unpaid family workers.
Source: Bureau of Labor Statistics

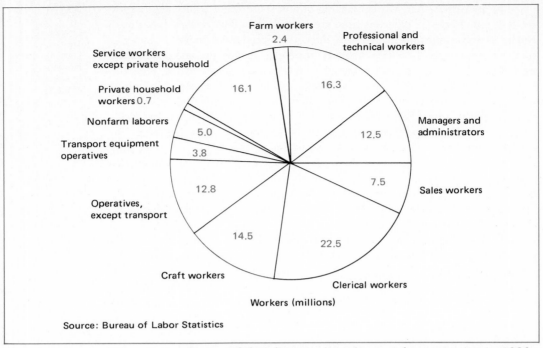

Figure 2–6. **Projected distribution of employment by occupation in 1990.**

changing characteristics of the labor force, but the employees comprising this new labor force must be able to adjust to the ever changing needs of organizations.

The Public

Members of society also exert considerable pressure upon personnel management. The public is no longer content to accept, without question, the actions of business. They have found that changes can be made through the pressures of their voices and votes and their influence is obvious by the large number of regulatory laws that have been passed since the early 1960s. If a firm is to remain acceptable to the general public, it must be capable of satisfactorily explaining its purpose.

A major point that management must consider is that the general public includes the firm's employees. For instance, if an organization has ten thousand employees, these individuals will have influence over a larger number of people who are not connected with the firm. They may be friends or members of an employee's family. Therefore, it behooves a firm to maintain clear communication with its employees so that the firm's side to a story is told.

The general public's attitude and beliefs can affect the firm's behavior. **Social responsibility** refers to an organization's basic obligation to ensure that its decisions and operations meet the needs and interests of society. Considerable pressure can be exerted upon a firm to alter its practices if the public believes

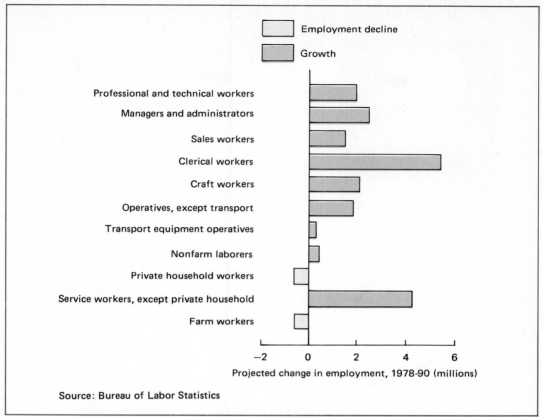

Figure 2–7. Replacement plus growth determine job openings.

that it is not operating in the best interest of society. If a firm is to be socially responsible, the interests and welfare of both the corporation and the public must be considered.

You may ask at this point, "Why should a business firm be concerned with the welfare of society? Its goal is to make a profit and grow." It is difficult to question that a business must make a profit in the long-run if it is to survive. But, a basic point should also be remembered: If the needs of society are not satisfied, a firm will ultimately cease to exist. A firm operates by public consent to satisfy society's needs. To compound the issue, goals, values, and attitudes are constantly changing. Some social responsibility areas include:

- Providing equal employment and educational opportunities regardless of race, color, sex, or age.
- Providing a sufficient number of jobs and career opportunities for all members of society
- Eliminating poverty
- Providing quality health care

Executive Profile

Drew M. Young, AEP
Vice President, Employee Relations
(Retired)
ARCO Oil and Gas Company
(Division of Atlantic Richfield
Company)

When the term *personnel professional* is used to suggest excellence in the field of personnel, the name of Drew M. Young must certainly come to mind. Throughout his career Drew has participated in professional and civic activities. He believes that a person should give something back to the profession and community of which he is a part. As a result of practicing this philosophy, Drew has held numerous leadership positions in professional associations including the national presidency of the American Society for Training and Development, the American Society for Personnel Administration, and the Personnel Accreditation Institute.

Drew's long and varied career began in the late 1930s after he received a B.A. degree in English and philosophy from Swarthmore College. He added to his education through the years by doing graduate studies in psychology and music at Temple University, graduating from the Executive Program at Columbia University's Graduate School of Business and participating in numerous seminars, training programs, and workshops in the human resources field. Drew's first position was that of director of music at Henry C. Conrad High School, Richardson Park, Delaware. The pay was higher for band directors than English teachers and he thoroughly enjoyed what he did.

During his five years in the U.S. Army, he taught training management at the Signal Corps Officer Candidate School (Ft. Monmouth, NJ) and was a training supervisor at the Army Signal Corps School AFWESPAC (Oro Bay, New Guinea and Manila, PI). These positions marked the beginning of his work in the field of training.

His transition to the world of business took place during the two years that he was an area training supervisor with the Veterans Administration. He and the training officers reporting to him were responsible for administering training for 12,000 veterans in Philadelphia, Chester, and Delaware Counties, Pennsylvania.

In 1947 he voluntarily took a cut in pay to enter the private sector as a training assistant with The Atlantic Refining Company (Philadelphia), one of the predecessor companies of Atlantic Richfield Company. As a member of the corporate training staff he found it somewhat frustrating to develop training programs for other company units and then not to see the results when not involved in implementing the programs. Thus, when

- Preserving the environment
- Improving the quality of the working life of employees[2]

[2]Adapted from the Committee for Economic Development and Sandra L. Holmes, "Corporate Social Performance and Present Areas of Commitment," *Academy of Management Journal* 20, no. 3 (1977): 435.

several years later he was asked to be the training supervisor on the personnel staff of the company's North American Producing Division (Dallas, Texas), he snapped at the opportunity. He found it challenging to initiate the Division's first supervisory training program and even more challenging to convince the management of the Atlantic Pipe Line Company that they needed such a program for their supervisors. One tool used to accomplish this objective was a morale survey of all of their employees. The survey results showed definite needs for improving supervisory skills and changing work procedures. Shortly thereafter their specially designed supervisory training program was implemented.

After six years as supervisor of an ever-growing training function, Drew was promoted to the position of personnel supervisor. His responsibilities included all of the personnel functions except safety and employment. After several years in this position, he accepted the assignment of manager of industrial relations for the Venezuelan Atlantic Refining Company (VARCO) in Caracas, Venezuela. During his almost four years in this position, he was responsible for all personnel functions plus the medical department which operated two hospitals, the schools for employees' children in field locations, and the travel and documentation section. Operating in a different culture with employees whose value systems varied somewhat from those of American employees, was a broadening and interesting experience. One thing he had to learn was to be able to say "no" in such a way that the other person could save face. He also found that negotiating collective labor agreements under

circumstances where the Ministry of Labor might make the final decisions was a whole new ball game. Drew said, "Working overseas provides valuable experience and is enriching in many ways. I would recommend it for anyone who is adaptable and has the opportunity. Many of the lessons that I learned there stood me in good stead in subsequent years."

Several years after returning to Dallas as general personnel supervisor, he was promoted to the position that he held until he retired in May of 1981. In addition to being responsible for all personnel functions, he was involved in many interesting special projects. Several projects that stood out in his mind were: working on a task force to plan the logistics and personnel requirements for ARCO operations on the North Slope of Alaska; chairing a task force to develop organizational and policy recommendations for the corporate medical department; and overseeing the development and implementation of an integrated personnel planning system.

Drew believes that personnel professionals should be well prepared to help their organizations meet three important needs:

- The need for greater, more creative contributions to productivity in the face of rising labor costs, stiffer competition, and economic changes.
- The need for more broadly skilled managers at the top of the company and stable executive succession.
- The need to plan and assimilate changes in status, work, and evolving relationships and expectations of employees.

Although the issues mentioned above are directed at the overall organization, it can easily be seen how Personnel might be expected to become involved in each. The organization is a member of the community in which it operates. Just as citizens may work to improve the quality of life in their community, the organization should also respect and work with the other members of its community. For instance, a high unemployment rate of a certain minority group may exist within the firm's service area. A philosophy of hiring workers who are capable of being trained as opposed to hiring only qualified applicants may work toward reducing unemployment. In the long-run this philosophy may actually improve profitability. It is extremely difficult for an individual to purchase the firm's products or services when he or she is unemployed. Human resources managers are becoming more involved in social responsibility issues.

Unions

Unions consist of organization members who have joined together for the purpose of presenting a united front in dealing with management. Unions are an external environmental factor because they essentially become a third party when dealing with the company. It is the union rather than the individual employee that negotiates an agreement with the firm. Unions are a major force which exerts pressure upon an organization. In the past, most unions have served blue collar workers. Although government estimates project some stabilization in the number of blue collar workers (see Figure 2–8), this should not be regarded as an indication of a coming decline in unionizing efforts. Job categories which have traditionally resisted unionization are not immune to such activity. For instance, inroads have been made into white collar and other professional jobs that heretofore were considered unlikely candidates for unionization. Unions have been formed in such traditionally nonunion professions as nursing and school teaching. Even though a firm is not currently un-

Figure 2–8. **Projected workers employed by white-collar, blue-collar, service, and farm.**

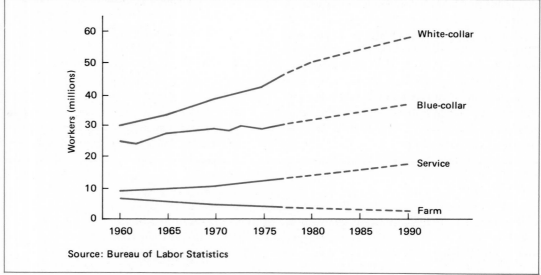

Source: Bureau of Labor Statistics

41

Chapter 2
The
Environment of
Human
Resources
Management

"My advice to the college senior who desires a career in the field of Personnel is to recognize that businesses are in business to achieve business-related goals. The personnel function should be performed in a way that supports and facilitates those goals. Enter the company in any job you can get. Line experience is very important; don't be afraid to start there or to spend time during your career in a line responsibility. For example, our most effective sales representative recruiters (who are part of our total personnel activities) have personal sales experience in their background. Perform every job to the very best of your ability, for this is the way you get the attention of management. Seek job changes that broaden your experience within and outside the personnel function. I personally believe we have not done enough cross–fertilization between our personnel function and line operations, specifically, and between staff, generally, and line operations."

Stanley W. Thiele, Senior Vice President,
Administrative Services 3M

ionized, its management must be alert to conditions within the firm which could provide a rallying point for a union's formation.

Stockholders/Owners

Individuals who share in a corporation's profit (or loss) are referred to as stockholders or owners. As such, these individuals are vitally interested in the firm's operating effectiveness. The price of the stock and the dividends paid are also of major concern to stockholders. Although managers operate the firm, they must constantly be sensitive to this group's needs, because they actually own the company.

Because of the monetary investment of stockholders/owners in the firm, programs considered beneficial to the organization may at times be challenged. Managers may be forced to justify the merits of a particular program in terms of how it will affect future profits. For instance, if it is recommended that $50,000 be spent for implementing a management development program, the program may need more justification than merely stating that "managers should become more open and adaptive to the needs of employees." Stockholders/owners will likely be more concerned with how this expenditure relates to increased revenues or reduced costs. Management must be prepared to explain the merits of a particular program in terms of cost/benefits.

Competition

Unless an organization is in the unusual position of monopolizing the market it serves, other firms will be producing similar products or services. For a firm

WANTED

- $1,000 in cash,* less taxes, for the referral and subsequent hire of all exempt engineers and any technically related positions of non-exempt Grade 9 or above; i.e., technical writers, drafts-persons, etc.

- In order to qualify, the person referred must indicate the Ampex employee's name on the Ampex employment application under the column headed "Referred By," and Ampex must be free of any obligation to pay an agency or any other fee upon employment of the person.

- Non-eligible persons for this "bounty" are Department Managers, exempt Personnel Department employees, and managers directly involved in the selection of the person for the opening to be filled.

- New employee must be employed 180 days before "bounty" is paid.

$1000 REWARD

* Redwood City and Sunnyvale employees only

Figure 2–9. A recruitment poster. (Source: Ampex Corporation.)

to succeed, grow, and prosper, it must be able to maintain a supply of competent employees. But other organizations are also striving toward the same general objective. A firm's major task is to ensure that it obtains and retains a sufficient number of employees in various career fields. A bidding war often results when competitors attempt to fill certain critical positions in their firms. Because of the strategic nature of their needs, firms are sometimes forced to resort to unusual means to recruit and retain critical employees. The poster you see in Figure 2–9 illustrates the extreme approaches that some organizations have used to recruit qualified workers.

On the other hand, because of the competitive nature of many businesses, organizations may feel that they are under considerable pressure to improve their compensation system. In order to meet this challenge, firms not only are improving their salaries but also are emphasizing other forms of rewards. Thus the overall working environment may need to be considered as a portion of the firm's total financial compensation program.

43

Chapter 2
The
Environment of
Human
Resources
Management

Customers

The people who actually use a firm's products and services also must be considered a part of the external environment. Because sales are critical to the firm's survival, management has the task of assuring that its employment practices do not antagonize the members of the market it serves. There have been instances of consumer boycotts when organizations have limited the number of minorities they employ. Thus, legal requirements are not the only consideration when determining the firm's workforce composition. If a certain minority or ethnic group purchases a large share of the firm's products, it may be in the best interests of the organization to make sure that a representative proportion of this group is included within its work force.

Customers are constantly demanding high quality products and improved service. Therefore, the firm must always strive to have a work force that is capable of providing these products and services. Sales are often lost or gained because of product quality which is directly related to the skills and qualifications of the organization's employees.

Technology: The State of the Art

Rapid change has been a significant factor in placing personnel managers in the forefront of organizational decision making. Few firms operate today as they did twenty years ago. Today, change is being experienced at an ever increasing pace. Of major concern is the effect that technological or state of the art changes have had on businesses. Frederick W. Bahl, director of personnel administration for Alumax, Inc., believes that "During the next decade, the most challenging area in personnel and human resources management will be training employees to stay up with rapidly advancing technology." Products that were not envisioned only a few years ago are now being mass produced. This has caused the task of all managers to be substantially enlarged. New skills are needed to meet new technology demands. These skills are typically not in large supply and it often becomes difficult to recruit qualified individuals.

As technological changes occur, certain skills are no longer required. This necessitates some retraining of the current work force. For instance, many colleges and universities have experienced enrollment decreases in certain fields of study. To offset these changes, some have begun to cross-train some of their instructors into fields that are experiencing a high level of demand. Math teachers, for instance, are taking additional courses to prepare themselves to teach data processing. Also because of the rapid change, some firms have been forced to emphasize job specialization. This process permits jobs to be broken down into smaller components in order that they may be performed by less skilled employees. However, this approach appears to be a two-edged sword. As jobs are specialized, employee motivation may become a problem.

The External Environment: Tying It Together

The external environment is comprised of those factors which affect a firm's human resources from outside the organizational boundaries. Predominant external factors include: legal considerations, the labor force, the public, unions, stockholders/owners, competition, customers, and technology. Each of these, considered separately or in combination, can result in constraints upon human resources management. For instance, if there are insufficient qualified applicants in the labor force, the firm may have to develop an extensive training program to prepare new workers to perform the required tasks. Or technology may change, requiring that the firm now select and train a new type of work force. The combinations are virtually unlimited. Without adequate attention to the external environment, effective human resources management would be virtually impossible.

THE INTERNAL ENVIRONMENT

The internal environment also exerts considerable pressure upon human resources management. As indicated in Figure 2–1, the primary internal factors include the firm's objectives (mission), company policies, and organizational climate. These factors determine the interaction between human resources management and other departments within the organization.

Company Objectives or Mission

Objectives are the end results which we strive to achieve. For an organization, the overriding objective which describes a firm's reason for existence is referred to as its mission. The specific **company mission** must be regarded as a major internal factor which affects the tasks of human resources management. Consider the following two broad-based company objectives and envision how related tasks might differ from one firm to another. Company A has the goal of being a leader in the industry with respect to technological advances. Growth occurs through the pioneering of new products and processes. On the other hand, Company B's goal is one of conservative growth with little risk taking. Only after another company's product or process has proven itself in the marketplace will Company B commit itself.

In Company A, the firm will need a creative environment which would encourage new ideas. Highly skilled workers must be recruited and selected to bring about technological advancement. Constant attention to the training and development of the work force is essential. A compensation program designed to retain and motivate the most productive workers is especially important.

45

Chapter 2
The
Environment of
Human
Resources
Management

The basic tasks of Personnel remain the same for Company B but the mission dictates that they be altered somewhat. A different kind of work force will likely be needed. Highly creative individuals may not want to work for Company B. Perhaps because the mission encourages little risk taking, most of the major decisions will be made higher in the organization. Thus, there may be less emphasis on management development at lower levels in the organization. The compensation program may be different to reflect the requirements of this particular work force.

As the above example illustrates, the overall company mission can exert a significant influence on Personnel's job. Personnel managers must have a clear understanding of the company mission before attempting to direct their departments' activities.

Policies

A general statement which guides thinking in decision making is referred to as a policy. **Policies** establish parameters which assist people in the organization as they go about accomplishing their jobs. Policies are also flexible in that they generally require some interpretation and judgment in their use. As such, they can exert significant influence on how managers accomplish their jobs. For instance, many firms have an "open door" policy which permits employees to bypass the immediate supervisor and take a problem to the next higher level in the organization. Knowing that a subordinate can speak to a higher level manager may encourage supervisors to try harder at resolving problems with subordinates.

Many larger firms have policies related to every major area of their operations. While policies are established for marketing, production, and finance, often the largest number of policies relate to human resources management. Some potential policy statements which could affect the work of the personnel manager are listed below:

- To provide employees with a place of work that is as safe as possible
- To encourage all employees to achieve as much of their human potential as possible
- To provide compensation which will encourage a high level of performance in the form of increased quality and quantity of production
- To work aggressively toward ensuring that all members of the labor force have equal opportunity for employment.
- To ensure present organizational members are considered first for any vacant position

The last policy listed above is often referred to as a "promotion from within" policy. This type of guideline aids managers when they are faced with promotion decisions. However, since policies have a degree of flexibility, the manager is not necessarily required to promote an employee currently with the firm. The supervisor may determine, for example, that no one in the firm is qualified and choose to look outside the firm for a replacement.

The tone of a policy can assist personnel managers as they perform their daily activities. Consider, for instance, the policy to ensure "that all members of the labor force have equal opportunity for employment." This policy implies more than merely adhering to certain government regulations. Confronted with this policy, the personnel manager will likely do more than merely conform to the laws. Perhaps a training program will be initiated to permit hiring of minorities or women who are not totally qualified to perform available jobs. Rather than just look for qualified applicants, a firm with this policy has gone beyond what is required by law.

Organizational Climate

Just as the climate of Hawaii may be described as warm and pleasant, the climate of Company XYZ may be generally open and supportive. There are also companies with climates comparable to Antarctica. As an internal environmental factor affecting Personnel, **organizational climate** is defined as the firm's psychological environment. An infinite number of possible climates exist and they might be viewed as a continuum. A closed and threatening climate is at one extreme. In this type of climate, decisions tend to be made higher in the organization. There tends to be a lack of trust and confidence in subordinates. Secrecy abounds throughout the firm, and workers are not encouraged to be creative and engage in problem solving activities. At the other extreme of the continuum there is an open climate in which decisions tend to be made at lower levels in the organization; a high degree of trust and confidence in subordinates exists; open communication is encouraged and workers are encouraged toward creativity and solution of problems with other team members.

Identification of the type of climate that exists within a firm is important because it affects job performance throughout the organization. A redeeming characteristic regarding organization climate is that it is determined by factors largely within the control of management.[3] Three major factors which influence a firm's organizational climate are communication effectiveness, motivational techniques, and leadership styles. There are ways by which communications in the firm can be improved. Motivational techniques and leadership styles can perhaps be tailored to meet specific organizational needs. The organization's climate, as perceived by the firm's employees, can either serve to encourage productivity or be potentially devastating to the organization's survival.[4] Because of the many different factors constantly confronting the personnel manager, it is likely that he or she could function better in the

[3]Abraham K. Korman, *Organizational Behavior* (Englewood Cliffs, NJ: Prentice-Hall, Inc., 1977), pp. 119–120.
[4]William R. LaFollette, "How is the Climate in Your Organization?" *Personnel Journal* 54 (July 1975): 376.

more open climate. The following sections will describe and illustrate the communication, motivational, and leadership factors of organizational climate.

47

Chapter 2
The
Environment of
Human
Resources
Management

Communication Effectiveness

Effective communication involves transmitting a message or idea in a manner that will be understood by the receiver. All managers must communicate effectively if they are to be successful. In fact, it has been estimated that 80 percent of poor management decisions occur because of ineffective communication.[5] Effective organizational communication has a positive influence on organizational climate. In addition, good communication in the organization enhances a manager's ability to accomplish his or her job successfully. Effective communication can have a substantial impact upon a firm's growth and profits. John Kasper, President of Elco Industries, stated, "We have our communication department, with a fulltime group working to refine communication with our people. They're going out on the plant floor to ask questions and get opinions."[6] To reinforce successful communication throughout the firm, Elco Industries has created a position of corporate director of communication which reports directly to the president.

Many companies, including Elco Industries, recognize that there are many ways communication can break down. Fortunately the ability to communicate effectively can be learned. Individuals who are willing to exert the effort to improve their communication ability can benefit from aids that are readily available. Some factors to be considered in improving a person's communication ability are described below.

Empathy. The ability to identify with another person's feelings and thoughts is referred to as **empathy.** As such, it is a quality that most successful managers possess. Empathy is reflected by this attitude: "Although I may not agree with you, I can understand why you think as you do." Managers may have different backgrounds, experiences, and personalities than their employees. However, when working with an employee they should attempt to view the situation as the worker does. Even if a worker is mad at the boss for a reason that the manager believes to be unfounded, a good communicator is able to relate to the employee's bitterness and perhaps work to ease existing tensions. For instance, a foreman who has recently been passed over for promotion may come to Personnel disappointed and with a feeling of failure. The personnel manager should be able to identify with this sense of defeat even though he or she realizes that a more qualified person was promoted.

Effective communication is significantly enhanced through development of empathy. The empathic individual identifies with people in order to understand why they behave as they do. You do not have to agree with the person's

[5]"If They Just Don't Seem to Get the Message," *Changing Times* 24 (June 1970): 39.
[6]Keith W. Bennett, "Communication and Costs Can Alter the Bottom Line," *Iron Age* 221 (June 26, 1978): 28.

views. But, if you are able to identify with an employee's perception of the situation, the stage is set for effective communication.

Listening. More problems are solved by listening than by talking. As such, listening is recognized as a useful communication facilitator. Listening consists of total involvement in what the speaker is saying. The effective listener hears the words that are spoken but also notices the different voice inflections and the body language used, as well as word selection. Effective listening requires that the full attention of the receiver be devoted to the sender.[7]

When an employee comes to the supervisor with a problem, the manager may find it best to allow the employee to describe the complete situation prior to commenting. Often workers will solve their own problems if they only have someone who will listen. But, even if employees are not capable of solving the problem themselves, the supervisor who listens attentively is in a much better position to assist in its solution.

Effective listening permits a manager to have the time to read between the lines of a conversation. For instance, the words that are said in committee meetings may take a different meaning than what was actually said. The statement, "We can get the work done without any more employees" can have significantly different meanings based strictly on voice inflections. Taken one way, the manager is saying that no problems are anticipated. Interpreted another way, the individual is stating, "I really don't think it can be done, but if you say it has to be accomplished with this number of employees, we will try."

Observation. It has been said that, "We see what we want to see." Most of us do not use our power of observation to its fullest even though it is a most effective form of communication. The husband who notices, or fails to notice, his wife's new hair style is communicating. The supervisor is communicating by observing that a particular worker keeps a clean shop and produces a good quality product. The art of observation is important for all managers. Merely walking through the plant or office and observing employees can uncover many problems. There may be an attitude of displeasure or unrest among workers even though they greet you cordially. If a person is able to combine the qualities of empathy, listening, and observation, the ability to communicate effectively is greatly enhanced.

Body Language. The nonverbal method of communication through which our physical actions—motions, gestures, and facial expressions—convey our thoughts and emotions is referred to as **body language.**[8] The need to understand the importance of body language in communication is closely tied to the need to be an effective observer. If a person understands the meaning of body language, communication can be significantly improved even though no words

[7]Warren K. Heckman, "How to Communicate With Meaning," *Pipeline and Gas Journal* 204 (July 1977): 48.
[8]George R. Parulski, Jr., "Silent Conversations: A Study of Nonverbal Communication," *Supervision* 41 (January 1979): 7.

are spoken. The astute manager can determine that an employee is upset over a situation without the worker saying that a problem exists. A worker's blank stare may mean that the individual's mind is on things other than the present job.

A manager should make a conscious effort to avoid sending unintentional signals that employees could misinterpret. For instance, even though on a given day the personnel manager may not feel as energetic as normal, he or she must realize that a depressed appearance might be interpreted by employees as suggesting that a problem exists. It has been said that personnel department members must think of themselves as working in a goldfish bowl. Whatever Personnel does, or fails to do, is noted by workers throughout the firm. A frown by the personnel director may take a different meaning than was intended. Employees often misinterpret these small signals, viewing them from different perspectives.

Word Choice. The words chosen by the sender must be understandable to the receiver if effective communication is to take place. Thus, simple or common words provide the best means of achieving effective communication. As a rule, the simpler the words and sentence structure, the likelier the message will be understood by a wide variety of people.

Motivation

Motivation refers to the goal-directed behavior of individuals. Management's job is to provide an organizational climate in which employee behavior can be constructively oriented toward task performance.

Around the turn of the century, employees were believed to be motivated entirely by money. This simplistic version of motivation seemed valid at the time and the idea is by no means dead today. However, managers of human resources in the 1980s must also consider other motivational factors. Employee needs and values have changed dramatically during the past three-quarters of a century. Individuals no longer work for pay alone. Rewards, in addition to pay, are expected from the employment relationship.

Managers do not actually motivate their employees. Motivation is internal to the individual and stems from perceived needs which serve as motives. These motives activate behavior that may result in the satisfaction of perceived needs. Motivation cannot be viewed directly; as with the wind, only the results are observed.

People in our society have a multitude of needs, many of which may be satisfied (or thwarted) on the job. Management has traditionally relied upon numerous theories of motivation to provide generalizations which have been helpful in understanding human motivation. Recently, however, greater attention has been directed toward understanding the wants and needs of individuals. What generally serves to motivate one person effectively may not apply to another worker. Today's personnel professionals recognize that in order to achieve an appropriate organizational climate conducive to productivity, em-

49

Chapter 2
The
Environment of
Human
Resources
Management

Robert L. Berra
Senior Vice President, Administration
Monsanto Company

There was never any doubt in Bob Berra's mind about what profession he would pursue as a career. "Personnel played to my strengths as I perceived them," he says. "I felt I had strong communcations skills and an ability to sense the meaning behind complex relationships—in other words, being able to cut through to what people really say and mean."

Mr. Berra received a B.S. degree in commerce and finance from St. Louis University in 1947 and an M.B.A. degree from the Harvard Graduate School of Business Administration that same year. "I took all the courses in personnel administration that Harvard offered at the time—both of them," he notes. He has also done graduate work in psychology at Washington University in St. Louis. He joined Monsanto in 1951 as assistant training manager for the company's Springfield, Massachusetts, plant and subsequently served there as employee relations manager, director of sales training, and director of sales administration. In 1959 he was appointed director of personnel for the Plastic Products and Resins Division. He was appointed director of administration for the division in 1966 and was named assistant director of the Corporate Personnel Department in 1967.

From 1970 to 1974, Mr. Berra was em-

ployees' personal needs must be reasonably satisfied. For example, the concept of flexible compensation, discussed in Chapter 12, involves allowing workers to essentially select their pay package from several options. Some employees may need additional insurance whereas others may desire additional vacations.

Leadership Styles

Leadership involves the directing and influencing of other individuals' activities. Managers have different personalities, backgrounds, goals, and experiences. Therefore, the manner in which they attempt to influence their employees may be quite different and can affect the organizational climate of the firm.

Many experts suggest that a "situational approach" to leadership is needed to cope with today's rapidly changing business environment. This means that the specific situation—comprised primarily of the interrelationships that exist between the manager, subordinates, and the tasks to be performed—dictates the best approach to leadership. The most effective leadership style is one which is best adapted to the particular situation (see Figure 2–10).

ployed by Foremost-McKesson, Inc., as corporate vice president of personnel and public relations. He rejoined Monsanto in 1974 as vice president of personnel and was named senior vice president, administration in 1980. As the "chief morale officer," as he describes it, for an organization of 57,000 employees worldwide, Mr. Berra is responsible for all personnel policies and programs, the Corporate Marketing Department, and the Corporate Public Affairs Department. He is a prolific author of articles in the area of management and motivation and has served as guest lecturer at numerous universities.

He is a past president of the Industrial Relations Association of Greater St. Louis and a past president and member of the Executive Committee of the American Society for Personnel Administration. "Monsanto gets first call on my time, but you have to feel strongly enough about your profession to take the time to contribute to it," he says. He also serves on the Board of Directors of Fisher Controls International, Inc., on the Advisory Council of St. John's Mercy Medical Center in St. Louis, and works with other civic organizations.

Mr. Berra has witnessed and participated in the evolution of the personnel function from specialty area to profession and senior management responsibility. "Today," he says, "the personnel executive wears many hats: manager, member of top management, advisor, employee representative, corporate officer, and professional. The successful human resources executive must be intelligent, sensitive, and healthy enough to handle the pressures. He has to be willing to stand up and be counted when the chips are on the line. Above all, he has to exercise good judgment and then make things happen." An essential element of good judgment, he says, is to seek "in-depth exposure to all parts of the organization to assure properly balanced decisions."

He stresses the importance of getting the right experience at the right time, forcing the issue if necessary. "In most careers, it's necessary to do this only once or twice; but when the need is obvious, don't delay."

The Leader. Leaders have different abilities, personalities, experiences, and expectations. They develop different approaches to accomplishing tasks because of these differences. They will likely continue to use a certain approach in the future if their experiences indicate that it was successful in the past. For ex-

Figure 2–10. **A situational approach to leadership.**

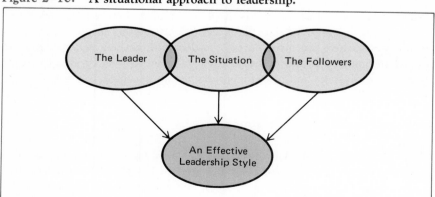

ample, a person who has been successful in utilizing the ideas of subordinates will tend to continue this leadership approach. Leaders should adapt their style to meet the needs of the followers and the situation. This does not mean that their basic assumptions about people change. They recognize that their effectiveness as a leader may be improved if they adapt their style to the situation.

The Followers. Followers also have different abilities, personalities, experiences, and expectations. They do not automatically obey orders given by supervisors. Followers accept orders when they believe them to be in their best interests. As a student, you will likely follow a teacher's instructions if you feel that it will assist you to prepare for the next exam.

The type of subordinates can affect a person's leadership style. If the followers are inexperienced and do not want more responsibility, an autocratic style may be most effective. Followers who are better educated and experienced and who seek responsibility will likely respond more readily to a participative style. A manager must consider the needs, goals, capabilities, and experiences of the followers in order to lead the group effectively.

The Situation. The situation that managers confront can also have a significant effect upon the type of leadership style that will prove most effective. Many of the external and internal environment factors may cause a leadership style to be altered. For instance, a firm's policies may encourage a more autocratic style among its managers. A manager may be forced to adapt his or her style to the needs of the situation.

We must also remember that each manager's style within the firm may be somewhat different due to a number of factors. An organization's overall leadership approach must be stated in general terms. For example, a firm may generally exhibit autocratic leadership even though there may be some highly participative managers in the company.

At the same time, when describing an individual manager's leadership style, we refer to a dominant style. A manager may, for example, normally stress employee participation. However, when the building is on fire, he or she may issue an order, "Get out of here *now* through exit number 2." The leader does not consult anyone about this decision and no committees are formed to study the problem. The leader has simply reverted to a more autocratic style. The situation has required that the leader quickly respond to the situation. In organizations, there are many "fires." Leaders who develop a high degree of mutual trust and confidence within their work group will be able to adjust their leadership styles and have them more readily accepted.

Organizational Climate: In Retrospect

We have already stated that a firm's psychological environment is referred to as organizational climate. We have also stressed the importance of effective communication, motivational techniques, and leadership styles as primary determinants of organizational climate. But you should remember that it is not just any one of these factors taken separately that determines a firm's climate. The means by which communication takes place in an organization can have an impact upon leadership styles and vice versa. Motivational techniques can affect communication. And, just to add another point of confusion to the understanding of climate, there may be other underlying factors that can affect climate. For instance, policy statements can be communicated in such a way that they may elicit either a negative or positive response. In any event, the type of climate existing in an organization can significantly influence human resources management.

53

Chapter 2
The
Environment of
Human
Resources
Management

QUALITY OF WORK LIFE

During the past decade, a concept which has many implications for human resources management has emerged and received much attention. This concept is called **quality of work life** (QWL). QWL is defined as the extent to which employees satisfy significant personal needs through their organizational experiences. The following description suggests the basic philosophy for many such programs. Improvements in quality of work life stem from activities occurring at every organizational level which seek greater effectiveness through enhancing human dignity and growth.[9]

Firms which have QWL programs must first determine the goals they wish to seek. Therefore, it is difficult to cite a list of appropriate activities as with, for example, management by objectives (MBO) programs. The goals and actions undertaken are the joint responsibility of management, the union, and members of the organization.

Certain guidelines may be helpful in initiating QWL efforts. These guidelines include:

- QWL improvement efforts are not short-term quick fix programs which should be undertaken lightly.
- Organizations must forge new definitions of "how we work in this organization" when initiating QWL efforts.
- QWL improvement efforts require the willing participation and involvement of people at all levels of the organization.
- QWL improvement efforts require the commitment of organization leaders. This goes beyond the rhetoric of endorsement and support and must be demonstrated daily.
- QWL improvement efforts enable organizations to communicate and integrate their strategic goals into the day-to-day operations of the business.
- QWL improvement efforts are most effective when management and labor leaders work with their constituencies to examine and resolve inter-

[9]Lee M. Ozley and Judith S. Ball, "Quality of Work Life: Initiating Successful Efforts in Labor-Management Organizations," *Personnel Administrator* 27 (May 1982): 27.

nal issues before moving to cooperative problem solving in joint committees. Management's demonstrated commitment in addressing its own issues and barriers contributes substantially to supportive and responsible behaviors and actions on the part of others within the organization.

- QWL improvement efforts represent new approaches and processes in most organizations. These processes are never static and require constant attentiveness and responsiveness to developments as they occur.[10]

As you can see, a multitude of activities might be considered appropriate for a specific QWL program. They might include everything from emphasizing performance appraisal systems to counseling programs or perhaps developing a more open approach to organizational communication.

SUMMARY

Human resources managers interact with other managers as they strive to achieve the goals of the organization. In a sense, all managers are managers of human resources. Personnel's job is not accomplished in a vacuum. There are many interacting factors affecting the performance of specific tasks which can be subdivided under two primary headings: (1) the external environment and (2) the internal environment.

The external environment consists of those factors which affect a firm's human resources from outside the organizational boundaries. Major external factors include: government legislation, customers, unions, the public, technology, the labor force, competition, and stockholders/owners. The primary internal factors include company objectives, company policies, and organizational climate. In addition, personnel professionals constantly work with people from other functional areas such as marketing, production, and finance. They must understand the different perspectives of people from various disciplines in order to perform their tasks.

Understanding the many interrelationships implied in the model is quite important as the personnel professional works with other managers to assist them in resolving their daily problems. The effect of a particular act must be considered in light of its impact upon the entire organization. The model provides a framework which emphasizes the big picture rather than concentrating upon a narrow phase of the company's operation.

The basic tasks assigned the personnel activity remain essentially the same no matter what impact is exerted from either the external or internal environments. However, the manner in which they are accomplished may be altered substantially. None of the personnel functions should be studied without considering the results of a decision on each of the other functions.

[10]*Ibid.*, p. 33.

Questions for Review

1. What is meant by the statement, "The personnel manager's job is not accomplished in a vacuum?"

2. What factors comprise the external environment of human resources management? Briefly describe each.

3. How is the labor force of the United States expected to change by 1990?

4. What internal environment considera-

obj, policy, climate

tions exert pressure upon the accomplishment of Personnel's job?

5. How could changes in an organizational policy affect the personnel professional's work? Give an example.

6. Define organizational climate. What affect could climate have upon human resources management?

Terms for Review

External environment
Social responsibility
Unions
Company mission
Policies
Organizational climate

Empathy
Body language
Motivation
Leadership
Quality of work life (QWL)

As the largest employer in Ouachita County, Arkansas, International Forest Products Company (IFP) is an important part of the local economy. Ouachita County includes a mostly rural area of south central Arkansas. IFP employs almost 10 percent of the local work force and there are few alternative job opportunities available.

Scott Wheeler, the personnel director at IFP, tells of a difficult decision he had to make in December 1982.

"Everything was going along pretty well despite the economic recession, but I knew that sooner or later we would be affected. I got the word at a private meeting with the president, Mr. Deason, that we would have to cut the work force by 30 percent on a crash basis. I was to get back to him within a week with a suggested plan. I knew that my plan would not be the final one, since the move was so major. But I knew that Mr. Deason was depending on me to provide at least a workable approach.

"First of all, I thought about how the union would react. Certainly, workers would have to be let go in order of seniority. The union would try to protect as many jobs as possible. I also knew that all management's actions during this period would be intensely scrutinized. We had to make sure that we had our act together.

"Then there was the matter of the impact on the surrounding community. The economy of Ouachita County had not been in good shape recently. Aside from the impact on individual workers

who were laid off, I knew that our cutbacks would further depress the area's economy. I knew that there would be a number of government officials and civic leaders who would want to know how we were trying to minimize the harm done to the public in the area.

"We really had no choice but to make the cuts, I believed. First of all, I had no choice because Mr. Deason said that we were going to do it. Also, I had recently read a news account that one of our competitors, Johns Manville Corporation in West Monroe, Louisiana, had laid off several hundred workers in a cost cutting move. To keep our sales from being further depressed, we had to ensure that our costs were just as low as those of our competitors. The wood products market is very competitive and a cost advantage of even 2 or 3 percent would allow competitors to take many of our customers.

"Finally, a major reason for the cutbacks was to protect the interests of our shareholders. A few years ago we had a shareholder group which disrupted the annual meeting to insist that IFP make certain anti-pollution changes. In general, though, the shareholders seem to be more concerned with the return on their investment than with social responsibility. At our meeting the president reminded me that, just like every other manager in the company, I should place the shareholders' interest foremost. I really was quite overwhelmed as I began to work up a personnel plan which would balance all of the conflicting interests that I knew about."

Questions

1. List the elements in the company's environment which will affect Scott's suggested plan. How legitimate is the interest of each of these?

2. Is it true that Scott should be concerned first and foremost with protecting the interests of the shareholders? Discuss.

As the personnel director for KBH Stores in St. Louis, Missouri, Virginia Knickerbocker knew that she had her work cut out for her. Company management had just announced a goal of opening ten new stores during the next twelve months. KBH employed 480 people in the thirty-five stores they then had in operation. Virginia knew that staffing the new stores would require hiring and training about 150 people. She felt that her own small office was inadequately funded and staffed to handle such a level of operations.

Virginia found out about the expansion plans from a friend who knew the president's secretary. While she didn't like being kept in the dark, she was not surprised that she had not been told. Glenn Sullivan, the president of KBH, was noted for his autocratic leadership style. He tended to tell subordinates what he wanted them to know. He expected everyone who worked for him to follow orders without question. He wasn't an unkind person,

though, and Virginia had always gotten along with him pretty well. She had never confronted Mr. Sullivan about anything so it was with some concern that she approached his office that day.

"Mr. Sullivan," she began, "I hear that we are going to be opening ten new stores next year." "That's right, Virginia," said Mr. Sullivan, "we've already arranged the credit lines and have picked out several of the sites." "What about staffing?" asked Virginia. "Well, I presume that you will take care of that, Virginia, when we get to that point."

"What about my own staff?" asked Virginia, "I think I am going to need at least three or four more people. We are crowded already, too, so I hope you plan to expand the personnel office." "Not really," said Mr. Sullivan, "You will have to get by with what you have for at least a year or so. It's going to be hard enough to afford the new stores and the people we need to staff them."

Questions

1. Evaluate the environment Virginia faces within the company.

2. How does the internal environment affect Virginia's ability to do her job?

•

____ Appendix to Chapter Two ____

There are many laws and court decisions pertaining to Personnel which organizations must consider. This appendix provides an overview of the major legislation which influences human resources management. The specific manner in which government legislation impacts each personnel function is provided in the appropriate chapter.

LAWS PRIOR TO 1960

The public often assumes that the major impact of government laws and regulations began with the highly visible legislation of the 1960s. These laws continue to exert a significant impact upon human resources management. While the legislation passed after 1960 is important, previous enactments laid the groundwork for government's increased intervention into business practices. A few of the most significant interventions are briefly described below. Some of them will be discussed in greater detail in appropriate chapters.

Civil Rights Acts of 1866 and 1871

The 1866 Civil Rights Act is based on the Thirteenth Amendment and prohibits race discrimination in hiring, placement, and continuation of employment. Private employers, unions, and employment agencies are covered. The 1871 act is based on the Fourteenth Amendment and prohibits deprivation of equal employment rights under coverage of state law. State and local governments are included. In the case of *Brown* v. *Gaston County Dyeing Machine Company* (1972), the court ruled that a black was entitled to back pay for the period during which discrimination occurred. The time period involved was between 1960 and 1961, three years prior to the 1964 Civil Rights Act. There is virtually no effective statute of limitation in filing charges under these acts.[1]

Railway Labor Act of 1926

This law provided procedures for collective bargaining and for settling disputes between labor and management within the railroad industry. Although the act pertained to only one industry, it is important because of its pioneering provisions in the area of collective bargaining and settling disputes between labor and management.

Davis-Bacon Act of 1931

The Davis-Bacon Act requires that businesses holding federal construction contracts in the amount of $2000 or more pay their employees the rates offered

---

[1]Howard C. Lockwood, "Equal Employment Opportunities," in *Staffing Policies and Strategies* edited by Dale Yoder and Herbert G. Heneman (Washington, DC: Bureau of National Affairs, Inc., 1979), p. 4–252.

for similar jobs in the community in which the work is being performed. This act resulted in the establishment of a high minimum wage for workers because "union scale" is normally taken to be the prevailing wage rate.

59

Chapter 2
The
Environment of
Human
Resources
Management

Anti-Injunction Act of 1932

This act, also known as the Norris-LaGuardia Act, severely restricts the use of injunctions in labor disputes. It defines permissible union activities in very broad terms. As a result of this act, the private injunction ceased to be used effectively as a means to defeat strikes. It also made the **"yellow dog" contract** legally unenforceable. These contracts between the employee and employer prohibited a worker from joining a union or engaging in union activities.

National Labor Relations Act of 1935

The National Labor Relations Act (NLRA) of 1935 was passed at a time when the United States was emerging from a severe depression. This act, referred to as the Wagner Act, has become the cornerstone of employer-employee relations in the United States. For the first time, a federal law supported union organization on a broad scale and required employers to recognize unions and to bargain collectively with them over wages, hours, and other terms and conditions of employment. The act also created the National Labor Relations Board (NLRB). This board was given responsibility for conducting representation elections and investigating and dealing with employers' unfair labor practices.

Social Security Act of 1935—As Amended

This act established a federal tax to be placed on payrolls and provided for unemployment and retirement benefits. The act also set up the Social Security Administration. Employers were to share equally with employees the cost of old age, survivors, and disability insurance. Employers were required to pay the full cost of unemployment insurance.

Walsh-Healey Act of 1936

The Walsh-Healey Act covers employers with federal contracts of $10,000 or more for the manufacture or furnishing of materials, supplies, articles, and equipment. As with the Davis-Bacon Act, employers must pay wages at the same rate paid for similar jobs in the community in which the work is being done. In addition, the act requires that time-and-one-half be paid for all work in excess of eight hours in one day or forty hours in one week.

Fair Labor Standards Act of 1938

This act, known also as the Wage and Hour Law, requires payment of a minimum wage to all workers except domestic and government employees. It also requires overtime pay at one-and-one-half times the regular rate for work beyond the established maximum number of hours per work week, typically forty hours. The act also sets a minimum employment age. Subsequent amendments have extended the coverage of the act to an increasing number of employees.

Labor-Management Relations Act of 1947

Twelve years after the labor-oriented Wagner Act, Congress attempted to provide a more balanced approach to labor relations by passing this piece of legislation, even overriding a presidential veto. Also known as the Taft-Hartley Act, this law is an amendment to the Wagner Act. The act gives employees the right to refrain from union activities and denies supervisors legal protection in obtaining union recognition. It also forbids any activity by management which tends to encourage or discourage membership in any particular labor union.

Labor-Management Reporting and Disclosure Act of 1959

During the late 1950s, a series of Congressional investigations uncovered evidence of racketeering, crime, violence, and corruption by labor organizations and employers. As a result, the Labor-Management Reporting and Disclosure Act of 1959 (Landrum-Griffin Act) was passed. This far-reaching law was based upon congressional findings of a "need to eliminate or prevent improper practices on the part of labor organizations, employers, labor relations consultants, and their officers and representatives which distort and defeat the policies of the Labor Management Relations Act, 1947, as amended, and the Railway Labor Act, as amended." The act established very detailed federal regulation of the internal affairs of unions.

LEGISLATION AFTER 1960

The laws passed prior to 1960 were important because they initiated a new era of labor-management relations. These laws paved the way for a proliferation of legislation which has had a significant effect upon human resources management. Major legislation passed after 1960 will be described next.

Equal Pay Act of 1963—Amended 1972

The Equal Pay Act (an amendment to the Fair Labor Standards Act of 1938) made it illegal to discriminate in pay on the basis of sex where jobs require equal skills, effort, and responsibility and are performed under similar working conditions. Exceptions are permitted if the payment is made based on a seniority system, a merit system, or a system that measures earnings by quality or quantity of production. Pay differentials are also permitted if they are based on factors other than sex.

The 1972 amendments expanded the act to cover employees in executive, administrative, professional, and outside sales force categories as well as employees in most state and local governments, hospitals, and schools. The act was originally administered by the U.S. Department of Labor but became the responsibility of the Equal Employment Opportunity Commission (EEOC) in 1979. In recent years, the act has been less significant because a violation of the Equal Pay Act is also a violation of Title VII of the Civil Rights Act.

61

Chapter 2
The
Environment of
Human
Resources
Management

Title VII of the Civil Rights Act of 1964— Amended 1972

One law that has had extensive influence upon human resources management is Title VII of the 1964 Civil Rights Act, as amended by the Equal Employment Opportunity Act of 1972. This legislation prohibits discrimination based on race, color, sex, religion, or national origin. Women and minorities comprise the majority of people in what are called "protected groups."

Title VII covers employers engaged in an industry affecting interstate commerce with fifteen or more employees for at least twenty calendar weeks in the year in which a charge is filed, or the year preceding the filing of a charge. Included in the definition of employers are state and local governments, schools, colleges, unions, and employment agencies.

The act created the Equal Employment Opportunity Commission (EEOC) which is responsible for its enforcement. Under Title VII, filing a discrimination charge initiates EEOC action. Charges may be filed by one of the presidentially appointed EEOC commissioners, by any aggrieved person, or by anyone acting on behalf of an aggrieved person. Charges must be filed within 180 days of the alleged act. However, the time is extended to 300 days if a state or local agency is involved in the case.

Although there are certain exceptions to the law such as bonafide occupational qualifications (BFOQ) for sex, religion, and national origin, the impact of the law has been felt by virtually every organization. In enforcing the act, the EEOC has the potential to affect human resources management in numerous ways, such as:

- Employers must now actively recruit those in protected classes such as minorities and women.

- Movement of organizational and plant facilities must be assessed for impact upon minority employment levels.

- Advertisements in such media as radio and television must be adapted to conform to legal requirements.

- Interviews, application blanks, and tests may require validation or evidence that they relate to job requirements.

- Job descriptions, job specifications, and employee performance appraisals must be analyzed with regard to their impact upon protected groups.
- Special efforts must be made to train minorities and women.
- Employment benefits must be provided on an unbiased basis.

Age Discrimination in Employment Act of 1967— Amended 1978

The Age Discrimination Act prohibits employers from discriminating against individuals who are at least forty but less than seventy years old. The act pertains to employers with twenty or more employees for twenty or more calendar weeks (either in the current or preceding calendar year), unions of twenty-five or more members, employment agencies, and federal, state, and local government subunits. Administration of the act was transferred from the U.S. Department of Labor to the EEOC in 1979.

Enforcement may begin once a charge is filed or the EEOC can review compliance even if no charge is filed. The Age Discrimination Act differs from Title VII in that it provides for trial by jury and there is a possible criminal aspect to a charge. The trial by jury is important in that the jury may have greater sympathy for older people who have possibly been discriminated against. The criminal aspect means that an employee may receive more than lost wages if discrimination is proven. In addition, under the 1978 amendment, class action suits are possible.

The Occupational Safety and Health Act of 1970

In recent years, no law has been as controversial as the Occupational Safety and Health Act (OSHA). The intent of the law was to make work and the work environment free of hazards. However, the manner of implementation has been questioned on many occasions, especially during the early years following its passage. The act established the Occupational Safety and Health Administration (Occupational Safety and Health Review Commission), an agency of the Department of Labor, to set up regulations and standards covering safety and health. OSHA has taken a broad view of interpreting health and safety factors and virtually all companies are affected. Results of the act will be described in detail in Chapter 13.

The Vocational Rehabilitation Act of 1973

This act covers government contractors or subcontractors or organizations which receive federal grants in excess of $2500. The Office of Federal Contract Compliance Program (OFCCP) administers the act. If the contract or subcontract exceeds $50,000, or if the contractor has fifty or more employees, an affirmative action program must be prepared. The contractor must indicate what reasonable accommodations are being made in hiring and promoting handicapped persons.

This act is expected to have even more impact in the future. The definition of what constitutes "handicapped" has not been thoroughly tested by the courts. In some court decisions, epilepsy and alcoholism have been held to be covered under the act.

63

Chapter 2
The
Environment of
Human
Resources
Management

Federal Privacy Act of 1974

The Federal Privacy Act of 1974 is designed to protect the privacy of individuals by restricting access to files containing personal information. Although the act applies primarily to government agencies, it has gained the attention of human resources managers because of the potential for future laws with broader coverage.

Vietnam Era Veterans Readjustment Act of 1974

This act relates only to government contractors or subcontractors who have contracts with the federal government in the amount of $10,000 or more. It covers honorably discharged persons who have served more than 180 days on active duty between August 5, 1964, and May 7, 1975. To be covered by the act, the veteran must have been separated from the service within forty-eight months prior to the alleged discriminatory action. The Department of Labor is responsible for administering the act.

A major provision of the act is that virtually all employment openings must be listed with the state employment office. Employers with fifty or more employees who have received contracts for over $50,000 must maintain an affirmative action program.

Employee Retirement Income Security Act of 1974

Passed in 1974, the Employee Retirement Income Security Act (ERISA) is one of the most complex pieces of federal legislation. The purpose of the act is described in this manner:

> It is hereby declared to be the policy of this Act to protect . . . the interests of participants in employee benefit plans and their beneficiaries . . . by establishing standards of conduct, responsibility and obligations for fiduciaries of employee benefit plans, and by providing for appropriate remedies, sanctions, and ready access to the federal courts.[2]

Note that the word "protect" is used because the act does not force employers to create employee benefit plans. It does set standards in the areas of participation, vesting of benefits, and funding for existing and new plans. Numerous existing retirement plans have been altered in order to conform to this legislation.

[2]U.S. *Statutes at Large 88*, Part I, 93rd Congress, 2nd Session, 1974, p. 833.

Pregnancy Discrimination Act of 1978

Passed as an amendment to Title VII of the Civil Rights Act, the Pregnancy Discrimination Act became effective October 31, 1978. The act prohibits discrimination in employment based on pregnancy, childbirth, or complications arising from either. Pregnancy and childbirth must rank equally with other disabilities covered by fringe benefits. One broad effect of the act is that firms must now equalize their health insurance programs. Failing to hire or terminating a woman strictly on the grounds of pregnancy are prohibited. Mandatory leaves because of pregnancy are illegal.

Civil Service Reform Act of 1978

The Civil Service Reform Act of 1978 had a great impact on the structure and practice of federal personnel management. The act, and two related agency reorganization plans, resulted in the abolishment of the U.S. Civil Service Commission, the creation of the Office of Personnel Management and the Merit Systems Protection Board, and an expanded affirmative action mission for the EEOC. It also included the first federal collective bargaining law enacted by Congress since 1955.

STATE AND LOCAL LAWS

There are numerous state and local laws which affect human resources management. Many individual states (particularly those which are highly industrialized) have legislation on the books many years before Congress passes a comparable law. In other situations, federal laws predate state enactments and set the pattern for state laws.

A number of states and some cities have passed fair employment practice laws prohibiting discrimination on the basis of race, color, religion, sex, or national origin. Several states also have antidiscrimination legislation relating to the aged and the handicapped. However, when EEOC regulations conflict with state or local civil rights regulations, the legislation more favorable to the protected class will be followed.

Almost all states have minimum wage legislation and equal pay laws. Every state has some form of workers' compensation law. These plans vary greatly and are constantly changing. They typically provide benefits to workers or dependents in the case of job-related injuries, diseases, or death. Medical care and rehabilitation services are also usually provided. The total cost is borne by the employers although the method of insuring may vary from state to state.

Each state also has an unemployment compensation law. These programs are financed by taxing employers according to the extent they have contributed to the unemployment rolls. Eligible unemployed workers receive an amount that varies by state. Compensation is provided for a limited number of weeks.

A few states have enacted versions of the Wagner and Taft-Hartley Acts. Many have adopted legislation relating to other specific aspects of labor relations.

65

Chapter 2
The
Environment of
Human
Resources
Management

Effect of Laws Upon Human Resources Management

Federal laws and regulations impact the personnel functional areas in varying degrees. Notice that Figure A2–1 lists the particular function affected by each law. It is easy to see why the human resources workload has expanded so dramatically in recent years.

Figure A2–1. Federal laws affecting human resources management.

MAJOR FEDERAL LEGISLATION	PLANNING, RECRUITMENT, AND SELECTION	TRAINING AND DEVELOPMENT	COMPENSATION	SAFETY AND HEALTH	EMPLOYEE AND LABOR RELATIONS	PERSONNEL RESEARCH
Railway Labor Act					X	
Davis–Bacon Act			X			
Norris–LaGuardia Act					X	
National Labor Relations Act	X	X	X	X	X	X
Social Security Act			X			X
Walsh–Healey Act			X			
Fair Labor Standards Act			X	X		X
Labor-Management Relations Act	X	X	X	X	X	X
Labor-Management Reporting and Disclosure Act					X	X
Equal Pay Act			X			X
Civil Rights Act of 1964	X	X	X	X	X	X
Age Discrimination in Employment Act	X	X	X	X	X	X
Occupational Safety and Health Act				X		X
Vocational Rehabilitation Act	X	X	X	X	X	X
Vietnam Era Veterans Readjustment Act	X	X	X	X	X	X
Employees Retirement Income Security Act				X		X
Federal Privacy Act	X					
Pregnancy Discrimination Act	X	X	X	X	X	X

An executive orders (EO) is a directive issued by the President which has the force and effect of a law enacted by Congress. Many executive orders affect private sector organizations doing business with the federal government.

Figure A2–2.   **Equal employment opportunity employer information report (EEO–1).**

Standard Form 100
(Rev. 12/78)
O.M.B. No. 124-R0011
Approval Expires 12/79
100-210

EQUAL EMPLOYMENT OPPORTUNITY
EMPLOYER INFORMATION REPORT EEO-1

Joint Reporting Committee

- Equal Employment Opportunity Commission
- Office of Federal Contract Compliance Programs

Section A — TYPE OF REPORT
Refer to Instructions for number and types of reports to be filed.

1. Indicate by marking in the appropriate box the type of reporting unit for which this copy of the form is submitted (MARK ONLY ONE BOX).

(1) ☐ Single-establishment Employer Report

Multi-establishment Employer:

(2) ☐ Consolidated Report
(3) ☐ Headquarters Unit Report
(4) ☐ Individual Establishment Report (submit one for each establishment with 25 or more employees)
(5) ☐ Special Report

2. Total number of reports being filed by this Company (Answer on Consolidated Report only)_____

Section B — COMPANY IDENTIFICATION (To be answered by all employers)

OFFICE USE ONLY

1. Parent Company
   a. Name of parent company (owns or controls establishment in item 2) omit if same as label

a.

Name of receiving office | Address (Number and street)

b.

City or town | County | State | ZIP code
b. Employer Identification No.

2. Establishment for which this report is filed. (Omit if same as label)
   a. Name of establishment

c.

Address (Number and street) | City or town | County | State | ZIP code

d.

b. Employer Identification No. | (If same as label. skip.)

3. Parent company affiliation

(Multi-establishment Employers.
Answer on Consolidated Report only)

   a. Name of parent—affiliated company | b. Employer Identification No.

Address (Number and street) | City or town | County | State | ZIP code

---

Section C — EMPLOYERS WHO ARE REQUIRED TO FILE (To be answered by all employers)

☐ Yes ☐ No   1. Does the entire company have at least 100 employees in the payroll period for which you are reporting?

☐ Yes ☐ No   2. Is your company affiliated through common ownership and/or centralized management with other entities in an enterprise with a total employment of 100 or more?

☐ Yes ☐ No   3. Does the company or any of its establishments (a) have 50 or more employees AND (b) is not exempt as provided by 41 CFR 60-1.5, AND either (1) is a prime government contractor or first-tier subcontractor, and has a contract, subcontract, or purchase order amounting to $50,000 or more, or (2) serves as a depository of Government funds in any amount or is a financial institution which is an issuing and paying agent for U.S. Savings Bonds and Savings Notes?

NOTE: If the answer is yes to ANY of these questions, complete the entire form; otherwise skip to Section G.

A major executive order affecting human resources management is EO 11246 as amended by EO 11375. EO 11246 prohibited discrimination on the basis of race, color, creed, or national origin by contractors doing business with the federal government. It was later amended by EO 11375 which changed the word "creed" to "religion" and added sex discrimination to the

67

Chapter 2
The
Environment of
Human
Resources
Management

Figure A2–2   *(cont.)*

Section D — EMPLOYMENT DATA

Employment at this establishment--Report all permanent, temporary, or part-time employees including apprentices and on-the-job trainees **unless** specifically excluded as set forth in the instructions. Enter the appropriate figures on all lines and in all columns. Blank spaces will be considered as zeros.

JOB CATEGORIES	OVERALL TOTALS (SUM OF COL. B THRU K)	MALE					FEMALE				
		WHITE (NOT OF HISPANIC ORIGIN)	BLACK (NOT OF HISPANIC ORIGIN)	HISPANIC	ASIAN OR PACIFIC ISLANDER	AMERICAN INDIAN OR ALASKAN NATIVE	WHITE (NOT OF HISPANIC ORIGIN)	BLACK (NOT OF HISPANIC ORIGIN)	HISPANIC	ASIAN OR PACIFIC ISLANDER	AMERICAN INDIAN OR ALASKAN NATIVE
	A	B	C	D	E	F	G	H	I	J	K
Officials and Managers											
Professionals											
Technicians											
Sales Workers											
Office and Clerical											
Craft Workers (Skilled)											
Operatives (Semi-Skilled)											
Laborers (Unskilled)											
Service Workers											
TOTAL											
Total employment reported in previous EEO-1 report											

(The trainees below should also be included in the figures for the appropriate occupational categories above)

| Formal On-the-job trainees | White collar | | | | | | | | | | | |
| | Production | | | | | | | | | | | |

1. NOTE: On consolidated report, skip questions 2-5 and Section E.
2. How was information as to race or ethnic group in Section D obtained?
   1 ☐ Visual Survey   3 ☐ Other — Specify ....
   2 ☐ Employment Record   ....
3. Dates of payroll period used –

4. Pay period of last report submitted for this establishment

5. Does this establishment employ apprentices?
   This year?   1 ☐ Yes   2 ☐ No
   Last year?   1 ☐ Yes   2 ☐ No

Section E — ESTABLISHMENT INFORMATION

1. Is the location of the establishment the same as that reported last year?
   1 ☐ Yes   2 ☐ No   3 ☐ Did not report last year   4 ☐ Reported on combined basis

2. Is the major business activity at this establishment the same as that reported last year?
   1 ☐ Yes   2 ☐ No   3 ☐ No report last year   4 ☐ Reported on combined basis

OFFICE USE ONLY

e.

3. What is the major activity of this establishment? (Be specific, i.e., manufacturing steel castings, retail grocer, wholesale plumbing supplies, title insurance, etc. Include the specific type of product or type of service provided, as well as the principal business or industrial activity.

Section F — REMARKS

Use this item to give any identification data appearing on last report which differs from that given above, explain major changes in composition or reporting units, and other pertinent information.

Section G — CERTIFICATION (See Instructions G)

Check one
1. ☐ All reports are accurate and were prepared in accordance with the instructions (check on consolidated only)
2. ☐ This report is accurate and was prepared in accordance with the instructions.

Name of Certifying Official	Title	Signature		Date
Name of person to contact regarding this report (Type or print)	Address (Number and street)			
Title	City and State	ZIP code	Telephone Area Code / Number / Extension	

All reports and information obtained from individual reports will be kept confidential as required by Section 709 (e) of Title VII
WILLFULLY FALSE STATEMENTS ON THIS REPORT ARE PUNISHABLE BY LAW, U.S. CODE, TITLE 18, SECTION 1001

other prohibited items. This amendment became effective in 1968 with enforcement of EOs being given to the Department of Labor.

The agency with the power and responsibility for implementing EO 11246 is the Office of Federal Contract Compliance Program (OFCCP). The degree of control the government will impose depends upon the size of the contract. There are three levels involved. First, the lowest level of regulation begins if the contract is $10,000 or more. Here, the contractor merely agrees to adhere to the EO. The second level of regulation occurs if the contract is for $50,000 or more. Organizations in this category must also file an EEO-1 report (see Figure A2–2) and comply with the affirmative action program requirements. The affirmative action program is the major focus of the executive order. The program requires specific steps to guarantee equal employment opportunity. Specific goals and timetables for achieving equal employment must be developed.

The third level for government contractors is when a contract or subcontract is for $1 million or more. All the previous requirements must be met. In addition, an on-site pre-award compliance review is required. Unlike Title VII, under EO 11246 an investigation can be initiated without a charge being filed.

In the public sector, federal labor relations are also regulated by executive orders. EO 10988, which President Kennedy signed in 1962, is a most significant one. This order greatly expanded unionism in the federal government. It was designed to permit collective bargaining in the public sector. However, in this EO a strong management-rights clause was included and strikes were banned. A major test of this ban occurred in 1981 when the Professional Air Traffic Controllers Organization (PATCO) was decertified as a bargaining agent. Approximately 11,500 striking controllers had previously been fired. In 1982, PATCO filed for bankruptcy.

EO 10988 has subsequently been modified by EO 11491 (1969) and EO 11838 (1975). EO 11491 established new procedures and agencies to oversee federal labor relations. It created the Federal Labor Relations Council which reviews decisions of the Department of Labor and interprets the executive order implementation. EO 11838 further extends and clarifies collective bargaining rules in the federal service. Federal agencies are required to bargain with employees on all issues unless the agency can show compelling reason not to negotiate.

IMPACT OF GOVERNMENT LEGISLATION: AN EXAMPLE

The total impact of government legislation is expressed exceedingly well by the following example. As the example will show, theoretically the person could lose in eleven forums, yet still receive relief from the employer in the twelfth (see Figure A2–3).[3]

[3]Kenneth J. McCulloch, *Selecting Employees Safely Under the Law* (Englewood Cliffs, NJ: Prentice-Hall, Inc., 1981), pp. 7–8.

Figure A2–3. **Impact of government legislation: an example**

A minority female with a heart murmur who is over 40 and working in New York City for an employer who is a government contractor can precipitate legal or administrative action, or both, against that employer in twelve different forums because of alleged discrimination. Theoretically, she could lose in eleven forums, yet still receive relief from the employer in the twelfth.

She could accuse the employer of discrimination on the basis of race or sex under Title VII.,[4] thereby precipitating "enforcement" either by EEOC or herself. In any event, she would precipitate an investigation by such a charge.

She could accuse the employer of discrimination on the basis of age, under the Age Discrimination in Employment Act of 1967,[5] and thereby precipitate court enforcement action by EEOC or herself. At a minimum, this would cause an attempted conciliation by EEOC.

She could file a lawsuit in federal court on the basis of race discrimination under the Civil Rights Act of 1866, 42 U.S.C. *1981.

She could file a claim of discrimination under the Equal Pay Act of 1963,[6] and thereby precipitate court enforcement action by either EEOC or herself. At a minimum, this charge would trigger an investigation.

She could file a claim of discrimination based upon her status as "handicapped"[7] and precipitate court enforcement action by the U.S. Department of Justice or herself[8] under the Rehabilitation Act of 1973. The same charge could also precipitate sanctions against the employer under the Rehabilitation Act of 1973, and the rules and regulations issued pursuant to that law.[9] Thus, this charge would trigger an investigation that could lead to an administrative hearing and, alternatively, a federal court proceeding[10]—as two possible forums.

By filing a charge of discrimination with OFCCP claiming race or sex discrimination in violation of Executive Order 11246,[11] she could precipitate sanctions against the employer because the employer is a government contractor. At a minimum, this charge would trigger an investigation, and it could precipitate an administrative hearing or a federal court action by the federal government[12]—again, two possible forums.

She could file a charge of discrimination on the basis of race, sex, disability, or age with the New York State Division of Human Rights and thereby precipitate an investigation.[13] She can either go to court directly herself, or await the administrative proceedings and then appeal an adverse determination to court. The New York statute offers her two distinct forums.[14]

[4]42 U.S.C. **2000e et seq.
[5]29 U.S.C. **621 et seq. (now enforced by EEOC).
[6]29 U.S.C. *206(d) (Now enforced by EEOC).
[7]29 U.S.C. *701.
[8]In Carmi v. St. Louis Sewer District, 20 FEP Cases 162 (E.D.Mo.1979), the court recognized the individual's right of action, but ruled against the plaintiff on the merits. Carmi discusses the cases which have split on the issue of whether there is an independent right of action available to a private party under the Rehabilitation Act.
[9]41 C.F.R. *60–741.
[10]See Davis v. Bucher, 451 F.Supp.791 (E.D.Pa.1978).
[11]3 C.F.R. *339.
[12]See United States v. New Orleans Public Services, Inc., 553 F.2d 459 (5th Cir.1977), vacated and remanded, 436 U.S. 942 (1978).
[13]N.Y. Exec. Law **290–301 (McKinney 1972); 3 Empl. Prac. Guide (CCH) **26000 et seq.
[14]Under Section 291 of the New York State Human Rights Law, the opportunity to obtain employment without discrimination because of age, race, creed, color, national origin, sex, or marital status was recognized and declared to be a civil right. As such, it is enforceable by direct court action. Additionally, a complainant may follow the procedures outlined in Section 297, which leads to administrative action and possible court review.

continued

She can file a charge of discrimination based on age, sex, race, or disability with the New York City Commission on Human Rights and thereby precipitate an investigation and an administrative determination, with court review.[15]

She can file a charge of discrimination based on age, sex, race, or disability under the Mayor's Executive Order, thereby precipitating sanctions against the employer because the employer is a city contractor. At a minimum, this charge would lead to another investigation.

If the woman were a disabled veteran, she could file a charge of discrimination with OFCCP on that basis, thereby precipitating possible sanctions against the employer because it is a government contractor and, possibly, court action initiated by either the Department of Justice or herself, or an administrative hearing.[16]

If the woman were covered by a collective bargaining agreement, she could precipitate an arbitration if there were a nondiscrimination clause in the agreement, or a lawsuit, under the Labor-Management Relations Act, against the union and the employer.[17]

If the employer were a New York State defense contractor, a charge of discrimination on the basis of race could lead to investigation and criminal conviction of a misdemeanor.[18]

---

[15]The New York City Commission on Human Rights and its powers are described in the Administrative Code of the City of New York, **B1–1.0 et seq. Commissions such as the New York City Commission are allowed to exist pursuant to the General Municipal Law, Article 12–D, **239 et seq. That law, apparently, did not grant to cities full hearing and court enforcement powers. See General Municipal Law, *239–R. However, in interpreting the law, the New York Court of Appeals has ruled that the New York City Commission on Human Rights does have jurisdiction to decide a controversy raised by a discrimination claim. See Maloff v. City Commission on Human Rights, 38 N.Y.2d 329, 342 N.E.2d.563, 379 N.Y.S.2d 788 (1975).

[16]The possibility of a court enforcement proceeding by the Department of Justice is indicated by 41 C.F.R. *60–250.28(b). The possibility of an administrative hearing is indicated by 41 C.F.R. *60–250–29 and 41 C.F.R. *60–250.26(g) (3). The possibility of an independent right of action for an individual claiming to be aggrieved by a violation of the Vietnam Era Readjustment Act of 1974 is enhanced by the Supreme Court's decision in University of California Board of Regents v. Bakke, 438 U.S. 265 (1978), 17 EPD (CCH) #8402 (June 28, 1978).

[17]29 U.S.C. **141 et seq.

[18]See N.Y. Civ. Rights Law **44, 44a (McKinney 1976); 3 Empl. Prac. Guide (CCH) #26,105.

Source: Kenneth J. McCulloch, SELECTING EMPLOYEES SAFELY UNDER THE LAW, © 1981, pp. 7–8. Reprinted by permission of Prentice-Hall, Inc., Englewood Cliffs, New Jersey.

Figure A2–3.   (cont.)

SIGNIFICANT SUPREME COURT DECISIONS

Knowledge of the law is important to the personnel practitioner. However, much more than the words in the law itself must be understood. The manner in which the courts interpret the law is vitally important. This is continuously changing even though the law itself may not have been altered. Some of the more significant U.S. Supreme Court decisions will next be identified. A more in-depth interpretation of some of these decisions will be made in appropriate chapters.

Griggs v. Duke Power Company

A major decision affecting the field of personnel and human resources management was rendered on March 8, 1971. A group of black employees at Duke

Power Company had charged job discrimination under Title VII of the Civil Rights Act of 1964. In an eight-to-zero vote, the Supreme Court voted against Duke Power Company and said, "If an employment practice which operates to exclude Negroes cannot be shown to be related to job performance the practice is prohibited." A major implication of this decision is that if personnel practices eliminate a higher percentage of minority applicants, or women, or any other member of a protected group, the burden of proof is on the employer to show that the practice is job related. This one court decision affected the personnel practices of many firms.

71

Chapter 2
The
Environment of
Human
Resources
Management

Phillips v. Martin Marietta Corporation

In this case, the Court ruled that the company had discriminated against a woman because she had young children. The company had argued that it did not preclude all women from job consideration. Only those women with school-age children were not considered and this was a business requirement. Because the company was hiring males with school-age children, the argument was rejected.

Albemarle Paper v. Moody

In this 1975 case, the Supreme Court reaffirmed the idea that any test used in the selection process or in promotion decisions must be validated if it is found that its use has had an adverse impact on members of protected groups. The employer has the burden of proof for showing that the test is valid. Therefore, the employer must be prepared to show that any selection or promotion device actually measures what it is supposed to measure.

University of California Board of Regents v. Bakke

This highly publicized 1978 case introduced the question of reverse discrimination. The University had reserved sixteen places at the start of each beginning class for minority applicants. Allen Bakke, a white male, was denied admission to the medical school, even though he scored higher on the admission criteria than some minority members who were admitted. The Supreme Court ruled 5 to 4 in Bakke's favor. At the same time, however, it reaffirmed that race may be taken into account in admission decisions. As a result, Bakke was admitted to the university and received his degree in 1982.

Kaiser Aluminum and Chemical Company v. Webber

Brian Webber, a white male steelworker, was employed by Kaiser Aluminum and Chemical Company. He sued his employer and his union, the United Steelworkers, charging both with reverse discrimination after he was allegedly denied a place in an on-the-job training program exclusively because of his race. The company and the union had agreed that 50 percent of the positions in the training program were reserved for blacks. Even though Webber had more seniority than some black workers who were admitted to the program, he was denied admission. Although lower courts ruled that Kaiser's actions were illegal because they fostered reverse discrimination, the Supreme Court reversed the decision. It stated that because the affirmative action plan was voluntarily agreed to by the company and the union, it did not violate Title VII.

Washington v. Davis

This 1976 Supreme Court decision involved the hiring of police officers in Washington, D.C. At issue was a reading comprehension and aptitude test which was given to all police officer position applicants. The test sampled material that the applicants would learn in the training program. Also, there was a positive correlation between success in the training program and success on the job. However, blacks and women failed the test at a much higher rate than white males.

The Supreme Court ruled that unfair discrimination did not occur because the test was job related. A major conclusion was that if a test is specifically job related, it is not illegal if it discriminates against members of protected groups.

Connecticut v. Teal

In a 1982 5 to 4 Supreme Court decision, the Court appeared to reject the "bottom line" defense of statistics which show an overall racial balance in a company's hiring process. Although the full impact of the decision is yet to be determined, the decision seems to imply that simply hiring more women and minorities will not cancel adverse impact claims.

Chapter Objectives

1. Describe the process of job analysis and explain why it is the most basic human resources management tool.
2. State the most common method for conducting job analysis.
3. Describe the type of data which are gathered through job analysis.
4. Explain the components of a well designed job description and job specification.
5. State some alternative methods for conducting job analysis.
6. Describe how job analysis helps to satisfy various legal requirements.

Chapter 3 _____

Job Analysis

I'm having trouble figuring out what kind of machine operator you need, Mary," said John Anderson, the personnel director, "I've sent four people down who seemed to meet the requirements of the job description and you have sent each of them back." "I haven't even read the job description, John," said Mary Blackett, the supervisor, "What I'm concerned with is finding someone who can do the job, not just meet the requirements of the job description. I don't believe any of the people you have sent me can do the job."

John got the job description and went over it point by point with Mary. They discovered that either the job description never fit the job or the job had changed a great deal since the description was written. For example, the job description specified experience on an older model drill press while the one in use was a new digital machine. The new one really required less skill, but of a completely different type.

After going over the job description with Mary, John said, "I think you and I should work together to make sure that the job description actually describes the job." "Yes," said Mary, "We could have both saved ourselves a lot of time if we had done this beforehand."

The above situation reflects a very common problem in human resources management. The job description did not adequately indicate what duties and skills were needed to perform the job. Therefore, it became virtually impossible for John Anderson, the personnel director, to do his job. Job analysis was critically needed if the problem were to be resolved. As will be stressed throughout the book, job analysis is the most basic function of human resources management.

The chapter begins with a definition of job analysis and a description of its importance to the performance of all personnel functions. Next, job analysis methods and types of data gathered through the process are discussed. The use of job analysis in the preparation of job descriptions and job specifications is then explained. Finally, the legal implications of thorough job analysis are given.

JOB ANALYSIS: A BASIC PERSONNEL TOOL

A **job** consists of a group of tasks that must be performed if an organization is to achieve its goals. The job may require the services of one person, such as that of president, or the services of two hundred, as might be the case with clerk typists in a large firm.

In a work group consisting of a supervisor, two senior clerks, and four stenographers, there are three jobs and seven positions. There is a **position** for every individual in an organization. For instance, a small company might have twenty-five jobs for their seventy-five employees, whereas in a large company 2000 jobs may exist for 50,000 employees.

The process of determining the duties and skills required for performing jobs in the organization is referred to as **job analysis**. Job facts are gathered, analyzed, and recorded as the job exists. Also identified are qualifications required to perform the job such as skills, education, and experience. Job analysis is conducted after the job has been designed and is being performed. The job analyst does not normally have the responsibility of recording job facts as the job should exist.[1] That function is most often assigned to such people as industrial engineers or methods analysts.

Job analysis is the most basic human resources management tool. Without properly conducted job analysis, it would be difficult, if not impossible, to perform the other personnel functions satisfactorily. As suggested in Figure 3–1, job analysis information is used to prepare both job descriptions and job specifications.

Job descriptions specify the duties and responsibilities associated with a job. Job specifications state the knowledges, skills, and abilities a person will need to perform the job. Both job descriptions and job specifications will be discussed in greater detail later in the chapter.

[1]John C. Crystal and Richard S. Deems, "Redesigning Jobs," *Training and Development Journal* 37 (February 1983): 45.

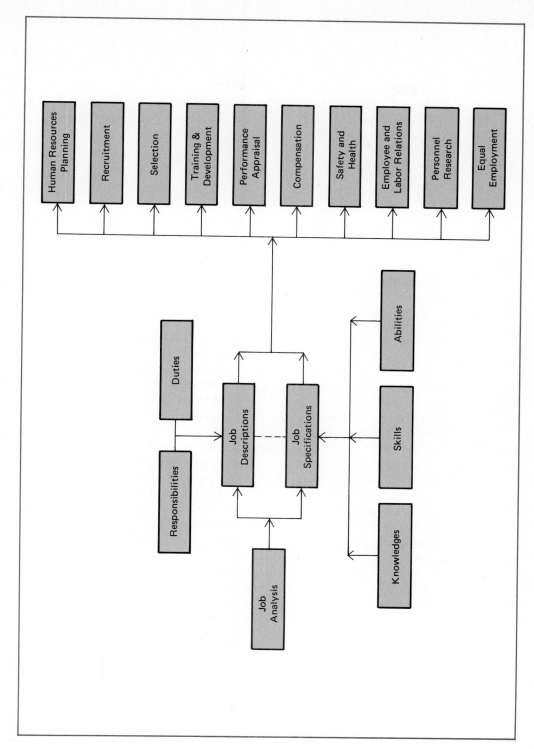

Figure 3–1. Job analysis: The most basic human resources management tool.

"In order to be effective as a personnel generalist, some solid operational/supervisory experience is essential. This helps the individual develop the ability to respond appropriately to issues involving the management of employees. Also, a record of success as a line manager helps the personnel executive establish credibility. It must be remembered that personnel people have little direct authority to exercise and that success is based on the ability to:

- Analyze
- Judge
- Influence or market judgments"

Mary Jean Wolf, Staff Vice President, Personnel and Compensation Trans World Airlines

Notice also in Figure 3–1 that job analysis information, in the form of job descriptions and job specifications, impacts virtually every aspect of human resources management. A major use of job analysis data is in the area of human resources planning. Merely knowing that the firm will need 1000 new employees to produce products and/or services to satisfy sales demand is insufficient. Each job requires different knowledges, skills, and ability levels. Planning must take this into consideration. Employee recruitment and selection would be haphazard if the qualifications needed to perform the job were not known. Without up-to-date job descriptions/specifications, employees would have to be recruited and selected for a job with no more guidelines than the implication that the new employee should be warm and breathing. Such a practice is unheard of in the procurement of raw materials, supplies, or equipment. Using the same logic, establishing specifications for human resources is also essential.

Job specification information often proves beneficial in identifying training and development needs. If the specification suggests that the job requires a particular knowledge, skill, or ability and the individual filling the position does not possess all of the qualifications required, T&D is likely in order. Training and development should be directed at assisting workers to perform duties specified in their present job descriptions or prepare them for promotion to higher level jobs.

With regard to performance appraisal, employees should be evaluated in terms of how well they accomplish the duties specified in their job description. An employer who evaluates an individual based upon factors not included in the job description is left wide open to allegations of discrimination.

In the area of compensation, we must know the relative value to the company of a particular job before a dollar value can be placed on it. The more significant the duties and responsibilities, the greater the job's relative worth. In addition, jobs that require greater knowledges, skills, and abilities should be worth more to the firm. For example, if the specification called for a masters degree as opposed to a high school diploma, the relative value would likely be higher.

Information initially derived from job analysis is also valuable to the safety and health function. Employers are required to state whether a job is hazardous. The job description/specification should satisfy this requirement. In addition, in certain hazardous jobs, workers may need specific information about the job in order to function safely in that environment.

Job analysis information is also important to employee and labor relations. When employees are considered for promotion, transfer, or demotion, the job description provides a standard for comparison of talent. Regardless of whether the firm is unionized, fair treatment is often based upon information obtained through job analysis.

When personnel research is undertaken, job analysis information provides the researcher with a starting point. For example, if we are trying to identify factors that distinguish successful from less successful employees, we need to study only those employees who have similar job descriptions/specifications. Otherwise it would be like mixing apples and oranges in performing the research.

Finally, the significance of having properly accomplished job analysis is particularly important when legal employment practices are considered. As will be seen in a later section of the chapter, job analysis data are needed in order to defend selection and promotion decisions. For this reason alone, job analysis is vital.

Thus far in our discussion, job analysis has been described as it pertains to each function of human resources management. In practice, there is considerable interrelationship among these functions. Job analysis is the basis for tying the functional areas together. It is insufficient to use job analysis information for compensation decisions and not use it for selection decisions. Job analysis is the foundation for a sound personnel program.

JOB ANALYSIS METHODS

Job analysis is performed on three occasions. First, it is needed when an organization is founded and the job analysis program is initiated. Second, it is used when a job is changed significantly as a result of new technology, methods, procedures, or systems. Third, it is performed when a new job is created. The U.S. Department of Labor projects that roughly one-third of the job openings during the 1980s will be for jobs that did not exist in the 1970s.[2]

Job analysis may be conducted in a number of ways. The most common methods are described next.

Questionnaires

Using questionnaires, the job analyst administers a structured questionnaire to employees who then identify the tasks they perform in accomplishing the job. Questionnaires are typically quick and economical to use. However, in some

[2]Robert E. Sibson, *Compensation* (New York: AMACOM, A Division of American Management Association, 1974), pp. 28–29.

Executive Profile

Joyce Lawson
Corporate Consultant—Human Resources Practice
General Electric Company

Human resources management has become increasingly complex, particularly in the past two decades. This complexity is reflected in the types of questions, concerns, and problems raised by management and employees, such as:

- Some of our businesses have job posting systems. Should we consider expanding open promotion systems to all businesses? What kinds of jobs should be included: hourly only, nonexempt and exempt salaried, some management, etc.? What are the key elements for a successful system?

- Turnover is increasing on job X. Why are employees leaving? Are there selection procedures we can use to identify those employees who will stay or those who will leave? Can a test publisher send something for us to use? What do the government's selection guidelines say about this?

- Companies with performance appraisal systems for professional employees usually have *one*. Our many businesses have developed their own, so we have *many* systems. Should we establish one system to be applied company-wide? Are the various systems working? Can they work more effectively?

- The cost of transferring an employee has increased dramatically. The cost to the employee has increased as well. "Quality of life" issues are affecting employees' willingness to transfer. Are these factors influencing the company's ability to transfer required skills? Should we be doing anything more or different?

These questions and others like them are asked of Joyce Lawson, a corporate consultant with General Electric Company, by operating business managers, personnel professionals, and corporate management. Her responses are based on twenty years of experience in virtually every function of the human resources management profession. As a corporate consultant, Ms. Lawson advises General Electric's operating businesses on such diverse procedures as reductions-in-force, performance appraisal systems, selection, promotion systems, and employee transfers.

---

cases employees may be lacking in verbal skills which detract from its usefulness. Also, there may be a tendency on the part of some employees to "build up" their jobs to suggest more responsibility than is actually possessed.

A portion of a job analysis questionnaire from First Interstate Bancorp is presented in Figure 3–2. Notice that the total questionnaire consists of six sections. We have shown only Section III which covers the skills and knowledge required to perform a job's tasks and activities.

"In the past two years, the questions which have demanded most of my time are the ones raised about employee relocation and performance appraisals." By 1980, changes in the economy and the housing market had made the transfer of employees a significant cost of doing business. General Electric had established a reputation for having one of the best transfer policies among its peers, and had recently introduced a new home sale assistance program and a mortgage interest differential allowance to increase its assistance to transferring employees. "Despite the new programs, recruiters were telling us they were not getting their first choices for jobs and that employees were turning down transfer opportunities. We had to find out why. Our finance and relocation people were as interested as we were in employee relations. So we went to recently transferred employees and asked them about their relocation experience. What we found was that moving was a stressful experience, created by a volatile housing market, high mortgage rates, a perceived lack of adequate information about the transfer process, and a need for spouse employment assistance.

"So our finance and relocation people made improvements in our home sale assistance program, and mortgage interest differential allowance. Additionally, we assigned the coordinating responsibility for a transfer to employee relations managers—many parties are involved and we have to ensure that they all work effectively. We established a checklist for them to help them do the coordinating job.

"We published an Employee Relocation Information Package spelling out what our policy was all about, the important parts of our program, and what was expected of the employees. And we established guidelines for spouse employment assistance for our operating divisions to follow. We haven't left it there; we now regularly survey employees after their transfer to ensure that we stay on top of their experiences, good and bad.

"The one thing we can be sure of in this business is that it never gets boring," Joyce says. "As soon as one concern is resolved, another interesting question comes along which can't be answered without a lot of research. That's what makes this a fascinating, worthwhile profession."

Joyce has served as a member of various employer group committees and currently serves on two specializing in selection procedures and equal opportunity. The professional association which receives most of her attention is the International Association for Personnel Women, and Ms. Lawson has served as a member of their executive board for a number of years and is a past president. "This organization has offered great opportunities for women to develop as professionals in their chosen career and, as the organization grows, so do the members—personally and professionally. I feel I've contributed a lot, but I have received more through my participation," Joyce relates.

Observation

When using the observation method the job analyst actually witnesses the work being performed and records his or her observations. This method is often used when manual skills are primarily required, such as with a machine operator. However, observation alone is typically insufficient as a sole means of job analysis. It is especially deficient when mental skills are dominant in a

First Interstate Bancorp

Job Analysis Questionnaire

Name _____

Position Title _____

Affiliate _____

Division / Group / Unit _____

City and State _____

Immediate Manager _____

General Instructions

This questionnaire is designed to provide information about your current position. It is *not* intended to measure your performance or productivity. It is a tool for analyzing and describing your job.

The questionnaire consists of six sections.

- **Section I** deals with the tasks and activities that comprise your job.
- **Section II** asks you to compare various job dimensions, which are groupings of similar tasks.
- **Section III** covers the skills and knowledge required to perform the tasks and activities of your position.
- **Section IV** identifies specific scope measures of your position.
- **Section V** focuses on individual factors that you bring to your job.
- **Section VI** includes additional factors which may have an impact on your position.

Because this questionnaire covers a broad range of affiliates and jobs, a number of the questions may not apply to your position. However, *if you perform tasks that are not covered by the questionnaire, space has been provided for you to write them in.* Whether you perform a large number of tasks or only a few is not important. What is essential is that you respond to *all* of the questions (for example, you may perform certain financial management tasks, although you are in a marketing function), and in a manner which best describes your position as it is typically performed by you.

In responding to the questions, please use the following definitions.

- **affiliate** refers to an individual bank (e.g., First Interstate Bank of Arizona) or a nonbank subsidiary (e.g., First Interstate Services Company).
- **customer** means any individual or group, inside or outside the company, with which you deal on a client or customer basis. For example, an affiliate bank can be a customer for the data processing unit, a small business can be a customer for the venture capital group, and an individual or a corporation can be a customer for a bank.
- **unit** is the organizational group in which you report or for which you have responsibility. This could be a functional group, a department, or a division of a company. For example, for a Cashier position, the unit might be the Cashier's Department; for a VP Operations, the unit might be the Operations Department; for a VP Administration, the unit might be the Administration Division; or for a Chief Executive Officer, the unit would be the entire bank.

The questionnaires will be returned directly to Towers, Perrin, Forster & Crosby (TPF&C), so all responses on this form will remain confidential. However, to ensure that the information about your position is accurate and consistent, you and your immediate manager will review the results of TPF&C's analysis of the questionnaire.

Please follow the specific instructions at the beginning of each section. Read each section in full before attempting to complete it so that you can respond as accurately as possible.

Thank you for your efforts in participating in this study.

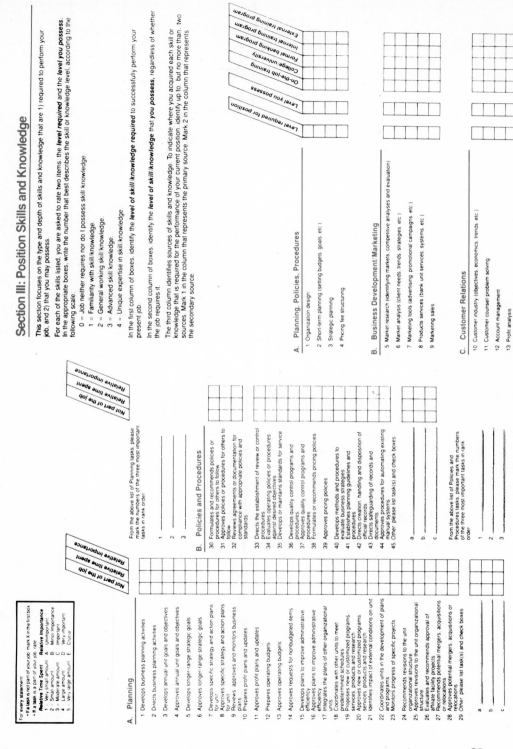

Figure 3-2. An example of a job analysis questionnaire.

83

job. Try observing a computer programmer at work sometimes and see what you can come up with.

Interview

An understanding of the job may also be gained through interviewing both the employee and the supervisor. Usually the employee is interviewed first and the job analyst assists the worker in describing the duties performed. Once the worker has been interviewed, the supervisor is normally contacted for additional information, check the accuracy of information obtained, and to clarify additional points.

Employee Recording

In some instances, job analysis information is gathered by having the employees describe their daily work activities in a diary or log. Again, the problem of employees exaggerating their jobs' importance may have to be overcome. For highly specialized jobs, however, valuable understanding of the job may be obtained through this method.

Combination

It is likely that no one job analysis method will be used exclusively. Rather, a combination is often more appropriate. For instance, in analyzing clerical and administrative jobs, the analyst might use questionnaires supported by interviews and limited observation. In studying shop jobs, interviews supplemented by a greater degree of work observation may provide the needed data.

CONDUCTING JOB ANALYSIS

The person(s) who conducts job analysis is interested in gathering data regarding what is involved in performing a particular job. The people who participate in job analysis should include the employee and the employee's immediate supervisor. In large organizations, there may be one or more job analysts. In smaller firms, line supervisors may have this responsibility. Outside consultants are often used if the organization lacks the expertise to perform the job analysis.

Before job analysis is conducted, the analyst (whatever the actual title) learns as much as possible about the job by such means as reviewing organizational charts and talking with individuals acquainted with the jobs to be studied. Before beginning, the analyst should be introduced to the employees by the supervisor, who should also explain the purpose of job analysis. Existing employee attitudes may be beyond the control of the job analyst. However, it

is imperative that the analyst attempt to develop a feeling of mutual trust and confidence with those whose jobs are being analyzed. Failure in this area will stifle an otherwise technically sound job analysis.

Considerable information is needed if job analysis is to be successfully accomplished. Examples of the types of data gathered through job analysis may be seen in Table 3–1. With regard to work activities, the job analyst attempts to determine the actual duties and responsibilities associated with the job. Worker-oriented activities are also important. What specifically are the demands of the job—energy expenditure and the like? In addition, the job analyst needs to know the forms of communication patterns that are required.

Knowledge of the types of machines, tools, equipment, and work aids that are used in performing the job are also important. This information is useful in later determining the skills needed for a person to perform the job. In ad-

Table 3–1. Examples of the types of data gathered in job analysis

---

Summary of Types of Data Collected Through Job Analysis*

---

1. *Work activities*
   a. Work activities and processes.
   b. Activity records (in film form, for example).
   c. Procedures used.
   d. Personal responsibility.
2. *Worker-oriented activities*
   a. Human behaviors, such as physical actions and communicating on the job.
   b. Elemental motions for methods analysis.
   c. Personal job demands, such as energy expenditure.
3. *Machines, tools, equipment and work aids used*
4. *Job-related tangibles and intangibles*
   a. Knowledge dealt with or applied (as in accounting).
   b. Materials processed.
   c. Products made or services performed.
5. *Work performance†*
   a. Error analysis.
   b. Work standards.
   c. Work measurements, such as time taken for a task.
6. *Job context*
   a. Work schedule.
   b. Financial and nonfinancial incentives.
   c. Physical working conditions.
   d. Organizational and social contexts.
7. *Personal requirements for the job*
   a. Personal attributes such as personality, interests.
   b. Education and training required.
   c. Work experience.

---

*This information can be in the form of qualitative, verbal, narrative descriptions or quantitative measurements of each item, such as error rates per unit of time or noise level.
†All job analysis systems do not develop the work performance aspects.
Source: McCormick, E. J. "Job and Task Analysis," in Marvin D. Dunnette (Ed.) *Handbook of Industrial and Organizational Psychology*. Chicago: Rand McNally, 1976. (By permission of the editor)

dition, the job analyst looks for job-related tangibles and intangibles. For instance, what knowledge must be dealt with or applied; what materials are processed; what products are made or services performed.

Some job analysis systems identify the standards that are established for the job. Work measurement studies may be conducted to determine, for example, how long it takes for a task to be performed. With regard to job content, the analyst studies the work schedule, financial and nonfinancial incentives, physical working conditions, and organizational and social contexts of the job. It is recognized that many jobs must be performed in conjunction with other workers.

Finally, the personal requirements of the job are identified. If a person needs to have a certain personality or interest, this qualification is noted. Also, specific education, training, and work experience pertinent to performing the job are identified. Once job analysis has been conducted, two of the most important personnel documents—job descriptions and job specifications—may be prepared.

JOB DESCRIPTION

Information obtained through job analysis is crucial to the development of job descriptions. The **job description** provides information regarding the duties and responsibilities of the job. The particular facts needed depend upon how the job description is to be used. Job descriptions are accurate, concise statements of what employees are expected to do on their jobs. They should indicate what employees do, how they do it, and the conditions under which the duties are performed. Among the items often included in a job description are:

- Major duties performed
- Percentage of time devoted to each duty
- Performance standards to be achieved
- Working conditions and possible hazards
- Number of persons working on each job and their reporting relationships
- The machines and equipment used on the job

The sections typically placed in the job description vary somewhat with the purpose for which it will be used. The most common sections included on a job description are described next.

Job Identification

This section includes a job title and a job number or code. A good title will closely approximate the nature of the work content and will distinguish that job from others. Job titles are often misleading. An "Executive Secretary" in one organization may be little more than a highly paid typist while a person with the same title in another firm may practically run the company. One of the authors, after receiving the B.B.A. degree, took his first job with a major tire and rubber company as an "Assistant District Service Manager." Because the primary duties of the job were to unload tires from trucks, check the tread wear, and stack the tires in boxcars, a more appropriate title would have been "Tire Checker and Stacker."

One information source which assists in standardizing job titles is the *Dictionary of Occupational Titles* (DOT).[3] The DOT includes standardized and comprehensive descriptions of job duties and relates information for over 20,000 occupations. This permits improved uniformity in the job titles and descriptions. Employers in different parts of the country are aided as they attempt to match job requirements with worker skills. The 1977 edition of DOT eliminated sex and age references.

An example of a DOT definition for a "Cloth Printer"—Occupational Code (652.382-010)—is provided in Figure 3–3. The first digit of the code identifies one of the following major job categories:

0/1	Professional, technical, and managerial occupations
2	Clerical and sales occupations
3	Service occupations
4	Farming, fishing, forestry, and related occupations
5	Processing occupations
6	Machine trade occupations
7	Bench work occupations
8	Structural work occupations
9	Miscellaneous occupations

In this instance, the major job classification would be "machine trade occupations." The next two digits represent further breakdowns of the specific job category.

Digits four through six describe the job's relationship to data, people, and things. For the "Cloth Printer" illustration, a code "3" for data would be "compiling," a code "8" for people would be "no significant relationship," and a code "2" for things would be "operating and controlling."

The final three digits of the occupational code indicate the alphabetical order of titles within the six digit code group. These codes assist in distinguishing a specific occupation from other similar ones. The alphabetical order for "Cloth Printer" is indicated by the digits 010.

Date of the Job Analysis

The job analysis date is placed on the job description to aid in identifying job changes which would make the description obsolete. It is often beneficial to place the following statement on the job description: "This document is valid

---

[3]U.S. Department of Labor, *Dictionary of Occupational Titles,* 4th ed. (Washington, DC: United States Government Printing Office, 1977).

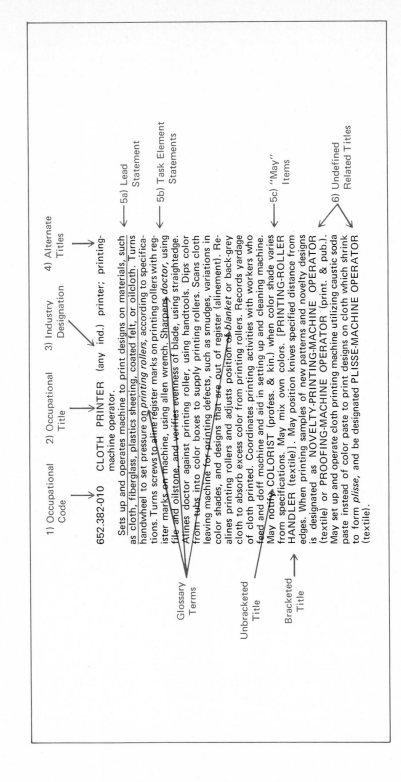

Figure 3–3. The parts of a DOT definition. (Source: U.S. Department of Labor, *Dictionary of Occupational Titles*.)

until June 1, 198X." This practice helps to ensure that the job content is reviewed periodically and to minimize the number of obsolete job descriptions.

Job Summary

The job summary provides the reader with a concise overview of the job. It is generally a short paragraph which states the job content.

Duties Performed

The body of the job description describes the duties performed. It is not meant to be all-inclusive but it should explain the major duties to be performed. Usually one sentence beginning with an action verb such as "receives," "performs," "establishes," or "assembles" can adequately describe each major duty.

JOB SPECIFICATION

Minimum acceptable qualifications that a person should possess to perform the job are included in the **job specification**. Some of the items often included in the job specification section are requirements for education, experience, personality, and physical abilities. Naturally, all specified qualifications should be directly related to abilities needed to perform the job. A General Mills, Inc. job description which includes a job qualification (specification) section is provided in Figure 3–4. As you can see, qualifications a person would need to perform the job of "Secretary II" include typing at least sixty words per minute and the shorthand skill of at least eighty words per minute. This type of information would be extremely valuable in the recruiting and selection process.

After jobs have been analyzed and the descriptions written, it is important that the results be reviewed with the supervisor and the worker. The job description needs to be clear and understandable. Also, the review assists in determining whether the information is complete and correct. The courtesy of reviewing results with employees assists in gaining acceptance. This single factor may well determine the success of the entire project.

In practice, both the job description and job specification are often combined into one form. Future reference, therefore, will be made only to the term "job description."

ALTERNATIVE METHODS FOR CONDUCTING JOB ANALYSIS

A large majority of the firms in the United States use some combination of the methods of job analysis previously presented. In recent years, there have

POSITION TITLE				POSITION NUMBER 217
SECRETARY II				APPROVAL RHS
DIVISION OR STAFF DEPARTMENT All	LOCATION All	REPORTS TO		EFFECTIVE DATE May, 1981
DEPARTMENT OR ACTIVITY	SECTION	POINTS 165	GRADE 6	REVISES

JOB SUMMARY

Performs clerical, stenographic, and administrative duties for a manager and often one or more staff members of a major function.

NATURE OF WORK

Performs a wide variety of office duties including most of the following:

a. Typing correspondence, reports, manuscripts, graphs, charts, etc., from shorthand notes, dictating machine tapes, and/or hand written drafts proficiently and with minimum direction and instructions.

b. Receiving telephone calls and visitors skillfully and handling incoming mail efficiently.

c. Originating routine correspondence and handling inquiries, and routing non-routine inquiries and correspondence to proper persons.

d. Establishing and maintaining department files and records.

e. Assuming responsibility for arranging appointments and meetings, screening calls, and handling personal and confidential matters for superior.

f. Assembling, organizing, processing, and evaluating data and reports; operating office machines needed for accomplishing this.

g. Performing administrative duties and special projects as directed, such as collecting and compiling general reference materials and information pertaining to company, division, or department practices and procedures.

Works independently, receiving a minimum of supervision and guidance on established office procedures. Relieves supervisor of minor administrative details. May have some light work direction over others in department. Structure is light and most work is not checked.

QUALIFICATIONS

High school education or its equivalent plus three years of clerical and stenographic experience, including one year with the Company, and a typing skill of at least 60 WPM. Demonstrated proficiency in English grammar, punctuation, spelling, and proper word usage. Must be able to anticipate problems and use sound judgment and tact in handling confidential matters, screening telephone calls and visitors, and scheduling superior's time. Must have the ability to acquire a thorough knowledge of the organization's policies, procedures, and personnel in order to relieve superior of specified administrative duties. A shorthand skill of at least 80 WPM is necessary if required in a specific position. A basic figure aptitude and/or a working knowledge of certain business machines may be necessary depending on the specific job.

Figure 3–4. A nonexempt job description. (Source: General Mills, Inc.)

been attempts to provide a more systematic approach in conducting job analysis. Several of these approaches will be described next.

Functional Job Analysis (FJA)

The United States Training and Employment Service (USTES) developed the concept of **functional job analysis** (FJA). The fundamental elements of FJA are provided as follows:

1. A major distinction is made between what gets done and what workers do to get things done. It is more important in job analysis to know the latter. For instance, a computer operator does not just keep the system running; there are a number of tasks that must be performed if his or her job is to be accomplished.

2. Each job is concerned with data, people, and things.

3. Workers function in unique ways relating to data, people, and things.

4. Each job requires the worker to relate to data, people, and things in some way.

5. There are only a few definite and identifiable functions involved with data, people, and things. These are identified in Table 3–2.

6. These functions proceed from the simple to the complex. Referring again to Table 3–2, the least complex form of data would be *comparing* while the most complex would be *synthesizing*. In addition, it is assumed that if an upper level function is required, all of the lower level functions are also required.

7. The three hierarchies for data, people, and things provide two measures for a job. First, there is a measure of relative complexity in relation to data, people, and things. In essence, how much interrelationship exists between the three functions. Second, there is a measure of proportional involvement for each function. For instance, 50 percent of a person's time may be spent in analyzing, 30 percent in supervising, and 20 percent in operating.[4]

Position Analysis Questionnaire (PAQ)

The **PAQ** is a a structured job analysis questionnaire which provides for the analysis of jobs in terms of 194 job descriptors. These job descriptors are analyzed according to six activities which include: information input, mental processes, work output, relationships with other persons, job context, and other

Table 3–2. Worker function scale of functional job analysis

Data (4th Digit)	People (5th Digit)	Things (6th digit)
0 Synthesizing	0 Monitoring	0 Setting-up
1 Coordinating	1 Negotiating	1 Precision Working
2 Analyzing	2 Instructing	2 Operating-Controlling
3 Compiling	3 Supervising	3 Driving-Operating
4 Computing	4 Diverting	4 Manipulating
5 Copying	5 Persuading	5 Tending
6 Comparing	6 Speaking-Signaling	6 Feeding-Offbearing
7 8 No Significant Relationship	7 Serving 8 No Significant Relationship	7 Handling 8 No Significant Relationship

[4]Ernest J. McCormick, "Job Information: Its Development and Application," in *Staffing Policies and Strategies*, edited by Dale Yoder and Herbert S. Heneman (Washington, DC: The Bureau of National Affairs, Inc., 1979), pp. 4–58.

job characteristics. Proponents of the PAQ believe that the nature of the job descriptors makes it possible to use this approach for virtually any type of position or job.[5]

Management Position Description Questionnaire (MPDQ)

This form of job analysis is designed for management positions and uses a checklist method to analyze jobs. There are 208 items which are related to managers' concerns and responsibilities.[6] These 208 items have been reduced to 13 primary job factors which include:

1. Product, market, and financial planning
2. Coordination of other organizational units and personnel
3. Internal business control
4. Products and service responsibility
5. Public and customer relations
6. Advanced consulting
7. Autonomy of action
8. Approval of financial commitment
9. Staff service
10. Supervision
11. Complexity and stress
12. Advanced financial responsibility
13. Broad personnel responsibility

The MPDQ has been used to determine training needs of individuals who are to move into managerial positions. It has also been used to evaluate and compensate managerial jobs and assign them to job families and place new managerial jobs in the proper job families.

JOB ANALYSIS AND THE LAW

A good job analysis system is needed as the firm recruits, selects, and moves employees through the organization. Recently, job analysis has become a focal point of Personnel because of the emphasis placed upon job-related selection methods by the Uniform Guidelines.[7] Legislation requiring thorough job analysis includes:

[5]E. J. McCormick and J. Triffin, *Industrial Psychology*, 6th ed., (Englewood Cliffs, NJ: Prentice-Hall, Inc., 1974), p. 53.
[6]W. W. Tornow and P. R. Pinto, "The Development of Management Job Taxonomy: A System for Describing, Classifying and Evaluating Executive Positions," *Journal of Applied Psychology 11* (1976): 410–18.
[7]Donald W. Myers, "The Impact of a Selected Provision in the Federal Guidelines on Job Analysis and Training," *Personnel Administration 26* (July 1981): 41–45.

- *Fair Labor Standards Act:* Employees are categorized as exempt or non-exempt. Job analysis is basic to this determination. Nonexempt personnel must be paid time and a half when they work over 40 hours per week. This is not required for exempt employees.
- *Equal Pay Act:* In the past, and to some extent today, men were often paid higher salaries than women even though essentially the same job was being performed. If jobs are not substantially different, similar pay should be provided. When pay differences exist, job descriptions can be used to show whether or not jobs are substantially equal in terms of skill, effort, responsibility, or working conditions.
- *Civil Rights Act:* As with the Equal Pay Act, job descriptions may provide the basis for adequate defenses against unfair discrimination charges. When job analysis is not performed, it is usually difficult to defend a qualification established for the job. For instance, stating that a high school diploma is required without having determined its necessity through job analysis leaves the firm open to discrimination charges.
- *OSHA:* Job descriptions are required to specify "elements of the job that endanger health, or are considered unsatisfactory or distasteful by the majority of the population." Showing the job description to the employee in advance is a good defense.

COST/BENEFITS ANALYSIS—JOB ANALYSIS

The most basic human resources management tool is job analysis. Without good job analyses, it would be difficult, if not impossible, to accomplish the various personnel functions successfully. But, there are costs associated with conducting and maintaining an effective job analysis program. Some individual in the firm must be available to conduct it. Management must be trained to support and assist in the process. A mechanism must be developed to maintain and update, when appropriate, job analysis data. The entire process can be time consuming.

But the benefits associated with having an effective job analysis system far surpass the costs. Every aspect of a personnel program is enhanced through thorough job analysis data. For instance, the recruitment and selection process is strengthened because job analysis points out what qualifications are needed for various positions. When individuals are considered for promotion, job analysis data shows what duties, responsibilities, and qualifications are required. Also, if we know what is required of a job, the T&D program can be tailored for specific needs. All aspects of Personnel are affected in some manner by job analysis.

SUMMARY

A job consists of a group of tasks that must be performed if an organization is to achieve its goals. There is a position for every individual in an organization.

The process of determining the duties and skills required for performing jobs in the organization is referred to as job analysis. Job analysis is the most basic human resources management tool. Without properly conducted job analysis, it would be difficult, if not impossible, to perform the other personnel-related functions satisfactorily.

Job analysis information is used to prepare both job descriptions and job specifications. Job descriptions specify the duties and responsibilities associated with a job. Job specifications state the knowledges, skills, and abilities a person will need to perform the job.

Job analysis may be conducted in a number of ways. Using questionnaires, the job analyst administers a structured questionnaire to employees who then identify the tasks they perform in accomplishing the job. The job analyst actually witnesses the work being performed and records his or her observations when the observation method is used. Also, an understanding of the job may be gained through interviewing both the employee and the supervisor. In some instances, job analysis information is gathered by having employees describe their daily work activities in a diary or log. Finally, a combination of any of the above methods may be used. The person(s) who conducts job analysis is interested in gathering data regarding what is involved in performing a particular job.

The most common sections included on a job description are: 1. job identification, 2. date of the job analysis, 3. job summary, and 4. duties performed. Some of the items often included in the job specification section are requirements for education, experience, personality, and physical abilities.

In recent years there have been attempts at providing a more systematic approach in conducting job analysis. Some of these approaches include: functional job analysis (FJA), position analysis questionnaire (PAQ), and management position description questionnaire (MPDQ). Recently, job analysis has become a focal point of Personnel because of the emphasis placed upon job-related selection methods by the Uniform Guidelines.

Questions for Review

1. Distinguish by definition between a "job," a "position," and "job analysis."

2. Discuss what is meant by the statement, "Job analysis is the most basic human resources management tool."

3. Describe the traditional methods that are used in conducting job analysis.

4. List and briefly describe the types of data that are typically gathered when conducting job analysis.

5. What are the basic components of a job description? Briefly describe each.

6. What are the typical items included in the job specification?

7. Briefly define each of the following: a. Functional job analysis (FJA) b. Position analysis questionnaire (PAQ) c. Management position description questionnaire (MPDQ)

8. How can effective job analysis be used to satisfy each of the following pieces of legislation? a. Fair Labor Standards Act b. Equal Pay Act c. Civil Rights Act d. Occupational Safety and Health Act

Terms for Review

Job

Position

Job analysis

Job description

Job specification

Functional job analysis

Position Analysis Questionnaire

Management Position Description Questionnaire

Shane Primeaux was excited as he told his dad about his plan for developing job descriptions at their family-owned company, Primeaux Gasket Company. Shane had been working with his father for some years after having completed a stint in the Air Force. He was taking over more and more of the responsibilities for management because they both knew that it would not be long before Mr. Primeaux retired. Shane had a degree in personnel administration from the University of Arkansas. In addition, he had just completed a symposium on job analysis. "Dad," said Shane, "in two years the work force here has gone from thirty to over fifty. I don't believe we can keep our finger on everything without a little more formality than we have had in the past." "I don't know son," said Mr. Primeaux. "The way you describe it, creating job descriptions is pretty complicated. I don't know how to conduct job analysis. For my part, I wouldn't do it unless you can figure out how it will help us make rubber gaskets better, faster, or with fewer work hours than we use now."

Primeaux Manufacturing Company is a small gasket maker near Monroe, Louisiana. Most of the jobs involve operating punch presses. The operators place pieces of fiber-reinforced rubber sheeting into their machines, press the footpedals, and remove the gaskets which have been cut. Some of the workers make nonstandard gaskets. They cut these using various kinds of punches and cutters which are hand operated. All workers are responsible for inspecting the items they make and packaging them for shipment. Even for standard items, it is seldom that a batch exceeds 2000 pieces. The gaskets are used throughout the country, primarily in the petrochemical industry.

Questions

1. Is Primeaux Gasket Company big enough to justify formal job analysis? Explain your answer.

2. If you were Shane, what kind of arguments would you use to convince Mr. Primeaux that formal job analysis is justified?

3. What method would you use for obtaining job analysis data?

4. What steps would you follow to accomplish formal job analysis at Primeaux Gasket Company?

As Professor Sharplin toured the Plymouth Tube Corporation plant in Pontiac, New Jersey, he became more and more impressed with his young guide, Jim Murdoch. Jim was the assistant personnel director at Plymouth Tube and was primarily responsible for job analysis. An industrial engineer was assigned fulltime to the Personnel Department to assist Jim in job design. Professor Sharplin had been retained by the personnel director to study Plymouth Tube's job analysis system and to make recommendations for improvements. He had gone through the files of job descriptions in the personnel office with Jim and found them, in general, to be complete and directly related to the jobs to be performed.

One of the first steps on the tour was the office of the weld mill supervisor, a 10-foot by 10-foot room out of the factory floor with glass windows on all sides. As Jim approached, the supervisor, Roger Dishongh, was outside his office. "Hi, Jim," he said. "Hello, Roger," said Jim. "This is Professor Sharplin. Could we look at your job descriptions and chat with you for a moment?" "Sure, Jim," said Roger, opening the door. "Come on in and have a seat and I'll get them out." From their vantage point, the men in the office could see the workers in the weld mill area. As they reviewed each job description it was possible to observe the worker actually performing the work described. Roger Dishongh was familiar with each of the jobs. He was very knowledgeable about the job descriptions themselves, having contributed to preparing or revising each of them. "How are the job descriptions related to the performance evaluations here?" asked Professor Sharplin. "Well," answered Roger, "I only evaluate the workers on the items specified in the job descriptions. These were determined through careful job analysis. Limiting performance evaluations to those

items helps to encourage me to correct the job descriptions when something changes and they don't accurately describe the job. Jim has conducted training sessions for all the supervisors so that we understand the relationship between job analysis, job descriptions, and performance evaluations. I think it's a pretty good system."

Jim and Professor Sharplin went on to several other areas of the plant and found similar situations. Jim seemed to have a good relationship with each of the supervisors as well as with the plant manager and the two or three mid-level managers they visited. As they headed back to the front office, Professor Sharplin was considering the comments which he would soon make to the plant manager.

Questions

1. What desirable attributes of job analysis do you see evident at Plymouth Tube Company?
2. What kind of report do you think Professor Sharplin should present to the plant manager?

3. Describe the relationship which might exist between the industrial engineer and the assistant personnel director regarding job analysis?

Section Case

PARMA CYCLE COMPANY: AN OVERVIEW

 Parma Cycle Company of Parma, Ohio, a Cleveland suburb, is one of only three companies which actually manufacture complete bicycles in the United States. Most of Parma's competitors import parts from other countries and simply assemble bicycles here. Parma Cycle employs about 800 workers, mainly machine operators and assemblers. The factory is laid out, coincidentally, like a bicycle wheel, with component manufacturing departments representing the tire and spoke area and assembly being done in the center of the factory, representing the hub.

Parma Cycle makes a line of bicycles and markets them under the Parma name. However, most of the bicycles Parma manufactures are purchased by large national retailers and marketed under those retailers' house names. A few bicycles are exported to Europe and South America but Parma has found it difficult to compete in the international market with Japanese and Italian manufacturers.

Parma Cycle Company, Inc. is a publicly held corporation, although 30 percent of its shares are controlled by a major recreational conglomerate corporation. There have been rumors of a take-over from time to time but none has materialized. Because of depressed earnings over the past two years, Parma's stock has declined from $27 per share to $13 per share. Interest rates have increased significantly during the same period. The company has found it costly, therefore, to raise funds to purchase the new machines which have been developed for bicycle manufacture. Included in Parma's line of bicycles is a high performance racing cycle. A research and development program aimed at improving the performance of that bicycle was cancelled because of the high cost of financing.

Jesse Heard is the personnel director. He has been with Parma Cycle for twenty-three years. His first job was as a painter, when painting was done with a hand-held spray gun. He was later promoted to supervisor and worked in several departments at the plant. Because the company paid for college tuition and fees as well as books to encourage supervisors to advance their education, Jesse had gone on to college. In 1970, he received his bachelor's degree in personnel administration from Case Western University in Cleveland. Jesse was immediately promoted to a job in the personnel department and three years later became the personnel director.

In May 1981, the Equal Employment Opportunity Commission received a complaint about employment practices at Parma. It was alleged that while the proportion of blacks in the Cleveland area approached 25 percent, only 8 percent of the Parma Cycle work force was black. There were only two black managers above the level of supervisor. Jesse Heard was advised of the complaint. He felt that the company was doing everything it should with regard to equal opportunity.

The company had an affirmative action plan and had a practice of encouraging managers to employ blacks and other minority group members as well as women. In fact, Jesse's efforts to encourage the employment of protected group members had provoked some managers to complain to the company president, his immediate supervisor.

In general, the working environment at Parma Cycle has been a good one. The company has a relatively flat organizational structure with few managerial levels, as shown in the organization chart.

Most of Parma's workers are of European stock and are fairly acclimated to working in a factory environment. Since 1975, the com-

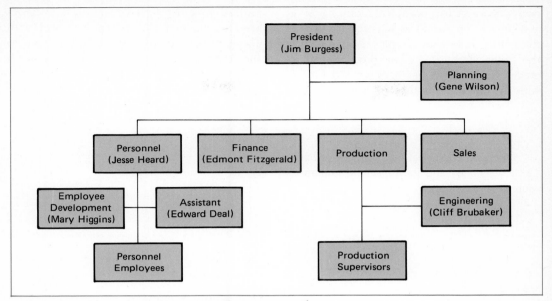

Figure I–1. **Parma Cycle Company: Organization chart.**

pany has had periodic management training seminars in which managers have been taught to be sensitive to workers and cooperative with one another. The management philosophy is one of decentralized authority. Managers, like Jesse Heard, are essentially responsible for their own operations.

As a result of an aggressive safety program, there has been only one fatal accident at Parma in the last ten years and work-related injuries are well below the industry average. Starting in about 1965 the ventilation system in the factory was modernized. The lighting is good, by Cleveland area standards, and the health and safety officer once remarked that the air is cleaner inside the factory than outside. Gene Wilson, the corporate planner, has said that he believes the company has spent too much money on employee safety and working conditions and that this is one reason for the declining profits Parma has seen. The company's mission has not been changed since 1960 when it was stated as: "To enhance the wealth of the common shareholder through efficient production and aggressive marketing of

bicycles while contributing to the well-being of our workers and the stability of the Cleveland economy."

Parma's work force is unionized, with the local union being a member of the National Association of Machinists. Employee recruitment is done primarily through referrals from current workers. Selection is based upon personal interviews, evaluation of job-related application forms and, for certain jobs, a basic skills test conducted by the supervisor. The supervisor makes the final hiring decision. Workers must join the union before the end of a three month probationary period. Over the years, the union has won wages and benefits which are about average for the Cleveland area.

The factory work at Parma Cycle is neither especially difficult nor complicated. Cycle technology has changed very little over the years and most of the jobs have become standardized. However, growing foreign competition and the economic recession which began in 1981 have caused an increasing emphasis upon productivity. Consequently, workers have been encouraged to put forth additional effort and production standards have been raised to the point where many employees complain of the faster work pace. The productivity improvement program has been carried forward with the union's assistance. This was felt to be justified in order to save jobs. There hasn't been a strike at Parma in ten years and, with unemployment in the area very high due to auto industry and other layoffs, one is considered unlikely.

Questions

1. Discuss the external environment of Parma Cycle Company and its impact on human resources management.

2. Is the internal environment at Parma Cycle a good one? Explain.

___ Experiencing Personnel Management ___

THE CHANGING LABOR MARKET

This is a role-playing exercise involving Jesse Heard, the personnel manager at Parma Cycle Company; Gene Wilson, the corporate planner; and Edmont Fitzgerald, the controller. Class members not assigned specific roles can be involved through participating in a question and answer session after the brief skit. The general background is provided in "Parma Cycle Company: An Overview" beginning on page 98. All participants should have studied that case thoroughly before reading the role descriptions below. The primary purpose of this exercise is to highlight a number of environmental concerns confronting personnel managers.

Role Descriptions

Jesse Heard. As the personnel manager, you are faced with a dilemma. On the one hand, you know you must represent the company's economic interest. You purchase labor and as is true for other resources, you are obligated to find the best quality at the best available price. The company's competitive position is already tenuous so this is even more important now. On the other hand, you are concerned about the workers, some of whom have been

with Parma Cycle for many years. Even though the highly favorable labor market allows you to replace many of them with lower paid workers, you hesitate to do so. Yesterday you received an angry call from the president, Mr. Burgess, who asked you to meet with the corporate planner and the controller and come up with a unified recommendation for taking advantage of the improved labor market and cutting labor costs. As you head for the meeting, you think about how different your view of the situation is from that of the controller.

Edmont Fitzgerald. An Ohio State University graduate in finance, you feel that above all things, the corporation is an economic entity. You believe that market forces will take care of those workers who really wish to contribute to the economy and that the general welfare is served by companies aggressively competing on every conceivable basis and purchasing all resources, including labor, at the lowest possible price. You agree with Milton Friedman, your idol, that "The only social responsibility of business is to earn a profit, within the rules of the game." You have little time for those like Jesse Heard, who would waste company resources trying to fulfill some kind of paternalistic role with regard to employees. Moreover, you believe that the union has coerced management into accepting wages and working conditions which have increased Parma's personnel costs unreasonably. This is the reason you believe that Parma has trouble competing in the international market. You see the current situation as an opportunity to decrease costs radically. The union is weak, jobs are scarce, and there is a surplus of skilled workers in the Cleveland area. If some of the more senior workers can be provoked to leave or can be fired for some semilegitimate reason, they can be replaced with experienced workers who will have no seniority at Parma and who, consequently, will draw a much lower wage. It was at your recommendation that the president decided to call the meeting which you are about to attend.

Gene Wilson. You never really had much power at Parma Cycle, although your title sounds impressive enough. Primarily, you maintain a chart room and keep track of various trends such as the cost of labor as a percent of total cost, fixed costs as opposed to variable costs in the plant, and trends in sales of the company's various products. You believe that a systematic corporate planning pro-

gram, while always important, is now a critical necessity. You think that Parma Cycle Company is headed downhill because of depressed markets and an inability on the part of company managers to decrease unit costs. In your opinion the most important asset which Parma Cycle has is a trained and loyal work force. While many of the workers could be replaced with lower paid workers, you are afraid that this would destroy the team spirit which now exists. You believe that, with the insecurity the workers all feel because of the growing number of layoffs in the Cleveland area, they are more likely than ever to respond to financial incentives. Therefore, you think it might be a good time to institute some kind of piece rate program or suggestion and bonus system to encourage worker productivity. If such a system could be set up at Parma, you feel productivity would increase and labor costs decrease without any reduction in wages. The work force would be reduced over a period of time through attrition. If you could be instrumental in solving the company's problem it would be a feather in your cap, and perhaps you would become the respected power wielder in the company which you believe the corporate planner—and you personally—deserves to be.

Questions

1. Is labor a resource, "just like other resources?" Explain.
2. How might internal politics enter into the anticipated meeting?

3. How might the weak union and job scarcity in the Cleveland area affect the day-to-day function of personnel management?

Part II _____

Human Resources Planning, Recruitment, and Selection

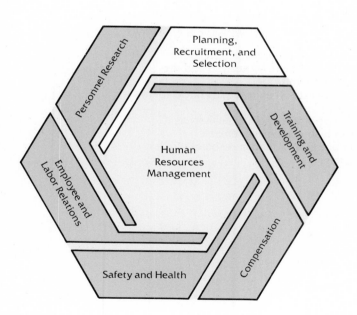

Personnel Research

Planning, Recruitment, and Selection

Training and Development

Human Resources Management

Employee and Labor Relations

Safety and Health

Compensation

Chapter Objectives

1. Explain the human resources planning process.
2. State the importance of demand forecasting in human resources planning.
3. Describe some demand forecasting techniques.
4. Express how personnel demand analysis and the planning process are interrelated.
5. State what a firm can do when a surplus of personnel exists.
6. Explain the concept of labor supply analysis as it relates to human resources management.
7. Describe what comprises a human resources information system.

Chapter 4 _____

Human Resources Planning

Mark Swann, the marketing director for a large manufacturing firm, raced into the executive meeting room bubbling with excitement. He exclaimed, "I have great news! We can get the large contract with Medord Corporation. All we have to do is complete the project in one year instead of two." Everyone was excited except one person, Linda Cane, vice president of personnel. She stunned the other members by saying, "There is no way we can meet that date, Mark. If we were going to bring on board the two hundred extra workers who would be needed to complete the project, planning should have started nine months ago." Everyone sat back in shock because they realized that Linda's analysis was correct.

106

Part II
Human
Resources
Planning,
Recruitment,
and Selection

In the above instance, all aspects of obtaining the contract had been considered except the staffing requirement. Human resources planning is the process which ensures that a sufficient number of employees possessing appropriate skills are available for achieving the firm's goals. Without human resources planning, the project completion date could not be achieved. Nevertheless, for many years companies gave only lip service to human resources planning. But this approach is changing rapidly.[1] Human resources planning is now an important company undertaking. The overall purpose of the chapter is to explain the importance and nature of human resources planning in organizations today.

THE HUMAN RESOURCES PLANNING PROCESS

As was previously mentioned, planning involves determining how the goals of the organization are to be achieved. Planning is particularly important if the firm is to fulfill its future human resources needs.[2] This function requires considerable time and effort in order to be accomplished effectively.

We have illustrated the human resources planning process in Figure 4–1. As you can see, organizational strategic planning—which requires consideration of both the external and internal environments—is first accomplished. Many of the external and internal factors mentioned in Chapter 2 must be considered here. **Strategic plans** are designed to help the firm achieve its primary objectives.[3] For instance, a major objective of Company A may be to produce the highest quality product in the industry. The strategic plan that must be developed to accomplish this goal will affect every major department in the firm. In the past, Personnel often did not become involved in strategic planning until these plans were developed. However, top management is beginning to recognize the necessity of including Personnel in the strategic planning process. The logic is sound. Corporate objectives and plans must reflect the firm's human resources capabilities.

After objectives and plans have been formulated, the demand for the firm's products and/or services should be forecasted. Once the demand for a firm's products and/or services has been established, the organization may then engage in human resources planning (HRP). Notice in Figure 4–1 that there are two sides to human resources planning—demand and supply. Also notice that job analysis is a prerequisite for both. On the demand side, the firm must identify the quantity and quality of employees needed to achieve its goals. This procedure is called personnel demand analysis. On the supply side, the organization needs to determine where workers may be found (whether from

[1]James W. Walker, "The New, More Substantive Approach to Manpower Planning," *Management Review* 66 (July 1977): 29 (hereinafter referred to as "Walker").
[2]William E. Bright, "How One Company Manages Its Human Resources," *Harvard Business Review* 54 (January-February 1976): 81–93 (hereinafter referred to as "Bright").
[3]George Steiner, *Top Management Planning* (New York: The Macmillan Company, 1969), p. 34.

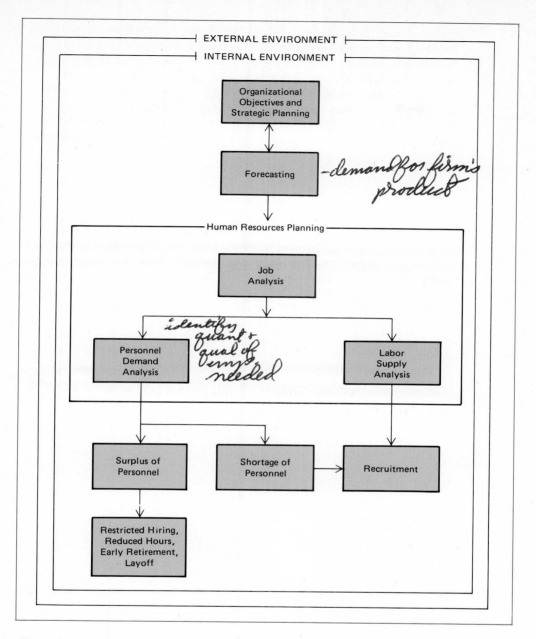

EXTERNAL ENVIRONMENT

INTERNAL ENVIRONMENT

Organizational
Objectives and
Strategic Planning

Forecasting

—demand for firm's product

Human Resources Planning

Job
Analysis

identify quant + qual of emp's needed

Personnel
Demand
Analysis

Labor
Supply
Analysis

Surplus of
Personnel

Shortage of
Personnel

Recruitment

Restricted Hiring,
Reduced Hours,
Early Retirement,
Layoff

Figure 4–1. **The human resources planning process.**

internal or external sources) to satisfy the firm's human resources requirements. This process is called labor supply analysis.

Once the demand and supply of future employees have been analyzed, the firm is in a position to determine whether it will face a surplus or shortage of employees. Means must be found to reduce the number of employees if a sur-

108

Part II
Human
Resources
Planning,
Recruitment,
and Selection

plus of workers is projected. Some of these methods include restricted hiring, reduced hours, early retirements, and layoffs. If a shortage is forecast, the firm must look to sources outside the organization to secure the proper quantity and quality of workers. External recruitment and selection are then required.

As you might expect, the human resources planning process is continuous. Conditions from either the external or internal environment can change in a short period of time. These changes could require that forecasts be extensively modified. Planning places managers in a much better position to anticipate and react to changing conditions.

FORECASTING

There are four basic terms used in forecasting. First the **long-run trend** line projects the demand for a firm's products, typically five years or more into the future.[4] As you can see in Figure 4–2, the long-run demand for Company A appears to be increasing. Sales are expected to virtually double in the next five years. Early recognition of such a trend is critical. You may not be able to fill some positions quickly. Considerable training may also be required. For instance, some employees may need several years of development before they are capable of assuming new responsibilities.

Second, **cyclical demand** varies around the long-run trend line. Cyclical variations may be due to such factors as war, political elections, economic

Figure 4–2. **Seasonal demand.**

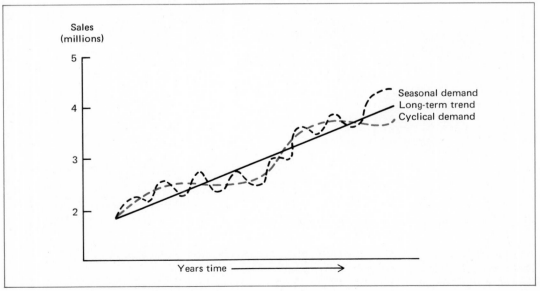

[4]Joseph E. Monks, *Operations Management: Theory and Problems* (New York: McGraw-Hill Book Company, 1977), p. 274.

"Be specifically aware of the changes taking place which affect personnel administration, changes such as ERISA, OSHA, and other new laws. Work hard to understand and fully grasp the basis of all disciplines within personnel administration, including employment, salary administration, and labor relations."

John M. DiEleuterio, Manager of Employment
Campbell Soup Company

conditions, and sociological pressures.[5] These variations are typically greater than one year and less than five years. Knowledge of cyclical demand is important because of the potential for severe peaks and valleys. Additional people may be required to meet cyclical demands even though a stable long-run demand is forecast. And, although the long-run forecast may be upward, there may be a temporary recession which would require a temporary work force reduction.

Third, **seasonal demand** varies around the cyclical demand and may fluctuate drastically (see Figure 4–2). This demand is the most immediate concern for many firms and occurs within a twelve-month period. Electric shavers are sold primarily during the holiday season while water ski boats are sold primarily in the Spring. Seasonal demands can have a major impact upon a firm as it attempts to integrate stability of labor force with production and inventory needs.

Finally, **random demand** follows no pattern. Even the most sophisticated forecasting techniques cannot anticipate it.[6]

RELATIONSHIP OF SALES VOLUME TO NUMBER OF EMPLOYEES

The relationship that tends to exist between demand and the number of employees needed is a positive one. A relatively simple means of forecasting is to prepare a scatter diagram.[7] As may be seen in the scatter diagram in Figure 4–3, the firm's sales units are depicted on the vertical axis and the number of employees actually required is shown on the horizontal axis. You can see in this illustration that a relationship exists between sales demand and the number of employees. Managers are able to approximate the number of employees who will be required at different demand levels. Such a relationship also exists in

[5]Richard B. Chase and Nicholas J. Aquilano, *Production and Operations Management* (Homewood, Ill.: Richard D. Irwin, Inc., 1973), p. 183.
[6]Elwood S. Buffa, *Modern Production Management*, 5th ed. (New York: John Wiley & Sons, 1977), p. 314.
[7]For a discussion of scatter diagrams, see John Neter and William Wasserman, *Applied Linear Statistical Models* (Homewood, Ill.: Richard D. Irwin, Inc., 1974), p. 24.

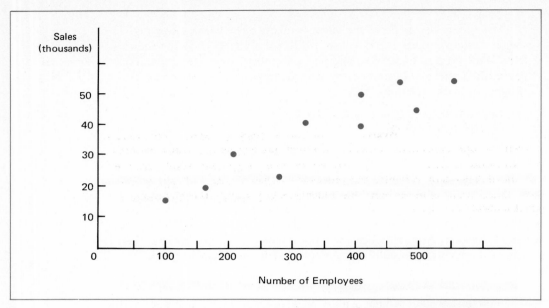

Figure 4–3. **The relationship of sales volume to number of employees.**

the public sector. For example, as the number of students increases in an educational institution, there is often an increased need for teachers.

It might initially appear that the approximation generated by the scatter diagram would be so unsophisticated as to render it virtually useless. However, experience has revealed a rough relationship between demand for a firm's products and services and the number of people required to produce them. Managers with experience in a particular firm or industry have come to trust this relationship.

DEMAND FORECASTING TECHNIQUES

We have already stated that a relationship tends to exist between the demand for a firm's products and/or services and the number of individuals the firm will need to employ. Several techniques are currently being used to determine the firm's projected employee demand. Three of the better known methods—the Delphi technique, regression analysis, and simulation—will next be described.

Delphi Technique

The Delphi technique is a nonquantitative method which was developed by the Rand Corporation. Using this approach, a series of questionnaires is sent to experts to be completed anonymously. Each questionnaire is based on the results of the previous one. This procedure continues until a consensus on forecasted demand is reached and a decision can be made.

Regression Analysis

With the increased use of high speed computers and sophisticated statistical packages, personnel managers have at their disposal a most useful forecasting tool—regression analysis. **Regression analysis** is used to predict one item (known as the dependent variable) through knowledge of other item(s) (known as the independent variables). When there is one dependent variable and one independent variable, the process is known as simple linear regression. When there is more than one independent variable, the technique is called multiple regression.

Using simple linear regression, a personnel manager might attempt to forecast employment level (dependent variable) based on sales (independent variable). If a strong relationship exists between sales and employment level, the personnel manager would be able to determine the number of workers needed by knowing the level of sales.

In most instances, the employment level is determined by several independent variables and multiple regression is required. Instead of predicting employment levels strictly through knowledge of sales, other variables such as efficiency level of the work force might be used. Multiple regression often produces superior results when compared to simple linear regression because it recognizes that a variety of factors may influence forecasted employment levels.

Simulation

In **simulation** the computer is used to assist in performing experiments on a model of a real system. A model is an abstraction of the real world. Thus, a simulation model is an attempt to represent a real world situation through mathematical logic in order to predict what will actually occur. Simulation assists the personnel manager by permitting him or her to ask many "What if . . ." questions without having to make the decision in the real world.

From a personnel viewpoint, a simulation model might be developed to show the many interrelations that exist between employment level and a variety of other variables. Then "What if. . ." questions could then be asked such as:

- What would happen if we put 10 percent of the present work force on overtime?
- What would happen if the plant went to two shifts? to three shifts?

Depending upon the purpose of the model developed, the personnel manager can derive considerable insight into a particular problem before making an actual decision.

L. R. Brice, AEP
President
Len Brice Associates

Len Brice's first real job after graduating from Baldwin-Wallace College was as director of a unique vocational school for Blacks in the South, and placing the graduates of the school aroused his interest in employment and employee relations. Thus began a career of some forty years in the personnel field—twenty-six years as a practitioner, most of which he spent as a top corporate personnel officer, followed by sixteen years as the executive vice president of the American Society for Personnel Administration which is the largest organization of its kind in the world.

Len's philosophy is simple: Every professional in a field should contribute to developing that profession. He practiced this philosophy by taking ASPA from a membership of 400 when he was the volunteer president, and 1100 members when he took over as executive vice president some years later, to a membership of more than 30,000, and from a budget of $64,000 his first year as ASPA's CEO to over $4,000,000 when he retired late in 1980.

Len helped to found the Personnel Accreditation Institute, formerly the ASPA Accreditation Institute. This organization created standards upon which people in the human resource management field could be accredited, and provided information upon which curricula in colleges and universities could be based or revised to meet current needs. One of the factors which contributed to the founding and growth of PAI was the publication of the *ASPA Handbook of Personnel and Industrial Relations*. Len wrote a chapter for this book and served as a member of its four-person advisory

PERSONNEL DEMAND ANALYSIS

Personnel demand analysis permits a firm to calculate the type and volume of work that needs to be completed if the firm is to achieve its goals. In order to accomplish demand analysis, the need for the firm's products or services must first be forecasted. This forecast is then converted into person-hour requirements. Various work activities are stated in terms of what will be required to meet this demand. For instance, if the firm is manufacturing hand calculators, activities might be stated in terms of the number of units produced, number of sales calls to be made, number of vouchers that will be processed, or a variety of other activities. These work activities are then translated into person-hours. For example, if 10,000 widgets are to be manufactured each week, it might require 5,000 hours of work by assemblers during a 40-hour week. If the 5,000 hours are divided by the 40 hours in the work week, we would need 125 assembly workers. Similar calculations are performed for the other jobs needed to produce and market the 10,000 widgets.

committee. This book brought together a body of knowledge not previously available.

Realizing early that the personnel field needed continued research and educational opportunities, Len was a founder of the ASPA Foundation which is dedicated to providing grants to promote appropriate work in the field. The Foundation recently published two books resulting from research it supported and sponsors many projects and awards in research. He continues to serve as the secretary treasurer of the Foundation.

One of Len's biggest satisfactions was the role he played as a founder of the World Federation of Personnel Management Associations. This organization now represents personnel groups in six regions throughout the world and includes some fifty countries and 150,000 personnel practitioners. He is serving his second four-year term as general secretary of WFPMA. His interests in personnel practices throughout the world motivated him to lead a team of personnel executives on a three-week trip to meet with counterparts in East Germany, the Soviet Union, Romania, and Yugoslavia some years ago, and recently

he took a team into the People's Republic of China, Hong Kong, and the Philippines to visit counterparts there.

An interest in continuing education for personnel and other management people led Len to be a member of the ASPA committee that established the Continuing Education Unit now accepted throughout the United States and Canada. This committee later became the Council on the Continuing Education Unit and Len is now the president of that organization. He also served for years on the board and was national chairman of the United States Chamber of Commerce's Institute for Organization Management.

Serving as he did, teaching in colleges and universities, serving on White House Advisory Committees as well as those of the National Association of Manufacturers, American Management Association, and others, Len feels he has lived up to his belief in the need to contribute to his profession. He hopes others in the field will share this philosophy.

As the principal in Len Brice Associates in Berea, Ohio, Len is actively involved as a consultant in human resources management.

When the analysis indicates a personnel shortage, the firm must initiate recruitment efforts. Recruitment will be the focus of the next chapter. When personnel demand analysis shows a personnel surplus, restricted hiring, reduced hours, early retirements, or layoffs may be required.

SURPLUS OF PERSONNEL

Planning is just as critical when demand for a firm's product is declining as when it is high. Managers must focus their attention upon maintaining sufficient people in the organization to produce the firm's goods or services while preparing to reduce the overall labor budget. If adequate planning has occurred, this process can take place with minimum hardships to the firm's current employees. Several means by which a firm may react to a decline in demand are discussed next.

114

Part II
Human
Resources
Planning,
Recruitment,
and Selection

Restricted Hiring

When a firm implements a restricted hiring policy, a work force reduction is made by failing to replace employees who leave the firm. New workers are only hired when overall performance of the organization may be affected. For instance, if a quality control department which consisted of four inspectors had one worker take a job with another firm, this individual would not likely be replaced. However, if the firm lost all of its inspectors, the firm would make an attempt to replace at least some of them to assure continued operation.

Reduced Hours

Reaction to a declining demand can also be made by reducing the total number of hours worked. Instead of continuing a forty-hour work week, management may decide to cut each employee's time to thirty hours. This process normally applies to hourly employees because management and professional staff members are not typically paid on an hourly basis.

Early Retirement

Early retirement of some present employees is another means of reducing the supply of personnel. Employees may be willing to accept early retirement if provided incentives such as adding certain benefits to the total retirement package.

Layoffs

At times, the firm has no other choice but to actually lay off a certain proportion of its workforce. A layoff does not have the same connotation as being fired, but it has the same short-term effect—the worker is no longer employed. When the firm is unionized, the procedures affecting a layoff are usually stated quite clearly in the labor-management agreement. Typically, the less senior members are laid off first. If the organization is nonunionized, a firm may lay off workers based on a combination of factors such as their seniority and their productivity level. When managerial and professional employees are laid off, it is very likely to be based upon ability, although politics may be a factor.

LABOR SUPPLY ANALYSIS

A large manufacturing firm on the West Coast was preparing to begin operations in a new plant. Analysts had already determined that there was a large long-term demand for the new product. Financing was available and equipment was in place. But production did not begin for three years! Management had made a critical mistake; they had studied the demand side of personnel and did not take the supply side into account. There were not enough qualified workers in the local labor force to operate the new plant. New workers had to receive extensive training before they would be capable of moving into the newly created jobs.

Personnel demand analysis provides the manager with the means of estimating how many and what kind of employees will be required. But there is another side of the coin. Management must also determine if they will be able to secure employees with the necessary skills and from what sources these individuals may be obtained. As suggested by the above example, **labor supply analysis** results in determining the availability of needed employees. The supply of employees may be met by obtaining people from within the company or the firm may decide to go outside the organization to meet its needs.

Internal Sources of Supply

Many of the workers that will be needed for future positions with the firm are already employed. If the firm is small, it is likely that management knows all workers well enough so that their skills and aspirations can easily be matched. If, for instance, the company is establishing a new sales position, it may be common knowledge that Mary Garcia, a five year employee with the company, has both the skills and desire to take over the new job. This unplanned process of matching demand with supply may be sufficient for smaller firms. As organizations grow, however, the matching process becomes increasingly difficult. Some of the tools available to identify internal sources of supply will next be discussed.

Management Inventories. As its name implies, management inventory information relates specifically to managers. An inventory would likely include data such as:

- Work history
- Strengths
- Weaknesses—identification of specific training that will be needed to possibly remove the weaknesses
- Promotion potential
- Career goals
- Personal data

A **management inventory** contains detailed data regarding each manager and can be used to identify individuals possessing the potential to move into higher level positions. In essence, the inventory provides information for preparing a management replacement chart. Detroit Edison calls their chart a Career Planning Inventory Organization Review Chart. As you can see in Figure

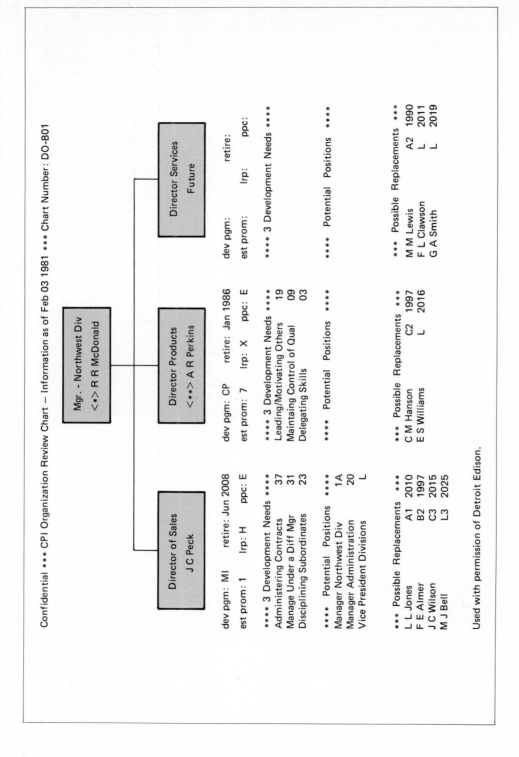

Confidential *** CPI Organization Review Chart — Information as of Feb 03 1981 *** Chart Number: DO-B01

Mgr. - Northwest Div
<*> R R McDonald

Director of Sales
J C Peck

dev pgm: MI   retire: Jun 2008
est prom: 1   lrp: H   ppc: E

**** 3 Development Needs ****
Administering Contracts   37
Manage Under a Diff Mgr   31
Disciplining Subordinates   23

**** Potential Positions ****
Manager Northwest Div   1A
Manager Administration   20
Vice President Divisions   L

*** Possible Replacements ***
L L Jones   A1   2010
F E Almer   B2   1997
J C Wilson   C3   2015
M J Bell   L3   2025

Director Products
<*> A R Perkins

dev pgm: CP   retire: Jan 1986
est prom: 7   lrp: X   ppc: E

**** 3 Development Needs ****
Leading/Motivating Others   19
Maintaing Control of Qual   09
Delegating Skills   03

**** Potential Positions ****

*** Possible Replacements ***
C M Hanson   C2   1997
E S Williams   L   2016

Director Services
Future

dev pgm: retire:
est prom: lrp: ppc:

**** 3 Development Needs ****

**** Potential Positions ****

*** Possible Replacements ***
M M Lewis   A2   1990
F L Clawson   L   2011
G A Smith   L   2019

Used with permission of Detroit Edison.

Figure 4–4. Career planning inventory organization review chart.

4–4, the chart displays a manager in the top box with up to four immediate subordinates in the lower boxes. Managers with more than four subordinates receive more than one chart. Information shown on the chart includes:

- *Position Box:* The position title and incumbent's name appear in each box. The symbol ` preceding the name identifies incumbents retiring between 1981–1985 and indicates that short-range planning is required. If the symbol `` precedes the name, the incumbent is identified as one who will retire between 1986–1992. In these cases, long-range planning is required. If the word OPEN appears in the box, the position is unfilled; if FUTURE appears, the position is anticipated but does not yet exist.
- *Dev Pgm:* Identifies the particular development program in which the employee participates.
- *Retire:* The month and year of the employee's planned retirement.
- *Est Prom:* Indicates the employee's estimated potential for promotion.
- *Lrp:* Indicates an estimate of the employee's long-range career potential in the Company.
- *Ppc:* Indicates the incumbent's current organizational level.
- *3 Developmental Needs:* Describes three priority developmental needs which have been identified.
- *Potential Positions:* The title of each position to which the incumbent is potentially promotable is shown along with codes which indicate an estimate of when the employee would be ready.
- *Possible Replacements:* The names of up to ten possible replacements for the position are shown with codes indicating when the replacements would be ready for promotion to this position.

Skills Inventories. While a management inventory includes information related specifically to managerial personnel, a **skills inventory** contains information regarding non-managerial employees. Although the process and the intent of the skills inventory is essentially the same as a management inventory, the information may differ somewhat. Possible information that might be included in a skills inventory is:

- Background and biographical data
- Work experience
- Specific skills and knowledge
- Supervisory evaluations
- Career goals

118

Part II
Human
Resources
Planning,
Recruitment,
and Selection

A properly designed and updated skills inventory system permits management to readily identify employees with particular skills in order to satisfy the changing needs of the company.

External Supply

Unless a firm is experiencing a declining demand, it may have to go outside the organization to obtain employees. By necessity, forecasting availability of employees is a continuous process and an important function of human resources management. Rapid employment of new employees is typically quite difficult. A firm must be capable of determining not only the number of employees required but also where they can be obtained. The best source of supply varies by industry, firms, and geographical location. Some organizations have found that their best source of future employees is colleges and universities, while others achieve excellent results from vocational schools, competitors, or unsolicited applications.

If the company has information revealing where their employees were recruited, statistics regarding present and past employees may be used to project the best sources. For instance, a firm may discover that graduates from a particular college or university adapt well to the firm's environment. One large farming equipment manufacturer has achieved excellent success in recruiting from schools located in rural areas. Managers in this firm believe that since many students come from a farming environment, they can adapt more quickly to the firm's method of operation.

Other firms have identified their employees' residences. They may discover from past records that the majority of their more successful employees lived no more than twenty miles from their workplace. This information may suggest that recruiting efforts should be concentrated in that particular geographical area.

Forecasting can assist not only in identifying where the supply of employees may be located but also in predicting what type of individuals will likely succeed in the organization. When a regional medical center located a great distance from a large metropolitan area reviewed its personnel files of registered nurses, it discovered that registered nurses who were born and raised in smaller towns adapted better to the small town environment than those who grew up in large metropolitan areas. After studying these statistics they modified their recruiting efforts.[8]

Examples of improper forecasting are numerous. Managers of one large convenience store chain were disturbed that their employee turnover rate was so high. When they analyzed their recruitment process, they discovered that the large majority of short-term employees had merely seen a sign in the store window that a position was available. These individuals were often unemployed and highly transient. The source of supply had a built-in mechanism to

[8]Wayne Mondy and Harry N. Mills, "Choice Not Chance in Nurse Selection," *Supervisor Nurse* 9 (November 1978): 35–39.

assure a high turnover rate. Once this fact was discovered, new sources of supply were found which significantly reduced turnover.

HUMAN RESOURCES PLANNING: AN EXAMPLE

The human resources planning model presented in Figure 4–1 is a generalized one. Each firm must tailor human resources planning to fit specific needs. The human resources planning process for Honeywell, Inc. is shown in Figure 4–5. Each element of the plan will next be discussed.

Organizational Goals

To be relevant, a human resource planning system needs to be clearly tied to the organization's business objectives. The plan must rest on a solid foundation of information about sales forecasts, market trends, technology advances, and major changes in processes or productivity. Considerable effort needs to be devoted to identifying reliable data on business trends and needs as the basic input which will "drive" the human resource plan in terms of quantity and quality of needed labor content.

Human Resource Needs Forecast

A second element in the planning process is the forecasting of human resource needs based on business objectives, production plans, and the various indicators of changes in technology or operating methods. This is usually accomplished utilizing historical data and reliable ratios (i.e.: indirect/direct labor) and adjusting them for productivity trends. The result of this forecast is a spread-sheet of employees needed to accomplish the organization's goals in terms of numbers, mix, cost, new skills or job categories, and numbers and levels of managers. Experience has shown that producing this forecast is the most challenging part of the planning process because it requires creative and highly participative approaches to dealing with business and technical uncertainties several years in the future.

Employee Information

A third element of the planning process is accurate information concerning the composition, configuration, and capabilities of the current work force. This includes information about job classifications, ages, sex, minority status, organization levels, salaries, and functions. Employee information may also include resume data such as skills, educational and training data, and career in-

120

Part II
Human
Resources
Planning,
Recruitment,
and Selection

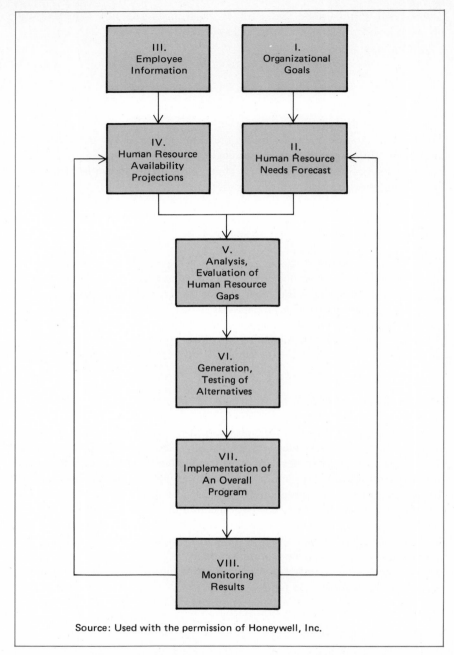

Figure 4–5. **Elements of a human resource plan at Honeywell, Inc.**

terests. Much of the data needed for human resource planning currently exists
in other personnel systems (i.e. payroll, talent review, or professional development data).

Human Resource Availability Projections

121

Chapter 4
Human
Resources
Planning

The fourth element of the planning process is to calculate what current human resources could be or will be available in terms of skills, numbers, age, deployment, etc. into the future. By projecting past data about the size, configuration, and composition of the work force and data about the flows of the human resources (turnover, aging, hiring) one can determine the probable availability at a specific future time. The result of this kind of activity is a picture of what human resources an organization currently has and how they will evolve over time due to turnover, retirement, obsolescence, etc.

Analyzing and Evaluating Human Resource Gaps

The fifth element of the planning process is to compare what is needed with what is available in terms of numbers, mix, skills, and technologies. This permits the personnel manager to determine gaps and to evaluate where the most serious mismatches occur. Such analysis should help the organization address issues such as:

- Are imbalances developing between human resource needs and projected availability?
- What is the effect of current productivity trends and pay levels on work force levels and costs?
- Do turnover problems exist in certain jobs or age levels?
- Are there problems of career blockage and obsolescence?
- Are there sufficient high-potential managers to fulfill future needs?
- Are we short any critical skills?

Such analysis will lead to the development of specific plans on a long-range basis for recruiting, hiring, training, transferring, and retraining appropriate numbers and types of employees.

Generating and Testing Alternatives

The analysis of the human resource system should have an impact on a wide range of policies and practices such as: staffing plans, promotion practices and policies, EEO plans, organization design, training and development programs, salary planning and career management systems. This merit phase of the process explores the implications of the analysis and generates alternatives to current practices and policies. Some more comprehensive human resource planning systems permit modeling the configuration and composition of human resources that would result from specific changes in staffing strategies or other personnel policies. This allows evaluation and testing of alternatives. If testing of anticipated consequences is not performed by a computer model, an equivalent manual system should be utilized.

122

Part II
Human
Resources
Planning,
Recruitment,
and Selection

Implementing an Overall
Human Resource Program

Once the best alternatives have been chosen to address the organization's human resource issues they need to become operational programs with specific plans, target dates, schedules, resource commitments, etc.

The analytical steps outlined above should shape an organization's staffing plan, EEO plan, training and development activities, mobility plans, productivity programs, bargaining strategies, and compensation programs.

Monitoring Results

The final element in any human resource planning process is to provide a means for management to monitor results of the overall program. This step should address such questions as:

- How well is the plan working?
- Is it cost effective?
- What is the actual versus planned impact on the work force?
- Where are the weak areas?
- What changes will be needed during the next cycle?

HUMAN RESOURCES INFORMATION
SYSTEMS

In order for Personnel to make sound decisions and recommendations related to human resources planning, information must be available on an accurate and timely basis. A **Human Resources Information System** facilitates obtaining such data in a logical, valid, and reliable manner in order to assist in managerial decision making.[9]

A problem that firms have historically confronted is the ability to make human resources decisions which meet these three requirements. For instance, suppose that the vice president of international operations called the personnel manager of a firm employing 10,000 workers with the following request: "Sam, this is Bill. I have a major problem. One of my managers was just killed in an automobile accident. I need someone immediately to take over that position. Hopefully, we can obtain someone from within the firm. The person I need must be able to speak Spanish fluently and be an electrical engineer with a working knowledge of electrical generators." If this type of search takes a month, Bill really has a problem. He needs the individual now! If the employee can be obtained in-house, the transition to this new position will likely be much faster than if the person must be brought in from outside the firm.

[9]William P. Anthony, "Get To Know Your Employees—The Human Resource Information System," *Personnel Journal* 56 (April 1977): 179.

Although the benefits of an HRIS are numerous and can affect all personnel functions, it is mentioned here because personnel planning relates to and precedes all other areas of Personnel. The many changes that have occurred during the past twenty years have created a need for useful information regarding potential employees and workers who are currently employed with the firm.[10]

Since the advent of high speed computers, management has been fascinated with the speed with which large amounts of data can be prepared. Large volumes of information can be stored in the computer and then be retrieved virtually instantly. However, an HRIS is not necessarily dependent upon a computer. A firm without a computer can also have a very efficient system. The computer has merely made it possible for some larger firms to obtain human resources data with increased speed. Whether the HRIS is computerized or performed manually is not the point we are concerned with here. The procedure for designing useful human resources information systems is essentially the same. The general steps that should be followed in the development of a useful HRIS are:

1. Study of the present system
2. Priority development of human resources information
3. Development of the new system
4. Installation of a computer, if necessary
5. Maintenance of the system

Study of the Present System

The first step in developing an effective HRIS is to study and identify the present system as it actually exists. This is important even if no formal system is currently in existence. An informal system may be used to obtain data, or each department or unit may have even developed separate systems to meet their needs. Whatever the situation, the future direction cannot be determined until a thorough appreciation is gained regarding the present system. Questions that may need to be answered are:

- What is the present flow of human resources data?
- How is the information used?
- How critical is the information that is available?
- What type of information is needed?
- Where is the information?
- How rapidly is the available information needed?

At one stage in his career, one of the authors was employed as a consultant to develop a human resources information system for a national forest

[10]Alfred J. Walker, Jr., "Personnel Uses the Computer," *Personnel Journal* 51 (March 1972): 204–205.

124

Part II
Human
Resources
Planning,
Recruitment,
and Selection

products firm. In studying the firm's existing system, the author was amazed to discover a large amount of duplication and wasted effort. Some weekly reports were essentially useless in the decision-making process. Two employees had to work a total of eight hours weekly to prepare one particular report. If the report was late, the vice president's secretary would send a strongly worded reprimand to the delinquent division chief. However, once the information arrived at headquarters, it was neatly filed and was never used. Numerous questions regarding this practice revealed that approximately five years ago this type of information was requested—as a one-time report. Preparation of the report had continued through the administration of three vice presidents.

Priority Development of Human Resources Information

The next step in developing an HRIS is to rank information according to its importance. Certain data are critical to the successful accomplishment of the personnel function, while other information may merely be nice to have. A properly designed human resources information system must be developed to provide the high priority information required in decision making. Lower priority reports and information will only be prepared as time and cost permit. For instance, a report describing the specific abilities of the firm's employees would likely be ranked high, whereas the available parking spaces report might be ranked quite low. Through the development of this priority list, one begins to realize that some information is critical to the successful operation of the firm while other data provide only marginal benefits.

Development of the New System

Once a priority has been assigned to specific reports and information, the human resources information system may next be developed. The system should meet the overall human resources management needs. Specific reports are designed which will provide the required information.

Figure 4–6 presents an overview of a human resources information system that was prepared for one organization. You will note that numerous types of input data are necessary. Information of these types is available from many sources. Through the HRIS, considerable output data then become available. These output reports have far reaching values ranging from personnel planning to operational uses. Some specific output reports will be described in a later section. The HRIS permits all areas related to human resources management to be tied together into a total information system. Data from several input sources are integrated to provide needed output data. Information critical to the firm's decision-making processes becomes available when the system is properly designed.

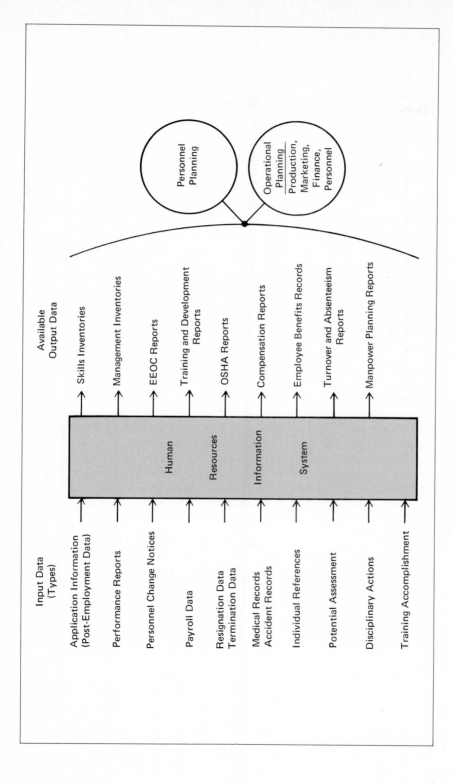

Figure 4-6. A human resources information system.

125

126

Part II
Human
Resources
Planning,
Recruitment,
and Selection

Installation of a Computer

One popular but mistaken assumption is that a human resources information system cannot function without a computer. A system should first be designed from the viewpoint of the optimum flow of data which will result in obtaining specific desired output. Many firms successfully use a manual system. A computer should only be considered when the speed and accuracy of a manual system are unacceptable. However, a computer should not be considered in the actual design phase, but should be chosen later when the actual system requirements are known.

Maintenance of the System

Workers in the data processing field have long had an expression called "GIGO," an acronym which means "Garbage-In-Garbage-Out." It certainly applies in maintaining an effective, timely, and accurate HRIS. It does not matter whether the system is manual or computerized. All sections and departments of the firm must be trained and made aware of the importance of forwarding source documents that are accurate and timely. The importance of each document to the overall system must be clearly understood and appreciated. When this occurs, the HRIS can benefit everyone in the organization.

HRIS: AN ILLUSTRATION

The desire for reliable, fast, and useful human resources data has been with managers for years. For a large number of firms this desire was relatively unfulfilled until the last ten or fifteen years. Computers capable of handling large data bases were quite expensive while software available to process the data was relatively unsophisticated. The use of computerized HRIS has become much more common because of the declining price of computers, the increasing sophistication and availability of software, and the growing need for human resources data.[11]

One firm that has pioneered the development of personnel information systems is Information Science Incorporated (InSci). Founded in 1965, InSci was the first company to engage in the commercial development of computer-based personnel information systems. An overview of The Human Resources System developed by InSci may be seen in Figure 4–7. As you can see, a large portion of the system is devoted toward dealing with government legislation. The system also provides information which aids management in planning for the future.

Information available from the HRIS may either be obtained through "hard copy" or through data display screens. An example of a hard copy of J. K. Robertson's career profile may be seen in Figure 4–8. As you can see,

[11]"Human Resources Has Its Own Computer," *Personnel* 55 (January-February 1978): 46.

considerable information is available which should be beneficial in evaluating Mr. Robertson's career interests and capabilities. A sample of some of the types of information available on data display screens may be seen in Figure 4–9. In this illustration, a person with access to the personnel file has requested a mini-profile of John Doe. When data display screens are used, files may be updated rapidly. These screens may be placed at critical areas in the firm to provide instant access to personnel information for individuals with a need to know. Decision-making information is available virtually immediately.

COST/BENEFITS ANALYSIS—HUMAN RESOURCES PLANNING

There are both costs and benefits associated with conducting effective human resources planning. In terms of time and money the costs can be substantial. To be effective, top-level management must be involved and this, in the past,

Figure 4–7. **The human resources system developed by Information Science Incorporated.**

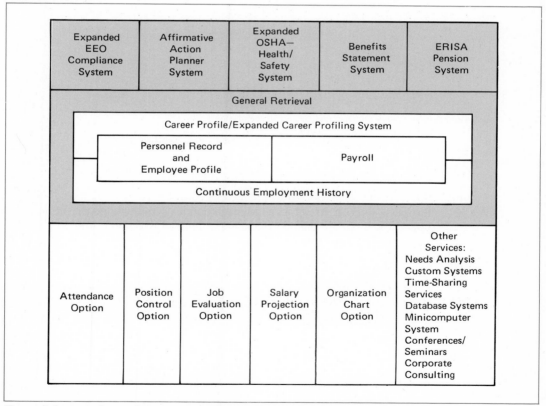

(Source: Information Science Incorporated. Used with permission.)

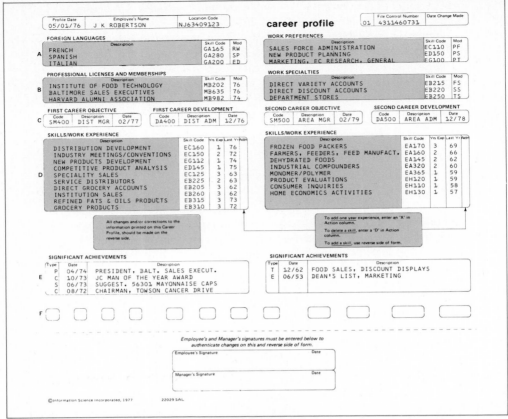

Figure 4–8. **An example of the hard copy available.**

has been difficult to achieve. Many individuals throughout the firm are involved in providing data to the system. Trained personnel professionals must be available to conduct the planning. Should a computer be needed, as is the case with most large firms, costs are associated with installing and using the computer system.

But the benefits of effective human resources planning usually far outweigh the costs. Management must consider the risk of not having qualified workers available at the proper time. It is difficult to have good recruitment and selection programs without planning. Human resources planning assists T&D by projecting what form of training and development will be needed in the future. Planning is also tied to compensation so the proper compensation packages can be prepared. Every aspect of human resources management is influenced by the need for planning.

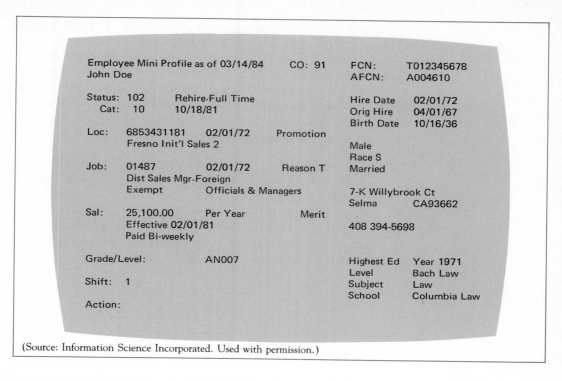

Employee Mini Profile as of 03/14/84   CO: 91   FCN: T012345678
John Doe   AFCN: A004610

Status: 102   Rehire·Full Time   Hire Date   02/01/72
   Cat: 10   10/18/81   Orig Hire   04/01/67
                                                  Birth Date   10/16/36
Loc: 6853431181   02/01/72   Promotion
        Fresno Init'l Sales 2   Male
                                                  Race S
Job: 01487   02/01/72   Reason T   Married
        Dist Sales Mgr·Foreign
        Exempt   Officials & Managers   7-K Willybrook Ct
                                                  Selma   CA93662
Sal: 25,100.00   Per Year   Merit
        Effective 02/01/81   408 394-5698
        Paid Bi-weekly

Grade/Level: AN007   Highest Ed   Year 1971
                                                  Level   Bach Law
Shift: 1   Subject   Law
                                                  School   Columbia Law
Action:

(Source: Information Science Incorporated. Used with permission.)

Figure 4–9. **Examples of the information available on data display screens.**

SUMMARY

Planning is the process by which management helps an organization achieve
its objectives. Planning is particularly important if the firm is to fulfill its future
human resources needs. Strategic plans are designed to help the firm achieve
its primary objectives. Personnel often did not become involved in strategic
planning until the plans were fully developed. However, top management is
beginning to recognize the necessity of involving Personnel in the strategic
planning process. The firm's human resources needs must reflect corporate objectives and plans. After objectives and plans have been formulated, the demand for the firm's products and/or services should be forecasted.

Once the demand for a firm's products and/or services has been established, the organization may then engage in human resources planning (HRP).
There are two sides to human resources planning—demand and supply. On
the demand side, the firm must identify the quantity and quality of employees
needed to achieve its goals. This procedure is called personnel demand analysis. The primary source for analyzing personnel demand is the firm's forecast of
the demand for its goods and/or services. A firm's human resources needed are
closely tied to this forecast.

On the supply side, the organization needs to determine where workers may be found (whether from internal or external sources) to satisfy the firm's human resources requirements. This process is called labor supply analysis.

A management inventory contains detailed data regarding each manager and can be used to identify individuals with the potential to move into higher-level positions. A skills inventory contains information regarding nonmanagerial employees. Although the process and the intent of the skills inventory is essentially the same as a management inventory, the information may differ somewhat.

A human resources information system facilitates obtaining useful data in a logical, valid, and reliable manner in order to assist in managerial decision making. The benefits of an HRIS are numerous and can affect all personnel functions. The general steps that should be followed in developing a useful HRIS are: 1. study of the present situation; 2. priority development of human resources information; 3. development of the new system; 4. installation of a computer, if necessary; and 5. maintenance of the system.

Questions for Review

1. Describe the human resources planning process.

2. Identify and define the basic terms appropriate to an understanding of demand forecasting. *determining projected emps. demand*

3. Describe the relationship between sales volume and the number of employees. Why is it important to understand this relationship in personnel planning?

4. Briefly describe the Delphi Technique, regression analysis, and simulation as they assist the personnel planning process. *demand forecasters*

5. Distinguish by definition and example between personnel demand analysis and labor supply analysis.

6. What are the primary actions a firm could take if it was experiencing a personnel surplus? *layoffs, restructuring hrs, early retire*

7. Distinguish between a management inventory and a skills inventory. What are the essential components of each?

8. What is the purpose of a human resources information system? What are the basic steps that should be considered in developing an HRIS? *1 study existing system 2 prioritize needs for info 3 dev new 4 install new, or comps, 5 maintain*

Terms for Review

Strategic plans *to achieve primary objectives*
Job analysis *prerequisite for both demand + supply analysis*
Long-run trend *need for firms products 5+ yrs into future*
Cyclical demand *> 1 yr < 5 yr - economics etc*
Seasonal demand
Random demand *no pattern in product need*
Delphi Technique *questionaire series → demand forecast*

Regression analysis *several variables → demand forecast*
Simulation *computer demand forecast*
Personnel demand analysis *type + # emp needed*
Labor supply analysis *where get "*
Management inventory *lists potential of mgrs for labor supply analyses*
Skills inventory *non-mgmt "*
Human resources information system *logical data → decisions*

demand + supply = HRP

Judy Anderson is the personnel recruiter for South Illinois Electric Company (SIE), a small supplier of natural gas and electricity for Cairo, Illinois and the surrounding area. The company has grown rapidly over the five years that Judy has worked there and the growth is expected to continue. She just heard that SIE purchased the utilities system serving a neighboring county. The company work force increased by 30 percent the previous year and Judy found it a struggle to recruit enough qualified job applicants. She knows that the new expansion will intensify the problem.

Meter readers are an area of particular concern. The tasks required in meter reading are relatively simple. A person drives to homes served by the company, finds the gas or electric meter, and records its current reading. If the meter has been tampered with it is reported. The reader performs no calculations; there is no decision making of any consequence associated with the job. The pay is $7.00 per hour. Even so, Judy has been having considerable difficulty in keeping the 37 meter reader positions filled.

One day recently Judy was thinking about how to attract more job applicants when she received a call from the personnel director, Sam McCord. "Judy," Sam said, "I'm unhappy with the job specification calling for only a high school education for meter readers. In planning for the future we need more educated people in the company. I've decided to change the education requirement for the meter reader job from a high school diploma to a college degree." "But, Mr. McCord," protested Judy, "the company is growing rapidly. If we are to have sufficient people to fill those jobs we just can't insist on finding college applicants to perform such basic tasks. I don't see how our plans for projecting our future needs for this job can be realized with such an unrealistic job qualification." Sam terminated the conversation abruptly by saying, "No, I don't agree. We need to upgrade all the people in our organization. This is just part of a general effort to do that. Anyway, I cleared this with the president before I decided to do it."

Questions

1. Should there be a minimum education requirement for the meter reader job? Discuss.
2. What is your opinion of Sam's effort to upgrade the people in the organization?

3. What legal ramifications, if any, should Sam have considered?

_____

David Johnson, personnel manager for Eagle Aircraft, was a little anxious as he checked through his in-basket that morning. He had just returned from a long weekend at Cozumel, Mexico. His friend Carl Edwards, vice president of marketing, had called the night before to tell him about a meeting of the company's executive council. "It was a great meet-

ing," Carl had said, "I don't think the future has ever looked brighter for Eagle."

Carl had gone on to tell about the president's decision to expand operations. He continued, "Everyone at the meeting seemed to be completely behind the president. Joe Davis, the controller, stressed our independent financial position; the production manager had done a complete work-up on the equipment we are going to need, including availability and cost information. And I have been pushing for this expansion for some time. So I was ready. I think it will be good for you too, David. The president said he expects employment to double in the next year."

David found nothing in his mail about the meeting. He decided not to worry about it. "I suppose they'll let me know when they need my help," he thought.

Just then he looked up to see Rex Schearer, a production supervisor, standing in the doorway. "David," said Rex, "the production manager jumped me Friday because maintenance doesn't have anybody qualified to work on the new digital lathe they are installing." "He's right," David replied, "we'd better get hot and see if we can find someone." David knew that it was going to be another busy Monday.

Questions

1. What deficiencies do you see in planning at Eagle Aircraft?

2. How might the planning situation at Eagle Aircraft be improved?

3. When should David start to work on finding the maintenance person for the digital lathe?

Chapter Objectives

1. Describe the recruitment process and explain why it is so closely related to human resources planning.
2. Identify actions a firm might consider before trying outside recruitment.
3. Describe the external and internal factors that can influence the recruitment process.
4. Explain the methods that are often used in internal recruiting.
5. Identify the various sources and methods available to an organization for external recruiting.
6. Relate the importance of the Uniform Guidelines to human resources management and describe what is meant by adverse impact.
7. Explain when firms must develop Affirmative Action programs.
8. State what should be done to ensure that recruitment efforts are appropriate to meet legal standards.
9. Explain what is meant by sexual harassment.

Chapter 5 _____

Personnel Recruitment

Scott Shelton is a college recruiter for Zipp Enterprises. On a recent recruiting trip to a university, Scott had a full schedule of student interviews. His first interviewee after lunch was a marketing major named Polly Stacy. Scott was tired and when Polly entered his office, he greeted her with, "O.K., let's get this over with as quickly as possible." Polly was infuriated with what appeared to her as a real putdown. The relationship between the two deteriorated even further as the interview continued. That evening Polly was talking with a group of friends about her experience. They all seemed to agree that Zipp Enterprises would be the last company they would want to work for.

Joyce Sather, recruiting supervisor for the Pluto Manufacturing Company, had been promoted to her position after serving years as a production supervisor. One of Joyce's first major assignments was to recruit a general foreman for Pluto. After considering various alternatives, Joyce decided to place the following ad in a local newspaper with a circulation in excess of 1,000,000:

Employment Opportunity
Growing firm has position available for person with managerial
experience. Contact Joyce Sather, Pluto Manufacturing Company.

More than 300 applications were received in the first week and Joyce was elated. However, when she reviewed the applications, it appeared that people with every conceivable type of work experience had applied. There were few if any good prospects in the group.

Mark Smith and Debra Coffee, two executives from competing firms, met at their annual product conference. They were discussing a hot topic, the effect of the government's civil rights activity in their firms. Mark said, "I don't think we have any difficulty at our company. I'm told that our employees are 35 percent minorities." "That's great," Debra replied, "How many of your minorities fill middle management positions?" After thinking a moment, Mark said, "I believe we have one over in maintenance." "Mark, you may have serious problems with EEO and not even realize it. I suggest that you do some checking."

136

Part II
Human
Resources
Planning,
Recruitment,
and Selection

Recruitment involves encouraging qualified people to apply for employment with a firm. Unless a sufficient number of qualified prospects apply for a job with the firm, you cannot have a truly selective employment system.[1] Scott, Joyce, Mark, and Debra are all associated with the recruitment process. If Scott continues to turn off applicants, as he did Polly, Zipp Enterprises' recruitment program may be severely damaged. Joyce, on the other hand, apparently did not tailor the recruitment message properly and obtained the wrong type of applicants. Mark may have difficulties because an insufficient number of minorities have progressed into management. Determining the proper means whereby future employees can be encouraged to apply for employment is important to every firm whether it is General Motors or Mr. Z's corner grocery store.

THE RECRUITMENT PROCESS

There is an old expression which states, "You can't turn down a job offer until one has been made." From the employer's side of this expression, it might be, "You can't make a job offer unless you have someone who wants the job." Personnel recruitment involves encouraging individuals, in sufficient quantity and quality, to apply for jobs with the organization. The best qualified applicants may then be selected from among a number of individuals. Obviously, personnel recruitment is an essential function of every firm. In most medium and large organizations, the personnel department is responsible for the recruitment process. In small firms recruiting will likely be conducted by individual managers.

The personnel recruitment process is shown in Figure 5–1. As you can see, both the internal and external environments continue to impact Personnel. Once human resources planning indicates a need for employees, the firm may then evaluate the possibility of using alternatives to meet the demand for its goods and services. When these alternatives are not appropriate, the recruitment process starts. Frequently recruitment begins when a manager initiates an employee requisition. The **requisition,** when used, specifies various details including job title, department, and the date the employee is needed for work. With this information, Personnel can refer to the appropriate job description to determine the qualifications needed by the person to be recruited. At times, firms continue their recruiting efforts even when vacancies do not exist. This practice permits them to maintain recruitment contacts and to identify and employ exceptional candidates.

The next step in the recruitment process is to determine whether qualified employees are available within the firm (the internal source) or must be recruited externally from sources such as colleges, universities, and other companies. Recruitment methods are the specific means through which potential

[1]Edwin S. Stanton, "The Sequential Selection System®: The Key to Hiring Better People," *Training and Development Journal* 33 (March 1979): 61.

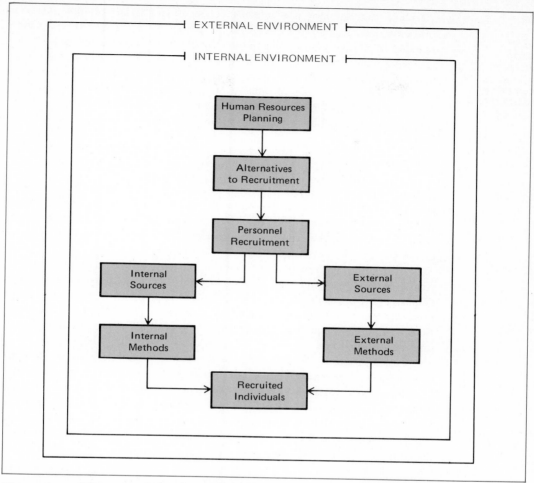

Figure 5–1. **The personnel recruitment process.**

employees are attracted to the organization. Appropriate methods for either internal or external recruitments are then used.

Because of the high costs of recruiting, organizations must be assured that they are utilizing the most productive sources and methods. It may be discovered that one recruitment method is superior to another for a given company in locating executive talent. For instance, one large equipment manufacturer determined that medium-sized state-supported colleges and universities located in rural areas were good sources for potential managers.

ALTERNATIVES TO RECRUITMENT

Even when human resources planning indicates a need for additional or re-placement employees, a firm may decide against immediately engaging in re-

138

Part II
Human
Resources
Planning,
Recruitment,
and Selection

cruitment. Recruitment and selection costs are high. For example, it costs some hospitals as much as $12,000 just to recruit and orient one nurse.[2] Often included in the calculation of costs are factors such as the search process, interviewing, agency fee payment, and relocation and inprocessing of the new employee. And, although decisions made in the selection process are not irreversible, once employees are placed on the payroll, they may be difficult to remove even if their performance is marginal. Therefore, a firm should consider its alternatives before engaging in recruitment.

Overtime

Perhaps the most common approach to meeting short-term fluctuations in work volume is through the use of overtime. Overtime can be useful to both employer and employee. The employer may benefit because the costs of recruiting, selection, and training are avoided. The employee benefits because higher pay may be received.

While there are obvious advantages in using overtime, there are also potential pitfalls. Many managers feel that when they are required to work their employees for unusually long periods of time, the company is paying more and receiving less in return. This condition may accelerate when excessive overtime is required. Employees may become fatigued and lack the energy to perform at a normal rate.

Two additional potential problems are related to prolonged overtime. Employees may, consciously or not, pace themselves so that their overtime will be assured. They may also become accustomed to the added income resulting from overtime payments. Employees may even elevate their standard of living to the level permitted by this additional income. Then, when overtime is no longer required, and the paycheck shrinks, the employees may become disgruntled.

Subcontracting

Even though an increased demand for its goods and/or services is anticipated, an organization may decide against expansion. Rather, the firm may decide to subcontract the work to another enterprise. This approach has much appeal when the increased demand is viewed as being of a short-range duration. Also, there are times when the subcontractor actually has greater expertise in producing a given product or providing the service. This arrangement may be mutually beneficial even for long periods of time.

Temporary Employees

When an anticipated increase in demand is of a short-range nature, another alternative to work force expansion is the use of temporary help. In the past

[2]"Re-entry Isn't Easy," *The Nurse Recruiter* 1, (February 1982): 1.

"Most importantly, a student in the senior year should prepare for an actual interview by anticipating the questions the professional recruiter might ask. Recruiters look for an applicant who has thoroughly researched their corporation, and who has a good understanding of the role of an employee relations department and its impact upon business operations. Students should also predetermine their specific interests within the employee relations profession, e.g., are they interested in a generalist assignment or a specialist position such as employment/placement; compensation; management development, etc?"

Robert E. Baillie, Manager-Employee Relations, Science and Technology, International Paper Company.

as many as nine out of ten companies in this country used temporary help services,[3] thereby saving the costs of fringe benefits. Savings may also be realized due to the lack of absenteeism and turnover. The expense of recruitment is also avoided. For instance, suppose Faye Brown, supervisor of the stenographic pool, has an immediate but short-range need for six secretaries. Rather than recruit and hire additional employees, Faye calls a local organization which supplies temporary workers. This firm immediately sends the employees needed. These people remain on the payroll of the temporary help organization and Faye's firm is billed later for their services. Firms specializing in providing temporary employees now comprise a $2 billion industry.[4]

Not all aspects of temporary help are positive. Since employees obtained in this manner are not on the client's payroll, they may not feel as loyal as fulltime employees. Also, temporary employees may lack required specialized training. Providing this training may take more time than can be justified.

EXTERNAL ENVIRONMENT OF RECRUITMENT

As with the other personnel functions, the recruitment process does not take place in a vacuum. Factors external to the organization can significantly affect the firm's recruitment efforts. Of particular importance is the supply and demand of specific skills in the labor market. If the demand for a particular skill is high relative to supply, an extraordinary recruiting effort may be required. For instance, the demand for computer programmers and accountants is likely to be higher than their supply, as opposed to the demand-supply relationship for nontechnical employees.

[3]Charles J. Sigrist, "Nine Out of Ten Firms Use Temporary Help," *The Office* 87 (January 1978): 90.
[4]Howard Rudnitsky, "A Cushion for Business," *Forbes* 123 (February 5, 1979): 78.

140

Part II
Human
Resources
Planning,
Recruitment,
and Selection

When the unemployment rate in a given area is high, the firm's recruitment process may be simpler. The number of unsolicited applicants is usually greater and the increased size of the labor pool provides better opportunities for attracting qualified applicants. On the other hand, as the unemployment rate drops, recruiting efforts must be increased and new sources explored.

Labor market conditions in a local area are of primary importance in recruiting for most nonmanagerial, many supervisory, and even some middle management positions. However, recruitment for executive and professional positions may be concerned more with the national market. Although the recruiter's day-to-day activities provide a feel for the labor market, accurate data regarding employment may be found in professional journals and Department of Labor reports.

Federal legislation also plays a significant role in recruitment practices in the United States. However, the individual and the employer first make contact during the recruitment process. Therefore, nondiscriminatory practices are absolutely essential at this stage of the employment relationship. Because EEO practices begin with recruitment, this vital topic will be discussed in a later section of this chapter.

The firm's corporate image is another important factor which affects the recruitment process. If employees believe that their employer deals with them in a fair manner, the positive word-of-mouth advertising they provide is of utmost value to the firm. It assists in establishing credibility with prospective employees. Good reputations earned in this manner can result in more and better qualified applicants seeking employment. Prospective employees are more inclined to respond positively to the organization's recruitment efforts. The firm with a healthy public image is one believed to be a "good place to work," and the recruitment efforts of such a firm are greatly enhanced.

INTERNAL ENVIRONMENT OF RECRUITMENT

While the labor market and the government exert powerful external influences on recruitment, the organization's own practices and policies also affect the recruitment effort. A major internal factor that can determine the success of a recruiting program is whether or not the firm engages in human resources planning. In most cases, a firm cannot attract prospective employees in sufficient numbers and with required skills overnight. It takes time to examine the alternatives regarding the appropriate sources of recruits and the most productive methods for obtaining them. Once the best alternatives have been identified, recruitment plans may be made. Effective human resources planning greatly facilitates the recruitment efforts.

An organization's promotion policy can also have a significant impact upon its recruitment program. Basically, there are two approaches an organization can follow. One stresses a policy of **promotion from within** its own ranks. The other involves filling positions from outside the organization. There is a logical rationale for each approach.

When an organization emphasizes promotion from within, its workers have increased incentive to strive for advancement. When employees witness promotions occurring within their units, they become aware of their own opportunities. The motivation provided by this practice is often accompanied by a general improvement in employee morale. However, a strictly applied promotion from within policy is not always possible and practical because the firm may need fresh ideas which can only come from outsiders. In any event, a promotion policy that first considers insiders is great for employee morale and motivation.

Another advantage of recruiting internally is that the organization is usually aware of its employees' capabilities. An employee's past performance in a given job may not, by itself, be a reliable criterion for promotion. Nevertheless, many personal and job related qualities may be known because the employee has established at least some track record as opposed to being an "unknown quantity." Also, the company's investment in the individual may be better utilized. Still another positive factor is the employee's knowledge of the firm, its policies, and its people.

Yet it is unlikely that a firm can or would even desire to adhere rigidly to a practice of promotion from within. The vice president of personnel and industrial relations for a major automobile manufacturer offers this advice: "A strictly applied 'PFW' policy eventually leads to inbreeding, a lack of cross-fertilization, and a lack of creativity. A good goal, in my opinion, is to fill 80 percent of openings above entry level positions from within." Management may believe that new blood is badly needed to provide new ideas and innovation that must take place for firms to remain competitive. In such cases, even organizations with promotion from within policies may opt to look outside the organization for new talent. One university's data processing manager routinely hired the school's best computer science graduates. She believed that this internal source provided the best qualified workers. But, because of this practice, new ideas were never brought into the data processing center. The procedures generated in the past were never challenged and many became quickly outdated.

Policies related to the employment of relatives may also affect a firm's recruitment efforts. While the content of such policies varies greatly, it is not uncommon for companies to have policies which discourage the employment of close relatives. This is often true when their assignments would be in the same chain of command.

There are two sides to the question of whether a firm should employ close relatives. On one hand, it may be disappointing for little Janet not to be able to follow in her father's footsteps. On the other, the possible concentration of a family in one organizational unit may result in favoritism and have other negative consequences. Favoritism shown to relatives in organizations is often referred to as nepotism.

Barbara Sullivan
President and co-Owner
Quest Personnel Services

Barbara Sullivan, President and co-owner of Quest Personnel Services in Los Angeles, was well on the road to becoming a social worker when she met her first personnel professional who inspired her to change her career goal. "Barbara, can you run the College Placement Service Office?" "Sure," was the answer of the naive second year graduate student at Tuskegee Institute in Alabama. Thus began a career in Personnel. While serving an internship in pupil personnel services at Tuskegee Institute, Ms. Sullivan was assigned to the Student Placement Office for her field project. When the director of the office became ill, Barbara was given the responsibility of coordinating the recruitment program. She talked to the various recruiters who came to interview on campus about the work they performed. As a result of that experience, after graduation from college, Barbara sought employment in the personnel field in Los Angeles, California.

However, she was surprised to discover that her master's degree in guidance and counseling and her related personnel experience did not eliminate the "need more experience" response from prospective employers. She wanted to be a recruiter, but in 1967, companies were not hiring many black female recruiters. After job searching for three months, Barbara finally accepted the only personnel related position offered to her. She became an employment counselor for an employment agency. After working there for one year, she felt that her agency interviewing experience qualified her to apply for an interviewer's position in the personnel department of Cedars Sinai Medical Center, where she was hired.

METHODS USED IN INTERNAL RECRUITING

Management needs to be able to identify current employees who are capable of filling positions as they become available. Helpful tools used for internal recruitment include management and skills inventories, and job posting and bidding procedures. As mentioned in Chapter 4, management and skills inventories permit organizations to determine whether current employees possess needed qualifications. As a recruitment device, these inventories have proven extremely valuable to organizations when they are maintained on a current basis. Inventories can be of tremendous value in locating internal talent. Also they support the concept of promotion from within.

The purpose of **job posting** is to communicate the fact that job openings exist. **Job bidding** permits individuals in the organization who believe that they possess the required qualifications to apply for the job. A procedure that might be used in a medium-sized business firm is shown in Table 5–1. Larger

While employed there, she held the positions of employment manager, EEO coordinator, and employee counselor/trainer.

Barbara was hired next as personnel director for a new medical facility, West Adams Community Hospital, where she organized and managed the personnel function. At West Adams, she and her staff of two employees was responsible for staffing, policy development, training, compensation, and benefits for over four hundred employees. Barbara also found herself responsible for fighting a union organizational drive that prepared her with the experience needed to face the same situation later in her career.

Barbara's career goals led her to seek an expanded work environment to further her personnel knowledge and experience. "I felt I was at the top of West Adams, yet I needed to learn more to sharpen my skills." She next joined Children's Hospital as assistant personnel director where she was mentored by two skilled, competent women in personnel and organizational development. "After three years at Children's Hospital, I knew I was professional-ready," states Barbara," and needed to move to the next challenge." She found that next challenge by responding to an advertisement in the *Los Angeles Times* for a personnel director for the City Attorney's Office, City of Los Angeles.

Barbara says, "The personnel function, more than any other area in a company, provides the opportunity and exposure for developing executive skills. The combination of people (staffing), project, and financial related tasks embodied in the daily duties of a personnel generalist are readily transferable to the executive suite." Barbara is currently proving this as she and her partner, Elaine Wegener (president of the personnel consulting firm PACT), continue to build the highly praised temporary and permanent placement agency, Quest.

"Because we are personnel professionals, we conduct our offices as extensions of our clients' personnel operations," states Barbara. She feels that there is a definite need for the services that agencies such as hers provide. Barbara envisions more of a cooperative spirit developing in the future between personnel agencies and companies as personnel agencies embrace a more professional posture toward service to the companies.

Table 5–1. Job posting and bidding procedure

Responsibility	Action Required
Personnel Assistant	1. Upon receiving *Form PR-12, Personnel Requisition,* write a memo to each appropriate supervisor stating that a job vacancy exists. The memo should include job title, job number, pay grade, salary range, a summary of the basic duties performed, and the qualifications required for the job (data to be taken from job description-specification).
	2. Ensure that a copy of this memo is posted on all company bulletin boards.
Supervisors	3. Make certain that every employee who might qualify for the position is made aware of the job opening.
Interested Employee	4. Contact the Personnel Department.

1. If you are interested in any of the opportunities listed below, please complete a "Job Opportunity Request" form and submit it to your Job Opportunity Office. Forms may be obtained from your personnel department.
2. Each opportunity will be held open for consideration of TIers for one week. To be considered, your Job Opportunity Request must be received in your site Job Opportunity Office by no later than seven days from the date of this bulletin.
3. To qualify for a job, you must satisfy all requirements of the job and you must list these qualifications on your Job Opportunity Request form. A resume or additional information may be attached if desired but the required qualifications as described in the job posting must be listed on the Job Opportunity Request form.
4. Each opportunity is coded to indicate payment of transfer expenses in accordance with Personnel Procedure PM 2-3-4 (Transfer Expenses of TI Personnel) as follows:
   CR—Candidates urgently needed. Transfer expenses including Home Guarantee Program paid.
   ER—Internal and external candidates are being sought locally and national. Transfer expenses paid as listed in PM 2-3-4.
   LR—Adequate local supply of qualified people. TIers in other locations may bid with understanding that no transfer expenses will be paid by TI.
   For details of transfer expenses paid for by each of the above classifications, see your personnel Administrator.
5. JOB GRADES—On jobs in locations other than your own, see your Personnel Adminstrator for comparison with your grading system.
6. If you do not receive an answer to your Job Opportunity Request by four weeks from the date of this Bulletin, call Job Opportunity at Dallas Expressway 5336. Remember the Job Number in requesting information about your Job Opportunity Request.

NON-EXEMPT
ADMINISTRATIVE

EQUIPMENT

CLK, GEN   (JPN)01DN2040
                         (JRC)0922723053
DUTIES: Prfm gen cler tasks; oper IBM key punch mach; oper calcul; some typg; maint logs, files, etc. MIN SKILL REQD: Prfm cler tasks. JG53:1-3 yrs rel expr. JG55: 3-5 yrs rel expr. SECURITY CLEARANCE REQD Grd 53/55 LR-CC922

CLK, GEN   (JPN)01DN2011
                         (JRC)0988723053
DUTIES: Oper various types of reprod/copy equip. Asst in oper of classified document contrl syst to include registration, transfer, filg % destruction of classified matl Typg ability reqd. Wrk hrs 10:30 a.m. – 7:00 p.m. MIN SKILL REQD: JG53: type 40-50 WPM, 1-5 yrs rel expr. JG55: type 50-60 WPM, 3-5 yrs rel expr. SECURITY CLEARANCE REQD. Grd 53/55 LR-CC988 s/lor Rotg

SECRETARY   (JPN)01DN2016
                         (JRC)0431731053
DUTIES: Sec duties f/Contract Admin includg hvy typg. filg, handlg classified documents, hvy phone liaison (cust/TI). JG53: over 1 yr dir rel expr. JG55: over 3 yrs dir rel expr MIN SKILL REQD: Typg 50-60 WPM. IBM Memory typg expr helpful. Abil to wrk under pressure & get along well w/others. Dependable, mature. Contracts or purchasing expr helpful. MIN EDUC REQD: Some bus sch &/or coll prefd. SECURITY CLEARANCE REQD. Grd 53/55 LR-CC431

WORD PROCESS   (JPN)01DN2032
OPER   (JRC)0713723053
DUTIES: Typg of draft copy, reprod copy & finished copy to meet contract data reqmts. Train on Word Procg Typg syst. Reqs attention to detail & sustained concentration f/long periods of time; abil to follow written, oral & mach-coded instructions. Prfm other rel duties as reqd. MIN SKILL REQD: JG53: 1-3 yrs rel expr & 40-50 WPM typg. JG55: 3-5 yrs rel expr & 60 WPM typg. SECURITY CLEARANCE REQD. Grd 53/55 LR-CC713

Figure 5–2. **An example of Texas Instruments Incorporated's job posting system. (Source: Texas Instruments Incorporated.)**

firms, including Texas Instruments, Inc., often provide their employees with a weekly list of jobs available within the company. Any qualified employee is encouraged to apply for these job openings. You can see an example of this approach in Figure 5–2. TI's procedure minimizes the common complaint heard in many companies that insiders never hear of a job opening until it has been filled. A job bidding and posting system attempts to avoid this problem. It reflects a management practice of openness that is generally highly valued by employees.

EXTERNAL SOURCES OF RECRUITMENT

At times, the firm must look to the outside to find additional sources of recruits. This is particularly important if a firm is in the process of expanding its work force. The following circumstances require external recruitment: (1) to fill entry level jobs, (2) to acquire skills not possessed by current employees, and (3) to obtain employees with different backgrounds to provide new ideas. As you see in Figure 5–3, even when promotions are made internally, entry level jobs must be filled from the outside. In this example, after the president retires, a series of internal promotions are made. Ultimately, however, the firm resorts to external recruitment to fill the entry level position of salary analyst. If the president's position had been filled from the outside, the chain-reaction promotions from within would not have occurred. Depending upon the qualifications desired, employees may be attracted from a number of sources.

High Schools and Vocational Schools

Organizations concerned with recruiting many operative employees look heavily to high schools and vocational schools. Many schools have designed outstanding programs for specific occupational skills and therefore are a valuable recruitment source.

Community Colleges

A number of community colleges have done an excellent job of defining the employment needs in their area. They have assembled necessary resources and are producing highly marketable products in the form of their students. Many employers have successfully used community colleges as a source for their recruiting efforts. In dealing with community colleges, recruiters should develop a good relationship with counselors, faculty, and administrators. If a placement office exists, its director will be a key to any recruitment efforts.

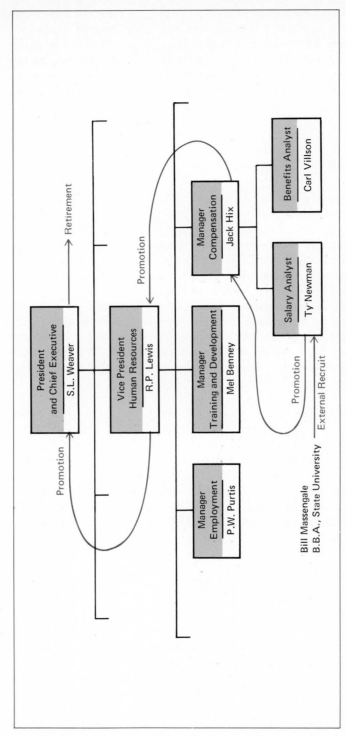

Figure 5–3. Internal promotion and external recruitment.

Colleges and universities represent a major source of recruitment for many organizations. Many of the professional, technical, and potential management employees are located in these institutions. Recruiters are commonly used to reach this important source. The following telephone conversation is not at all unusual.

> Professor Snow? This is Zack Whitmore. It's been a long time since I sat in the back row of your class. How are things at State U? You recall my telling you of my promotion to District Manager? Well, I'm trying to remember those things you taught me in your personnel class about recruiting employees. My problem is that I need four bright—no, not like me—young people very soon who can work effectively with our dealers. Our starting salary is extremely competitive and our compensation package includes a new car and all expenses paid. You know about our company's excellent benefits. Think you could come up with some good people for me? Thanks a lot, Dr. Snow. It's been nice talking with you. I'll get back to you next week.

Placement directors, faculty, and administrators are potentially helpful to organizations as they attempt to utilize this source of recruits. For instance, the large retailer, Bloomingdales, has improved its credibility on college campuses by making personal contacts with business professors and providing grants for studies and internships. The company has also used alumni to recruit and establish relationships with college placement offices.[5]

Since college recruitment is mutually beneficial, both employers and universities should take steps to develop and maintain close relationships. Once a recruiting program is established, especially with educational institutions, it is important that programs be continued year after year and that an effective and sound relationship be established with the school in question. It is important that the business know the school and that the school know the business.

Competitors and Other Firms

Competitors and other firms in the area or industry may be the most important source of recruits for positions where experience is highly desired. Even organizations which have strong policies of promotion from within must occasionally look to the outside (which includes competitors) to fill important positions. Several years ago when Cessna Aircraft entered the business jet market, they needed a top sales executive with experience in this field. Cessna was able to lure a successful executive from Pan American World Airways, Inc. to run their marketing operations.[6] Raiding other organizations for their high quality talent often occurs.

[5]"Combing Colleges for Exes," *Chain Store Age Executive* (July 1977): 27.
[6]Richard R. Conarroe, *Executive Search: A Guide for Recruiting Outstanding Executives* (New York: Van Nostrand Reinhold Company, 1976), p. 8.

148

Part II
Human
Resources
Planning,
Recruitment,
and Selection

Smaller firms in particular look for employees who have been trained by larger organizations which have the resources necessary to develop individuals.[7] For instance, one large optical firm believes that its own operation is not large enough to provide extensive training and development programs. It is likely that a person recruited by this firm would have at least two previous employers before being qualified for any significant management role.

Unsolicited Applicants

If an organization has the reputation of being a good place to work, it may be able to attract good prospective employees even without extensive recruitment efforts. Acting on their own initiative, high quality workers may seek out a specific company to apply for a job. Unsolicited applicants often prove to be a valuable source of recruits.

EXTERNAL METHODS OF RECRUITING

Through recruitment sources we are able to determine where the potential job applicants are located. Recruitment methods are the means by which job applicants may be enticed to seek employment with the firm. Recruitment methods such as advertising, employment agencies, and employee referrals may be effective in attracting virtually any type person. The use of recruiters, special events, and internships are designed primarily for students, especially those attending colleges and universities. Also, executive search firms and professional organizations are particularly beneficial in the recruitment of managerial and professional employees.

Advertising

The most inexpensive form of advertising which provides the broadest coverage is probably the newspaper advertisement. While help-wanted advertising is being used by an increasing number of firms, studies suggest that less than 40 percent of all jobs are filled through recruitment advertising.[8] Its greatest problem stems from many individuals responding who are not really qualified. The problem that Joyce Sather encountered when three hundred applicants applied for the job provides an excellent example of how a vaguely written advertisement can elicit responses from too wide a variety of managerial candidates. To write an effective ad, you must avoid generalities and provide as much information as possible about the job, the organization, and possibilities

---

[7]Patrick Crow, "Industry Scrambling To Get Adequate Manpower," *The Oil and Gas Journal* 76 (December 11, 1978): 33.

[8]James W. Schreier, "Deciphering Messages in Recruitment Ads," *Personnel Administrator* 28 (March 1983): 35.

PERSONNEL MANAGEMENT

SCHLUMBERGER-DOLL RESEARCH CENTER, a research facility developing new techniques for finding and evaluating underground hydrocarbons, is seeking a person to work in Personnel Management as an assistant to the Personnel Manager. This position is being filled for the first time and requires a personnel generalist. Responsibilities will include a combination of personnel administration, development and management while creating and maintaining a productive work environment for research physicists, engineers, mathematicians, computer scientists, and their support groups. Individual short-term and long-term projects will be encouraged. Specific areas of responsibility will be determined by the candidate's background and interests. Working as a generalist and participating in Schlumberger's Personnel Manager Training Program can lead to a Personnel Manager position within Schlumberger Limited.

The ideal candidate will be bright, creative, and articulate with a Master's or Ph.D. degree and proven performance in a company personnel function. Preparation in the field of organizational behavior or behavior analysis and some experience or knowledge of research or engineering environments are desired.

The Research Center supports the oil-field service activities of Schlumberger Limited, a $2^{1}/_{2}$ billion dollar corporation active in about 80 countries. People at the Center work closely with engineering groups located in Houston, Texas and Paris, France. The Personnel Department has a functional relationship to corporate offices in New York City.

If you are interested in an interview, please send a resume to:

Janet Curow, Ph.D.
Personnel Manager
SCHLUMBERGER-DOLL RESEARCH CENTER
P.O. Box 307
Ridgefield, Conn. 06877

— An Equal Opportunity Employer M/F —

(Source: Schlumberger-Doll Research Center. Used with permission.)

Figure 5–4. **A professional journal advertisement.**

for career mobility.[9] An examination of the Sunday edition of any major newspaper will reveal the extensive use of this medium for the recruitment of virtually every type employee.

Advertisements placed in publications such as the *Wall Street Journal* are generally for managerial, professional, and technical positions. The reading audience is comprised of those individuals who may be qualified for the position. Also there is less likelihood of receiving marginally qualified or even totally unqualified applicants.

Virtually every professional group publishes a journal which is widely read by its members. When advertising for personnel executive position, for example, *The Personnel Administrator* would be an excellent medium (see Figure 5–4).

Other media which can be used include telephone, radio, billboards, and television. While these methods may be more expensive than newspapers or journals, they have been used with success in specific situations. For instance, one large electronic firm has achieved considerable success in advertising for production trainees via radio spot advertisements.

[9]Van M. Evans, "Recruitment Advertising in the '80's," *The Personnel Administrator* 23 (December 1978): 23.

150   Employment Agencies

Part II
Human
Resources
Planning,
Recruitment,
and Selection

An **employment agency** is an organization that assists firms in recruiting employees and, at the same time, aids individuals in their attempt to locate jobs. They perform many recruitment and selection functions for the employer such as obtaining application blank data, holding screening interviews, and performing other selection functions for the employer.

Private agencies are utilized by firms for virtually every type of position. However, they are best known for their role in recruiting white collar employees. Although the industry has gained a bad reputation in some areas, a number of highly reputable employment agencies have been in operation for decades. Difficulties that occasionally occur stem from a lack of industry standards. The quality of a particular agency depends upon the professionalism of its management at each location. Even though problems may exist, private employment agencies present an important method for bringing qualified applicants and positions together. It is one which should not be overlooked by either the organization or the job applicant. Individuals are often turned off by agencies because of the fee they charge. However, the fee is often paid by the employer. An example of a typical employment agency fee schedule may be seen in Table 5–2. Fee percentages are based on gross salary.

An example of successful use of private agencies is provided by the Fulton Supply Company of Atlanta. "Over the years," says Ira B. Abernathy, presi-

Table 5–2.   Example of a typical employment agency fee schedule

Annual Gross Salary			Fee Percentage
$ 0	to	$ 9,999	10%
10,000	to	10,999	11%
11,000	to	11,999	12%
12,000	to	12,999	13%
13,000	to	13,999	14%
14,000	to	14,999	15%
15,000	to	15,999	16%
16,000	to	16,999	17%
17,000	to	17,999	18%
18,000	to	18,999	19%
19,000	to	19,999	20%
20,000	to	20,999	21%
21,000	to	21,999	22%
22,000	to	22,999	23%
23,000	to	23,999	24%
24,000	to	24,999	25%
25,000	to	25,999	26%
26,000	to	26,999	27%
27,000	to	27,999	28%
28,000	to	28,999	29%
29,000 +			30%

dent, "we've gotten to know them and they've gotten to know us and our particular needs." Fulton employs over one hundred people, and most of them, he says, "came to us through agencies. When we first started using agencies, they would send over people with almost any kind of background. It was up to us to weed them out. Now that the agencies know our business well enough, they do the weeding."[10]

While public employment agencies are operated by each state, they receive overall policy direction from the United States Employment Service. Public employment agencies are best known for their efforts in recruiting and placing individuals in operative jobs. But recently they have been increasingly involved with technical, professional, and managerial positions. Some public agencies utilize computerized job matching systems to aid in the recruitment process. The services provided by public employment agencies are without charge to either the employer or prospective employee.

Recruiters

The most common use of recruiters is with technical and vocational schools, community colleges, colleges, and universities. The key contact for recruiters on college and university campuses is often the director of student placement. This administrator is in an excellent position to arrange interviews with students possessing the qualifications desired. Placement services make it feasible for organizations to utilize their recruiters efficiently. Qualified candidates are identified, interviews are scheduled, and suitable physical locations are provided for the interviews.

The company recruiter obviously plays a vital role in attracting applicants. The recruiter's actions will be viewed as those reflecting the character of the firm. If the recruiter is dull, the company represented may be considered dull; if he or she is apathetic, discourteous, or vulgar, all these negative characteristics may well be attributed to the recruiting firm. Remember the reaction of Polly Stacy to the inept college recruiter, Scott Shelton.

Recruiters determine which individuals possess the best qualifications and who are to be encouraged to continue their interest in the firm. In achieving this purpose, the recruiter becomes involved in a two-way communication process by providing information about the company, its products and/or services, its general organizational structure, its policies, and a description of the job to be filled. The organization's compensation and benefits program may also be mentioned. The recruiter will also ask the prospect numerous questions which may range from, "What position do you want to occupy five years from now?" to, "How will your employment benefit our firm?" Questions such as these may be difficult to answer. However, the prospect is expected to respond in some logical manner. Other questions may be more predictable, such as those relating to grades, extracurricular activities, employment while attending school, and hobbies.

[10]"The Scramble for Talent," *Industrial Distribution* 66 (August 1976): 32.

152

Part II
Human
Resources
Planning,
Recruitment,
and Selection

Considering the importance of the occasion, the interview between the prospect and recruiter is often short—on the average about thirty minutes. It is therefore imperative that:

- The interview begin on time
- The recruiter be prepared, or at least have knowledge of the facts included on the prospect's data sheet
- The interview take place in a quiet, private area without outside disturbance[11]

The applicant must also prepare for the interview. If a good impression is to be made, the prospect must do some homework on the company. The Placement Service often has literature which describes the nature of the recruiting organization and gives other helpful information. In addition, library sources may provide such data as the company's sales volume, number of employees, products, and so forth. Prospects who possess facts such as these are in a good position to engage in a conversation with the recruiter for they can ask relevant questions. Other things being equal, an informed prospect has a competitive advantage.

Special Events

Special events recruiting involves an effort on the part of a single employer, or group of employers, to attract a large number of applicants for interviews. They often use job fairs, open houses, or visits to company plants or offices. An event is designed to bring together applicants and a wide variety of company representatives.

Internships

Internships represent a form of recruiting which has potential value to both the firm and the student. **Internships** typically involve a temporary job for the summer months or a part-time job during regular semesters. In many instances, students alternate their schedule by working full-time one semester and becoming full-time students the next. In the course of the internship, students are given the opportunity to view first hand the practice of businesses. At the same time, they contribute to the firm by performing needed tasks. Through this relationship, the student can determine whether the company would be a desirable employer. Likewise, the business firm can make better judgments regarding the candidate's qualifications.[12] Internships provide opportunities for students to bridge the gap from management theory to practice.

Internships have also proven useful in moving minorities into the work force. Bob Edwards, vice president for personnel, Southwestern Life Insurance Company, describes the program at his firm. "The successful integration of our

---

[11]Richard A. Fear, *The Evaluation Interview* (New York: McGraw-Hill Book Company, 1973).
[12]H. Felix Kloman, "The Student Intern," *Risk Management* 26 (February 1979): 10.

office work force after the Civil Rights legislation in 1964 required innovative approaches to selection as well as placement of minorities. The business leaders in Dallas were not yet confident that an acceptable solution could be found to answer the critics of integration or those advocates who did not want to weaken their companies' performance by active compliance. We elected to deal with this important issue by strengthening our high school internship program. Business-minded students in this program are provided full-time summer jobs in our home office prior to their senior year and are moved to part-time jobs through their final school term.

Our approach provides:

1. Summer employment to a predominantly minority population
2. Part-time employment without giving any employment test
3. Information to high school students that more accurately reflects the demands of an adult work environment
4. Maximum discretion for the student as the company requires no commitment beyond the school term
5. Maximum discretion for the company as full time employment can be offered to those students who performed well on the internship jobs
6. Up-to-date information for high school teachers and administrators on industry needs and hard data to motivate student development

"In summary, we integrated our work force with performers and minimized management reluctance to enter an unknown and, in some situations, a feared adventure with a population whose background is different from their own. Our success with this approach is evidenced by the size of our present employee minority population and their presence at all levels of responsibility."

Executive Search Firms

Organizations may use **executive search firms** to recruit experienced professionals and top level executives when other sources prove inadequate. Executive recruiters "are retained to search for the most qualified executive available for specific positions, only on assignment from the company seeking a specific type of individual."[13] "Executive search firms are a world apart from employment agencies and job advisory consultants," says Lester Korn, president and chief executive officer of Korn/Ferry International. "They do not work for individuals. They are retained by corporations and governmental bodies which pay the fees."[14] Korn/Ferry International has thirty-one offices around the world of which thirteen are in the United States. They concentrate on executives earning $60,000 or more, mostly more.[15]

[13]Richard J. Cronin, "Executive Recruiters: Are They Necessary?" *Personnel Administrator* (February 1981): 32.
[14]Beth Rosenthal, "Headhunters: (Women's Division)," *Across the Board* 14 (August 1977): 20.
[15]Interview with J. Alvin Wakefield, senior vice president, partner, Korn/Ferry International, August 9, 1982.

154

Part II
Human
Resources
Planning,
Recruitment,
and Selection

Firms in this business often visit their clients' offices to interview company management. This enables them to gain a clear understanding of the company's goals and the job qualifications required. After this information is obtained, potential candidates are contacted and interviewed, their references checked, and the best qualified are referred to the client for the selection decision. The search firm's fee is generally a percentage of the individual's first year's compensation. Fee and expenses are paid by the client.

Professional Associations

Associations in many business professions such as finance, marketing, data processing, and Personnel provide recruitment and placement services for their members. In the area of Personnel, the American Society for Personnel Administration is an example of an organization which operates a job referral service for members seeking new positions and employers with positions to fill.

Employee Referrals

Many organizations have found that their employees can assist in the recruitment process. Employees may actively solicit applications from their friends and associates. In some organizations, especially where certain skills are scarce, this approach has proven quite effective. For example, a few years ago the demand for engineers was so great that firms such as Ampex Corporation and TRW, Inc. were offering a $1,000 bonus to any employee who persuaded an engineer to join their organization.[16]

THE UNIFORM GUIDELINES AND ADVERSE IMPACT

Prior to 1978, employers were faced with complying with several different selection guidelines. In 1978, the **Uniform Guidelines on Employee Selection Procedures** were adopted. These guidelines cover the major federal equal employment opportunity statutes and orders including Title VII, Executive Order 11246, and the Equal Pay Act. The Uniform Guidelines do not apply to the Age Discrimination Act or the Vocational Rehabilitation Act. With regard to selection procedures, the Uniform Guidelines stated that a test was:

> . . . any measure, combination of measures, or procedures used as a basis for any employment decision. Selection procedures include the full range of assessment techniques from traditional paper and pencil tests, performance tests, testing programs or probationary periods and physical, education, and work experience requirements through informal or casual interviews and unscored application forms.

[16]"Engineering: Help Wanted," *Newsweek* 66 (January 1, 1979): 44.

Using this guideline, virtually any factor used in the selection decision could be considered a test.

Prior to the issuance of the 1978 Guidelines, the only way to prove job relatedness was through validation of each test. The new guidelines did not require validation in all cases. "It is essential only in instances where the test or other selection device produces an adverse impact on a minority group. Under the new guidelines, adverse impact has been defined in terms of selection rates, the selection rate being the number of applicants hired or promoted, divided by the total number of applicants."[17] **Adverse impact** occurs when members of protected groups receive unequal consideration for employment. As specifically defined by the 1978 Guidelines, adverse impact occurs if protected groups are not hired at the rate of at least 80 percent of the best-achieving group. This has also been called the **four-fifths rule**. The groups identified for analysis under the Uniform Guidelines are: (1) blacks; (2) American Indians (including Alaskan natives); (3) Asians; (4) Hispanics; (5) females; and (6) males.

In computing adverse impact for hiring, the following formula may be used:

$$\frac{\text{success rate for protected group applicants}}{\text{success rate for best-achieving group applicants}} = \frac{\text{determination of}}{\text{adverse impact}}$$

The success rate for protected group applicants is determined by dividing the number of members of a specific protected group *employed* in a period by a number of protected group member *applicants* in a period. The success rate for best-achieving group applicant is determined by dividing the number of people in the best-achieving group *employed* by the number of the best achieving group *applicants* in a period.

Using the above formula, let us determine if there has been adverse impact in a given organization. During 1983, 400 people were hired for a particular job. Of the total, 300 were white and 100 were black. There were 1500 applicants for these jobs of whom 1000 were white and 500 were black. Using the adverse impact formula we have:

$$\frac{100 \div 500}{300 \div 1000} = \frac{.2}{.3} = 66.67 \text{ percent}$$

Evidence of adverse impact is more than the total number of minority workers *employed*. The total number of *applicants* is also taken into consideration. For instance, assume that there were 300 blacks and 300 whites hired. But, there were 1500 black applicants and 1000 white applicants. Placing these figures into the adverse impact formula, you can see that adverse impact still exists.

$$\frac{300 \div 1500}{300 \div 1000} = \frac{.2}{.3} = 66.67 \text{ percent}$$

Clearly, firms must monitor their recruitment efforts very carefully.

[17]David E. Robertson, "New Directions in EEO Guidelines," *Personnel Journal* (July 1978).

Part II
Human
Resources
Planning,
Recruitment,
and Selection

Certain organizations must develop **Affirmative Action Programs** (AAP) to show that they hire members of protected groups in proportion to their representation in the relevant area of recruitment. Affirmative Action Programs may occur because of three different situations. The first situation leading to an AAP is for an organization to implement one voluntarily. Goals are established for hiring and promoting members of protected groups. In the second situation, if a federal procurement or federally assisted construction contract amounts to $50,000 or more, an affirmative action plan *must* be filed with the Office of Federal Contract Compliance Programs (OFCCP). Finally, an AAP may be required when a discrimination suit brought against a company by EEOC shows that discrimination exists. In this situation an AAP is usually a part of a consent decree.

An affirmative action plan "requires an employer to group its jobs, conduct a utilization analysis, identify cases of underutilization, and project goals and timetables to correct the situation.[18] In the analysis, the job titles and salaries of the various positions in the organization are ranked from lowest-paid to highest-paid within each department. The total number of workers in the unit is broken down by male, female, blacks, Hispanics, American Indians, and Orientals. If members of protected groups are underrepresented considering their number in the local work force, reasons for these deviations must be explained. Goals and timetables for correcting the discrimination must then be set up. The main elements for an affirmative action compliance program are listed below:

- Report of results of prior year's AAP
- Development or reaffirmation of EEO policy
- Internal and external dissemination of policy
- Establishment of responsibilities for implementation of the AAP
- Work force array
- Minority availability analysis
- Female availability analysis
- Identification of problem areas by organizational units and job group
- Establishment of goals and timetables
- Action programs to attain goals and objectives
- Internal audit and reporting systems
- Compliance of personnel policies and practices
- Support of programs to improve employment opportunities of minorities and women
- Consideration of women and minorities not currently in the work force
- Compliance with religion or national origin discrimination guidelines

[18]Kenneth J. McCulloch, *Selecting Employees Safely Under the Law* (Englewood Cliffs, N.J.: Prentice-Hall, Inc., 1981), p. 13.

Where courts have found discrimination, they have ruled that the remedial action taken must ensure equal opportunity. This action must also restore the rightful economic status of all individuals in the affected class. Discriminatory practices can become very expensive. Back pay may be rewarded to an entire affected class for as long as two years prior to the date a discrimination charge is filed. In addition to back pay, other expenses may be incurred related to investigation of the charges, attempted conciliation, and legal action. For instance, "The Household Finance Corporation paid more than $125,000 to white collar female employees who charged they were denied promotion because of their sex. Under terms of a consent decree, the company also agreed to hire 20 percent females for branch representative openings (subject to availability) until such representatives were 20 percent female. They also were required to hire 20 percent from specified minority groups for clerical, credit and branch representative jobs until total employees reached 65 percent of their population in the labor area. Household Finance Corporation also agreed to train female and minority employees to help them qualify for better jobs where they are underrepresented."[19]

One of the largest payment ever made was in an agreement signed by AT&T with EEOC and the Department of Labor. It provided for approximately $15 million to employees allegedly discriminated against. The agreement also called for additional affirmative actions and for an estimated $50 million in yearly payments for promotion and wage adjustments to minorities and female employees.[20]

RECRUITING EFFORTS UNDER THE LAW

In spite of existing equal opportunity laws, many past personnel practices have become deeply embedded in some organizations. These practices continue to have an unequal impact on protected groups. This has been the case even when the organization has not consciously discriminated. As in the case of Mark Smith and Debra Coffee, Mark may have some serious problems with EEO and not even realize it. Some traditional employment systems perpetuate the effects of past discrimination even after the original practices have been discontinued. The result is a continuation of what has been labeled "systemic discrimination." Courts have found that some employment practices, regardless of intent, have resulted in discrimination against members of protected groups.

To offset the momentum of past discrimination in employment, firms must resort to additional recruitment approaches. Members of protected groups, because of a lifetime of unequal opportunity, may not respond to traditional re-

[19]U.S. v. Household Finance Corporation, 4 EPD para. 7680 (N.D. Ill., 1972) (Consent decree).
[20]U.S. Equal Employment Opportunity Commission, Affirmative Action and Equal Employment: A Guidebook for Employers, vol. 1 (Washington, D.C.: U.S. Government Printing Office, January 1974), p. 10.

158

Part II
Human
Resources
Planning,
Recruitment,
and Selection

cruitment methods nor be a part of typical recruitment sources. Therefore, a recruitment program that is designed specifically to attract members of protected groups should be implemented.

Analysis of Recruitment Procedures

To ensure that an organization's recruitment program is nondiscriminatory, the firm must analyze its recruitment procedures. For example, it might be unwise to use employee referral as a primary method and unsolicited applicants as a main recruitment source. These actions may perpetuate the present composition of an organization's membership. And, where minorities and females are not well represented at all levels, the courts have ruled that reliance on these practices is discriminatory.

In identifying sources of continuing discrimination, it may be helpful to develop a record of applicant flow. This record would include personal and job related data concerning each applicant. It would also indicate whether a job offer was extended; if no job offer was made, an explanation should be provided. These records would enable the organization to analyze its recruitment and selection practices related to minority and female candidates and to take corrective action when necessary.

Utilization of Minorities and Women

Each individual who engages in recruitment should be trained in the use of objective, job related standards. These recruiters are in critical positions to either encourage or discourage protected group members in applying for jobs. Qualified minorities and women may be effectively utilized in key recruitment activities such as visiting schools and colleges and participating in career days. They are in an excellent position to provide valuable inputs for recruitment planning. And, they may effectively serve as referral sources. Pictures of minority and women employees in help-wanted advertisements and company brochures may assist in conveying the message, "We are an equal employment opportunity employer."

Advertising

With few exceptions, jobs must be open to all individuals. Therefore, sex-segregated advertisements, for example, cannot be used unless sex is a **bonafide occupational qualification** (BFOQ). The BFOQ exception provided in Title VII of the Civil Rights Act requires that the qualifications be job-related. This definition is narrowly interpreted by EEOC and the courts. The burden of proof is on the employer to establish that job requirements are essential for successful performance of the job.

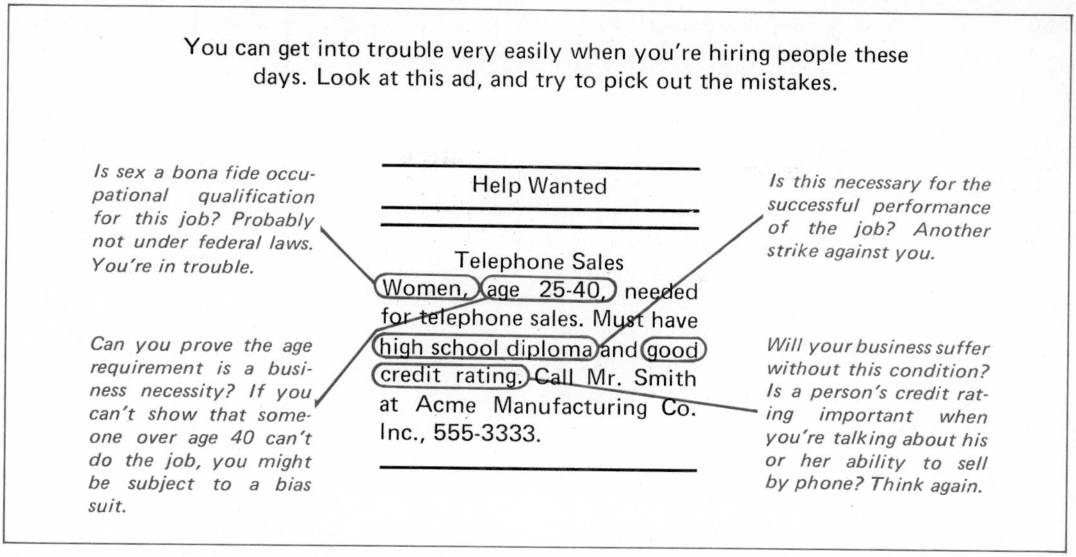

You can get into trouble very easily when you're hiring people these days. Look at this ad, and try to pick out the mistakes.

Is sex a bona fide occupational qualification for this job? Probably not under federal laws. You're in trouble.

Can you prove the age requirement is a business necessity? If you can't show that someone over age 40 can't do the job, you might be subject to a bias suit.

Help Wanted

Telephone Sales
Women, age 25-40, needed for telephone sales. Must have high school diploma and good credit rating. Call Mr. Smith at Acme Manufacturing Co. Inc., 555-3333.

Is this necessary for the successful performance of the job? Another strike against you.

Will your business suffer without this condition? Is a person's credit rating important when you're talking about his or her ability to sell by phone? Think again.

Figure 5–5. **A want ad that'll kill you.** (Source: Vivian C. Pospisil, "What Can You Ask a Job Applicant?" *Industry* Week, (March 1, 1976), p. 25. Used with permission.)

Other recruitment practices designed to provide equal opportunity include:

1. Ensuring that the content of advertisements does not indicate preference for any race, sex, or age or that these factors are a qualification for the job. For "A Want Ad That'll Kill You," see Figure 5–5.

2. Utilizing media that are directed toward minorities, such as soul radio stations.

3. Emphasizing the intent to recruit both sexes by including the phrase "Equal Employment Opportunity Employer, M/F" where jobs have tradi-

Figure 5–6. **A newspaper ad stressing equal employment opportunity for males and females.**

CORPORATE CONTROLLER

Sureway Development Company offers an outstanding opportunity for an individual with a degree in accounting and a minimum of 4 years experience. Background should include financial analysis and budgeting. Real estate development experience preferred and/or CPA. Please contact Bill Smith 318/255-1656.

Equal Opportunity Employer M/F

160

Part II
Human
Resources
Planning,
Recruitment,
and Selection

tionally been held by either males or females (see Figure 5–6). To many, EEO suggests only racial nondiscrimination.

Employment Agencies

An organization should emphasize its nondiscriminatory recruitment practices when placing job orders with employment agencies. While private agencies may be successfully utilized, jobs at all levels should be listed with the local public employment agency. State employment agencies can provide valuable assistance to organizations seeking to fulfill affirmative action goals.[21] In addition, agencies and consultant firms that specialize in minority and female applicants should be contacted.

Other Suggested Affirmative Recruitment Approaches

Personal contacts should be made with counselors and administrators at high schools, vocational schools, and colleges with large minority and/or female enrollments. These counselors and administrators should be made aware that the organization is actively seeking minorities and females for jobs that they have not traditionally held. Also, they should be familiar with the type of jobs available and the training and education needed to perform these jobs successfully. The possibilities for developing internships and summer employment for minorities and women should be carefully investigated.

Organizations should develop contact with minority, women's, and other community organizations. While the most productive sources may vary in each locality, some helpful organizations may include: National Association for the Advancement of Colored People, National Urban League, American Association of University Women, Federation of Business and Professional Women's Talent Bank, National Council of Negro Women, and the local Veteran's Administration. The EEOC's regional offices will assist employers in locating appropriate agencies.

SEXUAL HARASSMENT

It is anticipated that in the 1980s significant attention will be paid to solving the problem of sexual harassment. As previously mentioned, Title VII of the Civil Rights Act prohibits sex discrimination in employment. EEOC issued "Guidelines on Discrimination Because of Sex" in 1980 and the OFCCP issued similar guidelines the following year.

EEOC defined sexual harassment as "Unwelcome sexual advances, requests for sexual favors, and other verbal or physical conduct of a sexual nature

[21]William S. Hubbartt, "The State Employment Service: An Aid to Affirmative Action Implementation," *Personnel Journal* 56 (June 1977): 289.

that occur under any of the following situations:

1. When submission to sexual advance is a condition of keeping or getting a job, whether expressed in explicit terms or not.
2. When a supervisor or boss makes a personnel decision based on an employee's submission to or rejection of sexual advances.
3. When sexual conduct unreasonably interferes with a person's work performance or creates an intimidating, hostile, or offensive environment."[22]

The EEOC issued the guidelines because of the belief that sexual harassment continues to be a widespread problem.[23] In a 1979 study, 59 percent of the female employees reported experiencing one or more incidents of sexual harassment in their present place of employment.[24] In a 1982 study of recent female college graduates, 49.3 percent replied that they had experienced some form of sexual harassment.[25] One of the major implications of the guidelines is that they make the employer responsible for misbehavior by supervisory personnel, their assistants, coworkers, or outside personnel. It is quite clear that managers of both profit and not-for-profit organizations must be particularly alert to the issue of sexual harassment.

COST/BENEFITS ANALYSIS—RECRUITING

We have previously defined recruiting as the process of attracting qualified applicants to the firm. Without an effective recruiting program, the selection process cannot operate effectively. Each recruiting method, however, has a cost associated with it. To complicate the situation further, the most appropriate recruiting method will likely change depending on the particular job class involved. For example, the best recruiting method for skilled computer programmers may be quite different from the method used for entry-level machine operators.

It falls upon those in Personnel to analyze the recruiting process to determine the costs and benefits associated with each method. Cost itself is not the ultimate factor to consider. An expensive recruiting method may actually be more beneficial because it results in obtaining successful long-term employees. A method that results in getting many applicants but only a few successful employees may actually prove quite expensive. Each recruiting method must be analyzed with regard to its effectiveness for a particular job class.

[22]Eliza G. C. Collins and Timothy Blodgett, "Sexual Harassment: Some See It—Some Won't," *Harvard Business Review* 59 (March-April 1981): 79.
[23]Michelle Hoyman and Ronda Robinson, "Interpreting the New Sexual Harassment Guidelines," *Personnel Journal* 59 (December 1980): 996.
[24]Barbara Hagler, Testimony Before House Judiciary II Committee, State of Illinois, March 4, 1980, p. 5.
[25]Carolyn C. Dolecheck and Maynard M. Dolecheck, "Job-Related Sexual Harassment of Women with College Degrees in Business: How Serious Is It?" *NABTE Review* Issue Number 9 (Spring 1982): 17.

SUMMARY

Recruitment involves encouraging qualified people to apply for employment with a firm. Unless a sufficient number of qualified prospects apply for a job, the company cannot have a truly selective employment system. Once human resources planning indicates a need for new employees, the firm may then evaluate the possibility of using alternatives to hiring in order to meet the demand for its goods and services. Some alternatives include: overtime, subcontracting, and temporary help. The recruitment process must also consider the internal and external environments.

Frequently recruitment begins when a manager initiates an employee requisition. The requisition specifies various details including job title, department, and the date the employee is needed for work. The next step in the recruitment process is to determine whether qualified employees are available within the firm or must be recruited externally. Recruitment methods are the specific means through which potential employees are attracted to the organization.

Internal recruiting methods include job posting and job bidding. External sources of recruitment are: high schools and vocational schools, community colleges, colleges and universities, competitors and other firms, and unsolicited applicants. External recruiting methods include: advertising, employment agencies, recruiters, special events, internships, executive search firms, professional associations, and employee referrals.

In 1978, the Uniform Guidelines on Employee Selection Procedures were adopted. These guidelines cover the major federal equal employment opportunity statutes and orders. According to the guidelines, virtually any factor in the selection decision could be considered a test.

Adverse impact occurs when members of protected groups receive unequal consideration for employment. It occurs if protected groups are not hired at the rate of at least 80 percent of the best-achieving group. Certain organizations must develop Affirmative Action Programs to show that they hire members of protected groups in proportion to their representation in the relevant area of recruitment. Finally, it is anticipated that during the 1980s significant attention will be paid to correcting the problem of sexual harassment.

Questions for Review

1. Describe the components of the basic recruiting process.

2. What are some of the actions that could be taken prior to engaging in recruitment?

3. List and discuss the various external and internal factors which could affect the recruitment process.

4. What is meant by the term internal recruitment? Describe the advantages and disadvantages associated with internal recruitment.

5. Describe the methods often used in internal recruitment. Briefly define each.

6. Discuss the rationale for an external recruitment program.

7. Distinguish between sources and methods of external recruitment. Identify various sources and methods of external recruitment.

8. Distinguish between an executive search firm and an employment agency.

9. How is adverse impact computed? Give an example.

10. What situations can occur which would cause a firm to have an Affirmative Action Program?

11. How can a firm improve its recruiting efforts under the law?

12. How does EEOC define sexual harassment?

Terms for Review

Recruitment
Requisition
Promotion from within
Job posting
Job bidding
Employment agency
Special events recruiting
Internships

Executive search firm
Uniform Guidelines on Employee Selection Procedures
Adverse impact
Four-fifths Rule
Affirmative Action Programs
Bonafide occupational qualification

From the president on down, management at Epler Manufacturing Company in Greenfield, Wisconsin is committed to equal employment opportunity. According to Robert Key, the personnel manager, the commitment goes much deeper than posting the usual placards and filing an "affirmative action program" with the federal government. Still, the percentage of black employees at Epler is only 7 percent, while the surrounding community is 22 percent black.

Epler pays high wages and has a good training program. The main need is for machine operator trainees, who require training on Epler's specialized machines. The machines are not difficult to operate and there is no educational requirement for the jobs.

Robert was thinking of the problem of recruiting qualified blacks when Betty Alexander walked into his office. "Got a minute?" said Betty, "I need to talk to you about the recruiting trip to Michigan State next week." "Sure," said Robert, "but, first I need your advice about something. How can we get more qualified black people to apply for work here. We are running ads on WBEZ along with the classified ads in the *Tribune*. I think I've had you and John make recruiting trips to every community college within two hundred miles. We've encouraged employee referral, too, and I still think that's the most reliable source of new workers we have. But we just aren't getting any black applicants."

Questions

1. What is the basic problem associated with the low employment rate for blacks at Epler Manufacturing Company?

2. What do you believe would be the most effective way for Epler to recruit blacks?

———————————

Five years ago when Bobby Bret joined Crystal Productions as a junior accountant, he felt that he was on his way up. He had just graduated from college with a B+ average and was well liked both by his peers and by the faculty. He had been an officer in several student organizations. Bobby had shown a natural ability to get along with people as well as to get things done. He remembered what Roger Friedman, the controller at Crystal, had told him when he was hired, "I think you will do well here, Bobby. You've come highly recommended. You are the kind of guy that can expect to move right on up the ladder."

Bobby felt that he had done a good job at Crystal and everybody seemed to like him. In addition, his performance appraisals had been excellent. However, after five years he was still a junior accountant. He had applied for two senior accountant positions which had come open, but they were both filled by people hired from outside the firm. When the accounting supervisor's job came open two years ago, Bobby had not applied. He was surprised when his new boss turned out to be a hot shot graduate of State University whose only experience was three years with a "Big Eight" accounting firm. Bobby had hoped that Ron Greene, a senior accountant he particularly respected, would get the job.

On the fifth anniversary of his employment at Crystal, Bobby decided it was time to do something. He made an appointment with the controller. At that meeting Bobby explained to Mr. Friedman that he had worked hard to obtain a promotion and shared his frustration about having stayed in the same job for so long. "Well," said Mr. Friedman, "you don't think that you were all that much better qualified than the people that we have hired, do you?" "No," said Bobby, "but, I think I could have handled the senior accoun-tant job. Of course, the people you have hired are doing a great job too." The controller responded, "We just look at the qualifications of all of the applicants for each job and, considering everything, try to make a reasonable decision."

Questions

1. Explain the impact of a promotion from within policy upon outside recruitment.

2. Do you believe that Bobby has a legitimate complaint? Explain.

Chapter Objectives

1. List and explain the steps in the selection process.
2. State how the application blank is used in the selection process.
3. Explain the conditions that a test should meet before being used in the selection process.
4. Describe the various interview techniques that may be used in the selection process.
5. State why reference checks and background investigations are conducted.
6. Describe the current status of the use of polygraph tests.
7. Explain why an employment physical examination is administered.
8. Express the importance of new employee orientation.

Chapter 6 _____

Personnel Selection

Judy Thompson, the data processing manager for Ampex Manufacturing, called her friend, Bill Alexander in Personnel, to ask a favor. "Bill, I have a friend I'd like you to consider for the new sales manager's position. I really like the fellow and would appreciate anything you could do." "That's fine, Judy. Send me his resume and we'll look it over." A week later Bill called Judy with some bad news. "Judy, there's just no match between your friend's qualifications and our company's needs. After looking at the requirements of the new position and comparing them with your friend's background and experience, I'm certain that it would be a very poor match. It would be like putting you in charge of the production department where you've had no experience."

Jack Johnson, personnel manager for Zoomer Electronics, was speaking to the production manager, Phillip Lewis, regarding who should be hired to fill a newly created position. Jack started the conversation by saying, "Of all the applicants, Betty Jones scored highest on the tests. Her previous work experience is right in line with our needs and her references check out great. What do you think, Phillip?" Phillip replied, "I don't know. We've never had a woman in that position and I don't know if she could handle the job. It's a demanding one and you know that women don't always react well under pressure." Jack immediately interrupted Phillip by saying, "You'd better have a better reason than that if you reject Ms. Jones. We're already under pressure from the EEOC because we don't employ enough females. I hope that you'll reevaluate your thinking."

When Bobby Edwards applied for a job as an engineer with More Oil Company, he used Frank Edee as one of his references. Because More Oil's policy required that all references be checked prior to making a selection decision, a personnel specialist, Janet Adams, called Mr. Edee about Bobby's qualifications. After hearing the purpose of her call, Frank said, "You bet I know that worthless character. He worked for me for a time and was always coming in late and making some excuse to leave early. Still owes me $100. Can't believe he put my name down as a reference. He must have thought you didn't check references." Janet thanked Frank and completed her report, thinking, "We're going to have to check some more on Bobby before he's employed."

168

Part II
Human
Resources
Planning,
Recruitment,
and Selection

When Bill Alexander evaluated Judy Thompson's friend against the job description, there was no way he could justify selecting Judy's buddy for the position. Phillip Lewis is resisting hiring a woman to fill a position, an action which has serious legal implications. If Bobby Edwards is rejected, it may occur to him that many firms do conduct reference checks on prospective employees. These examples depict only a few aspects of the tasks that need to be accomplished in the selection process. The recruitment process encourages individuals to seek employment opportunities with the firm. The purpose of the selection program is to identify the best qualified workers who apply.

THE SELECTION PROCESS

Selection is the process of choosing from a group of applicants those individuals best suited for a particular position. As you might expect, the firm's recruitment efforts exert a significant impact upon the efficiency of the selection process. The organization may be forced to employ marginally acceptable workers if there are only a few applicants.

The effectiveness of the selection process can significantly impact, and is also affected by, the other functional areas of Personnel. For instance, if the selection process only provides the firm with marginally qualified workers, the organization may have to develop an extensive training program. If the compensation package is inferior to those provided by the firm's competition, it may be difficult to attract the best qualified applicants.

A generalized selection model is provided in Figure 6–1. The selection process typically begins with the preliminary interview where obviously unqualified candidates are rejected. Next, applicants complete the firm's application blank, then progress through a series of selection tests. This is followed by the employment interview and the reference and background checks. Once the selection decision has been made, the prospective employee is given a company physical examination. Naturally, there continue to be external and internal factors which impact the selection process.

ENVIRONMENTAL FACTORS AFFECTING
THE SELECTION PROCESS

The selection process would be greatly simplified if a standardized screening process could be developed which would never change. However, deviations from this precise sequence are often made to conform to the needs of a particular situation. As one personnel manager expressed it, "The only thing certain is that exceptions will be made." For instance, envision the differences in the

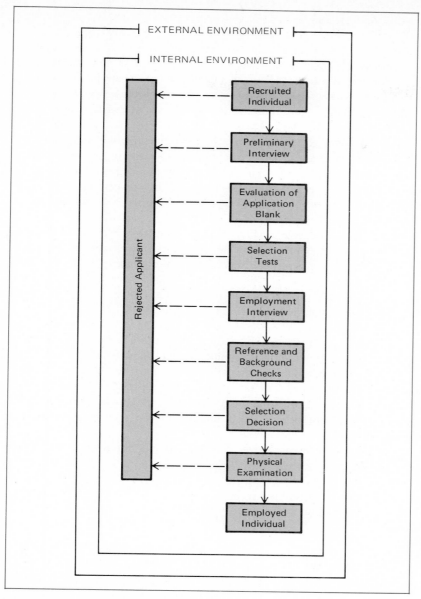

Figure 6–1. The selection process.

selection process that would be needed when hiring a top-level executive as opposed to hiring a person to fill a secretarial position. It is very doubtful that the executive candidate would complete an application blank or take selection tests.

Part II
Human
Resources
Planning,
Recruitment,
and Selection

As we described in Chapter 2 and its appendix, government legislation has had a major impact upon human resources management. It has particularly affected the selection process. Managers must be keenly aware of the impact of this legislation as they engage in selecting new employees. Specific effects of government legislation upon the selection process are described below.

Selection Tests. Although tests are often the most objective selection tool available, they have at times adversely affected employment of protected groups. For instance, test results for a person who grew up in a depressed area may not accurately indicate either intelligence or the ability to perform a job. The "language of the street" often does not prepare a person to compete successfully on a test.

Another point to consider when using selection tests is that a test may be valid for one group of employees, but not for another. For example, a test may be very effective in predicting job success for males but may be invalid when used to select females. Finally, when tests are deemed to be valid, they should be only one of several criteria used in the selection process. Other tools such as the employment interview should also be used.

Other Selection Tools. As previously mentioned, tests are not the only selection tools that may have potentially discriminatory questions. Selection techniques other than tests may be improperly used so as to have the effect of discriminating against racial, ethnic, or sex groups. Such techniques include, but are not limited to, unscored or casual interviews, unscored application forms, and unscored personnel history and background requirements not used uniformly as a basis for selection.

Human resources managers should also consider these questions at any stage of the selection process:

1. Does this question tend to have a disproportionate effect in the rejection of protected groups?

- "Determine if you really want to work in Personnel. Students frequently don't really know what it's all about. Talk to personnel people in different companies and at different levels.
- In considering what company you are going to work for, think beyond the initial job. Find out how personnel people typically move. What are the patterns? Is the environment conducive to growth?
- Determine how important the personnel function in the company is. Is it proactive? Are the personnel people really professionals?"

Gerald M. Groe, Director–Management Training and Development
American Express Company

2. Is this information necessary to judge this individual's competence for performing this particular job?

3. Are there alternate, nondiscriminatory ways to secure needed employment information?

Many questions traditionally asked during the selection process should be either eliminated or carefully reviewed to assure that their use is job related and nondiscriminatory. Potentially discriminatory areas in the selection process will next be briefly described.[1]

Race, national origin, religion: Questions regarding the applicant's race, national origin, and/or religion may be unlawful. For instance, questions regarding the applicant's religious denomination, religious affiliation, church, parish, pastor, or religious holidays observed are generally unlawful.

Education: Non-job-related educational requirements have been found by the courts to constitute illegal discrimination. Stating that a job requires a college degree when it could be accomplished effectively by a high school graduate may be discriminatory. A minority group member is less likely to have a college degree than a white male.

Arrest and conviction records: An individual's arrest record, which is not an indication of guilt, has been ruled by the courts to be an illegal basis for refusal to hire, unless a "business necessity" for such a policy can be shown. You should not ask, "Have you ever been arrested?" But you typically can ask, "Have you ever been convicted?" Jobs that require the person to handle large sums of money would fall into the business necessity category.

Credit rating: An individual's poor credit rating has been found to be an illegal basis for rejecting candidates where such practices have a disproportionate negative effect on minorities and the employer cannot show business necessity for such rejections. Inquiries about charge accounts, home or car ownership (unless the latter is required for the job) have been found to have an adverse effect on minorities and may be illegal.

Sex and marital and family status: Questions about a candidate's sex, marital status, and number and age of children rarely relate to job performance. Yet they have been used to discriminate against women. Questions such as, "Do you wish to be addressed as Mr., Mrs., Miss, or Ms.?" may be potentially discriminatory. Likewise, the question, "Are you married, single, divorced, or separated?" are in the same category. The name or other information regarding the applicant's spouse should not be asked.

Physical requirements: Questions about an applicant's height, weight, and other physical requirements should be asked only when these characteristics are necessary for performing a particular job. Decisions by the courts and EEOC have stated that height and weight requirements are illegal when they

[1]Specific questions in the following section regarding what questions are lawful and unlawful were extracted from the table in the article, "Attention Employers," *Across the Board* 14 (August 1977): 69–70.

172

Part II
Human
Resources
Planning,
Recruitment,
and Selection

result in the rejection of a disproportionate number of Spanish-surnamed persons, Asian-Americans, or women.

Experience requirements: Experience requirements should be reviewed to assure that they are necessary for specific jobs. For instance, requiring that a person have so many years of experience to secure a job may be discriminatory if this experience is not actually needed to perform the job.

Age or date of birth: Questions about an applicant's age or date of birth may violate the Age Discrimination in Employment Act. Also, questions about the ages of children, if any, could be potentially discriminatory. The organization may obtain this information after employment for such purposes as insurance.

Availability for Saturday or Sunday work: If it is necessary for the firm to obtain information about a candidate's availability for Saturday or Sunday work, it should be made clear that a reasonable effort will be made to accommodate the individual's religious needs.

Friends or relatives working for the company: Questions about an individual's friends or relatives working for the company may be unlawful if they result in reducing employment opportunities for protected groups. Discrimination could occur if the composition of the current workforce differs significantly from the proportion of the women or minorities in the relevant population area. Company rules that forbid both partners in a marriage from working for the employer may result in discrimination against women. For instance, a university in a small rural area which has a policy of not employing spouses of faculty members may discriminate against the wife when the faculty is predominately male. A woman may be better educated than her husband but be restricted from employment.

Appearance: Employment decisions based on such factors as length or style of hair, dress, and other aspects of appearance have been found to violate the law if they disproportionately affect employment of protected groups. Some courts have ruled that it is illegal to refuse to hire or fire males with long hair where the same practices are not followed with females. Hairstyle requirements also may be racially discriminatory.[2]

As you have seen from the above discussion, the type of information that may be used in the selection process is limited by federal laws and regulations. Nevertheless, a 1981 study revealed that discriminatory questions were still being asked by firms interviewing at college placement offices in the screening interview. Frequent "typical" illegal questions by discrimination area may be seen in Figure 6–2.

The selection process is also altered depending upon the type of position that is being filled. Suggested guidelines for five classes of jobs are provided in Table 6–1. You can see that the selection process may be affected by the specific position under consideration. As the job requirements increase, addi-

[2]Adapted from *Affirmative Action and Equal Employment: A Guidebook for Employers,* vol. 1 (Washington, D.C, U.S. Equal Employment Opportunity Commission, January 1974).

Discrimination Area	% of Total Number of Illegal Questions[1]	Examples of Typical Illegal Questions (in order of frequency of occurrence)[2]
Sex	34%	1. (Asked of Women) Do you have plans of having children/family? 2. (Asked of Women) What are your marriage plans? 3. (Asked of Women) What does your husband do? 4. (Asked of Women) What happens if you or your husband gets transferred or needs to relocate? 5. (Asked of Women) Who will take care of your children while you are at work? 6. (Asked of Men) How would you feel working for a woman?
Age	18%	1. How old are you? 2. What is your date of birth? 3. How would you feel working for a person younger than you?
National Origin	16%	1. Where were you born? 2. Where were your parents born? 3. Of what country are you a citizen?
Handicaps	12%	1. Do you have any handicaps? 2. As a handicapped person, what help are you going to need in order to do your work? 3. How severe is your handicap?
Religion	11%	1. What is your religion? 2. What church do you attend? 3. Do you hold any religious beliefs that would prevent you from working certain days of the week?
Race or Color	9%	1. Do you feel that your race/color will be a problem in your performing this job? 2. Are you of _____ heritage/race?

Source: Fredrick M. Jablin, "Use of Discriminatory Questions in Screening Interviews," *Personnel Administrator* 27 March 1982, p. 42. Used with permission.

[1]Represents percent of total number of illegal questions generated by respondents.
[2]The legality of a question is somewhat situational and may vary depending upon the context in which it was asked.

Figure 6–2. **Frequent "illegal" questions by discrimination area.**

tional information may be required to determine if the applicant is truly qualified to perform the necessary tasks associated with the position.

Speed of Decision Making

The time available to make the selection decision can have a major effect upon the selection process. Suppose, for instance, that Bobby Noles, the pro-

Part II
Human
Resources
Planning,
Recruitment,
and Selection

Table 6–1. Examples of the type information that can be asked

Production Workers:	Physical examination based on a completed physical demands form. No testing, no investigation, and no trick questions in the interview.
Office Workers:	Tests of typing and shorthand where relevant. Tests of intelligence and clerical ability may be used if provisions for test validation meet government regulations.
Skilled Mechanical Workers and Trainees:	Job sample tests where possible. Intelligence and mechanical aptitude tests are acceptable where provisions for test validations meet government regulations. Medical examination based on physical demands.
Banking and Retailing:	Careful investigation of previous employment. Interview bringing out interpersonal skills. Check of records acceptable for convictions, bankruptcies, and judgments. Polygraph or other physiological testing may be considered, but recent developments and changes in laws, public opinion, and validation studies should be taken into account. Only psychologically trained testers should be used.
Sales and Executive Applicants:	Interview for direct evidence of energy, drive, ambition, interpersonal skills, leadership, and organizing ability (where job-relevant). Personality testing by a psychologist, provided that there is no adverse impact on minorities and women. Personnel investigation by a qualified agency, when justified by costs of hiring and training.

Source: Reprinted by permission of the publisher, from "What Rights of Privacy Should Job Applicants Have?", Laurence Lipsett, SUPERVISORY MANAGEMENT (October 1977), © 1977 by AMACOM, a division of American Management Association, pages 35–36. All rights reserved. Used with permission.

duction foreman for a manufacturing firm, comes to the personnel manager's office and says, "My only quality control inspectors just had a fight and both quit. I can't operate until those positions are filled." Speed becomes a critical factor in this instance, and two interviews, a few phone calls, and a prayer may comprise the entire selection process. On the other hand, selecting a university dean may take an entire year, with considerable attention being devoted to careful study of resumes, intensive reference checking, and hours of interviews.

Organizational Hierarchy

The level in the organization at which a vacancy exists can also influence the selection process. Consider the differences in selecting an individual to fill a top level position for a major corporation as opposed to a machinist-trainee job requiring no work experience. Much more emphasis will be placed upon interviews and references for the high level position. Individuals making application for these jobs will not normally be required to take employment tests to prove their ability. Their track record will likely be more important in predicting future success. On the other hand, employment tests may be administered to the machinist-trainee, who may have no previous work experience from which to predict future performance. The level of the position in the organization must be considered when designing the optimum selection process.

Applicant Pool

The number of applicants for a particular job can also affect the selection process. The process can be selective if there are many applicants for a particular position. On the other hand, few applicants may be available for highly demanded skills. The selection process then becomes a matter of choosing whomever is available. Expansion and contraction of the labor market exert considerable influence upon the selection process.

The number of people hired for a particular job compared to the individuals in the applicant pool is often expressed as a **selection ratio**. The ratio is expressed as follows:

$$\text{Selection ratio} = \frac{\text{Number of individuals hired to fill a particular job}}{\text{Number of available applicants}}$$

If the ratio is consistently low, perhaps 1:2, selection must be made from a small number of applicants. People who might otherwise be rejected are often hired. On the other hand, a selection ratio of 1:10 indicates many available applicants.

Type of Organization

The segment of the economy where individuals are to be employed—private, governmental, or not-for-profit—can also affect the selection process. A business in the private sector is heavily profit oriented. Prospective employees are screened with regard to how they can help achieve this goal. The total individual, including personality factors, plays a role in the selection of future employees for this segment.[3]

The government's civil service system typically identifies qualified applicants through competitive examinations. Often, a manager can select from the top three applicants for a given position. A manager in this sector frequently does not have the prerogative to interview other applicants. On the other hand, individuals who are applying for positions in not-for-profit organizations (such as the Scouts or YMCA or YWCA) confront a different situation. The salary level may not be competitive with private and governmental organizations. Therefore, a person who fills one of these positions must not only be qualified but also dedicated toward this type of work.

[3]"Why Employers Turn Down Some Job Applicants," *The Office* 85 (May 1977): 151.

176

Part II
Human
Resources
Planning,
Recruitment,
and Selection

Probationary Period

Many firms use the **probationary period** which provides for evaluation of ability based upon performance. This may be either a substitute for, or supplement to, the use of tests. The rationale is that if an individual can successfully perform the job during the probationary period, tests may not be needed.

Even though a firm may be unionized, a new employee typically is not protected by the labor-management agreement until after a certain, probationary period. This period may be a month or longer. During this time, employee termination may occur with little or no justification. Once the probationary period is over, it may prove quite difficult to terminate a marginal employee. When a firm has a union, it becomes especially important for the selection process to be efficient in identifying the most productive workers. Once they fall under the union-management agreement, the power of the union must be considered in changing the status of a firm's union member.

PRELIMINARY INTERVIEW

The selection process begins with an initial screening of applicants to remove individuals who obviously do not fulfill the position requirements. At this stage, a few straightforward questions are asked. For instance, a position may require a college degree and considerable work experience. If an applicant has no experience and only a high school diploma, any further discussion regarding this particular position will prove useless for both the firm and the applicant.

In addition to eliminating obviously unqualified job applicants quickly, a preliminary interview may produce other positive benefits for the firm. It is likely that the position for which the applicant applied is not the only one available. A skilled interviewer who is up to date regarding other vacancies in the firm may be able to identify prospective employees who could fill other positions. The fact that a person does not qualify for one position does not mean that he or she would not be capable of performing well in another. For instance, the applicant may obviously be unqualified to fill the advertised position of senior programming analyst. But the individual might well be qualified to work as a computer operator. This type of counseling not only builds goodwill for the firm but also can maximize the recruitment and selecting efforts.

REVIEW OF APPLICATION BLANKS

The next step in the selection process involves having the prospective employee complete an application blank. The employer evaluates it with regard to whether there appears to be a match between the individual and the position. The specific type of information requested in an application blank may vary from firm to firm and even by positions within the organization. Sections of an application typically include personal data, physical condition, military service, education, work experience, and specific job qualifications.

An employment application blank must consider the firm's informational needs while reflecting legal requirements. An excellent illustration of a properly designed application form is provided in Figure 6–3. As you may note, potentially discriminatory questions have been eliminated from the form.

The information contained in a completed application blank is compared to the job description to determine whether a potential match exists between the firm and the applicant. As you might expect, this is often a difficult task. Applicants may attempt to present themselves in a positive light. Also, it is difficult to compare past duties and responsibilities with those needed with the job the applicant is seeking. A person with the title of "manager" in one firm may actually perform few managerial tasks while a person with the same title in another firm may have considerable managerial experience.

Over the years considerable effort has been devoted toward using application blank data to assist in differentiating between individuals who will be successful and less successful. Research during the past fifty years has suggested that the application blank can be a valuable predictive device in selection for certain types of positions. Personal factors such as number of dependents, hobbies (if not related to sex, race, religion, national origin, or age), years of education, and work experience have been found to be predictive of length of service and success on the job.[4] One large firm found that class standing was the primary factor related to the successful performance of its managerial jobs. Neither prestige of the university nor extracurricular activities were found to be significant in job success in this particular firm.

The best known technique for identifying factors which differentiate between successful and less successful employees is the **Weighted Application Blank** (WAB). When the WAB is used, an attempt is made to identify factors on the application blank which differentiate between such criteria variables as long- and short-term employees, productive and less productive workers, and satisfied and less satisfied employees. You can see one variable, "Years on the Last Job," in Figure 6–4. The percentage difference between short- and long-term workers is first computed. Then, a weight is assigned based upon the percentage point difference.[5] Once the weights for all variables on the application blank have been computed, applicants can be screened based on the point total they receive on the WAB. Using the WAB, applicants with the highest point total are considered to have the highest potential for success.

At times, the WAB has proven to be quite accurate and in other instances, its benefits have been marginal. Because the WAB approach has produced some unsatisfactory results, many personnel researchers have turned to other quantitative techniques to assist in evaluating data included on the ap-

[4]C. Harold Stone and Floyd L. Ruch, "Selection, Interviewing and Testing," in *ASPA Handbook of Personnel and Industrial Relations: Staffing Policies and Strategies* (Washington, D.C., The Bureau of National Affairs, Inc., 1974), pp. 4–131.

[5]Stanley R. Novack, "Developing an Effective Application Blank," *Personnel Journal* (May 1970): 422.

GENERAL ✦ ELECTRIC

An Equal Opportunity Employer

Application For Employment

It is the policy of the General Electric Company to provide employment, training, compensation, promotion and other conditions of employment based on qualifications, without regard to race, color, religion, national origin, sex, age, veteran status or handicap.

Print
Name _____
　　　　　Last　　　　　　First　　　　　　Middle

Address _____
　　　　　Number and Street

_____
City　　　　　　　State　　　　　　Zip Code

Telephone _____
　　　　　Area Code/Number

Social Security No. _____

Job Interest

Position Desired _____

Wages or Salary Expected $ _____ Per Hr. ☐ Week ☐ Month ☐
　　　　　　　　　　　　　　　　　　　　　　(Please Check One)

Other Positions for Which you are Qualified _____

Date Available for Employment _____

Were you Ever Employed by GE?　Yes ☐　No ☐

If Yes, Where? _____ Dates _____
　　　　　　　　　　　　　　　　　　　　　From ____　To ____

Education and Training

Circle Highest Grade Completed in Each School Category

	Grade School	High School	Tech School	College	Grad School
	1 2 3 4 5 6 7 8	9 10 11 12	1 2	1 2 3 4	1 2 3 4

	Name	Location	Course/Degree	Class Standing
Grade School				
High School				
College				
Graduate School				
Apprentice, Business, Technical, Military or Vocational School				

Other Training or Skills (Factory or Office Machines Operated, Special Courses, Military Training, etc.) _____

Other Job-Related Activities

List professional, trade, business or civic activities and offices held (exclude groups which indicate race, color, religion, sex or national origin). _____

To Be Detached by Employee Relations

Personal Data

Print
Name _____
　　　　　Last　　　　　　First　　　　　　Middle

Address _____
　　　　　Number and Street

_____
City　　　　　　　State　　　　　　Zip Code

Telephone _____
　　　　　Area Code/Number

Social Security No. _____

Date of Application _____

Is Your Age:　Under 18 ? _____　Yes ☐　No ☐
　　　　　　　　　　　　　　　　　　(Please Check One)
　　　　　　　Over 70 ? _____　Yes ☐　No ☐
　　　　　　　　　　　　　　　　　　(Please Check One)

Are you a citizen of USA? _____　Yes ☐　No ☐
　　　　　　　　　　　　　　　　　　　　　　(Please Check One)

If you are not a U.S. Citizen, have you a legal right to remain permanently in the U.S.? ____　Yes ☐　No ☐
　　　　　　　　　　　　　　　　　　　　　　(Please Check One)

Military

Were you in the U.S. Armed Forces? _____　Yes ☐　No ☐
　　　　　　　　　　　　　　　　　　　　　　(Please Check One)

If yes, what branch? _____

Date Entered _____ Date Discharged _____

Final Rank _____ Type of Discharge _____

Military experience should have been included in Employment History section on Page 2.

Convictions

Have you ever been convicted of a felony? _____　Yes ☐　No ☐
　　　　　　　　　　　　　　　　　　　　　　(Please Check One)

Have you been convicted of a misdemeanor committed within the past five years, or were you imprisoned for a misdemeanor which occurred more than five years ago? _____　Yes ☐　No ☐
　　　　　　　　　　　　　　　　　　　　　　(Please Check One)

If **Yes** to either of above questions, please explain fully. **This information will not necessarily bar an applicant from employment.**

_____

Additional Information

State any additional information you feel may be helpful to us in considering your application:

_____

Employment History

Please read carefully before starting. List all employment starting with **present** or **most recent** employer. Account for all periods, including unemployment and **service with the Armed Forces**. Also include relevant voluntary and/or part-time work experience. Use additional sheet if necessary.

	Dates		Hourly Rate/Salary	
Employer	From		Starting $	per
Address		Month Year	Final $	per
	To	Month Year		
Job Title	Describe Major Duties			
Department				
Supervisor	Reason For Leaving			

	Dates		Hourly Rate/Salary	
Employer	From		Starting $	per
Address		Month Year	Final $	per
	To	Month Year		
Job Title	Describe Major Duties			
Department				
Supervisor	Reason For Leaving			

	Dates		Hourly Rate/Salary	
Employer	From		Starting $	per
Address		Month Year	Final $	per
	To	Month Year		
Job Title	Describe Major Duties			
Department				
Supervisor	Reason For Leaving			

	Dates		Hourly Rate/Salary	
Employer	From		Starting $	per
Address		Month Year	Final $	per
	To	Month Year		
Job Title	Describe Major Duties			
Department				
Supervisor	Reason For Leaving			

Interviewer's Comments:

Interviewed By: _____   Date: _____

Affirmative Action

Special Employment Notice To Disabled Veterans, Vietnam Era Veterans And Individuals With Physical Or Mental Handicaps:

Government contractors are subject to Section 402 of the Vietnam Era Veterans Readjustment Act of 1974 which requires that they take affirmative action to employ and advance in employment qualified disabled veterans and veterans of the Vietnam Era (i.e. served more than 180 days between August 5, 1964 and May 7, 1975), and Section 503 of the Rehabilitation Act of 1973, as amended, which requires government contractors to take affirmative action to employ and advance in employment qualified handicapped individuals.

Please Check Below If You Are A:

☐ Vietnam Era Veteran

☐ Disabled Veteran

☐ Handicapped Individual

And wish to be considered under our Affirmative Action Program(s) **Submission of this information is voluntary.**

Please read this carefully before signing:

Employee Release and Privacy Statement

I understand that the General Electric Company requires certain information about me to evaluate my qualifications for employment and to conduct its business if I become an employee. Therefore, I authorize the Company to investigate my past employment, educational credentials and other employment-related activities. I agree to cooperate in such investigations, and release those parties supplying such information to the Company from all liability or responsibility with respect to information supplied.

I agree that the Company may use the information it obtains concerning me in the conduct of its business. I understand that such use may include disclosure outside the Company in those cases where its agents and contractors need such information to perform their functions, where the Company's legal interests and/or obligations are involved, or where there is a medical emergency involving me. I understand, however, that the Company intends to protect the confidentiality of personal information it obtains concerning me. Consequently, personal information in Company record-keeping systems, other than the fact and location of past or present Company employment, the dates of employment, or the job name or description of general duties, will not otherwise be disclosed outside the Company with a personal identifier without my consent. Further, the Company will require its agents and contractors to safeguard personal information disclosed to them by the Company.

I understand that any employment with the Company would not be for any fixed period of time and that, if employed, I may resign at any time for any reason or the Company may terminate my employment at any time for any reason in the absence of a specific written agreement to the contrary.

I understand that any false answers or statements made by me on this application or any supplement thereto or in connection with the above-mentioned investigations will be sufficient grounds for immediate discharge, if I am employed.

Applicant's Signature: _____   Date: _____

Figure 6–3.   An employment application. (Source: General Electric.)

180

Part II
Human
Resources
Planning,
Recruitment,
and Selection

	Percentage Responding			
Item	Short-term	Long-term	Difference	Weight
Years on the Last Job				
No response	4	12	+ 8	0
Less that 1	50	0	−50	−5
1–1 1/2	7	35	+28	+2
1 1/2–2 1/2	37	12	−25	−2
2 1/2–3	0	6	+ 6	0
More than 3	2	35	+33	+3

Figure 6–4. **An example of a weighted application blank question. (Source:** *Personnel Journal.*)

plication form. Two of these techniques, regression analysis and discriminant analysis, will be described in chapter 18.

ADMINISTRATION OF SELECTION TESTS

Selection tests are administered to assist in assessing the applicant's potential for success with the organization. They are used to determine a variety of attributes including the applicant's ability, aptitude, and personality. **Ability tests** (also called achievement tests) assist in determining how well an individual can currently perform tasks related to the job. An excellent illustration of this is a typing test given to a prospective employee for a secretarial job. This type of test may be designed to provide a validated measure of current performance.[6]

An individual may not currently possess the skills to perform the job. The purpose of an **aptitude test** is to determine a person's potential to learn in a given area. An example of such a test is the General Management Aptitude Test (GMAT) which many business students take prior to gaining admission to a graduate business school program. **Personality tests** are given to measure a prospective employee's ability to function in a particular working environment. For instance, a person with a particular type of personality may function best in a certain selling situation.

The Civil Rights Act of 1964 and its accompanying interpretations by the federal courts have had the effect of reducing the use of selection tests. For instance, in *Griggs, et al.* v. *Duke Power Company*, the U.S. Supreme Court ruled that preemployment requirements including tests must show a relationship to job performance, or, in other words, they must possess validity.[7] Also,

[6]Laurence Lipsett, "What Rights of Privacy Should Job Applicants Have?" *Supervisory Management* 22 (October 1977): 32
[7]Richard D. Arvez and Kevin M. Mossholder, "A Proposed Methodology for Determining Similarities and Differences Among Jobs," *Personnel Psychology* 30 (1977): 363.

in the case of *Albemarle Paper* v. *Moody*, the Supreme Court again ruled that any test used in the selection process or in promotion decisions must be validated if it is found that its use had an adverse impact on members of protected groups. Many selection tools discussed in this chapter are affected by this decision. For a selection test to be considered nondiscriminatory, it must conform to the guidelines set forth in Section 1607 of the *Code of Federal Regulations*.[8] Donald W. Vena, vice president-personnel relations for Western Airlines, Inc., stated, "I fully expect increased usage of 'valid' preemployment tests in the selection process. The usage of valid preemployment tests is a tremendous aid in selecting qualified applicants without regard to race, sex, etc." The fact that selection tests have at times been misused does not diminish their potential usefulness. However, there are certain conditions that should be met if they are to be used as a selection tool. Each of these conditions will next be described.

Reliability

The **reliability** of a selection tool is the extent to which it provides consistent results. If a person takes the same test a number of times, or parallel forms of the test, his or her scores will vary. This variance is called the standard error. When an individual is tested but once, only one of the many possible scores is achieved. The smaller the standard error, the more accurately Personnel can evaluate the individual's score. Reliability data reveal the degree of confidence that can be placed in a test. If a test has low reliability, its validity as a predictor will also be low.

Validity

Validity is the extent to which a test measures what it is designed to measure. It is commonly reported as a **correlation coefficient** which summarizes the relationship between two variables. For example, these variables may be the score on a selection test and some measure of employee performance. A coefficient of 0 shows no relationship while coefficients of either $+1.0$ or -1.0 indicate a perfect relationship. Naturally, no test will be 100 percent accurate. Yet organizations strive for the highest feasible coefficient. If a test is designed to predict job performance, and validity studies of the test indicate a high correlation coefficient, most prospective employees who score high on the test will later prove to be high performers. The ability to select better qualified individuals will help increase the firm's productivity.

In addition to improving selection decisions, a firm using validated instruments is addressing important legal considerations. Should charges of discrimination be made, and adverse impact established, the organization's legal defense will be much stronger.

[8]*Code of Federal Regulations*, 29 CFR Section 1607, July 1, 1978, pp. 921–927.

Catherine R. (Kay) Hildeen, AEP
Vice President
Drake Beam Morin, Inc.

Catherine Hildeen is vice president of a firm that "was founded almost two decades ago to help more effectively develop and manage the most valuable corporate resource—people." This philosophy of Drake-Beam Morin, Inc. matches perfectly the educational background, experience, and career aspirations of Kay Hildeen.

Kay studied personnel management at the University of Minnesota under the venerable Dale Yoder, author of one of the first personnel texts. A Phi Beta Kappa, she received her B.A. in psychology and economics, graduating magna cum laude. She was the only member of her class to have a straight "A" average. As to why she chose a career in Personnel, Kay says, "That was a choice I made in college after taking a variety of courses in liberal arts. I believed Personnel to be more fascinating than other phases of business. People are much more complicated than machines, paperwork, and accounting principles."

With the assistance of Professor Yoder, Ms. Hildeen launched her career in Personnel with the Continental Illinois National Bank in Chicago. In this initial position, she became involved with personnel research and organization analysis. She also validated selection tests, administered non-officer compensation, and analyzed costs and trends in personnel programs.

Kay became a personnel manager for her next employer—a large retailer—and quickly broadened her management background. She

There are several procedures for validating a test. Immediately following is a discussion of these types: criterion-related validity, content validity, and construct validity.

Criterion-Related Validity. When **criterion-related validity** is used, the scores on the tests are compared to some aspect of job performance as determined, for example, by performance appraisal. This measure might be such things as quantity and quality of work, turnover, and absenteeism. A high relationship between the score on the test and job performance suggests that the test is valid.

There are two basic forms of criterion-related validity, concurrent and predictive validity. With **concurrent validity**, the test scores and the criterion data are obtained at essentially the same time. For instance, all currently employed machine operators may be given a test. Through current company records information is available which identifies each operator's job performance. If the test is able to separate the productive from the less productive workers, it is said to be valid. A problem in using this validation procedure is that even was placed in charge of one department store's operations during the Christmas season while simultaneously recruiting employees for a new store.

In her next position, Kay became vice president personnel and labor relations for a fifty million dollar consumer cooperative that marketed domestic and imported goods and services. Serving here as one of four managing vice presidents, Kay participated in corporate planning, business strategies, and decision making in all phases of the company. In the area of labor relations, Kay negotiated over fifty union contracts within her firm's objectives. As a result of these experiences, her company suffered only one strike, which was settled within a week without additional concessions. As a testimonial to her professional expertise, she managed labor relations for over twenty years with only four grievances arbitrated. During this period, her employer overcame three organizing attempts. As an internal and external consultant, Kay became an expert in organization and manpower planning, labor relations, computer-based management information systems, and strategies for acquisitions, mergers, and divestitures. She developed a broad knowledge of marketing, corporate finance, and corporate and individual tax effects of management compensation systems.

Explaining why she left business and entered the management consulting field, Kay states, "People spend the bulk of their lives at work. As a personnel executive for a firm, my efforts were directed to improve the worklife of only that firm's employees. As a consultant, I have the opportunity to impact the lives of people in many organizations."

Regarding the need for a formal education, Ms. Hildeen says emphatically, "I don't think there is any substitute for it. It is important not only for success in a career, but also as it affects one's quality of life."

Kay has served as national vice president of the American Society for Personnel Administration and is currently vice president and board member of the Personnel Accreditation Institute. She has also been active in many civic and church activities.

the less productive workers have undergone the normal selection procedure. They were assumed to be able to do the job when hired. All applicants were not tested; only the ones who were hired.

Predictive validity involves administering a test and later obtaining the criterion information. For instance, a test might be administered to all applicants. However, the results of the test are not used in the selection decision. After employees' performance has been observed, the test results are analyzed to determine if they distinguish between successful and less successful employees. Predictive validity is considered a technically sound procedure. However, because of the time and cost involved, its use is often not feasible.

Content Validity. Although it is less statistically oriented, many personnel practitioners believe content validity provides a more commonsense approach to validating the selection process. When **content validity** is used, a person performs certain tasks (test) which are actual samples of the kind of work the job requires. Thorough job analysis and carefully prepared job descriptions are needed when using this form of validation.

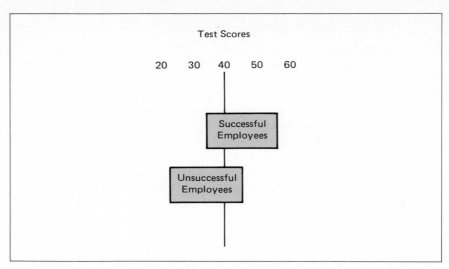

Figure 6–5. **Examples of the results of a validated test.**

The classic example of the use of content validity is giving a typing test to a secretary whose primary job would be to type. In the *Washington* v. *Davis* case mentioned previously, the Supreme Court gave support to the use of content validity. Its use will likely experience considerable growth in the future.

Construct Validity. **Construct validity** is used to determine whether or not a test measures certain traits or qualities identified as important in performing the job. For instance, if the job requires a large amount of persistence, such as in some forms of life insurance sales, a test would be used to measure persistence. However, traits or qualities needed on the job must first be identified through job analysis.

An example of what would likely occur when prospective employees are administered a validated test is provided in Figure 6–5. This firm's experience indicates that individuals who scored 40 and above on the test were successful. Those who scored below 40 were less successful. As noted in the figure, the test is not absolutely accurate. A small number of individuals who scored below 40 were good workers. Also, some applicants scoring above 40 were less successful. However, the test appears to be a good predictor a large portion of the time. It is because of this gray area that test results should serve as only one of several criteria in the selection decision.

Objectivity

When every grader can interpret the results of the same test and arrive at identical results, the test is said to have full **objectivity**. On the other hand, the more subjective the evaluation, the less the graders agree.

You are probably very familiar with multiple-choice and true-false tests. These are called objective tests because all scorers can use a key and agree per-

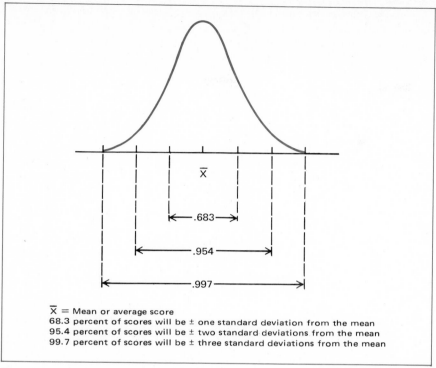

$\bar{X}$ = Mean or average score
68.3 percent of scores will be ± one standard deviation from the mean
95.4 percent of scores will be ± two standard deviations from the mean
99.7 percent of scores will be ± three standard deviations from the mean

Figure 6–6. A normal probability curve. (Source: John Neter, William Wasserman, and G.A. Whitmore, *Fundamental Statistics*.)

fectly on the result. An essay exam, however, is an example of a subjective test. This type of test may provide considerable room for disagreement among graders.

Standardization

A test that is standardized is "administered under standard conditions to a large group of persons who are representative of the individuals for whom it is intended.[9] The purpose of **standardization** is to obtain norms, or standards, in order that a specific test score can be meaningful when compared to other scores in the group. When a test is standardized, it is administered to a large number of people who are performing similar tasks. The scores will be distributed according to the normal probability curve presented in Figure 6–6. A normalized test will have the majority of the scores concentrated in the middle of the distribution. Individuals receiving scores in this range would be considered average for the population studied.

[9]Dale Yoder and Herbert G. Heneman, Jr., *Staffing Policies and Strategies, ASPA Handbook of Personnel and Industrial Relations*, vol. 1, (Washington, D.C.: The Bureau of National Affairs, Inc., 1974), pp. 4–135 to 4–136.

Where there are sufficient employees performing the same or similar work, employers can standardize their own tests. Typically, this is not the case and national norms for a particular test must be used. When national norms are used, a prospective employee takes the test and the score obtained is compared to national scores. The significance of the test score can be determined through this procedure.

Table 6–2. Examples of selection tests and their use

General Type	Name of Test	Purpose	Validated For
Ability	Thurstone Test of Mental Alertness	Measures general mental ability. Aids in determining if an applicant has the capacity for learning the requirements of the job, if a person's ability to understand meets the requirements of one job better than another, and if a present employee can change easily to another job and learn it quickly.	The TMA was validated in various companies and was found to be predictive of job success for the following jobs: Bank teller, Computer operator, Computer programmer, Clerical worker, Manager (retail store), Manager, assistant, Salesperson (retail store), Sales representative, Sales supervisor, Supervisor (insurance)
Ability	Adaptability Test	Measures mental adaptability or alertness. Distinguishes between persons who easily adapt to new situations and those who perform better on routine or repetitive jobs.	The Adaptability Test was validated in various companies and was found to be predictive of job success for the following jobs: Clerk, accounting, Clerk, adjustment, Clerk, Collector (credit), Finisher trainee, Inspector (quality control), Order processor (clerical), Secretary, Supervisor, first-line, Supervisor, industrial, Teletype trainee
Aptitude	Computer Programmer Aptitude Battery (CPAB)	Five subsets measure abilities related to success in computer programming and systems analysis fields.	The CPAB was found to be predictive of job success in validation studies conducted for the following organizations: Computer manufacturer training program, Insurance company, Railroad company, Research organization, Retail catalog company, Retail organization, Utility company

The number of available standardized selection tests is large and continues to grow. Illustrations of tests currently being used by organizations for a variety of jobs may be seen in Table 6–2. The specific jobs for which these tests have been validated are shown in this illustration.

All types of tests used in the selection process do not have the same degree of validity. For example, achievement tests tend to have relatively high

Table 6–2. *(cont.)*

General Type	Name of Test	Purpose	Validated For
Aptitude	Purdue Pegboard	Measures two kinds of finger dexterity related to productivity in routine manual jobs. Five separate scores can be obtained: right hand, left hand, both hands, right plus left plus both hands, and assembly.	The Purdue Pegboard was validated in various educational and industrial settings and was found to be predictive of success for: Assembler High school shop trainee Light machine operator Packer Proof-machine operator Radio tube mounter
Personality	Supervisory Index	Measures a person's attitude in typical supervisory situations. Four subscores (management, supervision, employees, and human relations practices) and a total score reflect how a person is likely to approach the supervisory job.	The Supervisory Index was validated in various companies and was found to be predictive of job success for the following jobs: Front-line supervisor Manager (retail chain) Manager, assistant (retail chain) Supervisor (duplicating machines manufacturer) Supervisor (insurance) Supervisor (technical construction) Vice president, assistant vice president, and executive trainee (bank)
Personality	Thurstone Temperament Schedule	Measures seven personality traits: active, vigorous, impulsive, dominant, stable, sociable, and reflective.	The TTS was validated in various educational and industrial settings and was found to be predictive of job performance for the following jobs: Manager of small retail store Office worker Retail store sales employee Sales supervisor Third and fourth grade teacher

Source: Adapted from *SRA Catalog for Business*, Science Research Associates, Inc., Chicago, Ill., 1978. Used with permission.

188

Part II
Human
Resources
Planning,
Recruitment,
and Selection

correlation coefficients whereas personality tests generally are notoriously low. Interest tests are normally much more useful in the areas of placement and career counseling. An important role of Personnel is to choose the best test for a specific purpose.

THE EMPLOYMENT INTERVIEW

Some jobs may be performed in isolation. However, the high degree of job specialization which has taken place since the turn of the century has created the need for persons to interact successfully with others. An excellent selection device for assessing a person's interpersonal competence is the employment interview. In fact, it has been described by some as the center of the selection process. It provides for the exchange of information between a company representative and the applicant. In fact, Donald W. Vena, vice president, personnel relations for Western Airlines, Inc., believes that, "The key element of a sound personnel selection program is highly trained employment interviewers." The interviewer obtains information about the candidate's qualifications as they relate to the job requirements. The subjective judgments which are often made during employment interviews sometime reduce their reliability. Some of the reasons for low interview reliability include:

- Asking different questions and using different interpretations of answers in response to given questions. This would include personal biases and prejudices as well as intuitive analyses of patterns of background or other information being processed by the interviewer.
- Using different techniques which have differing effects upon the interviewees. This would, of course, include the relative amounts of skill in eliciting responses from interviewees.
- Attempting to make judgments concerning nebulous and poorly defined characteristics or traits possessed by the interviewees. For example, in the absence of established objective indicators of a given trait, such as intellectual curiosity, interviewers must fall back upon their own intuition.
- Attempting to make judgments as to the possession or lack of certain traits based upon the behavior of the interviewee during the interview.[10]

Many possible errors can occur while interviewing candidates. Properly conducted interviews, however, can serve as useful selection tools.

Objectives of the Interview

Employment interviews have several basic objectives. It is important that the goals described below be successfully achieved.

[10]Robert L. Decker, "The Employment Interview," *Personnel Administrator* (November 1981): 72.

1. *Obtain additional information from the applicant.* It is essential that additional information be obtained about the applicant to complement the data provided by other selection tools. The interview is the only step in the selection process that permits clarification of certain points, the uncovering of additional information, and the elaboration of data which is needed to make a sound selection decision.

2. *Provide information regarding the firm.* General information about the job, company policies, its products, and its services should be communicated to the applicant during the interview. If the interviewee is adequately prepared, all of the information will not come as a surprise.

3. *Sell the company.* The employment interview provides an excellent opportunity for selling the company to the applicant. This should be accomplished in a realistic manner and the organization should not be presented by an interviewer who appears to view the firm through rose-colored glasses. Describing the company as a virtual utopia may well result in a disappointed employee or even an ex-employee.

4. *Make new friends.* The applicant should leave the interview with a positive attitude about the company. Hopefully this attitude will not change regardless of whether a job offer is made. The interview should never serve to make the applicant appear inadequate.

Content of the Interview

The specific content of employment interviews varies greatly by organization and the level of the job concerned. However, the following general topics are frequently included: academic achievement, personal qualities, occupational experience, interpersonal competence, and career orientation.[11] The interviewer should deal only with the information in these categories that represents bonafide occupational qualifications (BFOQ).

Academic Achievement. An employment interviewer might attempt to obtain additional insight into application blank data. At times, the applicant fails to record positive events that could affect employment decisions. The interviewer should attempt to discover any underlying factors related to academic performance. For example, a student who earned only a 2.28/4.0 GPA may turn out to be a very bright individual who, because of financial difficulties, might have worked virtually full time while still participating in a variety of activities. On the other hand, a student who received a 3.8/4.0 GPA may not be a well-rounded individual and may be a weak candidate for many jobs.

Personal Qualities. Personal qualities which would normally be observed during the interview include such factors as physical appearance, speaking ability, vo-

[11]Felix M. Lopez, "The Employment Interview," in *Handbook of Modern Personnel Administration*, ed. Joseph J. Farmularo (New York: McGraw-Hill Book Company, 1972), pp. 134, 135.

190

Part II
Human
Resources
Planning,
Recruitment,
and Selection

cabulary, poise, and assertiveness. Even though the "halo effect" occurs at times, efforts should be made to keep non-job-related personal qualities from biasing the selection process.[12]

Because of legal ramifications, it would obviously be unwise to permit personal qualities to influence the selection decision unless they were BFOQ. Physical appearance might very well be an occupational qualification if the job being filled was that of an actress who was to portray the early career of Brooke Shields. Speaking ability, vocabulary, and poise may be job related qualifications if the job is that of a sportscaster to work with Howard Cosell. The quality of assertiveness may be required for the successful performance of a credit collector's job.

Occupational Experience. Exploring an individual's occupational experience provides an indication of the applicant's skills, abilities, and willingness to handle assigned responsibilities. Job titles in one organization do not necessarily represent the same job content in another. And, good performance in one job does not guarantee that the individual will succeed in another. At the same time, past performance does provide some indication of the employee's ability and willingness to work.

Interpersonal Competence. To a degree an interviewer may observe an applicant's interpersonal competence. However, the interviewer may be witnessing an academy award performance by the candidate displaying an "I like people" nature. For this reason, the interview may need to consist of questions regarding the applicant's interpersonal relationship with family and friends plus how he or she behaves in other social and civic situations. The primary cause of failure in performing jobs is not due to the lack of technical ability but rather to shortcomings in interpersonal competence. Even though an individual may be a highly skilled worker, if he or she cannot work well with other employees, the chances for success are diminished.

Career Orientation. Questions about a candidate's career objectives may aid the interviewer in determining the degree to which an applicant's aspirations are realistic. The odds are rather great that a recent college graduate who expects to become a senior vice president within six months will become quickly dissatisfied with the company.

In addition to determining an applicant's career goals, the interviewer should present an honest and accurate description of career prospects in the organization. Deception on this point may prove counterproductive in that the applicant, if employed, may well become dissatisfied later as the truth unfolds. The firm may lose a substantial investment in the form of recruitment, selection, and training.

[12]Ray Jeffery, "Taking the Guesswork Out of Selection," *Personnel Management* 9 (October 1977): 40.

Many recruits have unrealistic expectations about their prospective job and employer. This inaccurate perception, which may have negative consequences, is often encouraged by firms which present themselves in overly attractive terms. To correct this situation, it is suggested that a realistic job preview be given to applicants early in the selection process and definitely before a job offer is made.

A **realistic job preview** (RJP) conveys important job information to the applicant in an unbiased manner including both positive and negative factors. This approach assists applicants in developing a more accurate perception of the job and the firm. Research studies suggest that newly hired employees who received RJPs have greater job survival and higher job satisfaction. At the same time, use of this technique does not reduce the flow of qualified applicants. A comparison of the results of traditional preview procedures as opposed to realistic preview procedures may be seen in Figure 6–7. Note that traditional procedures result in low job survival and dissatisfaction whereas RJPs overcome these difficulties.

Figure 6–7. Typical consequences of job preview procedures. (Source: *Personnel*.)

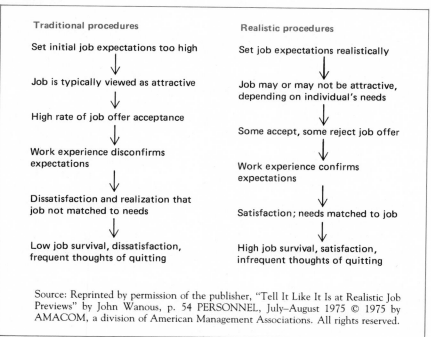

Traditional procedures	Realistic procedures
Set initial job expectations too high	Set job expectations realistically
↓	↓
Job is typically viewed as attractive	Job may or may not be attractive, depending on individual's needs
↓	↓
High rate of job offer acceptance	Some accept, some reject job offer
↓	↓
Work experience disconfirms expectations	Work experience confirms expectations
↓	↓
Dissatisfaction and realization that job not matched to needs	Satisfaction; needs matched to job
↓	↓
Low job survival, dissatisfaction, frequent thoughts of quitting	High job survival, satisfaction, infrequent thoughts of quitting

[13]John P. Wanous, "Tell It Like It Is at Realistic Job Previews," in *Current Issues in Personnel Management*, edited by Kendrith M. Rowland, Manuel London, Gerald R. Ferris and Jay. L. Sherman (Boston: Allyn & Bacon, Inc., 1980), pp. 41–50.

192

Part II
Human
Resources
Planning,
Recruitment,
and Selection

Types of Interviews

Interviews may be distinguished by the amount of structure or preplanned format they possess. Probing, open-ended questions are asked in the **nondirective interview**. The interview is comprehensive in nature and the interviewee is encouraged to do much of the talking. Usually only highly trained interviewers use the nondirective interview because it consists of a highly subjective appraisal of the job candidate. The nondirective interview is often more time consuming than one with more structure, yet some interviewers believe that it is more effective in obtaining significant information. The nature of the nondirective interview requires a highly trained and skillful interviewer who asks open-ended questions such as:

- What do you believe are your primary strengths? What are your main weaknesses?
- How will our company benefit by having you as an employee?
- Where do you want to be in this firm five years from now?
- What was your most significant contribution with your last employer?

The answer itself may not be as important to the interviewer as how the question is answered and the thought process that goes into developing the response.

The **patterned interview** consists of standardized questions that are asked of all applicants for a specific group of jobs. This standardization permits the candidates to be compared easily and greatly facilitates the validation process.

Table 6–3. Portion of a patterned interview guide

Work Experience	
Cover:	*Look for:*
Earliest jobs: part-time, temporary	Relevance of work
Military assignments	Sufficiency of work
Full-time positions	Skill and competence
Ask:	Adaptability
Things done best? Done less well?	Productivity
Things liked best? Liked less well?	Motivation
Major accomplishments? How achieved?	Interpersonal relations
Most difficult problems faced? How handled?	Leadership
Ways most effective with people? Ways less effective?	Growth and development
Level of earnings?	
Reasons for changing jobs?	
What learned from work experience?	
What looking for in job? In career?	

The advantages of structure may quickly become disadvantages if the interviewer asks each of the questions in a precise, mechanical manner. This approach could easily result in an overly formal environment and severely impair the candidate's ability or desire to respond.

A properly designed patterned interview will contain only those questions that are job related. In other words, it will be validated just as a selection test. An illustration of a patterned interview guide for discussing work experience is provided in Table 6–3. As you can see, each question is asked for a specific purpose.

Methods of Interviewing

Interviews may be conducted in several ways. A majority of employment interviews consist of the applicant meeting with an interviewer in a one-to-one situation. Since the interview itself may represent a highly emotional situation to the interviewee, the one-to-one interview if often less threatening.

Unlike a one-to-one interview, a **group interview** consists of several applicants interacting in the presence of one or more company representatives. This approach, while not mutually exclusive of the other types, may provide useful insights into the candidates' interpersonal competence as they engage in group discussion. The technique is often used because it saves the time of busy professionals and executives.

In a **board interview**, one candidate is quizzed by several interviewers. While a thorough examination of the applicant would likely result from this approach, the interviewee's anxiety level is often quite high. L. C. Barry, vice president of industrial relations for Gates Learjet said, "We use a three-person board to screen each applicant, asking a series of questions designed to ferret out the individual's attitudes toward former employers, jobs, etc. Then, a week later, we bring successful applicants and their spouses in for a family night meeting with top management and their spouses, where we further screen them while discussing the company and employee benefits." Naturally, the amount of time devoted to a board interview will differ depending on the type and level of job.

While most interview sessions are designed to minimize stress on the part of the candidate, the **stress interview** intentionally creates it. This type of interview is designed for jobs in which a great deal of anxiety is a part of the environment. The stress interview should only be attempted by highly trained and skilled interviewers. Interviewers for some types of sales jobs subject applicants to stress situations in order to determine how they will react under pressure. For instance, on the first interview, everything might progress extremely smoothly. The applicant is led to believe that all he or she has to do is come back for the second interview and the job offer will be made. However, on the second interview, events progress a bit differently. The individual might have to wait in the outer office for a considerable period of time before the interview begins. This tactic allows the interviewee's anxiety level to build up. Once with the interviewer, a statement might be made, "Mr. Noles, I ap-

194

Part II
Human
Resources
Planning,
Recruitment,
and Selection

preciate your time, but we just don't believe there is any need to continue this interview. Your qualifications just don't appear to match our needs." The purpose of this approach is to see how the applicant will react when confronted with an unexpected situation. The company has discovered that individuals who are able to turn this situation around will become successful sales representatives. Naturally, the majority of situations are not appropriate for the stress interview. However, a simulated situation may provide valuable insight regarding an applicant's ability to deal with a stressful situation.

The Interviewer, Interview Planning, and the Interview Process

The interviewer should possess a pleasant personality, empathy, and the ability to listen and communicate effectively. He or she should have a healthy respect for individuals who are different in terms of personal attributes and backgrounds. It is essential that interviewers be free of stereotyped views concerning the capabilities of females and minorities. Instead, they must be able to recognize the ability and potential possessed by individual candidates. Interviewers should also have a solid knowledge of actual job requirements so that they can properly assess the applicant's qualifications.

In addition, interview planning is essential for conducting effective employment interviews.[14] The physical location of the interview should be both pleasant and private. This type of environment provides for a minimum of interruptions. The interviewer should become familiar with the applicant's record by reviewing data provided by other selection tools.

The interview process should begin with a warm and sincere welcome for the candidate and rapport should be quickly developed. Since people can often talk most easily about themselves, it is a good practice for the interview to begin in this manner. After this initial ice breaking, the interviewer can proceed to ask relevant, job related questions. It is important that the interviewer avoid asking leading questions such as, "You didn't do too well in statistics, did you?" Rather, questions should be posed in a manner which permits the applicant some flexibility in answering the question.

When the necessary information has been obtained and the applicant's questions answered, the interview should be brought to a conclusion. At this point, the applicant should be told that he or she will receive notification of the selection decision within a short period of time. In reality this promise is often broken. Unfortunately, if this commitment is not kept, a positive relationship between the applicant and the organization can quickly break down.

REFERENCE CHECKS

Information contained in the completed application blank is at times incorrect or colored to present a more favorable image. The purpose of the **reference**

[14]"How Good Is Your Interviewing Style?" *International Management* 32 (December 1977): 56.

check is to provide additional insight into the information in the application blank and verify its accuracy. It is likely that if you have ever applied for a job you have had to provide a list of references. Reference checks are normally made either by letter, phone, or a combination of the two. When reference letters are used, the writer typically describes the nature of the job for which the applicant is being considered. Reference information is typically limited to dates of employment, job title, absentee record, promotions and demotions, compensation, and reasons for termination.[15] As you might expect, there are numerous problems associated with written reference checks.

Since the passage of the Federal Privacy Act of 1974, a person who has been employed by the federal government has the legal right to review reference checks that have been made regarding her or his employment unless the individual waives this right. There have been instances where applicants have sued and won court cases when it was proven that the reference was biased. Because of the possible expansion of the Privacy Act, many people are reluctant to provide negative reference information.[16] Often, a firm responding to a written reference check will only provide objective facts such as duration of employment, title of position when the individual left the firm, and his or her ending salary. Comments regarding the reason for termination and job performance are often not included in a letter.

Another difficulty of a letter of reference is that the job applicant provides the names of his or her references. Applicants will carefully select their references in order to present a more favorable image. For instance, it would appear unlikely that the applicant would choose a reference who would give an unfavorable report. Therefore, the majority of references are biased in a positive manner.

Perhaps because of the bias associated with a written reference letter, many firms use the telephone to obtain applicant information. They reason that a more objective appraisal will result if there is no documentation of the conversation. Still, managers must be conscious as to the type of questions that are asked. However, if the person desires to elaborate upon a particular topic, the reference checker would certainly encourage further discussion. For instance, the question might be asked, "How long was Bill with your firm? A response such as, "He was here ten years, but we should have fired him years ago," may reveal more information than a written reference. The reference checker should always remember that comments from a reference can be biased.

BACKGROUND INVESTIGATION

Although a reference check often provides information with which to verify certain statements on the application blank, there are many times when it does not. Often, it is important to perform a background investigation of the

[15]Scott T. Rickard, "Effective Staff Selection," *Personnel Journal* (June 1981): 477.
[16]J. David Jackson and Bruce W. Taylor, "A Scientific Approach to Management Selection," *CA Magazine* 110 (August 1977): 41.

196

Part II
Human
Resources
Planning,
Recruitment,
and Selection

applicant's past employment history. This **background investigation** may be helpful in determining if past work experience is related to the qualifications needed for the new position. For instance, job titles are quite deceptive when attempting to evaluate past work experience. A person with the title of "manager" in one firm may have only been an overpaid clerk while in another firm the person may have been in the mainstream of decision making.

Another reason for background investigations is that credential fraud has increased in recent years.[17] It has been found that between 7 and 10 percent of job applicants are not what they present themselves to be.[18] Some applicants are not even who they say they are. Properly conducted background investigations can confirm or disprove claims made by job applicants.

POLYGRAPH TESTS

Another means to verify background information is the polygraph, or lie detector test. One purpose of the polygraph is to confirm or refute the information contained in the application blank. The polygraph measures changes in a person's breathing, blood pressure, and pulse rate. Supposedly, if an individual tells a lie, a detectable change will occur, though actually, the polygraph can only measure tension and cannot measure honesty.

The person who is administering the polygraph will typically ask a series of questions that are known to be true and then ask questions relevant to the selection decision. For instance, questions such as, "Is your name Bobby Halmes? Do you live at 1401 Malloy Street? Are you married?" might be followed by the question, "Have you ever stolen anything from your employer?" If there was a major change on the polygraph when a "No" response was given, further probing would be needed. It could indicate that five years ago, Bobby took a pencil home and did not return it or it could mean that the prospective employee stole from his employer on a regular basis.

The polygraph has received considerable criticism from a variety of sources. In fact, by 1982, eighteen states prohibited the use of polygraphs either in selection or retention of workers. However, it continues to be used as a screening device in some organizations.[19]

SELECTION DECISION

Once information has been obtained from the preceding steps, the most critical of all of the steps—the actual decision of who to hire—must take place. The other stages in the selection process have been used to narrow the number of candidates. The final decision will be made from among the individuals who are still being considered after reference checks, selection tests, and back-

[17]Kenneth C. Cooper, "Those 'Qualified' Applicants and Their Phony Credentials," *Administrative Management* 38 (August 1977): 44.
[18]Scott T. Rickard, "Effective Staff Selection," *Personnel Journal* (June 1981): 477.
[19]"Business Buys the Lie Detector," *Business Week* (February 6, 1978): 100.

ground investigations have been evaluated. The individual with the best overall qualifications may not be hired. Rather, the person whose qualifications most closely conform to the open position should be selected.[20]

Personnel has been heavily involved in all phases leading up to the final employment decision. However, the person who normally makes the final selection decision is the manager who will be responsible for the performance of the new employee.[21] In making this decision, the operating manager may or may not solicit the advice of the personnel manager. The role of Personnel in this process is to provide service and counsel to the operating manager to facilitate the selection decision. The rationale for permitting the supervisor to make the final selection decision is simple: managers should be allowed the prerogative to select those individuals for whom they will be responsible.

There are, however, instances in which the personnel manager serves in a strong advisory capacity. For instance, if the organization is under pressure from the federal government to employ more individuals in a certain protected group, a recommendation by Personnel as to who should be employed may have the same impact as a directive from the president of the firm. However, the personnel manager should realize the dangers involved in this practice. The manager's authority may be severely undermined.

PHYSICAL EXAMINATION

Once a decision has been reached to make a job offer, the next phase of the selection process involves the successful completion of the physical examination. Typically, a job offer is contingent upon successful completion of this physical examination. The purposes of this examination are several. Obviously, one reason for requiring a physical is to screen out individuals who have a contagious disease. The exam also assists in determining if an applicant is physically capable of performing the work. For instance, if the work is very demanding and a physical examination uncovers a heart problem, the individual will likely be rejected. Finally, the physical examination information may be used to determine if there are certain physical capabilities which differentiate between successful and less successful employees. Because of the requirements of the Civil Rights Act, if a physical quality is specified in the job description, it must be shown to be job-related.

ACCEPTANCE OF JOB APPLICANTS

Assuming that no medical problems were discovered in the physical examination, the applicant can now be employed. The starting date of the job is typically based upon the needs of both the firm and the individual. If the individual is currently employed by another firm, it is customary for him or her to

[20]Hall A. Acuff, "Quality Control in Employee Selection," *Personnel Journal* 60 (July 1981): 563.
[21]A. Peter Fredrickson, "The Hiring Process: How It Works," *Supervisory Management* 20 (October 1975): 4.

198

Part II
Human
Resources
Planning,
Recruitment,
and Selection

give between two and four weeks notice. Even after this notice, the individual may need some personal time to prepare for the new job. It is particularly important if the new job requires a move to another city. The transition time before the individual can join the firm is often considerable.

The firm may also want the individual to delay the date of employment. If the new employee's first job upon joining the firm is to go to a training school, the organization may request that the individual delay joining the firm until perhaps a week before the school. This would keep the new employee from having nothing to do until school begins. Naturally, this practice cannot be abused, especially if the individual is unemployed and does not have money to survive.

REJECTION OF JOB APPLICANTS

Applicants may be rejected at any phase of the selection process. This section focuses upon the individuals who for various reasons were not offered employment with the firm.

When an individual makes application for employment, he or she is essentially saying, "I think I am qualified for the job. Why don't you hire me?" Tension builds as the applicant progresses through the selection process. If the preliminary interview shows that he or she is obviously not qualified, there is likely to be only a minimum amount of lost ego. The company may even be able to smooth over this by informing the individual of other jobs in the firm that better match his or her qualifications.

For most people, the employment interview is not one of the most enjoyable experiences. Taking a test which could affect your career often causes hands to become moist and perspiration to break out on the forehead. Suffering all of this only to be told "There does not appear to be a proper match between your qualifications and our needs" can be a painful experience. Most firms recognize this fact and attempt to let the individual down as easily as possible. But it is often difficult to tell people that they will not be employed. Where considerable time has been spent with the individual in the selection process, a company representative often sits down with the applicant and explains why another person was offered the job. On the other hand, if there were many applicants, time constraints may force the firm to notify individuals by letter that they were not chosen. A letter informing an applicant of his or her rejection can be personalized. A personalized touch will often reduce the stigma of a rejection and reduce the chance of the applicant having bad feelings for the company which a depersonalized letter could elicit. If the selection was made objectively, most individuals can, with time, understand why they were not chosen.

EMPLOYEE ORIENTATION

Orientation involves introducing new employees to their company, jobs, and members of the work group. Once an applicant has been selected and has joined the firm, his or her initial days may be spent in orientation. The purposes of orientation are threefold and include:

1. To create a favorable impression on the new employee of the organization and its work
2. To help ease the new employee's adjustment to the organization
3. To provide specific information concerning the task and performance expectations of the job[22]

Orientation programs should provide information needed for a good start with the company. A well-designed company orientation program can have a significant impact upon reducing costs associated with new employee recruitment, selection, and training.[23] One of the benefits of an effective orientation program is to reduce expensive turnover. Hall Marckwardt, president of Western Center, a Los Angeles management development firm, estimates that it takes $60,000 to $70,000 in training costs alone for an account executive with a brokerage firm. Turnover of a retail clerk can cost approximately $2000, he said.[24]

Employee orientation programs are designed basically for new workers. Here in itself is a problem. It has been estimated that between 60 and 80 percent of the current work force in an organization is "new" to the job market. This new work force includes either late or re-entries of women, men and women who were self-employed, recent graduates, and persons who have made radical career changes.[25] Many of these individuals have built up anxieties about entering the organization. An effective orientation program can do much to reduce these anxieties.

There are essentially three different stages in an effective orientation program.[26] In Stage I, general organization information is provided. Subjects that relate to all employees such as a company overview, review of company policies and procedures, and salary are covered. It is helpful for the new worker to know how the department fits into the overall scheme of the company's operations. Orientation programs should provide information concerning how the products or the services of the company benefit our society. Another purpose of Stage I is anxiety reduction. New workers are informed of some of the possible hazing games that older employees may play. Personnel may be heavily involved in this stage.

In Stage II, the employee's immediate supervisor is responsible for the orientation program. Topics included within this phase include a department overview, job requirements, safety, department tour, question and answer session, and an introduction to other employees. It is crucial that performance expectation and specific work rules be clearly understood by the newhire at

[22]Diana Reed-Mendenhall and C.W. Millard, "Orientation: A Training and Development Tool," *Personnel Administrator* 25 (August 1980): 40.
[23]*Ibid.*
[24] "Saying HELLO to New Employees," *Industry Week* 205 (May 26, 1980): 81.
[25]Mark S. Tauber, "New Employee Orientation: A Comprehensive Systems Approach," *Personnel Administrator* (January 1981): 65.
[26]Diana Reed-Mendenhall and C.W. Millard, "Orientation: A Training and Development Tool," *Personnel Administrator* 25 (August 1980): 42–44.

200

Part II
Human
Resources
Planning,
Recruitment,
and Selection

this point. It is also important that the supervisor work toward helping the newly hired individual to become socially accepted as quickly as possible.

The Stage III involves evaluation and follow-up. This is conducted in conjunction with Personnel and the immediate supervisor. The new worker does not merely go through the orientation program and become forgotten. During the first week or so the supervisor works with the new employee to clarify misunderstandings and make sure the worker has been properly integrated into the work group. Personnel works with the supervisor to ensure that this vital third step is accomplished.

COST/BENEFITS ANALYSIS—SELECTION

Each step in the selection process has a cost associated with it. If tests are to be used, they need to be validated. Professionals are required to administer, interpret the results, and explain the results to management. In addition, application blanks need to be developed which are job related for particular job classes. This takes time, effort, and money. Properly conducted reference checks and background investigations also have a cost associated with them. Even the preliminary interview requires that an individual be trained and time provided to perform the task properly.

Even though there are substantial costs involved with developing, implementing, and using a job-related selection process, there are likely many more benefits. If individuals are placed in positions for which they are not suited, dissatisfaction is inevitable.[27] There are also numerous hidden costs involved. For example, before discovering that the individual was wrong for the job, considerable supervisory effort may be involved. The quality and quantity of work in the department may suffer. And, the selected individual may have a negative impact on the other workers. Once the worker leaves the firm, a replacement must be found. If training has been provided, it is wasted and must be performed once again when a replacement is hired. Turnover costs associated with a poor selection process can be substantial.

SUMMARY

Selection is the process of choosing from a group of applicants those individuals best suited for a particular position. External and internal factors continue to influence the selection process—government legislation in particular. Managers must be keenly aware of the effect of this legislation as they engage in selecting new employees. Other factors which affect the selection process include: (1) the time that is available to make the decision, (2) the organizational hierarchy, (3) the number of people in the applicant pool, (4) the type of organization, and (5) the use of probationary periods.

[27]John C. Hafer and C. C. Hoth, "Selection Characteristics: Your Priorities and How Students Perceive Them," *Personnel Administrator* 28 (March 1983): 25.

The effectiveness of the selection process can significantly influence, and is itself affected by, the other functional areas of personnel. The selection process begins with an initial screening of applicants to remove individuals who obviously do not fulfill the position requirements. The next step in the selection process involves having the prospective employee complete an application blank. The employer evaluates it to determine whether there appears to be a match between the individual and the position.

Selection tests may next be administered to assist in assessing the applicant's potential for success with the organization. When tests are used as selection tools they should be reliable, valid, objective, and standardized. The employment interview is next considered. Interviews may be distinguished by the amount of structure or preplanned format they possess.

The purpose of the reference check is to provide additional insight into the information in the application blank and to verify its accuracy. The background investigation may be helpful in determining if past work experience is related to the qualifications needed for the new position. Once information has been obtained from the preceding steps, the actual decision of who to hire must be made. The person whose qualifications most closely conform to the open position should be selected. Once a decision has been reached to make a job offer, the next phase of the selection process involves the successful completion of the physical examination. Assuming that no medical problems are discovered in the physical examination, the applicant can then be employed.

Orientation involves introducing new employees to their company, jobs, and members of the work group. Orientation programs should provide information needed for a good start with the company. There are essentially three different stages in an effective orientation program. In Stage I, general information is provided. In Stage II, the employee's immediate supervisor is responsible for the orientation program. The Stage III involves evaluation and follow-up.

Questions for Review

1. What are the basic steps which are normally followed in the selection process?

2. Identify and describe the various factors outside the control of the personnel manager which could affect the selection process.

3. What would be the selection ratio if there were fifteen applicants to choose from and only one position to fill? Interpret the meaning of this selection ratio.

4. If a firm desires to use selection tests, what major points should be considered in their use to avoid discriminatory practices?

5. List and describe questions traditionally asked during the selection process which may

need to be either eliminated or reviewed to assure that their use is job related and nondiscriminatory.

6. What is the general purpose of the preliminary interview?

7. What types of questions should be included in an application blank?

8. What basic conditions should be met if selection tests are to be used in the screening process? Briefly describe each.

9. Briefly describe each of the basic objectives of the employment interview.

10. Define briefly each of the following types of interviews: a. Nondirective interview b.

Patterned interview c. One-to-one interview d. Group interview e. Board interview f. Stress interview

11. What is the purpose of reference checks and background investigations?

12. What are the reasons for administering a physical examination?

13. What are the purposes of orientation?

Terms for Review

Selection

Selection ratio

Probationary period

Weighted application blank

Ability test

Aptitude test

Personality test

Reliability

Validity

Correlation coefficient

Criterion related validity

Concurrent validity

Predictive validity

Content validity

Construct validity

Objectivity

Standardization

Realistic job preview

Nondirective interview

Patterned interview

Stress interview

Group interview

Board interview

Reference check

Background investigation

Orientation

As production manager for Thompson Manufacturing, Jack Stephens has the final authority to approve the hiring of any new supervisors who work for him. The personnel manager performs the initial screening of all prospective supervisors and then sends the most likely candidates to Jack for interviews.

One day recently, Jack received a call from Pete, the personnel manager. "Jack, I've just spoken to a young man who may be just who you're looking for to fill that final line supervisor position. He has some good work experience and it appears as if his head is screwed on straight. He's here right now and available if you could possibly see him." Jack hesitated a moment before answering. "Gee Pete," he said, "I'm certainly busy today but I'll try to squeeze him in. Send him on down."

A moment later Allen Guthrie, the new applicant, arrived at Jack's office and introduced himself. "Come on in, Allen," said Jack. "I'll be right with you after I make a few phone calls." Fifteen minutes later Jack finished the calls and began talking with Allen. Jack was quite impressed. After a few minutes Jack's door opened and a supervisor yelled, "We have a small problem on line number one and need your help." "Sure," Jack replied, "Excuse me a minute, Allen." Ten minutes later Jack returned and the conversation continued for at least ten more minutes before a series of phone calls again interrupted them.

This same pattern of interruptions continued for the next hour. Finally Allen looked at his watch and said, "I'm sorry, Mr. Stephens, but I have to pick up my wife." "Sure thing, Allen," Jack said as the phone rang again. "Call me later today."

Questions

1. What specific policies might a company follow to avoid interviews like this one?

2. Explain why Jack and not Pete should make the selection decision.

"Mrs. Peacock, I've decided that we should quit using selection tests altogether," said John Barnes, the personnel manager. "I'm not sure that there are any which could be defended if we ever got a discrimination complaint." John had just read a report of a court decision finding a large company nearby guilty of discriminatory employment practices. Essentially, the company had been using tests designed to measure general intelligence as a screening device for all kinds of employees. The court held that the tests caused certain protected groups to be eliminated from employment consideration.

The tests that John's firm, Miller Chemical Company, used were aptitude tests, carefully designed to apply to the specific job for which the applicant was applying. For example, the test for a certain mechanical mixer operator job included questions about the relative weights of various liquids and solids, about the ways in which emulsions are formed, and about the dangers involved in working with rotating machinery. No study had been done, however, to determine the relationship between performance on the test and success on the job. Most of the managers felt that the interviews and references were more valuable than the tests anyway. Besides, John thought that validation of the tests would be too expensive and time consuming.

As John was thinking about all of this, Nancy Peacock called back. "Mr. Barnes," she said, "I've been thinking about your decision to eliminate our tests. Do we still have enough to go on in making an employment decision?" "Not really," said John, "but I don't know what else we can do to be safe. A discrimina-tion suit could tie us up for months. The tests may not be any more discriminatory than interviews, but, I don't think that interviews can get us into trouble. The same thing is true of application blanks and reference checks. It would just be harder for the EEOC to attack us on those points." "Then I suppose the decision is final?" asked Nancy. "I've thought about it a lot, Mrs. Peacock," said John, "and I suppose it is."

Questions

1. Do you agree with the rationale for Mr. Barnes' decision? Explain.

2. Under what circumstances might Miller Chemical have been required to validate the tests?

PARMA CYCLE COMPANY: WORKERS FOR THE NEW PLANT

Gene Wilson, the corporate planner at Parma Cycle Company, was ecstatic as he talked with the personnel director, Jesse Heard, on Tuesday morning. He had just received word that the board of directors had approved the plan for Parma's new southern plant. "I really appreciate your help on this, Jesse," he said. "Without the research you did on the personnel needs for the new plant, I don't think that it would have been approved." "We still have a long way to go," said Jesse. "There's no doubt that we can construct the building and install the machinery, but getting skilled workers in Clarksdale, Mississippi may not be so easy." "Well," said Gene, "the results of the labor survey that you did in Clarksdale last year indicate that we'll be able to get by. Anyway, some of the people here at Parma will surely agree to transfer." "When is the new plant scheduled to open?" asked Jesse. Gene replied, "The building will be finished in February 1985; the machinery will be in by May; and the goal is to be in production by September 1985." "Gosh" said Jesse, "I had better get to work."

A few minutes later, back in his office, Jesse considered what the future held at Parma Cycle. The company had been located in Parma, Ohio, a Cleveland suburb, since its founding. It had grown over the years to become the nation's fourth largest bicycle manufacturer. The decision to open the Clarksdale, Mississippi plant had been made in hopes of decreasing production costs through lower wages. Although no one ever came right out and said it, it was assumed that the southern plant would be nonunion. The elimination of union work rules was expected to be a benefit.

The state of Mississippi had offered a ten year exemption from all property taxes. This was a significant advantage because tax rates for Cleveland area industries were extremely high. Jesse was pleased that he had been involved in the discussions from the time that the new plant was first suggested. Even with all the advanced preparation he had done, he knew that the coming months would be extremely difficult for him and his staff.

At that moment Jesse's assistant, Ed Deal, walked in with a bundle of papers. "Hi, Ed," said Jesse, "I'm glad you're here. The Clarksdale plant is definitely on the way and you and I need to get our act together." "That's great," said Ed. "It's quite a coincidence, too, because I was just going over this stack of job descriptions, identifying which ones might be eliminated as we scale back at this plant." Jesse said, "Remember, Ed, we are not going to cut back very much here. Some jobs will be deleted and others added. But out of the 800 positions here, I'll bet that not more than forty will actually be eliminated." "So, what you are saying is that we basically have to staff the plant with people we hire from the Clarksdale area?" Ed asked. Jesse replied, "No, Ed, we will have some people here who are willing to transfer even though their jobs are not being eliminated. We will then replace them with others we hire in the Cleveland area. Most of the workers at Clarksdale, though, will be recruited from that area."

"What about the management team?" asked Ed. "Well," said Jesse, "I think the boss already knows who the main people will be down there. They are managers we currently have on board plus a fellow we located at a defunct three wheeler plant in Mound Bayou, Mississippi."

"Who will be the personnel director down

there?" asked Ed. "Well," replied Jesse, "I don't think I'm talking out of school by telling you that I've recommended you for the job." After letting that soak in for a minute, Ed said, "It's no secret that I was hoping for that. When will we know for sure?" "There's really not much doubt," said Jesse, "I'm so sure that I've decided to put you in charge of personnel matters for that whole project. During the next two weeks I'd like you to put together a comprehensive plan. I want a detailed report of the people we will need, including their qualifications. Secondly, we will need a more complete knowledge of the labor supply in Clarksdale. Finally, I'd like you to come up with a general idea of who might be willing to transfer from this plant. They are really going to be the backbone of our work force at Clarksdale." "OK, Jesse, but I'll need a lot of help," said Ed as he gathered his papers and left. As Jesse watched Ed leave he thought he noticed a certain snappiness about Ed's movements that had not been there before.

Questions

1. What procedures do you feel should be followed in determining the personnel needs at the new plant?

2. How might Jesse and Ed go about recruiting workers in Clarksdale? Managers?

___ Experiencing Personnel Management ___

WRITING A JOB DESCRIPTION

During this exercise each participant will have an opportunity to prepare a rough draft of a job description from job analysis data. In addition to helping the student develop personnel skills, this exercise will help students make the connection between what is learned in the classroom and what is actually done in the workplace.

Your Role

As a senior personnel specialist at Parma Cycle Company you have been involved in job analysis planning for the new plant in Clarksdale, Mississippi. Most of the job analysis data have been gathered and now it is time to prepare specific job descriptions. You have been given a stack of job analysis information sheets and assigned responsibility for writing job descriptions for each of them. When the assistant personnel director, Ed Deal, handed you the data sheets, he said, "I'd like you to do the first one, then bring it to me then we will go over it together."

Illustrated below are the first job analysis sheet and a copy of the job description form which Parma uses. You are to complete the job description before Mr. Deal returns, thirty minutes from now.

Figure II–1. Parma Cycle Company's job analysis sheet.

Job Title: Marquette Spotwelder Operator

Work Activities:

Weld parts together as assigned by supervisor. All parts consist of thin steel pieces weighing less than two pounds each. The preformed pieces to be welded together are taken from numbered bins surrounding the spotwelder and placed in position on the machine. Then, the foot pedal is depressed to weld the pieces together. Completed pieces are next placed in a container for movement to another work station. The operator is responsible for ensuring that the settings on the machine are correct for the part being welded.

Relationship With Other Workers:

Job is located on the factory floor. Other machine operators running similar machines are within view, twenty to thirty feet away. The crane operator moves the parts bins to this work station and away as required, placing them where specified by the operator. There is little time for social interaction on the job.

Degree of Supervision:

The Spotwelder Supervisor supervises twelve operators, all doing essentially the same job. Operators are expected to do their jobs essentially without supervision, consulting with the supervisor only infrequently. Along with each job, the operator is provided a specification sheet showing the machine settings and describing the welding procedure. A sample prewelded part is also provided for each job and kept on a display board at the work station. The job instruction sheet shows the standard time that each job should take and the total time for each batch.

Records and Reports:

None.

Skill and Dexterity Requirements:

In order to meet the standard times, the worker must be able to take two parts from separate bins, place them together in the correct position, insert them into the machine against a prearranged jig, press the foot pedal, and put the completed part into the completed parts bin within 3.2 seconds.

Working Conditions:

The work station is relatively crowded because the parts bins have to be placed within armreach of the operator. Lighting is excellent. The operator is required to wear safety goggles because of the emission of an occasional hot spark from the welding machine. Ambient temperature varies from 60° F. in winter to 80° F. in summer. The noise level is about 60 decibels, distracting but safe.

Position Title				Position Number
				Approval
Division or Staff Department	Location	Reports To		Effective Date
Department or Activity	Section	Point	Grade	Revises

Job Summary

Nature of Work

Qualifications

Figure II–2. **Parma Cycle Company's job description form.**

Part III

Training and Development

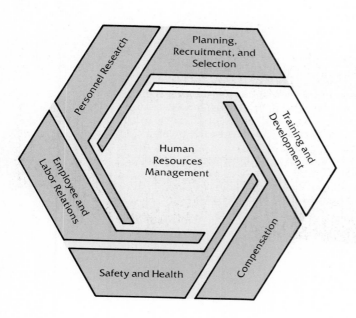

Personnel Research

Planning, Recruitment, and Selection

Training and Development

Human Resources Management

Employee and Labor Relations

Compensation

Safety and Health

Chapter Objectives

1. Define training and development (T&D) and distinguish between macro- and micro-level approaches.
2. Describe the general purpose of training and development.
3. State the various factors which influence the training and development process.
4. Discuss the nature of change and the steps involved in the change sequence.
5. Define organization development (OD) and explain the various approaches used in organization development.

Chapter 7 _____

Training and Development: Macro-Level Approaches

Marion Lilly recently graduated from high school and wants to work for Sweeny Manufacturing as a machine operator. However, Marion does not have the training or the experience to perform this job. Because the firm currently has vacancies for machine operators, and it is difficult to recruit skilled operators, Sweeny Manufacturing decides to hire Marion and train him to become a machine operator.

Webber Manufacturing Company's president, Gordon Vandergriff, has made a critical decision. His firm's production has declined steadily for the past few years. It appears that his first-line supervisors cannot motivate their employees to perform at higher levels. Gordon has employed a consulting firm to determine if his supervisors' leadership styles are contributing to the problem. If so, the consultants will likely conduct a supervisory training program.

Yantis Motor Corporation profits have declined over the past four years. Alyson Munson, the president, is especially concerned about several areas: the number of product recalls due to poor quality, unreasonably high sales costs, and excessive turnover in the firm. The problems do not appear to be limited to only a few of her departments. A decline in the general attitude throughout the firm seems to have occurred. Alyson recognizes that if productivity is to be improved, changes must be made throughout the organization.

In the first instance, it is evident that Marion lacks the skills necessary to perform efficiently as a machine operator. Through training, his skill level will be changed to that of a qualified operator. In the second illustration, training and development may take place on a group basis involving first-level supervisors. Gordon Vandergriff is prepared to engage in a supervisory training program if necessary. The Yantis Motor Corporation experience depicts an organization which needs to undertake training and development on an organizationwide basis. Every individual in the firm will become involved. T&D on the scale needed at Yantis Motors is often referred to as organization development (OD).

THE IMPORTANCE AND SCOPE OF
TRAINING AND DEVELOPMENT

Training and Development (T&D) is planned continuous effort by management to improve employee competency levels and the organization work environment. T&D's emphasis is on increased productivity within firms. Recent plant shutdowns coupled with rises in numbers of imported goods have made an impression on American workers. The connection between survival and efficiency has been made with the result that productivity is no longer considered a bad word.[1]

To improve productivity, desired changes must occur. T&D programs should be designed to accomplish such change. The change may include new approaches to managing people or it may simply involve upgrading skill levels required to operate a machine. It may focus upon individuals, groups, or the entire firm. Training and development is responsible for much of the planned change that occurs in a company. You can see an overview of a firm's response to the need for change in Figure 7–1. When management recognizes that change is needed for the entire organization, as with Yantis Motor Corporation, broad, **macro-level approaches** to T&D are indicated. Macro-level approaches are the focus of this chapter. The methods used to respond to change of less magnitude (as with Marion or the group of first-line supervisors) are referred to as **micro-level approaches** and will be discussed in the following chapter. Some methods become either macro- or micro-level depending upon the scope of their implementation.[2]

Referring once again to Figure 7–1, you can see that after T&D has taken place, the programs are evaluated. These evaluations, along with employee performance appraisals, assist management in determining the training and development needs of the firm, groups, and individual employees. Appraisal techniques provide feedback which complements other means used to identify training and development needs. Development of the organization's human resources must be continuous if the firm and its people are to achieve their goals.

[1]George J. McManus, "Team Concept Stressed in Productivity Confab," *Iron Age* 224 (December 7, 1981): 47.
[2]Rolf E. Rogers, *Organizational Theory* (Boston: Allyn and Bacon, Inc., 1975), p. 210.

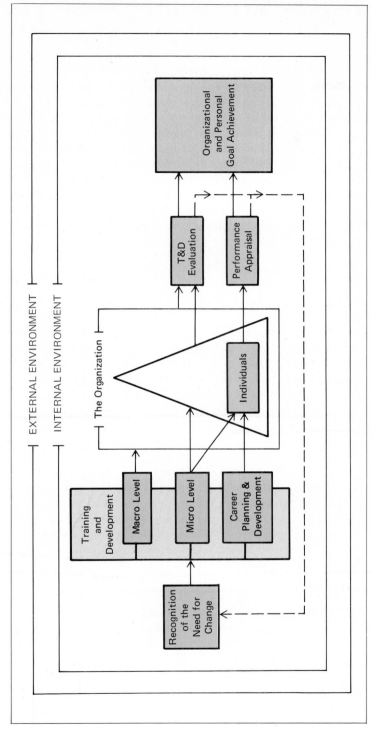

Figure 7–1. Organizational response to the need for change.

213

GENERAL PURPOSES OF T&D

The primary purpose of T&D is to improve worker productivity and the firm's profitability. Another major goal of T&D is to prevent obsolescence of skills at all levels in the company. Few employees operate anywhere near their full potential. In fact, there are estimates that most of us achieve only five percent of our total potential.[3] As Frederick Herzberg stated, "Resurrection is more difficult than giving birth."[4] While he was emphasizing the role of enriched jobs, effective T&D programs can also play a vital role in avoiding obsolescence.

Another purpose of T&D is to upgrade employees' skills in anticipation of their achieving higher positions in the organization. Opportunities for promotion from within must exist in order to maintain high employee morale. The organization is responsible for assisting employees in upgrading their skills based on their aptitudes and interests, in addition to the needs of the company. Training and development costs should be viewed as an investment in human resources.

FACTORS INFLUENCING T&D

As with all personnel functions, both external and internal factors can affect a T&D program. These factors are often beyond the personnel manager's control. Several of the most important factors which can influence a training and development program's effectiveness may be seen in Figure 7–2. These factors often determine the success of T&D objectives.

First and foremost, training and development programs must have top management's full support. The support must be real—not merely lip service—and it should be communicated to all concerned in the organization. True support becomes evident when the executive group provides the resources needed for the T&D function. The support is further strengthened when top executives actually take part in the training. These actions tend to convince employees of the significance of training and development programs.[5]

In recent years, changes in products, systems, and methods have occurred at increasingly rapid rates. These changes have had a significant impact on jobs that are required by the organization. Employees must constantly update their skills. Also, they need to develop an attitude that permits them not only to adapt to change, but also to accept and even seek it.

Organizations have grown to gigantic proportions in terms of the number of employees, sales volume, and diversity of products. This growth has also resulted in complex organizational structures. The resulting high degree of specialization necessitates greater interdependence of people operating in organi-

[3]Herbert A. Otts, "New Light on the Human Potential," in *Tomorrow's Organization*, ed. Jong S. Jun and William B. Storm (Glenview, Ill.: Scott, Foresman and Company, 1973), p. 112.
[4]*Motivation Through Job Enrichment*, BNA Films (Washington, D.C.: The Bureau of National Affairs, Inc., 1967).
[5]Dan R. Paxton, "Employment Development: A Lifelong Learning Approach," *Training and Development Journal* 30 (December 1976): 24–26.

215

Chapter 7
Training and
Development:
Macro-Level
Approaches

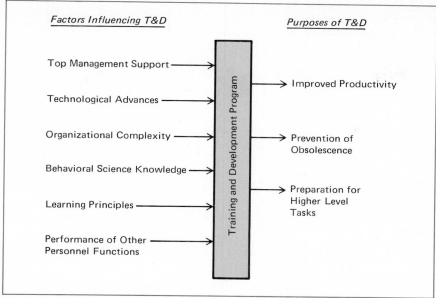

Figure 7–2. **Factors influencing training and development.**

zations. Individuals must interact with peers, subordinates, and superiors in groups to perform their jobs successfully.

During the past few decades, a vast amount of new knowledge has emerged from the behavioral sciences. A large portion of this information relates directly to the management of human resources. Today's managers must be aware of and capable of utilizing this new knowledge. The T&D activity has a substantial task in keeping pace with behavioral sciences developments and in imparting these developments to members of the organization.

As a T&D specialist, you must know more than the topic to be presented. There must be some understanding of basic learning principles. The purpose of training is to effect change in employee behavior. And, information must be learned if change is to take place. While there is still much to be discovered about the learning process, several generalizations may be helpful in understanding this phenomenon. Some general concepts—fundamentals related to learning—are shown in Table 7–1. Most of these concepts relate to the management and development of human resources. For example, behavior which is rewarded (reinforced) is more likely to recur. In applying this concept to managing people, you would want to ensure that your pay system rewarded good producers. As a T&D specialist, you would need to keep trainees advised of their performance. Failure to provide the desired feedback on their performance—according to this concept—would not encourage learning.

From the personnel manager's viewpoint, the successful accomplishment of other personnel functions can have a significant impact upon training and development. For instance, if recruitment and selection efforts only produce unskilled workers, an extensive T&D program may be needed to train entry

Table 7–1. General learning principles

- Behavior that is rewarded (reinforced) is more likely to recur.
- This reinforcement, to be most effective, must immediately follow the desired behavior and be clearly connected with that behavior.
- Mere repetition, without reinforcement, is an ineffective approach to learning.
- Threats and punishment have variable and uncertain effects on learning. Punishment may disturb the learning process.
- The sense of satisfaction that stems from achievement is the type of reward that has the greatest transfer value to other situations.
- The value of any external reward depends on who dispenses the reward. If the reward giver is highly respected, the extrinsic reward may be of great value; if not, it may be without value.
- Learners progress in an area of learning only as far as they need to in order to achieve their purposes.
- Individuals are more likely to be enthusiastic about a learning situation if they themselves have participated in the planning of the project.
- Autocratic leadership has been found to make members more dependent on the leader and to generate resentment in the group.
- Overstrict discipline tends to be associated with greater conformity, anxiety, shyness, and acquiescence; greater permissiveness is associated with more initiative and creativity.
- Many people experience so much criticism, failure, and discouragement that their self-confidence, level of aspiration, and sense of worth are damaged.
- When people experience too much frustration, their behavior ceases to be integrated, purposeful, and rational.
- People who have met with little success and continual failure are not apt to be in the mood to learn.
- Individuals tend to think whenever they encounter an obstacle or intellectual challenge which is of interest to them.
- The best way to help people form a general concept is to present an idea in numerous and varied situations.
- Learning from reading is aided more by time spent recalling what has been read than by rereading.
- Individuals remember new information that confirms their previous attitudes better than they remember new information that does not confirm their previous attitudes.
- What is learned is more likely to be available for use if it is learned in a situation much like that in which it is to be used, and immediately preceding the time when it is needed.
- The best time to learn is when the learning can be useful. Motivation is then at its strongest peak.

Source: Adapted from Goodwin Watson, "What Do We Know About Learning?" *N.E.A. Journal* 52 (March 1963): 20–22. (Reprinted by permission.)

level workers. T&D efforts may also be influenced by the firm's compensation package. A firm with a competitive program may find it easier to attract qualified workers, which substantially influences the form of training required. Also, a competitive compensation plan may help decrease the turnover rate, thereby reducing the need to train new workers.

A firm's employee relations efforts can also influence the T&D program. Workers want to feel that the company is interested in them. One way to express this interest is through management's support of good T&D programs. These programs can also train managers to deal more effectively with employees and their problems. Managers can be taught to treat employees as individuals and not merely as numbers.

The emphasis a firm places upon its employees' health and safety can also impact a T&D program. Heavy emphasis in the area can pave the way for extensive training programs throughout the firm. Providing a healthy and safe work environment can affect all other personnel functions as the firm gains a reputation as a healthful and safe place to work. From the above examples you can see how T&D affects, and is affected by, other personnel functions.

217

Chapter 7
Training and
Development:
Macro-Level
Approaches

CHANGE

At the beginning of the chapter the instances involving Marion Lilly, Gordon Vandergriff, and Alyson Munson all concerned the implementation of change. Change involves moving from one condition to another and it may affect individuals, groups, or an entire organization. Therefore, a person who desires to gain a better appreciation of T&D must understand the change sequence, the accompanying difficulties, and the means of reducing resistance to change.

The Change Sequence

Change for the sake of change is seldom justified. Some degree of stability is needed to allow employees to accomplish assigned tasks. Even too many rational changes over a short period of time may leave workers bewildered and confused.[6] There are, of course, circumstances in the internal or external environments which make change desirable or even necessary. Personnel, because of its primary role in T&D, must be especially alert to these factors. Basically, the impetus for change emanates from a belief that the organization and its human resources can be more productive and successful. But, if change is to be successfully implemented, it must be approached systematically.

The change sequence that typically occurs when T&D is implemented may be seen in Figure 7–3. As you can see, these steps appear to be relatively straightforward. However, their implementation is often quite complex. The first step in the change sequence is to recognize the need for change. You must become aware when there is a need for T&D. In practicing management, there is a tendency to feel that "we have always done it this way so why argue with success?" A firm's past success does not guarantee future success nor does it indicate that success has been maximized. There may have been a better

---

[6]H. Kent Baker and Stevan R. Holmberg, "Stepping Up to Supervision: Coping With Change," *Supervisory Management* 27 (March 1982): 23.

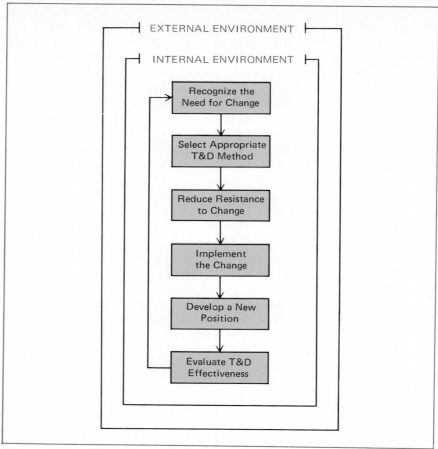

Figure 7–3.   **The change sequence.**

way all along. Managers should realize that the search for the "one best way" is unending.

Once we have recognized that change is needed, we must then select the most appropriate T&D method. The method chosen should be based upon the needs of the particular situation. Marion Lilly needed training to make him a better machine operator. The Yantis Motor Company needed training and development on a company-wide basis.

The next phase of the T&D process involves reducing resistance to change. At times, this may be an extremely difficult process. Although Marion Lilly will be unlikely to resist the change that will permit him to get the job, many times resistance is substantial. Consider, for instance, a machine operator who has been operating one piece of equipment and has just been told that another skill will have to be learned. Also, some company executives at Yantis Motors may resist change because they were able to rise to their present position under the old system. Any change may alter their power position in the firm.

Once resistance has been reduced, the change can then be implemented. Change may stem from an order or a suggestion, or it may be undertaken voluntarily. The change will be more satisfactorily accomplished if the person desires the change and feels that it is needed. The most successful approach to attitude change requires that a close relationship exist between the person attempting to implement the change (change agent) and the individual(s) to be changed.

219

Chapter 7
Training and
Development:
Macro-Level
Approaches

The change sequence does not end when the change is implemented. A new and flexible position must be developed. The new position must be capable of dealing with present requirements and of adapting to further change.[7] Once Gordon Vandergriff's supervisors have been taught to use the new motivational techniques, they must be encouraged to continue the process. If Gordon does not recognize and reward the use of these new techniques, the managers will likely revert to their former roles.

The final phase of the change sequence involves evaluating the effectiveness of the specific T&D method chosen. As previously mentioned, one primary measure of effectiveness is how the program impacted the firm's "bottom line." If Marion Lilly becomes a skilled machine operator, the training will be deemed effective. However, if Marion completes the training and still cannot operate the machine, this specific phase of the T&D program may need to be reevaluated. T&D is an on-going process because both internal and external conditions affecting the organization are never constant and are always changing.

Rationale for Resistance to Change

In business circles, there has been much discussion of employee's "natural" resistance to change. You cannot deny that change is often resisted, sometimes quite vigorously.[8] The opposition, however, is not due to employees' inborn characteristics. Rather, the resistance may be explained in terms of their expectations and past experiences. Individuals may resist change when they feel that it will result in their being denied satisfaction of their basic needs. For instance, one of the most frightening prospects for many people is the threat of being deprived of their employment. At times, methods and systems changes do result in the elimination of some jobs. They may also involve a drastic upgrading or downgrading of skills. Many employees believe that they lack the flexibility to adjust. Since most adults derive their primary income from their job, if they became unemployed they would be economically unable to obtain the basic necessities of life.

Many changes in organizations are perceived as disrupting established social groups. There may also be a fear that change will disturb established friendships. Because numerous social needs are satisfied on the job, any threat to these relationships may be resisted.

[7]Martin M. Broadwell, *The Supervisor as an Instructor,* 3d ed. (Reading, Mass.: Addison-Wesley Publishing Company, 1978), p. 85.
[8]Rensis Likert and Jane Gibson Likert, *New Ways of Managing Conflict* (New York: McGraw-Hill Book Company, 1976), p. 245.

Robert E. Edwards, AEP
Vice President, Personnel
Southwestern Life Insurance
Company

Bob Edwards' first job was as a caddie at the Ohio State University golf course at age eleven. From that time, he held diverse jobs as bundle boy in a textile mill, bank clerk, movie theater usher, and bag boy at a produce shop. Because of his father's failing health and the economic hardships of a depression era Bob was always moving and, of necessity, al-

ways working. When he reentered college after a four-year military commitment, he started work in the credit department of a large retailer where he became involved with collections and, occasionally, repossessions—one of the few tasks he disliked. However, at an early age Bob's breadth of work experience gave him an understanding of jobs and people performing jobs. This basic knowledge proved invaluable to him as his career progressed.

Bob joined Southwestern Life Insurance Company in 1957 after graduating from college with a concentration in personnel and industrial relations. Subsequently he earned a Masters of Science degree. Although he began his career in a general management training program assigned to the Agency Department, Bob knew that he ultimately wanted to be in Personnel. The opportunity presented itself in 1962. In 1965, he was promoted to assistant personnel manager. Four years later, he was named personnel director. In 1971, Bob assumed his present position, where as he puts it, "I am primarily concerned with improving the long-range profit-making ability of my company."

The potential threat to one's status in the organization may also become a powerful reason for resisting change. Many workers have literally invested their lives in their jobs. They are likely to resist any change effort which they perceive as disrupting their standing in the organization or their sense of importance. For instance, the master machinist, when faced with new automation in his firm, may fear that his high level skills will no longer be needed and his prestige lowered.

A classic example of resisting change has been repeated countless times in organizations planning computer installations. In some instances, many employees learned of the firm's plans through the grapevine. Employees may easily envision how the computer could accomplish all or a part of their work. They may fear unemployment, dispersion of their work group, or loss of status. The prospect of change can conceivably threaten every level of human need. This feeling often results in employees resisting change. The resistance is not "natural" but is based on reasons that appear quite logical to the employee.

When asked why he ignored sales work, Bob replies simply, "I haven't." He explains, "A good personnel executive must sell—she or he must have all the sales tools to deliver." To reinforce his point, Bob told a story about two of his top assistants who left Personnel to become Southwestern sales representatives. In their first year, both individuals received their company's top sales award.

Mr. Edwards says, "As a personnel executive, you view the organization as much like the chief executive as any other person. You don't miss a corner of it. You are in a unique position to shape the organization because you deal with both its people and its structure in a prime way. This challenge—if met—results in a tremendous amount of intrinsic satisfaction."

Bob believes that the knowledge gained from continuing academic curiosity coupled with a searching examination of company operations will determine the quality of the human resources department's contribution. He suggests that we should build an organizational climate that motivates individuals to perform to the best of their abilities. In explaining how this can be accomplished, he identifies one of the major areas, saying, "Training and development should be on a continuous basis. This permits employees to know that we care about them and that we are vitally concerned about their performance and mobility within the company."

Currently, Bob is a member of the American Society for Personnel Administration, Dallas Personnel Association, American Management Association, and Life Office Management Association. He is a past executive director of the North Texas Personnel Conference and past president of the Dallas Personnel Association. He has served as chairman of the National Chapter Awards Committee and assistant district director for the American Society for Personnel Administration. He currently is national chairman of the Personnel Accreditation Institute Management Practices Committee. He has also earned the AEP designation and a fellowship in the Life Office Management Association with a specialization in personnel administration.

Reducing Resistance to Change

If we are going to achieve wide acceptance of a needed change, management needs to be aware of the means through which resistance can be reduced. However, a firm cannot expect attitudes which cause resistance to be overcome overnight. It took one of the authors many years before he finally accepted his parents' suggestions that his grades would improve if he would not watch "Leave It to Beaver" while studying.

Building Trust and Confidence. The degree to which employees trust and have confidence in management directly relates to their past experiences. If they have suffered in the past as a result of change, they may well attempt to avoid future changes. When management has misrepresented the results of changes, by failing to level with employees, the resistance tends to become even greater. For instance, when faced with the prospect of having to reduce the work force, management may assure employees that layoffs will be based upon productivity. However, if previous layoffs appeared to be determined by favoritism or some other factor, employees may not believe that current actions will be different.

On the other hand, trust builds if management deals with employees in an open and straightforward manner. Workers who are told that they need additional training will accept the idea much more readily if they believe in their manager. The desired level of trust and confidence cannot be achieved overnight. Rather, it results from a long history of fair-dealing by the firm's management.

Developing Open Communication. It has been estimated that 90 percent of "confidential" information in most organizations is not truly confidential. It is withheld from employees because of an unwillingness to share information.[9] Managers who possess this attitude are likely to create a climate that breeds distrust and fear. In such an environment any rumor of planned changes may become extremely distorted and the firm's employees will often fear the worst.

By sharing information with employees, organizations can take a giant step toward developing open communications. In speaking to this point, Louis Lunborg once stated:

> People want to know several things. They want to know what their own job is all about, why they are doing what we ask them to do, what good it does anybody, and above all, how well they are doing it. And then they want to know what's going on—if they see strange things happening or hear rumors that something new is about to happen, they want to know about it.
>
> If you don't tell them, you're saying, "It's none of your business," and that in turn means, "I just don't think you are important enough." It is the deadliest thing you can do to people.[10]

As a manager, you must recognize that your subordinates are human beings and deal with them accordingly. Their needs should be recognized and reasonably met if possible.

Employee Participation

> Margaret Thomson is an experienced accountant. She competently handled the administrative tasks for an automobile agency for more than ten years and really knew the business. Two months ago the agency was sold to a young man with a background in data processing. He immediately leased a small-scale computer and automated every conceivable administrative function. Margaret was not consulted at any point in this process. She was, however, presented with an "Operating Manual" when the project was completed.

Margaret may well show considerable resistance to this change because she was not consulted. People are more inclined to accept changes if they have

[9]Justin G. Longenecker, *Principles of Management and Organizational Behavior*, 3d ed. (Columbus, Oh.: Charles E. Merrill Publishing Company, 1973), p. 479.
[10]Louis B. Lunborg, "Managing for Tomorrow," *Information and Records Management* (April 1971): 72. Reprinted by permission.

had an opportunity to participate in their development. For instance, suppose it has been determined that your departmental operating budget must be cut by 25 percent. You may more readily accept this change if you are permitted to help determine where the cuts should be made. Participation is also more effective when permitted in the early planning stages. For example, an employee might not feel too involved if brought in on a change the day before it is to be implemented.

Through participation, resistance to change can be minimized and in some cases eliminated. It is possible to develop a participative climate within which employees aggressively seek change. In order to achieve such an atmosphere, it is necessary to remove, or at least minimize, the fear that employees may have concerning their ability to satisfy their needs. Managers must be convinced that their own actions—not their employees' inherent nature—are most often responsible for attitudes about change. Only then can training and development programs—at either the macro or micro level—take place efficiently.

ORGANIZATIONAL CHANGE: AN EXAMPLE

Ronald C. Pilenzo, president of the American Society for Personnel Administration, tells of a major change he was involved with at International Multifoods Corporation. In 1979, the company was confronted with the challenge of how to actualize a human resource strategy to integrate women into its management ranks. The organization was very conservative and did not wish to create special opportunities (jobs) for women. It was seeking a way to (1) sensitize male managers, (2) create an awareness in female employees of job opportunities and their individual responsibilities for self-determination and self-development, and (3) achieve affirmative action goals.

After conducting extensive research on the subject, discussing the challenge with consultants and female experts in the field, and reviewing existing programs, Ronald made the following proposal to top management:

1. Design a program to fit the "organizational personality" of the company and its unique needs
2. Offer the program on a voluntary basis to *all* females regardless of position and rank, and male managers on a mandatory basis
3. Obtain full top management support and participation
4. Design and install a skills inventory system to identify available skills of both male and female employees nationwide to support the program

The program was accepted by top management. Over a two-year period, more than 700 female employees and 250 executives attended sessions designed for each group. The president of the company personally introduced the first four meetings for male managers to emphasize the company's commitment

223

Chapter 7
Training and
Development:
Macro-Level
Approaches

and goals. During the course of the program, fifteen to twenty high potential female candidates were identified for top management positions. An additional group of women began self-development programs. The financial cost of the program was significantly less than comparable programs in other companies fundamentally because of the use of existing company resources and available talent.

ORGANIZATION DEVELOPMENT

Our previous discussion has examined T&D from individual, group, and organizational viewpoints. For the remainder of this chapter we will focus on change efforts from a total organizational perspective. T&D effort which involves the entire organization is referred to as **organization development** (OD). For example, the conditions at Yantis Motor Company described at the beginning of this chapter reflect a need to make changes affecting the entire firm if it is to become more effective.

An OD program is designed to increase organizational effectiveness through planned interventions using behavioral science knowledge.[11] Some common OD techniques which will be discussed in the next section include team building, quality circles management by objectives, job enrichment, survey feedback, transactional analysis, and sensitivity training. From a practical viewpoint, some of these macro-level techniques may be combined to provide a strategic approach to organization development.[12]

Team Building

A conscious effort to develop effective work groups throughout the organization is referred to as **team building**.[13] While some activities may be more efficiently pursued by an individual, there are numerous occasions which present problems too broad and complex for one person. In these instances, management teams may be more effective.

Douglas McGregor identified some characteristics of effective management teams (see Table 7–2). His version of an effective group emphasizes an informal organizational climate that is relatively free of tension. There is much discussion and broad participation in the group's decision-making process. Communications are open and listening to the views of others is emphasized. Members feel free to disagree but do so in an atmosphere of acceptance. The

[11]Richard Beckhard, *Organization Development: Strategies and Models* (Reading, Mass.: Addison-Wesley Publishing Company, 1969), p. 9.
[12]Thomas H. Patten, Jr. and Peter B. Vaill, "Organization Development," in *Training and Development Handbook*, 2d ed., Robert L. Craig (New York: McGraw-Hill Book Company, 1976), pp. 20–10 to 20–16 (hereafter cited as Patten and Vaill).
[13]Edgar F. Huse, *Organization Development and Change* (St. Paul, Minn.: West Publishing Co., 1975), p. 230.

Table 7–2. Characteristics of effective groups

225

Chapter 7
Training and
Development:
Macro-Level
Approaches

1. The atmosphere, which can be sensed in a few minutes of observation, tends to be informal, comfortable, relaxed. There are no obvious tensions.

2. There is a lot of discussion in which virtually everyone participates, but it remains pertinent to the task of the group.

3. The task or the objective of the group is well understood and accepted by the members.

4. The members listen to each other! The discussion does not have the quality of jumping from one idea to another unrelated one. Every idea is given a hearing. People are not afraid of seeming foolish by putting forth a creative thought even if it seems fairly extreme.

5. There is disagreement. The group is comfortable with this and shows no signs of having to avoid conflict or to keep everything on a plane of sweetness and light. Disagreements are not suppressed or overridden by premature group action. Individuals who disagree do not appear to be trying to dominate the group or to express hostility. Their disagreement is an expression of a genuine difference of opinion, and they expect a hearing in order to find a solution.

6. Most decisions are reached by a kind of consensus in which it is clear that everybody is in general agreement and willing to go along.

7. Criticism is frequent, frank, and relatively comfortable. There is little evidence of personal attack, either openly or in a hidden fashion. The criticism has a constructive flavor in that it is oriented toward removing an obstacle that prevents the group from getting the job done.

8. People are free in expressing their feelings as well as their ideas on both the problem and the group's operation. There is little pussyfooting, there are few hidden agendas. Everybody appears to know quite well how everybody else feels about any matter under discussion.

9. When action is taken, clear assignments are made and accepted.

10. The chairman of the group does not dominate it, or, on the contrary, does the group defer unduly to him or her. In fact, as one observes the activity, it is clear that the leadership shifts from time to time, depending on the circumstances. At various times different members, because of their knowledge or experience, are in a position to act as "resources" for the group. The members utilize them in this fashion and they occupy leadership roles while they are thus being used. There is little evidence of a struggle for power as the group operates. The issue is not who controls but how to get the job done.

11. The group is self-conscious about its own operations. Frequently, it will stop to examine how well it is doing or what may be interfering with its operation. The problem may be a matter of procedure, or it may be that an individual whose behavior is interfering with the accomplishment of the group's objectives. Whatever the problem is, it receives open discussion until a solution is found.

Source: Adapted from Douglas McGregor, *The Human Side of Management* (New York: McGraw-Hill Book Company), 1960, pp. 232–235. (© 1960, McGraw-Hill Book Company. Reprinted by permission.)

effective group works as a team in pursuing goals which are understood and accepted.

Effective work groups focus on solving actual problems in building efficient management teams. The team-building process begins when the team leader defines a problem which requires organizational change (see Figure

7–4). After the group has received the problem, it is diagnosed to determine the underlying problem factors. These factors may be related to such areas as communication breakdowns, inappropriate leadership styles, or deficiencies in the organizational structure. Alternative solutions are proposed at the next step. Then, the group selects the most appropriate alternative. As a result of open and frank discussions, the participants are likely to be committed to the proposed course of action. The overall improvement in the interpersonal relations of group members enhances the implementation of the change.[14]

Figure 7–4.   **The team building process.**

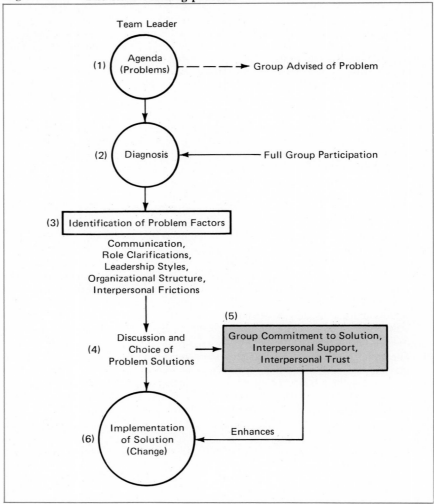

(Source: Reproduced by permission from *EFFECTIVE MANAGEMENT* by Michael A. Hitt, R. Dennis Middlemist and Robert L. Mathis. Copyright © 1979 by West Publishing Company. All rights reserved.)

[14]Michael A. Hitt, R. Dennis Middlemist, and Robert L. Mathis, *Effective Management* (St. Paul, Minn.: West Publishing Company, 1979), pp. 462–464.

227

Chapter 7
Training and
Development:
Macro-Level
Approaches

"Progress in Personnel and Industrial Relations is best assured by providing the person with a variety of projects and functional assignments at all levels in the organization. It is not enough to give a person an assignment in a specific area and then leave him or her in that assignment over some long period. People must be moved routinely and given a wide exposure if they are to grow."

John M. O'Hare, Vice President, Industrial Relations
The Bendix Corporation

Quality Circles

One approach to teamwork is the use of quality circles. **Quality circles are groups of employees who meet regularly with their supervisors to identify production problems and recommend actions for solutions.** These recommendations are then presented to senior management for review and the approved actions are implemented with employee participation.[15]

It is reported that in Japan over 10 million workers participate in quality circles which result in annual savings of from 20 to 25 billion dollars per year.[16] Even though the culture in the United States is different, an increasing number of firms are finding that the quality circle concept can be adapted to our society. To illustrate, according to the International Association of Quality Circles, more than 100 United States firms are now using quality circles, including thirty of the fifty largest companies. Westinghouse alone has over 700 circles.[17]

Quality circles are not a panacea for T&D and productivity problems. In fact, the concept has not worked for some firms.[18] To implement a successful program, these points should be considered:

- Establish clear goals for the program
- Obtain top management support
- Create an organizational climate which accepts the idea of participative management
- Select an enthusiastic and capable manager for the program
- Communicate the goals and nature of the program to all employees
- For the initial effort, select an area of the firm where cooperation and enthusiasm from participants can be expected
- Keep the program strictly on a voluntary basis
- Ensure that the participants receive adequate training in the operation of quality circles

[15]Robert J. Shaw, "From Skepticism to Support: Middle Management's Role in Quality Circles," *Peat Marwick/Management Focus* 29 (May-June 1982): 35.
[16]Sud Ingle, "How to Avoid Quality Circle Failure in Your Company," *Training and Development Journal* 36 (June 1982): 59 (hereafter cited as Ingle).
[17]Roy G. Folz, "QWL's Effect on Productivity," *Personnel Administrator* 27 (May 1982): 20.
[18]Ingle, 54.

• Start the program slowly and then let it proceed gradually but steadily[19]

Management by Objectives

Eileen Murphy, personnel manager for Red River Wholesale Company, stopped by Michael Wills's office to discuss a vacancy in her department. While she was waiting for Michael to return from lunch, she noticed that one of his employees appeared to be very busy at his desk. His desk was cluttered and he was filling out forms and talking on the phone at the same time. When Michael returned, Eileen mentioned this extremely busy person. "Yes," said Michael, "He's always very active. The only problem is that he's one of my least efficient employees. He has so many projects going at one time that nothing seems to get accomplished. He's active, yes. But productive, no!"

Michael Wills is keenly aware that activity is not necessarily a measure of productivity. An employee's ability to establish and attain measurable goals is a key to her or his success. **Management by objectives** (MBO) provides a systematic approach toward this end. It facilitates achievement of results by directing efforts toward attainable goals. MBO is a management approach which encourages managers to anticipate and plan for the future. It deemphasizes guessing or making decisions based upon hunches. Knowledge of MBO is especially important to the personnel manager as Personnel is often responsible for overseeing the entire company MBO program.

Because MBO emphasizes participative management approaches—incorporating Theory Y assumptions—it has been called a philosophy of management. Within this broader context, MBO becomes an important method of organization development. It focuses upon the achievement of individual and organizational goals. The participation of individuals in setting goals and the emphasis on self-control promote not only individual development but also development for the entire organization.

MBO as a means of organization development is a dynamic process. It must be continuously reviewed, modified, and updated. Top management's support is essential for its success.[20] It is top management that initiates the MBO process by establishing long-range goals (see Figure 7–5). For example, the president and vice president of personnel (superior-subordinate) jointly establish the firm's long-range plans regarding minority employment. When long-range goals have been formulated, it is then possible to determine intermediate and short-range objectives. Once individual performance goals have been formulated, intermediate and short-range objectives may be established. At this point, the subordinate's goals are mutually agreed upon. Action plans, which outline how the objectives will be achieved, are then established and the subordinate proceeds to work toward her or his goals. At the end of the appraisal period, both superior and subordinate review the subordinate's per-

[19]Ibid, 57–59.
[20]Jack Bucalo, "Personnel Directors . . . What You Should Know Before Recommending MBO," *Personnel Journal* 56 (April 1977): 476.

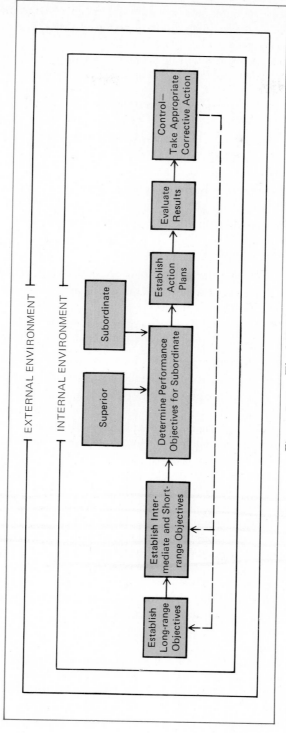

Figure 7-5. The MBO process.

229

formance and determine what can be done to overcome any problems that were encountered. Goals are then established for the next period and the process repeats itself.

From an organization development standpoint, MBO offers numerous potential benefits. Some of the more prominent ones are:

- MBO provides a golden opportunity for development for managers and employees.
- It facilitates the enterprise's ability to change.
- It provides a more objective and tangible basis for performance appraisal and salary decisions.
- It results in better overall management and the achievement of higher performance levels.
- It provides an effective overall planning system.
- It forces managers to establish priorities and measurable targets or standards of performance.
- It clarifies the specific roles, responsibilities, and authority of employees.
- It encourages the participation of individual employees and managers in establishing objectives.
- It facilitates the process of control.
- It lets individuals know what is expected of them.
- It improves communications within the organization.
- It helps identify promotable managers and employees.
- MBO increases motivation and commitment of employees.

As you can imagine, if these benefits are achieved, the entire organization will be positively affected. Viewed from this standpoint, MBO truly becomes a means of organization development.

But, certain problems have been associated with MBO. Without total support and commitment from top management, it is destined for failure. In addition, goals are at times difficult to establish and the system can create a seemingly insurmountable paper mill if it is not closely monitored. Another potential weakness is that there is a tendency to concentrate too much on the short-run at the expense of long-range planning. Short-term goals may be achieved while long-term goals are sacrificed. Finally, some managers believe MBO programs to be excessively time consuming. MBO forces people to think ahead and be capable of seeing how their goals fit into the big picture. This is not an easy task for some managers.

Use of the MBO Concept at Monsanto Company

Utilizing many MBO concepts, Monsanto Company has implemented its Management by Results (MBR) program throughout the corporation. While the initial direction came from top-level management, program implementation has since been decentralized and become part of the fabric of the management process.

231

Chapter 7
Training and
Development:
Macro-Level
Approaches

At Monsanto, MBR is one component of the management style used to accomplish corporate objectives. MBR's purpose is to motivate people, assist them in setting personal and unit direction, evaluate performance, provide equitable compensation, and ensure development for employees throughout the firm. MBR ensures that plans of individuals are properly integrated with those of their reporting unit and that involvement and cooperation are encouraged when seeking to achieve group goals. In addition, Monsanto's MBR system permits flexibility by focusing not on subordinates' specific activities, but rather on their progress on a broader basis. By emphasizing results for one year or longer, employees are encouraged to avoid short-term gains at the expense of longer-term results.

One mechanism for achieving these ends is the Job Results Analysis/Goals form—the basic document in the direction-setting phase of Monsanto's MBR system. The corporate guidelines for preparing this document are broad and flexible and emphasize that managers and units should use their best judgment as to the use of the form and its various sections. The first four sections constitute the Job Results Analysis and center on the job's longer-term definition and direction. The last five sections, the goals document, deal with coming-year expectations and performance (see Figure 7–6).

1. General conditions: In this section, employees state their assumptions about the environment in which they plan to operate for the coming year. For example, a salesperson would consider the growth rate of industries to be served and make projections about the health of the economy. If those assumptions later turn out to be off the mark, supervisor and subordinate are encouraged to review the document for possible change in overall direction or level of expectation.

2. Principal thrust: The most important thing to be done during the next year is stated in this section. It serves as a good check on the goals set later.

3. Results to be worked toward: Here, employees identify the areas of longer-term accomplishment which are important to the job and the unit.

4. Major results: An "X" is placed in this column to identify the most important results; this helps to establish priorities.

5. Goals: Here, the most important accomplishments for the coming year are set forth. Goals are considered milestones toward longer-term results. Normally, a Monsanto employee has from three to five goals for the year.

6. Joint accountability: The purpose of this section is to identify and gain commitment from those individuals—other than the supervisor or subordinates—who give or receive help in achieving each goal. Employees are encouraged to discuss their goals with others from whom support is required.

7. Basic/Outstanding: The range of performance for each goal is established and stated in this portion of the form. As an example, suppose a

Monsanto COMPANY CONFIDENTIAL | JOB RESULTS ANALYSIS — GOALS 19

Principal Thrust (2) | *Location* ______ *Name* ______
JRA — Date ______ *Goals Date* ______ *Title* ______

General Conditions Premises
(1)

Results To Be Worked Toward	Major Results	Goals	Joint Account Ability	Range		Weight
				Basic	Outstanding	
**relates to Principal Thrust* (3)	(4)	(5)	(6)	(7)		(8)

JRA Approved By ______ *Goals Approved By* ______

Date ______ *Date* ______

(9) *Goals represent* ______ *% of total performance*

Source: Used with the permission of Monsanto Company

Figure 7–6. **Monsanto's job results analysis/goals form.**

goal established was "to achieve new customer sales of $1,000,000 (expected)." In this case, $500,000 would be entered in the Basic Column and perhaps $2,000,000 in the Outstanding Column.

8. Weight: The entries in this column establish goal priorities for the coming year. The weight established indicates priority—not the amount of time to be spent on each goal. To accomplish this ranking process, 100 points may be allocated among the goals or the goals may be numerically ranked.

9. Goals represent ______% of your performance: The purpose of this entry is to show the relative importance of the stated goals to the entire job.

The MBR program at Monsanto provides a means for ensuring that employee training and development is accomplished on a continuous basis. This approach integrates training and development into the overall Monsanto management process.

Job Enrichment

233

Chapter 7
Training and
Development:
Macro-Level
Approaches

As was explained in Chapter 3, **job enrichment** is the deliberate restructuring of a job to make it more challenging, meaningful, and interesting. It emphasizes the accomplishment of significant tasks so that the employee can receive a sense of achievement. Job enrichment takes an optimistic view of employee capabilities. Its use presumes that individuals have the ability to perform more difficult and responsible tasks. Further, it assumes that most people will respond favorably if they are given the opportunity to perform challenging tasks. They will also be motivated to produce at higher efficiency levels. When job enrichment is applied on a broad scale, it becomes an important OD method.

An illustration of the implementation of job enrichment is provided by a department in which employees assembled a variety of hot plates. In this work unit, employees assembled hot plates in a normal assembly-line operation. Although management was satisfied with productivity, the supervisor and an engineer applied job enrichment principles which radically changed the work methods. Each employee was given responsibility for assembling the entire hot plate. Their reaction to this change was quite positive and controllable rejects decreased from 23 percent to 1 percent within six months. During the same period of time, absenteeism dropped from 8 percent to less than 1 percent. During the last six months of the year, productivity increased by 84 percent. The routine final inspection was later delegated to the assembly-line workers—a change that eliminated the need for a full-time quality control job.[21]

One of the more publicized experiences with job enrichment involves Sweden's leading car manufacturer, A. B. Volvo. Pehr Gyllenhammar introduced a drastic alternative to the traditional assembly line soon after assuming the presidency in 1971. Work at the new Kalmar plant was arranged in such a manner that groups of about twenty employees could assemble complete car components. This work arrangement permitted them to personally identify with their product. Gyllenhammar wanted his production employees to see a Volvo being driven down the street and say, "I made that car."[22]

When jobs within an organization are restructured to increase their responsibility and challenge, the employees continually develop while performing them. The nature of these jobs actually requires that employees keep their skills updated.

Survey Feedback

An old and widely used approach to organization development is the **survey feedback method.** It has been estimated that in the 1960s, survey feedback was used more frequently than all other methods combined, and its popularity continues.[23]

[21]Edgar F. Huse and Michael Beer. "Eclectic Approach to Organizational Development," *Harvard Business Review* 49 (September-October 1971).
[22]"Lessons from the Volvo Experience," *International Management* 33 (February 1978): 42.
[23]Michael E. McGill, *Organization Development for Operating Managers* (New York: AMACOM, A Division of American Management Associations, 1977), pp. 62–63 (hereafter cited as McGill).

Survey feedback involves three essential steps, as you see in Figure 7–7. In the first step, a consultant collects data from members of the organization. Normally, questionnaires are used and they are answered anonymously. It has been suggested that the survey include only those areas in which management is willing to make changes. Otherwise, the expectations of participating employees may not be realistic.[24]

The second step involves presenting the results of the study in the form of feedback to concerned organizational units. In the third step, the data are analyzed and action decisions are made. The decisions are directed at improving relationships in the organization. This is accomplished by revealing problem areas and dealing with them through straightforward discussions. Consultants facilitate this process by providing counsel.

An example of a survey feedback instrument is provided in Figure 7–8. This management diagnosis chart is widely used to analyze management performance in critical areas such as leadership, motivation, communication, decisions, goals, and controls. Employees are asked to check, along a continuum, the point that best describes their organization. They are also requested to in-

Figure 7–7.   **The survey feedback method.**

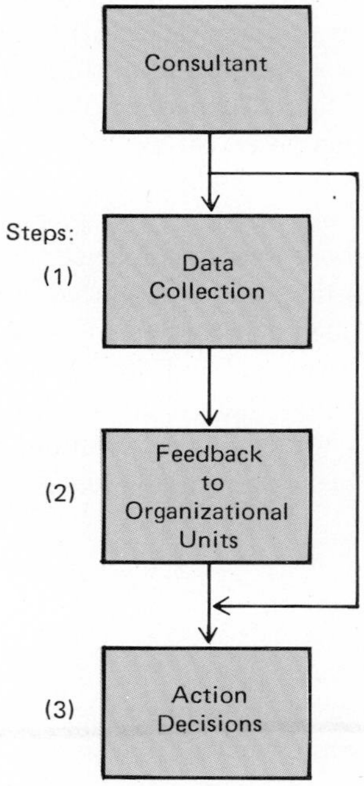

(Source: Adapted from Michael E. McGill, *Organization Development for Operating Managers.* (New York: AMACOM, a division of American Management Associations, 1977.)

[24]Don Hellriegel and John W. Slocum, Jr., *Organizational Behavior*, 2d ed. (St. Paul, Minn.: West Publishing Co., 1979), p. 591.

dicate their views of a desired state. An organizational profile is then prepared by averaging the responses and charting them. Referring again to Figure 7–8, you can see that the present state of leadership is perceived as being quite neg-

235

Chapter 7
Training and
Development:
Macro-Level
Approaches

Figure 7–8.   An example of a survey feedback questionnaire.

		Present State		Desired State	
LEADERSHIP	How much confidence is shown in subordinates?	None	Condescending	Substantial	Complete
	How free do they feel to talk to superiors about job?	Not at All	Not Very	Rather	Fully
	Are subordinates' ideas sought and used, if worthy?	Seldom	Sometimes	Usually	Always
MOTIVATION	Is predominant use made of (1) fear, (2) threats, (3) punishment, (4) rewards, (5) involvement?	1, 2, 3, Occasionally 4	4, Some 3	4, Some 3 and 5	5, 4, based on group-set goals
	Where is responsibility felt for achieving organization's goals?	Mostly at Top	Top and Middle	Fairly General	All Levels
COMMUNICATION	How much communication is aimed at achieving organization's objectives?	Very Little	Little	Quite a Bit	A Great Deal
	What is the direction of information flow?	Downward	Mostly Downward	Down and Up	Down, Up and Sideways
	How is downward communication accepted?	With Suspicion	Possibly with Suspicion	With Caution	With an Open Mind
	How accurate is upward communication?	Often Wrong	Censored for the Boss	Limited Accuracy	Accurate
	How well do superiors know problems faced by subordinates?	Know Little	Some Knowledge	Quite Well	Very Well
DECISIONS	At what level are decisions formally made?	Mostly at Top	Policy at Top, Some Delegation	Broad Policy at Top, More Delegation	Throughout but well integrated
	What is the origin of technical and professional knowledge used in decision making?	Top Management	Upper and Middle	To a Certain Extent Throughout	To a Great Extent Throughout
	Are subordinates involved in decisions related to their work?	Not at all	Occasionally Consulted	Generally Consulted	Fully Involved
	What does decision making process contribute to motivation?	Nothing, Often Weakens it	Relatively Little	Some Contribution	Substantial Contribution
GOALS	How are organizational goals established?	Orders Issued	Orders, Some Comment Invited	After Discussion, by Orders	By Group Action (Except in Crisis)
	How much covert resistance to goals is present?	Strong Resistance	Moderate Resistance	Some Resistance at Times	Little or None
CONTROL	How concentrated are review and control functions?	Highly at Top	Relatively Highly at Top	Moderate Delegation to Lower Levels	Quite Widely Shared
	Is there an informal organization resisting the formal one?	Yes	Usually	Sometimes	No—Same Goals as Formal
	What are cost, productivity and other control data used for?	Policing, Punishment	Reward and Punishment	Reward Some Self-guidance	Self-guidance Problem Solving

ative. These employees apparently feel that leadership in their firm is condescending. The consensus is that the leader should show "substantial" confidence in subordinates (the desired state).

Transactional Analysis[25]

The use of **transactional analysis** (TA) as an OD method is a relatively recent
development.[26] It has been used, however, for a number of years as a micro-
level technique for training and development programs.

Within the framework of TA, three separate sources of behavior (ego
states) are identified. These ego states—the "Parent," the "Adult," and the
"Child"—are constantly present and at work within each person. The manner
in which individual ego states interact can have a significant impact upon interpersonal relations and an organization's effectiveness.

The Parent ego state stores all the attitudes, beliefs, and values learned
from authority figures early in our lives. Everything seen or heard is recorded,
as on tape, and these messages influence our current behavior. The Parent ego
state may reflect nuturing behavior that is sympathetic, protective, and in-
structive or critical behavior that is punitive, prejudicial, and judgmental. The
boss who comes on as a critical parent tends to find fault excessively and to
punish rather than guide and develop subordinates.

The Adult, on the other hand, is the objective part of us. Through our
Adult, we analyze data and make independent, logical judgments. The Adult
serves as our internal computer, and behavioral changes occur through this ego
state.

The emotional side of individual behavior stems from the Child. This ego
state may take on different qualities—the Natural Child, the Little Professor,
or the Adaptive Child. When the Natural Child dominates, the individual is
expressive, self-centered, impulsive, and curious. The ego state of the Little
Professor centers around being intuitive, manipulative, and creative. The
manner in which the Adaptive Child behaves is determined by the parental
figures with whom the individual was associated.

The interaction of ego states can have a significant impact upon behavior
in organizations. If organizational members know which ego state a person is
in at a given time, they may be able to determine the best way to communicate. Various situations that a person may confront are presented in Figures
7–9 through 7–11. As Figure 7–9 shows, Frank's three ego states are shown on
the left and John's on the right. The two have engaged in an adult-to-adult
transaction. It is a *complementary transaction* because Frank's message gets the
expected response. When this occurs, communication remains open and there
is no conflict or difficulty between the parties.

A different situation is presented in Figure 7–10. Here, Frank speaks from
his parent ego state to John's child state. This also illustrates a complementary

---

[25]The material on Transactional Analysis that appears on these pages, is abridged and adapted from
I'm O.K.—You're O.K. by Thomas A. Harris, M.D. (© 1967, 1968, 1969 by Thomas A. Harris,
M.D. Reprinted by permission of Harper and Row Publishers, Inc.).
[26]McGill, p. 106.

transaction. However, while the lines of communication are open for the present, condescending behavior of this sort may have negative long-term consequences.

237

Chapter 7
Training and
Development:
Macro-Level
Approaches

Crossed transactions occur when the message sent gets an unexpected response. Notice that in Figure 7–11 Frank delivers a message from his parent ego state intended for John's child state, "I never want you to interrupt me again like you did in that meeting yesterday." Instead, John replies from his parent state, "Who the hell are you to hog the whole conversation?" Frank expected an apologetic response but instead received one that was unexpected. Here, the transaction was crossed. These types of transactions are generally unproductive and represent a breakdown in communication. While individuals should use all their ego states, the adult must remain in charge. As previously mentioned, it is through this state that behavioral changes occur.

At Bristol-Meyers Products, a development program uses transactional analysis as the model. Since its inception in 1975, this program has involved over 1000 managers, supervisors, professionals, and sales representatives. As Richard Crosbee, vice president, personnel, puts it, "The model is unique in that it teaches basic behavioral principles and does so in a down-to-earth, practical manner using words that all people know and understand. It can be successfully employed at all levels in the organization." Mr. Crosbee developed the program because, he states, "It was clear to me, as a personnel executive,

Figure 7–9. A complementary transaction.

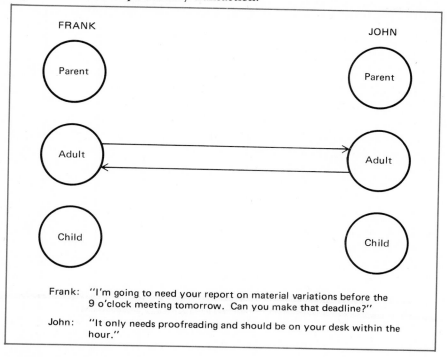

Frank: "I'm going to need your report on material variations before the 9 o'clock meeting tomorrow. Can you make that deadline?"

John: "It only needs proofreading and should be on your desk within the hour."

Source: Used with the permission of Bristol-Myers Products, A Division of Bristol-Myers Company.

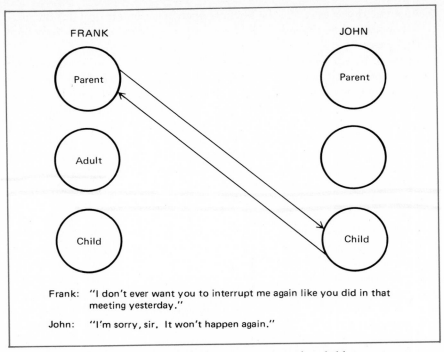

FRANK   JOHN

Parent   Parent

Adult

Child   Child

Frank: "I don't ever want you to interrupt me again like you did in that meeting yesterday."

John: "I'm sorry, sir. It won't happen again."

Figure 7–10. **A transaction involving a parent and a child ego state.**

Source: Used with the permission of Bristol-Myers Products, A Division of Bristol-Myers Company.

that the poor handling of people (self and others) was the primary reason for the failure of managers."

Applying TA concepts in T&D efforts on a broad basis may prove valuable in producing desired organizational change. As individuals in a firm learn to analyze their own social interactions, better communication and greater organizational effectiveness can follow.

Sensitivity Training

An organization development technique that is designed to make us aware of ourselves and our impact upon others is referred to as **sensitivity training.** It is quite different from the traditional form of training which stresses the learning of a predetermined set of concepts.[27]

Sensitivity training features a group—often called a training group or T-group—in which there is no preestablished agenda or focus. The trainer's purpose is merely to serve as a facilitator in this unstructured environment.

[27]James L. Gibson and John M. Ivancevich, *Organizations: Behavior, Structure, Processes,* Fourth Edition, (Plano, TX: Business Publications, Inc., 1982), pp. 580–581 (hereafter cited as Gibson and Ivancevich).

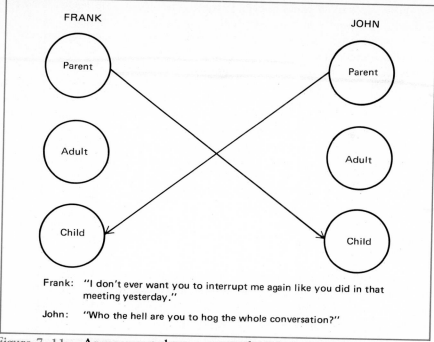

FRANK   JOHN

Parent   Parent

Adult   Adult

Child   Child

Frank: "I don't ever want you to interrupt me again like you did in that meeting yesterday."

John: "Who the hell are you to hog the whole conversation?"

Figure 7–11. **An unexpected response results in a crossed transaction.**
Source: Used with the permission of Bristol-Myers Products, A Division of Bristol-Myers Company.

Participants are encouraged to learn about themselves and others in the group. Some objectives of sensitivity training are to:

1. Increase self-insight and self-awareness concerning the participant's behavior and its meaning in a social context
2. Increase sensitivity to the behavior of others
3. Increase awareness and understanding of the types of processes that facilitate or inhibit group functioning and the interactions between different groups
4. Heighten diagnostic skill in social, interpersonal, and intergroup situations
5. Increase the participant's ability to intervene successfully in intergroup or intragroup situations so as to increase member satisfaction, effectiveness, and output
6. Increase the participant's ability to analyze continually his or her own interpersonal behavior in order to help himself or herself and others achieve more effective and satisfying interpersonal relationships[28]

[28]John P. Campbell and Marvin D. Dunnette, "Effectiveness of T-Group Experiences in Managerial Training and Development," *Psychological Bulletin* 70, no. 2 (August 1968): 73–104. (© 1968 by the American Psychological Association. Reprinted by permission.)

When sensitivity training begins, there is no agenda, no leaders, and no authority or power positions. Essentially a vacuum exists until participants begin to exchange dialogue. Through this feedback people begin to learn about themselves and others. Participants are encouraged to look at themselves as others see them. Then, if they want to change, they can.

Although the purpose of sensitivity training (to assist individuals to learn more about how they relate to other people) cannot by itself be questioned, the technique has received considerable criticism in recent years. Individuals may be encouraged to be more open and supportive in the T-group. Then when they return to their jobs, the environment there has not changed. In addition, there has been criticism about the emotional stress that participants must undergo. And finally, there are mixed results concerning sensitivity training leading to improved organizational effectiveness.[29]

CHANGE AGENTS

The preceding discussion presented the various techniques that might be used to bring about change on an organizational level. But precisely who is responsible for seeing that the change takes place properly? In many instances, the accountable individual is called a change agent.

A **change agent** is the person(s) responsible for assuring that the planned change in OD is properly implemented. The change agent may come from within the organization or be an external consultant. The role of consultants, or change agents, is to utilize specialized knowledge in the area of T&D in making interventions in the organization.[30] They assist managers in bringing about change in such areas as communication, leadership styles and motivational techniques.

Change agents are often consultants brought in from outside the organization. Management frequently believes that the outside expert brings objectivity to a situation and obtains acceptance and trust from organizational members. In many instances this belief continues. However, another school of thought seems to be developing. Lately, internal consultants (employees of the firm) have been serving as effective change agents. Proponents of this approach believe that because the internal consultant knows both the formal and informal nature of the organization, he or she can often produce desired results at a lower cost.

OD PROGRAM EVALUATION

Once an organizational effort has been implemented, the question must be asked, "Did anything happen as a result of this experience?" All too often the

[29]William J. Kearney and Desmond D. Martin, "Sensitivity Training: An Established Management Development Tool," *Academy of Management Journal* 17 (December 1974): 755–760.
[30]Patten and Vaill, pp. 20–5 to 20–6.

answer is "We don't know." We must admit that OD evaluation may be more difficult than determining if an employee has learned to operate a particular piece of equipment, but the evaluation should be accomplished. The company has likely expended considerable financial and human resources and deserves to know if the program has been effective.

One means by which the effectiveness of the program may be measured is through viewing changes in performance criteria.[31] Some of these factors might include: (1) absenteeism rate, (2) turnover rate, (3) accident rate, (4) costs, and (5) scrappage. An improvement in these and other criteria may mean that improvement has resulted from the OD method. For instance, if the turnover rate has declined, this might mean that workers are more satisfied with the work environment and have chosen to remain with the firm. If costs per unit produced have been reduced, it may suggest that workers are paying more attention to their work as a result of the OD program. Although this form of evaluative data is useful, it probably will not provide the entire answer as to program effectiveness.

An excellent means of determining what change has resulted in worker attitude is through the use of a survey questionnaire. This survey is administered to employees prior to OD efforts and after the development has occurred. A measurable difference in total employee satisfaction may well suggest the effectiveness of the system.

It should also be noted that measurement of effectiveness does not end once the program has been completed. It is necessary to continue to administer questionnaires on a periodic basis over an extended period of time. It is not a one-time event. And, in viewing the survey results, production criteria should be considered to gain a good appreciation of the effect of the change effort.

SUMMARY

Training and development is a planned, continuous effort by management to improve employee competency levels and the organization work environment. The overall purpose of T&D is to bring about desired change in organizations. When management recognizes that change is needed for the entire organization, broad, macro-level approaches to T&D are indicated. The methods used to respond to change of less magnitude are referred to as micro-level approaches.

The basic purposes of T&D are: (1) increased productivity, (2) prevention of obsolescence, and (3) preparation for higher level tasks. Numerous factors which influence T&D include: (1) top management support, (2) technological advances, (3) organizational complexity, (4) behavioral science knowledge, (5) learning principles, and (6) performance of other personnel functions.

The change sequence involves the following steps: (1) recognize the need for change, (2) select appropriate T&D method, (3) reduce resistance to change, (4) implement the change, (5) develop a new position, and (6) eval-

[31]Gibson and Ivancevich, pp. 547–548.

241

Chapter 7
Training and
Development:
Macro-Level
Approaches

uate T&D effectiveness. Some means of reducing resistance to change include: building trust and confidence, developing open communication, and employee participation.

Training and development efforts which involve the entire organization are referred to as organization development (OD). A conscious effort to develop effective work groups throughout the organization is referred to as team building. Management by objectives (MBO) provides a systematic approach to enable employees to establish and attain measurable goals. Job enrichment is the deliberate restructuring of a job to make it more challenging, meaningful, and interesting. An old and widely used approach to OD is the survey feedback method. The use of transactional analysis (TA) as an OD method is a relatively recent development. An OD technique that is designed to make us aware of ourselves and our impact upon others is referred to as sensitivity training.

A change agent is the person(s) responsible for assuring that the planned change in OD is properly implemented. The change agent may come from within the organization or be an external consultant. Once an organizational effort has been implemented, the question must be asked, "Did anything happen as a result of this experience?" One means by which the effectiveness of the program may be measured is through viewing changes in performance. Another method is through the use of survey questionnaires.

Questions for Review

1. Define training and development. Distinguish between macro- and micro-level approaches to training and development.

2. What are the general purposes of training and development?

3. Discuss the various factors that influence training and development.

4. What are the steps to follow in implementing organization change? Briefly describe each.

5. What are the possible reasons for a person to resist change? What means are available to reduce resistance to change?

6. Distinguish between team building and management by objectives as methods of organization development.

7. Why is the survey feedback method identified as an organization development method? Discuss.

8. Describe how transactional analysis and sensitivity training might be used as organization development methods.

9. How might organization development programs be evaluated?

Terms for Review

Training and development
Change

Macro-level approach
Micro-level approach

242

Organization development

Team building

Quality circles

Management by objectives

Job enrichment

Survey feedback

Transactional analysis

Sensitivity training

Change agent

Mr. Burt MacDaniel had been president and owner of MacDaniel Corporation for thirty years prior to his retirement. Burt had seen the firm grow from a three-person operation to an organization with over five hundred employees. He was a hard-working individual and had often been at his office for fifteen hours a day. Although Burt had made all major decisions, his pleasant personality had kept the managers from being alienated and they had accepted this arrangement.

When Mr. MacDaniel retired, his son Jim became president. Jim had a MBA degree and was eager to take over his father's business. He believed that his college training had prepared him well for this. One of the first things Jim wanted to do was to give decision-making authority to the managers. This would permit him to look at the big picture while the day-to-day problems were solved lower in the organization.

Jim called a meeting to tell the managers that the firm was going to implement an MBO program and that they would have more responsibility over their areas. They would not have to come to him for every decision. He spent over an hour that day describing how MBO works. Over the following week he spent an additional thirty minutes or so with each manager arriving at objectives.

Questions

1. What further steps will be involved in successful implementation of the MBO program?

2. Is MBO likely to produce the result Jim desires? Discuss.

For the past few years, sales at Glenco Manufacturing had been falling. The decline was industry wide. In fact, Glenco had actually been able to increase its share of the market slightly. Although forecasts indicated that demand for the products would improve in the future, Joe Goddard, the company president, believed that something needed to be done immediately to permit the firm to survive this temporary slump. As a first step he employed a consulting firm to determine if a reorganization might be helpful.

A team of five consultants arrived at the firm. They told Mr. Goddard that they first had to gain a thorough understanding of the current situation before they could make any recommendations. Mr. Goddard told them that the company was open to them. They could ask any questions that they thought were necessary.

The grapevine was full of rumors virtually from the day the consulting group arrived. One employee was heard to say, "If they shut down the company, I don't know if I could take care of my family." Another worker said, "If they move me away from my friends I'm going to quit."

When workers questioned their supervisors, they received no explanations. No one had told the supervisors what was going on either. The climate began to change to one of fear. Rather than being concerned about their daily work, employees worried about what was going to happen to the company and their jobs. Productivity dropped drastically as a result.

A month after the consultants departed, an informational memorandum was circulated throughout the company. It stated that the consultants had recommended a slight modification in the top levels of the organization to achieve greater efficiency. No one would be terminated. Any reductions would be the result of normal attrition. By this time, however, some of the best workers had already found other jobs and company operations were severely disrupted for several months.

Questions

1. Why do you believe that the employees tended to assume the worst about what was happening?

2. How could this difficulty have been avoided?

Chapter Objectives

1. Describe the training and development process.
2. Explain the role of training and development managers.
3. List and describe the various training and development methods.
4. State the amount of use and success associated with the various training and development methods.
5. Describe the implications associated with use of training and development media.
6. Explain the approaches that may be taken in evaluating training and development programs.

Chapter 8 _____

Training and Development: Micro-Level Approaches

Britt Swann, a recently retired Marine officer, has begun his second career. He is employed by the Texona Corporation as a production supervisor. Britt's military record was excellent and he was shocked when Jack Swilley, the plant superintendent, told him, "Britt, you have the potential to become a good manager, but your people resent your high-handed methods." Britt replied, "Jack, I have been successful twenty years managing people and using these exact methods." Before Jack turned to leave, he said, "I know, but you're not in the military now and times are changing. I think you should enroll in our basic supervisory management development seminar—and soon!"

The six press department employees of the Ajax Printing Company formed a congenial group. Most of them were hired two years ago when several key pressmen retired. Ajax's business was booming at the time but experienced people were not available. The company was forced to employ some young workers who were bright but inexperienced. Because business had been brisk, there was no time to devote specifically to training. But now, a long-term problem has become intolerable. The cost of "remakes" has continued to increase due to poor quality work. Company sales executives are afraid that Ajax may lose several good customers.

The previous chapter focused on bringing about change on a broad scale (macro level). However, in the above instances, training and development is suggested from a narrower viewpoint (micro level). Britt had been a good manager in the military, but obviously has not adjusted to his new working environment. A development program which could provide him with new leadership and motivation concepts might assist him in becoming a good manager with Texona. It also appears that the Ajax Company must now bite the bullet and provide the inexperienced workers with training in printing skills. Groups of individuals must be trained in this instance.

At the micro level, T&D permits employees and groups to learn something of value relative to present or future performance. T&D helps workers to change and to perform their jobs more effectively.

THE TRAINING AND DEVELOPMENT PROCESS

In this chapter we will focus on T&D as it is used to bring about change in both individuals and groups. First we will emphasize the broad scope of the training function by considering its three components: training, education, and development.[1] The term training describes those activities that serve to improve an employee's performance on a currently held job or one related to it.[2] Training a worker to operate a lathe or a supervisor to schedule daily production are examples. Education consists of activities that are conducted to improve the employee's overall competence in a specific direction and beyond the current job.[3] Seminars designed to develop communication or leadership skills are in this category.

Training and education both focus on either currently held jobs or predetermined different jobs within the firm. Development, on the other hand, includes activities that are designed to prepare employees to keep pace with the organization as it changes and grows.[4] University courses providing new insights for executives illustrate this T&D component.

The general training and development process is shown in Figure 8–1. The external and internal environments can affect this process. Alterations in the environment necessitate change; training should be the response to this need.[5] Recognition that a change is needed may come from a variety of sources. For instance, Britt Swann's supervisor noticed that his management

[1]Leonard Nadler, *Developing Human Resources*, Second Edition (Austin, Texas: Learning Concepts, 1979), 40.
[2]Leonard Nadler, 60.
[3]Leonard Nadler, 88.
[4]Dugan Laird, *Approaches to Training and Development* (Reading, Mass.: Addison-Wesley Publishing Company, 1978), 9.
[5]Chip R. Bell, "Criteria for Selecting Instructional Strategies," *Training and Development Journal* 31 (October 1977): 5.

249

Chapter 8
Training and
Development:
Micro-Level
Approaches

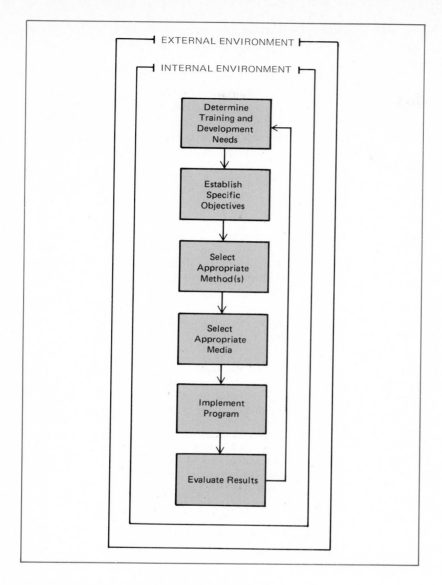

Figure 8–1. **The training and development process.**

style was not appropriate for the situation. In the second example, the cost of remakes had caused Ajax Printing to recognize the need for change.

The next phase of the process entails determining training needs and objectives. Essentially two questions must be asked. The first is "What are our training needs?" Second, "What do we want to accomplish through our T&D efforts?" The objectives might be quite narrow if limited to the supervisory ability of Britt Swann. Or, they might be so broad as to include improving the management skills of all first-line supervisors.

Once objectives have been stated, the appropriate methods and media which will accomplish the stated goals are determined. As you will see later in the chapter, there are a variety from which to choose. The actual implementation of the T&D program is where change actually occurs. Naturally, T&D must be continuously evaluated to determine if the training and development needs are being accomplished. George Odiorne has stated that training directors must move more toward economic evaluation of their training efforts.[6] Because numerous external and internal factors continuously affect training requirements, any effective training and development program must be a dynamic, ongoing process.

THE ROLE OF THE T&D MANAGER

Most personnel managers are highly involved in the training and development process. But, the T&D manager must play a key role if the firm's overall objectives are to be achieved. Views of some practitioners concerning the T&D manager's role are seen in Table 8–1. After studying these comments, some important conclusions regarding Personnel's responsibility in T&D can be made.

Table 8–1. Today's role of the training and development manager

Personnel Executive	Comments
Barry N. Lastra, Senior Advisor Personnel Development Chevron U.S.A., Inc.	Principal role is to be a consultant to managers to help identify (1) operating problems or potential problems, (2) scenarios or alternative courses of action to solve these problems or prevent them from occurring, and (3) feedback processes to see that on-job results are consistent with stated management goals.
Raymond Lee Director of Personnel Fotomat Corporation	The role varies greatly depending upon the industry and the individual in the job. My perception is that the role is becoming more important and is expanding into non-traditional training and development functions.
T. M. Fabek, District Manager Training Ohio Bell Telephone Company	The role of the training/development manager is a staff function that must prove to the line organization and users that the services provided are job relevant, and will improve productivity, lower costs, and increase profits.
Henry L. Dahl, Jr., Manager Employee Development and Planning The Upjohn Company	Plan, develop, and administer programs which meet the needs of line managers in assisting their people to obtain the knowledge and skills they need to perform their present job satisfactorily, prepare employees for future jobs in the company and assist them in achieving their personal goals.

[6]George Odiorne, *Training by Objectives*, (London: The Macmillan Company, 1970), p. 14.

251

Chapter 8
Training and
Development:
Micro-Level
Approaches

In the first place, the T&D manager operates essentially in a staff or advisory capacity. The responsibility for T&D belongs primarily to the line managers. Milton R. Scheiber, director/corporate management development for Lone Star Industries, Inc. said "The primary responsibility for training and development lies with the line manager, from the President and Chairman of the Board on down. T&D management merely provides the technical expertise, plus blood, sweat, and tears."

Another significant role of the T&D manager is to show management that there will be a predictable payoff if resources are expended toward this end. Merely stating, "I think this program will be good," is not sufficient because "training for training's sake doesn't work."[7] Some form of cost-benefit analysis must be made prior to implementing any program. The program should be job related, improve productivity, lower costs, and increase profits.

Finally, a major role of the T&D manager is to assist people in obtaining knowledge and skills needed for present and future jobs and to assist them in attaining personal goals. Learning is a self-activity and all employee development is self-development. The T&D manager explains the type of available training, shows how it can be accomplished, and provides encouragement to ensure successful accomplishment of the training.

DETERMINING TRAINING NEEDS AND OBJECTIVES

The first step in the training and development process is to determine training needs and establish related goals. In our competitive environment, "training for the sake of training" is no longer acceptable. Rather, bona fide needs must be addressed. Clearly stated goals will permit T&D specialists to design meaningful programs and will place them in a position to evaluate the results of their efforts.

Determining Training Needs

A traditional approach to determining training needs has included organizational analysis, operational analysis, and individual analysis.[8] In conducting an organizational analysis, the firm's goals and plans should be studied along with the results of human resources planning. Training needs may be indicated by information about new positions, retirements, turnover, absenteeism, grievances, quality control, accidents, and customer complaints. The results of an organization's MBO system might also reveal areas where the need for training is indicated.

[7]Dennis Dethlefs and Jerry L. Sellentin, "How to Be a 'Houdini' in Training," *Personnel Administrator* 24 (January 1979): 68.
[8]W. McGeehee and P. W. Thayer, *Training in Business and Industry* (New York: John Wiley, 1961).

Operational analysis relies largely upon the results of job analysis. Specific ability needs are reflected in job descriptions and specifications. Training managers may also refer to job performance standards as they observe work group performance. In addition, managers and operative employees may be interviewed or surveyed to obtain suggestions.

Individual analysis may be carried out by comparing actual employee performance against established standards. Training managers may utilize surveys, interviews, or observation in making these determinations. In addition, tests, role plays, and assessment centers may yield helpful information. Also, the results of career planning programs and performance appraisal systems may be quite revealing.

Establishing Specific T&D Objectives

We have stated that objectives are the end results we desire to achieve. In training and development, clear and concise objectives must be formulated. Without them, we could not design a T&D program nor, after it had been accomplished, would we have an important means for evaluating its effectiveness. The purposes and objectives of a segment of a training program designed by Chevron U.S.A., Inc. for "Employment Compliance" is provided below:

Employment Compliance

Purpose: To provide supervisor with:

1. Knowledge and value of consistent personnel practices
2. The intent of EEO legal requirements
3. The skills to apply them

Objectives: Be able to:

1. Cite the supervisory areas affected by EEO laws on discrimination
2. Identify acceptable and nonacceptable actions, according to EEO laws
3. State how to get help on EEO and Affirmative Action matters
4. Describe why we have discipline and grievance procedures
5. Describe our discipline and grievance procedures including who is covered

As you can see, the purpose is first clearly established. Managers would have little difficulty in determining whether this is the type of training a subordinate needs. The specific learning objectives leave little doubt of the knowledge that should be obtained from the course. Action words such as "cite," "identify," "state," and "describe" are used to tell the specific content of the program. With these types of objectives, evaluation of whether a person has achieved the necessary knowledge may be made. For instance, a trainee can either state how to get help on EEO and Affirmative Action matters or he or she cannot.

Rosemarie Ramirez
Employee Development Officer
The St. Paul Property and Liability
Insurance

After graduating from the University of Minnesota and Minnesota School of Business in 1963, Rose was employed by 3M Company as a secretary in sales development. After several promotions—including working for twenty different people during the first two years—Rose was promoted to executive secretary to a division head. Because of her firsthand knowledge of the product line, she accepted the opportunity to train customers in the use of 3M Brand Overhead Projector and Transparencies. While traveling 60–80 percent of the time from 1967–1969, she discovered that industrial adult education training was exciting and fulfilling for herself and beneficial to others.

She proposed to the corporate education department that they expand their program and curriculum for 3M employees. They agreed, and Rose joined the Education, Training, and Development Department as a trainer in June 1970. Rose said, "It didn't take me long to understand that I needed to expand the job for continued self-growth." Within a short time she was promoted to supervisor and in 1975 became manager. During this time, she devel-

oped total training programs in office skills, affirmative action, interpersonal communications, group dynamics, time management, problem solving, decision making, women in management, minority in the corporate world, career development, and handling conflicts. Again this came about by continuing to take on more responsibility to show others what she was capable of doing. While developing program content, Rose expanded her administrative management skills by managing the corporate tuition refund program, an office staff of fifteen, the training facility, and the budget for the total department of sixty people.

Knowing that practical experience alone would not be sufficient to further her career, Rose became active in the International Association of Personnel Women (IAPW) to broaden her "personnel" expertise, and returned to school to complete her BA in personnel management in 1978. She knew this had paid off when St. Paul Companies (property and casualty insurance company) recruited her as their employment development officer. Rose joined the organization in 1980 to manage career and management development units, library, underwriting-marketing, and claims training units. Also in 1980 Ms. Ramirez was selected as the Outstanding Woman in Business by the St. Paul YWCA.

When asked to describe a major problem she had overcome, Rose replied, "While at 3M for seventeen years, I had to overcome the image of being female and a secretary. I had to demonstrate that I was capable and interested in assuming greater responsibility and that what my unit performed was adding to the bottom line by helping employees (management and non-management) be more productive. My way of handling this was to constantly look for opportunities, i.e., turning problem areas into challenges especially those no one else thought of or wanted to tackle or solve."

Table 8–2. Training and development methods

Method	Utilized For			Conducted	
	Managers and Entry Level Professionals	Operatives	Both	On-The-Job	Off-The-Job
Coaching			X	X	
Business games	X				X
Case study	X				X
Conference/discussion	X				X
In-basket training	X				X
Internships	X			X	
Role playing	X				X
Job rotation			X	X	
Programmed instruction			X		X
Computer assisted instruction			X		X
Classroom lecture			X		X
Apprenticeship training		X		X	
Simulators		X			X
Vestibule training		X			X

TRAINING AND DEVELOPMENT METHODS

When a person is working on a car, some tools are more appropriate in performing certain functions than others. The same logic applies when considering the many T&D methods. You can see a list of various methods in Table 8–2. Notice that some apply strictly to managers, others to operative employees, and several can be used in the training and development of both managers and operative workers. As we discuss these various methods, we will present the topics under the headings "Management Development," "Training for Entry Level Professional Employees," and "The Training of Operative Employees." Methods which apply to both manager and operative training will be included under management development.

Again referring to Table 8–2, you can see that T&D methods are broken down by whether they are conducted on or off the job. Often it is not feasible to learn while doing. Therefore, while a large portion of training and development takes place on the job, many T&D programs occur away from the job.

MANAGEMENT DEVELOPMENT

A firm's future lies primarily in the hands of its management. This group performs the essential functions necessary for the organization to survive and prosper. Managers of an organization must have a good batting average in the numerous decisions they make. Otherwise, the firm will not grow and may even succumb to competitive pressures. For these reasons, it is imperative that managers continue to be developed. They must remain attuned to the latest knowledge in their various fields and be capable of managing an ever changing work force within a dynamic environment. To assist in this process, many organizations emphasize training and development programs for managers. **Management development** consists of all learning experiences provided by an organization for the purpose of providing and upgrading skills and knowledge required in current and future positions. Firstline supervisors, middle-managers, and executives may all be expected to participate in programs. Management development programs are offered through in-house programs, professional organizations, or colleges and universities. In-house programs are those which are planned and presented by a firm's own members, who are often assigned to a T&D unit within Personnel. Line managers are also frequently utilized to conduct segments of a program.

Outside the company, professional organizations and universities are additional sources used to provide management development. Organizations such as the American Society for Personnel Administration and the American Management Association are active in conducting conferences, seminars, and other programs. The American Management Association offers courses in a number of areas including supervisory development. One such program covers a number of topics. For example, the nature of management and the managerial functions of planning, organizing, directing, and controlling are presented. Also, communications, leadership, motivation, and decision making are featured.[9]

Numerous universities provide management training and development programs for industry, as they are often staffed with capable faculty and have adequate facilities. At times, colleges and universities possess expertise not available within organizations. Another possible advantage is that T&D programs may be provided at less expense. In some cases, it is advantageous for academicians and management practitioners to jointly present T&D programs.

Regardless of whether programs are presented in-house or by an outside source, a number of methods are utilized in imparting knowledge to managers. A discussion of these methods follows.

Coaching

Coaching is an on-the-job approach to management development in which the manager—on a one-to-one basis—is given an opportunity to teach by example. Some firms create "Assistant to" positions for this purpose. An individual placed in this type of staff position becomes an understudy to his or her boss. In addition to having the opportunity to observe, the subordinate will also be assigned significant tasks requiring decision-making skills. To be pro-

[9]Debra Gottheimer, "A Manager's Training Film Festival," *Administrative Management*, vol. 38, no. 7 (July 1977): 25.

255

Chapter 8
Training and
Development:
Micro-Level
Approaches

ductive, coach/counselor managers must have a thorough knowledge of the job as it relates to the firm's goals. They should also have a strong desire to share information with the understudy and be willing to take the time—which can be considerable—for this endeavor. The relationship between the supervisor and subordinate must be based on mutual trust and confidence.

Business Games

Simulations which represent actual business situations are referred to as **business games**. These simulations attempt to duplicate selected parts of a particular situation which are then manipulated by the participants.[10] Business games involve two or more hypothetical organizations competing in a given product market. The participants are assigned such roles as president, controller, and marketing vice president. They make decisions affecting price levels, production volume, and inventory levels. The results of their decisions are manipulated by a computer program with the results simulating those in an actual business situation. Participants are able to see how their decisions affect other groups and vice versa. The best part about learning in this environment is that if you make a decision which costs the company $1 million, you won't lose your job.

Case Study

When the **case study** is used, the student is provided with a simulated business problem. The individual is expected to study the information given in the case and make decisions based upon the situation. If the student is provided a case involving an actual company, he or she would be expected to research the firm to gain a better appreciation of its financial condition and environment. Typically, the case study method is used in the classroom with an instructor who performs as a facilitator.

Conference Method

The **conference method,** or discussion method, is a widely used instructional approach which can be highly effective. The purpose of this method is to bring together individuals with common interests to discuss and attempt to solve problems. Often the leader of the group is the supervisor. The group leader's role is to keep the discussion on course and avoid some people's tendency to get off the subject. As problems are discussed, he or she listens and tries to permit group members to solve their own problems. When this is not possible, the group leader may serve as a facilitator of learning. Individuals engaged in

---

[10]Larry C. Coppard, "Gaming Simulation and the Training Process," in *Training and Development Handbook: A Guide to Human Resources Development,* 2d ed., ed. Robert I. Craig (New York: McGraw-Hill Book Company, 1976), pp. 40–42.

257

Chapter 8
Training and
Development:
Micro-Level
Approaches

"A student should determine if he or she wants to specialize in a field like labor relations or industrial relations or instead be a generalist in the personnel field. Besides taking all the coursework offered, practical work experience during the summer or an internship is a decided advantage."

**Richard A. Morse, Recruitment Associate
Shell Oil Company**

the conference method may not even perceive that they are in training. They are working to solve problems which are occurring in their everyday activity.

Behavior Modeling[11]

A training process permitting managers to receive training in interpersonal skills is called **behavior modeling**. More than three hundred companies—including such giants as Exxon, Westinghouse, Union Carbide, and Federated Department Stores—are now using it. In this technique, videotapes are prepared specifically to illustrate how managers function in various situations. The trainees then observe the "model's" actions. For example, a supervisor may act out his or her role in disciplining an employee who has been consistently late in reporting to work. Since the situations presented are typical of their firm's problems, the participants are able to relate the behavior to their own jobs. Although it is a relatively new approach, behavior modeling seems to have outstanding potential as a training and development method.

In-Basket Training

When **in-basket training** is used, the participant is given a number of business papers such as memoranda, reports, and telephone messages that would typically come across a manager's desk. The papers, presented in no particular order, call for actions ranging from urgent to routine handling. The participant is required to act on the information contained in these papers. Prioritizing each particular matter is initially required.

Internships

In an **internship** program involving university students, students divide their time between attending classes and working for an organization. From the employer's point of view, the internship provides an excellent means of viewing

[11]Bernard L. Rosenbaum, "Common Misconceptions About Behavior Modeling and Supervisory Skill Training (SST)," *Training and Development Journal* 33 (August 1979): 40–44.

a potential permanent employee at work. The internship normally provides much more information than can be obtained in an employment interview. Management is then in a better position to make selection and placement decisions.

Internships also provide advantages for students. The experience they obtain through working enables them to integrate theory learned in the classroom with the practice of management. At the same time, interns may gain knowledge of the organization which will help them determine whether the firm would be a good place to work.

Role Playing

Role playing is a technique in which some problem—real or imaginary—involving human interaction is presented and then spontaneously acted out.[12] Participants may assume the roles of specific organizational members in a given situation and then act out their roles. For example, a trainee might be assigned the role of a supervisor who is required to discipline an employee for excessive absences. Another participant would assume the role of the employee. The individual in the supervisory role would then proceed to take whatever action is deemed appropriate. This action then provides the basis for discussion and comments by the group. Role reversal—an exchange of roles by the participants—is an effective version of role playing. This exchange provides trainees with a different perspective of the problem. It helps them to develop empathy, a quality vitally needed by managers.

Job Rotation

Job rotation involves moving employees from one job to another for the purpose of providing them with broader experiences. This added knowledge may be needed for performing higher level tasks. Consider this example:

> Roy Reid's firm is grooming him to fill the position of plant controller at the company's new branch plant. Roy is expected to assume his new responsibilities within the next six months. In preparing Roy for his new job, the vice president for finance and the personnel director have decided that he needs additional experience in credit operations and accounts receivable. They have scheduled him to spend three months in each of these departments prior to his move to the new plant.

As might be expected, Roy's temporary assignment will not make him an expert in either area. He will, however, gain an overview of these functions which will assist him in his new position.

There are several potential problems related to job rotation. Individuals are often not permitted to remain on a job long enough to really learn its es-

[12]Wallace Wohlking, "Role Playing," in *Training and Development Handbook: A Guide to Human Resources Development*, 2nd ed., ed. Robert I. Craig (New York: McGraw-Hill Book Company, 1976), p. 36–1.

sential elements. Because these assignments are typically temporary, individuals may not be very productive during this time. In fact, they may even be detrimental to the productivity of the work group. In addition, department employees who witness an individual coming aboard on a job rotation basis may jealously resent the so-called "fair-haired" employee.

259

Chapter 8
Training and
Development:
Micro-Level
Approaches

Programmed Instruction

A teaching method which provides instruction without the intervention of an instructor is called **programmed instruction** (PI).[13] In PI, information is broken down into small portions (frames). The learner reads each frame in sequence and responds to questions, receiving immediate feedback as to response accuracy. If correct, the learner proceeds to the next frame. If not, the learner repeats the frame. Primary features of this approach are immediate reinforcement and the ability of learners to proceed at their own pace. Programmed instruction material may be presented in a book or in more sophisticated forms, such as teaching machines which mechanically advance frames.

Computer Assisted Instruction

An extension of programmed instruction concepts is **computer assisted instruction** (CAI). The speed, memory, and data manipulation capabilities of the computer permit greater utilization of basic PI concepts. For example, the student's response may determine the difficulty level of the next frame.

The increased speed of presentation plus a lesser dependence on an instructor are advantages of both PI and CAI. However, some students object to the absence of a human. Another primary disadvantage is the cost of developing programs. One source estimated that up to two hundred hours of preparation time is required for each hour of CAI student instruction.[14] However, if there is a sufficient number of trainees, the cost may quickly reach an acceptable level. It appears that CAI is much more than a fad. A recent survey indicated that more than 20 percent of training departments use it.[15]

Classroom Lecture

The classroom lecture provides effective employee training in certain areas. A great deal of information may be transmitted in a relatively short time. The lecture seems to be most appropriate when new information is to be presented.

[13]Leonard Silvern, "Training: Man-Man and Man-Machine Communications," in *Systems Psychology*, ed. Kenyon De Greene (New York: McGraw-Hill Book Company, 1970), p. 383.
[14]Walter Goodman and Thomas F. Gould, *New York State Conference on Instructional Uses of the Computer: Final Report*, U.S. Educational Resources Information Center, ERIC Document ED 035 291, 1968.
[15]William R. Neher and Leopold Hauser III, "How Computers Can Help Adults Overcome the Fear of Learning," *Training: The Magazine of Human Resources Development* 19 (February 1982): 49.

The passive role of students is perhaps the major disadvantage of the typical lecture. Lecture effectiveness can be improved when groups are small enough to permit discussion. The instructor's ability to capture the imagination of the class is another significant factor. Also, lectures can be assisted through timely and appropriate use of audio-visual equipment (AV).

MANAGEMENT DEVELOPMENT PROGRAMS AT IBM

At IBM, formal management development programs are conducted for three groups of individuals: new managers, middle managers, and executives. These groups are described as follows:

- New Managers—those appointed to their first level of management responsibility.
- Middle Managers—those whose responsibility it is to manage managers.
- Executives—those who have reached executive-level positions and those who are considered to have potential for such responsibility.

An overview of the programs provided for these management groups is provided in Figure 8–2. In addition to providing training early in the manager's career, IBM emphasizes regular and continuous development. Annual training programs have been initiated to ensure that managers at all levels have an opportunity to receive at least one week of formal training each year.

TRAINING FOR ENTRY-LEVEL PROFESSIONAL EMPLOYEES

As previously mentioned, firms have a special interest in college-trained employees hired for entry-level professional positions, including management trainees. As an example, General Electric has programs which are conducted for new employees in numerous fields. One such program is their Information Systems Manufacturing Program (ISMP). ISMP is a two-year program combining rotational work assignments with graduate level seminars. It prepares employees to design, program, and implement integrated computerized and manual information systems.

GE's ISMP emphasizes challenging work assignments in such areas as programming, systems analysis and design, computer center operation, project management, and functional work. The length of these assignments varies and individual progress is determined by employee performance and demonstrated potential.

Figure 8–2. **IBM's management development programs.**

New Manager School

All individuals appointed to the initial level of management responsibility, after receiving basic orientation to their job by their immediate managers, are enrolled, usually within one month, in a one-week basic training program.

The objectives of this training are:

Developing a deeper awareness of the basic policies and practices by which the company is managed.

Learning the practical application of these policies and practices.

Acquiring the basic management concepts, skills and techniques.

Included in the program are such subjects as A Business and Its Beliefs, Performance Planning, Counseling and Evaluation, and Managing Individuals.

Middle Management Training

Individuals newly appointed to the responsibility of managing managers attend, usually within ninety days, a week-long program.

The objectives of such training are:

Defining the role of the manager of managers.

Learning the organization, delegation, and control skills required of this level of management.

Understanding the interrelationship of the various business functions within the company.

Acquiring a knowledge of, and appreciation for, the issues and challenges of the business environment.

Included in the program are such subjects as Transition to Middle Management, Business Management Issues, People Management, and Leadership Styles.

Executive Development

Managers who have been appointed to executive-level positions, and those identified as having potential to be promoted to such positions, receive formal training at internally conducted programs as well as out-company programs.

The earliest of this series of company-conducted internal programs is scheduled within a year of the individual being included in the executive resource category. These classes, usually of three to four weeks duration, have objectives related to these areas:

The IBM Company: its organization, missions, management system; its policies, practices, and strategies; and its current issues and challenges.

Management Practices: leadership and decision making, general management concepts, functional integration, and management of change.

External Environment: international economic, political, and social changes; the current relationship of business, government, and other institutions.

Included in the programs are such courses as Finance, Marketing, Personnel, Environmental Analysis and Strategic Thinking, Goals and Means of Our Economy, and Business Ethics.

In addition, individuals attend external training programs conducted by colleges, universities, and other institutions. Such programs include concentration on general management, leadership, government relations, and the humanities. Attendance at such internal and external executive development programs is scheduled at intervals to complement on-the-job experiences.

Source: Used with the permission of International Business Machines Corporation.

Candidates for ISMP must have taken at least two computer science courses in college and have bachelor's degrees in one of the following majors or related fields: computer science, industrial engineering, accounting, mathematics, business administration, industrial management, or management information systems. Selection to the ISMP is based on a careful review of the employee's course curriculum, academic records, leadership in extra-curricular activities, and work experience.

Other training programs for college graduates may have more or less structure than GE's ISMP. However, most other programs also emphasize training provided on-the-job. "Hands on" experience, alone or in combination with other methods, appears to be an essential component.

TRAINING FOR OPERATIVE EMPLOYEES

Unlike managers, operative employees do not make their contribution to the firm through the efforts of other people. They are, always, the "other people." Their contribution is direct and, collectively, of utmost significance to any organization. Organizations rely heavily upon their executive secretaries, senior clerks, leadmen, and other individuals occupying operative positions. Every position in an organization is necessary or it would not (or should not) exist. Therefore, training and development for operative employees must also be given high priority by firms.

In this section we will present T&D methods which apply to the training of operative employees. However, as you remember, these are not the only available methods. You may recall that Figure 8–2 listed methods which are available to both management and operative employees.

On-the-Job Training (OJT)

A supervisor once told a young applicant, "We have the best training program in our industry. Our company emphasizes OJT." This reply led the applicant to believe the firm had a formal training program. Actually, with **on-the-job training,** the person learns job tasks by actually performing them.

Although some may not consider OJT a separate method, it is the most commonly used approach to T&D. With OJT, there is no problem in later transferring what has been learned to the task. Individuals may also be more highly motivated to learn because they are acquiring knowledge needed to perform their jobs. At times, however, the emphasis on production may tend to detract from the training process. The trainee may feel pressure to perform to the point where learning is negatively affected. To improve the effectiveness of OJT, three requirements must be kept in mind:

1. OJT is a joint effort involving both the superior and the subordinate.

2. The superior is responsible for creating a climate of trust.
3. The superior must be a good listener.[16]

263

Chapter 8
Training and
Development:
Micro-Level
Approaches

Apprenticeship Training

One approach to operative training is **apprenticeship training**. This method combines classroom and on-the-job training and is traditionally used in craft jobs such as plumber, barber, carpenter, machinist, and printer. While in training, the employee earns less than the master craftsperson who is the instructor. The training period varies according to the craft, as you see in Table 8–3. For instance, the apprenticeship training for barbers is two years while machinists take four years, and pattern makers five years.

Simulators

Simulators are training devices of varying degrees of complexity which duplicate the "real world." They range from simple paper mock-ups of mechnical devices to computerized simulations of total environments. T&D specialists often simulate sales counters, automobiles, and airplanes.[17] While simulator training may be less valuable than on-the-job training for some purposes, it

Table 8–3. Selected apprenticeable occupations classified by length of apprenticeship

Two years	Barber Cosmetician	Four years	Boilermaker Carpenter
Two to three years	Brewer Butcher Roofer		Machinist Printing pressman Tailor
Two to four years	Bindery worker	Four to five years	Electrical worker
Three years	Baker Bricklayer Photographer		Lithographer Mailer
		Four to eight years	Die sinker
Three to four years	Airplane mechanic Leatherworker	Five years	Lead burner Pattern maker
	Operating engineer Sheet-metal worker	Five to six years	Electrotyper Photoengraver
Three to five years	Draftsman-designer		Stereotyper

Source: U.S. Department of Labor. *The National Apprenticeship Program.* (Washington, D.C.: U.S. Government Printing Office, 1972), pp. 9–27.

[16]Delbert W. Fisher, "Educational Psychology Involved in On–The–Job Training," *Personnel Journal* 56 (October 1977): 519.
[17]Dugan Laird, *Approaches to Training and Development* (Reading, Mass.: Addison-Wesley Publishing Company, 1978): 206–7.

provides certain advantages. A prime example is the training of airline pilots; simulated training crashes neither take lives nor deplete the firm's fleet of jets.

Vestibule Training

Vestibule training utilizes equipment which closely resembles the actual equipment used on the job. However, the training takes place away from the production area. For example, a group of lathes may be located in a training center where the trainees will be instructed in their use. A primary advantage of vestibule training is that it removes the employee from the pressure of having to produce while learning. The emphasis is on learning the skills required by the job.

USE AND SUCCESS OF VARIOUS T&D METHODS

Selecting an appropriate method is a crucial step in developing any training program. To aid in this decision, some insight is provided by a study of training directors' perceptions. These specialists were employed by the 200 U.S.

Table 8–4. Training directors' ratings of effectiveness of alternative training methods for various training objectives

Training Method	Knowledge Acquisition Mean Rank	Changing Attitudes Mean Rank	Problem- Solving Skills Mean Rank	Inter- personal Skills Mean Rank	Participant Acceptance Mean Rank	Knowledge Retention Mean Rank
Case study	4	5	1	5	1	4
Conference (discussion) method	1	3	5	4	5	2
Lecture (with questions)	8	7	7	8	8	3
Business games	5	4	2	3	2	7
Movie films	6	6	9	6	4	5
Programmed instruction	3	8	6	7	9	1
Role playing	2	2	3	1	3	5
Sensitivity training (T-group)	7	1	4	2	6	9
Television lecture	9	9	8	9	7	8

Note: 1 = highest rank
Source: Adapted from John W. Newstrom, "Evaluating the Effectiveness of Training Methods," p. 58. Reprinted from the January 1980 issue of *Personnel Administrator,* 30 Park Drive, Berea, OH 44017.

Table 8–5. Frequency of use of instructional methods

265

Chapter 8
Training and
Development:
Micro-Level
Approaches

	Number of Using Firms	Percent of Firms in Study
Lectures	99	73
Discussions	98	73
Reading books	39	29
Textbooks	108	80
Films/audio-visual materials	15	11
Cases	54	40
Incidents	36	27
Experiential exercises	46	34
Guest speakers	7	5
Internships/co-op programs	7	5

Source: Adapted from "Newsletter of Personnel/Human Resources Division," Academy of Management, Volume 3, Issue 1 (December, 1978), p. 3. (Reprinted by permission.)

firms identified by *Forbes* as having the largest number of employees. The results of this study may be seen in Table 8–4.

The case study was ranked highest for both *Problem-Solving Skills* and *Participant Acceptance*. The conference (discussion) method topped the list for *Knowledge Acquisition*. Programmed instruction was rated best for *Knowledge Retention*. Role playing was ranked highest for *Interpersonal Skills* and was perceived as being the best overall method. Sensitivity training, while no longer a popular training method, topped the list for *Changing Attitudes*. The most-criticized lecture method generally did not fare well. However, it was ranked a respectable "3" for *Knowledge Retention*, following only programmed instruction and the conference method for this training goal. The television lecture was rated the poorest overall method. Generally, methods requiring participant involvement were rated higher than those requiring a more passive role.

Another study revealed the frequency of instructional methods usage (see Table 8–5). Comparing the results of this study to the one just mentioned, the lecture method (rated low for most training objectives) is apparently one of the most frequently used instructional methods. On the other hand, the highly rated methods of role playing and case study are used much less. (It is assumed that role playing is included as part of experiential exercises.)

TRAINING AND DEVELOPMENT MEDIA

Many organizations have found it beneficial to utilize various forms of media to enhance training program effectiveness. As used in this context, **media** are special methods of communicating ideas and concepts. These media include

Table 8–6. Audio-visual media

Films

Films are heavily relied upon because of their versatility. Films can combine many elements such as color, motion, action, plot, and musical scoring. Films provide a wide range of topics available for rental at a relatively low cost but are very expensive for an organization to produce.

Filmstrips

A series of still pictures, usually 35 mm, on a strip of film may be accompanied by a sound program using records, cassette tapes, etc. Each picture may be advanced manually or automatically depending on the projector and the system. The production cost is much less than for films.

Slide Projectors

Slide projectors are commonly used, with slide-tape presentations becoming more popular. In these programs, the projector may be advanced automatically by an inaudible signal from one stereo channel.

Overhead and Opaque Projectors

An overhead projector, providing an image on a screen by passing light through a transparency, can be used to provide colorful visual presentations. The trainer can maintain eye contact in an undarkened room and the trainees may take notes.

An opaque projector does not require transparencies but can project from opaques such as organizational charts or pages from a book.

Audio Tapes

While there are several types of audio tape systems on the market, the compact cassette is becoming increasingly popular. The running time varies from sixty minutes (thirty minutes per side) to two hours.

Video

The instant-replay capability of video makes it a potentially valuable medium for use in training programs. Most of the advantages of film are inherent in video but, as with film, costs may be a factor; especially the secondary costs associated with production, maintenance, operating personnel, etc.

Flip Charts, Chalkboards, and Slap Boards

These relatively inexpensive pieces of equipment can assist the trainer in emphasizing major points. A new type of chalkboard permits the use of a colored ink pen which may be easily erased.

Source: Adapted from O'Sullivan, Devin, "Audiovisuals and the Training Process," *Training and Development Handbook, A Guide to Human Resource Development, Second Edition,* edited by Robert L. Craig (New York: McGraw-Hill Book Company, 1976). (Reprinted by permission.)

videotapes, films, closed-circuit television, slide projectors, overhead and opaque projectors, flip charts, chalkboards, and slap boards.

While some critics have referred to audio-visual aids as "gadgetry for its own sake," these devices have filled a useful role in training and development programs.[18] Criticism of the use of audio-visual aids is placed in proper perspective when you realize that approximately 75 percent of what you learn is by sight while about 75 percent of what you hear is forgotten within two days.[19] These facts underlie the importance of using visual aids in training programs. Consider, for instance, the impact a film might have in dramatizing the role of informal groups as they affect the formal organization.

[18]Max H. Forster, "Training and Development Programs, Methods, and Facilities," in *ASPA Handbook of Personnel and Industrial Relations: Training and Development,* ed. Dale Yoder and Herbert G. Heneman, Jr. (Washington, D.C.: The Bureau of National Affairs, Inc.), 1977, pp. 5–53.

[19]Martin M. Broadwell, *The Supervisor as an Instructor,* 3rd ed. (Reading, Mass.: Addison-Wesley Publishing Company, 1978), p. 85.

An overview of the various forms and uses of audio-visual media may be seen in Table 8–6. Audio-visual aids are valuable supplements to training methods. For example, a lecture might be greatly enhanced by use of an overhead projector or a short film. These various media can assist in gaining and maintaining trainee interest and attention. Audio-visual media are not mutually exclusive. The use of more than one type of audio-visual aid (multimedia) may be appropriate for many training sessions. An example would be the use of a slide-tape presentation.

267

Chapter 8
Training and
Development:
Micro-Level
Approaches

IMPLEMENTATION OF T&D PROGRAMS

A perfectly conceived training program can fail if the participants are not sold on its merits. They must be convinced that the program has value and that it will assist them in achieving their personal and professional goals. The credibility of T&D specialists may come only after a string of successful programs.

The implementation of T&D programs is often difficult. One of the reasons is that many managers are action oriented and frequently say they are too busy to engage in training efforts. As one management development executive stated, "Most busy executives are too involved chopping down the proverbial tree to stop for the purpose of sharpening their axes. . . ." Another difficulty in program implementation is that qualified trainers must be available. In addition to possessing communications skills, the trainers must know the company's philosophy, its objectives, its formal and informal organization, and the training program's goals. Training and development requires a higher degree of creativity than perhaps any other personnel specialty.

In implementing a new program it is very important that it be monitored carefully, especially during the initial phases. Training implies change which, as we know, is often vigorously resisted. There are some who may even sit back waiting, perhaps even hoping, that the program will fail. Participant feedback is vital at this stage because there will be "bugs" in any new program. The sooner these problems are solved, the better the chances for success.

The T&D manager has specific problems associated with implementation. For example, it is often difficult to schedule the training around present work requirements. Unless the employee is new to the firm, he or she probably has prescribed duties to perform. Although it is the line manager's job to have positions covered while an employee is in training, the T&D manager must assist with this problem.

Another difficulty in implementing T&D programs is record keeping. For instance, records need to be maintained as to how well the trainee performed in the training. This information may prove beneficial as the trainee progresses in the company.

When the training is conducted outside the organization, considerable coordination must take place. Consider the magnitude of this problem if managers are coming from all parts of the country to participate in a T&D program in Houston, Texas. The logistics involved in this type of undertaking can be significant, and Personnel is typically charged with the responsibility.

The credibility of T&D is greatly enhanced when it can be shown that the organization has benefited tangibly. Also, effective training directors will attempt to evaluate all their training efforts.[20] Organizations have taken several approaches in attempting to determine the worth of specific programs. These involve evaluations of: (1) participants' opinion of the program, (2) the extent to which they have learned the material, (3) their ability to apply the new knowledge, and (4) whether the stated training goals have been achieved.

Evaluation of training programs is often attempted by determining how well the participants enjoyed training sessions. This information helps T&D specialists to fine tune the program. However, results of these inquiries may not always reflect a high degree of objectivity. For example, Charlie Dixon has just completed a three-day executive seminar in Honolulu. At the conclusion of the program, Charlie was given a brief questionnaire which, in essence, asked him if the seminar was beneficial. It is difficult to imagine Charlie or any of his fellow participants downgrading this training program. Even if it had been conducted in a less exotic location, a brief break from the hectic pace of an executive's job can be a welcome relief. Participants' perceptions of the value of such programs should be viewed in proper perspective.

Some organizations resort to administering tests in an attempt to determine what participants in a training program have learned. The most widely accepted evaluation procedure is referred to as the _pre-test/post-test, control group design._[21] This procedure requires that the same test be used before and after training. It also calls for both a control group (which does not receive the training) and an experimental group (which does). Trainees are randomly assigned to each group. Differences that are shown to exist between the pre- and post-tests and between groups are then attributed to the training provided.

While tests may provide fairly accurate indications of what has been learned, they give little insight into desired behavioral changes. For example, it is one thing for a manager to learn about motivational techniques. It is quite another matter for this same individual to apply the new knowledge.

> Max Johnson sat in the front row at the supervisory training seminar his company sponsored. The primary topic of the program was delegation of authority. As the lecturer made each point regarding effective delegation techniques, Max would nod his head in agreement. He thoroughly understood what was being said over the three-day period of the seminar. At the end of the program, Max returned to his department and continued the management style he had followed for ten years—a style which involved little delegation of authority. Max had learned the material presented in the seminar, but the learning of the material in this instance was of little value to the organization.

Still another approach to the evaluation of T&D programs involves determining the extent to which stated training goals have been achieved. For in-

[20]Donald L. Kirkpatrick, "Evaluation of Training," in _Training and Development Handbook: A Guide to Human Resources Development,_ 2d ed., ed. Robert I. Craig (New York: McGraw-Hill Book Company, 1976), p. 18–1.
[21]John H. Zenger and Kenneth Hargis, "Assessing Training Results: It's Time to Take the Plunge!" _Training and Development Journal_ 36 (January 1982): 13–14.

stance, if the goal of an accident prevention program is to reduce the number and severity of accidents by 15 percent, a comparison of accident rates before and after training provides useful evaluation data. However, many programs dealing with broader topics are somewhat more difficult to evaluate. A group of executives may, for example, be sent to a state university for a one-week course in management and leadership development. "Before" and "after" performance appraisals of the participants may be available. Yet, a number of other factors could impact the managers' performance following the training. The managers may actually be better prepared to perform their jobs, but other variables may distort the picture. For instance, a mild recession forces the lay-off of several key employees; a competing firm's success in luring away one of the department's top engineers or the company president could pressure the employment director to hire an incompetent relative. These and many other factors could cause the performance level of the group to decline, even though the managers had benefited from the training.

In evaluating training programs, a past president of the American Society for Training and Development suggested that you should strive for proof that the program is effective. But, at times, evidence of a sound program is sufficient and proof is not possible.[22] Nevertheless, in spite of problems associated with evaluation, Personnel must continue to strive for solid evidence of T&D's contributions in achieving organizational goals.

269

Chapter 8
Training and
Development:
Micro-Level
Approaches

SUPERVISORY TRAINING PROGRAM: AN ILLUSTRATION

Numerous firms conduct supervisory training programs. They view this training as necessary if their first-line managers are to perform to their maximum potential. An overview of a supervisory training program developed by Chevron U.S.A., Inc. for their first-level managers is shown in Figure 8–3. This program is designed to provide new supervisors with skills and knowledge needed to manage people. The training program is also available to long-service supervisors to update their knowledge. The program has three phases: pre-session activities; a five-day, live-in session; and post-session activities.

Several weeks prior to the live-in session, participants are asked to engage in activities that will prepare them for program involvement. The participants are asked to do the following:

1. Identify their productive and nonproductive activities
2. Discuss the basic elements of their jobs with their bosses
3. Select a major opportunity or problem that both the participant and the boss are committed to deal with (this becomes an Action Plan)
4. Send a sample of an employee evaluation to the training program coordinator

[22]Donald L. Kirkpatrick, "Evaluating Training Programs: Evidence vs. Proof," *Training and Development Journal* 31, no. 11 (November 1977): 12.

Five-Day, Live-In Session Activities

Presession Activities	Support Subjects	Key Course Subjects	Program Evaluation	Postsession Activities
Time Analysis	Why We Are Here	Performance Planning and Review	Formulate an Action Plan Project	Approval and Implementation of an Action Plan Project
Work Analysis	Analyzing Performance Problems	Documentation Skills		
Performance Planning Discussion	Training	Employee Ranking	Rank Session's Topics	Possible Performance Planning and Review Discussions
Selecting an Action Plan Project	Special Health Services	Salary Administration	Evaluate Program	Follow-up Questionnaire to Participant and Boss
Writing a Performance Evaluation	Time Management	Employee Development		
Interview with Coordinator	Employment Compliance			
Time:	Time:	Time:	Time:	Time:
Completed Prior to Start of Program	1 1/2 days	2 1/2 days	1 day	2–4 months after program

Figure 8–3. An overview of Chevron U.S.A., Inc.'s supervisory training program.

The five-day live-in session comprises the heart of the program. It begins on a Sunday night with a social get-together, dinner, and business meeting. Participants are asked to tell briefly about their jobs and discuss their Action Plan. A top management member meets with the group during this initial meeting to discuss the role of the supervisor, the purpose of the program, and what on-job results are expected.

271

Chapter 8
Training and
Development:
Micro-Level
Approaches

During this main session, a number of support subjects and key course subjects are presented. At the same time, information is provided concerning laws, company policies and practices, and situations which affect typical decisions. A brief description of the purposes of support subjects and key course subjects are presented in Table 8–7. Action Plan Projects are worked with during the program evaluation. The results of these projects are used to measure the program's value.

The post-session phase of Chevron's Supervisory Training Program consists of implementing the Action Plan. Further attempts are also made to relate the program's impact to the supervisor's job performance. At this point, train-

Table 8–7. Chevron U.S.A., Inc.'s supervisory training program's purpose for a five-day live-in session

Support Subjects	Key Course Subjects
Why We Are Here	*Performance Planning and Review*
To orient participants with top management views of the role of a supervisor, the purpose of this program, and what on-job results are expected to occur.	To increase supervisory productivity and efficiency by creating better: • Communications • Understanding of the job • Planning and allocation of time • Data for evaluating employees' work performance
Analyzing Performance Problems	
To provide supervisors with the skills necessary to analyze a performance discrepancy so that they can determine the best solution.	*Documentation Skills*
	To improve writing skills of supervisors in order that they may better manage their human resources
Training	
To provide supervisors with the skill and knowledge to effectively train others.	*Employee Ranking*
	To provide supervisors with the skill and knowledge needed to objectively evaluate employee performance on the job.
Special Health Services	
To provide supervisors with an expanded awareness of their responsibilities in the area of Special Health Services and with information and skills to deal with the troubled employee.	*Salary Administration*
	To review the basics of salary administration so that supervisors can provide meaningful inputs to higher management and provide feedback to employees about salary decisions.
Time Management	
To provide skills in how to better manage and use time.	*Employee Development*
Employment Compliance	To assist supervisors in their role of developing employees both within their current jobs and for future jobs as appropriate.
To teach supervisors the value of consistent personnel practices and the skills to apply them, as well as the intent of EEO legal requirements.	

Source: Used with the permission of Chevron U.S.A., Inc.

ing needs which are not being met are emphasized. Appropriate changes are made to ensure that the training program maintains practical worth to both the employee and the company.

COST/BENEFITS ANALYSIS— TRAINING AND DEVELOPMENT

The purpose of training and development is to improve employee competency levels and the organization work environment, and the overall focus should be on increasing productivity within the firm. If this objective is to be accomplished, there will be various costs involved. Individuals must be available to conduct the training. Workers who are being trained may not be available to perform their normal work activities. Training may actually disrupt, and temporarily lower, a unit's productivity level. In addition, there will likely be a need for continuous monitoring of the T&D function. Decisions have to be made regarding what type of training to provide and to whom.

But, the benefits of an effective T&D program far outweigh the costs. Every area of human resources management is affected. A firm that has gained a reputation for having a good T&D program will likely experience better results in their recruitment efforts, thereby being able to select better qualified employees. Most individuals enjoy the prospect of having an opportunity to grow and develop on their job.

In addition, as was mentioned earlier in the book, compensation involves more than merely the money in a person's paycheck. Many workers may view an effective T&D program as part of the compensation package. Health and safety also benefit from T&D. As workers are trained, a safer, healthier work environment may develop.

Finally, T&D typically has a major impact upon employees and labor relations. Should a firm desire to remain nonunion, all managers must be trained and developed to incorporate the philosophy of remaining nonunion. Supervisors need to have the necessary behavioral skills to deal with today's workers.

SUMMARY

The term "training" may be used to describe methods for influencing the knowledge needed to improve current job performance. Development is often viewed as dealing with predicted future needs and efforts to prepare individuals so they can keep pace with the organization as it changes and grows. Education deals with possible future needs aimed at preparing employees for higher level positions in the firm.

The external and internal environment can exert considerable pressure upon the training and development process. Shifts in the environment necessitate change. Once specific needs for change have been identified, the next phase entails determining training needs and objectives. The appropriate methods and media which will accomplish the stated goals are next determined. The real implementation of the T&D program comes when change actually occurs. Any successful training and development program must be a dynamic, ongoing process.

273

Chapter 8
Training and
Development:
Micro-Level
Approaches

Management development programs help managers remain attuned to the latest knowledge in their various fields and capable of managing an ever changing work force within a dynamic environment. These programs are offered through in-house programs, professional organizations, or colleges and universities. Some management development methods include: on-the-job training, business games, case studies, conference method, behavior modeling, in-basket training, internships, role playing, job rotation, programmed instruction, computer assisted instruction, and classroom lecture. Unlike managers, operative employees do not make their contribution to the firm through the efforts of other people. Some of the means of training operative employees include apprenticeship training, simulators, and vestibule training.

Effective training directors will attempt to evaluate all their training efforts. Organizations have taken several approaches in attempting to determine the worth of specific programs. These involve: (1) an inquiry into the participants' enjoyment of the program, (2) the extent to which they have learned the material, (3) their ability to apply the new knowledge, and (4) whether the stated training goals have been achieved.

Questions for Review

1. Define the terms *training, development,* and *education.*

2. Describe the training and development process.

3. What is the role of Personnel in training and development?

4. Describe management development. Why is it important to a firm?

5. List and define the primary methods used in management development.

6. What training methods are used primarily to train operative employees?

7. Describe the major factors that should be considered in the implementation of training and development programs.

8. What are some major means by which training and development programs are evaluated? Discuss.

Terms for Review

Training
Development
Education
Management development
Coaching
Business games
Case study
Conference method
Behavior modeling
In-basket training

Internship
Role playing
Job rotation
Programmed instruction
Computer assisted instruction
On-the-job training
Apprenticeship training
Simulators
Vestibule training
Media

"I'm a little discouraged," said Susan Matthews to the training officer. "I keep making mistakes running the new printing press. It's a lot more complicated than the one I operated before and I just can't seem to get the hang of it." "Well, Susan," responded George Duncan, "Maybe you're just not cut out for the job. You know that we sent you to the two-week refresher course in Atlanta to get you more familiar with the new equipment." "Yes," said Susan. "They had modern equipment at the school but it wasn't anything like this machine." "What about the factory rep," asked George. "Didn't he spend some time with you?" "No, I was on vacation at that time," said Susan. "Have you asked your boss to get him back for a day or two?" "I asked him," said Susan, "but he said training was your responsibility. That's why I'm here." After she was gone George got a yellow legal pad and began to write a letter to the printing press manufacturer.

Questions

1. What steps in the training and development process had the company neglected?
2. Is George taking the proper action? What would you do?
3. Who should have primary responsibility for training and development? Why is this true?

_____

As the initial training session began, John Robertson, the hospital administrator, spoke of the tremendous benefits he expected from the management development program the hospital was starting. He also complimented Brenda Short, the personnel director, for her efforts in arranging the program. As he finished his five minute talk, he said, "I'm not sure what Brenda has in store for you, but I know that management development is important, and I'll expect each of you to put forth your best efforts to make it work." Mr. Robertson then excused himself from the meeting and turned the program over to Brenda.

For several years Brenda had been trying to convince Mr. Robertson that the supervisors could benefit from a management development program. She believed that many problems within the hospital were management-related. Reluctantly, Mr. Robertson had agreed to authorize funds to employ a consultant. Through employee interviews and a self-administered questionnaire completed by the supervisors, the consultant attempted to identify development needs. The consultant recommended twelve four-hour sessions emphasizing communication, leadership, and motivation. Each session was to be repeated once so that supervisors who missed the first session could attend the second.

Mr. Robertson had signed the memo which Brenda prepared directing that all supervisors support the management development program. There was considerable grumbling, but all the supervisors agreed to attend. As Brenda replaced Mr. Robertson on the podium, she could sense the lack of interest in the room.

Questions

1. Have there been any serious errors up to this point in the management development program? What would you have done differently?

2. What advice do you have for Brenda at this point to help make the program more effective?

Chapter Objectives

1. Define the process of career planning and development.
2. Describe factors affecting career planning.
3. Explain the importance of individual career planning and how conducting a thorough self-assessment is crucial to career planning.
4. Explain the nature of career planning.
5. Relate the importance of career planning from an organization's viewpoint.
6. Discuss career paths and identify methods of organization career planning and development.

Chapter 9 _____

Career Planning and Development

Bob Allen and Thelma Gowen, both supervisors at Sharpco Industries, were speaking to each other one day last week. Bob said, "I'm really frustrated. I spoke with the boss last week about career opportunities at Sharpco and all he kept saying was, 'there are all kinds of opportunities.' I need more than that. I'm not sure if I want to spend my life in production or if there are better career opportunities." Thelma replied, "I'm having the same trouble. He told me that 'the sky was the limit.' I'd like to know where I might end up if I decide to stay with Sharpco."

It seems obvious from the above discussion that Sharpco Industries has no career planning and development program. Bob is frustrated and Thelma wants to know what career avenues are available to her. Lacking this knowledge, they may decide not to remain with Sharpco. Career planning and development is important to both the individual and the company to ensure that people with the necessary skills and experiences will be available when needed.

In this chapter we will first introduce the concept of career planning and development. Next, some factors affecting career planning will be identified. The nature of career planning will then be described. This will be followed by a discussion of individual career planning and a section on the reasons why organizations get involved in career planning. Types of career planning that organizations conduct will then be described followed by a section on methods used in career planning and development. Finally, we will discuss how a person might begin a career in Personnel.

CAREER PLANNING AND DEVELOPMENT DEFINED

When we were children people asked, "What are you going to do when you grow up?" Some of us had the right answer, such as "doctor," "lawyer," or "nurse." But, as a rule, we did not know what we wanted to do with our lives. Later, more serious thought was given to what we wanted from a career. A **career** is a general course of action a person chooses to pursue throughout life. **Individual career planning** is a process whereby goals are set and the means to achieve them are established.

Individual and organizational careers are not separate and distinct. A person whose individual career plan cannot be carried out within the organization will probably leave the firm sooner or later. Thus, organizations should assist employees in career planning so that both can satisfy their needs. **Career paths** are flexible lines of progression through which employees typically move. Following established career paths, the employee can undertake career development with the firm's assistance. **Career development** is a formalized approach taken by the organization to ensure that people with the proper qualifications and experience are available when needed. Individual career planning and human resources planning are highly interrelated.

Career planning and development benefits both the individual and the organization. For example, a large bank estimated that it saved $1.95 million in one year through its career counseling program. Turnover was reduced by 65 percent. There was an 85 percent improvement in performance, a 25 percent increase in productivity, and a 75 percent increased opportunity for promotion.[1]

[1]Milan Moravec, "A Cost-Effective Career Planning Program Requires a Strategy," *Personnel Administrator* 27 (January 1982): 28 (hereafter referred to as "Moravec.").

There are several factors which affect a person's view of a career. Two of these, life stages and career anchors, are described below.

Life Stages

People are constantly changing, and thus view their careers differently at various stages of their lives. Some of these changes are caused by the aging process, but others result from factors such as the opportunity for growth and status. The basic life stages may be seen in Figure 9–1.

The first stage is that of establishing identity. This stage is typically reached between the ages of ten and twenty. In this stage, career alternatives are explored and an attempt is made to move into the adult world. Stage two involves growing and getting established in a career and typically lasts from ages twenty to forty. During this stage a person chooses an occupation and establishes a career path. The third stage, maintenance and adjustment to self, generally lasts to age fifty and beyond. A person either accepts life as it is or makes adjustments. Career change and divorce often occur at this stage when people have serious questions about the quality of their lives. The final stage is that of decline. Diminishing physical and mental capabilities may bring on this stage. Aspiration and motivation may be lowered. In some instances, this stage is induced by forced retirement.

Figure 9–1. **Life stages.**

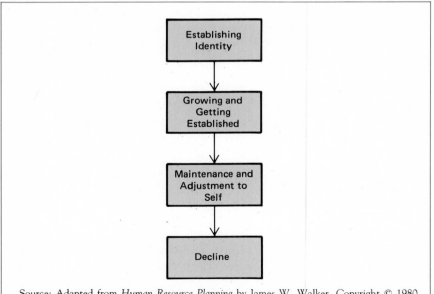

Source: Adapted from *Human Resource Planning* by James W. Walker. Copyright © 1980 by McGraw-Hill Book Company. Used with the permission of McGraw-Hill Book Company.

In many firms, career development programs concentrate upon the second life stage. Still, good older employees may be lost because career planning is not available to them. The Age Discrimination Act may encourage employers to exert more effort on career planning for the 40–70 age group.[2]

Career Anchors

All of us have different aspirations, backgrounds, and experiences. Our personalities are molded, to a certain extent, by the results of our interaction with our environment. Edgar Schein's research identified five different motives which account for the way people select and prepare for a career. He called these "**career anchors**."[3] His five career anchors are set forth below.

1. *Managerial Competence:* The career goal of managers are to develop qualities of interpersonal, analytical and emotional competence. People using this anchor want to manage people.
2. *Technical/Functional Competence:* The anchor for technicians is the continuous development of technical talent. These individuals do not seek managerial positions.
3. *Security:* The anchor for these security conscious individuals is to stabilize their career situation. They often see themselves tied to a particular organization or geographical location.
4. *Creativity:* Creative individuals are somewhat entrepreneurial in their attitude. They want to create or build something that is entirely their own.
5. *Autonomy and Independence:* The career anchor for independent people stresses a desire to be free of organizational constraints. They value autonomy and want to be on their own and work at their own pace.

One of the implications of these career anchors is that different career paths will be needed. Companies must be flexible enough to provide alternative paths to satisfy people's varying needs. Firms must recognize that not everyone is motivated by the need for managerial competence. Individuals may be valued employees without managerial aspirations.

INDIVIDUAL CAREER PLANNING

The primary responsibility for career planning rests with the individual. Career planning begins with gaining a realistic understanding of oneself. Better self-understanding will help a person see which career anchor may be predomi-

[2]James W. Walker, *Human Resource Planning* (New York: McGraw-Hill Book Company, 1980) pp. 331–332.
[3]Edgar Schein, "How 'Career Anchors' Hold Executives to Their Career Paths," *Personnel* (May–June 1975): 11–24.

nant. Once this has taken place, a person is in a position to establish realistic goals and is then able to determine what must be done if these goals are to be achieved. This action also lets us know if our goals are realistic.

Getting to know ourselves is not a one-time occurrence. As we progress down the path of life, our priorities change. You may know yourself at one stage of your life and later begin to see yourself differently. Gaining self-insight involves conducting a thorough self-assessment. Some tools which have proven useful in this endeavor include preparing a Strengths/Weaknesses Balance Sheet and a Likes and Dislikes Analysis.

Strengths/Weaknesses Balance Sheet

Each of us is unique. This situation is good, but it does create problems in decision making. As individuals, we have different strengths and weaknesses which may change somewhat as we grow older. In making career decisions, it is critical to understand both our strengths and weaknesses. By recognizing strengths, a person may be encouraged to pursue a particular career path. Awareness of weaknesses may discourage a certain career path or encourage training or development to remove deficiencies.

The **Strengths/Weaknesses Balance Sheet** (SWBS) is a technique which one of the authors developed as he was making his own career path decisions. Many have found this procedure beneficial when confronting career decisions. The procedure involves identifying both strengths and weaknesses as they are perceived. If people believe that they have a certain strength or weakness, whether real or not, it may affect their choice of a career.

The first step in preparing a SWBS is to draw a line down the middle of a sheet of paper. One side is headed *Strengths* and the other *Weaknesses.* Perceived strengths and weaknesses are then listed. The process is not complete after only one attempt, however, it must be repeated several times. For most people, the first listing will probably produce more weaknesses than strengths. As people understand themselves better, perceived weaknesses may be seen in a different light as strengths. For example, a perceived weakness such as, "I cannot bear to look inactive," may also be viewed as a strength if considered from a different perspective. An illustration of an actual SWBS is presented in Figure 9–2. The most important consideration in completing the SWBS is that a person be totally honest. No one except the person completing the SWBS will have access to the information. It should be used strictly as a means of gaining better understanding of factors which could affect career path decisions. Remember also that items on the SWBS can change at different stages of our lives.

Likes and Dislikes Analysis

Similar to the SWBS, the **Likes and Dislikes Analysis** provides a person with a tool for assessing certain factors that could have an impact upon the devel-

STRENGTHS	WEAKNESSES
Hard worker	Tend to be close-minded
Responsible	Inefficient time manager
Honest	Tend to nitpick
Religious	Hot tempered (sometimes)
High morals	Nervous in unfamiliar places
Take criticism well	Can't stay put in one place very long (i.e. desk, classroom, etc.)
Give constructive criticism	Very opinionated
Patient	Put things off until last minute
Very prompt	Bog down on detail in interesting subjects and overlook detail in less interesting subjects
Dependable	
Conservative	
Enjoy people	Poor in mathematics
Active	Allow friendship to affect decisions and judgment at times
Like to work	
Work well under pressure	Too serious at times
Good judgment	Possessive
Slow to anger	Bored easily
High degree of empathy	Tend to preach at times
Help others	Stubborn
Go an extra mile	Daydream at times
Kind	Judgmental
Very neat and orderly	Quick to speak out before rationally analyzing facts
Confident	Open mouth without engaging brain
Persistent	Have hard time remembering names
Like to read	Tend to overemphasize and exaggerate
Like to work with hands	Spelling
Like to travel	On occasion make snap judgments about situations and people's characters
Like to make friends	
Do things my own way	Tend to downgrade myself
Write well	Like to spend money
Don't smoke, drink, etc.	Like to chase girls
Don't hold grudges	Quick to correct people (even superiors) when they are wrong
	Impatient reading technical material; skim through, missing important detail
	Clock watcher

Figure 9–2. **A strengths/weaknesses balance sheet.**

LIKES	DISLIKES
Like to travel	Do not want to work for a large firm
Would like to live in the State of California	Will not work in the North
Like to be my own boss	Do not like to work behind a desk all day
Would like to live in a large city	Do not like to wear suits all the time
Enjoy watching football and baseball	
Enjoy playing golf and tennis	

Figure 9–3. **A likes and dislikes analysis.**

opment of a career path. An illustration of a Likes and Dislikes Analysis may be seen in Figure 9–3. Dislikes should be considered as restrictions that we place upon ourselves. For instance, if an individual is unwilling to relocate outside of a certain region, this item should be listed as a dislike. Likewise, a disdain for a desk job should be placed in the same category. On the other hand, likes are things that we have discovered to be enjoyable. An example of a "like" might be enjoyment of working for a large company, a medium-sized company, or even a small company. There are advantages and disadvantages associated with any of the choices. It is a matter of personal preference as to which size firm should be placed in the likes category.

As with a person's strengths and weaknesses, likes and dislikes can also change over time. People might enjoy extensive traveling at one stage of their career and at a later phase find it quite distasteful. In any event, likes and dislikes should certainly be taken into consideration in establishing individual career paths.

The self-assessment helps a person understand his or her basic motives or career anchors. Understanding yourself may set the stage for progressing into management or seeking further technical competence. A person with no desire to progress into management would be foolish to accept such a promotion. People who know themselves can make the needed rational decisions that are necessary for successful career planning. Many people get sidetracked because they choose careers based strictly on the wishes of others and not on what is best for them personally.

THE NATURE OF CAREER PLANNING

Career planning does not cease after an individual obtains that first job. Firms should recognize this and should be vitally interested in career planning. From the organization's viewpoint, career planning involves a conscious attempt to maximize a person's potential contribution. Firms which actively engage in career planning programs for their employees reap at least two important benefits. First, they give recognition to each individual for being an important part

Executive Profile

Gayla S. Godfrey, APD

*Personnel Specialist/EEO
Coordinator
International Telephone and
Telegraph*

When Gayla first entered college in 1966, she jokingly referred to her major as "fun." Ms. Godfrey said, "It was several years before I recognized the true value of a formal education and it was twelve years later before I did something about it. After graduating from Northeast Louisiana University in General Studies, I was hooked. I began pursuing, on a part-time basis, a degree in management with emphasis in personnel and human resources. I must admit, I was shocked to find that the college students today seem to be much more serious about their education. They appear to know what career paths they want to follow. I hope this will continue to hold true, especially for my two sons." Because the personnel field is dynamic, Gayla believes that professionals working in this area must keep abreast of the expanding knowledge and current laws through a continuing process of career growth and development. In view of this, she has attended and completed over forty personnel-related courses and seminars and was accredited by the Personnel Accreditation Institute as an Accredited Personnel Diplomat (APD).

Gayla has a varied work history including experience in government, private industry, service organizations, and direct selling. Oddly enough, her first job was in Personnel. She was fresh out of college (the first time) and went to an employment agency which could not place her because of lack of work experience, so they hired her. From there she worked in several traditional female secretarial positions in a bank and a savings and loan association. But deep down, she always wanted a little bit more. Ms. Godfrey became one of

of the organization. This results in improved motivation and loyalty. In the second place, the firm is investing in a resource which has a potentially high rate of return. The firm's productivity will be improved if employees maximize their abilities.

You can see the career planning process depicted in Figure 9–4. It is a continuous endeavor which begins with a person's placement in an entry-level job and initial orientation. Job performance will then be observed and compared with the job standards. At this stage, strengths and weaknesses will be noted which will enable management to assist the employee in making a tentative career decision. Naturally, this decision can be altered at a later date as the process continues. This tentative career decision is based on a number of factors which include personal needs, abilities, and aspirations as well as the needs of the organization. Management can then schedule training and development programs which relate to the employee's specific needs. For instance, the first interior decorator displayers to work in Northeast Louisiana and Mississippi for Home Interiors and Gifts, Inc. Being highly motivated by the challenge and reward of selling, she rose to the top 1 percent of 16,000 saleswomen nationwide for three years. "Mary Crowley, owner of Home Interiors, inspired me with her famous quotation, 'Be somebody. God doesn't have time to make a nobody.' "

Gayla says, "I've been extremely fortunate to have worked for people who have expressed confidence in me and who have given me the opportunity to grow professionally. I set my goals high and was promoted through the ranks to the position of personnel director for the Ouachita Parish Police Jury (local government)." In that position she directed all activities of the Personnel Department, including planning, organizing, developing, and coordinating all the functions (recruitment, selection, evaluation, classification, EEO compliance, grievance, training, and all fringe benefits for approximately 285 employees) of the department. She also developed the Personnel Management System for the Ouachita Parish Public Libraries, which included conducting a job analysis study; writing all job descriptions, the policy manual, and the employee hand-book; and developing the classification and compensation plan.

Next, Gayla became personnel director for G. B. Cooley Hospital for Retarded Citizens. She participated in the development and implementation of the first personnel department for the hospital. Duties included management of all personnel records, supervision of the employment process and employee benefits, recruitment and interviewing, and development of an employee performance appraisal system.

In 1981 she went to work for ITT Pneumotive, a unit of International Telephone and Telegraph, as personnel specialist/EEO coordinator. She said, "During my first interview with ITT I was asked if I considered this position a step backward in my career from my current position of director. I told my future boss that I considered it a side-step, as I was really applying for his job. I further explained that my intentions were to be hired as personnel specialist and do such an outstanding job that he would be promoted and I would be in line for his position of industrial relations/personnel manager. Besides, it's difficult to consider working for one of the world's largest corporations as anything but a step forward."

"If the senior has a degree in Personnel or a comparable major, no stone should be left unturned in seeking a job in the field. If the senior has some other major, steps should be taken to secure a Masters degree in Personnel or a comparable major. In either event, the student should achieve the best credentials possible and the job search should be aggressively conducted, since entry positions in Personnel are scarce. If direct entry into personnel work is not available, students should secure supervisory work in an area appropriate to their interests. The supervisory function includes many personnel activities and can lead to an eventual career as a staff personnel specialist."

D. M. Bates, Sr. Coordinator, United States Steel College Relations

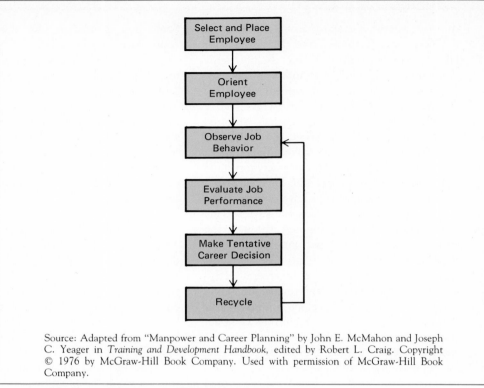

Source: Adapted from "Manpower and Career Planning" by John E. McMahon and Joseph C. Yeager in *Training and Development Handbook*, edited by Robert L. Craig. Copyright © 1976 by McGraw-Hill Book Company. Used with permission of McGraw-Hill Book Company.

Figure 9–4. **The career planning process.**

a person who desires to progress upward in the field of labor relations may require additional legal training.

Notice again in Figure 9–4 that career planning is an ongoing process. It takes into consideration the changes that occur in people and organizations. This type of flexibility is absolutely necessary in today's dynamic organizational environment.[4] Not only do the firm's requirements change, but individuals may choose to revise their career progression. An employee might believe, for instance, that he or she could be more productive in Personnel than in marketing or vice versa. Rather than lose a valued employee, the firm may attempt to facilitate this change.

WHY ORGANIZATIONAL CAREER PLANNING?

If an organization is to be successful, it must be capable of ensuring that properly qualified people are available when vacancies occur. We have already dis-

[4]John E. McMahon and Joseph C. Yeager, "Manpower and Career Planning," *Training and Development Handbook*, Robert L. Craig, ed. (New York: McGraw-Hill Book Company, 1976) pp. 11–18.

cussed recruitment and selection as means of accomplishing this goal. However, if a company stresses promotion from within, a procedure is needed which will identify job progression possibilities and establish the required qualifications for each position. The process of establishing career paths within a firm is referred to as organizational career planning.

Career planning programs should be implemented only when they contribute to the accomplishment of basic organizational goals. Therefore, the rationale for career planning programs varies among firms. In most organizations, career planning programs are expected to achieve one or more of the following goals:

- More effective development of available talent
- Self-appraisal opportunities for employees considering new or nontraditional career paths
- More efficient deployment of human resources within and between divisions and/or geographic locations
- A demonstration of a tangible commitment to EEO, affirmative action, and the corporate image
- Satisfaction of employees' personal development needs
- Improvement of performance through on-the-job training experiences provided by horizontal and vertical career moves
- Increased employee loyalty and motivation, leading to decreased turnover
- A method of determining training and development needs[5]

All of the above options may be desirable in view of the organization's primary goals. But, successful career planning depends upon a firm's ability to satisfy those goals which are considered to be most crucial.

As may be seen in Figure 9–5, a career planning program may cause some employees to develop more realistic expectations. This ultimately leads to enhanced performance, improved retention, and improved utilization of talent. Although certain benefits are associated with career planning, there are also risks involved. Difficulties occur when the career planning program raises employee expectations to unrealistic levels. When this occurs, organizational disruption, diminished performance, and turnover may result. Therefore, the focus of a career planning program should be on developing realistic expectations.[6] If employees believe that they have better opportunities than actually exist, disappointments are inevitable.

CAREER PATHS

In the past, and to a certain extent today, organizational career planning has been informal. A person might casually discuss career possibilities with his or

[5]Moravec, p. 29.
[6]James W. Walker, "Does Career Planning Rock the Boat?" *Human Resource Management* (Spring 1978): 3.

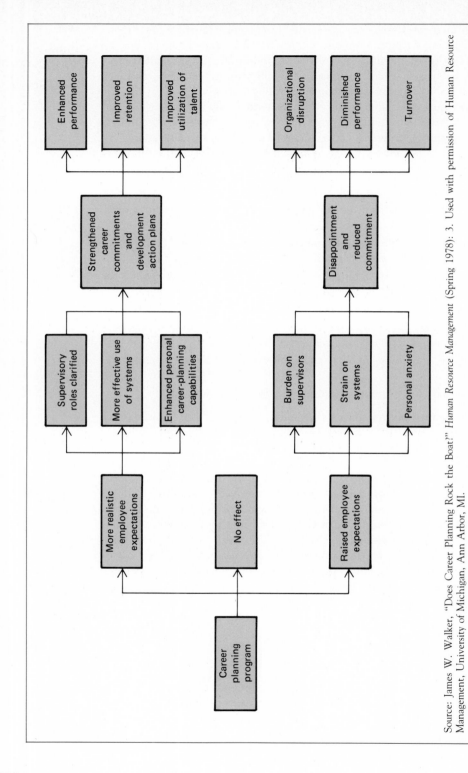

Figure 9–5. The effects of career planning.

Source: James W. Walker, "Does Career Planning Rock the Boat?" *Human Resource Management* (Spring 1978): 3. Used with permission of Human Resource Management, University of Michigan, Ann Arbor, MI.

her boss. Today a more systematic approach to career planning seems reasonable. Firms are going to great lengths to show employees progression possibilities and the qualifications they need if they are to be qualified to assume certain positions. Naturally, a well-developed job analysis program is needed to permit effective organizational career planning.

Traditionally, career paths have focused upon upward mobility within a particular occupation. There might be several paths for one employee leading to a high-level position. A career path chart showing progression steps from an entry-level personnel position to corporate personnel director is shown in Figure 9–6. As you see, there are many avenues a person may choose if his or her ultimate goal is to be the corporate personnel director. Through studying the job descriptions, a person should be able to determine the developmental needs required to achieve a higher-level position.

Some enlightened firms have recognized that not everyone wants to follow traditional vertical career movements within specific functions. Career paths have been developed which take into consideration lateral, diagonal, and even downward career progression. Not all employees want promotions. Some, after analyzing their career goals, may prefer to try something new and make a lateral move. Others may want to change career fields. Still others have reached a stage in their lives where they desire less responsibility and more personal time. These individuals may seek a downward career progression.[7] Although the needs of the organization must first be taken into consideration, it is often possible to retain and motivate valued employees through these forms of career paths.

METHODS OF ORGANIZATION CAREER PLANNING AND DEVELOPMENT

There are numerous means through which individuals can be assisted in their career planning and development. Some currently used methods will next be identified and described. Most of these are used in various combinations.

- *Management by Objectives (MBO):* MBO provides an excellent means of assisting in career planning. Remember in our previous discussion of MBO that the superior and subordinate jointly agree upon goals that can be accomplished during a certain time frame. Also, you may recall that needed resources are made available. These resources may well include developmental programs. In addition, when goals are not achieved, future developmental needs may be identified.
- *Career Counseling:* Persons either inside or outside the organization may counsel employees as to the most beneficial career path. Personnel

[7]Richard D. Conner and Robert L. Fjerstad, "Internal Personnel Maintenance," in *Staffing Policies and Strategies ASPA Handbook of Personnel and Industrial Relations* Vol. I, ed. by Dale Yoder and Herbert G. Heneman (Washington, DC: The Bureau of National Affairs, Inc., 1979), pp. 4-226–4-227.

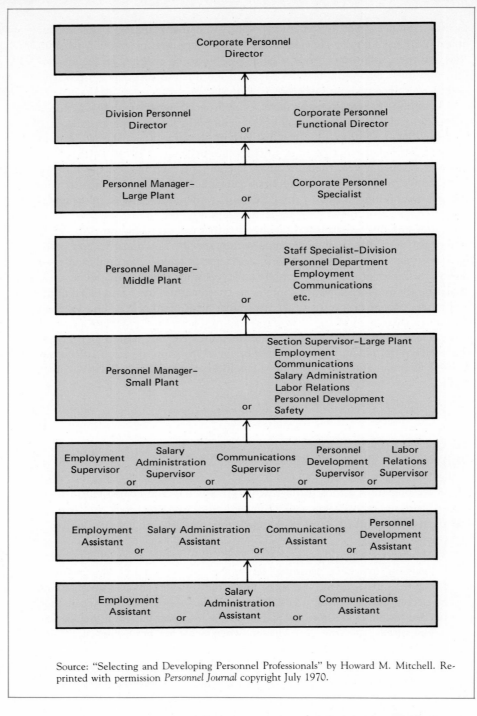

Source: "Selecting and Developing Personnel Professionals" by Howard M. Mitchell. Reprinted with permission *Personnel Journal* copyright July 1970.

Figure 9–6. **From entry level position to corporate personnel director.**

professionals are often called upon to assist in this endeavor. Psychologists or guidance counselors are also used. Colleges and universities are also at times sources of counseling efforts.

- *Company Material:* Some firms provide material specifically developed to assist their workers in career planning. Such material is tailored to the firm's special needs.

- *Performance Appraisal System:* The firm's appraisal system can also be a valuable tool in career planning. Because strengths and weaknesses are typically noted, developmental needs may be discovered from this process. At times it may be difficult or even impossible to overcome a particular weakness and an alternate career path may have to be chosen.

- *Workshops:* Some organizations conduct workshops lasting two or three days for the purpose of helping workers develop careers within the company. It helps them to match their specific career goals with the needs of the company.

Career planning and development is becoming increasingly necessary in order for firms to retain their effectiveness. These and other methods are currently being used to assist in this endeavor.

CAREER DEVELOPMENT PROGRAM: AN EXAMPLE

Realizing that highly skilled employees hold the key to corporate growth, Detroit Edison has designed the Initial Professional Development Program. The program helps build individual careers and, in so doing, assures the development of employees required to satisfy future personnel needs.

Detroit Edison's program is available to most entry-level professionals who possess a bachelor's degree and have less than three years experience related to their college degree preparation. If selected for the program, participants assume the primary responsibility for their professional growth and are expected to take advantage of various opportunities provided.

The Initial Professional Development Program takes place over a three year period and involves a number of specific developmental activities (see Figure 9–7). The major activities include rotational work assignments and participation in company seminars. Work assignments involve the participants in stimulating and productive projects. Assistance is given by seasoned professionals who answer questions and provide guidance. Attendance at three formal seminars gives trainees the opportunity to expand skills and interact with employees from other functional areas of the company.

Additional developmental opportunities are provided in-house through courses covering such subjects as communication skills, power systems engineering, economic analysis, and problems and challenges faced by public utilities. Also, although not required, program participants are encouraged to take

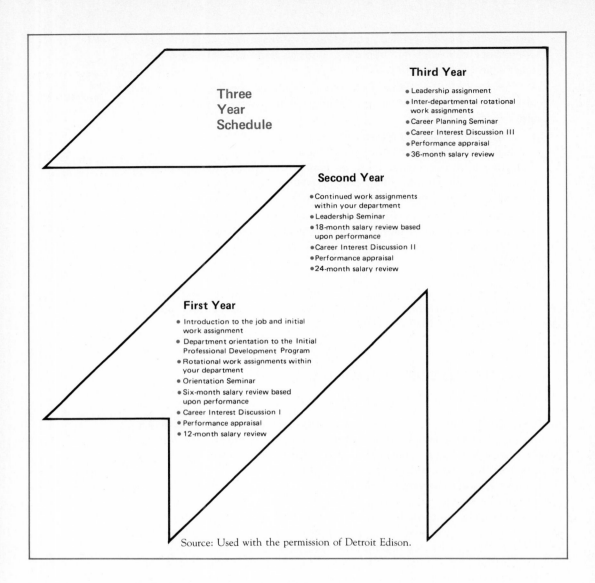

Three Year Schedule

Third Year
- Leadership assignment
- Inter-departmental rotational work assignments
- Career Planning Seminar
- Career Interest Discussion III
- Performance appraisal
- 36-month salary review

Second Year
- Continued work assignments within your department
- Leadership Seminar
- 18-month salary review based upon performance
- Career Interest Discussion II
- Performance appraisal
- 24-month salary review

First Year
- Introduction to the job and initial work assignment
- Department orientation to the Initial Professional Development Program
- Rotational work assignments within your department
- Orientation Seminar
- Six-month salary review based upon performance
- Career Interest Discussion I
- Performance appraisal
- 12-month salary review

Source: Used with the permission of Detroit Edison.

Figure 9–7. Detroit Edison's professional development program.

advantage of educational opportunities at local colleges and universities. Many employees have earned advanced degrees with the aid of the Detroit Edison Educational Assistance Program.

BEGINNING A CAREER IN PERSONNEL

For individuals desiring a career in Personnel there are two basic ways of entering the field. You may enter the firm of your choice in another department and later transfer to Personnel. Or, you may secure a beginning position in Personnel. There appears to be no uniform agreement as to the best means to obtain an entry-level personnel position. However, the second approach is often the more difficult. In order to assist us in solving this dilemma, personnel practitioners from a wide variety of firms were asked the following questions:

1. Which entry-level position in your firm would be most helpful if a person desires to progress into Personnel?

2. What types of education or experience are most desirable for these entry-level positions?

3. Which Personnel entry-level position would best assist a person's career progression in your firm?

As you can see from Table 9–1, there is no consistency in the responses to these questions. However, it is clear that some firms stress work in other functional areas before moving into Personnel, while others believe in direct entry into Personnel.

Entry-Level Positions in Other Functional Areas

Executives in some firms believe that experience should be gained in positions other than Personnel before moving into the human resources function. They reason that future personnel professionals need wide company exposure to be effective in personnel positions. This exposure may increase their credibility in dealing with other managers.

Numerous firms have this philosophy. For instance, Trans World Airlines selects personnel staffing specialists from among their experienced reservation sales agents. The best route for an individual to move into Personnel with the Chicago, Rock Island and Pacific Railroad Company is from the position of "trainman." Experience in this job permits an individual to learn the operations from the ground up.

Entry-Level Positions in Personnel

Not all firms require broad-based experience prior to entering Personnel. In fact, the number of individuals entering Personnel directly appears to be increasing. Perhaps this trend is due to the high degree of specialized knowledge currently expected. Some firms need people who can produce very quickly after being placed in Personnel. These organizations apparently do not feel that time is available to provide basic training.

Several firms believe that the compensation specialty provides excellent entry-level positions. For example, Grumman Aerospace Corporation identifies salary administration as the best entry-level position "because it affects almost every aspect of personnel work and company operations." Teledyne McKay Corporation believes that "starting in wage and salary provides an individual with exposure to relationships of job classifications throughout the company," and that this background is helpful to the personnel practitioner.

Table 9–1. Careers in personnel management

Company	Entry-Level Positions	Education/Experience
A. B. Dick Company	*Assistant Hourly Employment Manager Shop Foreman Assistant Salary Administrator	Bachelor's degree for all positions
Bristol-Myers Products	Personnel Assistant	Bachelor's degree with two or three years experience in general personnel work
Chicago, Rock Island and Pacific Railroad Company	*Trainman Operations Analyst Cost/Engineering	Bachelor's degree for all positions
Conoco Inc.	*Personnel Trainee Any position with Conoco	Bachelor's or master's degree in personnel administration, industrial relations, organizational development, business, or engineering
Denny's Incorporated	*Interviewer	Bachelor's degree in business or two years in personnel interviewing
	Wage and Salary Analyst	Bachelor's degree and one year experience in personnel, preferably with compensation experience
	Personnel Administrator	Bachelor's degree and/or two years experience in personnel
GAF Corporation	*Production Supervisor Industrial Engineer Wage and Salary Analyst Safety Specialist	B.S.I.E., B.S.M.E., B.B.A. B.A. with relevant coursework B.S. with relevant coursework
General Cable Technologies	Assistant Plant Industrial Relations Manager Compensation Analyst	B.S. in industrial relations B.S. in industrial relations
Gerber Products Company	*Supervisor Trainee *Administrative Trainee	Four years of college Four years of college
Grumman Aerospace Corporation	*Salary Analyst Employment Interviewer Career Development Analyst	Bachelor's degree in any of a variety of concentrations including psychology, business, and data processing
Hart Schaffner & Marx	Personnel Assistant Compensation Assistant Employee Relations Assistant Personnel Director (small plant or store)	Bachelor's or master's degree in business, personnel, or employee relations

*Indicates best entry-level position

Table 9–1. (continued)

Company	Entry-Level Positions	Education/Experience
International Paper Company	*Supervisor–Employee Relations Administrator–Industrial Relations Entry level specialist assigned to the Corporate Human Resources Department	B.S. or B.A. in personnel or industrial management B.S. or B.A. in industrial or labor relations, or B.S. in industrial management
Johns-Manville Corporation	*Employee Relations Supervisor *Plant Supervisor *Benefits Clerk	Bachelor's degree and some plant experience desirable
Motorola Inc.	*Employment Interviewer	B.S. or B.A.; no experience
Nabisco, Inc.	*Personnel Assistant (Field)	Bachelor's degree in such fields as business or psychology
Rockwell International	Supervisory Trainee (Field) Personnel/Industrial Relations Trainee	M.B.A. in personnel or industrial relations
Shell Oil Company	Employee Relations Analyst	Bachelor's or master's degree in personnel or industrial relations preferred
Squibb Corporation	Personnel Assistant (nonexempt recruiting)	Two or three years experience of personnel related activities preferred
Standard Oil Company of California	Employee Relations Trainee	M.B.A. (industrial relations) with up to two years experience
Stokely-Van Camp, Inc.	Employee Relations–Management Trainee	Master's degree (preferably in personnel)
Teledyne McKay	*Wage and Salary Representative Labor Relations Representative	B.A. or personnel or financial administrative experience B.A. or general plant or personnel administrative experience
Trans World Airlines	Reservation Sales Agent	High school diploma, customer contact, and sales experience
U.S. Steel Corporation	Labor Relations Trainee Employee Relations Trainee Line Operations Management Trainee	Law degree Master's degree, accreditation, experience Technical degree plus leadership
Walt Disney Productions	*Personnel Interviewer Personnel Assistant Wage and Salary Analyst	People skills; B.A. and/or equivalent People skills; B.A. and/or equivalent Salaried experience and statistical orientation

*Indicates best entry-level position

The nature of the firm's business may also affect the best personnel entry-level position. Labor intensive organizations—those which have high labor costs relative to total operating costs—appear to emphasize staffing and recruiting positions where interviewing skills are quite important. For instance, Denny's Inc. lists the "interviewer" as being the best personnel entry-level position. Walt Disney Productions also identifies the "personnel interviewer" position as one of the best.

Entry-Level Positions: An Overview

Practitioners do not agree as to the most appropriate entry-level position for individuals aspiring to a job in Personnel. A position considered best by one firm may not be viewed the same by another. The nature of the firm's business or its management's personnel philosophy may account for these differences. Some firms stress the need for operating experience before entering Personnel. Others believe that direct entry into Personnel provides a more suitable beginning. People with ability who truly desire to obtain a position in Personnel will likely be given the opportunity.

SUMMARY

A career is a general course of action a person chooses to pursue throughout life. Individual career planning is a process whereby goals are set and the means to achieve them are established. Career paths are flexible lines of progression along which employees typically move through an organization. Career development is a formalized approach taken by the organization to ensure that people with the proper qualifications and experience are available when needed.

There are several factors which affect a person's view of a career such as career anchors and life stages. The five career anchors are: (1) managerial competence, (2) technical/functional competence, (3) security, (4) creativity, and (5) autonomy and independence. The basic life stages are: (1) establishing identity, (2) growing and getting established, (3) maintenance and adjustment to self, and (4) decline.

The primary responsibility for career planning rests with the individual. Career planning begins with gaining a realistic understanding of oneself. Gaining insight involves conducting a thorough self-assessment.

Career planning does not cease after an individual obtains his or her first job. Firms are also vitally interested in career planning. From the organization's viewpoint, career planning involves a conscious attempt to maximize employees' potential ability. Career planning programs should be implemented only when they contribute to the accomplishment of basic organizational goals.

Traditionally, career paths have focused upon upward mobility within a particular occupation. Some firms have recognized that not everyone wants to follow traditional vertical career movements within specific functions. Career paths have been developed which take into consideration lateral, diagonal, and even downward career progression.

There are numerous means through which individuals can be assisted in their career planning and development. Some of these means include: Management by Objectives, career counseling, company material, performance appraisal systems, and workshops. Most of these are used in combination with each other.

There are two basic means for entering Personnel. A person may be required to enter the firm of his or her choice in another department and later transfer to Personnel. Or, a beginning position in Personnel may be secured. There appears to be no uniform agreement as to the best means of obtaining an entry-level Personnel position.

Questions for Review

1. Define the following terms: a. Career b. Individual career planning c. Career paths d. Career development

2. List and briefly define the five types of career anchors.

3. Identify the basic stages that people enter at various points in their lives?

4. How should a Strengths/Weaknesses Balance Sheet and a Likes and Dislikes Analysis be prepared?

5. Describe in your own words the stages in the organizational career planning process.

6. Why is it important for firms to engage in organizational career planning?

7. Identify and describe some of the methods of organizational career planning.

8. What are the two basic means for entering Personnel? Why do you think firms might favor one means over another?

Terms for Review

Career
Individual career planning
Career paths
Career development

Career anchors
Strengths/Weakness Balance Sheet
Likes and Dislikes Analysis

Marsha Smith was exceptionally happy the day she received word of her appointment as assistant personnel director at Nelson Electronics in Boise, Idaho. Marsha had joined Nelson Electronics as a recruiter three years earlier. Her degree from the University of Missouri was in personnel administration and she had four years of experience as a personnel specialist.

As she walked back to her office, she thought about how much she had learned while working as a recruiter. The first year she was with Nelson she went on a recruiting trip to Southern Idaho State College only to find the placement director there extremely angry with her company. She was visibly upset when the placement director said, "If you expect to recruit any of our students you at Nelson had better get your act together." Questioning of the placement director revealed that a previous recruiter had failed to show up for a full afternoon of scheduled interviews with Southern's students. This trip ended amicably, though, and Marsha eventually recruited a number of excellent employees from the college.

Another important lesson began when the production manager asked for some help. "I need you to find me an experienced quality control inspector," he said. "I want to make sure that the person has a degree in statistics.

Beyond that, you decide on the qualifications." Marsha advertised the position and checked through dozens of resumes in search of the right person. She sent each promising applicant to the production manager. This went on for six months with the production manager giving various obscure reasons for not hiring any of the applicants. Finally, the production manager called Marsha and said, "I just hired a QC person. He has a degree in history but he seems eager. Besides, he was willing to work for only a thousand a month."

Marsha learned more with each passing day. She feels that one of her greatest accomplishments is having improved the firm's minority recruiting program. Her ability to do this was based on something of a coincidence. One of her close friends in school had become a leader in the Black Chamber of Commerce. With his advice she was able to develop a recruiting program which attracted blacks to Nelson Electronics.

As Marsha began to clean out her desk, she suddenly realized that the learning process was just beginning. As assistant personnel director, she would not only be responsible for matters related to recruiting but to all aspects of personnel management. It was a little scary but she felt ready.

Questions

1. What are the lessons that can be learned from each of the three incidents described above?

2. How will the problems Marsha faces as an assistant personnel director differ from those she has handled as a recruiter?

___

"Could you come to my office for a minute, Bob?" asked Terry Geech, the plant manager. "Sure, be right there," said Bob Glemson. Bob was the plant's quality control director. He

had been with the company for four years. After completing his degree in mechanical engineering, he worked as a production supervisor and then as maintenance manager, prior to promotion to his present job. Bob thought he knew what the call was about.

"Your letter of resignation catches me by surprise," began Terry. "I know that Wilson Products will be getting a good man, but we sure need you here, too." "I thought about it a lot," said Bob, "but there just doesn't seem to be a future for me here." "Why do you say that," asked Terry. "Well," replied Bob, "the next position above mine is yours. With you only 39 I don't think it's likely that you'll be leaving soon." "The fact is that I am leaving soon," said Terry. "That's why it's even more of a shock to know that you are resigning. I think I'll be moving to the corporate offices in June of next year. Besides, the company has several plants which are larger than this one and we need good people in those plants from time to time. Both in quality control and in general management." "Well, I heard about an opening in the Cincinnati plant last year," said Bob, "but by the time I checked, the job had already been filled. We never know about job opportunities in the other plants until we read about the incumbent in the company paper."

"All this is beside the point now. What would it take to get you to change your mind?" asked Terry. "I don't think I can change my mind now," replied Bob, "I've already signed a contract with Wilson."

Questions

1. Evaluate the career planning and development program at this company.

2. What actions might have prevented Bob's resignation?

THE SEARCH FOR THE RIGHT COMPANY

It is a basic truism that a person cannot start a career until a job offer is made. Thus, this appendix will concentrate upon the steps you should take in order to obtain desirable job offers.

The Resume

In many instances a resume is a prospective employee's first contact with the person in charge of employment. As such, the resume becomes an extension of an individual's personality. The resume sells the person in that person's absence. It should be designed to present an individual in the best possible perspective.

The importance of proper attention to resume preparation was vividly illustrated to one of the authors immediately after receiving his doctoral degree. He had been divorced for seven years and thought nothing of placing "divorced" in the marital status category. However, he discovered that some colleges and universities remain quite conservative, and his divorced status often meant that his resume was not read. In addition, the author had received three degrees from one university (which is not acceptable to many employers) and this item was placed directly following career objectives. The author had ten years of business experience with major corporations and had published numerous articles, but this fact would not be known unless the entire resume was read.

It did not take long to recognize that a problem existed. The fact that the telephone did not ring, accompanied by numerous letters of rejection, contributed to this realization. This prompted a few modifications in the resume so as to present the author's qualifications in a different perspective. His ten years of business and consulting experience were highlighted immediately following career objectives. Biographical data were moved to the back of the resume and "divorced" was changed to "Dependents: one, Alyson Lynn." The author was amazed at the change in responses. He received many invitations to visit campuses and was able to obtain the position of his choice.

The illustration provides an excellent example of the importance of a clearly thought out resume where strengths are emphasized. College seniors preparing to enter the job market should follow the same approach. Remember that your resume must be developed to present you in the best possible image. Whereas you can explain deficiencies during the interview, your resume cannot talk back. It must stand on its own merits.

Some helpful guidelines in resume preparation have been developed through experience and contacts with personnel directors. Consider these points:

1. Present your most significant accomplishments and attributes. If something is the truth, it is not bragging.

2. The order of the presentation of items on a resume should be dictated by your strengths. If you have high grades, stress them; if you have a significant amount of work experience, give it top priority.

3. Many companies emphasize activities outside the classroom such as membership and offices held in social and business organizations. If you have been particularly active in one or more campus organizations, highlight these achievements.

4. The amount of college expenses that you personally paid is also receiving increased attention. A statement such as "paid 50 percent of college expenses" is often viewed as being positive.

5. If you are willing to be mobile, stress this fact. For a company with operations throughout the United States, stating a geographical preference of "none" would likely attract greater attention than stating "West Coast." Naturally, if you have a strong geographical preference, you should state it.

6. A person who has had work experience while attending college should stress this fact. Firms recognize that individuals who are working to finance their education will probably not have fancy job titles. They are interested in determining how you performed while employed. It is highly advantageous for a recruiter to call one of your past employers and receive statements such as, "He's a hard worker," or "She didn't constantly watch the clock."

7. If you have had work experience, describe the functions that you performed on the job. Merely listing the position titles does not give the recruiter significant insights into the type of work you actually did. Action phrases such as "was responsible for," "coordinated the activities of," and "in charge of" are much more descriptive.

8. If names of references are to be placed on a resume, you should obtain permission from the references even if they are good friends.

Sample resumes of two individuals who have entirely different backgrounds are presented in Figures A9–1 and A9–2. As you see, Philip Anders has considerable work experience. His grades may not be anything to write home about, so his resume emphasizes other attributes. Beth Johnson, on the other hand, has had time to concentrate on her studies. Her grades reflect her intense dedication to her coursework and her acceptance into numerous honor societies. Both Philip and Beth have the potential to develop good resumes, but their format will likely be different. In developing a resume, there is no standard sequence for information. Formats vary because people are different.

Matching Yourself with the Right Company

The next step in searching for the right company is to identify the firm(s) that offer the greatest opportunity to achieve your career objectives. However, re-

PHILIP D. ANDERS
1706 W. Birge St.
Los Angeles, California 90050
(213-387-8017)

PERSONAL DATA

Height: 6'4"
Weight: 210 pounds
Date of Birth: April 4, 1957

Dependents: John, Tera, and wife Maryanne
Physical Limitations: None
Hobbies and Interests: Fishing, sports, and most outdoor activities

CAREER OBJECTIVES

My goal is to obtain a supervisory position in an aggressive industry which can fully utilize my experience and abilities. My five-year goal is to obtain a middle management position in Personnel with a growing manufacturing firm.

SIGNIFICANT BUSINESS EXPERIENCE

California Instruments, Inc., Los Angeles, California. May 1979 to present. Production Control Supervisor in charge of high volume and commercial products. Developed forcasts and budgets in both job shop and high volume products. Interfaced with manufacturing on product performance through tracking and presentation of performance. Instigated plans and schedules to shop both monthly and quarterly so staffing and material requirements are met to sustain forcast and plan.

Hale and Hasel Food Stores, Assistant Manager. August 1977 to May 1979. In charge of developing work schedules, and supervising and training approximately 20 employees. Maintained the store accounts and made weekly and monthly summaries and recommendations to division head.

EDUCATION

Bachelor of Business Administration, UCLA
Expected date of graduation: December 15, 1984

PROFESSIONAL SCHOOLS

California Instruments, Inc.: Management Training Program (10 weeks)
Supervisors Training Programs, Phase I & II (16 weeks)
Work Simplification Classes (8 weeks)

GEOGRAPHICAL PREFERENCE: West or Southwest

Figure A9–1. **Philip Anders's resume.**

member what the old philosopher said, "You can never turn down a job until an offer has been made." Identifying these firms is a task that often proves difficult for students seeking their first job. But, it is a task that must be done. Here you will be attempting to identify firms that can provide the opportunity for you to meet your specific needs.

Numerous sources are available which provide the names of outstanding firms. A great deal of information can be found in trade journals (see Table 1) that apply to the particular industry in which you are interested. Also, a large amount of useful data may be found in *Standard and Poors, Fortune, Forbes,* and

```
                              BETH JOHNSON
                               P.O. Box 3695
                                LSU Station
                           Baton Rouge, LA  70821
                               318-275-7621


    CAREER OBJECTIVE

        My goal is to obtain a position in Personnel with the ultimate objective  of progressing into a
        position of managerial responsibility.

    EDUCATIONAL BACKGROUND

        Bachelor of Science, Louisiana State University
           Graduated with High Honors May 1983
           Honors Thesis Title: "A Comparison of the Academic Achievement at Louisiana State
           University of Students Who Graduated From Small and Large High Schools"
           Grade Point Average: 3.63/4.00

    HONORS

        Listed in Who's Who Among Students in American Colleges and Universities (1982, 1983)
        Alpha Chi National Honor Scholarship Society
        Dean's List
        Cap and Gown Honorary Society
        President's List

    MEMBERSHIPS IN ORGANIZATIONS

        Phi Chi Theta Business Fraternity, President
        Zeta Phi Beta Social Sorority, Inc., Vice President and Corresponding Secretary
        Young Democrats of Louisiana, Baton Rouge Chapter, Vice President
        American Society for Personnel Administration, President

    PERSONAL DATA

        Marital Status: Single
        Physical Limitations: None
        Date of Birth: December 6, 1961


    GEOGRAPHICAL PREFERENCE: None
```

Figure A9–2.   Beth Johnson's resume.

The Wall Street Journal. A person should select only the firms that have the potential for fulfilling specific needs. For instance, if your goal is to be employed by a medium-sized firm headquartered in the Southwest, you might not consider Coca-Cola, with headquarters in Atlanta. Dr Pepper, a smaller firm headquartered in Dallas, might meet your requirements. It is beneficial to select approximately twenty-five companies representing several industries from which to continue the job search.

Once your list of prospective employers has been developed, you are still not in a position to send out a resume. A certain amount of research remains. Data concerning each company should be obtained to assist you in writing a personal cover letter to each firm. This information includes the name of the person to whom your letter will be addressed. The cover letter should state your reason for wanting a job with that particular company. Remember that

Table A9–1. Examples of trade journals

Building and Construction

Builders' Merchants' Journal
Building and Contract Journal
Building Supply Dealer
California Licensed Contractor
Cleaning Management
Concrete Construction
Demolition Age
Educational Building Digest
Excavating Contractor
Fence Industry
Home Improvement Contractor

**Business and Economics—Marketing
and Purchasing**

American Salesman
Auctioneer
Buyers and Buying
Industrial Marketing
Industrial Purchasing Agent
Sales Executive
Sales Manager's Bulletin
Southern Purchaser
Vending Times

**Computer Technology and
Applications**

American Journal of Computational
   Linguistics
Computer Age

Computer Graphics
Computer News
Computers and People
Data Processing Digest
Data Processor
IBM Systems Journal (International
   Business Machines)
Micrographics Today
Software Digest

Hospitals

ACHA News (American College of Hospital Administrators)
Aid Newsletter
Hospital Financial Management
Hospital Practice
Hospital Supervisor's Bulletin
Southern Hospitals
Washington Developments

Hotels and Restaurants

Chef Institutional
HSMA World (Hotel Sales Management
   Association)
Host
Restaurant News

Insurance

American Agent and Broker
Business Insurance

the only reason a firm will consider you for employment is that they believe you can provide services which will make money for the company. A copy of a sample cover letter is presented in Figure A9–3.

The job search does not stop here. Now the waiting process begins, which is often a difficult time. But, if you have done your homework, you can reasonably assume that you will receive an invitation to visit a company. Before making this visit, additional research, or at least a review of your previous research, may be necessary. You need much more information than last year's sales statistics. In addition, it may be wise to develop a list of questions that you, as a prospective employee, would like to ask about the company. The interview is a two-way street; the interviewee is attempting to determine if the particular company is a good place to work, while the firm is evaluating the individual for potential to fit into the organization.

If the interview goes well and you believe that the company has the potential to satisfy your career objectives, it is customary to write a letter expressing your sincere interest. In this letter you should also tell them precisely why

Table A9–1. (continued)

305

Chapter 9
Career Planning
and
Development

Equinews
Factory Mutual Record
Health Insurance Underwriter
Independent Adjuster
Insurance Journal
Risk Management

Manufacturing

American Industry
Businessmen's Expectations
Current Industrial Reports
Ideas That Made Millions
Industrial Development and Manufacturers
  Record
Industrial Organization Review
International New Product Newsletter
Manufacturing and the Law
Manufacturing Developments in Virginia
New Products News
Production
U.S. Federal Trade Commission Quarterly
  Financial Report for Manufacturing,
  Mining and Trade Corporations

Printing

American Inkmaker
Business Forms Reporter
Engravers Journal
Fine Print
Graphics

Inland Printer/American Lithographer
Print
Print Review
Printing and Publishing
Printing Journal
Reproduction Bulletin
Screen Printing

Retailing

Catalog Showroom Merchandiser
Checkout
Commerce Business Daily
Department Store Economist
Discount Store News
Installment Retailing
Journal of Retailing
Marketeer
Retailer
Retailer and Marketing News

Transportation—Automobiles

Bulletin (American Association of Motor
  Vehicle Administrators)
American Clean Car
Auto Trim News
Automobile Quarterly
Automotive Fleet
Economical Driver
Mobile Home Merchandiser

you feel qualified to take a position with their company. A comment such as, "The work that a job analyst with your firm performs appears extremely interesting and challenging. I am confident that I possess the ability necessary for getting the job done." On the other hand, if you discover during your visit that the position is not what you expected, a courteous letter should be written thanking them for their interest, but telling the company representative that you do not believe a proper match exists.

The follow-up phone call is a technique that may further enhance your chances of obtaining the desired position. Approximately one day after the follow-up letter has been received by the company, a phone call might be placed to the person who interviewed you. During this call, you should ask intelligent, searching questions as well as again expressing interest in the firm. Once the call has been completed, you have had the opportunity to visit with the company representatives four times: by resume, in person, by letter, and by phone.

If you receive a job offer, you must decide whether it should be accepted or rejected. This usually poses no problem unless several equally desirable of-

November 16, 1984

Mr. Paul C. Abrams
Director of Personnel
Taxco Industries, Inc.
3 Mancion Center
San Francisco, CA 94111

Dear Mr. Abrams:

**Tell the Position
You Want**

Enclosed is a copy of my resume. I would like to be considered for the position of personnel interviewer with your firm.

**Tell Why You Are
Qualified**

Both my college training and work experience have been directed toward obtaining a position in personnel. My degree is in human resources management and I have a minor in psychology. For the past two years I have participated in an internship program at Loud Chemical Company where I have performed duties as a job analyst trainee.

**Tell Why this Company
Interests You**

Taxco Industries has the reputation of being a leader in its field and is well respected for its advanced employee relations programs. It is the type of company that would offer me an excellent opportunity for growth and development.

**Reinforce Your
Qualifications**

I am confident that I possess the qualifications to be successful as a personnel practitioner. If you have any questions or desire further information, please contact me at (214) 886-5699. Thank you for your consideration.

Sincerely,

S. Rene Scott

Shelley Rene Scott

Enclosure

Figure A9–3. **An example of a cover letter to introduce the resume.**

fers are received. Hopefully, since your homework has been done, this will be the case. In making your decision as to which job to take, remember this major point: the job with the greatest long-run potential—rather than one with the highest starting pay—may be the better choice. It is often tempting to take the highest salary offer without considering all factors. But, success on the first job after graduation can have a tremendous impact upon an entire career. It should be chosen with care.

Chapter Objectives

1. Describe the performance appraisal process and identify its basic objectives.
2. Identify who may typically be responsible for performance appraisal.
3. Identify the various traditional methods that have been used in the appraisal process.
4. List the weaknesses that have been associated with the traditional methods of performance appraisal.
5. State how management by objectives is used as a performance appraisal method.
6. Describe how assessment centers are used to assess an employee's management potential.
7. List the actions a firm may take to defend its performance appraisal system in court.

Chapter 10 _____

Performance Appraisal

"Tim, we've got to get more production out of the people in this plant," exclaimed Doug Parsley, vice president of production. "Our productivity is declining while our costs are skyrocketing." Tim Overbeck, production superintendent, nodded his head in agreement and replied, "I couldn't agree with you more, Doug. What these people need is a good swift kick." "No," Doug countered, "we've tried that approach before. I think you'd better talk with the personnel office first thing tomorrow and see if we can come up with a reasonable system of evaluating employee performance. If this is possible, we can then pay people according to how well they perform. Maybe that would give our people some incentive."

Doug Parsley was beginning to realize a need for identifying his top producers. All managers need to be able to recognize differences in job performance. Employees can then be rewarded on the basis of their contributions toward organizational goals. The appraisal method used must be perceived as being fair and equitable and it should also serve to identify employee development needs. The overall purpose of this chapter is to emphasize the importance of performance appraisal as it relates to human resources management and its special implications for training and development of the firm's human resources.

PERFORMANCE APPRAISAL DEFINED

Nothing is more discouraging for a top producer in a work group than to receive the same pay increase as a marginal employee. In such a situation, the incentive to do superior work certainly declines. While employees at all levels, management and nonmanagement alike, are appraised continuously, it is desirable to summarize these evaluations periodically. The process which leads to this formalized activity is referred to as **performance appraisal,** performance rating, employee performance review, personnel appraisal, performance evaluation, employee evaluation, and (perhaps the oldest of the terms used) merit rating. A properly designed performance appraisal system will develop an accurate yet concise evaluation of an individual's work performance over a given period of time.

While most firms recognize the need for an appraisal system, many do not have a satisfactory program. When the authors requested copies of performance appraisal forms from a large number of personnel managers, many replied, "We would be happy to do so but we are in the process of developing a new one." James H. Kennedy, editor and publisher of *Consultant News* magazine, stated that finding a workable appraisal system "seems like a search for the Holy Grail."[1] Developing a sound performance appraisal method continues to be a significant management challenge. But, a systematic appraisal method is needed to assure that a firm's human resources are properly developed and utilized.

OBJECTIVES OF PERFORMANCE APPRAISAL

The overriding purpose of any performance appraisal system is to improve the overall effectiveness of the organization. In order to accomplish this purpose,

---

[1]"The Rating Game," *The Wall Street Journal,* May 23, 1978, p. 1 (hereafter cited as "The Rating Game"). Reprinted by permission of *The Wall Street Journal,* © Dow Jones & Company, Inc. (1978). All rights reserved.

a number of specific objectives need to be attained. But, there appears to be no universal agreement as to the precise objectives to be pursued. As you see in Table 10–1, comments from several personnel executives suggest that specific appraisal goals differ from firm to firm. There are, however, several areas within which objectives may be achieved. It is very unlikely that a single system can effectively serve all of these purposes. As will be shown later, some appraisal systems are more appropriate in achieving certain objectives than other systems.

Human Resources Planning

You recall that one aspect of human resources planning is an analysis of the firm's labor supply. This process includes the determination of the skills and qualifications of its employees. Managers must have information, often contained in skills inventories, which reveals the promotability and potential of members of the work force. The source for much of this information is the organization's performance appraisal system.

Employee Selection and Recruitment

Performance evaluation ratings may be helpful in predicting the future performance of job applicants. It may be found, for example, that a significant number of successful managers received their training from certain schools or majored in particular fields. Knowledge of this type could certainly influence the direction taken in recruitment. Also, in validating selection tests, the employee's rating is often used as the variable against which test scores are compared. The validity of the selection test in this case depends upon the accuracy of the performance appraisal results.

Communication

Most of us have a strong need to know how well we are performing. A good appraisal system provides the desired feedback. You would find it quite difficult to improve your course grade if you did not know what your instructor expected. A worker in business has a similar problem. Sound appraisal programs can improve communication between superiors and their subordinates. The appraisal interview presents an excellent opportunity for both parties to express their opinions. While the formal appraisal interview should not serve as a substitute for day-to-day communication, it does provide a unique opportunity for an information exchange related to the individual's job performance and the overall work situation.

Table 10–1. Performance appraisal objectives

Company	Name and Title of Person Responding	
Sea-Land Service, Inc.	Thomas M. Jordan Vice President Personnel	• Performance measurement and correction • Identify training and development needs • Merit pay
Owens-Illinois, Inc.	David A. Miron, Ed.D. Director Human Resources Management	• Employee/supervisor interaction • Clarify job elements and standards of performance • Evaluate performance and potential • Document career interests and readiness for other positions • Establish plans for career development and/or improved performance • Computer entry for internal searches
General Mills, Incorporated	F. E. Westervelt, Jr. Coordinator Executive Development	• Individual development • Assessment of potential • Compensation
New York Times	Peter M. Spinner Manager Training/Staff Development	• Establish performance goals • Analyze performance problems • Plan for performance improvement
Inland Container Corporation	David J. Harrison Vice President Employee Relations/ Staff Services	• Measure performance against previously determined quantitative/qualitative objectives • Provide useful performance feedback to ratee • Develop action plan for ratee to improve weak areas of performance

A completed appraisal form should point out employees' specific needs for training and development which will lead to their improved performance.[2] For instance, if Mary Jones receives a marginal evaluation with regard to her written communication abilities, additional training in this area is suggested. If the personnel manager detects that a number of first-line supervisors were rated low in communication skills, a communication improvement session for all first-line supervisors may be needed. By identifying these deficiencies, Personnel is able to develop T&D programs which permit individuals to build on their strengths and minimize their deficiencies. The existence of an appraisal system does not guarantee that employees will be properly trained and developed. However, the task of determining training and development needs is simplified when appraisal data are available.

Compensation

The results of a performance appraisal system provide the basis for administrative decisions affecting pay increases, promotion, demotion, and transfers. With regard to pay, most managers feel that outstanding job performance should be rewarded tangibly through increased financial compensation. They believe that "what you reward is what you get." This may be the difficulty with the compensation practice described at the beginning of the chapter by Doug Parsley, the production vice president. He has discovered that a good swift kick does not encourage people to produce at their highest level of efficiency over the long run. And, when poor performers are given the same pay increases as top producers, chances are good that the organization will begin to receive marginal performance even from its previously productive employees. To encourage good performance, a firm should design and implement a fair performance appraisal system and then reward the most productive workers.

Assessment of Employee Potential

Some organizations attempt to assess employee potential as they appraise job performance. It has been said that the best predictors of future behavior are past behaviors.[3] However, an employee's past performance in a given job may not accurately indicate future behavior in a higher level position. The best salesperson in the company may not become a successful district sales manager. The best computer programmer may, if promoted, be a disaster as a data pro-

[2]Thomas N. Baylie, Carl J. Kujawski and Drew M. Young, "Appraisals of 'People' Resources," in *ASPA Handbook of Personnel and Industrial Relations, Staffing Policies and Strategies*, vol. 1, eds. Dale Yoder and Herbert G. Heneman, Jr. (Washington, D.C.: The Bureau of National Affairs, Inc., 1974), pp. 4–168.
[3]L. L. Cummings and Donald P. Schwab, "Designing Appraisal Systems for Information Yield," *California Management Review*, 20 (Summer 1978): 22.

Kathryn D. McKee, APD
Vice President
First Interstate BanCorp.

Kathryn D. McKee, former president of the International Association of Personnel Women says, "The field of Personnel is on the cutting edge of major social change." In today's highly complex environment, Ms. McKee believes that the programs developed and the decisions made by Personnel can profoundly impact a business firm's profits.

Kathryn's extensive background in Personnel includes experience with several orga-

nizations. After she graduated from college, her first assignment was as an employment clerk for a major aerospace firm in southern California. After this job, she obtained a position as employment security officer with the State of California, and, as she puts it, she was "out from behind the typewriter at last!" At this job she received a solid foundation for her career in human resources management. Kathryn obtained invaluable experience in job classification, employment interviewing, unemployment claims determination, and vocational counseling.

Ms. McKee next joined Mattel, Inc., as an employment interviewer. She progressed rapidly to salary analyst and later to corporate compensation manager. While at Mattel, Kathryn demonstrated that raising a family and being a business executive are not mutually exclusive—her employment with Mattel was interrupted briefly for two maternity leaves.

The next phase of Ms. McKee's career began when the president of a small firm sought her out to serve as director of industrial relations. Three weeks into her job, the Teamsters were trying to organize the office employees.

cessing manager. Overemphasizing technical skills and ignoring other equally important skills is a common error in promoting employees into management jobs. Recognition of this problem has led some firms to separate performance appraisals from the assessment of potential. These firms have established "assessment centers" which will be discussed in a later section.

THE PERFORMANCE APPRAISAL PROCESS

Many of the external and internal environmental factors discussed in Chapter 2 can influence the appraisal process. Governmental legislation, for example, requires that appraisal systems be nondiscriminatory. In the 1977 case of *Mistretta* v. *Sandia Corporation* (a subsidiary of Western Electric Company, Inc.),

"Ironically they picked the day we were to implement the new salary administration plan for *all* nonunion employees to pass out the signature cards, almost as if they knew we were starting to create programs. After a few harried hours of panic and some counsel from our labor attorney, we proceeded to implement our programs and face down the Union. Anyone who has been through that experience will attest to the exhileration and the anxiety it creates. There are so many things employers can't do in such situations. The episode came to a head when, on advice of counsel, we held an open meeting for all nonunion employees and the new President in effect said, 'We're new and we're here to make this company run better. Give us six months to make improvements. If, after that time, you feel you need a union to make it better, then do what you want, but at least give us a chance.' The upshot of that was, acting upon a request from an employee, top management held a series of small-group, open meetings to air problems and respond with what we could do to solve them. The problems ranged from 'The carpet is dirty' to 'We have lousy benefits,' both of which were true at that time. After three months, we had all the issues resolved, the teamsters had no show of interest, and the organizing attempt was moot."

When Twentieth Century Fox needed to fill the position of corporate compensation manager, they selected Kathryn McKee. After a year of developing, organizing, and implementing a compensation program, she embarked on still another major project which encompassed designing the company's corporate equal opportunity program. Later she moved from compensation to establish a management development function as well.

Kathryn's newest career opportunity came when First Interstate BanCorp recruited her as vice president of compensation and benefits, responsible for designing and implementing benefit programs which affect over 32,000 employees, and for developing corporate compensation policies and administrative tools such as a state of the art quantitative job evaluation plan used to analyze and evaluate senior executive positions. "It is in this position I am able to draw on all the human resources experience I have. Compensation and benefits planning affects and is affected by all aspects of our profession."

a district judge ruled against the company stating that "there is sufficient circumstantial evidence to indicate that age bias and age based policies appear throughout the performance rating process to the detriment of the protected age group.[4] The *Albemarle Paper* v. *Moody* case supported validation requirements for performance appraisals in addition to selection tests. Organizations must avoid any appraisal method which results in discriminatory decisions related to training opportunities, pay increases, promotions, or other areas of employment.[5]

The labor union is another external factor that might affect a firm's appraisal process. Unions have traditionally stressed seniority as the basis for promotions and pay increases. They may vigorously oppose the use of a manage-

[4]James W. Walker and Daniel E. Lupton, "Performance Appraisal Programs and Age Discrimination Law," *Aging and Work* 2 (1978): 73–83.
[5]Dena B. Schneir, "The Impact of EEO Legislation on Performance Appraisals," *Personnel* 55 (July-August 1978): 24.

ment designed performance appraisal system which would be used for these purposes.

There are also factors within the internal environment which can affect the performance appraisal process. For instance, the type of organizational climate can serve to assist or hinder the process. In today's highly complex organizations, employees must often rely upon co-workers in performing their tasks. A closed, nontrusting climate may discourage the cooperation that is so often needed to successfully complete the job. In such an environment, performance may suffer even though the worker would like to do a good job.

Figure 10–1. **The performance appraisal process.**

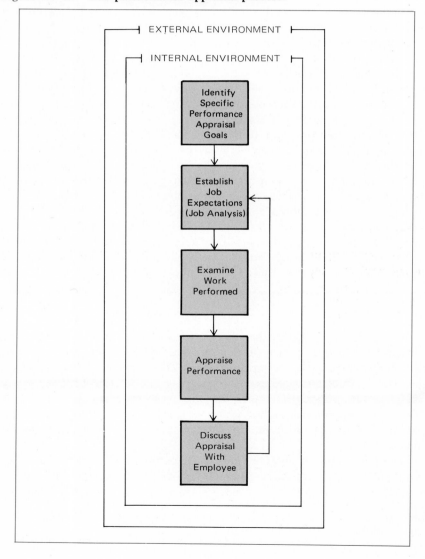

And, it may be quite difficult to recognize the true contribution of an individual worker.

Identification of specific goals establishes the starting point for the performance appraisal process (see Figure 10–1). In the previous section, we identified areas within which performance appraisal goals may be set. Because an appraisal system cannot effectively serve all purposes, a firm must select those specific goals it desires to achieve. For example, some firms may want to stress training and development goals whereas other organizations may wish to focus on administrative decisions such as pay adjustments. It is entirely possible that a firm may require more than one system if multiple goals are desired.

Once specific appraisal goals have been established, workers must then understand what is expected from them in their jobs. This normally takes the form of discussions with their supervisors to review the major duties determined through job analysis and contained in the job description.

Once the work has been performed, the results are examined and performance is then evaluated based upon previously established job performance standards. The results of evaluation are then communicated to the worker. The performance evaluation discussion serves to reestablish job requirements in the employee's mind. As previously stated, performance appraisal is a dynamic, ongoing process.

RESPONSIBILITY FOR APPRAISAL

In most organizations, Personnel is responsible for designing and overseeing the appraisal programs. The person who conducts performance appraisals varies from company to company. However, direct participation by line management in the operation of the program is necessary for success.[6] Several possibilities exist as to who will actually rate the employee.

Immediate Superior

An individual's immediate superior commonly conducts the performance appraisal. There are several valid reasons for this choice. In the first place, the superior should be in an excellent position to observe an employee's performance. No one is likely to know the subordinate's capabilities better than his or her superior. Another reason is that the superior has the responsibility for managing a particular unit. When the task of evaluating subordinates is given to another person, the supervisor's authority may become seriously undermined. Finally, training and development of subordinates is an important element in every manager's job. Because appraisal programs are often closely re-

[6]William F. Lloyd, Jr., "Performance Appraisal: A Shortsighted Approach for Installing a Workable Program," *Personnel Journal* 56 (September 1977): 446–450.

lated to T&D, the immediate superior may be the logical choice to conduct the performance evaluation.

On the negative side, immediate superiors may emphasize certain aspects of employee performance to the neglect of others. Also, managers have been known to manipulate evaluations to justify their decisions on pay increases and promotions. The immediate superior will probably continue to be the most likely person to evaluate employee performance. Organizations will seek alternatives, however, because of the weaknesses mentioned plus a desire to broaden the perspective of the appraisal.

Subordinates

Managers in a few firms have concluded that subordinate evaluation is feasible. They reason that subordinates are in a good position to view their superior's managerial effectiveness. Advocates of this approach believe that supervisors will become especially conscious of the work group's needs and will do a better job of managing. Others argue that evaluation by subordinates may cause the supervisor to become excessively concerned with popularity.

Peers

Another possible practice is to have employee's evaluated by their peers. Proponents of this approach believe that peer evaluation need not result in popularity contests. Peer appraisal, they feel, may be reliable if the work group is stable over a reasonable period of time and performs tasks that require interaction. However, little research has been conducted to determine how peers establish standards for evaluating others or the overall effect of peer appraisal on the group's attitude.[7]

Group Appraisal

When **group appraisal** is used, several managers who know the employee work with a coordinator to appraise the worker's performance. For instance, if a person regularly works with the data processing manager and the financial manager, these two individuals might participate in the evaluation. An advantage of this approach is that it maintains as much objectivity as possible. A disadvantage is that it diminishes the role of the immediate supervisor. Also, it may be difficult to get managers together and to schedule the group appraisal.

Self-Appraisal

Employees become actively involved in thinking about their work contributions when they engage in **self-appraisal**. Also, because employee develop-

[7]Angelo S. DeNisi and Jimmy L. Mitchell, "An Analysis of Peer Ratings as Predictors and Criterion Measures and a Proposed New Application," *Academy of Management Review* 3 (April 1978): 369–374.

"I advise you to become knowledgeable about the operations of a personnel department before going out on job interviews. Then be willing to accept a personnel job offer that may seem to be non-personnel oriented, such as salary administration analyst, pension analyst, benefits analyst, or systems analyst. These areas are important and they are often the most difficult to fill with qualified candidates. Be prepared to offer the employer a variety of skills such as counseling, research techniques, and familiarity with computer operations. If the student has the opportunity, he or she should take a course in statistics, research, or computer language. If possible, seek a two-day-a-week internship with a company personnel department. (This should become a course requirement within the university program just as student teaching is a requirement for education majors.)"

**Joelyn Iannone, Manager, Career Education and Training
Grumman Aerospace Corporation**

ment is self-development, they may become more highly motivated. Self-appraisal has great appeal to managers primarily concerned with employee participation and training and development.

Combinations

In seeking an answer to the question, "Who shall evaluate?", we should recognize that the approaches previously cited are not mutually exclusive. Many are used in combination. For example, "RCA Corporation tries to minimize subjectivity by having each RCA manager rated separately by a group of fellow workers, generally including his immediate superior, two or three higher level managers, two or three peers and one of two workers in lower positions. This multiple assessment, RCA feels, gives a better-rounded indication of a manager's performance."[8] This unique approach illustrates the importance some organizations place upon the appraisal process. The use of combination methods may provide greater insight into an individual's actual performance.

THE APPRAISAL PERIOD

The performance evaluations are typically reduced to write-ups at specific time intervals. In most organizations, this time period is either annual or semi-annual.[9] Additional evaluations are often made just before the end of an individual's probationary period. It is also common practice for new employees

[8]"The Rating Game," p. 1.
[9]Robert C. Ford and Kenneth M. Jennings, "How to Make Performance Appraisals More Effective," *Personnel* 54 (April 1977): 51.

to be evaluated several times during their first year of employment. The following are examples of the evaluation periods for three companies:

- The New York *Times* evaluates all its guild and non-union employees annually. Craft unions are not included in this process.
- Cessna Aircraft Company appraises all monthly salaried employees and all weekly salaried supervisors approximately once a year.
- General Mills, Inc. evaluates all employees on an annual basis except for operative, nonexempt employees, who are evaluated each six months.

The appraisal period may begin with the employee's hiring-in date, or all employees may be evaluated at the same time. While there are advantages to both practices, the staggered appraisal period seems to have greater merit. There may not be sufficient time to evaluate each employee adequately if all evaluations are conducted at the same time. The problem would be especially acute in larger departments.

TRADITIONAL METHODS OF APPRAISAL

There are a number of appraisal methods from which to choose. The particular objectives that a firm emphasizes and the expense it is willing to incur are primary factors in deciding which appraisal method to use. Appraisal methods can be classified in a number of different ways. In this book we will use two classifications: traditional methods and results-oriented methods such as management by objectives. Traditional employee performance appraisal includes some methods which have been used by organizations for many years.

Rating Scales

Rating scales are probably the most commonly used method of appraising employee performance. According to one study, the rating scale method is used more than all other appraisal methods combined (see Table 10–2). With this method, employees are evaluated according to defined factors. These factors are divided into a number of degrees from the highest to the lowest level. The factors chosen are typically of two types: job related and personal characteristics (see Figure 10–2). As you see, job related factors include quantity and quality of work, while personal factors consist of such attributes as dependability, initiative, adaptability, and cooperation. The rater completes the form by indicating the degree of each factor which is most descriptive of the employee or her or his performance.

Notice that this illustration is—as a reviewer of this book candidly noted—a good example of a poor form. There are no behaviors to refer to and the rater is forced to make judgments on vague criteria. While the form is ad-

Table 10–2. Usage of performance appraisal methods

Method	Small Organizations	Large Organizations	All
Rating scale	59.5%	54.2%	56.7%
Essay	25.8	24.2	24.9
MBO	8.5	16.6	12.7
All others	6.2	5.0	5.7
Total	100.0	100.0	100.0

Source: "Performance Appraisal—A Survey of Current Practices" by Alan H. Locher and Kenneth S. Teel. Reprinted with permission *Personnel Journal* copyright 1977.

mittedly deficient, it unfortunately resembles all too closely many used by organizations today. It could be dramatically improved by exclusively using evaluation factors which are job related and determined through job analysis.

Some firms provide space for the rater to comment on the evaluation given for each factor. This practice may be especially encouraged when either the highest or lowest rating is given. For instance, if an employee is rated "Unsatisfactory" in the "Initiative" category, the rater must provide written justification for this low evaluation. The purpose of this activity is to avoid arbitrary and hastily made judgments.

Again referring to Figure 10–2, you can see that each factor and each factor degree has been defined. In order to receive an "Exceptional" rating for the factor "Quality of Work," a person must consistently exceed the prescribed work requirements. The more precisely the various factors and degrees are defined, the better the rater can evaluate worker performance. Evaluation consistency throughout the organization is achieved when each rater has the same interpretation of the various grades.

Many rating scale performance appraisal forms also provide for an assessment of the employee's growth potential. As you can see in Figure 10–2, there are four categories for evaluating a person's potential for future growth and development. They range from "Now at or near maximum performance in present job" to "No apparent limitations." Although there are weaknesses in attempting to evaluate both past performance and future potential at the same time, this practice is often followed.

Critical Incidents

The **critical incident** method of performance appraisal requires written records of highly favorable and highly unfavorable actions occurring in an employee's work. When an employee's action significantly impacts the department's effectiveness—either positively or negatively—the manager writes it down. This is a critical incident. At the end of the appraisal period, the rater has relevant data to use in evaluating employee performance. An example of the use of this method related to an employee's "Ability to Perform the Job with Available

Employee's Name _____

Job Title _____

Department _____

Supervisor _____

Evaluation Period:
   From _____ to _____

Instructions for Evaluation:
1. Consider only one factor at a time. Do not permit rating given for one factor to affect decision for others.
2. Consider performance for entire evaluation period. Avoid concentration on recent events or isolated incidents.
3. Remember that the average employee performs duties in a satisfactory manner. An above average or exceptional rating indicates that the employee has clearly distinguished himself or herself from the average employee.

EVALUATION FACTORS	Unsatisfactory. Does not meet requirements.	Below average. Needs improvement. Requirements occasionally not met.	Average. Consistently meets requirements.	Good. Frequently exceeds requirements.	Exceptional. Consistently exceeds requirements.
QUANTITY OF WORK: Consider the volume of work achieved. Is productivity at an acceptable level?					
QUALITY OF WORK: Consider accuracy, precision, neatness, and completeness in handling assigned duties.					
DEPENDABILITY: Consider degree to which employee can be relied on to meet work commitments.					
INITIATIVE: Consider self-reliance, resourcefulness, and willingness to accept responsibility.					
ADAPTABILITY: Consider ability to respond to changing requirements and conditions.					
COOPERATION: Consider ability to work for and with others. Are assignments, including overtime, willingly accepted?					

POTENTIAL FOR FUTURE GROWTH AND DEVELOPMENT:
☐ Now at or near maximum performance in present job.
☐ Now at or near maximum performance in this job, but has potential for improvement in another job, such as:

_____

☐ Capable of progressing after further training and experience.
☐ No apparent limitations.

EMPLOYEE STATEMENT: I agree ☐   Disagree ☐ with this evaluation
   Comments: _____

Employee _____   Date _____

Supervisor _____   Date _____

Reviewing Manager _____   Date _____

Figure 10–2.   **Rating scales method of performance appraisal.**

Table 10–3. Critical-incident method example

Ability to Perform the Job with Available Resources			
Negative Impact		**Positive Impact**	
March 25	Overran budget for the Holmes production report by $500 as a result of inefficient time management.	January 29	Completed the Thompson project on time and within budget in spite of two key employees being ill.

Resources" is shown in Table 10–3. As you can see, the report focuses only on unusual facts as they relate to organizational effectiveness.

Essay

In the **essay method** of evaluation, the rater simply writes a brief narrative describing the employee's performance. This method tends to focus on extreme behavior in the employee's work rather than routine day-to-day performance. Ratings of this type depend heavily upon the evaluator's writing ability. As the evaluations are reviewed, a positive evaluation may be negatively received if the evaluator misspells words or cannot write a good paragraph. Some supervisors, because of their excellent writing ability, can make even a marginal worker appear to be excellent. There might also be difficulty in comparing evaluations. However, some managers believe that the essay method is the best approach to employee evaluation.

Ranking and Paired Comparison

In using the **ranking method** of performance appraisal, the rater simply ranks employees in a given group on the basis of their overall performance. For instance, the best employee in the department will be ranked number one and the poorest will receive the lowest ranking. A major difficulty occurs when a department consists of individuals who possess comparable abilities.

Paired comparison, a variation of the ranking method, involves comparing the performance of each employee with every other employee in the group. As you can see in Figure 10–3, Mary Bone's performance was compared with that of five other employees. She was considered to be more productive than Bill Massey, Bob Marshall, and Wanda Parker (a check mark (✔) was placed in the box under each of these employee's names). Mary was considered to be less productive than George Magellan and Dorothy Bryan. The "3" in the total column indicates that Mary was rated higher than three employees and lower than two.

The same procedure is followed for the other employees. An examination of the total number of checks received by each employee gives a rank order. The highest performance ranking was given to George Magellan (who received five checks), the next highest to Dorothy Bryan (four checks), and so on.

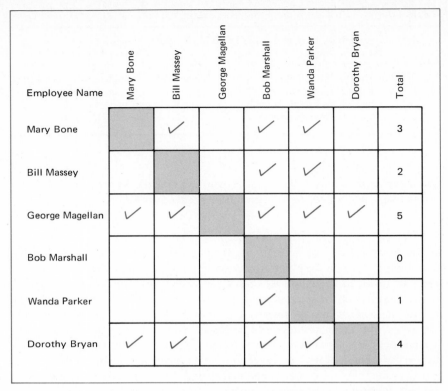

Figure 10–3. **A worksheet for the paired comparison method of appraisal.**

Forced Distribution

Using **forced distribution,** the rater is required to assign individuals in the work group to a limited number of categories similar to a normal frequency distribution. As an example, employees in the top 10 percent are placed in the highest group; the next 20 percent in the next highest group, the next 40 percent in the middle group, the next 20 percent in the next group, and the remaining 10 percent in the lowest category. This approach makes the rather questionable assumption that all groups of employees will have the same distribution of excellent, average, and poor performers. If one department has all outstanding workers, the supervisor would likely be hard pressed to decide who should be placed in the lower categories.

Forced-Choice and Weighted Checklist Performance Reports

In **forced-choiced performance reports,** the individual performing the appraisal is given a series of statements about an individual. These statements are arranged in blocks of two or more and the rater indicates which statement is most or least descriptive of the employee. A difficulty often arises because the two statements may appear to be virtually identical in describing the employee.

With the **weighted checklist method,** the rater completes a form similar to the forced-choice performance but the various responses have been assigned different weights. The form includes questions related to the employee's behavior and the evaluator answers each question either positively or negatively. The evaluator is not aware of how each question is weighted.

As with forced-choice performance reports, the weighted checklist is expensive to design. While both methods strive for objectivity, they have the mutual problem of the evaluator not knowing the items which contribute most to successful performance.

Behaviorally Anchored Rating Scales

The **Behaviorally Anchored Rating Scale** (BARS) method combines elements of the traditional rating scales and critical incidents methods. In addition, BARS typically requires considerable employee participation which may increase its acceptance by supervisors and subordinates. In BARS, various performance levels are shown along a scale and described in terms of an employee's specific job behavior. Table 10–4 illustrates a BARS system which was developed to evaluate interviewers and claims deputies for the employment service of a state Department of Labor. Notice that the factor "Ability to Absorb and Interpret Policies" is job related and carefully defined. Each point on the scale is also described in terms which are more meaningful than, for example, "excellent," "average," or "unacceptable." BARS was developed to overcome weaknesses in other evaluation methods, and researchers have been comparing BARS to other methods such as rating scales. While the results of this research are mixed, BARS had not been shown to be superior in overcoming rater errors or in achieving psychometric soundness.[10] Although the reasons are not clear, there are indications that it has not lived up to earlier expectations.[11]

A CRITIQUE OF TRADITIONAL APPRAISAL METHODS

Many of the traditional performance appraisal approaches have received considerable criticism. Because the rating scales method is so commonly used, it

[10]Stephen J. Carroll and Craig E. Schneier, *Performance Appraisal and Review Systems: The Identification, Measurement, and Development of Performance in Organizations* (Glenview, IL: Scott, Foresman and Company, 1982), p. 117.
[11]Robert S. Atkin and Edward J. Conlon, "Behaviorally Anchored Rating Scales: Some Theoretical Issues," *Academy of Management Review* 3 (January 1978): 119.

Table 10–4. BARS for factor: "Ability to absorb and interpret policies"

Interviewers and claims deputies must keep abreast of current changes and interpret and apply new information. Some can absorb and interpret new policy guides and procedures quickly with a minimum of explanation. Others seem unable to learn even after repeated explanations and practice. They have difficulty learning and following new policies. When making this rating, disregard job knowledge and experience and evaluate ability to learn on the job.

Very Positive	9	This interviewer could be expected to serve as an information source concerning new and changed policies for others in the office.
	8	Could be expected to be aware quickly of program changes and explain these changes to employers.
	7	Could be expected to reconcile conflicting policies and procedures correctly to meet immediate job needs.
	6	Could be expected to recognize the need for additional information to gain better understanding of policy changes.
Neutral	5	After receiving instruction on completing ESAR forms, this interviewer could be expected to complete the forms correctly.
	4	Could be expected to require some help and practice in mastering new policies and procedures.
	3	Could be expected to know that there is a problem, but might go down many blind alleys before realizing they are wrong.
	2	Could be expected to incorrectly interpret program guidelines, thereby referring an unqualified person.
Very Negative	1	Even after repeated explanations, this interviewer could be expected to be unable to learn new procedures.

Source: Adapted from Cheedle W. Millard, Fred Luthans, and Robert L. Ottemann, "A New Breakthrough for Performance Appraisal," *Business Horizons* 19 (August 1976), 69. Copyright, 1976, by the Foundation for the School of Business at Indiana University. Reprinted by permission.

has perhaps received the greatest attention. In all fairness, many of the problems commonly mentioned are not inherent in the various methods. Rather, they reflect an improper use of the method. For example, raters may be improperly trained or not trained at all. Also, the appraisal device may not be job related.

Lack of Objectivity

A potential weakness of traditional methods of appraisal is that they lack objectivity. In the rating scales method, for example, commonly used factors such as attitude, loyalty, and personality are difficult to measure accurately. In addition, these factors may have little to do with an employee's performance.

A degree of subjectivity will probably exist in any appraisal method. However, to emphasize objectivity, job related factors should be stressed. Employee appraisal based primarily on personal characteristics may place the evaluator and the company in untenable positions relative to both the employee and EEO guidelines. They may have to show that the factors used are job related.

Halo Error

A **halo error** occurs when the evaluator perceives one factor as being of paramount importance and gives a good overall rating to an employee who rates high on this factor. Of course, this type of error could work in the opposite direction as well. For example, David Edwards, accounting supervisor, placed a high value on "neatness," which was a factor used in the company's performance appraisal system. As David was evaluating the performance of his senior accounting clerk, Carl Curtis, he noted that Carl was not a very neat individual and gave him a low ranking on this factor. David also permitted, consciously or unconsciously, the low ranking on neatness to carry over to other factors with the effect that Carl received undeserved low ratings on all factors.

Leniency

The giving of undeserved high ratings is referred to as **leniency**. Thomas M. Jordan, vice president of Personnel for Sea-Land Service, Incorporated, stated that one of the major problems encountered in his company's appraisal system is "getting managers to be objective and honest, especially where poor performance is involved." Research tends to support the belief that evaluations will be inflated if a supervisor is required to discuss them with employees.[12] In many situations the evaluating supervisor simply gives the employee the benefit of the doubt. One study revealed that over 50 percent of the employees in one organization were rated in the most favorable category, "Excellent."[13] These actions are often motivated out of a desire to avoid controversy over the appraisal. This practice is more prevalent where highly subjective factors are used as performance criteria.

Central Tendency

Central tendency is a common error that occurs when employees are incorrectly rated near the average or middle of the scale. Some rating scale systems require the evaluator to justify in writing extremely high or extremely low ratings. In these instances, the rater may avoid possible controversy or criticism by giving only average ratings.[14]

Recent Behavior Bias

Anyone who has observed the behavior of young children several weeks before Christmas can readily identify with the problem of recent behavior bias. All

[12]Hubert S. Field and William H. Holley, "Subordinates' Characteristics, Supervisors' Ratings, and Decisions to Discuss Appraisal Results," *Academy of Management Journal* 20 (June 1977): 315–321.
[13]William H. Holley, Hubert S. Field, and Nona J. Barnett, "Analyzing Performance Appraisal Systems: An Empirical Study," *Personnel Journal* 55 (September 1976): 458
[14]Marion G. Haynes, "Developing an Appraisal Program: Part I," *Personnel Journal* 57 (January 1978): 17.

of a sudden, it seems, the wildest hellions in the neighborhood develop angelic personalities in anticipation of the rewards they expect to receive.

Individuals in the workforce are not children, but they are human. Almost every employee will be able to tell you the exact time he or she is scheduled for a performance review. The employees' actions may not be conscious. But, behavior often improves and productivity tends to rise several days or weeks before the scheduled evaluation. It is only natural to remember recent behavior more clearly than actions from the more distant past. However, performance appraisals generally cover a specified period of time. Therefore, an individual's performance should be considered for the entire period.

Personal Bias

It is possible for appraising supervisors to have biased feelings about anything from the way employees part their hair to the style of clothes they wear. Unfortunately, some supervisors may also display partiality toward a member of a certain race, religion, sex, or age group. While federal legislation protects employees in these groups, discrimination continues in at least isolated cases.

Judgmental Role of Evaluator

Supervisors using traditional performance evaluation methods have been accused of "playing God" with their employees. The rating supervisors often control virtually every aspect of the process. They make decisions about the ratings and typically try to tell or sell their version to their employees. This highly judgmental role often places employees on the defensive. The results of such a relationship are hardly conducive to employee development.

The manager or supervisor tends to serve as a judge in appraising employees in traditional performance rating approaches. These and other factors have resulted in mounting criticism of these methods. As a result, many organizations have begun using a results oriented approach such as management by objectives.

MANAGEMENT BY OBJECTIVES (MBO)

Although the concept of management by objectives was set forth in Peter F. Drucker's *The Practice of Management*,[15] published in 1954, it was described only a few years ago as the "latest rage" in performance appraisal.[16] As previously discussed, the MBO concept reflects a management philosophy which values and utilizes employee contributions. It is also an effective method of evaluating an employee's performance and we now discuss it in this context.

[15]Peter F. Drucker, *The Practice of Management* (New York: Harper and Row, Publishers, 1954).
[16]"The Rating Game," p. 1.

In traditional approaches to performance appraisal, personal traits of employees are often used as criteria for evaluating performance. In addition, the role of the evaluating supervisor is similar to that of a judge. With MBO, the focus of the appraisal process shifts from the worker's personal attributes to job performance. The supervisor's role changes from that of an umpire to that of a counselor and facilitator. Also, the employee's function evolves from that of a passive bystander to an active participant. Individuals jointly establish goals with their superiors and then are given some latitude in the means used to achieve their objectives.

At the end of the appraisal period, the employee and supervisor meet for an appraisal interview. They first review the extent to which the goals have been achieved and second, the actions needed to solve remaining problems. Under MBO, the supervisor keeps two-way communications channels open throughout the appraisal period. The problem-solving discussion during the appraisal interview is merely another conversation designed to assist the worker in progressing according to plan. At this time, goals are established for the next evaluation period and the process repeats itself.

It should be obvious that not all leadership styles are compatible with the participative concept of MBO. It probably would not be successful in an organization run by highly autocratic managers. An attempt to implement an MBO appraisal system in such a firm would likely result in top management believing that, "MBO is OK in theory but no good in practice." In this case, the theory is quite sound. Implementation problems often stem from the incompatibility of the theory with the organization's climate.

MBO: AN ILLUSTRATION

The Dr Pepper Company is a highly successful soft-drink manufacturer. The company recognizes that its plans for future growth require, not only sufficient capital, but also adequate human resources. Dr Pepper views its management by objectives system as the glue which holds its rapid change management process together.

Ray Ackerman (former director of management development for Dr Pepper) was brought into the company over a decade ago for the purpose of implementing an MBO system. However, his plans received a temporary setback when the results of an attitude survey became known. The study revealed that Dr Pepper's prevalent management style was not compatible with the participative philosophy inherent in MBO systems. Knowledge of this situation inspired the creation of extensive management training and development programs which were conducted over a period of four to five years. Only then did the company's management believe that it had progressed to the stage where it could effectively implement an MBO system. A successful plan is currently in operation at Dr Pepper. The company's MBO program is considered to be an evolutionary process which is sufficiently flexible to adapt to meet the company's changing needs.

NAME _____   JOB TITLE _____   TIME IN POSITION _____

DEPT/DIV_____   BRANCH LOCATION _____

I. Indicate what you and employee consider special accomplishments and/or performance since the last review.

II. What were the results achieved for the objectives agreed upon during the last performance review? (If more space is required use separate page and attach appropriate number of copies.)

A. Objective   B. Result
   1.   4.   1.   4.

   2.   5.   2.   5.

   3.   6.   3.   6.

C. Mark on scale an overall evaluation of employee performance compared to expected results; 1 is substandard 5 is typical and 9 is special requiring recognition.

1	2	3	4	5	6	7	8	9

III. List any special assignments that could be assigned to or volunteered by the employee that could improve performance and/or personal development.

_____

(Personnel Department)

(Management Development Center)

(Supervisor)

(Employee)

Figure 10–4. Dr Pepper's supervisory/exempt performance review form. (Source: Dr Pepper Company.)

At regular intervals throughout Dr Pepper, superiors and subordinates discuss and negotiate specific performance objectives. The process of meshing the goals of each may require several discussion sessions. The end result—mutually established objectives—constitutes the performance standards against which the subordinate will be evaluated.

A sample of the forms used in Dr Pepper's MBO program for supervisory employees may be seen in Figure 10–4. A statement summarizing the employee's special accomplishments since the last performance review is provided in Part I. Note that the statement seeks the opinion of both superior and sub-

IV. Listed below are the routine, problem solving and innovative objectives that we have agreed should be accomplished during the next time period. (If more space is required use separate page and attach appropriate number of copies.)

A. Agreed Upon Objective

1.　　　　4.

2.　　　　5.

3.　　　　6.

B. Desired Result

1.　　　　4.

2.　　　　5.

3.　　　　6.

V. List assistance, aid and/or training that you will provide or recommend for the employee to ensure that desired results are achieved.

1.　　　　　　　　　4.

2.　　　　　　　　　5.

3.

Rated Employee _____ Date_____

Supervisor/Manager _____ Date_____

Reviewed By _____ Date_____

(Personnel Department)

(Management Development Center)

(Supervisor)

(Employee)

Figure 10–4.　*(cont.)*

ordinate. Part IIA is provided for restating the objectives established during the last performance review. A description of the extent to which the objectives were achieved may be given in Part IIB. Results are compared against each previously agreed upon objective. Part IIC provides for an overall evaluation of how well the employee has achieved goals in the form of a nine degree rating scale.

Parts I and II of the performance review relate to the employee's past performance. Data related to future performance begin with Part III. Part III requires that consideration be given to any actions that can be taken by either the superior or the subordinate which could assist the employee in improving his or her performance and personal development.

The mutually agreed upon objectives for the next period are stated in Part IVA and the desired results are given in Part IVB. In Part V, a commitment is required from the superior as to the resources that the subordinate needs to accomplish the required goal. As with a legal contract, consideration is required of both parties. The subordinate agrees that the stated goals are reasonable and that they can be achieved. The superior approves the goals and makes a commitment to provide the needed support. The subordinate, the superior, and a reviewing third party sign the form. All three become actively involved in achieving goals which, ultimately, contribute to the attainment of Dr Pepper's overall goals.

The objectives established at Dr Pepper do not exist in a vacuum. Rather they are communicated throughout the company. Copies of the performance review forms are distributed to (1) the employee, (2) the supervisor, (3) Personnel, and (4) the Management Development Department. The objectives are also channeled upwards in the company to ensure that they support overall corporate plans. These routing procedures facilitate the communication and coordination of the corporation's management activities.

Performance review data are sent to the Management Development Department to permit a search for areas in which individuals or groups may need developmental assistance. This assistance may be provided in the form of management development courses, extra coaching, or counseling from the superior, or perhaps a new approach suggested by the appraisal information.

The results of Dr Pepper's efforts are an organization and its management mobilized toward achieving a common goal. And, equally important for the future, the system represents a structure by which employees learn from experience.

Management by objectives has a number of advantages over traditional approaches to employee appraisal. It is not, however, a perfect system and there are shortcomings. The positive and negative aspects of MBO were discussed in Chapter 7.

THE APPRAISAL INTERVIEW

As illustrated in the Dr Pepper Company system, at the end of an employee's appraisal period it is common practice for the evaluating supervisor to conduct a formal **appraisal interview**. This interview is essential for achieving employee development. The key to a successful interview is to structure it so that both the manager and subordinate will approach it as problem solving rather than fault finding.[17]

The interview should be scheduled soon after the end of the appraisal period. Employees usually know when their interview should take place, and

---

[17]Randall Brett and Alan J. Fredian, "Performance Appraisal: The System is Not the Solution," *Personnel Administrator* (December 1981): 62.

their anxiety tends to increase when it is delayed. Interviews with top performers are often pleasant experiences. However, many supervisors are reluctant to meet face to face with poor performers. There is often a tendency to postpone these anxiety-provoking interviews.

The amount of time devoted to an appraisal interview varies considerably due to company policy and the position of the evaluated employee. While interviewing costs must be considered, there is merit in conducting separate interviews for discussing: (1) employee performance and development and (2) pay increases. Many managers have learned that as soon as pay is mentioned in an interview it tends to dominate the conversation. For this reason, it is now a rather common practice to defer pay discussions until a second interview can be conducted. This brief second interview should be held within one or two weeks of the first.

Conducting an appraisal interview requires tact and patience on the part of the supervisor. It is often one of management's more difficult tasks. Praise should be provided when warranted, but it can have only limited value if not clearly deserved.

Criticism is especially difficult to apply. So called "constructive" criticism is often not perceived as such by the employee. Yet, it is difficult for a manager at any level to avoid criticism when conducting appraisal interviews. The supervisor should realize that all individuals have some deficiencies which may not be changed easily, if at all. Continued criticism may lead to frustration and have a damaging effect on employee development. Again, this does not mean that undesirable employee behavior should be ignored. However, discussions of sensitive issues should focus on the deficiency and not the person. Threats to the employee's self-esteem should be minimized.[18]

A serious error that is sometimes committed is for the supervisor to surprise the subordinate by bringing up some past mistake or problem. For example, if an incident had not been previously discussed, it would be most inappropriate for the supervisor to state, "Two months ago, you failed to properly coordinate your plans for implementing the new accounts receivable procedure." Good management practices and common sense dictate that this type of situation should be dealt with as it occurs and not be saved for the appraisal interview.

The entire performance appraisal process should be a positive experience for employees. In practice, however, it often is not. Negative feelings can often be traced to the appraisal interview and the manner in which it is conducted by the supervisor.[19] Ideally, appraised employees will leave the interview with positive feelings about the supervisor, the company, the job, and themselves. The prospects for improved performance will be bleak if the employee's ego is deflated. While past behavior cannot be changed, future performance can. Specific plans for the employee's development should be clearly outlined and mutually agreed upon. Cessna Aircraft has developed several

[18]Herbert H. Meyer, "The Annual Performance Review Discussion—Making it Constructive," *Personnel Journal* 56 (October 1977): 508–511.
[19]Bob Wooten, "Using Appraisals to Set Objectives," *Supervisory Management* (November 1981): 31.

hints for supervisors which have been found helpful in conducting appraisal interviews (see Figure 10–5).

Figure 10–5. **Suggestions for conducting appraisal interviews**

1. Give the employee a few days notice of the discussion and its purpose. Encourage the employee to give some preparatory thought to his or her job performance and development plans. In some cases, have employees read their written performance evaluation prior to the meeting.
2. Prepare notes and use the completed performance appraisal form as a discussion guide so that each important topic will be covered. Be ready to answer questions employees may ask about why you appraised them as you did. Encourage your employees to ask questions.
3. Be ready to suggest specific developmental activities suitable to each employee's needs. When there are specific performance problems, remember to "attack the problem, not the person."
4. Establish a friendly, helpful and purposeful tone at the outset of the discussion. Recognize that it is not unusual for you and your employee to be nervous about the discussion and use suitable techniques to put you both more at ease.
5. Assure your employee that everyone on Cessna's management team is being evaluated so that opportunities for improvement and development will not be overlooked and each person's performance will be fully recognized.
6. Make sure that the session is truly a discussion. Encourage employees to talk about how they feel they are doing on the job, how they might improve, and what developmental activities they might undertake. Often an employee's viewpoints on these matters will be quite close to your own.
7. When your appraisal differs from the employee's, discuss these differences. Sometimes employees have hidden reasons for performing in a certain manner or using certain methods. This is an opportunity to find out if such reasons exist.
8. These discussions should contain both constructive compliments and constructive criticism. Be sure to discuss the employee's strengths as well as weaknesses. Your employees should have clear pictures of how you view their performance when the discussions are concluded.
9. Occasionally the appraisal interview will uncover strong emotions. This is one of the values of regular appraisals; they can bring out bothersome feelings so they can be dealt with honestly. The emotional dimension of managing is very important. Ignoring it can lead to poor performance. Deal with emotional issues when they arise because they block a person's ability to concentrate on other issues. Consult Personnel for help when especially strong emotions are uncovered.
10. Make certain that your employees fully understand your appraisal of their performance. Sometimes it helps to have an employee orally summarize the appraisal as he or she understands it. If there are any misunderstandings they can be cleared up on the spot. Ask questions to make sure you have been fully understood.
11. Discuss the future as well as the past. Plan with the employee specific changes in performance or specific developmental activities that will allow fuller use of potential. Ask what you can do to help.
12. End the discussion on a positive, future-improvement-oriented note. You and your employee are a team, working toward the development of everyone involved.

Source: Used with the permission of Cessna Aircraft Company

ASSESSMENT CENTERS

Many employee performance appraisal systems evaluate an individual's past performance and at the same time attempt to assess his or her potential for advancement. Other organizations have developed a separate approach for assessing potential. This process often takes place in what is appropriately referred to as an **assessment center**.

The assessment center method requires employees to participate in a series of activities similar to what they might be expected to do in an actual job. The situational activities exercises are developed as a result of thorough job analysis.[20] Such activities include in-basket exercises, management games, leaderless group discussions, mock interviews, and tests. The assessors observe the employees in a secluded environment, usually separate from the work place, over a certain period of time. The assessors selected are typically experienced managers who participate in the exercises and evaluate the performance of the candidate.

Assessment centers are used increasingly for purposes of: (1) identifying employees who have higher level management potential, (2) selecting first level supervisors, and (3) determining employees' developmental needs. Assessment centers are used by over one thousand organizations[21] including small firms and such large corporations as General Electric, J.C. Penney, Ford Motor Company, and AT&T. A typical schedule for General Electric's Supervisory Assessment Center (SAC) is shown in Table 10–5. The SAC program is used for selecting new employees and assessing current employees' management potential. As you see, a number of exercises are utilized in evaluating a participant's behavior.

An evaluation of the General Electric SAC process revealed these results:

• The SAC was based on a job analysis of a supervisor's job and is considered to have content validity.[22]

• The SAC provides all candidates an equal opportunity to demonstrate their skills and does not discriminate against any employee group. For example, a study of over one thousand candidates from fourteen company locations shows the following success ratios in the SAC:

Caucasian   39%
Minority   43%
Female   46%

• Those individuals who scored highest in the SAC are the same individuals who have subsequently received the greatest number of job promotions. Thus, one area of predictive validity of the SAC was demonstrated.

There often are as many as a half dozen assessors evaluating each participant, as is the case at General Electric. The participants' position in an organ-

---

[20]Cabot L. Jaffee and Joseph T. Sefcik, Jr., "What is an Assessment Center?" *Personnel Administrator* 25 (February 1980): 40–43.

[21]*General Electric Assessment Center Manual,* General Electric Company.

[22]Content validity is inherent in the assessment center process when the exercises developed are based upon proper job analysis. This type of validity is acceptable according to the new guidelines on employee selection.

TABLE 10–5. General Electric Company's supervisory assessment center's (SAC) typical schedule

Day 1

Approximately four hours per candidate are required for the background interview and an in-basket exercise. The interview covers such traditional areas as work experience, educational background, and leadership experience. The in-basket exercise provides an opportunity for the individual to demonstrate how he or she would handle administrative problems including day-to-day "fire-fighting." All Day 1 activities are scheduled on an individual basis and are typically administered by persons in Employee Relations.

Day 2

An additional four hours are devoted to group and individual exercises. Group exercises related to reallocation of resources allow an individual's performance to be observed as the candidate solves problems in peer group situations. In the individual exercises each candidate assumes the role of a supervisor to handle four typical work-related problems. Six operating managers serve as the SAC staff for Day 2 activities. They observe and evaluate the performance of six candidates. The staff completes structured rating forms on each candidate's performance immediately following each exercise. After all exercises have been completed and the candidates dismissed, the staff conducts an overall evaluation of each individual's potential for a supervisory position. Over fifty pieces of data from each candidate's performance are reviewed along with information obtained from the interview. The staff then arrives at a consensus decision and a recommended course of action for each candidate.

Source: Used with permission of the General Electric Company.

ization often determines the amount of time spent in the center. First-level supervisory candidates may only spend a day or two, while more time may be needed for those being considered for middle management and executive jobs. The participants return to their jobs after the session is completed. The assessors then prepare their evaluation. Interestingly, because the assessors are often not full-time members of the training and development staff, they also often gain improved insights as to how managers in their organization should function. Also, while the primary purpose of assessment centers is to identify management potential, J.C. Penney's experience indicates that the "participants gain valuable insights into their own strengths, weaknesses and interests." This permits the organization and the individual to make plans for the employee's development.

LEGAL IMPLICATIONS

It has been estimated that during the first year of this decade over 30 million workers had their performance formally appraised. While appraisals have been and are widely used in industry and government, the process contains many potential sources for error.[23] Mistakes in appraising performance can have serious repercussions in various areas of human resources management, such as the improper allocation of money for merit increases. In addition, mistakes

[23]N. B. Winstanley, "Legal and Ethical Issues in Performance Appraisals," *Harvard Business Review* 58 (November–December 1980): 186.

can result in costly legal action being taken against a firm. In settling cases, courts have considered the employer liable for back pay, court costs, and other costs related to training and promoting protected group members. While the point has been made before, we want to emphasize that the *Uniform Guidelines on Employee Selection Procedures* apply to all methods used to make employment decisions, including performance evaluations. Therefore, employers must be aware of pitfalls in designing and implementing performance evaluation systems.

Certain practices have been found to be associated with the successful legal defense of employers' appraisal systems. These recommendations include:[24]

1. Conduct a thorough job analysis and use the results in developing the content of appraisal systems. The Uniform Guidelines *require* job analysis for all content and construct validation studies.

2. In designing an appraisal system, use specific, objective, or job-related standards. Because of the potential for bias, avoid the use of trait-oriented criteria.

3. Establish an affirmative action program to minimize the possibility of adversely impacting members of minority groups. This reduces the chance that a *prima facie* case of discrimination can be established by the employee.

4. Give written instructions to all individuals who will be performing appraisals. The instructions should be rather detailed and include the need for raters to be objective and unbiased.

5. Ensure that individuals who rate performance maintain sufficient employee contact and have the opportunity for observations to be able to rate accurately.

6. Provide employees with feedback on the results of their appraisals. Hold evaluation interviews on a timely basis.

7. Provide training for those individuals in the organization who will be evaluating performance. The training should include how to rate and how to conduct appraisal interviews.

8. Provide for meaningful due process. Employees should have the means for pursuing their grievances and having them addressed objectively.

Naturally, an organization cannot avoid the possibility of legal action even if all these suggestions are followed. However, positive action by a firm can substantially improve its position in court if this becomes necessary.

COST/BENEFITS ANALYSIS— PERFORMANCE APPRAISAL

Maintaining an effective ongoing performance appraisal system has certain costs attached. Merely getting a system started will likely require many hours

---

[24]Winstanley; and William H. Holley and Hubert S. Field, "Will Your Performance Appraisal System Hold Up in Court?" *Personnel* (January–February 1982): 59–64.

of developmental costs. Managers at all levels must be trained to use the system. Workers need to be "sold" on the merits of the program. Because of the legal implications of performance appraisal, the appraisal form needs to be validated to show job relatedness. In addition, it takes time to complete the appraisal form and conduct the evaluation interview. Record keeping is also a very important part of any appraisal system. The total hours associated with an effective system can be substantial.

The benefits associated with having a workable appraisal system far outweigh the costs. Virtually every aspect of human resources management is affected. Because a well designed appraisal program will be job related, compensation decisions can be based on actual job performance. Training and development decisions can focus upon the actual needs of the members of the organization. Promotion decisions can be made more rationally. Also, recruitment and selection may be enhanced because future workers may see the firm as being fair. Finally, for nonunion firms, a well conceived appraisal system can reduce favoritism complaints, a major factor should a firm desire to remain nonunion.

SUMMARY

The process which leads to a formalized evaluation of employees is referred to as performance appraisal. The overriding purpose of any performance appraisal system is to improve the overall effectiveness of the organization. The performance appraisal process begins by considering the external and internal environment. Government legislation and labor unions are prime external factors.

Identification of specific goals establishes the starting point for the performance appraisal process. Because an appraisal system cannot serve all purposes, a firm must select those specific goals it desires to achieve. Once specific goals have been established, workers must then understand what is expected from them in their jobs. This normally takes the form of discussions with their supervisors to review the major duties contained in the job description.

Once the work has been performed, the results are examined and performance is then periodically evaluated based upon previously established job performance standards. The results of the evaluation are then communicated to workers. The performance evaluation discussion serves to reestablish job requirements in the employee's mind. The process is dynamic and ongoing; each appraisal discussion results in reestablishing job performance standards.

Personnel is responsible for designing and overseeing the appraisal program. The person who conducts performance appraisals varies from company to company. Direct participation by line management in the operation of the program is necessary for success. Several possibilities exist as to who will actually rate the employee which include: immediate superior, subordinates, peers, group appraisal, self-appraisal, and combinations.

There are a number of appraisal methods from which to choose. Traditional methods include: (1) rating scales, (2) critical incidents, (3) essay, (4) ranking and paired comparison, (5) forced distribution, (6) forced-choice and weighted checklist performance reports, and (7) behaviorally anchored rating scales. Management by objectives has proven to be an effective method to evaluate employees' performances. With MBO, the focus of the appraisal process shifts from the worker's personal attributes to job performance. The supervisor's role changes from that of an umpire to that of a counselor and facilitator.

At the end of an employee appraisal period it is common practice for the evaluating supervisor to conduct a formal appraisal interview. This interview is essential for achieving employee development. The key to a successful interview is to structure it so that both the manager and subordinate will approach it as problem solving rather than fault finding.

The assessment center method requires employees to participate in a series of activities similar to what they might be expected to do in an actual job. Assessment centers are used increasingly for the purpose of: (1) identifying employees who have higher level management potential, (2) selecting first level supervisors, and (3) determining employees' developmental needs.

Certain practices have been found to be associated with the successful legal defense of employers' appraisal systems. Mistakes can result in costly legal action being taken against a firm.

Questions for Review

1. Define and give the basic purposes of performance appraisal. Briefly discuss.

2. What are the basic steps involved in the performance appraisal process?

3. Briefly describe the various alternatives as to who should conduct performance appraisals.

4. Briefly describe each of the following traditional methods of performance appraisal: (a) rating scales, (b) critical incidents, (c) essay, (d) ranking and paired comparison, (e) forced distribution, (f) forced-choice and weighted checklists, and (g) behaviorally anchored rating scales.

5. What are the basic weaknesses associated with the traditional methods of performance appraisal? Briefly describe each.

6. Describe how management by objectives could be used as an effective method of performance appraisal.

7. What is the purpose of an appraisal interview? Discuss.

8. Describe how an assessment center could be used as a means for performance appraisal.

9. What could an employer do with regard to performance appraisal to improve its position in court if this becomes necessary?

Terms for Review

Performance appraisal

Group appraisal

Self-appraisal

Rating scales

Critical incidents

Essay method

Ranking method

Paired comparison

Forced distribution

Forced-choice performance report

Weighted checklist

Behaviorally anchored rating scale

Halo error

Leniency

Central tendency

Appraisal interview

Assessment center

It was performance appraisal time again and Alex Funderburk knew that he would receive a low evaluation this time. Janet Stevens, Alex's boss, opened the appraisal interview with this comment, "The sales department had a good increase this quarter. Also, departmental expenses are down a good bit. But, we nowhere near accomplished the ambitious goals you and I set last quarter." "I know," said Alex. "I thought we were going to make it, though. We would have, too, if we had received that big Simpson order and if I could have gotten us on the computer a little earlier in the quarter."

"I agree with you, Alex," said Janet. "Do you think we were just too ambitious or do you think there was some way we could have made the Simpson sale and speeded up the computerization process?" "Yes," replied Alex, "we could have gotten the Simpson order this quarter." I just made a couple of concessions to Simpson and their purchasing manager tells me he can issue the order next week. The delay with the computer was caused by a thoughtless mistake I made. I won't let that happen again."

The discussion continued for about thirty minutes longer. Alex discovered that Janet was going to mark him very high in all areas despite his failure to accomplish the goals that they had set.

Prior to the meeting, Janet had planned to suggest that the unattained goals for last period be set as the new goals for the coming quarter. After she and Alex had discussed matters, however, they both decided to establish new goals which were somewhat higher. As he was about to leave the meeting, Alex said, "Janet, I feel good about these objectives but, I don't believe we have more than a 50 percent chance of accomplishing them." "I believe you can do it," replied Janet. "If you knew for sure, though, the goals wouldn't be high enough." "I see what you mean," said Alex, as he left the office.

Questions

1. What was wrong or right with Janet's appraisal of Alex's performance?

2. Should the new objectives be higher or lower than they are? Explain.

As the production supervisor for Sweeney Electronics, Mike Mahoney was generally well thought of by most of his subordinates. Mike was an easygoing individual who tried to help his employees any way he could. If a worker needed a small loan until payday, he would dig into his pocket with no questions asked. Should an employee need some time off to attend to a personal problem, he would not dock the individual's pay; rather, he would take up the slack himself until the worker returned.

Everything had been going smoothly, at least until the last performance appraisal period. One of Mike's workers, Bill Overstreet, had been experiencing a large number of personal problems for the past year. Bill's wife had been sick much of the time and her medical expenses were high. Bill's son had a speech impediment and the doctors had recommended a special clinic. Bill, who had already borrowed the limit the bank would loan, had become upset and despondent over his general circumstances.

When it was time for Bill's annual performance appraisal, Mike decided he was going to do as much as possible to help him. Although Bill could not be considered more than an average worker, Mike rated him outstanding in virtually every category. Because the firm's compensation system was tied heavily to the performance appraisal, Bill would be eligible for a merit increase of 10 percent in addition to the regular cost of living raise he would receive as an average worker.

Mike explained to Bill why he was giving him such high ratings and Bill acknowledged that his performance had really been no better than average. Bill was very grateful and expressed this to Mike. As Bill left the office he was excitedly looking forward to telling his friends about what a wonderful boss he had. Seeing Bill smile as he left gave Mike a warm feeling.

Questions

1. From Sweeney Electronic's standpoint, what difficulties might Mike Mahoney's performance appraisal practices create?

2. What can Mike do now to diminish the negative impact of his evaluation of Bill?

Section Case

PARMA CYCLE COMPANY: TRAINING THE WORK FORCE

 As the date for the new plant opening drew near, Mary Higgins, director of employee development at Parma Cycle Company in Parma, Ohio, grew increasingly nervous. With only six months to train the work force for the new Clarksdale, Mississippi plant, Mary knew that there was little room for error.

Mary had already arranged to lease a building near the factory site and some of the machinery for the new plant was being installed in that building for training purposes. Most of the machinery was similar to that being used at Parma and Mary had selected trainers from among the supervisory staff at the Parma plant. One machine, however, a robotized frame assembler, was entirely new. The assembler was being purchased from a Japanese firm. Mary had arranged to have two operators trained in the Japanese factory.

In connection with all of this activity, Mary had personnally made two trips to Clarksdale. She had also retained a training consultant, a management professor from the University of Mississippi. The training consultant had agreed to help Mary plan the training program and to evaluate the program as it went along. It was at the consultant's suggestion that Mary decided to use a combination of vestibule training and classroom lectures in developing a trained work force prior to factory startup time. In the past, Parma Cycle had used on-the-job training almost exclusively. This was not feasible, she felt, at the new plant.

As Mary was thinking about how short the time was, the phone rang. It was the personnel director, Jesse Heard, telling her that he was ready for their meeting. When she got to his office she found him studying a training report she had prepared a few days earlier. "Mary," said Jesse, "It looks like you have things well under control for the Clarksdale plant. But I don't see anything here about training the workers who are going to be transferred down from this plant." "Well," said Mary, "they have all been working in bicycle manufacture for quite a while. I thought it might not be necessary to have any formal training for them." "That's true," said Jesse, "but most of them will be taking different jobs when they move to Clarksdale." "I'll get on it right away," said Mary.

"What are we going to do about supervisory training at the Clarksdale plant?" asked Jesse. Mary replied, "I think we'll use the same system we use here for the long haul. We'll bring our supervisors up through the ranks and have quarterly off-site seminars. To start, the supervisors who move down from Parma can help train the others." Jesse asked, "What do you think about bringing the supervisors hired in Clarksdale up here for a few days to help them learn how we do things?" "That's a good idea," said Mary. "We can pair them off with some of our better people at Parma."

"That won't help us with performance evaluations, Mary," said Jesse. "You know we're going to use a different system down there. We've decided to use management by objectives down to the supervisory level and a new three-item rating scale for the workers." "I know," answered Mary. "I'd planned classroom training on that beginning the month after startup at the Clarksdale plant. I'm going to conduct those sessions myself. Because the performance scores will be used to allocate incentive bonuses, I want to make sure that they are consistently assigned."

"Mary," said Jesse, "I'm really impressed with the way you are taking charge of our training effort for the Clarksdale plant. Just keep up the good work." "Thank you, Jesse," said Mary. "I'll get back to you next week on the training I recommend for the workers who will transfer down from Parma."

Questions

1. Describe how an untrained person hired in Clarksdale could become a competent machine operator by the time the new plant opens.

2. Do you think Mary needed the training consultant? Why or why not?

3. What do you think of Jesse's idea to have the supervisors for the new plant trained by those transferred from Ohio? Explain your answer.

—— Experiencing Personnel Management ——

AN IN-BASKET EXERCISE

In-basket exercises are becoming increasingly popular, both as a selection tool and for training managers at several levels. Essentially the exercise consists of prioritizing pieces of correspondence and determining how to respond to them. The way the present or prospective manager handles various items gives some insight into that manager's competence and helps to prepare managers for situations which may arise.

Your Role

You are Jesse Heard, personnel director at Parma Cycle Company, and you have been away for four days attending a seminar on "New Developments in Personnel Manage-ment" at Northeast Louisiana University. It is Friday morning and you have come in at 7:00 o'clock so that you can go through your in-basket and plan for the busy day you expect. The basket is piled high with correspondence, forms, reports, computer printouts, etc. After laying aside a number of the voluminous reports which you always receive but never read, you place the remainder of the items on your desk and begin to go through them. Your objective is to prioritize them according to when you will take action, and then to determine what action to take on each. You have decided to sort them into four stacks: "Immediate Action Required," "Action Required Sometime Today," "Delay Until Next Week," and "Ignore." The first three items are on pages 344–345.

Questions

1. In the long run, what should you do about the reports you "always receive, but never read"?

2. Was it ethical for Jim Burgess's friend to call Jim about Edward Deal's job-seeking efforts?

3. What information would you normally provide a prospective employer about a previous employee?

CONFIDENTIAL

MEMORANDUM

TO: Jesse Heard
FROM: Jim Burgess
DATE: December 16, 19--
SUBJECT: Edward Deal

I had a call from a friend the other day who said that Edward Deal is on the job market. I thought he was excited about the job down in Clarksdale. If he's not, we'd better start scrambling. Check it out and get with me Monday or Tuesday. I'll be out of town until Sunday afternoon. I would have waited to talk with you personally but I didn't think this should wait.

Jim

To _Jesse Heard_

Date _12/16_   Time _3:00_

WHILE YOU WERE OUT

M _Mary Higgins_

of _Training_

Phone _____
     Area Code   Number   Extension

TELEPHONED	✓	PLEASE CALL	✓
CALLED TO SEE YOU		WILL CALL AGAIN	
WANTS TO SEE YOU		URGENT	✓
	RETURNED YOUR CALL		

Message _____

_____

_____

_____

                    Operator

December 16, 19--

Parma Cycle Company
301 West 31st Street
Parma, OH 40127

Dear Mr. Heard:

I have tried to call you several times, but could never get through to you. Since I have
been traveling, I did not leave a message. Perhaps you will kindly respond to this letter
right away.

Mr. Claude L. Simpson, who used to work in your office as a personnel specialist, has
applied for a job with us as Assistant Personnel Manager. Could you please provide the
following information about Mr. Simpson. For your convenience just fill it in on this
letter and return it in the enclosed envelope.

Length of time employed by Parma. _____

How would you evaluate his ability to get along with others? _____

_____

Rate of pay at time of discharge. _____

Reason discharged. _____

Record of disciplinary offenses, if any. _____

_____

Your overall recommendation as to whether Mr. Simpson would make a reliable
employee. _____

I assure you that the information which you provide will be held in strictest confidence.
I must make a decision on Mr. Simpson's employment within a few days, so if you could
do this while you have it before you, I would appreciate it.

Sincerely,

Ryan Chappell,
Plant Manager

RC:ds

Enclosure

Part IV

Compensation

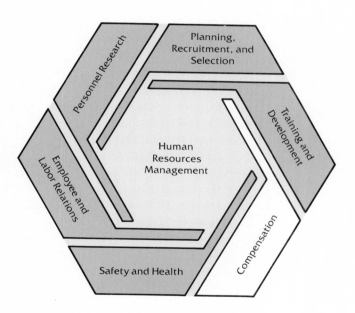

Chapter Objectives

1. Identify and describe the components of a total compensation program.
2. Explain job evaluation and the concept of pay equity.
3. Explain the factors associated with job pricing.
4. Describe how the employee's characteristics affect the compensation decision.

Chapter 11 _____

Financial Compensation

Earl Louis and his wife are full of excitement and anticipation as they leave their home for a shopping trip. Earl had recently found a job after several weeks of unemployment and the paycheck he received today will enable them to make a downpayment on a much needed refrigerator.

Inez Scroggin's anxiety over scheduled minor surgery was somewhat relieved. Her supervisor has assured her that 90 percent of her medical and hospitalization costs will be covered by her firm's health insurance plan.

Trig Abrahamson, executive director of the local YMCA, returns home from his job each evening no earlier than six o'clock. He is dead tired and his salary is small compared with the salaries of many other managers in the local area who have similar responsibilities. Yet, Trig is an exceptionally happy person who feels that his work with youth, civic leaders, and other members of the community is extremely important and worthwhile.

Joanne Marshall has been employed by a large manufacturing firm for eight years. Although her salary is not what she would like it to be, her job in the accounts payable department enables her to have contact with some of her best friends. She likes her supervisor and considers the overall working environment to be great. Joanne would not trade jobs with anyone she knows.

The above instances reflect an example of each of the components of a total compensation program (see Figure 11–1). Earl Louis has just received his paycheck and wants to purchase a needed item for his family. **Direct financial compensation** consists of the pay a person receives in the form of wages, salaries, bonuses, and commissions. Inez Scroggins is receiving indirect financial compensation because her company pays ninety percent of all medical and hospitalization costs. **Indirect financial compensation** includes all financial rewards which are not included as direct. As you can see from Figure 11–1, this form of compensation includes a wide variety of rewards which are normally received indirectly by the employee.

Trig Abrahamson and Joanne Marshall are receiving important forms of **nonfinancial compensation**. Trig is extremely satisfied with the job he performs. This type of nonfinancial compensation involves satisfaction that a person receives by performing meaningful job related tasks. On the other hand, Joanne's job permits her to have contacts with her best friends. This form of nonfinancial compensation involves both the psychological and physical environment in which the job is performed.

All of the above types of compensation comprise a total compensation program. Naturally, financial compensation—both direct and indirect—comprises the heart of such a system. However, nonfinancial forms are becoming increasingly important as firms reach the saturation point in pay and benefits. In designing a total compensation program which will attract, retain, and motivate employees, all types of rewards should be considered.

This chapter emphasizes direct financial compensation. Other financial compensation considerations such as incentives as well as the unique aspects of managerial, professional, and sales compensation will be discussed in Chapter 12. Benefits and nonfinancial compensation will also be described in the next chapter.

COMPENSATION: AN OVERVIEW

Compensation refers to every type of reward that individuals receive in return for performing organizational tasks. Each of us has different reasons for working. When people are responsible for providing food and clothing for their families, money may well be the most important reward. Yet, how do you explain why some people work many hours each day, receive little pay, and yet love their work? To a large degree, adequate compensation is in the mind of the receiver. It is often more than the dollar a person receives in the form of a paycheck. Because a total compensation package includes more than the actual paycheck you receive, compensation administration is one of the most difficult and challenging areas confronting managers of human resources.[1]

[1]Robert E. Sibson, *Compensation* (New York: AMACOM, A Division of American Management Associations, 1974), p. vii (hereafter cited as "Sibson").

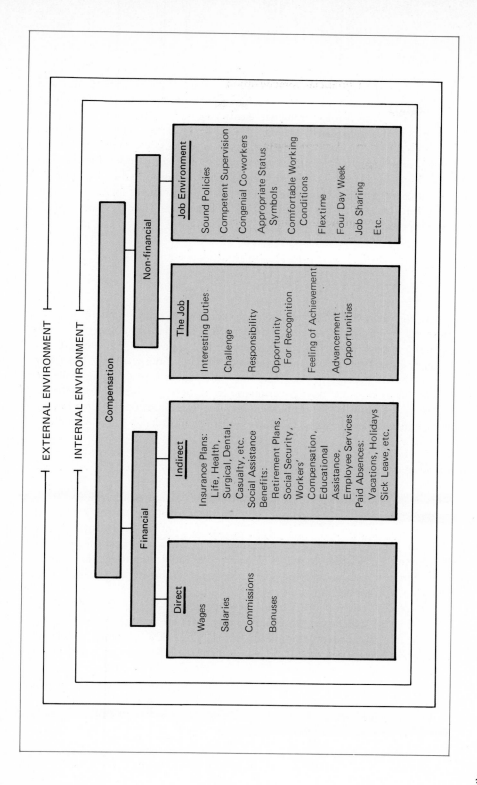

Figure 11–1. The components of a total compensation program.

DETERMINANTS OF FINANCIAL COMPENSATION

As we emphasize throughout the book, many factors interact with and affect human resources management. Again, external and internal environmental factors exert considerable influence—this time in determining the financial compensation a person will receive. Notice some of the major factors shown in Figure 11–2. As you see, the job itself is a primary determinant of pay. Computer programmers are likely to be paid more than janitors. Once a dollar value has been placed on the job through job pricing, other factors related to the employee interact before we know what an individual's financial compensation will be. All of the topics shown in Figure 11–2 are described later in this chapter.

THE EXTERNAL ENVIRONMENT

When you were hired for your first job, there were probably many factors in the external environment which influenced your financial compensation. For example, if every person in your hometown had applied for the same job, your pay may have been less than if you were the only one available. If your employer was unionized, this also may have affected your pay. If your skills were limited, it is possible that government legislation provided a floor for your wages in the form of a minimum wage. In determining a person's pay, the firm's external environment can have a distinct impact.

The Labor Market

The geographical area from which employees are recruited for a particular job is referred to as a **labor market**. Labor markets for some jobs may extend far beyond a local area. Human resources management of an aerospace firm in Orlando, for example, may be concerned about the labor market for engineers in Wichita or Seattle. Managerial and professional employees are often recruited from a wide geographical area. In fact, recruitment on a national basis is not unusual for certain skills.[2]

Moreover, pay for jobs within these markets may vary considerably. The job "executive secretary", for example, may carry an average salary of $20,000 per year in a large, urban community but only $12,000 in a small, rural town. Compensation managers must be aware of these differences in order to compete successfully for employees. The going wage, or prevailing rate, is an important guide in determining pay, and many employees view it as the standard for judging the fairness of their firm's compensation practices.

Large organizations routinely conduct compensation surveys to determine prevailing pay rates within labor markets. These studies provide information

---

[2]R. E. Hollerbach, "Determining Wage and Salary Policy," *Handbook of Wage and Salary Administration*, ed. Milton L. Rock (New York: McGraw-Hill Book Company, 1972), p. 4–12.

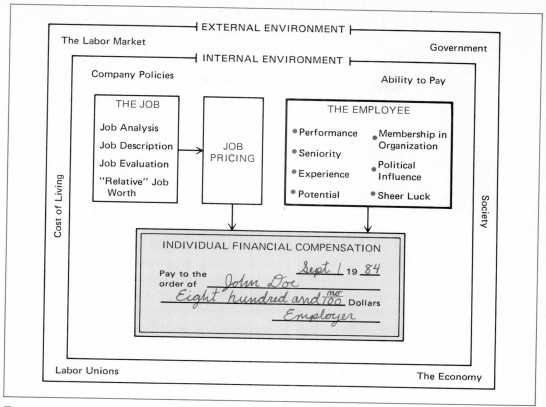

Figure 11–2. The primary determinants of financial compensation for individual employees.

for establishing both direct and indirect compensation. The decisions that must be made prior to conducting a compensation survey include determining: (1) the geographic area of the survey, (2) the specific firms to contact, and (3) the jobs to include. The geographic area to be included in the survey is often determined from personnel records. Data from this source may indicate maximum distance or time employees are willing to travel to work. Also, the firms that are to be contacted for the survey are often from the same industry. But, they also include those that compete for the same type of skills. Because it may not be feasible to obtain data on all jobs in the organization, Personnel often surveys only key jobs. A **key job** is one which is well known in the company and industry and one that can be easily defined.

The primary difficulty in conducting a compensation survey involves determining comparable jobs. There are many different ways of organizing work and designing jobs. A job in one company may only roughly resemble a comparable job in another. For this reason, job titles are of little value in making surveys. Instead, well written job descriptions must be used when requesting compensation data.

There are alternatives for obtaining compensation data in a given labor market. Some professional organizations periodically conduct surveys. The Bu-

Executive Profile

Ronald C. Pilenzo
President and Chief Operating Officer, American Society for Personnel Administration

During the early 1950s when Ronald C. Pilenzo was trying to decide upon a career, the personnel field was only beginning to emerge and make its presence felt. But, he says, "I wanted a career that offered personal growth and financial reward. I also wanted a career that offered wide scope and diversity, as opposed to a highly structured job that offered very narrow career ranges. Through Personnel I feel that I have achieved this goal."

After graduation from the University of Detroit, Ronald joined Ford Motor Company, where he progressed to the position of personnel director, Industrial and Chemical Products Division. Later, Mr. Pilenzo became a principal consultant with the international consulting firm of Raymond E. Danto, where he was responsible for all personnel and organization consulting. He subsequently joined Allied Supermarkets, Inc. as director, corporate recruiting, compensation, and manpower planning. In this position he was responsible for 18,000 employees in eleven major divisions covering forty-three states. Ronald next served as director, manpower and organization development with Evans Products Company for five years before he joined International Multifoods as director, corporate compensation and management development, corporate human resource staff in 1975. In 1980, Ronald was selected to become president and chief operating officer of the American Society for Personnel Administration (ASPA), the world's largest professional personnel organization.

When asked what were some critical moments in his career, Mr. Pilenzo replied, "They involved making career decisions that

---

reau of Labor Statistics makes yearly surveys and provides data by area, industry, and job type. A number of journals such as *Compensation Review* and *Hospital Administration* also produce periodic compensation information. Some organizations choose to use other sources even though they are large enough to afford a survey. Southwestern Life Insurance Company, for example, uses compensation data provided by the Life Office Management Association along with survey data supplied by A. S. Hansen, Hay Associates, the American Society for Personnel Administration, and American Management Associations.

Cost of Living

The logic for using cost of living as a pay determinant is simple. When prices rise over a period of time and pay does not, "real pay" is actually lowered. A pay increase must be roughly the equivalent to the cost of living increase if a person is to maintain a previous level of real wages. If Jack Findley earns

354

related to the kind and type of organization where I was to be employed. For example, at least three times in my career I have been offered opportunities to create a professional organization where either one did not exist or one existed that was not performing satisfactorily." Ronald accepted all three challenges, but says, "Interesting challenges present high risk situations." He did not fail and has become one of the most respected professionals in his field.

When asked about the qualities needed for success, he replies, "Personnel executives need to be tough-minded, intelligent, capable of working within and outside the personnel function, and not in a vacuum. They must be individuals who can work comfortably in a changing environment that involves complex problems with no readily available solutions. The successful personnel executive will probably have a personality profile that is comparable to an operating executive."

Asked to comment regarding the earning potential of personnel executives, Mr. Pilenzo stated, "It is interesting to note that in the past five years salaries for personnel executives have risen substantially faster than salaries for almost any other functional management group. It is not unusual today to find major corporations' top personnel executives earning salaries and bonuses in the six figure range."

Ronald also believes that company loyalty is not the same as in the past. He says, "In today's changing world, and with people's obviously shifting value systems, loyalty to an organization is an interesting dilemma. The days of employees who dedicated their entire lives to the organization are probably at an end. This does not mean that while people are employed in an organization that they should not give their best possible effort. What it does mean, however, is that people now place a different value on company loyalty. This means that younger people today generally consider loyalty to self above loyalty to company."

Finally, Mr. Pilenzo states, "It is no longer sufficient or desirable for organizations to employ personnel people who desire a career in personnel simply because they 'like people' and 'helping others.' In fact, people who see this as their primary role are usually unsuccessful as professional personnel managers."

$24,000 during a year in which the average rate of inflation is 10 percent, a two hundred dollar per month salary increase will be necessary merely to maintain his standard of living.

People living on fixed incomes (primarily the old and the poor) are especially hard hit by inflation. But they are not alone, as most employees also suffer financially. In recognition of this problem, some organizations grant pay increases which are tied to the inflation rate. Some firms will sacrifice "merit money" to provide across-the-board increases designed to offset the results of inflation.

Labor Unions

An excerpt from the Wagner Act prescribes the areas of mandatory collective bargaining between management and unions as "wages, hours, and other terms and conditions of employment." The broad bargaining areas outlined in the above phrase illustrate the potential impact of unions on compensation decisions. The words of Samuel Gompers, the first president of the American Federation of Labor (AFL), "more, more, now!" still ring in the ears of company representatives sitting at bargaining tables as they try to stem the tide of union demands. The union affects company compensation policies in three important areas. It influences the standards used in making compensation decisions, the wage differentials, and wage payment methods.[3]

When the union uses comparable pay as a standard for making compensation demands, the employer must obtain accurate labor market data. When cost of living is emphasized, management may be persuaded to include a **cost-of-living allowance (COLA)** or escalator clause in the labor agreement which automatically increases wages as the Bureau of Labor Statistics cost of living index rises.

Unions may also attempt to create, preserve, or even destroy pay differentials between wages for craft workers and unskilled workers. The politics of a given situation will determine the direction taken. For instance, if the unskilled workers have the strongest membership, an attempt may be made to eliminate pay differentials.

Incentive plans may be desired by management as a means of providing greater employee motivation. However, decisions to implement such plans may be scrapped if the union strongly opposes this method. Employee acceptance of such plans is essential for successful implementation, and union opposition may make the plan unworkable.

Government Legislation

The amount of compensation a person receives can also be affected by certain government legislation.

Fair Labor Standard Act of 1938. The most significant law affecting compensation is the Fair Labor Standards Act of 1938 (FLSA) as amended. This act, which was described in the appendix to Chapter 2, is also called the Wage and Hour Law. It establishes a minimum wage, requires overtime pay, and provides standards for child labor. This act is administered by the Wage and Hour Division of the Department of Labor. It affects more than 50 million full-time and part-time workers.[4]

As of January 1981, the act provided for a minimum wage of not less than $3.35 an hour. It also required overtime payment at the rate of one and one-half times the employee's regular rate after forty hours of work in the work week. Although most organizations and employees are covered by the Act, certain classes of employees are specifically exempt from the minimum wage and overtime provisions.

[3]Cyril Curtis Ling, *The Management of Personnel Relations* (Homewood, IL: Richard D. Irwin, Inc., 1965), pp. 146–151.
[4]Handy Referency Guide to the Fair Labor Standards Act, U.S. Department of Labor Employment Standards Administration, Wage and Hour Division, W. H. Publication 1282, Revised October 1978.

Exempt employees are categorized as executive, administrative, professional employees and outside salespersons. An executive employee is essentially a manager (such as a production manager) with broad authority over subordinates. An administrative employee, while not a manager, occupies an important staff position in an organization and might have a title such as systems analyst or assistant to the president. A professional employee performs work requiring advanced knowledge in a field of learning normally acquired through a prolonged course of specialized instruction. This type of employee might have a title such as company physician, legal counsel, or senior statistician. Outside salespeople sell tangible or intangible items, away from the employer's place of business. Employees in jobs not conforming to these definitions are considered nonexempt. Nonexempt employees, many of whom are paid salaries, are covered by both the minimum wage and overtime provisions of the act.

During fiscal year 1981, the Wage and Hour Division received over 46,000 wage complaints and conducted more than 68,000 investigations. The agency recovered $745 million in unpaid overtime wages due to 291,000 employees. An employer must be aware of the minimum wage level, maintain accurate payroll records, and accurately identify workers covered by the act.[5]

Equal Pay Act of 1963. The Equal Pay Act of 1963 (an amendment to the FLSA) has also influenced the field of compensation. The purpose of this legislation is to prohibit discrimination on the basis of sex. As evidence that the act does have teeth, female employees have received millions of dollars to compensate for past discrimination in pay policies.

The Equal Pay Act applies to all organizations and employees covered by the FLSA including the exempt categories. The act requires equal pay for equal work for both sexes. Equal work is defined as work requiring equal skill, effort, and responsibility which is performed under similar working conditions. This act does not prohibit the establishment of different wage rates which are based on seniority or merit systems. Also permitted are pay systems which are based on the quantity or quality of production and differentials based on any factor other than sex.

One of the most controversial issues in the personnel field today is that of comparable worth.[6] While the Equal Pay Act requires equal pay for equal work, advocates of **comparable worth** prefer a broader interpretation requiring equal pay for comparable work. When females dominate a particular occupation, the pay rates for jobs in that field appear to be lower than pay for men in jobs within male-dominated occupations. For example, some individuals question whether nurses should be paid the same as plumbers or whether office clerks should be compensated equally with assembly workers. The basic problem stems from segregated occupations.

---

[5]William S. Hubbartt, "The Ten Commandments of Salary Administration," *Administrative Management* 4, (April 1982): 60.
[6]George L. Whaley, "Controversy Swirls Over Comparable Worth Issue," *Personnel Administrator* 27 (April 1982): 51.

In the case of *County of Washington* v. *Gunther*, the plaintiffs claimed that their wages were depressed because of sex discrimination. Female jail matrons were paid $200 per month less than male jailers. The jailers supervised over ten times as many inmates as the matrons while the matrons spent much more time performing clerical duties. Because the work assignments were not "equal", the plaintiffs were not protected by the Equal Pay Act.[7] The court's decision did not clarify the question of comparable worth. However, the court did rule that the case could be tried in a lower court under the broader provisions of Title VII of the Civil Rights Act.[8] Therefore, while the comparable worth issue is still unsettled, it poses serious challenges to many existing pay systems.

Davis-Bacon Act of 1931. The Davis-Bacon Act of 1931 was the first national law to deal with minimum wages. It requires federal construction contractors with projects valued in excess of $2000 to pay at least the prevailing wages in the area. The Secretary of Labor has the authority to make this determination and the prevailing wage is often the average local union rate. Davis-Bacon has been under fire because critics claimed that it resulted in construction cost overruns approaching 20 percent. Charges have also been made that the act is inflationary and obstructs minority hiring due to its limitations of one apprentice for every three full-time journeymen on a job.[9]

Walsh-Healy Act of 1936. The Walsh-Healy Act of 1936 requires firms with federal contracts exceeding $10,000 to pay prevailing wages. The act also requires the payment of overtime for hours worked over eight per day or 40 per week.

Society

Compensation paid to employees in a given firm often affects that firm's pricing of its goods and/or services. For this reason, the consuming public is also interested in compensation decisions. Public sentiments are often reflected in legislation. At times, the government responds to public opinion and steps in to encourage business to keep wages in line. The process of "jawboning" (as initiated by President John F. Kennedy in the early 1960s) involves using the prestige of the presidency to informally pressure large companies to hold wages and prices down.

Businesses in a given labor market are also concerned with the pay practices of competitors. For instance, when the management of a large electronics firm announced plans to locate a branch plant in a relatively small community, it was confronted by local civic leaders. Their questions largely concerned the wage and salary rates that would be paid. Subtle pressure was ap-

[7]Richard I. Henderson, *Compensation Management: Rewarding Performance*, 3rd Edition, (Reston, Virginia: Reston Publishing Company, Inc., 1979), p. 171.
[8]James T. Brinks, APD, "The Comparable Worth Issue: A Salary Administration Bombshell," *Personnel Administrator* 26 (November 1981): 38.
[9]George Fowler, "Davis-Bacon Needs a Decent Burial," *Nations Business* 67 (March 1979): 57.

plied to keep the wages in line with other wages in the community. The electronics firm agreed to begin operations with initial compensation at a lower level than it usually paid. But, the firm's management made it clear that a series of pay increases would be given over a period of two years to maintain its own "pay leader" policy.

The Economy

While it is possible for some firms to thrive in a recession, there is no question that the economy affects compensation decisions. For example, a depressed economy will probably increase the labor supply. This, in turn, should serve to lower the going wage rate.

In most cases, the cost of living will rise in an expanding economy. Because the cost of living is commonly used as a pay standard, the economy's health exerts a major impact upon pay decisions. Labor unions, government, and society are all less likely to press for pay increases in a depressed economy.

THE INTERNAL ENVIRONMENT

Each firm's personality is a major influence upon an individual's financial compensation. An organization often establishes—formally or informally—compensation policies which determine whether it will be a pay leader or a pay follower, or strive for an average position in the labor market. The leaders pay higher wages and salaries than the other firms competing in the labor market. Organizations with this leadership philosophy expect to have lower per unit labor costs. They feel that they will be able to attract high quality employees who will be very productive. Higher-paying firms usually attract not only more applicants, but more qualified applicants than do lower-paying companies in the same industry.[10]

A person who is paid the **"going rate"** receives the average wage that most employers pay for the same job in a particular labor market. Most organizations have a policy which calls for paying the going rate. The managements of these firms believe that they will be able to employ qualified people and still remain competitive by not having to raise the price of their goods and/or services. Employers with this policy may be overlooking the possibility of hiring more proficient workers. Yet, there are a number of firms with jobs which require only average qualified employees. An assembly line worker who is assigned the job of tightening four bolts every minute and a half is an example. In this situation, an excellent employee would not likely be much more productive than one with only average ability.

Charlie Davis managed a large but financially strapped farming operation in the Southwest. Although no formal policies were established, Charlie had a

[10]Gene Milbourn, Jr., "The Relationship of Money and Motivation," *Compensation Review* 12, Second Quarter 1980, p. 33

tendency to pay the lowest wage possible. One of his farm hands, Ron Poole, was paid the minimum wage. During a period of three weeks, Ron wrecked a tractor, severely damaged a combine, and stripped the gears in a new pickup truck. Ron's actions prompted Charlie to remark, "Ron is the most expensive darned employee I've ever had."

Some companies choose to pay below the going rate because of a poor financial condition (as with Charlie's farm) or a belief that they simply do not require highly capable employees. These firms may experience a high turnover rate as their most qualified employees join organizations offering higher pay. Regardless of their reasons for paying below the going rate, such firms will most likely experience a lower productivity level in addition to a higher turnover rate.

The organizational level where compensation decisions are made can also have an impact. Compensation decisions are often made at a high management level to ensure consistency. However, there are advantages to making pay decisions at lower levels where more information may exist regarding employee performance. Top level executives could make major errors if they made decisions that should be handled at lower levels. The example described below involving Ruby Kelly illustrates this point.

Ruby Kelly was the manager of a rapidly growing data processing center in a medium-sized petroleum company. Although she had eight department managers reporting to her, Ruby insisted on making all pay increase decisions. Recently she gave a $200 a month raise to the poorest producing employee in the programming department. The manager of this department, Clyde Murphy, was outraged. He told his wife at supper, "Honey, I can't live with this situation much longer. Ruby is so far removed from our operations that she couldn't tell our best performer from our worst. I may lose half my people."

An organization's assessment of its ability to pay is also an important factor in determining pay levels. Financially successful firms are often under pressure from both employees and the union to pay higher wages. In fact these firms tend to provide higher than average compensation.[11] However, an organization's financial strength establishes only the upper limits of what it will pay. To arrive at a specific pay level, other factors must be considered.

THE JOB

All of the external and internal factors comprising an organization's environment are important. As mentioned in Chapter 3, a job consists of a group of tasks that must be performed if an organization is to achieve its goals.

The job people are given to do is a major determinant of the amount of financial compensation they will receive.[12] Organizations pay for the value

---

[11]David W. Belcher, *Compensation Administration*, (Englewood Cliffs, NJ: Prentice-Hall, Inc., 1974), p. 487 (hereafter cited as "Belcher").
[12]"Is Inflation Wrecking Salary Structures?" *Industry Week*, 199 (October 30, 1978): 55.

"In evaluating the candidates for professional employee relations positions, we look for people who have a strong academic record, good communications skills, a willingness to move around in terms of job assignments, good analytical skills, and the potential, as best this can be evaluated at the time, to progress into a managerial position in the personnel function."

**W. F. Hoeppner, Manager, Personnel Development
Standard Oil Company (Indiana)**

they attach to certain duties, responsibilities, and other job related factors such as working conditions. Factors which must be considered in the process of determining a job's relative worth include job analysis, job descriptions (discussed in Chapter 3), and job evaluation.

Before a company can determine the relative difficulty or value of its jobs, it must first define their content. This is normally achieved through job analysis. You may recall that job analysis involves gathering, analyzing, and recording job facts in the form of job descriptions. The job description is the primary by-product of job analysis and consists of a written document describing the duties and responsibilities associated with the jobs. Job descriptions are used for many different purposes including job evaluation. They are essential for all job evaluation methods, with the success of a job evaluation program depending largely upon their accuracy and clarity.

JOB EVALUATION

A systematic approach to determining the relative value or worth of each job in an organization is referred to as **job evaluation**.[13] The basic purpose of job evaluation is to eliminate pay inequities which exist because of illogical pay structures. For example, a pay inequity exists if the person who delivers the mail earns more money than the accounting supervisor.

The concept of pay equity is closely related to the purposes of job evaluation. **Pay equity** refers to the relationship between what employees believe they should receive and what they believe they are actually receiving. Generally speaking, people believe that their pay should be related to their contributions to the firm. They quickly become unhappy when they perceive that someone in their organization receives more pay for performing the same or lower level work.

Within The Bendix Corporation, the precise method of implementing job evaluation programs is left to the discretion of individual business groups and divisions. However, corporate philosophy serves as a basic guide to these operating units. This philosophy includes the belief that the job evaluation pro-

[13]Richard I. Henderson, *Compensation Management: Rewarding Performance*, 2d ed. (Reston, Virginia: Reston Publishing Company, Inc., 1979), p. 209.

cess is the foundation of a sound compensation system. The job evaluation process must in turn satisfy these requirements:

- Provide a consistent measure of job worth which can be easily understood by everyone concerned
- Involve managers from its inception through its administration and subsequent revision
- Protect employees from favoritism, biases, and resultant internal pay inequities
- Measure the job and not the performance of the employee doing the job
- Adapt to broad job clusters within functional groups

The personnel department is usually responsible for the administration of job evaluation programs. However, the evaluation of jobs is typically accomplished through a committee. The committee is often comprised of managers from different functional areas. A typical committee might include the personnel director as chairperson and the vice presidents for finance, production, and marketing. The composition of the committee usually depends upon the type and level of the jobs that are being evaluated. In all instances, it is important for the committee to keep personalities out of the evaluation process. As the Bendix statement indicated, it is the job which should be evaluated, not the person(s) performing the job.

Small- and medium-sized organizations often lack job evaluation expertise. Therefore, they may elect to use an outside consultant. While many qualified consultants are available, management should require that they develop a job evaluation program and train company employees so that they will be able to administer the system successfully.

There are four basic job evaluation methods used in organizations: the ranking method, the classification method, the factor comparison method, and the point method.[14] In selecting a method, many firms choose a plan and modify it to fit their particular needs. The ranking and classification methods are nonquantitative while the factor comparison and point methods are quantitative approaches.

Ranking Method

The simplest of the four job evaluation methods is the **ranking method.** The procedure is essentially the same process discussed in Chapter 10 regarding the ranking method for performance evaluation. The only difference is that we are now talking about evaluating jobs, not people. The first step in this method—as with all methods—is conducting job analysis and writing job descriptions. The most straightforward approach to ranking is to have the raters examine

[14]Sibson, p. 38.

the descriptions of jobs being evaluated and simply arrange them in order according to their difficulty.

363

Chapter 11
Financial
Compensation

Classification Method

In the **classification method** a number of classes, or grades, are defined which describe a group of jobs. The best-known example of this method is the federal government's classic Civil Service System. In this system, there are eighteen grades (GS-1 to GS-18) with GS-1 being the lowest level. At the bottom of the scale (GS-1), the nature and typical duties of the job are very simple and routine. Jobs become progressively more difficult up through GS-18, where high-level executive tasks are required.

In evaluating jobs by the classification method, the job description is compared with the class description. The class description which most closely agrees with the job description determines the classification for that job. For example, in evaluating the job of clerk typist, the description might include these duties:

1. Type letters from prepared drafts.
2. Address envelopes.
3. Deliver completed correspondence to unit supervisor.

Assuming the remainder of the job description includes similar routine work, this job would most likely be classified as a GS-1 job. The description of that job class best matches the job description.

It is difficult to clearly define grade descriptions for many diverse jobs. For this reason, the federal government is now implementing a new system called Factor Evaluation System (FES). This system combines three methods of job evaluation: the ranking method (which has previously been discussed), the factor comparison method and the point method (which are covered next).[15]

Factor Comparison Method

The basic version of the **factor comparison method** was developed by Eugene Benge and is somewhat more complex than the two previously discussed qualitative methods. It differs in several respects: (1) raters need not keep the entire job in mind as they evaluate, (2) raters make decisions on separate aspects, or factors, of the job, and (3) the method assumes the existence of five universal job factors. These factors are:

- *Mental requirements:* Reflect mental traits such as intelligence, reasoning, and imagination

[15]Arch S. Ramsay, "The New Factor Evaluating System of Position Classification," *Civil Service Journal* 16 (January–March 1976): 15–19.

Table 11–1. Average ranks of key jobs by difficulty

Job	Factor				
	Mental	**Skill**	**Physical**	**Responsibility**	**Working Conditions**[*]
Systems analyst	1	4	2	1	3
Keypunch operator	4	1	1	4	1
Programmer	2	3	3	2	4
Console operator	3	2	4	3	2

[*]The poorer the working conditions, the higher the rating. (The highest rating is 1.)

- *Skill:* Pertains to facility in muscular coordination and training in the interpretation of sensory impressions
- *Physical requirements:* Involved in such activities as sitting, standing, walking, lifting, etc.
- *Responsibilities:* In such areas as raw materials, money, records, and supervision
- *Working conditions:* Reflect the environmental influences of noise, illumination, ventilation, hazards, and hours[16]

The first step requires that selected key jobs be ranked by the five factors according to their difficulty. The job description serves as a basis for making these decisions. An example of this initial ranking is shown in Table 11–1. As you see, the jobs are first ranked according to mental requirements where it was determined that the systems analyst job ranked highest. Next in the ranking of mental requirements was the job of programmer (2), followed by console operator (3), and keypunch operator (4). The same ranking procedure was followed for the other four factors.

The committee must next allocate pay rates for each job to each factor. This allocation is based upon the importance of the respective factor to the job. An example of allocating the systems analyst's average pay rate ($12.00 per hour) to each of the five factors is shown in Table 11–2. This step is probably the most difficult to explain satisfactorily to employees because the decision is highly subjective.

Table 11–2. Allocation of pay to factors

Job: Systems analyst	Mental	$4.00
	Skill	2.00
Average pay per hour: $12.00	Physical	.80
	Responsibility	4.00
	Working conditions	1.20

[16]John A. Patton, C. L. Littlefield, and Stanley Allen Self, *Job Evaluation: Text and Cases*, 3d ed. (Homewood, IL: Richard D. Irwin, Inc., 1964), p. 115. (Hereafter cited as "Patton et al.").

Table 11–3. Average ranks of key jobs by pay rates

Job	Mental	Skill	Physical	Responsibility	Working Conditions	Pay Rate
Systems analyst	4.00(1)	2.00(4)	.80(2)	4.00(1)	1.20(3)	12.00
Keypunch operator	1.50(4)	2.70(1)	1.00(1)	1.30(4)	1.40(1)	7.90
Programmer	3.40(2)	2.50(3)	.70(3)	3.00(2)	1.00(4)	10.60
Console operator	2.30(3)	2.60(2)	.60(4)	1.80(3)	1.30(2)	8.60

After pay rates have been assigned to each factor for each job, the results may be placed in a format similar to the one shown in Table 11–3. You may note that this procedure results in a ranking of jobs within each factor on the basis of pay rates. (Rank order is shown in parentheses.)

By comparing the first ranking of jobs on the basis of difficulty (DR) with the last ranking achieved on the basis of pay (PR), the committee's consistency in making judgments may be determined. A side-by-side comparison of the two separate rankings is seen in Table 11–4. You see that no differences exist. If there had been a ranking inconsistency, the jobs affected would not be used in the next step.

A job comparison scale consisting of the five universal factors is constructed next (see Figure 11–3). This scale is used to rate other jobs in the group being evaluated. The raters compare each job, factor by factor, with those appearing on the job comparison scale. They then place them on the chart in an appropriate position. For example, assume that the committee is evaluating the job of programmer analyst (which was not used as a key job). It determines that this job requires fewer mental requirements than systems analyst and more than a programmer. The job would then be plotted on this chart between these two jobs at a point agreed upon by the committee. In this example, the mental requirements factor was evaluated at $3.80. This procedure would be repeated on the remaining four factors.

The factor comparison method provides a systematic approach to job evaluation. However, there are some problems that should be recognized. The assumption that the five factors are universal has been questioned. Certain factors may be more appropriate to some job groups than others. Finally, while

Table 11–4. Comparison of difficulty ranking (DR) and pay ranking (PR) by factor

Job	Factor				
	Mental DR PR	Skill DR PR	Physical DR PR	Responsibility DR PR	Working Conditions DR PR
Systems analyst	1 1	4 4	2 2	1 1	3 3
Keypunch operator	4 4	1 1	1 1	4 4	1 1
Programmer	2 2	3 3	3 3	2 2	4 4
Console operator	3 3	2 2	4 4	3 3	2 2

Scale	Mental	Skill	Physical	Responsibility	Working Conditions
$4.00	Systems Analyst			Systems Analyst	
3.80	(Programmer Analyst)				
3.50	Programmer			Programmer	
3.00		Keypunch Operator / Console Operator / Programmer			
2.50	Console Operator			Console Operator	
2.00		Systems Analyst			
1.50	Keypunch Operator			Keypunch Operator	Keypunch Operator / Console Operator / Systems Analyst
1.00			Keypunch Operator / Systems Analyst / Programmer / Console Operator		Programmer
.50					
.00					

Figure 11–3. A job comparison scale.

the steps are not overly complicated, they are somewhat detailed and may be difficult to explain.

Point Method

The majority of job evaluation plans in use today is some variation of the **point method.**[17] This method requires that job factors be selected according to the nature of the specific group of jobs being evaluated. Point method plans are used by both large and small companies. Their use has been encouraged by associations such as the National Electrical Manufacturers' Association, the Life Office Management Association, and the Administrative Management Society.

Normally, organizations develop a separate plan for each group of similar jobs **(job clusters)** in the company. Shop jobs, clerical jobs, and sales jobs are examples of job clusters. The procedure for establishing a point method is illustrated in Figure 11–4. The first activity that takes place—after determining the group of jobs to be studied—is conducting job analysis and writing job descriptions. The job evaluation committee will later use these descriptions as the basis for making evaluation decisions.

The next activity involves selecting and defining the job factors to be used in measuring job value. These factors become the standards used for the evaluation of jobs. They can best be identified by individuals who are thoroughly familiar with the content of the jobs under consideration. Education, experience, job knowledge, mental effort, physical effort, responsibility, and working conditions are examples of typically used factors. Each factor should be significant in helping to distinguish between jobs. Factors which exist in equal amounts in all jobs would obviously not serve this purpose. As an example, in evaluating clerical jobs in a company, the factor "working conditions" would be of little value in distinguishing between jobs if all jobs in the cluster had approximately the same working conditions. The number of factors used varies, with the average being approximately eleven.[18]

Factor weights must next be established according to their relative importance in the jobs to be evaluated. For example, if experience is considered quite important for a particular job cluster, this factor might be weighted as much as 35 percent. Physical effort (if used at all as a factor in an office cluster) would likely be low, perhaps less than 10 percent.

The next consideration entails determining the number of degrees for each job factor and providing each degree with a definition. Degrees represent the number of distinct levels associated with a particular factor. The number of degrees needed for each factor depends upon job requirements. If a particular cluster required virtually the same level of formal education (a high school diploma, for example), then fewer degrees would be appropriate than if some jobs in the cluster required advanced degrees.

[17]J. Gary Berg, *Managing Compensation* (New York: AMACOM, A Division of American Management Associations, 1976), p. 104.
[18]See Belcher for a detailed discussion of job factors and compensable factors.

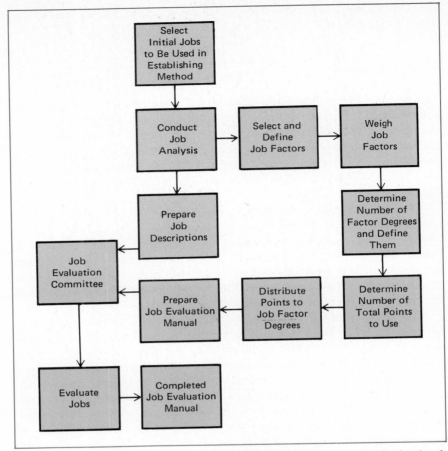

Figure 11–4. **The procedure for establishing the point method of job evaluation.**

The number of total points to use in the plan is next determined. The exact number may vary but typically 500 or 1,000 points are used. The use of a smaller number of points (for example, 50) would not likely provide the proper distinction between jobs, while a larger number (such as 50,000) would be unnecessarily cumbersome. The total number of points in a plan indicates the maximum points any job could receive.

The next step in the point method is to distribute point values to job factor degrees (see Table 11–5). As you see in this example, factor number 1 has five degrees; factor 2 has four; factor 3 has five and factor 4 has three. The maximum number of points is easily calculated by multiplying the maximum points in the system by the assigned weights. For education, the maximum points would be 250 (50 percent weight multiplied by 500 points). The points for the minimum degree could take the percentage weight assigned to the factor (50 points). The degree interval may be calculated by subtracting the minimum number of points (50) from the maximum number (250) and dividing

Table 11–5. Overview of the point system (500 point system)

Job Factors	Weight	Degrees of Factors				
		1	2	3	4	5
1. Education	50%	50	100	150	200	250
2. Responsibility	30%	30	70	110	150	
3. Physical effort	12%	12	24	36	48	60
4. Working conditions	8%	8	24	40		

by the number of degrees used minus one. For example, the interval for factor 1 (education) was calculated as follows:

$$\text{Interval} = \frac{250 - 50}{5 - 1} = 50$$

The above approach to determining the number of points for each degree is referred to as arithmetic progression. An arithmetic progression is simple to understand and to explain to employees. It makes sense when the factors have been defined in such a manner that there is equal distance between the degrees.[19] In other instances, the firm may choose to use a geometric or even an irregular progression to conform to the manner in which degrees have been defined.

The next step involves preparing a job evaluation manual. While there is no standard format, the manual often contains an introductory section, factor and degree definitions, and job descriptions. As a final step, the job evaluation committee then evaluates jobs in the cluster by comparing each job description with the factors in the job evaluation manual. A portion of a large appliance manufacturer's job evaluation manual is illustrated in Figure 11–5. Assume the job of personnel interviewer is being evaluated. After studying the job description, it is decided that the job requirements closely match degree IV of the factor "contacts." The job receives 79 points for this factor. After the point values of all factors have been determined, they are totalled and the numerical value of the job is obtained. Values of all other jobs in the cluster are determined in this manner.

While it takes considerable time and effort to design a point plan, a redeeming feature of the method is that once it is developed, the plan may be useful over a long period of time. The procedure for using an established point method is presented in Figure 11–6. As new jobs are created and the contents of old jobs substantially changed, job analysis must be conducted and job descriptions rewritten. The job evaluation committee evaluates the jobs and updates the manual. Only when job factors change, or for some reason the weights assigned become inappropriate, does the plan become obsolete.

[19]Other alternatives exist, such as geometric progression and irregular progression. For a detailed discussion of methods of progression, see Patton, et al., pp. 153–154.

Factor: Contacts

This factor considers the responsibility for working with other people to get results, either interdepartmental or outside the plant. In the lower degrees, it is largely a matter of giving or getting information or instructions. In the higher degrees, the factor involves dealing with or influencing other persons. In rating this factor, consider how the contacts are made, the duration of the contacts, and their purposes.

LEVEL (DEGREE)	POINTS
IV Usual purposes of the contacts are to discuss problems and possible solutions, to secure cooperation or coordination of efforts, and to get agreement and action; more than ordinary tact and persuasiveness required.	79
III Usual purposes of the contacts are to exchange information or settle specific problems encountered in the course of daily work.	46
II Contacts may be repetitive but usually are brief and with little or no continuity.	27
I Contacts normally extend to persons in the immediate work unit only.	16

Factor: Complexity of Duties

This factor considers the complexity of duties in terms of the character of the tasks to be performed, the scope of independent action allowed, and the exercise of perception and judgment required.

LEVEL (DEGREE)	POINTS
IV Performs work where only general methods are available. Independent action and judgment are required regularly to analyze facts, evaluate situations, draw conclusions, make decisions, and take or recommend action.	91
III Performs duties working from standard procedures or generally understood methods. Some independent action and judgment are required to decide what to do, determine permissible variations from standard procedures, review facts in situations, and determine action to be taken, within limits prescribed.	53
II Standard procedure limits independent action and judgment to decisions not difficult to make since choices are limited. Duties require deciding when to ask for assistance.	31
I Little or no independent action or judgment. Duties are so standardized and simple as to involve little choice as to how to do them.	18

Figure 11–5. The point method as used in a job evaluation manual.

Legal Implications for Job Evaluation

The primary pay criterion of most organizations is the market price of labor.[20] Because of the potential threat that the comparable worth issue poses to this traditional approach to pricing jobs, it has been suggested that job evaluation systems should emphasize market data along with internal equity considera-

[20]Belcher, p. 458.

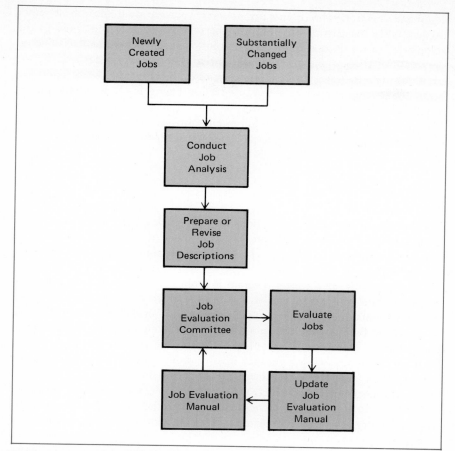

Figure 11–6. **The procedure for using an established point method of job evaluation.**

tions and that this balanced approach be explained to employees.[21] Some firms are becoming reluctant to use market data only, however, in the belief that this approach might result in perpetuating past discrimination in the labor market.[22]

JOB PRICING

The process of job evaluation results in a job hierarchy. It might reveal, for example, that the job of senior accountant is more valuable than the job of

[21]Brinks, p. 39.
[22]Robert J. Greene, APD, "Thoughts on Compensation Management in the '80s and '90s," *Personnel Administrator* 25, (May 1980): 27.

computer operator, which, in turn, is more valuable than the job of senior invoice biller. At this point, we know the relative value of these jobs to the company, but we do not know their absolute value. Placing a dollar value on the worth of a job is referred to as **job pricing**. It may take place once the job has been evaluated and the relative value of each job in the organization has been determined. However, as you observed in Figure 11–2, additional factors should be considered in determining the job's absolute value. Firms often use pay grades and pay ranges in the job pricing process. These topics along with problems associated with pay rate adjustments are discussed next.

Pay Grades

Many organizations group similar jobs into **pay grades** (sometimes called labor grades) to simplify the pricing process. It is much more convenient to price fifteen pay grades as opposed to two-hundred separate jobs. The point plan readily lends itself to this practice.

Plotting jobs on a scatter diagram is often useful in determining the appropriate number of pay grades. In Figure 11–7, each point on the scatter diagram represents one job as it relates to pay and the evaluated points reflecting its difficulty. By following this procedure, it will likely be found that a certain point spread will work satisfactorily (100 points are used in this illustration). Each dot represents one job but may involve dozens of individuals who fill that one job. The large dot at the lower left corner of the diagram represents the job of keypunch operator, which was evaluated at 75 points. The keypunch operator's hourly rate of $7.90 represents either the average wage currently being paid the job or its market rate. This decision depends upon how the organization wants to price its jobs.

A **wage curve** is fitted to the plotted points in order to create a smooth progression between pay grades. The line which is drawn to minimize the distance between all dots and the line—a line of best fit—may be straight or curved. However, when the point system is used (normally considering only one job cluster), a straight line is the usual result, as in Figure 11–7. Two approaches used in drawing this wage line are the least squares line (a statistical version) and the less sophisticated "eyeball" approach.[23] Some compensation specialists use the latter because of its simplicity.

Rate or Pay Ranges

A decision must next be made as to whether all individuals performing the same job will receive equal pay or whether pay ranges will be used. A **pay range** includes a minimum and maximum rate with enough variance between the two to allow some significant pay difference. Pay ranges are generally pre-

[23]For a discussion of the least squares method, see Morris Hamburg, *Statistical Analysis for Decision Makers* (New York: Harcourt, Brace and World, Inc., 1970).

Figure 11–7. **A scatter diagram of evaluated jobs illustrating the wage curve, pay grades, and rate ranges.**

ferred because they allow employees to be paid according to experience and performance levels. Pay can then serve as a positive incentive. When pay ranges are used, some method must be employed to advance individuals through the range. Referring again to Figure 11–7, you can readily determine the minimum, midpoint, and maximum rates per hour for each of the five pay grades. For example, for pay grade 5, the minimum rate is $12.20, the midpoint, $13.50, and the maximum, $14.80.

The minimum rate is normally the "hiring in" rate that a person receives when joining the firm.[24] The maximum rate represents the most pay an employee can receive regardless of how well the job is performed. A person who is at "tops" will have to be promoted to a job in a higher pay grade in order to receive a pay increase unless an across-the-board adjustment is made or the job is reevaluated and placed in a higher pay grade. This situation has caused

[24]Howard Risher, "Inflation and Salary Administration," *Personnel Administrator* 26 (May 1981): 36.

numerous managers anguish as they attempt to explain the pay system to an employee who is doing a tremendous job but is at the maximum of the pay grade. Consider this situation:

> Everyone in the department realized that Beth Smith was the best secretary in the company. At times she appeared to do the job of three secretaries. Bill Merideth, Beth's supervisor, was especially impressed. Recently he had a discussion with the personnel manager to see what could be done to get a raise for Beth. After Bill described the situation, the personnel manager's only reply was, "Sorry, Bill. Beth is already at the top of her pay grade. There is nothing you can do unless you can have her job upgraded or promote her to another position."

Situations such as Beth's present personnel managers with a perplexing problem. Many would be inclined to make an exception to the system and give Beth a salary increase. However, this action would be contrary to a basic principle which holds that there is a maximum value for every job in the organization, regardless of how well it is performed. In addition, making exceptions to the compensation plan could soon result in pay inequities.

The rate ranges established should be large enough to provide incentive to do a better job. At times, pay differentials may need to be greater to be

Figure 11–8. **Rate ranges based on a percentage spread.**

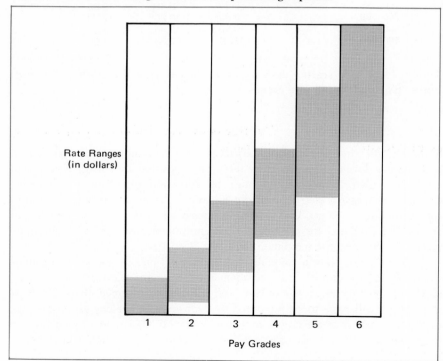

Rate Ranges
(in dollars)

Pay Grades

1   2   3   4   5   6

meaningful, especially at higher levels. There may be logic in having the rate range become increasingly wide at each consecutive level (see Figure 11–8). Consider as an example, what a $50 per month salary increase would mean to a file clerk earning $600 per month (an 8.3 percent increase) and to a senior cost accountant earning $1,500 per month (a 3.3 percent increase). Assuming an inflationary rate of 8 percent, the file clerk would be able to retain his or her real pay while the cost accountant would obviously fall behind.

Some workplace conditions do not favor pay ranges. For instance, in a situation where all or most jobs are routine, with little opportunity for employees to vary their productivity, a single rate, or fixed rate, system may be more appropriate. When single rates are used, everyone on the same job receives the same pay regardless of seniority or productivity.[25]

Adjustments in Pay Rates

When rate ranges have been determined and jobs assigned to pay grades, it may become obvious that some jobs are overpaid and others underpaid. Underpaid jobs are normally brought to the minimum of the pay range as soon as possible. Referring again to Figure 11–7, a job evaluated at about 225 points and paid $9.00 per hour is represented by a circled dot immediately below pay grade 3. The job was determined to be difficult enough to fall in pay grade 3 (200 to 299 points). However, employees working in the job are being paid 60 cents per hour less than the minimum for the pay grade ($9.60 per hour). Some jobs in pay grade 2 and even in pay grade 1 are paid more. A good management practice would be to correct this inequity as rapidly as possible by placing the job in the proper pay grade.

Overpaid jobs present more of a problem. An illustration of an overpaid job for pay grade 4 is provided in Figure 11–7 (note the circled dot above pay grade 4). Employees in this job earn $14.00 per hour or 50 cents more than the maximum for the grade. This type of overpayment (and underpayment as well) is referred to as "red circle" rates.[26]

An ideal solution to the problem of an overpaid job is to promote the employee. This might be a reasonable approach if he or she is qualified for a higher rated job and a job opening is available. Another possibility would be to bring the job rate and employee pay into line through a pay cut. This type of action may appear logical, but it is not consistent with good management practice. This action would punish employees for a situation they did not create. Somewhere between these two possible solutions is a third—to freeze the rate until across-the-board pay increases bring it into line. If the past thirty years are an indication of the future, rising pay levels will eventually solve this problem.

[25]Robert J. Greene, "Which Pay Delivery System is Best for Your Organization?" *Personnel* 58 (May–June 1981): 52.
[26]J. D. Dunn and Frank M. Rachel, *Wage and Salary Administration: Total Compensation Systems* (New York: McGraw-Hill Book Company, 1971), p. 228.

PAY SECRECY

For various possible reasons, organizations tend to keep their pay rates secret. If a firm's compensation plan is illogical, secrecy may indeed be appropriate. Only a well-designed pay system can stand the light of full disclosure.[27] An open system would almost certainly require managers to provide many explanations to subordinates.

Secrecy has curious results, however. For example, managers who are unaware of pay rates in their firm tend to overestimate the pay of managers around them and to underestimate what higher level employees make. Such perceptions destroy much of the motivation intended in a differential pay system and indirectly contribute to turnover.[28]

Ideally, a firm will strive to develop a logical pay system which reflects both internal and external equity. In the process, employee participation should be fully utilized. Compensation managers should then take necessary action to ensure that employees understand the basis for their pay. Obviously, happiness for all employees cannot be guaranteed. The dissatisfaction and costs associated with a secret pay system, however, seem to make that approach highly questionable.

PAY COMPRESSION

Pay compression is another potentially troublesome problem which occurs when pay differences between jobs of different levels of importance become small. It can be created in several ways, including by hiring new employees at pay rates which are comparable to pay rates for current employees who may have been with the firm for several years. Pay adjustments made at the lower end of the job hierarchy without commensurate adjustments at the top are common causes of pay compression. Consider, for example, pay rates for college graduates in the data processing field. These employees are able to command top salaries because of a shortage of qualified workers.[29]

Pay compression can also result from the granting of pay increases on a flat cents-per-hour basis over a long period of time. Percentage increases, on the other hand, maintain relative differences in pay rates. The result of compression is dissatisfaction on the part of employees in higher level jobs. With the slope of the pay curve flattened, there is less incentive to be promoted.[30]

[27]Roy G. Foltz, "Compensation Communications," *Personnel Administrator* 25, (May 1980): 22.
[28]Edward E. Lawler III, *Pay and Organizational Effectiveness: A Psychological View* (New York: McGraw-Hill Book Co., 1971), pp. 174–175, 196–197.
[29]William S. Hubbartt, "The Ten Commandments of Salary Administration," *Administrative Management* 4, (April 1982): 24.
[30]Bruce R. Ellig, "Pay Inequities: How Many Exist Within Your Organization?" *Compensation Review* 12 (Third Quarter 1980): 42.

Even after a job has been priced, other factors determine how much a specific employee will receive. These factors range from sheer luck to the manner in which he or she actually performs a job. Some factors may seem inappropriate, but, in real life, they are often major determinants of an individual's pay.

Performance

Nothing is more demoralizing to outstanding employees than to be paid the same as a less productive worker. Therefore, management generally prefers a merit system based on employee performance. Such an approach permits individuals to be rewarded according to their productivity. Further, such a system permits pay to serve as a motivator of performance. It gives employees the incentive to put forth their best efforts.

Seniority

The length of time an employee has been associated with the company, division, department, or job is referred to as seniority. While management prefers performance as a basis for compensation changes, labor unions tend to favor seniority, which they believe provides an objective and fair basis for pay increases. Many union leaders believe performance evaluation systems are too subjective and permit management to reward their favorites arbitrarily.

At one personnel conference, a compensation consultant pointed out the possibility of permitting employees to receive pay increases to midpoint of their pay grade on the basis of seniority.[31] The rationale is that workers performing at an acceptable level should eventually receive the average wage or salary of their pay grade. However, progression beyond the midpoint should be based on performance. This practice would permit only the outstanding performers to reach the maximum rate for the grade. It reflects the initial rationale for rate ranges. However, this concept has fallen by the wayside in organizations where many of the employees are near the top of their respective grades. An increasing number receive pay above the midpoint.[32]

Experience

"Experience has taught our best racquetball players how to really play the game," the director of a state university's recreational facility recently ex-

[31]Brooks Bernhardt, President, Brooks Bernhardt Associates, 37th North Texas Personnel Conference, Dallas, Texas, September 1978.
[32]"The Tightening Squeeze on White-Collar Pay," *Business Week* 2500 (September 12, 1977): 83–84.

claimed. No doubt it was a true statement. But, as someone else put it, "Experience has also taught our worst racquetball players how to play." The point is, that while experience is invaluable, not all experience is good experience. You can play golf for ten years (without lessons from a pro, of course), have a hook that almost returns to the tee box, and be further away from being a good golfer than you were before you started playing. Although not always realized in business circles, the same is true of management experience. How much ahead of the game is the manager who has been a poor manager for two decades? Managers who comment, with considerable confidence and pleasure, that they have had twenty years of management experience may actually have (because of the duplication involved) only ten years experience two times, or five years experience four times. Heaven forbid the possibility of having six months experience forty times!

Experience is truly indispensable. And, in many cases, management does compensate employees on this basis. Sometimes the practice is justified because of the invaluable insights that can only be acquired through experience on the job. Occasionally, experience is irrelevant even though it may still be rewarded.

Membership in the Organization

Some components of individual financial compensation are given employees without regard to the particular job they perform or their level of productivity. These rewards are provided because employees are members of the organization. As an example, an average performer occupying a job in grade 1 may receive the same number of vacation days, the same amount of group life insurance, and the same reimbursement for educational expenses as a superior employee working in a job classified in pay grade 10. In fact, the worker in pay grade 1 may get more vacation time if he or she has been with the firm longer. Rewards based on organizational membership are intended to maintain a high degree of stability in the work force.

Potential

Potential is useless if it is never realized. Yet, organizations do pay some individuals based on their potential. In order to attract talented young people to the firm, the overall compensation program must appeal to the person with no experience or any immediate ability to perform difficult tasks. Many young employees are paid because they possess the potential to become a first-level supervisor, manager of compensation, vice president of marketing, or possibly even the chief executive officer.

College graduates typically do not have significant business experience for employment managers to examine. Lacking this track record, organizations turn elsewhere for factors to predict the success of the graduate. Grades in college are often considered. Although there is controversy about the relationship between grades and performance on the job, personnel recruiters and line managers often have no alternative but to emphasize a student's academic success. Of course, there are other factors that might indicate potential. Some questions commonly asked of college prospects are:

- What percent of your school expenses did you pay?
- What class offices did you hold?
- To what professional student associations did you belong, such as American Society for Personnel Administration, Society for Advancement of Management, Pi Sigma Epsilon, Delta Sigma Pi, or Alpha Kappa Psi? Did you hold offices in these organizations?
- Were you a member of a social sorority or fraternity? What leadership positions did you occupy?

These and many other questions may be asked as organizations attempt to identify individuals who will provide the future leadership for their firm. The people sought are those with potential.

Political Influence

Before this topic is discussed, we want you to know that this factor should not be considered a bona fide determinant of financial compensation. However, to deny that it exists would be like playing ostrich by sticking our heads in the sand. It is disheartening to hear someone say, "It's not what you know, it's who you know." Yet, there is an unfortunate element of truth in the statement. To varying degrees in business, government, and not-for-profit organizations, a person's pull or political influence may influence both pay and promotions. It may be natural for a manager to favor a friend or relative in granting a pay increase or promotion. Whether it is natural or not, if the person receiving the reward is not truly deserving, this fact will become known by the peer group. This practice can have a devastating impact upon employee morale. Employees want, and are beginning to demand, fair and equitable treatment. There is nothing either fair or equitable about a person receiving a promotion and/or pay increase based strictly on politics.

Sheer Luck

We have all heard people say, "It certainly helps to be in the right place at the right time." There is more than a smattering of truth in this statement as it relates to the determination of one's compensation. The situation we are describing might be termed sheer luck. Positions are continually opening up in firms. Realistically, there is no way for managers to foresee many of the changes that occur. For instance, who could have known that the purchasing agent, Joe Flynch, an apparently happily married man, would suddenly quit his job, take off with his neighbor's wife, and never be heard from again? Although the company may have been grooming several managers for Joe's position, none may be capable of immediately assuming the increased responsibility. The most experienced person, Tommy Foy, has been with the company only six months. Tommy had been an assistant buyer for a competitor for four years. Because of his experience, Tommy receives the promotion and the increased financial compensation. Tommy Foy was in the right place at the right time.

When asked to explain their most important reasons for success and effectiveness as managers, two chief executives responded candidly. One said, "Success is being at the right place at the right time and being recognized as having the ability to make timely decisions. It also depends on having good rapport with people, a good operating background, and the knowledge of how to develop people." The other replied, "My present position was attained by being in the right place at the right time with a history of getting the job done."

In determining individual compensation, other factors may be unique to specific organizations. Although there is currently no perfect system, human resources managers are charged with constantly striving to improve their compensation systems.

SUMMARY

Compensation refers to every type of reward that individuals receive in return for performing organizational tasks. The primary components of a total compensation program include: (1) direct financial compensation, (2) indirect financial compensation, and (3) nonfinancial compensation. Direct financial compensation consists of the pay a person receives in the form of wages, salaries, bonuses, and commissions. Indirect financial compensation includes all financial rewards which are not included as direct. Nonfinancial compensation consists of the satisfaction that a person receives by performing meaningful job tasks or the psychological and physical environment in which the job is performed. In designing a total compensation program which will attract, retain, and motivate employees, management should consider all types of rewards.

The external and internal environment can influence an individual's financial compensation. External factors include: (1) the labor market, (2) cost of living, (3) labor unions, (4) government legislation, (5) society, and (6) the economy.

A systematic approach to determining the relative value or worth of each job in an organization is referred to as job evaluation. There are four basic job evaluation methods used in organizations: the ranking method, the classification method, the factor comparison method, and the point method. In selecting a method, many firms choose a plan and modify it to fit their particular needs. The ranking and classification methods are nonquantitative while the factor comparison and point methods are quantitative approaches.

Placing a dollar value on a job's worth is referred to as job pricing. Many organizations group similar jobs into pay grades to simplify the pricing process. A pay range includes a minimum and a maximum rate with enough variance between the two to allow some significant pay difference. Even after the job has been priced, other factors determine how much a specific employee will receive. These factors range from sheer luck to the manner in which he or she actually performs the job.

Questions for Review

1. What are the primary factors that should be considered when a total compensation program is designed? Briefly describe each.

2. Distinguish between a pay follower, a pay leader, and a "going rate" organization.

3. What are the external factors that affect compensation decisions? Discuss each factor briefly.

4. Give the primary purpose of job evaluation.

5. Distinguish between the four basic methods of job evaluation: the ranking method, the classification method, the factor comparison method, and the point method.

6. What is the purpose of "job pricing"? Briefly discuss.

7. What is the basic procedure for determining pay grades?

8. What is the purpose for establishing pay ranges for jobs?

9. List and describe the various factors concerning the individual employee as they relate to the determination of pay and benefits.

Terms for Review

Compensation
Direct financial compensation
Indirect financial compensation
Nonfinancial compensation
Labor market
Key job
Cost-of-living allowance
Exempt employees
Comparable worth
Going rate
Job evaluation

Pay equity
Ranking method
Classification method
Factor comparison method
Point method
Job cluster
Job pricing
Pay grades
Wage curve
Pay range
Pay compression

David Rhine, compensation manager for Farrington Lingerie Company, was generally a relaxed and good natured individual. Although he was a no-nonsense, competent executive, David was one of the most popular managers in the company. This Friday morning, however, David was not his usual self. As chairperson of the company's job evaluation committee, he had called a late morning meeting at which several jobs were to be considered for reevaluation. The jobs had already been rated and assigned to pay grade 3. But the office manager, Ben Butler, was upset that one was not rated higher. To press the issue, Ben had taken his case to two executives who were also members of the job evaluation committee. The two executives (production manager Bill Nelson and general marketing manager Betty Anderson) then requested that the job ratings be reviewed. Bill and Betty supported Ben's side of the dispute and David was not looking forward to the confrontation that was almost certain to occur.

The controversial job was that of receptionist. There was only one receptionist position in the company and it was held by Beth Smithers. Beth had been with the firm twelve years, longer than any of the committee members. She performed her tasks in an unusually efficient manner and her outstanding work was noticed by virtually all the executives in the company, including the president. Bill Nelson and Betty Anderson were particularly pleased with Beth because of the cordial manner in which she greeted and accommodated Farrington's customers and vendors who frequently visited the plant. They felt that Beth's professionalism projected a positive image of the company.

When the meeting began, David said, "Good morning. I know that you are busy so let's get the show on the road. We have several jobs to evaluate this morning and I suggest we begin. . ." Before he could finish his sentence, Bill interrupted, "I suggest we start with Beth." Betty nodded in agreement. When David regained his composure, he quietly but firmly asserted, "Bill, we are *not* here today to evaluate Beth. Her supervisor does that at performance appraisal time. We're meeting to evaluate jobs based on job content. In order to do this fairly with regard to other jobs in the company, we must leave personalities out of our evaluation." David then proceeded to pass out copies of the receptionist job description while Bill and Betty appeared to be most irritated.

Questions

1. Do you feel that David was justified in insisiting that the job, not the person, be evaluated? Discuss.
2. Do you believe that there is a maximum for every job in an organization, regardless of how well the job is being performed? Justify your position.
3. Assuming that Beth is earning the maximum of the range for her pay grade, in what ways can she obtain a salary increase?

Harry Neal had been employed with Trimark Data Systems, Inc. (TDS) for five years and had progressed to his current position of senior programmer analyst. He was generally pleased with the company and thoroughly enjoyed the creative demands of his job.

One Saturday afternoon during a golf game with his friend and coworker Randy Dean, Harry discovered that his department had hired a recent State University graduate as a programmer analyst. Harry really became upset when he learned that the new man's starting salary was only $30 a month lower than his own. Although Harry was a good natured fellow, he was bewildered. He was upset because he felt that he was being treated unfairly.

The following Monday morning Harry confronted Dave Edwards, the personnel director, and asked if what he had heard was true. Dave apologetically admitted that it was and attempted to explain the company's situation: "Harry, the market for programmer analysts is very tight and in order for the company to attract qualified prospects, we have to offer a premium starting salary. We desperately needed another analyst and this was the only way we could get one." Harry asked Dave if his salary would be adjusted accordingly. Dave answered, "Your salary will be reevaluated at the regular time. You're doing a great job, though, and I'm sure the boss will recommend a raise." Harry thanked Dave for his time but left the office shaking his head and wondering about his future.

Questions

1. Do you feel that Dave's explanation was satisfactory? Discuss.

2. What action do you think the company should have taken with regard to Harry?

Chapter Objectives

1. Describe the various incentive compensation programs that are available in many organizations.
2. Describe how compensation for managers is determined and some of the types of managerial compensation.
3. Explain how compensation for professionals and sales personnel is determined.
4. Describe the importance of benefits to the total compensation program.
5. Identify the benefits the law requires and the voluntary benefits organizations provide.
6. Identify the many forms of nonfinancial compensation that members of organizations are beginning to expect.

Chapter 12 _____

Additional Compensation Considerations

Arnold Thompson, Joe Minnis, and Randy Anderson are all employed as shipping clerks for Mainstreet Furniture Company. Arnold and Joe are energetic young people who consistently work hard each day. Both earn about $6.50 per hour. Randy is a "good ole boy" who spends most of his time flipping quarters with dock workers and talking with the department secretary. Yesterday, work was piling up in the department and Arnold and Joe were working furiously to keep up. Randy was nowhere to be found. "Arnold," Joe said disgustedly, "the pay here just isn't fair. We do twice as much work as Randy yet he makes as much as we do." "I know," Joe acknowledged, "but he punches in and out at the same time we do."

Mac Lewis—a college dropout—was a senior credit clerk at Ajax Manufacturing Company. A bright young man, Mac had been with Ajax for four years. He had received excellent performance ratings in each of several positions he had held with the firm. However, during his last appraisal interview, Mac's supervisor implied that promotion to a higher level job would require additional formal education. Because he appeared to be receptive to the idea, Mac's supevisor suggested that he check with Personnel to learn the details of Ajax's educational assistance policy.

Liz Brown was a divorcee and the mother of three elementary school children. She worked as an illustrator for Busiform Company to support her family. Her normal working hours were from 8:00 A.M. to 5:00 P.M., Monday through Friday. The children's school began each weekday morning at 9:00 A.M. and ended at 3:30 P.M. Satisfactory arrangements had been made for the children after school. However, she faced an almost impossible task of transporting them to school in the morning and arriving at her job on time. The school's principal permitted the children to enter the building at 7:45 each morning to wait until classes began, but Liz was afraid she could not count on this practice to continue indefinitely. When Busiform management announced implementation of a new system of flexible working hours, Liz was delighted.

While these anecdotes may seem to have little in common, each relates to the broad area of compensation. Arnold Thompson and Joe Minnis are not on an incentive system and are angry because they do more work than Randy Anderson. Mac is investigating the possibility of continuing his education through his company's educational assistance program. While Liz could use additional money, her primary concern is the well-being of her children. She believes that the new flexible working hours will solve her most difficult problem.

The overall purpose of this chapter is to emphasize the many and varied aspects of compensation. The chapter begins with a discussion of incentive compensation plans and the special pay considerations required by managers, professionals, and sales personnel. Next, we refer to benefits and the various forms they may take. The final section covers nonfinancial compensation which emanates from the job and the environmental factors surrounding the job.

INCENTIVE COMPENSATION

According to the 1978 Economic Report to the President, one of the most significant economic problems of recent years has been the slowdown in United States productivity. There is evidence that this productivity problem, which affects both the public and private sectors of our economy, has become increasingly serious over the past few years.[1] While compensation is most often determined by how much time an employee spends at work, there are circumstances which encourage organizations to relate pay to productivity. Compensation based upon this concept is referred to as **incentive compensation.** A primary purpose of such a plan is to encourage greater productivity from individuals and work groups. The management assumption is that money will serve to motivate performance. It is likely that more productive workers such as Arnold Thompson and Joe Minnis would prefer to be paid on the basis of their output.

Money can serve as a most important motivator for those who value it, which most of us do. The organization must reward employees according to their productivity. A clear relationship must exist between performance and pay if money is to serve as an effective motivator.

Output standards must be established before any type of incentive system can be applied. This standard is a measure of work that an average well-trained employee, working at a normal pace, should be able to accomplish in a given

[1]Edward M. Glaser, "Productivity Gains Through Worklife Improvement," *Personnel* 57, (January–February 1980): 71.

period of time. For example, a firm may determine that employees in a particular department should be able to produce five finished parts per hour. The standard then becomes five. Time study specialists (who generally report to industrial engineering or methods departments) are often responsible for establishing work standards. A more direct approach to balancing pay and performance is to pay incentive compensation which can be offered on an individual, group, or company-wide basis.

Individual Incentive Plans

Many individual incentive plans have been used in an attempt to improve worker productivity and the firm's profitability. If Arnold Thompson produces more than Randy Anderson (another employee performing the same job) he will receive a greater financial reward because of his greater productivity. The straight piecework plan and the standard hour plan are the most commonly used individual plans.

A predetermined amount of money is paid for each unit produced in the **straight piecework plan.** The piece rate is calculated by dividing the standard hourly output into the job's pay rate. For example, if the standard output is 25 units per hour and the job's pay rate is $5 per hour, the piece rate would be $.20. In this example, an employee who produced at the rate of 35 units per hour would earn $56 in an eight hour day (35 units × 8 hours × $.20). Most incentive plans in use today have a guaranteed base. In the example above, it would be the $5 per hour rate.

The straight piecework plan is simple and easily understood by employees.[2] One possible weakness (which is minimized by the use of today's computers) is that any change in the overall pay scale necessitates computing new piece rates for every job. The standard hour plan was devised to overcome this problem.

Time allowances, rather than piece rates, are calculated for each unit of output the **standard hour plan** is used. Again, assume that 25 units per hour is the standard output, $5 the hourly job rate and eight hours the time worked per day. Under these assumptions, an employee would have an allowance of 2.4 minutes per unit of output (instead of a piece rate of $.20 per unit). The allowance is calculated by dividing 60 minutes (the basis for the standard) by the output standard of 25 units.

An employee producing at the rate of 35 units per hour would receive an allowance of 2.4 minutes per unit for the 10 units over the standard. This allowance would total 192 minutes (3.2 hours) for the eight hour shift [10 (units over standard) × 8 (hours in shift) × 2.4 (minutes allowance per unit)].

---

[2]David W. Belcher, *Compensation Administration* (Englewood Cliffs, NJ: Prentice-Hall, Inc., 1974), p. 315 (hereafter cited as Belcher).

The pay for the day would be:

Guaranteed base rate ($5 × 8 hours)	$40.00
Pay for 192 minutes ($5 × 3.2 hours)	16.00
Total pay	$56.00

The standard hour plan has the characteristics of a straight piecework plan. An advantage is that piece rates need not be recalculated for every pay rate change.

One potential problem with both the straight piecework plan and the standard hour plan is related to the output standard. The standard is typically established by industrial engineers and may be distrusted by the workers. Any change in the standard, although justified in the eyes of management, may be viewed with considerable skepticism.

When individual output cannot be easily distinguished, group and company-wide plans offer alternatives to individual incentive plans. These approaches will be discussed next.

Group Incentive Plans

As we suggested earlier, it is not always feasible to pay individual incentives. Work is often organized in such a manner that productivity results from group effort. It is then difficult, if not impossible, to determine each individual's contribution, so incentives must be provided to the group. For example, if the group produced one hundred units over standard, each member would receive incentive compensation on a pro rata basis.

There are advantages and disadvantages to group incentive. For instance, in the assembly of electrical transformers, there may be ten employees working on one phase of the operation. They must work together if the overall task is to be successfully accomplished. If nine employees perform their task but one does not, the productivity of the entire group may suffer. The peer pressure exerted in such a situation can be so great that the affected individual will either conform to the group's standards or leave the group. Group incentive plans tend to foster teamwork. They often encourage peers to serve as counselors and coaches for new members. There is a tendency for group members to lend a helping hand when it is needed.

Company-wide Plans

On a baseball team it does not matter that you have an outstanding pitcher or a great outfield. The standard by which the team is evaluated is the overall win/loss record. Just as with the baseball club, some managers believe that incentive plans encourage competition between individuals and groups. Company-wide plans then offer a viable alternative. These plans may be based on

Richard G. Jamison, APD
Director of Compensation
Rockwell International

Dick Jamison joined the Vick Chemical Division of Richardson-Merrell as a co-op student from Drexel University. Upon graduation in 1953, he was asked, "Would you mind working in Personnel for a while?" Dick remembers that he was not terribly enthusiastic about this proposal because his major in college had been statistics. He accepted the position of assistant employment manager, however, and quickly discovered the reason for the request. His boss was terminated almost before Dick was shown to his desk and he soon became personnel supervisor for the entire plant. This was the turning point in his career. Looking back, Dick has no regrets about his career, and his record of success provides the evidence. In 1956, he was promoted to the position of personnel director of the National Drug Division of Richardson-Merrell. Eight years later, he was named director of compensation and benefits for General Mills.

Dick joined Rockwell International in 1974 as director of compensation, a position which he holds today. In this capacity, he is responsible for compensation throughout Rockwell, including executive compensation.

In connection with this specialized area, Dick says, "Executives know when they perform well. And, when they do, they expect to be rewarded. If your compensation system does this, fine. If not, you will lose your best people."

Dick believes that the field of compensation is extremely exciting. He says, "It has a direct and important impact on the bottom line of company results." When asked what difficulties a compensation manager might face, he said, "It's managing compensation practices in a multi-industry corporation where the economy is having an adverse affect on one business unit while another is growing. Although internal consistency is desirable, salaries cannot be overmanaged to the point of forcing all units to ignore the competitive demands of their particular business."

Jamison believes that Personnel is broadening its scope and that to be a successful practitioner, one needs a good understanding of the total operations of the business. "We need to avoid becoming so enthralled with our specialty that we lose sight of the total business picture," Jamison says.

Dick is past president of the Pittsburgh Personnel Association, Philadelphia Chapter of ASPA, and the Twin Cities Personnel Association. He has held several leadership positions within ASPA, including regional vice president, national treasurer, and national vice president. He also served as treasurer of the Personnel Accreditation Institute and is the past chairman of the steering committee for the Conference Board Council on Compensation. He is a member of the American Compensation Association. In 1979, Richard received the Distinguished Service Award at West Virginia University. He has been elected to Who's Who in Finance and Industry each year since 1977.

the organization's productivity, cost savings, or profitability. To illustrate the concept of company-wide plans, we will discuss profit sharing plans, employee stock ownership plans, and the Scanlon plan.

Profit Sharing. **Profit sharing** is a compensation plan which results in the distribution of a predetermined percentage of the firm's profits to employees. Many organizations use this type of plan to integrate the employee's interests with those of the company. Profit sharing plans can aid firms in recruiting, retaining, and motivating employees to be more productive. There are three basic forms of profit sharing plans: current, deferred, and combination.[3]

- *Current plans* provide payment to employees in cash or stock as soon as profits are determined.
- *Deferred plans* involve placing company contributions in an irrevocable trust to be credited to the account of individual employees. The funds are normally invested in securities, and become available to the employee (or his or her survivors) at retirement, termination, or death.
- *Combination plans* permit employees to receive part of their share on a current basis while a portion of it is deferred.

Normally, most full-time employees are included in a company's profit sharing plan after a specified waiting period. Vesting rights are the amount of "profit" an employee actually owns in his or her account. It is often established on a graduated basis. For example, an employee may become 25 percent vested after being in the plan for two years; 50 percent vested after three years; 75 percent vested after four years; and 100 percent vested after five years. You can see that this approach to vesting may tend to reduce turnover by encouraging employees to remain with the company.

In summarizing the merits and disadvantages of profit sharing, one consultant stated: "Profit sharing has a lot of pluses, but its minus is it's subject to stock market performance and the company's experience, and they are unpredictable."[4] For example, if the company does not make sufficient profits for several years, employees may not benefit through the plan. This may be a special problem when employees have become accustomed to receiving the added compensation.

[3]J. D. Dunn and Frank M. Rachel, *Salary Administration: Total Compensation Systems,* (New York: McGraw-Hill Book Company, 1971), pp. 261–262 (hereafter cited as *Dunn*).
[4]Kathryn McIntyre Roberts, "Sears, Xerox Acts Spotlight Decline in Profit Sharing," *Business Insurance* (May 2, 1977): 34.

Employee Stock Ownership Plan. Another type of company-wide incentive plan is the **Employee Stock Ownership Plan** (ESOP). Using this plan, a company provides its employees with company stock. Allocation of the stock is assigned to each participant on the basis of her or his base pay. Currently, contributions made to ESOPs are tax-deductible expenses.

Many of the benefits of profit sharing plans have also been cited for ESOPs. Specifically, ESOP advocates have suggested that employees obtain a stake in the business and become more closely identified with the firm—a relationship which theoretically increases motivation. Also, employees may acquire a second income without increasing the firm's compensation costs. Finally, from a company viewpoint, capital may be raised for expansion.[5]

While the potential advantages of ESOPs are impressive, critics point out the dangers of employees having all their eggs in one basket. Employees would be in a vulnerable position should their company fail.

The Scanlon Plan. The **Scanlon Plan** is a cost savings plan which, like profit sharing, features participation by the firm's employees.[6] The plan was developed by Joseph Scanlon in 1937, and it continues to be a successful approach to group incentive, especially in smaller plants. The financial reward provided employees is based on savings in labor cost, resulting largely from employee suggestions. These suggestions are evaluated by employee-management committees. Calculation of the savings is based on a ratio of payroll costs to the sales value of what that payroll produces. If the company is able to reduce its payroll costs through increased efficiency in operation, the savings are shared with the employees. In reflecting upon his company's experience with the Scanlon Plan, George Sherman (vice president of human resources for Midland-Ross), stated: "American workers want and, in my judgement, are entitled to a piece of the action when, through their own efforts and ingenuity, they are able to help the company do better."[7]

COMPENSATION FOR MANAGERS

Management performance has a significant impact on a firm's success and survival. For this reason, it is vital for organizations to provide appropriate compensation for their managers. Managerial efficiency and the firm's welfare are closely related. Therefore, it is not unusual for a large portion of management

[5]Donald E. Sullivan, "ESOP's: Panacea or Placebo?" *California Management Review* 20 (Fall 1977): 55–56.
[6]Dunn, p. 253.
[7]"Scanlon Plan Puts Everyone on the Team," *Iron Age* 218 (August 9, 1976): 18.

compensation—especially for top executives—to be linked to the company's performance.

Determination of Managerial Compensation

A recent survey of Fortune 200 Companies indicated that these firms prefer to relate salary growth for the highest level executives to overall corporate performance. For the next management tier, an integration of overall corporate performance with market rates and internal considerations is desired. For lower level managers, the tendency is to determine salaries on the basis of market rates, internal pay relationships, and individual performance.[8] As a generalization, the higher the managerial position, the greater the flexibility managers have in designing their jobs. Management jobs are often difficult to define because of their complexity. And, when they are defined, they are often described in terms of anticipated results rather than what or how the work is accomplished. One management consultant has suggested the "entrepreneurial approach," or market pricing, to determine managerial compensation.[9] In this approach, organizations use compensation survey data to determine pay levels for a representative group of jobs. These data may be obtained from such sources as the American Management Association and Sibson & Company, Inc. Some organizations also adapt point and factor comparison methods of job evaluation to determine the relative value of management jobs.

The Hay Guide Chart-Profile Method

This method has long been an extremely popular approach, and today more than two thousand firms throughout the world use it.[10] This method enables firms to determine the relative difficulty and importance of jobs using these factors: know-how, problem solving, accountability, and where appropriate, working conditions. Point values are assigned to these factors to determine the final point profile for any job.

The popularity of the Hay Plan provides it with an important advantage by facilitating comparison of jobs within one firm with those of others. Thus, the plan serves not only to permit determination of internal equity — by ascertaining relative worth within the firm — but external equity as well.[11]

Types of Managerial Compensation

Managers typically prefer to have the bulk of their compensation in the form of salary. Salary is especially important because it determines their standard of

[8]James T. Brinks, APD, "Executive Compensation: Crossroads of the '80s," *Personnel Administrator* 26 (December 1981): 23.

[9]Robert E. Sibson, *Compensation* (New York: AMACOM, A Division of American Management Associations, 1974), p. 141 (hereafter cited as Sibson).

[10]Richard I. Henderson, *Compensation Management: Rewarding Performance*, Third Edition, (Reston, VA: Reston Publishing Company, Inc., 1979), p. 222 (hereafter cited as "Henderson").

[11]Henderson, 225.

living. It also provides the basis for other indirect forms of compensation. For example, an executive might receive life insurance protection based on 2½ times salary. In addition, bonus payments may be related to the executive's salary. These payments supplement the salary; they may be paid on a current or deferred basis. Bonuses are paid by organizations whose managers believe in their incentive value. According to one compensation expert, "average bonus levels range from 80 percent of base salary at the top to 20 percent for the lowest level participant."[12]

The stock option is another form of compensation which is designed to integrate the interests of management with the organization. Although various types of plans exist, the typical **stock option plan** gives the manager the option to buy a specified amount of stock in the future at or below the current market price. This form of compensation is advantageous when stock prices are rising. There are potential disadvantages to stock option plans. The manager may feel uncomfortable investing money in the same organization in which he or she is building a career. Also, as with profit sharing, this method of compensation is popular when a firm is successful. But, during periods of decline when stock prices fall, the participants may become disenchanted.

Deferred compensation—pay which is held in trust for a manager until retirement—is often used to provide a delayed reward for executives. This permits them to receive income when they are taxed at a lower rate.

An interesting, although extreme case of executive compensation occurred a number of years ago. A large electronics firm allegedly lured a brilliant executive away from a competitor by offering him virtually everything but the "kitchen sink." It was contended that the following inducements were offered: an annual salary of $120,000 (an increase of $30,000), an immediate payment of $250,000 or equivalent stock options, an option to buy 90,000 shares of company stock, and a loan at no interest for ten years of $5.4 million with which to exercise his stock option.[13]

Perquisites (perks) are benefits designed exclusively for top level executives. In addition to status, these benefits provide rewards that either are not considered as earned income or are taxed at a low level. Some of the more common perks are shown below:[14]

- Company provided car for both business and personal use
- Accessible, no cost, parking
- Limousine service—the chauffeur may also serve as a bodyguard
- Kidnap and ransom protection
- Tax assistance and financial counseling
- Use of company plane and yacht
- Membership in country clubs
- Special dining room facilities

[12]Belcher, p. 545.
[13]Reprinted from *Electronics* (August 19, 1968): 47. © McGraw-Hill Book Company, 1968. All rights reserved.
[14]Henderson, pp. 463–464.

"Realize that Personnel does not possess much corporate authority
and that results will depend on personal influence and leadership
rather than authority.

Understand that many of the rewards in personnel work are psychic
and be sure that this is your bag before you enter the field.

Be prepared to cope with managers who from time to time may not
be totally appreciative of the people needs of the staff and may be
more concerned with economics.

Learn to handle the feeling of loss that occurs when other managers
assume they are 'personnel experts' in their own eyes."

**Richard C. Crosbee, Vice President of Personnel
Bristol-Myers Company**

- Season tickets to entertainment and sporting events
- Use of company credit card
- College tuition reimbursement for children

Perquisites extend a firm's benefit program on an individual basis. They
seem to be more popular in smaller firms than in major organizations.[15]

Some of us often criticize the high level of executive pay and benefits.
However, a firm's success depends upon executives who possess the ability to
utilize the organization's resources effectively. When you consider this, executive compensation is better understood.

Some of the special compensation features available for managers apply to
other exempt employees in an organization, especially professional employees.

COMPENSATION FOR PROFESSIONALS

People in professional jobs are compensated primarily for the knowledge they
bring to the organization. Because of this, the administration of compensation
programs for professionals is somewhat different than for managerial staff.
Many professional employees eventually become managers. For those who do
not desire this form of career progression, some organizations have created a
duel track of compensation. The duel track provides a separate pay structure
for professionals which may overlap a portion of the managerial structure. It is
indeed a sad situation when high performing professionals are required to accept management positions in order to increase their compensation. For instance, in some organizations, the only way to increase professionals' pay is to
promote them into management. However, a real problem is created when it

[15]Bruce R. Ellig, "Perquisites: The Intrinsic Form of Pay," *Personnel* 58 (January–February 1981):
23–31.

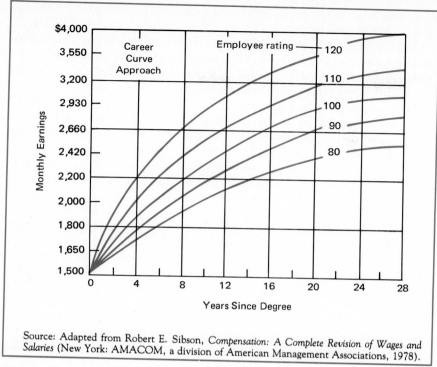

Source: Adapted from Robert E. Sibson, *Compensation: A Complete Revision of Wages and Salaries* (New York: AMACOM, a division of American Management Associations, 1978).

Figure 12–1. **Professional career curves.**

is discovered that a top performing professional is not able to perform satisfactorily as a manager.

The professional career curve, shown as Figure 12–1, is an approach which has been developed especially for determining compensation for professional jobs. In preparing career curves, it is assumed that the more experience an individual has, the higher the earnings. However, as you see in this figure, career curves may be drawn to reflect varying performance levels. In this particular field a professional employee who has twenty years' experience and performs at a level 10 percent above the average, would presumably earn $3200 per month. On the other hand, a person with the same experience performing at the 80 percent level, would be assumed to earn about $2400 dollars a month. Some type of performance appraisal system is obviously necessary in order to make these productivity distinctions.

SALES COMPENSATION

Because compensation programs for sales employees constitute a unique set of considerations, some organizations assign this responsibility to the sales staff rather than to Personnel. Still, many general compensation practices also apply to sales jobs. For example, job content, relative job worth, and job market value should be determined.

The straight salary approach is at one extreme in sales compensation. This involves salespersons receiving a fixed salary regardless of their sales levels. Organizations use this method primarily when continued service after the sale is stressed.[16] For instance, many sales representatives who deal largely with the federal government are compensated in this manner. At the other extreme, the person whose pay is totally determined as a percentage of sales is on straight commission. An example of a salesperson in this category might be door-to-door sales workers. Richard H. Swanson, director of compensation for General Mills, Inc., has stated that, "the only 'pure' nondeferred compensation plan is the 100 percent sales commission plan. This type of pay is probably the most effective one to motivate salespeople. Unfortunately, straight commission is inappropriate for most of the selling that is done today."

Between these extremes, there are endless combinations of part salary-part commission. The possibilities increase when various types of bonuses are added to the basic compensation package. The emphasis given to either commission or salary depends upon several factors, including the organization's philosophy toward service, the nature of the product, and the time period required for closing a sale.

In addition to salary, commissions, and bonuses, salespersons often receive other forms of compensation which are intended to serve as added incentives. Sales contests which offer television sets, refrigerators, or all-expense vacations to exotic locations are not uncommon.

If any one feature sets sales compensation apart from other programs, it is the emphasis placed on incentives. The nature of sales work often simplifies the problem of determining individual output. Sales volume can usually be related to specific individuals, a situation which encourages payment of incentive compensation. Also, experience in sales compensation practices over the years has supported the concept of relating rewards to performance.

BENEFITS OR INDIRECT FINANCIAL COMPENSATION

Most organizations recognize a responsibility to their employees by providing "benefits" for their health, safety, security, and general welfare (see Figure 12–2). **Benefits** include any financial compensation cost borne by the employers—in addition to pay—that can be given to individual employees. Benefits cost the firm money but employees usually receive them indirectly. For example, an organization may spend $500 a year to pay the health insurance premiums for each nonexempt employee. The employee does not receive money but does obtain the benefits of the health insurance coverage. This type of compensation has two distinct advantages. First, it is generally nontaxable to the em-

[16]Sibson, p. 141.

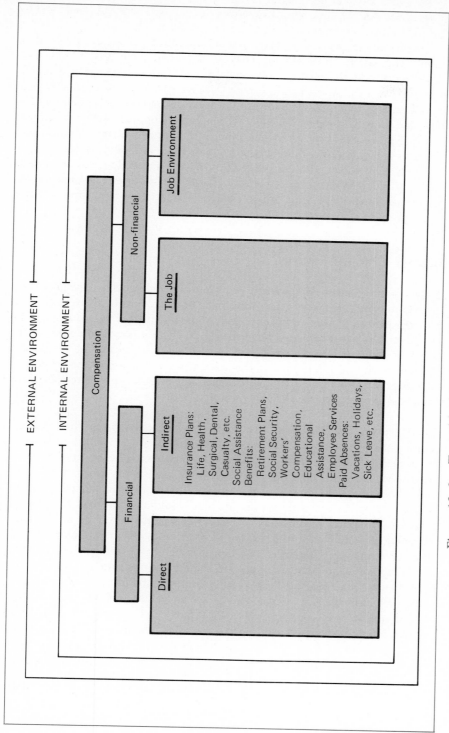

Figure 12–2. Typical benefits in a total compensation program.

ployee. Second, in the case of insurance, the premium rates are much less for large groups of employees as opposed to individual policies.

Generally speaking, benefits are provided employees as a result of their membership in the organization. They are typically not related to employee productivity and therefore do not serve as motivation for improved performance. However, an attractive benefit package can assist an organization in recruiting and retaining a quality workforce. The price for this assistance is high and growing rapidly. Benefits cost employers approximately $350 billion a year. They account for about one-third of total financial compensation provided by organizations and are growing almost twice as rapidly as direct pay.[17]

A typical worker who earns $24,000 per year indirectly receives approximately $12,000 in the form of benefits. These facts no doubt account for the less frequent use of the term "fringe" benefits. In fact, the term fringe benefits ". . . has become a misnomer in most organizations."[18]

Benefits Required by Law

Some organizations would probably provide mandated benefits regardless of legal requirements. However, most firms have no choice in the matter and must provide their employees certain benefits. Some might say, "If it is required by law, then it is not a benefit." Nevertheless, in these instances the firm is contributing additional money on behalf of the employee because he or she is a member of the organization. For this reason, we will consider these items to be benefits. These legally required benefits are social security, unemployment compensation, and workers' compensation.

Social Security. The Social Security Act of 1935 created a system that provided retirement benefits only. Subsequent amendments to the act added other forms of protection such as disability insurance, survivors benefits, and most recently, Medicare. Today, approximately nine out of ten employees in the United States are covered by social security. Disability insurance protects employees against loss of earnings due to total disability. Survivors benefits are provided to certain members of an employee's family when he or she dies. These benefits are paid to the widow, widower, and unmarried children of the deceased employee. Unmarried children may be eligible for survivors benefits until they are eighteen years of age. In some cases, students retain eligibility until they are nineteen. Medicare provides hospital and medical insurance protection for individuals sixty-five years of age and older or those who have become disabled.

While employees must pay a portion of the cost, the employer makes an equal contribution for Social Security coverage. It is this part which is considered a benefit. As may be seen in Table 12–1 the tax rate paid by both em-

---

[17]"The Hidden Paycheck: Employee Benefits Average $90 a Week," *Nation's Business* 66 (October 1978): 78.
[18]Richard C. Huseman, John D. Hatfield, and Russell W. Driver, "Getting Your Benefit Programs Understood and Appreciated," *Personnel Journal* 57 (October 1978): 560.

Table 12–1. Social Security taxes 1977–1986

Year	Maximum Taxable Wage	Tax Rate	Maximum Tax
1977	$16,500	5.85%	$ 965.25
1978	17,700	6.05	1,070.85
1979	22,900	6.13	1,403.77
1980	25,900	6.13	1,587.67
1981	29,700	6.65	1,975.05
1982	32,400	6.70	2,170.80
1983	35,700	6.70	2,351.70
1984*	37,500	7.00	2,625.00
1985	40,500	7.05	2,855.25
1986	43,800	7.15	3,131.70

*The amounts shown for 1984 and later are projected on the basis of assumptions of the 1982 Trustees Report.
Source: *Social Security Administration Program Circular,* Public Information Number 884, June 1982.

ployee and employer and the maximum wage taxable is increasing sharply. Between the years 1977 and 1986, the maximum social security tax will have more than tripled if current projections prove accurate. This dramatic increase, coupled with a continuing debate over the fiscal soundness of the system, leaves many employees with mixed feelings about its desirability.

Table 12–2 provides examples of monthly social security payments which may be received. As you see, a retired employee with average earnings of $8000 may receive monthly social security payments of $482.60. The same employee may retire at age 62, but with reduced benefits ($386.10). As a result of legislation passed in 1972, social security benefits will automatically increase in the future as the cost of living rises.

Unemployment Compensation. If an individual is laid off from employment by an organization covered by the Social Security Act, he or she may receive **unemployment compensation** for up to twenty-six weeks. While the federal government provides certain guidelines, unemployment compensation programs are administered by the states. As you might expect, the benefits vary by state. A federal payroll tax paid by the employer furnishes the funds for unemployment compensation.

Workers' Compensation. **Workers' compensation** benefits provide a degree of financial protection for employees who incur expenses resulting from job related accidents or illnesses. As with unemployment compensation, the various states administer individual programs subject to federal regulations. Employers pay the entire cost of workers' compensation insurance. Their premium expense is directly tied to their past experience with job related accidents and illnesses. This situation should encourage employers to actively pursue health and safety programs—topics we will discuss in the next chapter.

Table 12–2. Monthly retirement benefits for workers and dependents

Average Yearly Earnings	For Workers Retirement at 65	at 64	at 63	at 62	For Dependents[1] Spouse at 65 or child	at 64	at 63	at 62	Family[2] benefits
1,200	156.70	146.30	135.90	125.40	78.40	71.90	65.40	58.80	235.10
2,600	230.10	214.80	199.50	184.10	115.10	105.50	95.90	86.40	345.20
3,000	251.80	235.10	218.30	201.50	125.90	115.40	104.90	94.50	384.90
3,400	270.00	252.00	234.00	216.00	135.00	123.80	112.50	101.30	434.90
4,000	296.20	276.50	256.80	237.00	148.10	135.70	123.40	111.10	506.20
4,400	317.30	296.20	275.00	253.90	158.70	145.40	132.20	119.10	562.50
4,800	336.00	313.60	291.20	268.80	168.00	153.90	140.00	126.00	612.70
5,200	353.20	329.70	306.20	282.60	176.60	161.80	147.20	132.50	662.70
5,600	370.60	345.90	321.20	296.50	185.30	169.80	154.40	139.00	687.10
6,000	388.20	362.40	336.50	310.60	194.10	177.80	161.70	145.60	712.10
6,400	405.60	378.60	351.60	324.50	202.80	185.80	169.00	152.10	737.10
6,800	424.10	395.90	367.60	339.30	212.10	194.30	176.70	159.10	762.30
7,200	446.00	416.30	386.60	356.80	223.00	204.30	185.80	167.30	788.90
7,600	465.60	434.50	403.60	372.50	232.80	213.30	194.00	174.60	814.70
8,000	482.60	450.50	418.30	386.10	241.30	221.10	201.10	181.00	844.50
8,400	492.90	460.10	427.20	394.40	246.50	225.80	205.40	184.90	862.60
8,800	505.10	471.50	437.80	404.10	252.60	231.40	210.50	189.50	883.80
9,200	516.00	481.60	447.20	412.80	258.00	236.40	215.00	193.50	903.00
9,400	520.40	485.80	451.10	416.40	260.20	238.40	216.80	195.20	910.40
9,600	524.60	489.70	454.70	419.70	262.30	240.30	218.50	196.80	918.00
9,800	530.40	495.10	459.70	424.40	265.20	243.00	221.00	198.90	928.00
10,000	534.70	499.10	463.50	427.80	267.40	245.00	222.80	200.60	935.70

[1]If a person is eligible for both a worker's benefit and a spouse's benefit, the check actually payable is limited to the larger of the two.
[2]The maximum amount payable to a family is generally reached when a worker and two family members are eligible.
Source: U.S. Department of Health and Human Services, Social Security Administration, SSA Publication No. 05-10088, June 1982.

Voluntary Benefits

There seems to be an endless number of benefits provided voluntarily by organizations. These benefits may be classified according to the following categories: (1) payment for time not worked, (2) employee health and security benefits, (3) services to employees, and (4) premium pay. Benefits provided within these categories are not legally required. While they are provided "voluntarily," in some firms many have no doubt resulted from union-management negotiations.

Payment for Time Not Worked. In providing payment for time not worked, employers recognize employees' need for some time away from the job. For instance, paid vacations provide workers with time to rest and become rejuvenated, while also encouraging them to remain with the firm. A person in an operative job will normally receive two weeks annual vacation. Paid vacation time typically increases with seniority, with most senior employees receiving one month paid vacation annually. For example, employees with six months service may receive one week vacation; employees with one year service, two weeks; ten years service, three weeks; and fifteen years service, four weeks.

A senior executive with a month vacation and an annual salary of $96,000 would receive approximately $8,000 each year while not working. A junior employee earning $24,000 a year might receive two weeks of vacation time worth about $1,000.

Each year many firms allocate employees a certain number of days of sick leave which can be used when they are ill. The employees continue to receive their pay up to a maximum number of days if they cannot report to work. As with vacation pay, the number of sick leave days typically depends upon seniority. Some sick leave programs have been severely criticized. At times they have been abused by individuals calling in sick when all they really wanted was additional paid vacation. In order to counter this situation, some firms require a doctor's statement after a certain number of sick leave days have been taken.

There are other occasions on which employees are paid though they are not working. Holidays, coffee breaks, rest periods, jury duty service, voting time, clean-up time, and bereavement time are in this category.

Employee Welfare. Benefits which provide for general employee welfare may be of several kinds. Health insurance typically includes hospital room and board costs, service charges, and surgical fees. This increasingly costly benefit is often paid in part, or totally, by the employer. Many plans provide for major medical benefits to cover extraordinary expenses. The use of "deductibles" is a common feature of major medical benefits. For example, the employee may pay the first $100 of the health care cost before the insurance becomes effective.

Group life insurance is a common benefit provided to protect the employee's family in the event of his or her death. The cost of group life insurance is low even when the employee must contribute toward payment of the premium. Some plans call for a flat amount of coverage, say $10,000. Other plans base the coverage on the employee's annual earnings. For example, a worker earning $12,000 per year may have $24,000 worth of group life coverage. Typically, members of group plans do not have to show evidence of insurability. This provision is especially important to older employees and those with physical problems. Many of these employees may find the cost of insurance on an individual basis to be prohibitive.

Private retirement plans provide income for employees who retire after reaching a certain age or having served the firm for a specific period of time. Pension plans are vitally important to employees because Social Security was not designed to provide complete retirement income. The Employee Retirement Income Security Act of 1974 (ERISA) was passed to strengthen existing and future retirement programs. The Act also ensures that retired employees receive deserved pensions.

Supplemental Unemployment Benefits (SUB) first appeared in automobile labor agreements in 1955.[19] They are designed to provide additional income for employees receiving unemployment insurance benefits and have spread to many other industries. These plans are usually financed by the company. They tend to benefit newer employees because layoffs are normally determined by seniority. For this reason, employees with considerable seniority are often not enthusiastic about SUB.

Employee Services. Organizations offer a variety of benefits that are classified under employee services. These include company subsidized food services, financial assistance for employee operated credit unions, legal and income tax aid, club memberships, athletic and recreational programs, discounts on company products, moving expenses, parking spaces, and tuition rebates for educational expenses. These benefits have the potential for greatly enhancing the employment relationship.

Premium Pay. **Premium pay** is compensation given employees for working long periods of time or working under dangerous or undesirable conditions. As mentioned in Chapter 11, payment for overtime is required for nonexempt employees who work beyond forty hours in a given week. However, some firms pay overtime for hours worked beyond eight in a given day and pay double time—or even more—for work on Sundays and holidays.

Additional pay provided to employees who work under extremely dangerous conditions is called **hazard pay.** A window washer on skyscrapers in New York City might well be given extra compensation because of dangerous working conditions. Military pilots receive extra money in the form of "flight pay" because of the hazards associated with flying.

Shift differentials are paid to reward employees for the inconvenience of working undesirable hours. This type of pay may be provided on the basis of additional cents-per-hour. For example, employees who work the second shift ("swing" shift) from 4:30 P.M. until midnight might receive $.25 per hour above the base rate. The third shift ("graveyard" shift) often warrants an even greater differential. For example, an extra $.32 per hour may be given. Shift differentials are sometimes based on a percentage of the employee's base rate.

A Comprehensive Voluntary Benefits Program

International Business Machines Corporation offers a comprehensive voluntary benefits program. IBM's program is non-contributory; that is, the company bears the full cost of the benefits. The growth of the IBM benefits program is shown in Figure 12–3. You can see that since its inception the program has been improved and enlarged to meet changing employee needs. Two of the

[19]Belcher, pp. 358–359.

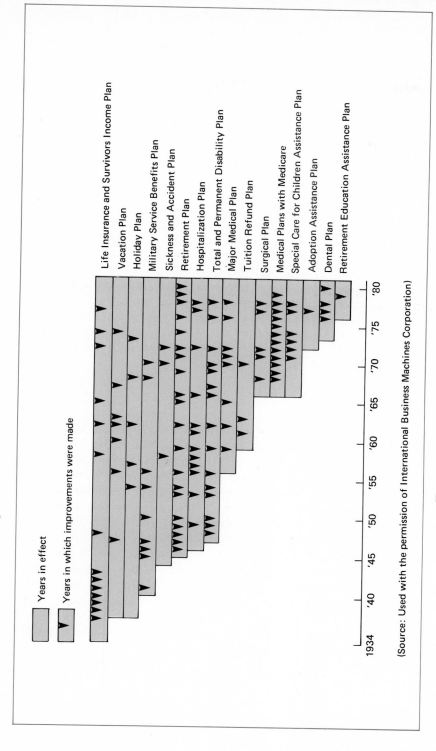

Figure 12–3. IBM benefits: A history of growth.

(Source: Used with the permission of International Business Machines Corporation)

403

most recent additions are particularly interesting: the Adoption Assistance Plan and the Retirement Education Assistance Plan.

Under the Adoption Assistance Plan, IBM will reimburse employees for 80 percent of eligible charges up to a maximum of $1000 for each adoption. Eligible charges include:

- Adoption agency fees
- Placement fees
- Lawyers' fees and other required legal fees
- Maternity fees (child's natural mother)
- Temporary foster care charges (immediately preceding placement of the child with the adopting family)

The IBM Retirement Education Assistance Plan is designed to help employees and their spouses prepare for activities and personal fulfillment in their retirement years. Under this plan, IBM will reimburse tuition costs for retirement courses—up to $2500 per individual—upon evidence of course completion. This plan covers any course offered by nationally accredited colleges and post-secondary schools, as well as adult continuing education courses conducted by state certified schools or educational organizations. Other courses which appear to meet the intent of the plan are also considered for reimbursement. The employee's eligibility in this plan continues until two years after the actual date of retirement.

New Benefits

Several new benefits have recently appeared on the scene in addition to those included in IBM's innovative plan. One of these is subsidized day care centers. In such centers, the firm provides facilities for young children of employees for a modest fee. Parents typically transport the children to and from the Center. While there, the children engage in supervised play and receive meals. This benefit is a good recruitment aid and helps to reduce absenteeism. To indicate the need for such programs, consider that in 1980 almost half of American women with children under six years of age were in the work force.[20]

In an attempt to conserve energy and relieve traffic congestion some firms have begun transporting workers to and from work. In these programs, participating employees pay a portion of the costs to ride in company vans or buses. Some employees find this benefit very convenient and a means to avoid "fighting traffic."

Massachusetts Mutual Life Insurance Company has initiated two new benefits in the health care area.[21] One of these programs serves to detect and treat high blood pressure. Once each year, all employees are offered a physical examination. When a case of high blood pressure is detected, the employee is

---

[20]"The New Corporate Goodies," *Dun's Review* 118 (July 1981): 49 (hereafter cited as *Dun's Review*).

[21]*Dun's Review.*

referred to his or her own physician for further diagnosis and treatment. The company pays all medical costs for this treatment. It is believed that this program literally saves lives and, for this reason, it is a very popular benefit.

Another Mass Mutual program encourages employees to stop smoking. The company will reimburse any person on the payroll who consults a hypnotist for treatment. Although the program is very new, about half of the employees in the program have stopped smoking cigarettes.

405

Chapter 12
Additional
Compensation
Considerations

Communicating the Benefits Package

Employee benefits can help a firm recruit and retain a quality work force. Management depends upon an upward flow of information from employees in order to know when benefit changes are needed.[22] In addition, because employee awareness of benefits is often severely limited, the essential aspects of programs must be communicated downward.[23] Regardless of a benefits program's technical soundness, a firm simply cannot get its money's worth if its employees don't know what they are receiving. It has been suggested that workers may even become resentful if they are not frequently reminded of benefit plan values. They may resent their obligation to pay for a portion of some benefits while overlooking the larger picture of what they receive and the substantially greater costs borne by their employer.[24]

The Employee Retirement Income Security Act provides still another reason for communicating a firm's benefits program. This act requires organizations with a pension or profit sharing plan to provide employees with specific data at specified times. It further mandates that the information be presented in an understandable manner. ERISA's basic requirements are that each person in the firm be given this information:

- the kind of plan
- eligibility requirements
- amount of benefits due at specific times and payment options
- surviving dependents' benefits
- how the pension trust is invested
- who is responsible for managing the plan[25]

Naturally organizations can go beyond what is legally required. In fact many firms, such as Southwestern Life Insurance Company, have done so even before ERISA's enactment. As you see in Figure 12–4, Southwestern's report shows each employee the total amount of money contributed for his or her

[22]Richard C. Huseman, John D. Hatfield and Russell W. Driver, "Getting Your Benefits Program Understood and Appreciated," *Personnel Journal* (October 1978): 564.
[23]Jeffery C. Claypool and Joseph P. Cangemi, "The Annual Employee Earnings and Benefits Letter," *Personnel Journal* (July 1980): 563.
[24]Robert M. McCaffery, "Employee Benefits: Beyond the Fringe?" *Personnel Administrator* 26 (May 1981): 30.
[25]Robert Krogman, "Is Your Company Getting the Most Out of Its Benefits Program?" *Personnel Administrator* 25 (May 1980): 45–46.

Your Future Financial Security

YOUR RETIREMENT BENEFITS (YOU ARE 100% VESTED)

$ 669.42 Credited monthly income at age 65 from the Southwestern Retirement Plan

On AUGUST 1, 2007, your normal retirement date, you will receive....

Projected Monthly Income

$ 1,799.60	Southwestern Retirement Plan
$ 632.00	Social Security
$ 2,400.60	Total Projected Monthly Income
$ 259,070	is approximately the amount you would have to accumulate by age 65 to provide the projected monthly income from the Southwestern Retirement Plan.

Continued Insurance During Retirement

$ 5,000 Group term life insurance continued at no cost to you

PLUS Group medical protection on yourself and your eligible dependents continued at no cost to you.

YOUR SURVIVORS' BENEFITS

$ 64,200	Group Life Insurance
$ 64,200	Accidental Death and Dismemberment Insurance
$ 255	Social Security death benefit (IF ELIGIBLE)
$ 110.24	Monthly benefit for surviving spouse from Southwestern's Retirement Plan based on 03/02/44 as your spouse's date of birth

PROGRESS SHARING PLAN

903.03336 SHARES OF TENNECO COMMON STOCK
37.55068 SHARES OF TENNECO PREFERENCE STOCK

Additional Benefits

PLUS Monthly Income from Social Security

PLUS Continuation of Group Medical Coverage for eligible dependents

---

To Fellow Southwesterners:

This report reflects the increasing importance and value of your Southwestern benefits to your present and future financial security. All of your benefits are covered in this one combined statement so you can evaluate the full range of benefits as a total benefits program.

Your individual position in each of the benefit plans grows in dollar value annually as you accrue additional years of service and as you receive salary increases. To help keep you up to date on changes in your benefits, a new report will be provided to you each year.

It will only take a few minutes of your time to review this updated benefits information. We hope this statement will keep you abreast of your employee benefits and help you in your personal financial planning.

William H. Seay

Jon B. White

STATEMENT PREPARED AS OF:

DECEMBER 31, 1981

JOHN DOE
APT. 38
1234 STATE ST.
ANYTOWN TX 77777

406

Your Employee Benefits in Perspective

Southwestern employees and their families enjoy the benefit and protection of:

- Hospital and Medical Expense Benefits
- Group Life Insurance
- Accidental Death and Dismemberment Insurance
- Long-Term Disability Insurance
- Retirement Annuity Plan

- Christmas Bonus
- Progress Sharing Plan
- Vacations
- Holidays
- Social Security

Total estimated annual cost of these benefits $ 13,435.12

Less your estimated annual cost
Contributions for Group Benefits $ 373.76
Your one-half of the Social Security Tax $ 1,975.05

Total estimated annual contribution by Southwestern to provide your benefits $ 10,586.51

The value of other benefits is not included in the figures above. Some of these benefits are:

- Sickness and Accident Benefits
- Professional Educational Allowances
- Cafeteria and Medical Facility

- Transportation Assistance
- Employee Activities and Services
- Service Recognition Awards

PROGRESS SHARING PLAN

...to provide you a tax-sheltered means of accumulating capital while you participate in the progress and growth of the company through ownership of Tenneco Inc. stock.

Southwestern's Contributions to Your Account

Total contributions as of   DECEMBER 31, 1980 $ 11,826.40

Contributions on   DECEMBER 10, 1981 $ 2,407.50

Total contributions as of   DECEMBER 31, 1981 $ 14,233.90

Shares of Stock Credited to Your Account

Total shares of Common stock credited as of   DECEMBER 31, 1980   437.43072

Purchases and dividends credited during the year   125.25316

Total shares of Common stock credited as of   DECEMBER 31, 1981   563.03368

Total shares of $11 Preference stock credited to your account   97.55063

You have a 100% vested interest in your Progress Sharing Plan Account.

Your Financial Security Today

HOSPITAL AND MEDICAL BENEFITS

100%   of the first $500   of covered hospital charges

30%   of remaining covered expenses, however,

100%   of those exceeding $5000   in each calendar year will be payable

$ 250,000   lifetime maximum benefit for each covered person

$ 50   calendar year deductible for each covered person for the above benefits ($150 maximum deductible per family)

$ 300   special accident expense benefit

SICKNESS AND DISABILITY INCOME BENEFITS

If you become sick or disabled and are unable to work, you will be eligible for:

6 MONTHS   AT FULL SALARY FOLLOWED BY
6 MONTHS   AT ONE-HALF SALARY

$ 1783.33   After   12   months of total disability you may receive a month in long term disability income. This amount includes any benefits payable under our Long Term Disability Plan, Retirement Annuity Plan, Social Security and other statutory programs.

Figure 12–4. An example of the value communicating of benefits. (Source: Southwestern Life Insurance Company.)

benefits. A summary of this type helps employees to become aware of their total benefits package and assists the firm in achieving its compensation objectives.

NONFINANCIAL COMPENSATION

In recent years, most Americans have been able to satisfy their basic physiological and safety needs, so their interests have tended to shift somewhat away from money as the primary form of compensation. As employees receive sufficient cash to provide for basic necessities (and then stereoes and color televisions), they tend to desire rewards which will satisfy higher order needs. Specifically, social, ego, and self-actualization needs are becoming more important. These needs may be satisfied through the job that employees are given to perform and the environment of that job. The basic nonfinancial elements of the total compensation package are illustrated in Figure 12–5.

The Job

One of Personnel's major goals is to satisfactorily match job requirements and employee abilities and aspirations. Although the task of job design is typically performed by other organizational units, Personnel does have a responsibility in recruiting, selecting, and placing individuals in those jobs. A good case could even be made for directly involving Personnel in the task of job design. Having a "good" job has the potential for becoming an important part of nonfinancial compensation. Because of this, a number of organizations have become actively engaged in job enrichment, as was discussed in Chapter 8.

The job is a central issue in many theories of motivation and we believe that it is also a vital part of a total compensation program. Employees may receive important rewards by performing meaningful jobs. While this type of reward is intrinsic in nature, a firm's management determines job content. Therefore, the job's compensation possibilities are to a degree under the organization's control. The selection and placement processes are extremely important in this context. A job which is challenging to one person may be quite boring to another.

The Job Environment

The job's environment is also an important part of nonfinancial compensation. The significance of a warm, supportive organizational climate was discussed in Chapter 2. While organizations have often paid mere lip service to making jobs more rewarding, a concerted effort has frequently been made to improve many of the factors which surround the job.

Sound Policies. Personnel policies expressing management's sincerity in its employee relationships can serve as positive rewards. For example, policies and

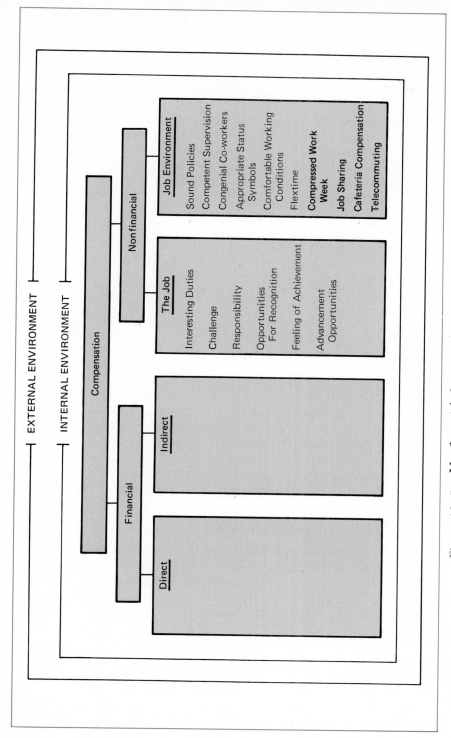

Figure 12–5. Nonfinancial elements of a total compensation program.

practices related to providing stable employment reflect a company's true respect for its human resources. IBM is such a firm. In almost forty years, despite severe recessions and dramatic technological changes, no IBM employee has been laid off because of economic necessity. If a firm's policies show respect—rather than disrespect, fear, doubt, or lack of confidence—the result can be rewarding to both employees and the organization.

Competent Supervision. Nothing in organizational life can be so demoralizing to employees as to have an incompetent supervisor. It is demeaning for an individual to work for an incompetent manager. Successful organizations have continuing programs emphasizing supervisory and executive development. These programs exist to maximize the probability of providing sound leadership and management.

Congenial Co-Workers. Although a few individuals in this world may be quite self-sufficient and prefer to be left alone, this is not the prevalent attitude. Most of us possess in varying degrees a desire to be accepted by our work group. This acceptance helps us to satisfy basic social needs. Management, in its staffing efforts, should be concerned with developing compatible work groups.

Appropriate Status Symbols. Employees may engage in activities such as comparing the size of their office with that of a peer, or measuring the distance from his or her office to the chief executive's. When this extreme behavior occurs, it is time to examine the firm's policy regarding status symbols. While these symbols may be appropriate in achieving certain purposes—such as providing incentive for employees to progress in the firm—care must be taken to assure that they are not overemphasized. However, status symbols (such as office size, the size and quality of the desk, other office furnishings, floor covering, office location, title, parking space, or make of company car) can serve as compensation because they often appeal to employees' ego needs. While some organizations tend to minimize the use of status symbols, other firms use them liberally. A critical point to consider in providing such rewards is that they be provided equitably.

Comfortable Working Conditions. Good working conditions are for the most part taken for granted in many organizations today. However, a brief return to non-air-conditioned offices would quickly remind us of their importance. The view that working conditions can be a form of compensation is reinforced by pay plans which increase the financial reward for jobs with relatively poor working conditions.

Flextime. The practice of permitting employees to choose, with certain limitations, their own working hours is referred to as **flextime**. It was introduced in Germany in the late 1960s and has since spread throughout Europe and the United States. In a flextime system, employees work the same number of hours as on a standard schedule. However, they are permitted to acquire these hours

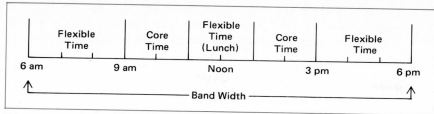

Figure 12–6.   **An illustration of flextime.**

within what is called a band width, which is the maximum length of the work day (see Figure 12–6). Core time is that part of the day when all employees must be present. Flexible time is the time period within which employees may vary their schedules.[26] A typical schedule permits employees to begin work between 6:00 a.m. and 9:00 a.m. and complete their workday between 3:00 p.m. and 6:00 p.m.

Perhaps flextime's most important feature is its ability to schedule time to minimize conflicts between personal needs and job requirements. This advantage would be quite attractive to individuals with problems such as Liz Brown. She now has the opportunity to arrive later after dropping her children off at school. Personal needs can be accommodated without resorting to sick leave. Flextime also permits employees to work at hours when they feel they can function best. It caters to those who are early risers or those who prefer to work later in the day. The public also seems to reap benefits from flextime. Transportation services, recreational facilities, medical clinics, and other services can be better utilized as a result of reduced competition for service at conventional peak times.

Flextime is not suitable for all types of organizations. Its use may be severely limited in assembly line operations and companies utilizing multiple shifts. However, flextime seems feasible in a number of situations. Many organizations that use it feel that both employees and employers benefit. Clearly, the use of plans such as flextime are compatible with desires of employees (especially younger ones) to participate in decisions that affect their work.

The Compressed Work Week. Any arrangement of work hours which permits employees to fulfill their work obligation in fewer than the typical five-day work week is referred to as the **compressed work week.** The most common approach to the compressed work week has been four ten-hour days. Working under this arrangement, some employees have reported an increase in job satisfaction. In addition, the compressed work week offers them the potential for better use of leisure time for family life, personal business, and recreation.[27] Employers, in some instances, have cited such advantages as increased productivity and reduced turnover and absenteeism. On the other hand, problems have been encountered in such areas as work scheduling and employee fatigue.

[26]Tim Burt, "Making the Most of Time with Flexible Working Hours," *Personnel Executive* 1 (March 1982): 37.
[27]Simcha Ronen and Sophia B. Primps, "The Compressed Work Week as Organizational Change: Behavioral and Attitudinal Outcomes," *Academy of Management Review* 6 (January 1981): 61.

In some cases, these problems have resulted in lower quality products and reduced customer service. Some firms have reverted to the conventional five-day
week. It seems clear that the overall acceptance of the compressed work week
is not as clearcut as with flextime.

Job Sharing. **Job sharing** is a relatively new approach to work that is attractive
to people who wish to work fewer than forty hours per week. According to
this plan, two part-time people split the duties of one job in some manner and
are paid according to their contributions. From the employer's viewpoint,
compensation is paid for only one job, but creativity is obtained from two employees. The total financial compensation cost may be greater due to additional benefits provided, however, this expense may be offset due to increased
productivity. Job sharing may be especially attractive to individuals who have
substantial family responsibilities and to older workers who wish to fade gradually into retirement.

Cafeteria Compensation (Flexible Compensation). **Cafeteria compensation** plans
permit employees to decide, from among many alternatives, how their financial compensation will be allocated. They are given considerable latitude in
determining how much of the financial compensation will be given in the form
of such items as salary, life insurance, and pension contributions. Cafeteria
plans permit flexibility in allowing each employee to determine the compensation package which would best satisfy his or her particular needs.

The rationale behind cafeteria plans is that employees have individual
needs and preferences. A sixty-year-old male employee would probably not desire maternity benefits in an insurance plan. At the same time, a twenty-five
year old female who regularly jogs six miles each day might not highly value
parking facilities located near the firm's entrance. Some of the possible compensation vehicles utilized in a cafeteria approach are shown in Table 12–3.

Obviously, organizations cannot permit employees to "spend" all their financial compensation as they choose. The mandatory benefits required by law
must be provided. Also, one compensation expert believes that, "It is usually
best to mandatorily give each employee a basic 'core' of coverage—especially
in the medical insurance area."[28] Some guidelines would likely be helpful for
most employees in the long run. However, the freedom to select highly desired
benefits would seem to maximize the value of an individual's compensation.
Involvement in the determination of tailored compensation plans should also
effectively communicate the cost of benefits to employees.

TRW Systems Group has had a flexible compensation program since
1974. The program was inspired by a general belief that employees should
have more flexibility and self-determination shaping their compensation package. The plan developed at TRW is based on these principles:

- The core plan will be available to each employee at the Company's
  expense.

[28]David J. Thomsen, "Introducing Cafeteria Compensation in Your Company," *Personnel Journal*
56 (March 1977): 130.

Table 12-3. Compensation vehicles utilized in a cafeteria compensation approach

Accidental death, dismemberment insurance

Birthdays (vacation)

Bonus eligibility

Business and professional memberships

Cash profit sharing

Club memberships

Commissions

Company medical assistance

Company-provided automobile

Company-provided housing

Company-provided or subsidized travel

Day care centers

Deferred bonus

Deferred compensation plan

Deferred profit sharing

Dental and eye care insurance

Discount on company products

Education costs

Educational activities (time off)

Employment contract

Executive dining room

Free checking account

Free or subsidized lunches

Group automobile insurance

Group homeowners insurance

Group life insurance

Health maintenance organization fees

Holidays (extra)

Home health care

Hospital-surgical-medical insurance

Incentive growth fund

Interest-free loans

Layoff pay (S.U.B.)

Legal, estate-planning, and other professional assistance

Loans of company equipment

Long term disability benefit

Matching educational donations

Nurseries

Nursing home care

Opportunity for travel

Outside medical services

Paid attendance at business, professional, and other outside meetings

Parking facilities

Pension

Personal accident insurance

Personal counseling

Personal credit cards

Personal expense accounts

Physical examinations

Political activities (time off)

Price discount plan

Private office

Professional activities

Psychiatric services

Recreation facilities

Resort facilities

Retirement gratuity

Sabbatical leaves

Salary

Salary continuation

Savings plan

Scholarships for dependents

Severance pay

Shorter or flexible work week

Sickness and accident insurance

Social Security

Social service sabbaticals

Split-dollar life insurance

State disability plans

Stock appreciation rights

Stock bonus plan

Stock options plan (qualified, non-qualified, tandem)

Stock purchase plan

Survivors benefits

Tax assistance

Title

Training programs

Vacations

Wages

Weekly indemnity insurance

Source: "Introducing Cafeteria Compensation in Your Company," by David J. Thomsen. Reprinted with permission *Personnel Journal* Copyright March 1977.

- Plans that are better, but more costly than the current plan, will be developed and made available at the employee's expense.
- Plans that provide less coverage, and are less costly than the current plan, will be developed and an employee given credit toward other benefits or given the difference in cash.
- The core plan will be reviewed annually and will be maintained at a competitive level.
- Additional choices will be added as experience is gained and as new elements of the total compensation package can be defined on a choice basis.

Choices in the current plan include benefits in these areas: health care, hospital, surgical, maternity, supplemental accident, and major medical. As mentioned earlier, TRW will continue to consider expanding areas of choice for its employees. Future possibilities are vacation, retirement supplement, group auto and home owners' insurance, and long-term disability.

Telecommuting. **Telecommuting** is an approach to work which permits employees to work at home. In keeping with this concept and to combat the steady increase in employment costs, Control Data Corporation has developed a program it calls HOMEWORK. This innovative approach is a home-based training and employment program for persons seeking a non-traditional work environment.

Using a cathode ray tube (CRT) located in the employee's home and connected by telephone to CDC's computer network, both training and job duties are carried out without reduction in efficiency and quality. Business application programmer is an example of a HOMEWORK job. Initially, HOMEWORK was available only to a few severely disabled employees. It has now been expanded and the program has great potential for employees who have no disability. Additional HOMEWORK programs are being developed by CDC that have wide-range implications for other employers in both private and public sectors. These advantages have been cited for both employee and employer:

- Permits effective use of human resources.
- Eliminates the need for office space.
- Provides flexible working hours.
- Eliminates costs associated with travel to work.
- Enhances intellectual functioning.
- Helps establish strong bonds and company loyalty.
- Permits a higher level of self-care for severely disabled employees.
- Reduces costs of health care (CDC's costs decreased from between 50 to 75 percent for most of its participants).
- Increases employees' self-concept and confidence levels.
- Provides a means for re-entering a traditional work environment.

It has been predicted that programs such as the CDC's HOMEWORK will involve as many as 15 million workers by the mid-1990s.[29] While ties between employees and their firms may be weakened, successful programs will require a higher degree of trust between employees and their supervisors. One thing seems certain, the size of the work force should be expanded due primarily to the increased utilization of handicapped workers and workers with small children.

COST/BENEFITS ANALYSIS—COMPENSATION

As the preceding sections have explained, compensation involves much more than the pay a person receives. Direct financial compensation, indirect financial compensation, the job, and the job environment are all involved in a total compensation program. Because of the broad nature of compensation in today's organizations, there are often substantial costs associated with maintaining a sound, ongoing compensation program. Workers must be available and trained to maintain the program. Surveys may need to be conducted to ensure that compensation is in line with what other firms are providing for similar positions. The wide variety of positions required in today's business often makes this a difficult task. Many work hours are required if a firm is to have an effective compensation program.

The benefits of a sound compensation system certainly outweigh the costs. A reputation for providing an equitable reward system will enhance recruitment. This will likely enable the firm to selecting a better-qualified work force. In addition, because the firm obtains higher caliber employees, training efforts can be advanced accordingly. Furthermore, firms that desire to remain non-union have a better chance of achieving this goal if compensation is perceived as being fair. Finally, turnover may decrease because there will be less incentive for workers to leave the firm for better paying jobs.

SUMMARY

Compensation based upon productivity is referred to as incentive compensation. The most commonly used individual incentive plans are the straight piecework plan and the standard hour plan. When work is organized in such a manner that productivity results from group efforts, group incentive plans are often utilized. Company-wide incentive plans are used to integrate the interests of employment and management. These plans may take the form of profit sharing, employee stock ownership plans, or the Scanlon Plan.

[29]"If Home Is Where the Heart Is," *Business Week* 2737 (May 3, 1982): 66.

Management performance has a significant impact upon a firm's success and survival. A large portion of management compensation is linked to company performance. Some types of managerial compensation include salaries, stock option plans, and deferred compensation.

People performing in professional jobs are compensated primarily for the knowledge they bring to the organization. Some organizations have created a dual track of compensation for this group of employees. This approach permits a person who has no desire to become a manager to be rewarded appropriately.

Because compensation programs for sales employees constitute a unique set of circumstances, some firms assign this responsibility to the sales function rather than to Personnel. Compensation for the sales employees takes the form of straight salary, commissions, bonuses, or various combinations of the three.

Benefits include any financial compensation cost (other than pay) borne by the employer. Generally speaking, benefits are provided to employees as a result of their membership in the organization, and, while some benefits are required by law, others are provided voluntarily by the organization.

In recent years, Americans have been able to satisfy many of their basic physiological and safety needs. Therefore, social, ego, and self-actualization needs are becoming more important. These needs may be satisfied through the jobs that employees are given to perform and through the environment of those jobs.

Questions for Review

1. What is meant by the term *incentive compensation*? When would an individual incentive plan, as opposed to a group incentive plan, be used?

2. Define the following terms: (a) *straight piecework,* (b) *standard hour plan,* (c) *profit sharing,* (d) *employee stock ownership plan,* (e) *Scanlon Plan.*

3. What are major determinants of compensation for managers? List and define the primary types of managerial compensation.

4. Define *benefits.* What are the general purposes of benefits?

5. Describe the various benefits that are required by law.

6. In terms of voluntary benefits, what are the basic categories of benefits? Give an example of each type of benefit.

7. Distinguish between overtime pay, hazard pay, and shift differential pay.

8. Why are nonfinancial compensation considerations becoming such a major part of an individual's pay? What are some of the basic types of nonfinancial compensation?

Terms for Review

Incentive compensation
Straight piecework plan
Standard hour plan

Profit sharing
Employee stock ownership plan
Scanlon Plan

A number of years ago Electrojet Corporation, of Atlanta, Georgia, implemented a comprehensive profit sharing plan. The company manufactures a group of patented jet engine components which it sells to companies such as Boeing, Lockheed, and some European companies. The decision to share profits was made after several years of rapidly increasing sales and profits. It was largely based upon an attitude survey of the employees at Electrojet which showed that they strongly preferred profit sharing over other fringe benefits.

The compensation plan at Electrojet provides for wages before profit distributions that are about 20 percent below wage levels for similar jobs in Atlanta. Half of company profits are paid out each quarter as a fixed percentage of employee wages. Over the past few years distributed profits have averaged more than 50 percent of base wages. Because of the high total wages, Electrojet has been a popular employer and has been able to take its pick from a long waiting list of applicants.

Other benefits have been kept to a minimum at Electrojet. There is no retirement plan and a very limited medical plan designed to cover catastrophic illnesses only.

The recession of 1981–1982 hit the airline industry especially hard. Profits were down for all major arilines and one, Braniff, even declared bankruptcy. As a result, aircraft sales were greatly depressed. Few new orders were received by the manufacturers and many existing orders were cancelled or scaled back. As a supplier to the aircraft manufacturing industry, Electrojet Corporation's sales plummeted.

The profit sharing bonus for 1981 was only about 25 percent of base wages. Profits declined further for the first two quarters of 1982. By mid-year, it was clear that the company would be in the red for the entire second half. A board meeting was called in late August to discuss the profit sharing program. One director made it known that he felt the company should drop the profit sharing plan. The personnel director, Vince Harwood, was asked to sit in at the board meeting and to make a presentation suggesting what the company should do about compensation.

Questions

1. Evaluate the compensation plan at Electrojet.

2. If you were Mr. Harwood, what would you recommend for the short term? For the long term?

Wayne McGraw greeted Robert Peters, his next interviewee, warmly. Robert had an excellent academic record and appeared to be just the kind of person Wayne's company, Beco Electric, was seeking. Wayne is the university recruiter for Beco and had already interviewed six graduating seniors at Centenary College.

Based on the application form, Robert appeared to be the most promising candidate to be interviewed that day. He was 22 years old. He had a 3.6 grade point average and a 4.0 in his major field, Industrial Management. He was the vice president of the Student Government Association and was activities chairman for Kappa Alpha Psi, a social fraternity. The reference letters in Robert's file revealed that he was very active socially although a rather intense and serious student. One of the letters, from Robert's employer the previous summer, expressed satisfaction with Robert's work habits.

Wayne knew that discussion of pay could be an important part of the recruiting interview. But he could not decide what aspect of Beco's compensation program would appeal most to Robert. The company has an excellent profit sharing plan, although 80 percent of profit distributions are deferred and included in each employee's retirement account.

Health benefits are also good. The company's medical and dental plan pays almost 100 percent of costs. A company cafeteria provides meals at about 70 percent of outside prices, although few managers take advantage of this. Employees get one week vacation after the first year and two weeks after ten years with the company. In addition there are twelve paid holidays each year. Finally, the company encourages advanced educational efforts, paying for tuition and books in full and often allowing time off to attend classes during the day.

Questions

1. What aspect of Beco's compensation and benefits program are likely to appeal to Robert? Explain.

2. Is the total compensation package likely to be attractive to Robert? Why or why not?

PARMA CYCLE COMPANY: THE PAY PLAN

At Parma Cycle Company in Parma, Ohio, wage rates for hourly workers are established by a three-year labor-management agreement. The agreement provides for cost of living adjustments (COLA) based upon changes in the Federal Consumer Price Index. Wage rates vary according to job class and by seniority within each class. For example, a machine operator with two to four years seniority earns $8.75 per hour. With four to eight years seniority the rate increases to $10.60 an hour. A company-paid health plan provides medical and dental care for employees. The company contributes 6½ percent of wages to a retirement plan administered by the machinists union.

Salaried workers at Parma Cycle are paid straight salaries based upon a forty-hour work week. For first- and second-level managers and clerical workers, work beyond forty hours in any week is compensated on a pro rata basis. For managers above the second level there is no additional compensation for work after forty hours per week. Cost of living adjustments are applied semi-annually to all wages and salaries.

Only in the sales department at Parma is any kind of incentive compensation program in effect. The sales representatives are paid a commission averaging about 2 percent of sales in addition to straight salary. The sales manager assigns the sales representatives to particular territories; they are generally given a choice of territories according to seniority. Once a sales representative has become accustomed to a given territory, however, requests to change are usually turned down. As older sales representatives have left the company some of the younger ones have moved into the better sales areas. This has caused some of the more senior sales representatives to request territory changes to increase their sales potential. This has been done in a few cases but no consistent policy has been developed.

Parma Cycle Company was building a new plant in Clarksdale, Mississippi in 1981–1982. The new plant was to employ about 600 people, two-thirds the number working at the main plant in Parma, Ohio. About two months before the new plant was scheduled to open, Jesse Heard, the personnel director, was asked to meet with the president to discuss the compensation policies that would be followed in Clarksdale. Jesse knew that Jim Burgess, the president, tended to take a personal hand in matters relating to pay, so he prepared thoroughly for their meeting.

Mr. Burgess had a reputation for getting right to the heart of the matter. "I'm worried about the pay differentials that we are going to have between this plant and the one in Clarksdale," he began. "As I see it, some of the people down there won't be paid half as much as similar workers here." "That's true," said Jesse. "Really that is the main reason for the move to Clarksdale. Without the union and with the low wage rates in that area, we will be able to pay just what the market requires. Most of the helpers and trainees will be available, we think, at minimum wage." "How will the pay classifications down there compare to those up here?" asked Mr. Burgess. "Well," said Jesse, "up here we have 'workmen' and 'machine operators' and the pay within classes is by seniority. Down there we plan to have helpers/trainees, grades 1 and 2, and machine operators, grades 1, 2, and 3. Seniority won't count. We will promote workers based upon the recommendations of their supervisors and their performance evaluation scores."

"I liked the incentive plan when you told me about it before, Jesse," said Mr. Burgess. "Let's go over it again. As I understand it, we are going to take 30 percent of the cost savings below standard and pay it out as semi-annual bonuses." "Yes," said Jesse. "An individual's bonus will be a certain percentage of the gross wages paid during that period. But we will multiply that by the person's performance evaluation score." "Will the standard costs be the same as the ones we have here at the Parma plant?" asked Mr. Burgess. "Yes, at first they will," answered Jesse. "But after a time, it will be the average of costs at the two plants."

Mr. Burgess continued, "The last time we talked I think you said that we would save money in Clarksdale on the benefits package too." "Yes," replied Jesse, "For one thing, the tradition in that area is for the company to pay a health insurance premium for a worker and for the worker to pay the portion applicable to any dependants. Also, we won't have a dental plan down there, just medical. Finally, I don't think that we will even have a retirement program for those workers, at least not for a few years." "I think I know the answer," said Mr. Burgess, "but, what about the ones who transfer down from Parma?" "They'll have the same benefits they have here," replied Jesse. "We will keep them covered under the same insurance plan and guarantee them that their wages will keep pace with those of similar workers here at Parma."

Questions

1. What are the pros and cons of paying workers on the basis of seniority?
2. How do cost of living adjustments (COLA) work?
3. Is anything legally wrong with Parma's plan for paying salaried workers? Explain.

4. Are the pay and benefits differentials between the plants likely to create problems? Why?

___ Experiencing Personnel Management ___

JOB EVALUATION BY "POINTS"

The following two job descriptions (Figure IV-1 and Figure IV-2) are for two new jobs created at Parma Cycle Company's Parma, Ohio plant. As a personnel specialist you have been asked to evaluate the jobs according to the company's point system. Study the job descriptions carefully and complete a job evaluation matrix (see Figure IV-3) provided for each job. Assume that each job factor has five degrees and compute the point total for each job.

In actual practice you would normally have more information available than just the job descriptions. In this case, though, you must work with what you have. This information will be used to determine the initial job classification, and therefore the pay rate for the job.

Position Title				Position Number
Personnel Office Receptionist				
				Approval
Division or Staff Department	Location	Reports to		Effective Date
Personnel		Assistant		
		Person. Dir.		
Department or Activity	Section	Point	Grade	Revises

Job Summary

Greets visitors to the Personnel Office; directs them to the appropriate desks. Operates Personnel Office switchboard, with four incoming lines and twelve extensions. Performs miscellaneous clerical work as directed by Assistant Personnel Director.

Nature of Work

1. Welcome visitors to Personnel Office and direct them to appropriate desk or person.

2. Maintain familiarity with all office procedures to facilitate above.

3. Answer incoming calls politely, switching them to the appropriate desk.

4. Perform miscellaneous clerical and administrative work as directed by Assistant Personnel Director.

5. Type outgoing letters and other correspondence as directed by Assistant Personnel Director.

Qualifications

High school education
Pleasing voice
Typing 60 words per minute
Ability to operate PCD 16 switchboard

Figure IV–1. **Parma Cycle Company's job description: Personnel office receptionist.**

Questions

1. What additional factors would you include in evaluating clerical jobs?

2. What job factors would you include for machine operators at Parma Cycle?

3. How would you change the relative weights assigned to the job factors? Why?

Position Title		Position Number
Personnel Clerk, II		
		Approval

Division or Staff Department Personnel	Location	Reports To Records Supervisor	Effective Date

Department or Activity	Section	Point	Grade	Revises

Job Summary

Maintain performance evaluation records and miscellaneous clerical work as required.

Nature of Work

1. Every six months, and as required in special cases, distribute about 800 performance evaluation forms along with form memoranda describing how to complete the performance evaluations to the respective supervisors.

2. File completed forms in respective personnel records.

3. Insure timely completion of performance evaluation forms by follow-up memoranda, phone calls, and personal visits to supervisors.

4. Do miscellaneous typing of forms, reports, and records as directed by supervisor.

5. Fill in for personnel office receptionist when required.

Qualifications

High school education, or equivalency certificate
Typing, 50 words per minute
Familiarity with IBM Selectric III typewriter
Score of 50 or better on company filing and records retrieval test

Figure IV–2. **Parma Cycle Company's job description: Personnel clerk, II.**

Job Factors	Weight	Requirement for each job factor on this job				
		1	2	3	4	5
Reasoning & Creativity	40%					
Physical skill & Coordination	25%					
Strength & Stamina	15%					
Complexity of Duties	20%					

Total Points: ☐

Figure IV–3. A job evaluation matrix.

Part V

Safety and Health

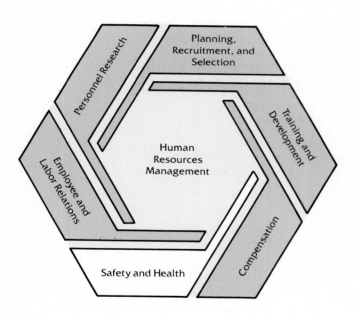

Chapter Objectives

1. Describe the nature of the safety and health field and its role in organizations.
2. Describe the Occupational Safety and Health Act and the impact it has had upon American business.
3. Relate the nature of stress and the importance of stress management in business today.
4. Describe burnout and explain why it is a major concern to management.
5. Identify the various sources of stress.
6. Explain the approaches organization and individuals take in coping with stress.
7. State the rationale for and the role of physical fitness, alcohol, drug, and employee assistance programs.

Chapter 13 _____

Safety and Health

Dionne Martin, safety engineer for Sather Manufacturing, was walking through the plant when she spotted a situation that immediately got her attention. Someone had spilled a large quantity of oil on the floor and had not cleaned it up. Just at that moment, Ron Moore, one of the firm's employees, stepped on the oil. His feet went out from under him and the packages he was carrying scattered everywhere. Ron landed squarely on his back and for a moment did not move. Although he got up slowly, it appeared that Ron was not injured. Dionne was relieved, but became quite disturbed when she realized the many possible consequences of the accident.

Bob Byroms, production foreman for King Electronics, is concerned about the health of one of his best workers, Cecil Weeks. For the past several months Cecil has been relatively ineffective on the job. He has been doing sloppy work and many of his coworkers have complained about his poor disposition. Recently, Bob observed Cecil at his locker during a work break take a bottle from a brown bag and drink from it. The odor on Cecil's breath suggested to Bob the cause of Cecil's changed work habits. Bob believes that Cecil may be an alcoholic. He wonders what should be done.

Dionne and Bob are each involved with but a few of the many critical areas related to employee safety and health. Dionne realizes that safety is a major concern in an organization and that she must constantly work to ensure that accidents such as the one she just witnessed are reduced or eliminated. Bob has just discovered that the poor performance of one of his employees may be caused by a stress-related drinking problem.

In our discussion, **safety** involves protecting employees from injuries due to work related accidents. **Health** refers to the employees' freedom from physical or emotional illness. Many people may wonder why Personnel should be concerned with such a wide range of responsibilities. The answer becomes quite clear, however, when you realize that safety and health are a major aspect of human resources management. Problems in these areas can seriously affect productivity. As will be discussed, employee accidents and illnesses can have a dramatic effect upon a firm's effectiveness. Although line managers are primarily responsible for safety and health within the firm, Personnel provides needed expertise through its staff assistance. In addition, Personnel is frequently responsible for coordinating and monitoring specific safety and health programs.

The chapter begins with a discussion of the impact of the Occupational Safety and Health Act upon today's businesses. Safety and health programs will then be discussed. This will be followed by a presentation on stress management. Topics included in this section are burnout, physical fitness, alcoholism, drug addiction, and employee assistance programs. Also covered are stress sources and means used to combat stress. The overall purpose of this chapter is to provide you with an understanding of the importance of safety and health in organizations today.

THE OCCUPATIONAL SAFETY AND HEALTH ACT

Industrial safety has, for years, been a major problem that has seemingly resisted solution. The problem's magnitude can best be understood by considering these statistics. During World War II, 292,000 American servicemen were killed in action, and over 17,000 servicemen lost major limbs. During the same period, approximately 90,000 people were killed in factory accidents; there were approximately 9,000 permanent injuries, 500,000 partial permanent injuries, and 10,000,000 temporary injuries.[1]

Prior to 1971, industrial safety was regulated primarily by the worker's compensation laws of the various states. This changed in 1970 when Congress passed the **Occupational Safety and Health Act** (OSHA). It quickly became one of the most controversial laws affecting personnel management and has

[1]*Handbook of Labor Statistics*, 1947 ed., U.S. Department of Labor, Bureau of Labor Statistics, p. 164.

dramatically altered management's role in the area of safety and health. The purpose of the act was to assure "so far as possible that every man and woman in the nation has a safe and healthful working condition." Basic requirements of the act may be seen in Table 13–1.

CRITICISM OF THE ACT

Critics immediately attacked the law in spite of an apparent need for safety and health legislation. One detractor stated, "The act wasn't needed, it is being implemented too rapidly with a hard hand, and the cost of compliance is so high that it threatens our corporate competitive position."[2] This comment continues to represent many employers' views. However, the act does have considerable support from unions, public interest groups, and some employers.

The purpose and intent of the act have rarely been questioned. However, OSHA has received a great deal of criticism. Most of it has dealt with the trivia of some requirements and the general manner in which the law has been administered. In fact, the horror stories that have been associated with OSHA are numerous. Some are factual, others fictitious.

In one instance, Joe Pinga, who operated a bakery in West Warwick, Rhode Island, was charged by OSHA with twelve violations including having a safety rail that was four inches too low. Pinga took the case to court where he spent $1500 in legal fees to avoid a $90 fine. During the trial, the young OSHA inspector admitted that her only qualification as an inspector was a forty-hour series of OSHA seminars.[3] Another story involved the owner of a small business in a Western state. He was told by an OSHA inspector to install separate men's and women's restrooms for his employees. "He had but one employee: his wife."[4]

One citation was given for "allowing ice to come in direct contact with water." Another story that some still like to tell involves a standard which was strictly enforced. It called for U-shaped toilet seats in workside washroom facilities.[5] The above two standards have been eliminated as well as a number of other trivial provisions.[6]

CURRENT TRENDS

There is little doubt that OHSA's intent is justified and that many businesses have neglected safety and health. Changes have been made in recent years to

[2]Fred K. Foulkes, "Learning to Live with OSHA," *Harvard Business Review* (November-December 1973): 57.
[3]"Rage Over Rising Regulations," *Time* 111 (January 2, 1978): 48.
[4]"Why Nobody Wants to Listen to OSHA," *Business Week* (June 14, 1976): 64.
[5]Ibid.
[6]"OSHA Drops 928 Nitpicking Standards," *Nation's Business* 66 (December 1978): 17 (hereafter cited as "OSHA Drops 928").

Table 13–1. Job safety and health protection

The Occupational Safety and Health Act of 1970 provides job safety and health protection for workers through the promotion of safe and healthful working conditions throughout the nation. Requirements of the act include the following:

Employers:

Each employer must furnish to each of his employees employment and a place of employment free from recognized hazards that are causing or are likely to cause death or serious harm to his employees; and shall comply with occupational safety and health standards issued under the act.

Employees:

Each employee shall comply with all occupational safety and health standards, rules, regulations, and orders issued under the act that apply to his own actions and conduct on the job. The Occupational Safety and Health Administration (OSHA) of the Department of Labor has the primary responsibility for administering the act. OSHA issues occupational safety and health standards, and its Compliance Safety and Health Officers conduct jobsite inspections to ensure compliance with the act.

Inspection:

The act requires that a representative of the employer and a representative authorized by the employees be given an opportunity to accompany the OSHA inspector for the purpose of aiding the inspection. Where there is no authorized employee representative, the OSHA Compliance Officer must consult with a reasonable number of employees concerning safety and health conditions in the workplace.

Complaint:

Employees or their representatives have the right to file a complaint with the nearest OSHA office requesting an inspection if they believe unsafe or unhealthful conditions exist in their workplace. OSHA will withold, on request, names of employees complaining. The act provides that employees may not be discharged or discriminated against in any way for filing safety and health complaints or otherwise exercising their rights under the act. An employee who believes he has been discriminated against may file a complaint with the nearest OSHA office within thirty days of the alleged discrimination.

Citation:

If upon inspection OSHA believes an employer has violated the act, a citation alleging such violations will be issued to the employer. Each citation will specify a time period within which the alleged violation must be corrected. The OSHA citation must be prominently displayed at or near the place of alleged violation for three days, or until it is corrected, whichever is later, to warn employees of dangers that may exist there.

Proposed Penalty:

The act provides for mandatory penalties against employers of up to $1,000 for each serious violation and for optional penalties of up to $1,000 for each nonserious violation. Penalties of up to $1,000 per day may be proposed for failure to correct violations within the proposed time period. Also, any employer who willfully or repeatedly violates the act may be assessed penalties of up to $10,000 for each such violation. Criminal penalties are also provided for in the act. Any willful violation resulting in death of an employee, upon conviction, is punishable by a fine of not more than $10,000 or by imprisonment for not more than six months, or by both. Conviction of an employer after a first conviction doubles these maximum penalties.

Voluntary Activity:

While providing penalties for violations, the act also encourages efforts by labor and management, before an OSHA inspection, to reduce injuries and illnesses arising out of employment. The Department of Labor encourages employers and employees to reduce workplace hazards voluntarily and to develop and improve safety and health programs in all workplaces and industries. Such cooperative action would initially focus on the identification and elimination of hazards that could cause death, injury, or illness to employees and supervisors. There are many public and private organizations that can provide information and assistance in this effort, if requested.

Source: *OSHA Bulletin*

make the agency more responsive and to overcome its negative image. In the late 1970s, Jimmy Carter directed OSHA to "get back to basics." OSHA has now begun to change its role from a policeperson to a guidance counselor for industry.[7] In many instances, the agency is working with businesses to solve health and safety related problems.

OSHA has also begun to concentrate its resources on high risk industries, such as construction, where the payoff will be greater (see Figure 13–1). As Eula Bingham, head of the Occupational Safety and Health Review Commission stated, "Right now, we are targeting 95 percent of our resources on higher-hazard industries."[8] Industries with lower accident and illness rates will not receive as much attention as before. While safety has received the primary emphasis in the past, OSHA has been moving into areas that affect health. Inspectors trained in these areas are now being employed.

Many of OSHA's rules have been simplified. For instance, instead of requiring that a fire extinguisher be so many inches from the floor, the rule now states that it has to be readily accessible. In addition, almost 1000 inappropriate rules have been eliminated.[9] This trend is expected to continue. OSHA leaders are expected to retain their heavy emphasis on both health and safety, but they appear to be taking a more positive and realistic viewpoint.

SAFETY

Many workers are killed or injured each year as a result of job related accidents. The cost of these accidents has been substantial—over $32 billion in 1981, as you can see in Table 13–2. These expenses are often passed along to the consumer in the form of higher prices. Everyone, directly or indirectly, is affected as accident rates go up. Although many foward looking businesses had elaborate safety programs for years before OSHA was passed, a large number of firms established formal safety programs following its enactment.

The Focus of Safety Programs

Safety programs may be designed to accomplish their purposes through two primary avenues. In the first, the firm works toward creating an environment and attitudes that promote safety. Accidents can be reduced by employees consciously or unconsciously thinking about safety. This attitude must permeate each and every phase of the firm's operations. A strong company policy which emphasizes safety and health is critical. For example, a major chemical firm's policy states: "It is the policy of the company that every employee be assigned to a safe and healthful place to work. We strongly desire accident prevention in all phases of our operations. Toward this end, the full cooperation of all

[7]"OSHA: Hardest to Live With," *Business Week* (April 4, 1977): 74.
[8]"Out Go 'Silly' Rules on Worker Safety," *U.S. News & World Report* 84 (January 16, 1978): 65.
[9]OSHA Drops 928.

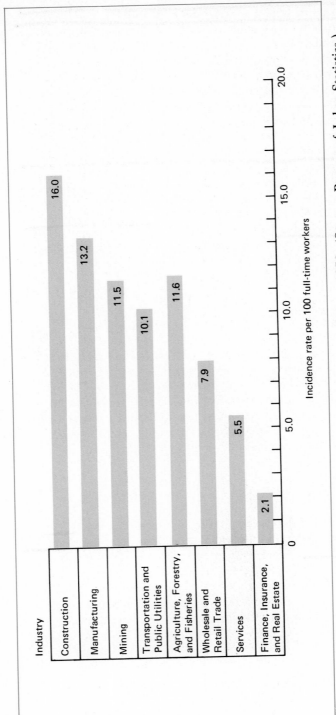

Figure 13–1. Injury and illness incidence rates by industry, 1978. (Source: Bureau of Labor Statistics.)

Table 13–2. Work accident costs

Compensation paid to all workers in the nation who are under workers' compensation laws was approximately $13,359,000,000 in 1980 (latest figures reported by the Social Security Administration). Of this amount, $3,860,000,000 was for medical and hospital costs and $9,499,000,000 for wage compensation. These figures are not comparable to Council cost estimates due to differences in coverage of workers and types of cases.

Total Cost In 1981 _____ $32,500,000,000

Visible Costs _____ $15,100,000,000

Includes wage losses of $5,100,000,000 insurance administrative costs amounting to about $6,600,000,000 and medical costs of $3,400,000,000.

Other Costs _____ $15,100,000,000

Includes the money value of time lost by workers other than those with disabling injuries, who are directly or indirectly involved in accidents. Also included would be the time required to investigate accidents, write up accident reports, etc.

Fire Losses _____ $2,300,000,000

Cost Per Worker _____ $330

This figure indicates the value of goods or services each worker must produce to offset the cost of work injuries. It is *not* the average cost of a work injury.

Source: National Safety Council, *Accident Facts* (Washington, DC: U.S. Government Printing Office, 1982) p. 24.

employees will be required." As the policy infers, no one person is assigned the task of making the workplace safe. It is the job of everyone from top management to the lowest level employee. All members of the firm are encouraged to devise innovative solutions to safety problems.[10]

Following a second approach to safety program design, organizations develop and maintain a safe working environment. The previously described approach to accident prevention was more psychological in nature. Here, the physical work environment is altered to prevent accidents. Even if Joe Smith, a machine operator, has been partying all night and can barely open his eyes, the safety devices on his machine will keep him safe. It is in this area that OSHA has had its greatest influence. For instance, OSHA's guidelines for power transmission apparatus may be seen in Table 13–3. Through procedures such as these and the ones developed by individual organizations, an attempt is made to create an environment where accidents cannot occur.

Developing Safety Programs

Organizational safety programs reflect planning that was designed to prevent workplace accidents. Plans may be relatively simple, as would be the case for

[10]Jeff Ball, "Do-It-Yourself Safety: A Federal Agency Stresses Worker Participation," *Job Safety and Health* 5 (November 1977): 16.

Executive Profile

Richard C. Crosbee
Vice President-Personnel
Bristol-Myers Products

As vice president, personnel, Dick Crosbee is responsible for a wide variety of personnel programs. "Just about anything you could conceive of as being people related is my responsibility," he says.

Dick joined a Bristol-Myers subsidiary in 1948. After a year with the company, he entered Personnel and on his first assignment served as editor of the company paper. He quickly obtained experience in a number of Personnel areas including employment, union relations, job evaluation, and recreation. He later became personnel assistant, personnel manager, and, later, personnel director for two plants. Eight years ago he was named to his current position.

When Dick began work in Personnel he quickly realized the need for additional education. However, his formal training came the hard way. After working eight years at night on a degree program, he graduated from Seton Hall University with a major in management. Still feeling the need for additional knowledge, Dick completed a master's degree program in behavioral sciences in May, 1982. He believes that a broad education is necessary because personnel people deal with many disciplines. "Having said 'broad,' " Dick says, "I don't mean formal necessarily. I don't think it's necessary to have a master's degree in personnel work. It may not even be important to have a bachelor's degree. But I think, somehow, the education and the broad view of humanity and the understanding of different disciplines have to be acquired. Whether you acquire them on your own or in an academic program makes no difference, just as long as they are acquired—that is the important thing."

When asked to describe a major business problem he has confronted and to tell how he solved it, Mr. Crosbee said, "A real problem for me early in my career was stage fright when facing an audience. I found that my desire to avoid making a mistake in public was at the root of the fear. This fear implied that there was a standard or ideal way to make a speech, and any deviation would be unacceptable and,

a small retail store. A large automobile assembly plant would likely develop a highly sophisticated program. Regardless of the organization's size, top management's support is essential if safety programs are to be effective. The top executives in a firm must be shown how accident prevention can affect the organization's profits. They must recognize the tremendous economic losses which can result from accidents. Some of the logical reasons for top management support of a safety program may be seen in Table 13–4. As you can see, the lost productivity of a single injured worker is not the only factor to consider. Every phase of human resources management is involved. For instance, the firm may have difficulty in recruiting if it becomes known for its hazardous hence, a mistake. I finally conquered this fear when I realized that we are all unique individuals and thus must have a unique contribution to make to the world. If we are all unique, then there is no standard or ideal to be measured against, and my way of delivering a presentation was just as acceptable as the next person's. I could only be me, and if that wasn't good enough, there was no one else I could be. Since I realized that, I have never feared facing any group of any size and 'doing my thing'."

Dick admits that his career in Personnel began more as an accident than as a result of career planning. He believes that for him it has been "natural." "I have always been interested in dealing with people rather than things and concepts. And, I have found that I have been able to express that interest in the personnel profession." Dick states that while pay is somewhat lower in personnel than other professions, it has increased dramatically in recent years. He adds, "I think I have had rewards in Personnel that could not have been paid for—rewards from helping people grow, helping people in difficulty, helping people think better of themselves. These kinds of rewards are meaningful to me and to many people in Personnel. They don't have a monetary value."

Mr. Crosbee feels that personnel people do not have a great deal of formal authority in most organizations. But, he says, "I think that is mitigated somewhat by the person in charge whose skills, abilities, leadership, and influence may be strong enough to overcome the lack of authority inherent in any well-run personnel position. The personnel executive can't have the authority; it must be with line management if the task is to be completed."

There are three important qualifications for success, according to Mr. Crosbee:

- Knowledge of the job, the organization, and the industry.
- Flexibility
- Personal skills

The field of Personnel is currently in transition, Dick says. While Personnel has traditionally focused on maintenance and hygiene factors, he remarks, "I think we are beginning to see the emergence or more and more emphasis on training and development of our people resources and a de-emphasis on the maintenance functions. I think most people have more potential than we have been able to unleash and I think that the proper kind of leadership and the proper kind of development programs—and they are really the same—can help us tap the potential that most people possess. I think that if we can do that, we can unleash productivity, and maybe more important, we can increase the satisfaction and quality of people's working lives."

working conditions. Employee relations may be seriously hampered if workers do not believe that management cares enough about them to make their workplace safe. Even compensation may be affected if the firm must pay more to attract and retain qualified applicants.

Companies with effective safety programs have likely involved virtually everyone in the firm. Line managers are normally responsible for controlling conditions that encourage accidents. As part of this responsibility, they must set the proper safety example for other employees. If the supervisor fails to use safety devices when demonstrating use of the equipment, the subordinates may feel that the device is not really necessary. The line manager's attitude can

Table 13–3. OSHA guidelines for power transmission apparatus

Power Transmission Apparatus

All belts, pulleys, shafts, flywheels, couplings, and other moving power transmission parts must be securely guarded.

A flywheel located so that any part is seven feet or less above a floor or platform must be guarded with an enclosure of sheet, perforated or expanded metal, or woven wire. It must also be fenced in with guard rails.

All exposed parts of horizontal shafting must be enclosed in a metal or wire cage on a frame of angle iron or iron pipe securely fastened to the floor or frame of the machine. If wire mesh forms the enclosure, it should be the type in which the wires are strongly fastened at every cross point, either by welding, soldering, or galvanizing.

Projecting shaft ends must be guarded by nonrotating caps or safety sleeves.

Pulleys or sheaves seven feet or less from the floor must be guarded with metal or wire mesh enclosures.

Horizontal, vertical, and inclined belt, rope, and chain drives must be enclosed in metal or wire mesh cages. The same applies to chains, sprockets, couplings, and gears.

Guards for horizontal overhead belts must run the entire length of the belt and follow the line of the pulley to the ceiling. This also applies to overhead rope and chain drives.

Source: *Essentials of Machine Guarding*, U.S. Department of Labor, Office of Safety and Health Administration, OSHA no. 2227 (July 1975), pp. 10, 12.

also affect a worker's attitude toward safety training. Comments such as "Let's go to that worthless safety meeting," are not likely to elicit enthusiastic support from subordinates. The supervisor can show support for the safety program by conscientiously enforcing safety rules and cooperating with the staff people who monitor the program.

In many companies, a staff position exists to coordinate the overall safety program. Some major corporations have risk management departments, which anticipate losses associated with safety and so prepare adequate legal defenses.[11] Titles such as safety director, safety engineers, and safety committees are common. One of the safety director's primary tasks is to provide safety training for company employees. This involves educating line managers as to the merits of safety in addition to teaching them how to recognize and eliminate unsafe situations. Although the safety director operates essentially in an advisory capacity, a well informed and assertive director may have considerable power in the organization.

Accident Investigation

At times, even in the most safety conscious firms, accidents happen. Each accident should be carefully evaluated to ensure that it does not recur. Both the safety engineer and the line manager participate in investigating accidents. One of the responsibilities of any supervisor is to prevent accidents. To accomplish this, the supervisor learns—through active participation in the safety

- *Personal loss.* Most individuals strongly prefer not to be injured. The physical pain and mental anguish associated with injuries is unpleasant. Of much greater concern is the possibility of permanent disablement or even death.
- *Financial loss to injured employees.* Most employees are covered by company insurance plans or personal accident insurance. However, an injury may result in financial losses not covered by the insurance.
- *Lost productivity.* When an employee is injured, there will be a loss of productivity to the firm. In addition to obvious losses, there are often hidden costs. For example, a replacement may need additional training to replace the injured employee. Even when a person can be moved into the injured employee's position, efficiency may suffer.
- *Higher insurance premiums.* Workers' compensation insurance premiums are based on the employer's history of insurance claims. The potential for savings related to employee safety provides a degree of incentive to establish formal programs.
- *Possibility of fines and imprisonment.* Since the enactment of OSHA, a willful and repeated violation of its provisions may result in serious penalties.
- *Social responsibility.* Many executives feel responsible for the safety and health of their employees. A number of firms had excellent safety programs years before OSHA. Thus, safety is in the best interest of the firm.

program—why accidents occur, how they occur, where they occur, and who is involved. Surprisingly, it has been estimated that 10 percent of the workforce is responsible for 70 percent of the accidents.[12] Supervisors will gain much knowledge in the area of accident prevention by assisting in the preparation of accident reports.[13]

A safety program also needs to be reflected in the training and orientation of new employees. The early months of employment are often critical. As you can see in Table 13–5, work injuries decrease substantially with length of service.[14] Notice that this pattern is consistent for both men and women. Knowledge of the relationship between length of service and accidents should be particularly important to supervisors as new employees are trained.

Evaluation of Safety Programs

Perhaps the best indicator of the success of any safety program is checking to find out if accidents have been reduced. But, there is more involved than this question suggests. The number of accidents may have been reduced, but the ones that occurred may have been more severe. Therefore, measures of per-

[11]John L. Pickens, "Effective Loss-Control Management," *Management Review* 66 (December 1977): 41–42.
[12]Milton Layden, "Whipping Your Worst Enemy on the Job: Hostility," *Nation's Business* 66 (October 1978): 87 (hereafter cited as Layden).
[13]W. H. Weiss, "Accident Investigation: A Major Responsibility of Supervisors," *Supervision* 40 (July 1978): 1.
[14]Norman Root and Michael Hoefer, "The First Work-Injury Data Available from New BLS Study," *Monthly Labor Review* 102 (January 1979): 77.

Table 13–5. Pattern of accident rates by length of service

Length of Service	Men	Women
1 month	10.64	8.78
2 to 3 months	5.90	5.47
4 to 6 months	3.41	3.31
7 to 12 months	1.72	1.84
2 to 3 years	.84	.95
4 to 5 years	.43	.46
6 to 10 years	.21	.23
11 to 25 years	.06	.05
26 to 35 years	.02	.01

The above tabulation shows the average percent per month of work injuries, by length of service, for 218,446 men and 52,136 women in ten states, 1976–77.
Source: Norman Root and Michael Hoefer, "The First Work-Injury Data Available from New BLS Study," *Monthly Labor Review* 102 (January 1979), 77. Reprinted by permission.

formance must first be established. Statistics such as frequency rates and severity rates are often used. The **frequency rate** is expressed by the following formula which computes the number of lost-time accidents per million people-hours worked:

Nat'l Safety Counsel Formula

$$\text{Frequency Rate} = \frac{\text{Number of lost-time accidents} \times 1,000,000}{\text{Number of people-hours worked during period}}$$

Although the above formula is often used, OSHA has developed a frequency rate which is conceptually different.[15] This formula is provided below:

$$\text{Incidence Rate} = \frac{\text{Number of injuries and/or illnesses}}{\text{Total hours worked by all employees during reference year}} \times 200,000 \text{ (Base for 100 full-time equivalent workers who are working 40 hours per week, 50 weeks per year.)}$$

The major differences between this formula and the first are that both injuries and illnesses are considered and that the base for reporting injury frequency rates is 100 full-time employees (as opposed to the million employee hours in the previous formula).

The **severity rate** supplies an indication of the number of days lost because of accidents per million people-hours worked. It is expressed by the formula:

$$\text{Severity Rate} = \frac{\text{Number of people-days lost} \times 1,000,000}{\text{Number of people-hours worked during period}}$$

[15]Lyle R. Schauer and Thomas S. Ryder, "New Approach to Occupational Safety and Health Statistics," *Monthly Labor Review* 95 (March 1972): 18–19.

Not only must criteria be available to evaluate the program, a reporting system must exist which ensures that accidents will be recorded. At times, when a new safety program is initiated, safety figures show a significant decrease in the number of accidents. However, some supervisors may have ceased reporting some accidents so the statistics will look better for their unit. The ability to evaluate a safety program depends upon the reporting and recording of accurate data.

To be of value, the conclusions derived from safety evaluation must be used to improve the program. Gathering data and permitting them to collect dust on the safety director's desk does not solve problems or prevent accidents. The results of the evaluation should be transmitted upward to top management and downward to line managers in order for improvements to be made.

HEALTH

The reason a firm is concerned with its employees' health becomes crystal clear when economic values are placed on the employees' worth. For instance, how valuable is a highly qualified executive who has developed and implemented a new marketing program? Or, what value could be placed on a skilled engineer trained by the firm for five years? Consider, for example, the bright, forty-year-old executive who succumbs to alcoholism because of job stress. Or consider the machinist, who because of job boredom, turns to drugs to brighten up his day. The designer who pushes herself so hard that she dies of cardiac arrest while walking out of the building is but another illustration. Loss of an individual's productivity because of health problems definitely affects an organization's profitability.

Union support has also hastened the establishment of more effective health programs. Today, unions are placing industrial health issues high on their list of demands in collective bargaining.[16] Rather than concentrating primarily upon pay, unions now seek items such as a safer work environment and recreational facilities.

A formal company health program involves more than merely dispensing aspirins and bandages. As with the safety program, it should reflect a company philosophy which emphasizes the value of its human assets and which has top management support. Many of the procedures used in establishing a sound safety program are also applicable to a company health program. A firm with the reputation of having a healthy work environment is in a stronger position to perform many of the other personnel functions. For instance, recruiting may be easier because applicants want to work for the company. Employee and management relations may be improved when workers view the company as having their best interests in mind.

A health program starts when applicants are initially screened and continues throughout the worker's employment. It typically is concerned with a wide variety of potential health hazards. Certain fumes, dust, gases, liquids, and solids have proven harmful to workers' health. At times a health program em-

[16]"The New Activism on Job Health," *Business Week* (September 18, 1978): 146.

phasizes reducing the noise level in a plant. Loss of hearing has resulted from excessive and prolonged exposure to noise. In recent years, one of the major health concerns has related to workers' exposure to hazardous substances such as asbestos. In addition to monitoring traditional health problems, many organizations have expanded the scope of their health concerns to include stress management.

STRESS MANAGEMENT

Increasingly, firms are beginning to become concerned about their employees' emotional, as well as physical, health. In fact, it is becoming common to view them together. Programs dealing with stress and its related problems are becoming popular.

Stress is your body's reaction to any demand made upon it. Our perceptions of events, whether positive or negative, activates stress. It is therefore a highly individual matter. Certain events may be quite stressful to one person but not to another. Mild stress actually improves productivity.[17] For example, it can be helpful as it assists you in developing creative ideas. All of us live under a certain amount of stress. In fact, the only people without stress are dead.[18] But, if stress is severe enough and persists for long periods of time, it can be harmful. Stress can be as disruptive to an individual as any accident. It can result in poor attendance, excessive use of alcohol, poor performance on the job, or even overall poor health. In fact, there is increasing evidence that undue stress is related to diseases which are leading causes of death—coronary heart disease, stroke, hypertension, cancer, emphysema, diabetes, and cirrhosis—and also to suicide.[19] The results of stress have been estimated to cost American industry between $20 and $50 billion each year.[20] The cost to a single firm may account for as much as 6 percent of total sales.[21]

Aside from humanitarian reasons, the economic factor is sufficient to gain management interest in helping employees manage stress. A legal factor may provide still another reason. One manager recently filed suit against his company charging that his physical ailments, including a heart attack, were caused by the pressure of his job. The man won his case and the company was ordered to make a cash settlement.[22]

The National Institute for Occupational Safety and Health (NIOSH) is one organization that has studied stress as it relates to work. This organization's research indicates that some jobs are more stressful than others. The twelve most stressful jobs are listed in Table 13–6. The central theme that ties

[17]Michael Pesci, "Stress Management: Separating Myth from Reality," *Personal Administrator* 27 (January 1982): 59 (hereafter cited as Pesci).
[18]Hans Selye, "Secret of Coping with Stress," *U.S. News & World Report* 82 (March 21, 1977): 1.
[19]John M. Ivancevich and Michael T. Matteson, "Optimizing Human Resources: A Case for Preventive Health and Stress Management," *Organizational Dynamics* 9, (Autumn 1980): 5–8 (hereafter cited as Ivancevich and Matteson).
[20]Oliver L. Niehouse and Karen B. Massoni, "Stress—An Inevitable Part of Change," *Advanced Management Journal* 44 (Spring 1979): 17 (hereafter cited as Niehouse and Massoni).
[21]Randy Weigel and Sheldon Pinsky, "Managing Stress: A Model for the Human Resource Staff," *Personnel Administrator* 27 (February 1982): 56.
[22]Ivancevich and Matteson, p. 6.

Table 13–6.   Stressful jobs

Where the Pressure Builds Up

12 Jobs With Most Stress . . .

1. Laborer
2. Secretary
3. Inspector
4. Clinical lab technician
5. Office manager
6. Foreman
7. Manager/administrator
8. Waitress/waiter
9. Machine operator
10. Farm owner
11. Miner
12. Painter

Other High-Stress Jobs . . . (In alphabetical order)

• Bank teller	• Machinist	• Railroad switchman
• Clergyman	• Meatcutter	• Registered nurse
• Computer programmer	• Mechanic	• Sales manager
• Dental assistant	• Musician	• Sales representative
• Electrician	• Nurses' aide	• Social worker
• Fireman	• Plumber	• Structural-metal worker
• Guard/watchman	• Policeman	• Teachers' aide
• Hairdresser	• Practical nurse	• Telephone operator
• Health aide	• Public relations person	• Warehouse worker
• Health technician		

Source: From a ranking of 130 occupations by the federal government's National Institute for Occupational Safety and Health.

these jobs together is lack of employee control over their work.[23] People in these jobs may feel trapped and that they are more like machines than people. Some of the less stressful jobs involve workers who have more control over their jobs, such as college professors and master craftspersons. Because certain jobs are beginning to be identified as more stressful than others, there are some serious implications for management. Managers must be responsible for recognizing deviant behavior and referring affected subordinates to health professionals for diagnosis and treatment. (Refer to Figure 13-2 for behavior that may indicate problems.) In addition, managers should monitor their employees' progress and provide them with the motivation to succeed.[24] While stress may result in many complex problems, the good news is that it can generally be handled successfully.[25] The bad news is that it often is not. The following section describes a condition which may result from organizational and individual failure to deal with stress effectively.

[23]Niehouse and Massoni, p. 41.
[24]Pesci, p. 67.
[25]Ibid., p. 58.

- Reduced clarity of judgment and effectiveness
- Rigid behavior
- Medical problems
- Strained relationships with others due to irritability

- Increasing excessive absence
- Addictive behaviors emerging (e.g., drugs, alcohol, smoking)
- Expressions of inadequacy and low self-esteem
- Apathy or anger on the job

Source: Michael Pesci, "Stress Management: Separating Myth from Reality." Reprinted from the January 1982 issue of *Personnel Administrator*, 30 Park Drive, Berea, OH 44017.

Figure 13–2. **Signs of stress: What managers should look for.**

Burnout

Sheryl Weaver supervised fifty people in the administrative department of a large insurance firm. She was a competent and conscientious manager with a reputation for doing things right and on time. Until recently, Sheryl had been strongly considered as a candidate for the position of vice president—administration. However, things have changed. Sheryl behaves differently. She can't seem to concentrate on her work and appears to be a victim of "battle fatigue." "Oh, Sheryl," a coworker advised, "You'll make it. You've always been so strong." But Sheryl surprised her associate when she responded, "I don't want to be told I'll make it on my own. I already know I can't."

Sheryl doesn't know exactly what has caused her run-down condition. She only senses that she is at her wits end and desperately needs assistance. Sheryl apparently is the victim of an increasingly publicized phenomenon known as burnout. **Burnout** has been described as a state of fatigue or frustration which stems from devotion to a cause, way of life, or relationship that did not provide the expected reward.[26] It is often found in a mid-life or mid-career crisis but it can happen at different times to different people.[27] Individuals in the helping professions such as teachers and counselors seem to be susceptible to burnout, whereas others may be vulnerable because of their upbringing, expectations, or their personalities.[28] The burnout syndrome is frequently associated with people whose jobs require close relationships with others under stressful and tension-filled conditions.[29] While any employee may experience this condition, perhaps 10 percent of managers and executives are so affected.[30] The dangerous part of burnout is that it is contagious. A highly cynical and pessimistic burnout can quickly transform an entire group into burnouts. Therefore,

[26]Herbert J. Freudenberger, *Burnout: The High Cost of High Achievement* (Garden City, NY: Anchor Press, Doubleday and Company, Inc., 1980): 13.
[27]John G. Nelson, "Burn Out—Business's Most Costly Expense," *Personnel Administrator* 25 (August 1980): 82.
[28]Dick Friedman, "Job Burnout," *Working Woman* 5 (July 1980): 34.
[29]Christina Meslach and Susan E. Jackson, "Burned-Out Cops and Their Families," *Psychology Today* 12 (May 1979): 59.
[30]Beverly Norman, "Career Burnout," *Black Enterprise* 12 (July 1981): 45.

it is important that the problem be dealt with quickly. Once it has begun, it is difficult to stop.[31]

Some of the symptoms of burnout include: (1) chronic fatigue; (2) anger at those making demands; (3) self-criticism for putting up with demands; (4) cynicism, negativism, and irritability; (5) a sense of being besieged; and (6) hair-trigger display of emotions.[32] Other symptoms might include recurring health problems, such as ulcers, back pain, or frequent headaches. The burnout victim is often unable to maintain an even keel emotionally. Unwarranted hostility may occur in totally inappropriate situations.

Burnout is a problem which must be dealt with preferably before it occurs. In order to do so, managers must be aware of potential sources of stress. These sources exist within and outside the organization and are discussed next.

Sources of Stress[33]

Regardless of its origin, stress possesses the same devastating potential. Some factors are controllable to varying degrees whereas others are not. In the following sections we shall discuss some of the primary sources of stress.

The Family. Although a frequent source of happiness and security, the family can also serve as a significant stressor. Consider that nearly one-half of all marriages end in divorce. Divorce itself is also quite stressful. When it leads to single parenthood, the difficulties may be compounded.

Children are another of life's sources of happiness. Yet, consider the effect of an infant awakening parents in the middle of the night with a severe asthmatic attack! Anxiety levels rise significantly as the parents watch their child struggle for each breath. Academic problems or extreme social adjustment difficulties for a teenager can also create much anguish for all concerned.

A relatively recent phenomenon is the dual career family. When both husband and wife have job and family responsibilities, traditional roles are altered. What happens when one partner is totally content with a job and the other is offered a sought-after promotion requiring transfer to a distant city? At best, these circumstances are beset with difficulties.

Financial Problems. Problems with finances may place an unbearable strain on the family. Such difficulties are frequently related to divorce. For some, these problems are persistent and never quite resolved. Nagging, unpaid bills and bill collectors can create much tension.

Living Conditions. Stress levels may also be increased for people who live in densely populated areas. These people face longer lines, endure more hectic

[31]Cary Cherniss, "Job Burnout: Growing Worry for Workers, Bosses," *U.S. News & World Report* 88 (February 1980): 72.
[32]Harry Levinson, "When Executives Burn Out," *Harvard Business Review* 59 (May–June 1981): 76.
[33]Certain portions of this section were adapted from unpublished working papers of Robert M. Smith, Professor of Student Personnel and Guidance, East Texas State University, 1982.

traffic jams, and contend with higher levels of air and noise pollution. Metropolitan life has many advantages. However, the benefits provided are not without costs often in the form of stress.

Life Changes. Life change events have been weighted according to the stress they produce. As you see in Table 13–7, the most stressful life event is the death of a spouse. One study determined that persons who registered more than 300 life change units (LCUs) in a year had an illness during the following year in 70 percent of the cases. It was also noted that these illnesses tended to be multiple.[34]

Organizational Climate. Generally speaking, an organizational climate characterized by a lack of freedom is strongly pervaded with stress. The CEO's leadership style often sets the tone. If he or she is autocratic and permits little input from subordinates, a stressful environment may result. If the CEO is too weak, internal conflicts may result as subordinates compete for power. Certain firms have even been cited as having stressful climates because the CEO insists on superior performance.

Even in the healthiest organizational climate, stressful relationships among employees can occur. Employee personality types vary and these, combined with differing values and belief systems, may so impair communication that stressful situations occur. Also, competition encouraged by the organization's reward system for promotion, pay increases, and status may add to the problem.[35]

Role Ambiguity and Role Conflict. **Role ambiguity** exists when employees lack clear information about the content of their jobs. This condition can be quite threatening to an employee and produce feelings of insecurity.

Role conflict occurs when an individual is placed in the position of seeking opposing goals. For example, a manager may be expected to increase production while having to decrease the size of his or her labor force.[36] When this happens, both objectives may not be reached and stress stems from the resulting conflict. A nationwide survey emphasized the pervasiveness of these problems by revealing that 35 percent of the respondents had complaints about role ambiguity and 48 percent felt they were victims of role conflict.[37]

Job Overload. When employees are given more work than they can possibly handle, they become victims of **job overload**. A critical aspect of this problem is that often the best performers in the firm are the ones affected. These individuals have proven that they can perform more so they are given more to do. At its extreme, work overload becomes burnout.

[34]E. K. Eric Gunderson and Richard H. Rahe, editors, *Life Stress and Illness* (Springfield, IL: Charles C Thomas Publishing, 1974): 62.
[35]"Can You Cope With Stress?" *Duns Review* 106 (November 1975): 90.
[36]Arthur P. Brief, "How to Manage Managerial Stress," *Personnel* 57 (September/October 1980): 27.
[37]Peter J. Frost, Vance F. Mitchell and Walter R. Nord, *Organizational Reality: Reports from the Firing Line, 2nd Edition* (Glenview, IL: Scott, Foresman and Company, 1982): 446.

Working Conditions. The physical characteristics of the workplace, including the machines and tools, can create stress. Overcrowding, excessive noise, poor lighting, and poorly maintained work stations and equipment can all adversely affect employees morale and increase stress levels.

Table 13–7. Life change events

		LCU Values
Family:	Death of spouse	100
	Divorce	73
	Marital separation	65
	Death of close family member	63
	Marriage	50
	Marital reconciliation	45
	Major change in health of family	44
	Pregnancy	40
	Addition of new family member	39
	Major change in arguments with wife	35
	Son or daughter leaving home	29
	In-law troubles	29
	Wife starting or ending work	26
	Major change in family get-togethers	15
Personal:	Detention in jail	63
	Major personal injury or illness	53
	Sexual difficulties	39
	Death of a close friend	37
	Outstanding personal achievement	28
	Start or end of formal schooling	26
	Major change in living conditions	25
	Major revision of personal habits	24
	Changing to a new school	20
	Change in residence	20
	Major change in recreation	19
	Major change in church activities	19
	Major change in social activities	18
	Major change in sleeping habits	16
	Major change in eating habits	15
	Vacation	13
	Christmas	12
	Minor violations of the law	11
Work:	Being fired from work	47
	Retirement from work	45
	Major business adjustment	39
	Changing to different line of work	36
	Major change in work responsibilities	29
	Trouble with boss	23
	Major change in working conditions	20
Financial:	Major change in financial state	38
	Mortgage or loan over $10,000	31
	Mortgage foreclosure	30
	Mortgage or loan less than $10,000	17

Source: From E. K. Eric Gunderson and Richard H. Rahe, editors, *Life Stress and Illness,* 1974. Courtesy of Charles C Thomas Publisher, Springfield, Illinos.

It is important for managers to be aware of stress sources. It is equally vital that they implement programs to deal with it effectively. Programs and techniques which may serve as means for coping with stress are discussed next.

Coping With Stress

A number of organizational programs and techniques may be effective in either preventing or relieving excessive stress. These are shown in Table 13–8. General organizational programs, while not specifically designed to cope with stress, may nevertheless play a major role. These programs are discussed in the chapters indicated. When properly implemented, they will achieve these results:

- An organizational climate is created which holds anxiety and tension to an acceptable level. Employee inputs are sought and valued by all levels of management. Generally, individuals are given greater control over their work. Communication is emphasized.
- Each person's role is defined, yet care is taken not to discourage risk-takers and those who want to take on greater responsibility.
- Individuals are provided with the training and development needed to assist them in the successful performance of current and future jobs. Equal consideration is given to the need for achieving personal and organizational goals. Individuals are encouraged to plan and exercise greater control over their own work. They are trained to work as effective team members and to develop an awareness of how they relate to others.
- Employees are assisted in planning for career progression.
- Organizational members participate in making decisions which affect them. They are made aware of their company's plans and their particular

Table 13–8. Organizational programs and techniques which may be effective in coping with stress

		Chapter
General Organizational Programs	Effective communication, motivation and leadership styles (Organizational climate)	2
	Job analysis	3
	Organization development	7
	Training and development	8
	Career planning and development	9
	Performance appraisal	10
Specific Techniques	Compensation	11 & 12
	Hypnosis, Transcendental meditation, Biofeedback, and the Relaxation response	13
Specific Organizational Programs	Physical fitness, Alcoholism, Drug addiction and Employee assistance programs	13

role in implementing these plans. They know what is going on in the firm and how well they are peforming their jobs.

- Employee needs—financial and non-financial—are met through an equitable reward system.

Again referring to Table 13–8, you will note several techniques that may be specifically utilized by organizations or individuals in dealing with stress. These methods include hypnosis, biofeedback, Transcendental Meditation, and the Relaxation Response.

Hypnosis is "an altered state of consciousness which is artificially induced and characterized by increased receptiveness to suggestions." A person in a hypnotic state may therefore respond to the hypnotist's suggestion to relax.[38] Hypnosis can help many people cope with stress. The serenity achieved through dissipation of anxieties and fears can restore an individual's confidence. A principal benefit of hynotherapy is that peace of mind continues after awakening from an hypnotic state. This tranquility continues to grow, especially when the person has been trained in self-hypnosis.[39]

Biofeedback is a method of learning to control involuntary bodily processes such as blood pressure or heart rate.[40] For example, using equipment to provide a visual display of blood pressure, individuals may learn to lower their systolic blood pressure levels.

In **Transcendental Meditation** (TM) a secret word or phrase (mantra) provided by a trained instructor is mentally repeated while an individual is comfortably seated. Repeating the mantra over and over helps prevent distracting thoughts. It has been found to produce these physiologic changes: decreased oxygen consumption, decreased carbon-dioxide elimination, and decreased breathing rate. TM results in a decreased metabolic rate and a restful state.[41]

The Relaxation Response is another technique for dealing with the stressful consequences of living in our modern society. This approach to dealing with stress was developed at Harvard's Thorndike Memorial Laboratory and Boston's Beth Israel Hospital. The technique has its roots in ancient Eastern and Western religious, cultic, and lay practices such as Yoga. Use of this method was found to produce the same kind of physiologic changes as Transcendental Meditation. The feelings associated with this altered state of consciousness have been described as ecstatic, beautiful, and totally relaxing. Other individuals have felt a sense of well-being similar to that experienced after exercise but without the fatigue.[42] The Relaxation Response technique procedures are shown in Figure 13–3.

Referring again to Table 13–8, organizational programs are listed which are designed specifically to deal with stress and related problems. These include physical fitness, alcoholism, drug addiction, and employee assistance programs. A discussion of these approaches is presented in the balance of the chapter.

[38]Herbert Benson, *The Relaxation Response* (New York: William Morrow and Company, Inc., 1975): 72 (hereafter cited as Benson).
[39]E. M. Cherman, *Stress and the Bottom Line: A Guide to Personal Well-Being and Corporate Health* (New York: AMACOM, A Division of American Management Associations, 1981): 273.
[40]Benson, 55–56.
[41]Benson, 60–62.
[42]Benson, 75, 112–114.

1. Sit quietly in a comfortable position.

2. Close your eyes.

3. Deeply relax all your muscles, beginning at your feet and progressing up to your face. Keep them relaxed.

4. Breathe through your nose. Become aware of your breathing. As you breathe out, say the word, "ONE," silently to yourself. For example, breathe IN . . . OUT, "ONE": IN . . . OUT, "ONE": etc. Breathe easily and naturally.

5. Continue for 10 to 20 minutes, You may open your eyes to check the time, but do not use an alarm. When you finish, sit quietly for several minutes, at first with your eyes closed and later with your eyes opened. Do not stand up for a few minutes.

6. Do not worry about whether you are successful in achieving a deep level of relaxation. Maintain a passive attitude and permit relaxation to occur at its own pace. When distracting thoughts occur, try to ignore them by not dwelling upon them and return to repeating "ONE." With practice, the response should come with little effort. Practice the technique once or twice daily, but not within two hours after any meal, since the digestive processes seem to interfere with the elicitation of the relaxation response.

Source: From pp. 114–5 (under your title "Procedures for The Relaxation Response") in THE RELAXATION RESPONSE by Herbert Benson, M.D. with Miriam Z. Klipper. Copyright © 1975 by William Morrow and Company, Inc. By permission of the publisher.

Figure 13–3. **Procedures for the relaxation response.**

PHYSICAL FITNESS PROGRAMS

More and more American businesses are providing fitness programs for their employees.[43] From management's viewpoint, this trend is sensible. Loss of productivity resulting from coronary heart disease totals approximately $32 billion annually.[44] The total cost to society is even higher because of lost tax revenue, health care costs, and the expense involved in finding and training replacements. Absenteeism, accidents, and sick pay are often reduced through company sponsored fitness programs. Employees who are physically fit are more alert and productive, and their morale is higher.[45]

A number of organizations have developed physical fitness programs for their employees. Xerox Corporation currently has nine in-house physical fitness laboratories at locations throughout the United States. The Xerox programs are designed to help employees avoid coronary heart diseases and other degenerative disorders. A fitness program, carefully designed for each individual, helps people feel and look better. As an added benefit, it also enhances their self-concept. Jim Post, program manager of executive fitness at Xerox, has stated: "We are concerned about the ever increasing costs of medical and

[43]Jack Martin, "The New Business Boom—Employee Fitness," *Nation's Business* 66 (February 1978): 68.
[44]Robert Kreitner, "Employee Physical Fitness: Protecting an Investment in Human Resources," *Personnel Journal* 55 (July 1976): 340.
[45]Kenneth H. Cooper, *The New Aerobics* (New York: A Bantam Book/Published by arrangement with M. Evans and Company, 1970): 13.

insurance premiums, but beyond that, we have an obligation to our people as people."

The Xerox Executive Fitness Program emphasizes four areas: (1) cardiovascular fitness, (2) flexibility, (3) relaxation by means of biofeedback, and (4) weight conditioning. In the cardiovascular training program, the motorized treadmill is the primary tool. The bicycle ergometer is also used along with biofeedback training. Biofeedback, which was described earlier, is a process which permits an individual to monitor his or her own physiological states (such as pulse rate, skin temperature, blood pressure, muscular tension, and brain waves) through the use of bioinstruments. Electrodes are placed over selected muscles during exercise. They indicate the level of a person's tension. By listening to an audio tone, individuals can actually measure and relax the tension existing in a specific muscle.

Flexibility (the range of movement in a joint or joints) is achieved by using static methods. Static stretching holds muscles and connective tissues at their greatest length, thus helping to relax them. Joint flexibility helps prevent the aches and pains that are common with aging. Finally, relaxation, by means of biofeedback, is an important aspect of the exercise program. Appropriate exercise, it has been shown, can have a greater effect on relaxation than the use of tranquilizers.

Xerox's weight conditioning program is used to strengthen major muscle groups and joints. The lifting of heavy weights, especially for middle-aged individuals, is carefully avoided as relatively light weights and frequent repetitions are emphasized.

At Kimberly-Clark Corporation, approximately 1200 employees participate in a health management program. A staff of twenty-three full-time health care professionals administers this program utilizing a $2.5 million facility. Prior to admission, employees undergo a physical and medical history exam. Each employee then receives an individualized health prescription. The program at Kimberly-Clark was begun after its top management made a commitment to reduce health care costs.[46]

Programs such as the ones at Xerox and Kimberly-Clark are expected to increase dramatically in the future. Firms now recognize how healthy workers contribute directly to the profitability of the organization.

ALCOHOLISM PROGRAMS

Alcoholism is a significant problem which may result from excessive stress. The American Medical Association defined **alcoholism** as a treatable disease in 1956.[47] The disease is characterized by uncontrolled and compulsive drinking that interferes with normal living patterns.

An individual may feel that drinking improves his or her ability to cope. Alcohol rarely improves performance, however; rather, it impairs it. As a per-

[46]Ivancevich and Matteson.
[47]W. David Gibson, "They're Bringing Problem Drinkers Out of the Closet," *Chemical Week* 123 (November 15, 1978): 85.

son starts to drink excessively, the drinking itself results in greater stress. This increased stress is dealt with by more drinking, making it a most vicious circle.[48] Alcoholism affects people at every stratum within our society, from top-level managers to the skid row bum. It is also one of the most difficult diseases to detect. Sometimes a person progresses to advanced stages of alcoholism before perceiving that he or she may actually be an alcoholic. By then, the person's career may be on the verge of destruction. Early signs of alcoholism are especially difficult to identify. Often the symptoms are nothing more than an increasing number of absences. Productivity may, over a period of time, begin to decline. Accidents may occur more frequently.[49] A normally pleasant person can become highly disagreeable.

An increasing number of firms are establishing alcoholism programs. From fifty programs in 1950, the number had expanded to nearly 2400 by 1977. Supervisors are being trained to cope with this health problem. No longer does alcoholism result in automatic termination. Some of the warning signs that supervisors look for with regard to alcoholism are provided in Table 13–9. Any one of these signs taken individually does not suggest the excessive use of alcohol. It is when they are observed as a pattern that potential difficulties may exist.

Table 13–9.   Warning signs of alcoholism

Warning Signs

The New York City Affiliate, Inc., National Council on Alcoholism, considers the following work related problems to be possible indications of alcoholism:

- Absenteeism
- Ineffectiveness on the job
- Tardiness (particularly mornings and after lunch)
- Careless and sloppy work
- Accidents on the job
- Unexplained absences from the workplace
- Inability to remember details and commitments
- Leaving work early
- Avoidance of co-workers and supervisors
- Unpredictable and inappropriate behavior
- Customers' complaints
- Co-workers' complaints
- Unreasonable resentment
- Overreaction to criticism
- Borrowing money from co-workers
- Grandiose, aggressive, belligerent behavior
- "Jekyll and Hyde" personality

Source: "They're Bringing Problem Drinkers Out of the Closet," *Chemical Week* 123 (November 15, 1978): 85. Reprinted by permission.

[48]Derek Rutherford, "Alcoholic Solution," *The Accountant* 182 (August 21, 1980): 310.
[49]Kenneth P. Camisa, "How Alcoholism Treatment Pays for Itself," SAM *Advanced Management Journal* 47 (Winter 1982): 55.

There are indications that drug use in industry has increased during the past decade. Society has become more concerned with this health problem. Numerous firms have recognized that drug problems exist and have taken positive action to deal with them. One such formal program is illustrated in Figure 13–4. There are two sides to the program: (1) safeguards which identify drug problems or prevent them from occurring, and (2) mechanisms which eliminate drug users from the firm.

A major purpose of the program is to ensure that drug abusers are not hired. However, if a person becomes addicted after employment, a supervisor can use progressive discipline for work related irregularities such as absenteeism and low productivity. A supervisor should be trained to look for signs of drug usage.

If drug usage is suspected, the supervisor requires that the employee report to the medical department. Failure to comply may result in discharge. The

Figure 13–4. Some safeguards and mechanisms used to eliminate employee drug usage.

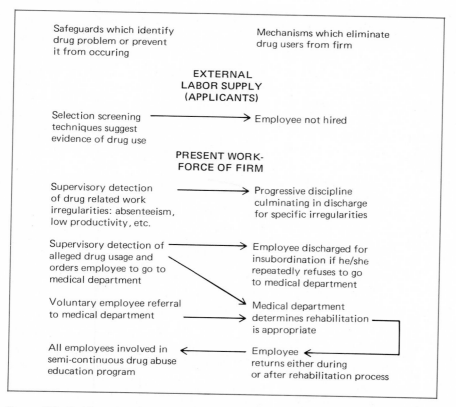

Source: "The Problem of Employee Drug Use and Remedial Alternatives" by Ken Jennings. Reprinted with permission *Personnel Journal* copyright November 1977.

> "It seems to me that today's employer, who says he has no problem drinkers in his organization, is not unlike the employed alcoholic who insists he has no problem with alcohol. Neither is facing the realities of his situation. They are alike, too, in that each is paying a heavy and needless penalty for his illusion."
>
> **James S. Kemper, Jr., Chairman of the Board**
> **Kemper Group**

medical department works with the individual or refers him or her to appropriate agencies for treatment. At all times, there is an ongoing educational program which constantly advises employees of the disadvantages of drug use.

EMPLOYEE ASSISTANCE PROGRAMS

One comprehensive approach that some organizations have taken to deal with burnout, alcoholism, drug abuse, and other emotional disturbances is to implement an **employee assistance program (EAP).** In an EAP, a firm either provides in-house professional counselors or refers employees to an appropriate community social service agency. Typically, most or all of the costs are borne by the employer up to a predetermined amount. The purpose of EAPs is to provide emotionally troubled employees with the same consideration and assistance given employees having physical illnesses.

Every firm has employees with health and personal problems and, during the 1970s, U.S. businesses implemented approximately 2000 EAPs.[50] One such program has been initiated at American Coil Spring Company. L. C. Barry, employee relations director, describes the program by saying, "Its intent is to help employees whose personal problems are affecting their work. Frequently, drinking, drugs, impending divorce, finances, etc. will adversely affect a person's attendance, productivity, or relationship with fellow employees. Often they result in disciplinary action with ultimate termination. The intent of the EAP is to catch these problems early on and refer the employee to counseling before his or her job is in jeopardy."

Kemper Group has one of the better known EAPs. At Kemper, the following guidelines assist in the administration of its employee assistance program. These principles are:

1. We believe that alcoholism, drug addiction, and emotional disturbances are illnesses and should be treated as such.

2. We believe the majority of employees who develop alcoholism, other drug addiction, or emotional illness can be helped to recover, and the company should offer appropriate assistance.

[50]William J. Sonnenstuhl and James E. O'Donnell, "EAPs: The Whys and Hows of Planning Them," *Personnel Administrator* 25 (November 1980): 35.

3. We believe the decision to seek diagnosis and accept treatment for any suspected illness is the responsibility of the employee. However, continued refusal of an employee to seek treatment when it appears that substandard performance may be caused by any illness is not tolerated. We believe that alcoholism, or drug addiction, or emotional illness should not be made an exception to this commonly accepted principle.

4. We believe that it is in the best interest of employees and the company that when alcoholism, other drug addiction, or emotional illness is present, it should be diagnosed and treated at the earliest possible date.

5. We believe that the company's concern for individual alcohol drinking, drug taking, and behavioral habits begins only when they result in unsatisfactory job performance, poor attendance, or behavior detrimental to the good reputation of the company.

6. We believe that confidential handling of the diagnosis and treatment of alcoholism, or other drug addiction, or emotional illness is essential.

EAPs are justified on the basis of improvements that may be made in employees' quality of life by successfully dealing with internal and external stressors. In turn, this may result in increased organization productivity by lowering turnover and absenteeism rates, creating better communication, and generally improving labor relations.[51]

COST/BENEFITS ANALYSIS—SAFETY AND HEALTH

The costs associated with having company programs in safety and health are small when compared to the benefits. Nevertheless, there are costs. Individuals must be available to implement the programs. Time must be taken to train managers and workers regarding safety and health. It is an ongoing process and not merely a one-time occurrence. Costs are also associated with developing and maintaining a safe and healthy workplace. The physical work environment may actually have to be altered to prevent accidents or to remove health hazards. For some firms, this may be a very expensive process.

But, the benefits of an effective safety and health program certainly outweigh the costs. In most instances, when a useful safety and health program is available, productivity losses decrease. Recruitment and selection are enhanced because the firm has gained a reputation for having a safe and healthy work environment. Having such a program may even relate to compensation because, as previously mentioned, the job environment is part of the total compensation package. Workers may even accept less pay in exchange for a safe and healthy work environment. In addition, relationships with both union and nonunion workers are likely to improve. As you remember, unions were a primary force in advocating safety and health in the workplace. Taking

[51]Luis R. Gomez-Mejia and David B. Balking, "Classifying Work-Related and Personal Problems of Troubled Employees," *Personnel Administrator* (November 1980): 27.

all these factors into consideration, the benefits of a sound safety and health program are substantial.

SUMMARY

Safety involves protecting employees from injuries due to work related accidents. Health refers to the employees' freedom from physical or emotional illness. Industrial safety has been a major problem that has seemingly resisted solution. In 1970, Congress passed the Occupational Safety and Health Act.

Many workers are killed or injured each year as a result of job related accidents. Safety programs may be designed to accomplish their purposes through two primary avenues. In the first, the firm works toward creating an environment and an attitude that promote safety. Following a second approach to safety program design, organizations develop and maintain a safe working environment.

The reason a firm is concerned with its employees' health becomes clear when economic values are placed on the employees' worth. A formal company health program should reflect a company philosophy which emphasizes the value of its human assets and which has top management support. A health program starts when applicants are initially screened and continues throughout the workers' employment.

In addition to monitoring traditional health problems, many organizations have expanded the scope of their health concerns to include stress management. Stress refers to physiological and psychological reactions to any event or situation that requires more of us than usual. If stress is severe enough and persists for long periods of time, it can be harmful. Stress can be as disruptive to an individual as any accident.

Burnout has been described as a state of fatigue or frustration which stems from devotion to a cause, way of life, or relationship that did not provide the expected reward. Burnout is a problem which must be dealt with preferably before it occurs. In order to do so, managers must be aware of potential sources of stress. Some of the primary origins of stress include: the family, financial problems, living conditions, life changes, organizational climate, role ambiguity and role conflict, job overload, and working conditions. There are a number of organizational programs and techniques that may be effective in either preventing or relieving excessive stress.

There are organizational programs that are designed specifically to deal with stress and related problems. These include physical fitness, alcoholism, drug addiction, and employee assistance programs.

Questions for Review

1. Distinguish by definition between safety and health.

2. What are the reasons that the Occupational Safety and Health Act has received so

much criticism? What is the current attitude toward OSHA?

3. What are the primary ways in which safety programs are designed? Discuss.

4. What are some measurements that would suggest the success of a firm's safety program?

5. Why should a firm attempt to identify stressful jobs? What could an organization do to reduce stressful situations associated with a job?

6. What are some signs that a supervisor might look for in identifying alcoholics?

7. Why should a firm be concerned with employee burnout?

8. Describe why employee assistance programs are being established.

Terms for Review

Safety

Health

Occupational Safety and Health Act

Frequency rate

Severity rate

Stress

Burnout

Role ambiguity

Role conflict

Job overload

Hypnosis

Biofeedback

Transcendental Meditation

The Relaxation Response

Alcoholism

Employee assistance program

Wanda Zackery was extremely excited a year ago when she joined Landon Electronics as its first safety engineer. She had graduated from Florida State University with a degree in electrical engineering and a strong desire to enter business. Wanda had selected her job at Landon Electronics over several other offers. She believed it would provide her with a broad range of experiences which she could not receive in a strictly engineering job. Also, when she was interviewed by the company president, Mark Lincoln, he promised her that the firm's resources would be at her disposal to correct any safety related problems.

Her first few months at Landon were hectic but exciting. There were numerous safety problems which she immediately identified. One of the most dangerous involved a failure to install safety guards on all exposed equipment. Wanda carefully prepared her proposal, including the expected costs to make the minimum changes that were needed. She estimated that it would take approximately $50,000 to complete the necessary conversions. Wanda then presented the entire package to Mr. Lincoln. She explained the need for the changes to him and her presentation was cordially received. Mr. Lincoln said he would like to think it over and would get back to her.

But that was six months ago! Every time Wanda attempted to get some action on her proposal, Mr. Lincoln was friendly but still wanted some more time to consider it. In the meantime, Wanda had become increasingly anxious. Recently, a worker barely avoided a serious injury because of the lack of a safety guard. Some workers had also become concerned. She heard through the grapevine that someone had telephoned the regional office of OSHA.

Her suspicions were confirmed the very next week when an OSHA inspector appeared at the plant. No previous visits had ever been made to the company. Although Mr. Lincoln was not overjoyed, he permitted the inspector access to the company. Later he might have wished he had not been so cooperative. Before the inspector left, violations had been written up for each piece of equipment that did not have the necessary safety guards. The fines were to total $5,000 if the problems were not corrected right away. The inspector cautioned that repeat violations could cost $50,000 and possible imprisonment.

As the inspector was leaving, Wanda received a phone call. "Wanda, this is Mark. Get up to my office right now. We need to get your project underway."

Questions

1. Discuss Mr. Lincoln's level of commitment to occupational safety.

2. Is there a necessary tradeoff between Landon's need for low expenses and the workers' need for safe working conditions? Explain.

"Will you just leave me alone and let me do my job," said Manuel Gomez. Taken aback, Bill Brown, Manuel's supervisor, decided to "count to ten" before responding to Manuel's fury. As he walked back to his office, Bill thought about how Manuel had changed over the past few months. He had been a hard worker and an extremely cooperative one when he went to work for Bill two years earlier. The company had sent Manuel to two training schools and had received glowing reports about his performance in each of them.

Until about a year ago, Manuel had a perfect attendance record and was a practically ideal employee. At about that time, however, he began to have personal problems which resulted in a divorce six months later. Manuel had requested a day off several times to take care of personal problems and Bill had tried to help in every way he could. He tried not to get involved in Manuel's personal affairs. But he was aware of the strain Manuel must have felt as his marriage broke up and he and his wife engaged in the inevitable disputes about child custody, alimony payments, and so forth.

During the same time period, top management initiated a push for improving productivity. Bill found it necessary to put additional pressure on all of his workers, including Manuel. He tried to be considerate but he had to become much more numbers oriented, insisting upon increased output from every worker.

As time went on, Manuel began to show up late for work and actually missed two days without calling Bill in advance. Bill attributed Manuel's behavior to extreme stress and because Manuel had been such a good worker for so long he excused the tardiness and absences, only gently suggesting that Manuel should try to do better.

Sitting at his desk, Bill thought about what caused Manuel's outburst of a few minutes earlier. Bill had simply suggested to Manuel that he shut down the machine he was operating and clean up the surrounding area. This was a normal part of Manuel's job and something he had been careful to do in the past. Bill thought the disorderliness around Manuel's machine might account for the increasing number of defects in the parts he was making. "This is a tough one, I think I'll talk to the boss about it," thought Bill.

Questions

1. What do you think is likely to be Manuel's problem? Discuss.

2. If you were Bill's boss, what would you recommend that he do?

PARMA CYCLE COMPANY: SAFETY AND HEALTH AT THE NEW PLANT

"I want the new plant to be a model of safety and health," said Mr. Burgess, the president of Parma Cycle Company in Parma, Ohio. "I do too," said Jesse Heard, the personnel director, "but you have to be aware that it's going to cost a lot." "Remember now, Jesse," the president replied, "we're putting the plant in Clarksdale, Mississippi primarily to reduce costs. I believe that the main thing we can do for safety is to train our workers to be safety conscious. That doesn't cost much." "That's the main thing, I know," said Jesse, "but we'll also have to spend some money. There are several areas where safety can be improved by installing hand rails. Also, a good number of the machines will come in without chain and belt guards. We'll have to have those fabricated." "Well," said Mr. Burgess, "let's just try to meet the OSHA requirements on those kinds of things. I'd like to see a cost benefit analysis of anything that goes beyond the OSHA standards."

At about that time, Cliff Brubaker, the chief engineer at Parma, who had also been summoned to the meeting, came in. After a few niceties, Cliff asked, "Mr. Burgess, making sure that all the machinery and the machine layouts meets OSHA requirements has made engineering the new plant a lot more difficult. We won't be able to use our floor space nearly as efficiently at Clarksdale as we do here at Parma. Also, the workflow is going to be less efficient because I had to separate machines to keep the area noise level below standard. Don't you think we could fudge a little on some of this? The Parma plant doesn't come close to meeting OSHA requirements and we have only had one $5000 fine since I've been here."

"I don't think you can trade off personal safety against a few dollars of cost savings," Jesse said. "You remember when Joe Blum lost his arm last year? The company came out okay on that because Joe didn't sue us. But what about Joe? How much was his arm worth?" "Don't get upset, Jesse," said Cliff. "I know what you mean and I really feel the same way. But we can go to extremes." Mr. Burgess spoke up, "I don't think that meeting OSHA standards is going to extremes. Besides, if companies like Parma Cycle don't take some initiative in protecting workers, we're going to see even more enforcement efforts in the future. I want to make sure that you both understand my position. Everything in the plant at Clarksdale is to meet OSHA requirements for safety and health as a minimum. If the requirements can be exceeded with no additional cost, I want to opt for maximum safety. If you have to spend extra money to improve safety or health at the Clarksdale plant, I want to see a cost benefit analysis on each item." "I think that that's clear enough," said Jesse. "Me too," said Cliff, "but I'll have to get back with you on a number of the modifications we had planned."

Questions

1. What do you think of Mr. Burgess' insistence on using OSHA standards as a goal?

2. Do you agree with Jesse that, "you can't trade-off personal safety against a few dollars of cost savings?"

Experiencing Personnel Management

TRANSFERRING A WORKER FOR SAFETY

This is a role playing exercise involving Roger Graves, an abrasive cut-off saw operator at Parma Cycle Company's Parma, Ohio plant, and Roy Brinson, his supervisor. The exercise is designed to highlight the kind of problems created when suspected alcoholism or drug abuse produces a safety concern.

Role Descriptions

Roger Graves. You have been operating the abrasive cut-off saw for three years. The saw consists of an electric motor with a very thin, 24-inch diameter, reinforced grinding wheel, or "blade," attached. The grinding wheel spins at a high rate of speed, but is covered by a protective guard. You wear goggles as further protection and the vacuum system takes away the dust created by the spinning wheel.

You cut 3/4 to 1-inch diameter steel tubing to various lengths. To do this, you slide a long length of tubing under the cut-off wheel until it contacts a spot that you have set at the appropriate distance from the saw. Then you grasp the handle on the saw and pull it downward until the wheel contacts the metal and cuts through it. You release the handle, allowing the saw to be pulled upward by a heavy spring. Then you move the piece of tubing you have cut and slide the tubing down for another cut. This continues throughout the day with periodic changes in the diameter and length of the pieces you are cutting.

You don't consider your job particularly dangerous, although you realize that the saw blade would cut through anything which came in contact with it including a hand or arm. You have also seen a saw blade explode when an operator pulled down rapidly, causing the blade to contact the metal being sawed too sharply. If this should happen and the operator were not wearing safety goggles and a leather apron, the flying pieces of abrasive disk could cause injury.

Recently you have been having family problems. Your wife has moved to her mother's home and taken your two children with her. You have tried to keep it from affecting your work. A few times, however, you have stayed up all night trying to work things out, driving to your wife's mother's home, and so forth. Thus, you sometimes arrive at work the next day in pretty bad condition. Your supervisor has spoken to you a time or two about looking tired or being careless. You like and respect him; you really want to do a good job; but you think the personal problems you have may last for a long time. Your supervisor came by a little while ago and asked you to come to his office. The woman who operates your saw on the next shift has just shown up. As you head for the supervisor's office you think, "I sure hope there's no problem. All I need now is problems at work too."

Roy Brinson. You have been a supervisor at Parma for eight years and have been working in your present department for four of those years. Recently you have observed Roger Graves with increasing concern. Several times you have seen Roger barely miss his hand when bringing the cut-off saw into contact with the metal he was cutting. The OSHA inspector has complained about the safety of the machine but no way has been found to make it completely safe without seriously hampering productivity. Roger has been a safe operator until very recently. You suspect that he is an alcoholic now. He has come to work a number of times looking disheveled, red-eyed, and uncommunicative. He failed to show up for work one day without even calling. When you questioned him about it, he avoided a direct answer and you didn't press the matter. You think that Roger may need professional help.

Your immediate problem, though, is that you have decided you have to transfer him to a safer job. You have decided to assign him to the frame painter. There he will hang the bicycle frames on a conveyer which moves through a spray painting enclosure where the frames are automatically painted and baked dry. He will be responsible for adjusting the painting equipment, maintaining the conveyors, etc. The job is at the same skill level as his present job but it involves no significant danger. He will have to learn some new skills. You have talked this matter over with the personnel director. He agrees that you have no choice but to transfer Roger immediately. As you see Roger approaching the office you try to think of how you can tell him of your decision.

Questions

1. How should Roy Brinson break the news to Roger?

2. Discuss, pro or con, Roy's decision to transfer Roger. Suggest alternatives.

3. Do you have enough information to suggest that Roger has an alcohol problem? Defend your answer.

Part VI

Employee and Labor Relations

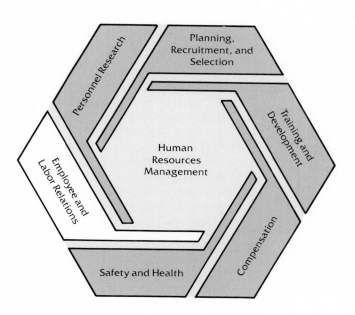

Chapter Objectives

1. Describe the history of the labor movement.
2. List the most significant union objectives.
3. Identify the reasons why employees join unions.
4. Describe the basic structure of union organization.
5. State the basic steps involved if a union desires to become the bargaining representative.
6. Explain the various strategies that a union may use in gaining bargaining unit recognition.

Chapter 14 _____

The Labor Union

Since the turn of the century, no single factor has exerted more influence on human resources management than organized labor. Through the process of collective bargaining, organized labor has established patterns of employee-management relations that have influenced not only unionized companies but also those that strive to maintain nonunion status. Wage levels, benefits, and working conditions for millions of employees now reflect decisions made jointly by unions and management. Human resources policies and practices can no longer be determined unilaterally by management in many organizations.

Unions have become not only a formidable political force in America but they are also active in the general social and economic spheres of individual communities and the nation as a whole. They attempt to influence the decisions of state legislatures and Congress in such areas as employee recruitment and selection, training and development, compensation, and health and safety. Because of the prominent role that unions play in many organizations and in our society as a whole, human resources management has become much more complex. An understanding of the labor movement is essential for practitioners and students of personnel management.

Unions are not a recent development in American history. The earliest unions originated at the end of the eighteenth century about the time of the American Revolution. Although these early associations had few characteristics of present-day labor unions, they did bring workers together to consider problems of mutual concern. These early unions were local in nature and usually existed for only a short time.[1]

The labor movement has not had a simple and straightforward line of development. Instead, it has had as much failure as success. Employer opposition, the impact of the business cycle, the growth and development of American industry, court rulings, and government legislation have exerted their influence in varying degrees at various times. As a result, the labor movement's history has somewhat resembled the swinging of a pendulum. At times, the pendulum has moved in favor of labor and at other times, it has swung toward the advantage of management.

Prior to the 1930s, the trend definitely favored management. The courts strongly supported employers in their attempts to thwart the organized labor movement. This was first evidenced by use of criminal and civil conspiracy doctrines which were derived from English common law. A **conspiracy,** generally defined, exists when two or more persons band together to prejudice the right of others (i.e., by refusing to work or demanding higher wages). The essence of the doctrine is that what one employee can do legally becomes an illegal conspiracy if several employees join together for the same purpose. From 1806 to 1842 there were seventeen trials in which labor unions were charged as conspiracies.[2] These cases resulted in the demise of several union organizations and certainly discouraged union activities by other groups of employees. The conspiracy doctrine was considerably softened by the decision reached in the landmark case *Commonwealth* v. *Hunt* in 1842. In that case Chief Justice Shaw of the Supreme Judicial Court of Massachusetts contended that labor organizations were legal organizations. In order to be convicted under the conspiracy doctrine, it must be shown that the objectives of the union are unlawful or the means employed to gain a lawful end are unlawful.[3]

Other tactics used by employers to stifle union growth were injunctions and yellow dog contracts. The **injunction,** a prohibiting legal procedure, was used by employers to prevent certain union activities such as strikes and unionization attempts. The **yellow dog contract** was a written agreement between the employee and the company made at the time of employment. It prohibited a worker from joining a union or engaging in union activities. Each of these defensive tactics was used by management and supported by the courts, and they severely limited union growth.

In the latter half of the nineteenth century the American industrial system started to grow and prosper. Factory production began to displace handi-

[1]*Brief History of the American Labor Movement,* U.S. Department of Labor, Bureau of Labor Statistics, Bulletin 1000, 1970 ed., p. 1.
[2]Benjamin J. Taylor and Fred Witney, *Labor Relations Law,* 3d ed. (Englewood Cliffs, N.J.: Prentice-Hall, Inc., 1979), pp. 17–18.
[3]Ibid., p. 21.

craft forms of manufacturing. The Civil War gave the factory system a great boost. Goods were demanded in quantities which only mass production methods could supply. The railroads developed new networks of routes to span the continent and knit the country into an economic whole. Employment was high and unions sought to organize workers in the new and expanded enterprises. Most unions during this time were small and rather weak, and many did not survive the economic recession of the 1870s. Union membership rose to 300,000 by 1872 and then dropped to 50,000 by 1878.[4] This period also marked the rise of radical labor activity and increased industrial strife as unions struggled for recognition and survival.[5]

Out of the turbulence of the 1870s emerged the most substantial labor organization that had appeared in the United States. The Noble Order of the Knights of Labor was founded in 1869 as a secret society of the Philadelphia garment workers. After its secrecy was abandoned and other crafts were invited to join, it grew rapidly, reaching a membership of more than 700,000 by the mid-1880s. Internal conflict among the Knights' leadership in 1881 gave rise to the nucleus of a new organization which would soon replace it on the labor scene.[6] That organization was the **American Federation of Labor (AFL)**.

Devoted to "pure and simple unionism," Samuel Gompers, of the Cigarmakers Union, led some twenty-five labor groups representing the skilled trades to found the American Federation of Labor in 1886. Gompers was elected the first president of the AFL, a position he held for thirty-seven years. He is probably the single most important individual in American trade union history. The AFL began with a membership of some 138,000 and doubled that number during the next twelve years.[7]

In 1890, Congress passed the Sherman Anti-Trust Act. This marked the entrance of the federal government into the statutory regulation of labor organizations. Although the primary stimulus for this Act came from public concern over business's monopoly power, court interpretations soon applied its provisions to organized labor. Later, in 1914, Congress passed the Clayton Act (an amendment to the Sherman Act) with the intent of removing labor from the purview of the Sherman Act. Again, judicial interpretation nullified that intent and left labor even more exposed to legal suits.[8] Nonetheless, the AFL grew to almost five million members by 1920.[9]

During the 1920s labor faced legal restrictions on union activity and unfavorable court decisions. The one exception to such repressive policies was the passage and approval of the Railway Labor Act of 1926. This was the first time that the government declared unqualifiably the right of private employees to join unions and bargain collectively through representatives of their own choosing without interference from their employers. It also set up special machinery for the settlement of labor disputes. Although the act covered only

[4]*Brief History of the American Labor Movement*, p. 9.
[5]See Foster Rhea Dulles, *Labor in America*, 3d ed. (New York: Crowell, 1966): 114–125.
[6]Ibid., pp. 126–149.
[7]*Brief History of the American Labor Movement*, pp. 15–16.
[8]E. Edward Herman and Alfred Kuhn, *Collective Bargaining and Labor Relations* (Englewood Cliffs, N.J.: Prentice-Hall, 1981): 37–39.
[9]*Brief History of the American Labor Movement*, p. 27.

**Jerry L. Sellentin, Ph.D.,
AEP**

*Director of Human Resources
Bryan Memorial Hospital
Lincoln, Nebraska*

Jerry's initial experience in Personnel was with Central Telephone and Utilities Corporation, which was no place for the weak-hearted. In addition to other personnel tasks, he was responsible for the administration of twenty-four labor union contracts! In 1968, he became personnel manager for a major retail store employing six hundred employees (eight hundred during the Christmas season). His major responsibilities were aimed at reorganizing and directing the personnel department.

As a result of his experience in reorganizing a personnel department, Dr. Sellentin entered the health care field in 1970 as director of personnel with Bryan Memorial Hospital, a 339-bed hospital. Today, the hospital employs 1465 employees and Jerry has a staff specializing in personnel administration, training, EEOC, and labor relations. He views his role as that of a consultant for both management and employees. In this capacity, he helps management in selecting and effectively utilizing its people to achieve organizational objectives while meeting the employees' needs in their work. Dr. Sellentin says, "My responsibilities for Personnel must be related to the bottom line of the hospital's balance sheet. This concept will continue to be a major factor in the personnel manager's job."

Jerry feels that the personnel function, once taken for granted as a catch-all department, is now making inroads in most organizations. When asked to describe a human resources management problem and how it is

employees in the railroad industry (a later amendment extended coverage to the airline industry) it foreshadowed the extension of similar rights to other classes of employees in the 1930s.

THE LABOR MOVEMENT AFTER 1930

The 1930s found the United States in one of the worst depressions in history. The unemployment rate rose as high as 25 percent.[10] The sentiment of the country began to favor organized labor as many people blamed business for the

[10]*Historical Statistics of the United States, Colonial Times to 1970, Bicentennial Edition, Part 1* (Washington, D.C.: U.S. Bureau of the Census, 1975): 126.

solved, he replied, "A major issue I have recently grappled with involves our Wage and Salary Administration Program. The Human Resources office is responsible for submitting to the hospital's Board of Trustees a yearly proposed plan for changes in the Wage and Salary Program. In preparing our recommendations it has been our practice to do salary surveys. The organizations we have contacted for exchange of information have been in the immediate area and limited to the State of Nebraska as established by guidelines from the Board of Trustees. Finding a shortage of key personnel—including registered nurses and specialized technicians—in our local recruitment, we began to recruit from other parts of the United States. Therefore, we had to show the Board of Trustees that our wage and salary recommendations should be based on salary information obtained from a regional area instead of limited to the local area. Our Board wanted to have competitive salaries, but believed strongly that we could continue to recruit and retain good employees by maintaining our local salary survey practice. Through discussion and evaluation of data, including turnover rates, we were able to show the trustees that a regional salary survey consisting of six states was more meaningful and helpful to our overall Wage and Salary Administration Program in reducing turnover and training costs and in recruiting qualified applicants."

Dr. Sellentin believes that the personnel manager must be active in professional, civic, and community organizations. He is currently past chairman of the American Society for Personnel Administration and serves on the executive committee of this organization. He has been a board member of the American Society for Hospital Personnel Administration and chairperson of the Nebraska Equal Opportunity Commission (an appointed position by the Governor of Nebraska). Dr. Sellentin has also been appointed by the Governor of Nebraska as a member of the State Personnel Board and Merit Council. He is active in the United Way of Lincoln, the Chamber of Commerce, the YMCA, the Lincoln Public Schools, Junior Achievement, and the Lincoln Better Business Bureau.

---

agony that accompanied the depression. The pendulum began to swing away from management and toward labor.

Anti-Injunction Act (Norris-LaGuardia Act)—1932

The Great Depression of the 1930s brought about a substantial change in American thinking relative to the place of unions in contemporary society. Congress reflected this thinking in 1932 with the passage of the Norris-LaGuardia Act. The act affirms that United States public policy sanctions collective bargaining and approves the formation and effective operation of labor unions.[11] While this act did not outlaw the use of injunctions, it severely re-

[11]Taylor and Witney, *Labor Relations Law*, pp. 84–85.

stricted the federal courts' authority to issue them in labor disputes. It also made yellow-dog contracts unenforceable in the federal courts. These then passed from the labor relations scene.

National Labor Relations Act (Wagner Act)— 1935

In 1933 Congress made an abortive attempt to stimulate economic recovery by the passage of the National Industrial Recovery Act (NIRA). Declared unconstitutional by the Supreme Court in May, 1935, the NIRA did provide the nucleus for legislation which followed it. Section 7a of the NIRA proclaimed the right of workers to organize and bargain collectively. Congress did not, however, provide procedures to enforce these rights.[12]

Undeterred by the Supreme Court decision and strongly supported by organized labor, Congress speedily enacted a comprehensive labor law, the National Labor Relations Act (Wagner Act). This act, approved by President Roosevelt on July 5, 1935, is one of the most significant pieces of labor-management relations legislation. Drawing heavily on the experience of the Railway Labor Act of 1926 and Section 7a of NIRA, the act declared legislative support, on a broad scale, of the right of labor to organize and engage in collective bargaining. The spirit of the Wagner Act is stated in Section 7, which defines the substantive rights of employees:

> Employees shall have the right to self-organization, to form, join, or assist labor organizations, to bargain collectively through representatives of their own choosing, and to engage in other concerted activities, for the purpose of collective bargaining or other mutual aid or protection.

The rights defined in Section 7 were protected against employer interference by Section 8, which detailed and prohibited five practices deemed to be unfair to labor. These are:

1. Interfering with or restraining or coercing employees in the exercise of their right to self-organization
2. Dominating or interfering in the affairs of a union
3. Discriminating in regard to hire or tenure or any condition of employment for the purpose of encouraging or discouraging union membership
4. Discriminating against or discharging an employee who has filed charges or given testimony under the act
5. Refusing to bargain with chosen representatives of employees

In order to administer and enforce the provisions of the act, the National Labor Relations Board (NLRB) was created. The NLRB has been given two principle functions: (1) to establish procedures for holding bargaining unit elections and to monitor the election procedures, and (2) to investigate com-

[12]Ibid., pp. 156–157.

plaints and prevent unlawful acts involving unfair labor practices. Much of its work is delegated to regional offices located throughout the country.

Following the Wagner Act, union membership increased from approximately three million to fifteen million between 1935 and 1947.[13] You can see this rapid growth depicted in Figure 14–1. The increase was most conspicuous in the mass producing industries. New unions in these industries were organized on an industrial basis rather than a craft basis, and members were primar-

Figure 14–1. **The growth of union membership. (Source: Bureau of Labor Statistics, _Directory of National Unions and Employee Associations._)**

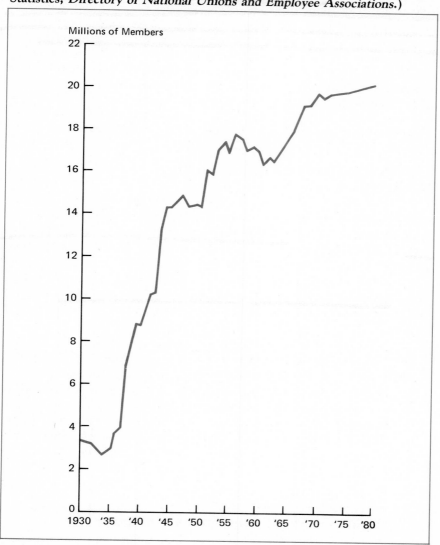

[13]I. Bernstein, "The Growth of American Unions," _American Economic Review_ 44 (1954): 308–317.

ily unskilled or semiskilled workers. An internal struggle developed within the AFL over the question of whether unions should be organized to include all workers in an industry, or organized strictly on a craft or occupational basis. In 1935 six AFL-affiliated unions and the officers of two other AFL unions formed a "Committee for Industrial Organization" to promote the organization of workers in mass production and unorganized industries. The controversy grew to the point that in May 1938 the AFL expelled the Committee for Industrial Organization unions. In November 1938 the expelled unions held their first convention in Pittsburgh and reorganized as a federation of unions under the name of **"Congress of Industrial Organizations"** (CIO). The new federation included nine unions expelled from the AFL and thirty-two other groups established to recruit workers in various industries.[14] John L. Lewis, president of the United Mine Workers, was elected the first president.

The rivalry generated by the two large federations stimulated union organization efforts in each group. With this growth, the labor movement gained considerable influence in the United States. However, many individuals and groups began to feel that the Wagner Act was too prolabor. This shift in public sentiment was in part related to costly strikes following World War II. Whether justified or not, unions were blamed for these disruptions.

Labor Management Relations Act (Taft-Hartley Act)—1947

In 1947, with public pressure mounting, Congress overrode President Truman's veto and passed the Labor Management Relations Act (Taft-Hartley Act). The Taft-Hartley Act extensively revised the National Labor Relations Act which became Title I of the new law. A new period in public policy began. The pendulum had again begun to swing toward a position which reflected a more balanced approach between labor and management.

Some of the important changes introduced by the Taft-Hartley Act included:

1. Modified Section 7 to include the right of employees to refrain from union activity as well as engage in it.
2. Prohibited the closed shop (the arrangement requiring that all workers be union members at the time they are hired) and narrowed the freedom of the parties to authorize the union shop (the employer may hire anyone he chooses, but all new workers must join the union after a stipulated period of time).
3. Broadened the employer's right of free speech.
4. Provided that employers need not recognize or bargain with unions formed by supervisory personnel.
5. Stated that employees may initiate decertification petitions.
6. Provided for government intervention in "national emergency strikes".

[14]*Brief History of the American Labor Movement*, pp. 31–33.

A significant change in the act was to extend the concept of unfair labor practices to unions. Labor organizations were to refrain from:

1. Restraining or coercing employees in the exercise of their guaranteed collective bargaining rights.

2. Causing an employer to discriminate in any way against an employee in order to encourage or discourage union membership.

3. Refusing to bargain in good faith with an employer regarding wages, hours, and other conditions of employment.

4. Engaging in certain types of strikes and boycotts.

5. Requiring employees covered by union-shop contracts to pay initiation fees or dues "in an amount which the Board finds excessive or discriminatory under all circumstances".

6. "Featherbedding", i.e., requiring that an employer pay for services not performed.

One of the most controversial elements of Taft-Hartley was its section 14b. According to this section, states are permitted to enact "right-to-work" legislation. This legislation prohibits management and unions from developing agreements which require union membership as a condition of employment. Some twenty states, located primarily in the South and West, have adopted such laws, which have been a continuing source of irritation between labor and management. Much of the impetus behind the right-to-work movement is provided by the National Right to Work Committee, based in Fairfax, Virginia. Some estimates are that this group receives $10 million in annual contributions (and sends out approximately 25 million letters to and on behalf of its 1.25 million members).[15]

For about ten years after the passage of the Taft-Hartley Act, union membership expanded at about the same rate as nonagricultural employment. But, all was not well within the organized labor movement. Ever since the creation of the CIO, the two federations had engaged in a bitter and costly rivalry. Both the CIO and the AFL recognized the increasing need for cooperation and reunification. In 1955, following two years of intensive negotiations between the two organizations, the merger agreement was ratified and the AFL-CIO became a reality. In the years following the merger, however, the AFL-CIO faced some of its greatest challenges.

Labor-Management Reporting and Disclosure Act (Landrum-Griffin Act)—1959

Corruption had plagued organized labor since the early 1900s. Periodic revelations of graft, violence, extortion, racketeering, and other improper activities aroused public indignation or invited governmental investigation. Even

[15]Arthur A. Sloane and Fred Witney, *Labor Relations*, 4th edition (Englewood Cliffs, N.J.: Prentice-Hall, Inc., 1981): 378.

though the number of unions involved was small, every disclosure undermined the public image of organized labor as a whole.[16]

Scrutiny of union activities intensified after World War II and ultimately led to the creation in 1957 of the Senate Select Committee on Improper Activities in the Labor or Management Field, headed by Senator McClellan of Arkansas. Between 1957 and 1959 the McClellan Committee held numerous hearings, many of which were nationally televised, which alarmed the entire country. As evidence came to light the AFL-CIO moved to take action.

In 1957 the AFL-CIO expelled three unions (representing approximately 1.6 million members) for their practices. One of them, the Teamsters, was and is the largest in the country. In 1959, largely as a result of the recommendations of the McClellan Committee, Congress enacted the **Labor-Management Reporting and Disclosure Act (Landrum-Griffin Act)**. This act marked a significant turning point in the involvement of the federal government in internal union affairs. The Landrum-Griffin Act spelled out a "Bill of Rights of Members of Labor Organizations" which is designed to protect certain rights of individuals in their union relationships. The Act also requires extensive reporting on numerous internal union activities and contains severe penalties for violations. In addition, the Act amended the Taft-Hartley Act by adding additional restrictions on picketing and secondary boycotts.

In 1974 Congress extended coverage of the Taft-Hartley Act to private not-for-profit hospitals and health care institutions. This amendment brought within the jurisdiction of the National Labor Relations Board some 2 million employees. Proprietary (profit-making) health care organizations were previously under NLRB jurisdiction. The amendment does not cover government-operated hospitals; it applies only to the private sector.

The labor movement has experienced membership problems since the mid-1950s. In 1968 the second largest union in the country, the United Auto Workers, disaffiliated with the AFL-CIO. The UAW reaffiliated with the AFL-CIO in 1981. From 1956 to 1968 union membership dropped from about 30 percent to 23 percent of the total labor force.[17] As may be seen in Figure 14-2, this percentage has continued to decline even though total membership has remained relatively stable.

A trend is also developing regarding the ability of unions to gain recognition as collective bargaining agents in companies. In 1968 unions won 57.1 percent of the certification elections held by the NLRB. By 1981 union victories had dropped to 44 percent.[18] This is graphically presented in Figure 14-3. Although union growth appears to have stabilized, the labor movement continues to be a major force in our society.

THE PUBLIC SECTOR

Government employees are generally considered a class apart from other workers. This is reflected in their exclusion from the coverage of general labor leg-

[16]Dulles, *Labor in America*, pp. 382–383.
[17]*Brief History of the American Labor Movement*, p. 67.
[18]Ann M. Reilly, "Big Labor's Crumbling Clout," *Dun's Review*, 112 (October 1978): 53.

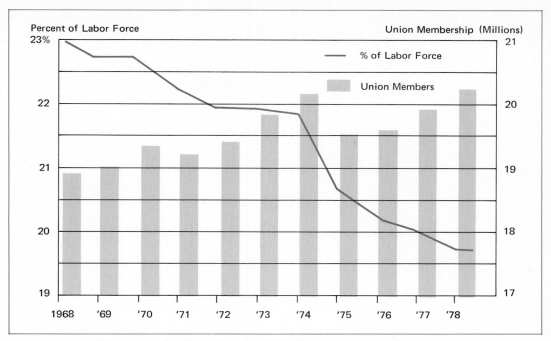

Percent of Labor Force

23%

22

21

20

19

Union Membership (Millions)

21

20

19

18

17

— % of Labor Force

Union Members

1968 '69 '70 '71 '72 '73 '74 '75 '76 '77 '78

Figure 14–2. **Union membership. (Source: U.S. Department of Labor.)**

islation.[19] However, like their counterparts in private industry, government employees have demonstrated a persistence in organizing for an effective voice in the manner and terms of their employment.

For many years the federal government had no well-defined policy on employee-management relations regarding its own employees. On January 17, 1962, President John F. Kennedy issued Executive Order 10988. Section 1 (a) of the Order stated:

Employees of the federal government shall have, and shall be protected in the exercise of, the right, freely and without fear of penalty or reprisal, to

"The head of a personnel and industrial relations function must know more than just Personnel. You must understand the overall operation and work within the objectives of the operation. To do a good job you have to be able to understand both sides of the people problems that a company faces. It takes much more than just liking people to do a good job."

**Stuart J. Levey, Director of Industrial Relations
Teledyne, Inc.**

[19]Examples include the Social Security Act, Fair Labor Standards Act, and the National Labor Relations Act and its amendments.

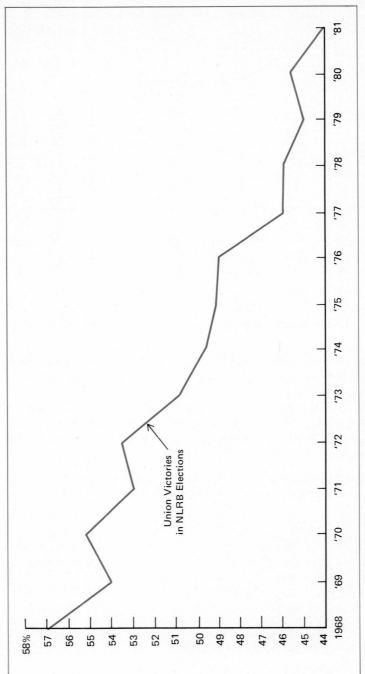

Figure 14–3. Union victories in NLRB elections. (Source: National Labor Relations Board.)

474

form, join and assist any employee organization or to refrain from any such activity.

For the first time in the history of the federal civil service, a uniform, comprehensive plan for cooperation between employee organizations and management in the executive branch of government was established. Employees were permitted to organize and negotiate on personnel policies and practices and matters affecting working conditions so long as they were within the administrative discretion of the agency officials concerned. Employees could not strike, however. Public Law 84-330, passed in 1955, had made it a felony to strike against the United States government.

E.O. 10988 has been substantially amended and clarified over the years. While each subsequent order has brought about changes in definitions and procedures, the basic rights of government employees to organize remains intact. Although federal employees do not have rights equal to their counterparts in the private sector, they are much closer than at any other time in history. Even though federal employees are prohibited from striking, eight states provide their workers with a limited right-to-strike provision. These states include Alaska, Hawaii, Minnesota, Montana, Oregon, Pennsylvania, Vermont, and Wisconsin.

EMPLOYEE ASSOCIATIONS

The Bureau of Labor Statistics lists thirty-seven major professional and state employee associations representing a membership of over 2.6 million people.[20] The largest of these, the National Education Association, has over 1,600,800 members. Others include the Civil Service Employees Association, Inc. of New York, 220,000 members, and the Fraternal Order of Police, 150,000.

In the past, employee associations were primarily concerned with the professional aspects of employment and avoided any semblance of unionism. In recent years, this has changed as public and private sector unions have actively organized both professional and government employees. Many employee associations are now enthusiastically pursuing organized dealings with management. In 1974 they had negotiated more than 12,500 agreements for their members.

OBJECTIVES OF UNIONS

As previously indicated, the labor movement has a long history in the United States. Yet, each union within the movement is a unique organization seeking varying goals. However, several broad objectives characterize the labor movement as a whole. These include:

[20]*Directory of National Unions and Employee Associations,* U.S. Department of Labor, Bureau of Labor Statistics, Bulletin 1937 (1977).

1. To secure and, if possible, improve the living standards and economic status of its members

2. To enhance and, if possible, guarantee individual security against threats and contingencies that might result from market fluctuations, technological change, or management decisions

3. To influence power relations in the social system in ways that favor and do not threaten union gains and goals

4. To advance the welfare of all who work for a living, whether union members or not.[21]

In order to accomplish the above objectives, most unions recognize that they must strive for continued growth and power. Although growth and power are related, they will be discussed separately.

Growth

To maximize a union's objectives, its membership must strive for continued growth. Members pay dues which are vitally needed to promote the union cause. Thus, an overall goal of most unions is continued growth. But, as we previously mentioned, the percentage of union members in the workforce is declining. Many union leaders are concerned about this trend. Much of a union's ability to accomplish its objectives is derived from strength in numbers. For this reason, unions must continue to explore new areas for potential members. They have recently directed much of their attention toward white collar groups and government employees.

Power

Power is defined here as the amount of external control an organization is able to exert. As such, the union's power is influenced to a large extent by the size of its membership. However, other facts must be considered.

The importance of the jobs held by union members significantly affects union power. For instance, an entire plant may have to be shut down if unionized machinists performing critical jobs decide to strike. A few strategically located union members may exert a disproportionate amount of power. A union's power can also be determined from the type of firm that is unionized. Unionization of such key workers as truckers, steelworkers, or farm workers can affect the entire country. Through control of key industries, the union's power may extend to firms that are not unionized. For instance, the power of the trucking unions extends well beyond firms that the truckers serve. Firms that depend upon deliveries by the trucking industry often yield to union pressures in order to continue receiving services.

[21]Edwin F. Beal and James P. Begin, *The Practice of Collective Bargaining*, 6th edition (Homewood, Ill.: Richard D. Irwin, Inc., 1982): 91.

Through achievement of growth and power, a union is capable of exerting its force in the political arena. The political arm of the AFL-CIO is the **Committee on Political Education** (COPE). Founded in 1955, its purpose is to support politicians who are friendly to the cause of organized labor. The union recommends and assists those candidates who best serve its interests. Union members also encourage their friends to support their candidates. The larger the voting membership, the greater the union influence with politicians. With "friends" in government, the union is in a much stronger position to maneuver against management.

WHY EMPLOYEES JOIN UNIONS

The reasons individuals join unions are many and varied, and they tend to change over time. They may involve job, personal, social, or political considerations. It would be impossible to discuss them all. However, the following are some of the major reasons: dissatisfaction with management, need for a social outlet, need for avenues of leadership, forced unionization, and social pressure from peers.

Dissatisfaction with Management

Every job holds potential for real dissatisfactions. Each individual has a boiling point that can trigger him or her to consider a union as a solution to real or perceived problems. Unions look for problem situations in organizations and then emphasize the advantages of union membership. Some of the more common reasons for employee dissatisfaction are described below.

Compensation. Employees want their compensation to be fair and equitable. Wages are important to them because they provide both the necessities and pleasures of life. If they are dissatisfied with their wages, employees may look to the union for assistance in raising their standard of living.

There is also a psychological aspect associated with compensation administration. The amount of compensation an individual receives in relation to other workers performing similar work may be all important. If he or she perceives that management has shown favoritism by paying someone else more to perform the same or a lower level job, dissatisfaction will likely result. Union members know precisely the basis of their pay and how it compares with others.

Job Security. When an employee is young, job security is often less important than for older workers. She or he may feel that, "If I lose this job, I can always get another." But, if employees see management consistently terminating older employees to make room for younger, more aggressive workers, they may begin to think in terms of job security. If the firm does not provide its employees with a feeling of job security, the workers may turn to the union.

Management's Attitude. People like to feel they are important. They do not like to be considered a commodity which can be bought and sold. In some firms, management's attitude becomes insensitive to the needs of its employees. When this situation occurs, employees may perceive that they have little or no influence or control in job related matters. Workers who feel that they are not really part of the organization are prime targets for unionization.

Management's attitude may be reflected in such small things as how notices on the bulletin board are written. Memos addressed "To All Employees" instead of "To Our Employees" may indicate a management attitude of indifference to employee needs. This attitude will likely stem from top management. But it is initially noticed in the actions of first line supervisors. Workers may begin to observe that the supervisors are judging people entirely on what they can do, how much they can do, and when they can do it. Because of this attitude, employees may be treated more as machines than people. Supervisors may fail to give reasons for unusual assignments and may expect employees to dedicate their entire lives to the firm without providing adequate rewards. The prevailing philosophy may be, "If you don't like it here, leave." When management does not consider the needs of the employees as individuals, the firm is ripe for unionization.

A Social Outlet

People, by nature, have strong social needs. They generally enjoy being around others who have similar interests and desires. Some employees join a union for no other reason than to be able to go down to the union hall and socialize with their peers.

To promote a closeness among members, unions often have active programs of social activities such as picnics, dances, and parties. Some unions now offer day care centers and other services which appeal to working men and women and increase their sense of solidarity with other union members. People who develop close personal relationships will likely stand together in difficult times.

Providing Avenues of Leadership

Certain individuals aspire to leadership roles. It is not always easy for an operant employee to progress into management. Many individuals may not even desire to enter management of the firm. However, those employees with leadership aspirations can often satisfy these ambitions through the union. As with the firm, the union also has a hierarchy of leadership, and individual members have the opportunity to work their way up through the various levels. Employers often notice employees who are leaders in the union and it is not uncommon to find them promoted into managerial ranks as supervisors.

Forced Unionization

It is generally illegal for management to require that an individual join a union prior to employment. However, in the thirty states without right-to-work laws, it is legal for an employer to agree with the union that a new employee must join the union after a certain period (generally thirty days) or be terminated. This is referred to as a union shop agreement. Data are not available indicating the number of employees who become union members because of these compulsory agreements.

Peer Pressure

Many individuals will join a union simply because they are urged to do so by other members of the work group. Friends and associates may constantly remind an employee that he or she is not a member of the union. This social pressure from one's peers is difficult to resist. Failure to join the union may result in the employee being completely rejected by other workers. In extreme cases, union members have threatened nonmembers with physical violence and have sometimes even carried out these threats.

UNION STRUCTURE

The labor movement has taken on a multilevel organizational structure over time. This complex of organizations ranges all the way from local unions to the principal federation, the AFL-CIO. Each level has its own government or ways of managing its operations. Many national unions have intermediate levels between the national and the local levels. In this section, however, we will describe the three basic elements of union organization. They are (1) the local union, (2) the national union, and (3) the federation or AFL-CIO.

The Local Union

The basic element in the structure of the American labor movement is the **local union**. To the individual union member, it is the most important level in the structure of organized labor. Through the local, the individual deals with the employer on a day-to-day basis. There are approximately 70,000 local unions in the United States, most of which are affiliated with one of the 175 national unions. Local unions vary in size, ranging from a few members to 20,000 to 30,000 members.[22]

There are two basic kinds of local unions: craft and industrial. **Craft unions,** such as the Carpenters and Joiners, are typically composed of members of a particular trade or skill in an area or locality. Members usually acquire

[22]*Directory of National Unions and Employee Associations*, p. 77.

their job skills through an apprenticeship type of training program. **Industrial unions** generally consist of all the workers in a particular plant or group of plants. The specific kind of work they do or the level of skill they possess is not a condition for membership in the union. An example of an industrial union is the United Auto Workers.

The local union's functions are many and varied. Administering the collective bargaining agreement and representing the workers in handling grievances are two important activities. Other functions include keeping the membership informed on labor issues, promoting increased membership, maintaining effective contact with the national union, and when appropriate, negotiating with local level management.

National Unions

The most powerful level in the union structure is the national union. As previously stated, most locals are affiliated with national unions. Some national unions are called "international" because they have affiliated locals in Canada.

A **national union** is composed of local unions which it charters. As such it is the parent organization to the local unions. The local union—not the individual worker—holds membership in the national union. The national union is supported financially by each local union, whose contribution is based on its membership size.

The national union is governed by a national constitution and a national convention of local unions, which usually meets every two to five years. The day-to-day operation of the national is conducted by elected officers aided by an administrative staff. The national union is active in organizing any unorganized workers within its jurisdiction, engaging in collective bargaining at the national level, and assisting its locals in their negotiations. In addition, the national union may provide numerous educational and research services for its constituent locals, dispense strike funds, publish the union newspaper, provide legal counsel, and actively lobby at national and state levels.

AFL-CIO

The American Federation of Labor and Congress of Industrial Organizations (AFL-CIO) is the central trade union federation for the United States. It represents the interest of labor and its member national unions at the highest level. The federation engages in no collective bargaining; however, it provides the means through which the member unions can cooperate to pursue common objectives and attempt to resolve internal problems faced by organized labor. The federation is financed by its member national unions and is governed by a national convention which meets every two years.

As shown in Figure 14-4 the structure of the AFL-CIO is complex. The federation has central bodies in all fifty states. In addition, national unions can affiliate with one or more of the trade and industrial departments. These departments seek to promote the interests of specific groups of workers who are

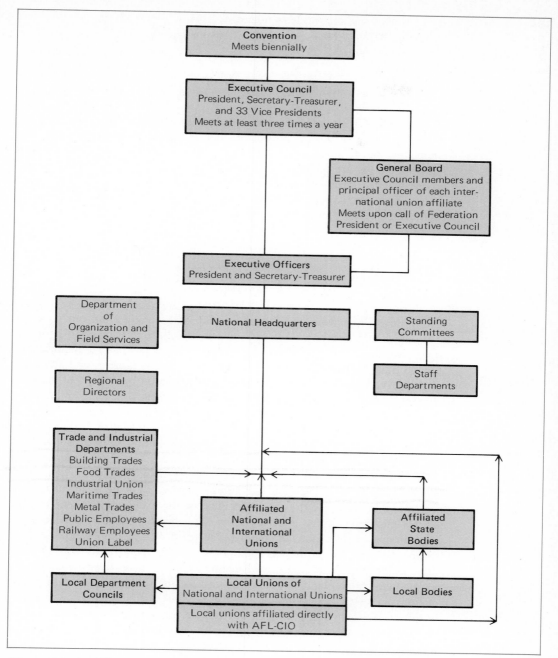

Figure 14–4. **The structure of the AFL-CIO. (Source: Bureau of Labor Statistics,** *Directory of National Unions and Employee Associations.***)**

in different unions but who have common interests. Among the federation's major activities are:

1. Improving the image of organized labor
2. Extensive lobbying in behalf of labor interests
3. Political education through COPE (Committee on Political Education)
4. Resolving disputes between national unions
5. Policing internal affairs of member unions

The AFL-CIO is a loosely knit organization of some 108 national unions. It has little formal power or control. The member national unions remain completely autonomous and decide their own policies and programs. Not all national unions are members of the federation. In fact, one of the largest unions is not a member; the Teamsters were expelled in 1957. The affiliated unions, however, do represent approximately 17,076,000 workers, or about 75 percent of all union members in the United States.[23]

ESTABLISHING THE COLLECTIVE BARGAINING RELATIONSHIP

The primary law governing the relationship of companies and unions is the National Labor Relations Act, as amended. Collective bargaining is one of the keystones of the Act. Section 1 of the Act declares that the policy of the United States is to be carried out "by encouraging the practice and procedure of collective bargaining and by protecting the exercise by workers of full freedom of association, self-organization, and designation of representatives of their own choosing, for the purpose of negotiating the terms and conditions of their employment or other mutual aid or protection."

As defined by the Act, **collective bargaining** requires an employer and the representative of its employees to meet at reasonable times, to confer in good faith about certain matters, and to put into writing any agreement reached if requested by either party. The Act further provides that the designated or selected representative of the employees shall be the exclusive representative for all the employees in the unit for purposes of collective bargaining. A **bargaining unit** consists of a group of employees recognized by an employer or certified by an administrative agency as appropriate for representation by a labor organization for purposes of collective bargaining. A unit may cover the employees in one plant of an employer, or it may cover employees in two or more plants of the same employer. Although the Act requires the representative to be selected by the employees, it does not require any particular procedure to be used so long as the choice clearly reflects the desire of the majority of the employees in the bargaining unit. The employee representative is normally chosen in a secret election conducted by the National Labor Relations Board (NLRB). The series of events that typically transpires when a union desires to become the bargaining representative may be seen in Figure 14–5. As you can

---

[23]Daniel Quinn Mills, *Labor-Management Relations*, 2nd edition (New York: McGraw-Hill Book Company, 1982): 219.

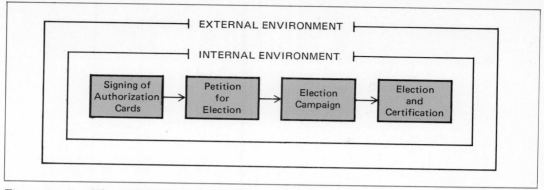

Figure 14–5. **The steps that lead to becoming a bargaining unit.**

see, there are external and internal factors which can affect the process. The primary external factors include government legislation and the union, while the prevailing organization climate can affect the internal environment.

Signing Authorization Cards

The first prerequisite to becoming a recognized bargaining unit is to determine if there is a sufficient amount of interest. Evidence of this interest is sufficiently expressed when at least 30 percent of the employees in a work group sign an **authorization card**. This card includes a statement that the individual desires a particular union to bargain for him or her. (Figure 14–6 gives an example of an authorization card used by the International Association of Machinists.) However, most union organizers will not press the issue further unless at least 50 percent of the workers in the group sign the cards.

Petition for Election

After at least 30 percent of the workers have signed authorization cards, a petition for an election may be made to the appropriate Regional Office of the NLRB. Once the petition has been received, the NLRB must conduct an investigation to determine the following:

1. Whether the Board has jurisdiction to conduct an election
2. Whether there is a sufficient showing of employee interest to justify an election
3. Whether a question of representation exists (for example, the employee representative has demanded recognition which has been denied by the employer)
4. Whether the election includes appropriate employees in the unit (for instance, the Board is prohibited from including plant guards in the same unit with the other employees)

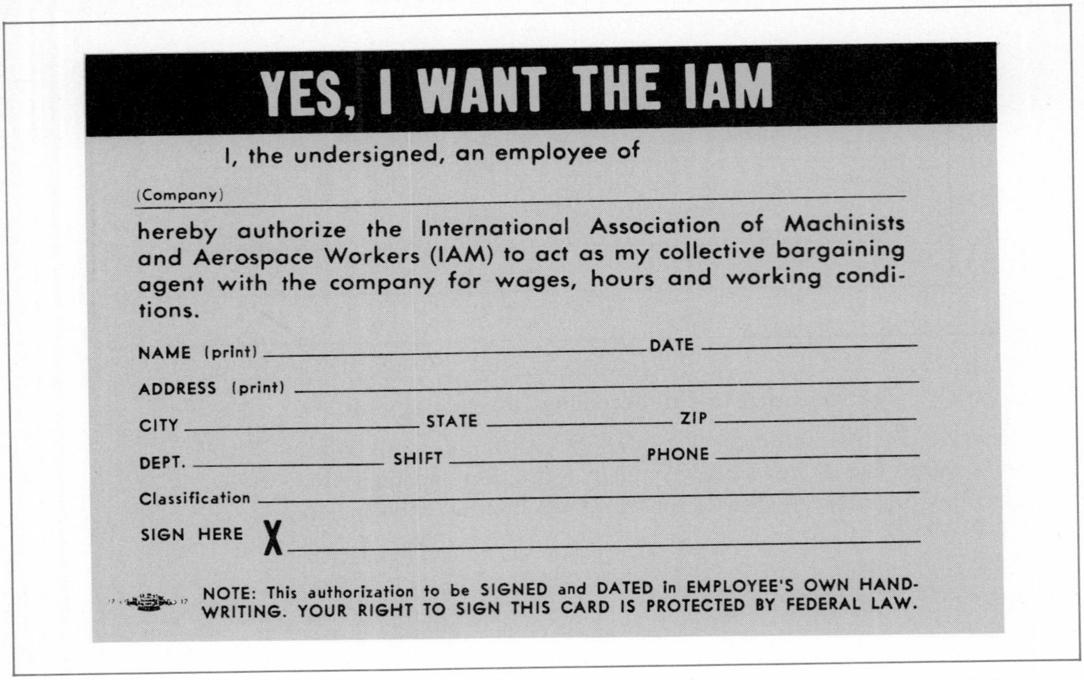

YES, I WANT THE IAM

I, the undersigned, an employee of

(Company) _____

hereby authorize the International Association of Machinists and Aerospace Workers (IAM) to act as my collective bargaining agent with the company for wages, hours and working conditions.

NAME (print) _____ DATE _____

ADDRESS (print) _____

CITY _____ STATE _____ ZIP _____

DEPT. _____ SHIFT _____ PHONE _____

Classification _____

SIGN HERE **X** _____

NOTE: This authorization to be SIGNED and DATED in EMPLOYEE'S OWN HANDWRITING. YOUR RIGHT TO SIGN THIS CARD IS PROTECTED BY FEDERAL LAW.

Figure 14–6. An authorization card. (Source: The International Association of Machinists and Aerospace Workers.)

5. Whether the representative named in the petition is qualified (for example, a supervisor or any other management representative may not be an employee representative)

6. Whether there are any barriers to an election in the form of existing contracts or prior elections held within the past twelve months.[24]

Assuming that the above conditions are met, the NLRB will ordinarily direct that an election be held within thirty days. Election details are left largely to the Regional Director. At this time, management is prohibited from making unusual concessions or promises which would encourage workers to remain nonunion.

Campaign

Once the election has been ordered, both the union and management will likely make strong attempts to promote their causes. Unions will continue to encourage workers to join the union. Management may begin a campaign to tell workers the benefits of remaining nonunion. Theoretically, both the union

[24]A Guide to Basic Law and Procedures under the National Labor Relations Act (Washington, D.C.: U.S. Government Printing Office, 1976), pp. 11–12.

and management are permitted to tell their stories without interference from the other side. It is the obligation of the NLRB to monitor the process and keep illegal activities from occurring. At times, the campaign becomes quite intense. An election will be set aside if it was accompanied by conduct that the NLRB considers to have interfered with the employee's freedom of choice. Examples of such conduct are:

- An employer or a union threatening loss of jobs or benefits to influence employees' votes or union activities
- An employer or a union misstating important facts in the election campaign when the other party does not have a chance to reply
- Either an employer or a union inciting racial or religious prejudice by inflammatory campaign appeals
- An employer firing employees to discourage or encourage their union activities or a union causing an employer to take such an action
- An employer or a union making campaign speeches to assembled groups of employees on company time within the twenty-four hour period before an election

Election and Certification

The NLRB monitors the secret ballot election on the date set. NLRB representatives are responsible, first, for seeing that only eligible employees vote and, second, for counting the votes. Where a valid election is held, the Board will issue a certification of the results to the participants. If a union has been chosen by a majority of the employees voting in the bargaining unit, it will receive a certificate showing that it is the official bargaining representative of the employees in the unit.

UNION STRATEGIES IN BARGAINING-UNIT RECOGNITION

Unions use various strategies to obtain recognition by management. The key factor that unions have in their favor is that they generally make the first move. This places management in the position of having to react to union maneuvers. The search for potential firms to organize is a continuous, ongoing effort conducted by union leaders. To begin a drive, unions often look for festering wounds. Union organizers recognize that if management's house is in order, the firm will be extremely difficult to organize. Some indications of a firm that is ripe for organizing include:

- A history of unjustified and arbitrary management decisions
- Compensation below the industry average
- Lack of concern for the welfare of the firm's employees

The union does not normally look at isolated conditions of employee unrest. Rather, it attempts to locate general patterns of employee dissatisfaction. Whatever the case, the union will probably not make a major attempt at organizing unless it feels that there is a good chance for success.

The union may take numerous approaches in getting authorization cards signed. One effective technique is to first identify workers who are not only dissatisfied, but who are also influential in the firm's informal organization. These individuals can assist the organizers in developing an effective organizing campaign. Information is obtained through the grapevine regarding such facts as who was hired, who was fired, and management mistakes in general. Such information is beneficial to union organizers as they approach company employees. Statements such as this are common: "I hear Bill Adams was fired today. Understand he was a good old boy and well liked. No way that would have happened if you had a union."

Ultimately, the union must abandon its secret activities. Sooner or later, management will discover the organization attempt. At this point, union organizers may station themselves and other supporters at company entrances and pass out "throwsheets" or campaign literature proclaiming the benefits of joining the union and emphasizing the weaknesses of management. They will talk to anyone who will listen in their attempt to identify union sympathizers.

Employees who sign an authorization card are then encouraged to convince their friends to sign also. It becomes a mushrooming effort. Often a sufficient number of authorization cards have been signed before management has time to react effectively.

Union efforts continue even after the election petition has been approved by the NLRB. Every attempt is made by the organizers to involve as many workers from the firm as possible. The outside organizers would like to take a backseat and let company employees convince their peers to join the union. Peer pressure typically has much more effect in convincing a person to join a union than outside influence can, for peers are the individuals who are keenly aware of the problems of the firm.

SUMMARY

Since the turn of the century, no single factor has exerted more influence upon human resources management than organized labor. Through the process of collective bargaining, organized labor has established patterns of employee-management relations affecting both unionized companies and those which strive to maintain nonunion status. Wage levels, benefits, and working conditions for millions of employees now reflect decisions made jointly by unions and management.

In order to accomplish objectives, most unions recognize that they must strive to increase their size and power. The reasons individuals join unions are many and varied and they tend to change over time. They may involve dissatisfaction with management, a social outlet, a need for avenues of leadership, forced unionization, and social pressure from peers.

The labor movement has taken on a multilevel organizational structure over time. This complex of organizations ranges all the way from local unions to the principal federation, the AFL-CIO. Each level has its own government or way of managing its operations. Many unions have intermediate levels between their national and local levels.

Collective bargaining requires an employer and the representative of its employees to meet at reasonable times, to confer in good faith about certain matters, and to put into writing any agreement reached if requested by either party. The series of events that typically transpires when a union desires to become the bargaining representative includes: (1) signing of authorization cards, (2) petition for election, (3) election campaign, and (4) election and certification. The external environment and internal environment both impact this process.

Questions for Review

1. Describe the development of the labor movement in the United States.

2. List the unfair labor practices that were prohibited by management in the Wagner Act. _NLRA 1935 rt to org + collectively bargain_

3. What union actions were prohibited under the Taft-Hartley Act? _Revised NLRA, Prohibit closed shop, emps. may decertify. Emps._

4. In what way does unionization of the public sector differ from unionization of the private sector? _general labor leg. doesn't effect 1962 executive order: can have unions, can't strike vs. U.S. gov't_

5. Why would unions strive for continued growth and power? Discuss.

6. What are the primary reasons that employees join labor unions?

7. Explain the structure of the AFL-CIO.

8. What steps must a union take in attempting to form a bargaining unit? Briefly describe each step.

9. Identify and describe various strategies that unions often use in gaining bargaining unit recognition.

Terms for Review

Conspiracy _2 or more persons + rts of others_
Injunction _↓ union growth_
Yellow dog contract _at time of empl. union membership_
American Federation of Labor _1886 S. Gompers from Nobe order of Kn of L._
National Labor Relations Board _NLRA or Wagner act created._
Congress of Industrial Organizations _1938 splt off_
Right to work _1947 clause of Taft Hartley or LMRA._
Committee on Political Education _part of AFL-CIO_

Local union
Craft union
Industrial union
National union
Collective bargaining _empl. + empl. rep — reasonable times, confer, writing_
Bargaining unit _group of emps rec by emp or act._
Authorization card _bay agency to rep. employes_

★ elections, + prevent unfair

Jerry Sharplin eagerly drove his new company pickup onto the construction site. He had just been assigned by his employer, Lurgi-Knost Construction Company, to supervise a crew of sixteen equipment operators, oilers, and mechanics. This was the first unionized crew Jerry had supervised. As he approached his work area, he noticed one of the "cherry pickers" (a type of mobile crane with an extendable boom) standing idle with the operator beside it. Jerry pulled up beside the operator and said, "What's going on here?"

"Out of gas," the operator said.

"Well, go and get some," Jerry said.

The operator reached to get his thermos jug out of the tool box on the side of the crane and said, "The oiler's on break right now. He'll be back in a few minutes."

Jerry remembered that he had a five gallon can of gasoline in the back of his pickup. So he quickly got the gasoline, climbed on the cherry picker, and started to pour it into the gas tank. As he did, he heard the other machines shutting down in unison. He looked around and saw all the other operators climbing down from their equipment and standing to watch him pour the gasoline. A moment later, he saw the union steward approaching.

Questions

1. Why did all the operators shut down their machines?

2. If you were Jerry, what would you do now? Explain.

In late 1982, a vigorous union organizing campaign was underway at Dodge Tube Company in Rochester, North Carolina. The management at Dodge was strongly anti-union and made no bones about it. Roger Verdon was a general foreman at Dodge, with the responsibility for four supervisors and about eighty machine operators and helpers. Roger had become increasingly incensed as the union's organizing attempts became more apparent.

At first, fliers and other promotional literature had been handed out at the plant gates. There had been an increasing number of complaints and Roger felt that many of them were caused by the union organizing activity. The workers in general had become more belligerent, Roger thought, and he saw more and more secret communication. Workers who had been his friends before seemed to have pulled away. While they were not unfriendly, they typically limited their conversation with him to official matters.

Roger felt that Dodge was a good employer and treated its people fairly. Discipline was administered by supervisors on the spot. Helpers were paid minimum wage, but few stayed in that position for very long. Most helpers were either fired or promoted to machine operator within about six months. The machine operators were placed into grade 1, 2, or 3 at the discretion of the supervisor. Supervisors were encouraged to base pay grade assignments only upon proficiency in doing the job. Most of the supervisors were required to participate in the company's management training program. The ones who were not college graduates were required to complete a correspondence course in management from the University of Maryland during their first six months as a supervisor.

The company had an aggressive health and safety program. Workers in noisy areas were required to wear ear plugs and a worker who failed to do so was immediately fired. The same was true of safety glasses in areas involving grinding, drilling, or chipping. The workers in and around the tube cleaning area were required to wear respirators after an OSHA inspector cited the company for the amount of particulate matter in the air.

One day in early December, Roger observed what he considered to be the "last straw." He saw a worker from another part of the plant walking through his area handing out cards to the workers. Bob asked to see one of the cards and saw that it was a union authorization card. He decided to have a meeting with his supervisors.

Questions

1. What factors could have produced unionizing activity?

2. What can Roger do about it?

Chapter Objectives

1. Explain the collective bargaining process.
2. Describe what is involved as unions and management prepare for negotiation.
3. Name and define the basic topics that are included in virtually all labor agreements.
4. Relate the typical procedure that is involved as union and management attempt to negotiate a new labor agreement.
5. Identify the means through which breakdowns in negotiations may be overcome.
6. Describe current trends in collective bargaining.

Chapter 15 _____

Collective Bargaining

Robert Billup, president of Surefine Productions, was angry and disappointed. He had just been informed by the NLRB that a majority of his employees had voted to have the union represent them. He looked at the personnel manager, Max Lewis, and said: "I don't know what to do. The union will demand so much we can't be competitive." Max replied: "Don't forget, Mr. Billup, just because the union has won the right to be represented doesn't mean that we have to agree to all their terms. I'm sure we can negotiate a good contract."

We saw in the previous chapter how a union gains the right to act as the bargaining representative for a group of employees. But, as Max Lewis told Mr. Billup, the mere fact that a union has gained this right does not mean that an unfavorable union-management agreement will automatically be forthcoming. The process through which union and management negotiators reach a contractual agreement is referred to as collective bargaining. The purpose of this chapter is to show you the many factors involved in the collective bargaining process.

THE COLLECTIVE BARGAINING PROCESS

Diversity is probably the key characteristic of collective bargaining in the United States. There is no precise format regarding what to do or how to do it. A generalized collective bargaining process model may be seen in Figure 15–1. As you can see, the external and internal environmental factors influence the process. For instance, the form of bargaining structure that exists between the union and the company can affect how collective bargaining is conducted. The four major types of structure are: (1) one company dealing with a single union, (2) several companies dealing with a single union, (3) several unions dealing with a single company, and (4) several companies dealing with several unions. Although most contract bargaining is of the first type, one can easily envision how the process could become quite complicated when several companies and unions are involved.

Another environmental factor influencing collective bargaining is the type of union-management relationship which exists. Sloane and Witney listed five types which generally cover the spectrum.[1] They are:

1. *Conflict.* Each challenges the other's actions and motivation; cooperation is nonexistent; union militancy is present.

2. *Armed truce.* Each views the other as antagonistic, but tries to avoid head-on conflict; strict interpretation of bargaining obligations and contract interpretations.

3. *Power bargaining.* Management accepts the union; each side tries to gain advantage from the other.

4. *Accommodation.* Each side tolerates the other in a live and let live atmosphere, and attempts to reduce conflict without eliminating it.

5. *Cooperation.* Each side accepts the other and works together to resolve personnel and production problems as they occur.

Depending upon which of the above types of relationship exists, the collective bargaining process may be relatively simple or it may be a long, tense experience for both parties.

[1]Arthur A. Sloane and Fred Witney, *Labor Relations* (Englewood Cliffs, N.J.: Prentice-Hall, Inc., 1967), pp. 27–31.

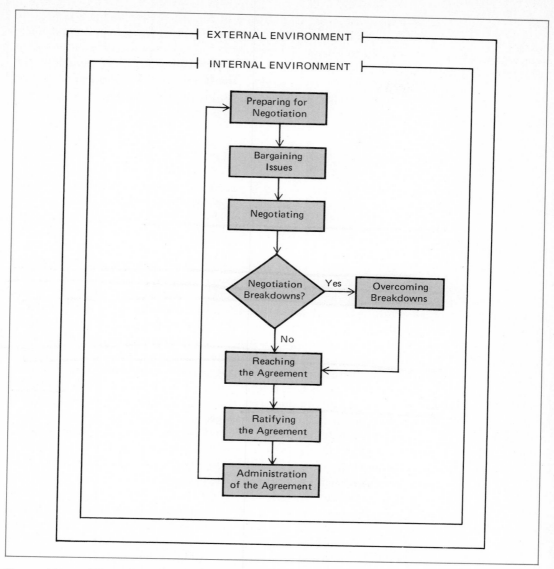

Figure 15–1. **The collective bargaining process.**

Considering both the external and internal factors, the first step in the collective bargaining process is preparing for negotiations. This is often an extensive and ongoing process for both union and management. Issues which will be negotiated are determined. Negotiating involves the two sides attempting to decide upon a mutually acceptable contract. But, at times breakdowns in negotiations occur. Both labor and management have at their disposal tools which can be used to convince the other side to accept their view. Eventually, however, management and the union reach an agreement that defines the rules of the game for labor and management to abide by for the duration of the contract. The next steps consists of the union membership ratifying the agreement. You should also note that there is a feedback loop from administration of the agreement to preparing for negotiations (see Figure 15–1). In many instances, preparing for the next negotiations begins virtually from the time the present contract is ratified. The steps depicted in this collective bargaining process model form the basic outline for the remainder of the chapter.

PREPARING FOR NEGOTIATIONS

Because of the complex issues facing labor and management today, careful advance preparations must be made before any formal negotiations begin. The duration of a typical labor agreement is three years. Since the last signing, both sides may have discovered a number of issues that need to be added, deleted, or modified.

Bargaining issues can be divided into three categories: mandatory, permissive, and prohibited. **Mandatory issues** are those which fall within the definition of wages, hours, and other terms and conditions of employment (see Table 15–1.) These are issues that generally have an immediate and direct effect on the workers' jobs. A refusal to bargain in these areas could lead to an unfair labor practice charge. **Permissive** or **voluntary issues** are those which may be raised, but neither side may insist that they be bargained over. For example, the union may want to bargain over health benefits for retired workers or union participation in establishing company pricing policies. **Prohibited issues** are those that are outlawed, such as the closed shop or demands that the employer use only union-produced goods.

The union must constantly gather information regarding membership dissatisfaction. The union steward is normally in the best position to gather this data. Because stewards are elected by their peers, they must be well informed regarding union members' attitudes. The union steward constantly funnels information up through the union's chain of command where the data are compiled and analyzed. Union leadership attempts to uncover any areas of dissatisfaction because the general union membership must approve any agreement before it becomes final. It would be foolish for union leaders to demand management concessions and have the members reject their proposals. Union leaders will lose their positions if the demands they make of management do not represent the desires of the general membership.

Management also spends long hours working in preparation for negotiations. A model which presents the many interrelated tasks that need to be accomplished is presented in Figure 15–2. The firm in this illustration allows twenty-two weeks to prepare for negotiations. All facets of the current contract are considered. Management also studies the present contract to determine if it contains flaws that should be corrected.

A considerable amount of useful information with which to develop a plan of action may be obtained from first-line supervisors. There are the indi-

Table 15–1. Mandatory issues for bargaining

Wages

Hours

Discharge

Arbitration

Paid holidays

Paid vacations

Duration of agreement

Grievance procedure

Layoff plan

Reinstatement of economic strikers

Change of payment from hourly base to salary base

Union security and checkoff of dues

Work rules

Merit wage increase

Work schedule

Lunch periods

Rest periods

Pension plan

Retirement age

Bonus payments

Cancellation of seniority upon relocation of plant

Discounts on company products

Shift differentials

Contract clause providing for supervisors keeping seniority in unit

Procedures for income tax withholding

Severance pay

Nondiscriminary hiring hall

Plant rules

Safety

Prohibition against supervisor doing unit work

Superseniority for union stewards

Partial plant closing

Hunting on employer's forest reserve where previously granted

Plant closedown and relocation

Change in operations resulting in reclassifying workers from incentive to straight time, or cut work force, or installation of cost saving machinery

Price of meals provided by company

Group insurance—health, accident, life

Promotions

Seniority

Layoffs

Transfers

Work assignments and transfers

No-strike clause

Piece rates

Stock purchase plan

Workloads

Change of employee status to independent contractors

Motor carrier—union agreement providing that carriers use own equipment before leasing outside equipment

Overtime pay

Agency shop

Sick leave

Employer's insistence on clause giving arbitrator right to enforce award

Management rights clause

Plant closing

Job posting procedures

Plant reopening

Employee physical examination

Bargaining over "bar list"

Truck rentals—minimum rental to be paid by carriers to employee-owned vehicles

Musician price lists

Arrangement for negotiation

Change in insurance carrier and benefits

Profit sharing plan

Company houses

Subcontracting

Discriminatory racial policies

Production ceiling imposed by union

Most favored nation clause

Source: Reed Richardson, "Positive Collective Bargaining," Chapter 7.5 of *ASPA Handbook of Personnel and Industrial Relations*, copyright © 1979 by The Bureau of National Affairs, Inc., Washington, D.C., pp. 7–120, 121. Reprinted by permission.

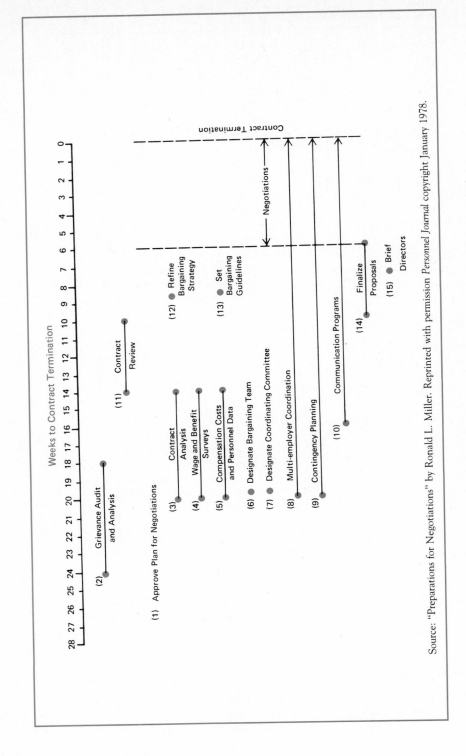

Figure 15–2.   An example of how a company may prepare for negotiations.

Source: "Preparations for Negotiations" by Ronald L. Miller. Reprinted with permission *Personnel Journal* copyright January 1978.

viduals who must administer the labor agreement on a day-to-day basis. They must live with any error that management makes in negotiating the contract. An alert first-line supervisor is also able to inform upper management of the demands unions may make in future negotiating efforts.

Management also attempts to obtain information periodically regarding the attitudes of the workforce. Surveys are often administered to workers on a regular basis to determine their feelings toward their jobs and job environment. When union and management representatives sit down at the bargaining table, both sides likely know a great deal about employees' attitudes.

Another part of actual preparation for negotiations involves identifying various positions that both union and management will take as the negotiations progress. Each takes an initial position representing "Utopia"—the conditions union or management would prefer. It is likely that the two sides will determine an absolute limit to their offers or demands before a breakdown in negotiations occurs. Preparations for negotiations include considerable detailed planning because clear minds often do not prevail during the heat of negotiations.

Finally, a major consideration in preparing for negotiations is the creation of the bargaining teams. The make-up of the management bargaining team is usually dependent upon the type of firm and its size. Normally, bargaining is conducted by labor relations specialists with the advice and assistance of operating managers. In some instances top executives are directly involved, particularly in smaller firms. Larger companies utilize staff specialists (a personnel manager or industrial relations executive), managers of principal operating divisions, and in some cases an outside consultant such as a labor attorney.

The responsibility for conducting negotiations for the union is usually entrusted to union officers. At the local level, the bargaining committee will normally be supplemented by rank-and-file members elected specifically for this purpose. In addition, the national union will often send a representative to act in an advisory capacity or even participate directly in the bargaining sessions. The real task of the union negotiating team is to develop and obtain solutions to the problems raised by the union's membership.

BARGAINING ISSUES

The collective bargaining agreement that is to be negotiated by the union and the employer is usually a detailed and complicated document. Each agreement

"Try to work the first three to five years in operating departments (production, engineering, sales, and accounting) to learn what the people really do and how the organization functions."

S.G.F. De Chant, Personnel Director
Georgia-Pacific Corporation

Art E. Hobbs
Vice President, Employee Relations/
Administration
E-Systems, Inc.

In 1970, Art Hobbs graduated from the University of Texas at Arlington with a degree in business management. Twelve years later he was named vice president, employee relations/administration for E-Systems, Inc., Greenville Division. Art's meteoric rise in the field of human resources management is a tribute to his pursuit of excellence and the skillful execution of a professional career plan. His first job upon graduation was with Texas Power and Light Company as a field account manager. In this position, he was placed in various assignments of increasing responsibility in the area of field accounting. While with TP&L, Art received training in all facets of district level operations including personnel, accounting, and marketing. That initial training continues to have a major impact on his career. In 1973 he joined Frito-Lay, Inc. as a training specialist and was quickly recognized for his overall grasp of the personnel function. Less than a year later, Art was promoted to personnel manager for the Lubbock, Texas and Denver, Colorado operations. Early in 1978, Mr. Hobbs returned to the Dallas headquarters of Frito-Lay as employee relations manager and, later, as the manager of Management Institute. In this position he was responsible for developing and implementing a centralized "Institute" approach to management skills training.

When the position of director, employee relations became open at E-Systems, Inc., Art was asked to apply. He did so, and was offered the position which he accepted in late 1979. In that capacity he was accountable for all employee relations functions including staffing, compensation, benefits, administrative services, labor relations, EEO, and training/management development. One year later Art was promoted to director of administration where his responsibility was expanded to include security and public relations in addition to employee relations. In September of 1982, Mr. Hobbs was named vice president, employee relations/administration.

is unique and there is no standard or universal model. In spite of the dissimilarity, there are certain topics which are included in virtually all labor agreements. These include recognition, management rights, union security, compensation and benefits, grievance procedure, employee security, and job-related factors.

Recognition

This section usually appears at the beginning of the labor agreement. Its purpose is to identify the union which is recognized as the bargaining represent-

When asked to describe a major problem he had encountered in the area of personnel and how he ultimately resolved it, Art replied, "For many years, the working relationship between organized labor and management at the Greenville Division of E-Systems was best described as adversarial. During previous contract negotiations, the adversary, or win-lose approach, had resulted in an extended strike, the results of which have lingered on to the present time. Day-to-day activity involving labor and management was characterized by one-upmanship and very little true problem solving was achieved. I developed a pro-active labor relations program emphasizing problem prevention rather than reaction. Some specific elements of this program include:

- Building a responsible relationship with union representatives.
- Holding regular meetings with union officials to discuss issues and concerns before they become grievance problems.
- Increasing "floor time" for labor relations representatives.
- Striving for win-win solutions to problems.
- Orientation and training for supervisors on how to administer the day-to-day aspects of the labor agreement.

- Communicating with supervisors/ managers on a regular basis regarding contract interpretation, grievance settlements, etc.
- Administering a new employee orientation program with a special section on how to resolve problems, questions, and concerns."

Art notes that as a result of implementing this new pro-active labor relations program, several positive results have been achieved. These results include: reduced number of grievances, reduced number of arbitrations, reduced time spent by company and union representatives on grievances, a new labor agreement negotiated with no strike vote taken, and an improved working climate among supervisors and the bargaining unit.

While new challenges lie ahead, Art takes great pride in his accomplishments in the field of human resources management. "My only regret," he says, "is that I did not recognize my interest in Personnel while in college. But, there were not that many personnel courses available while I was in school. Today's graduates have a much better opportunity to be exposed to the advantages of a major in personnel and human resources management."

---

ative and to describe the bargaining unit, that is, the employees for whom the union speaks. A typical recognition section might read, "The XYZ Company recognizes the ABC Union as the sole and exclusive representative of the company's employees for the purpose of collective bargaining with regard to wages, hours, and other conditions of employment."

Management Rights

A section which is often but not always placed into the labor agreement spells out the rights of management. If it is excluded, management may reason that it retains control of all topics not described as bargainable in the contract. The precise content of the management rights section will vary by industry, company, and union. When included, **management rights** generally involve:

1. Freedom to select the business objectives of the company
2. Freedom to determine the uses to which the material assets of the enterprise will be devoted
3. Power to discipline for cause[2]

In a brochure it publishes for all its first-line supervisors, Southwestern Bell describes management's rights when dealing with the union. The brochure includes the following:

> You should remember that management has all such rights except those restricted by law or by contract with the union. You either make these decisions or carry them out through contact with your people. Some examples of these decisions and actions are:
>
> - To determine what work is to be done and where, when, and how it is to be done
> - To determine the number of employees who will do the work
> - To supervise and instruct employees in doing the work
> - To correct employees whose work performance or personal conduct fails to meet reasonable standards. This includes administering discipline
> - To recommend hiring, dismissing, upgrading, or downgrading employees
> - To recommend employees for promotion to management[3]

Union Security

Union security is typically the first item negotiated in a collective bargaining agreement. There are several forms of union recognition. One of the main factors that will determine the type of recognition is whether the firm or bargaining unit is located in a right-to-work state. Some primary types of union security are discussed below.

Closed Shop. Under a **closed shop** arrangement union membership is a prerequisite for employment. Such arrangements are prohibited by the Taft-Hartley Act.

Union Shop. As mentioned in the previous chapter, a **union shop** requires all employees to become members of the union within a specified time after being hired (usually thirty days) or after a new union shop provision has been negotiated. They must remain members of the union as a condition of employ-

[2]Edwin F. Beal and James P. Begin, *The Practice of Collective Bargaining,* 6th edition (Homewood, IL: Richard D. Irwin, Inc., 1982): 295–298 (hereafter cited as *Collective Bargaining*).
[3]*Management/Employee/Union Relations,* (Dallas: Southwestern Bell Telephone Company, December 1971), p. 3.

ment. The union shop is generally legal in the United States except in right-to-work states.

Maintenance of Membership Shop. Employees who are members of the union at the time the labor agreement is signed, or who later voluntarily join, must continue their memberships until the termination of the agreement, as a condition of employment. This form of recognition is also prohibited in most right-to-work states and is rarely utilized now.

Agency Shop. When an **agency shop** exists, employees are not required to join the union, However, the labor agreement requires that as a condition of employment, each nonunion member of the bargaining unit must "pay the union the equivalent of initiation fees and dues as a kind of tax, or service charge, in return for the union acting as the bargaining agent."[4] The agency shop is outlawed in most right-to-work states.

Exclusive Bargaining Shop. Thirteen of the twenty right-to-work states allow only exclusive bargaining shop provisions. Under this form of recognition, the company is legally bound to deal with the union that has achieved recognition, but employees are not obligated to join or maintain membership in the union.

Open Shop. A closed shop describes the absence of security rather than its presence. The open shop, strictly defined, is open on equal terms to union members and nonmembers. If members are less than the majority, no collective bargaining occurs and no contract is signed. The shop or organization is nonunion.

Another type of security that unions attempt to achieve is the checkoff of dues. A checkoff agreement may be used in addition to any of the previously mentioned "shop" agreements. When the **checkoff of dues** is in effect, the company agrees to withhold union dues from members' checks and to forward the money directly to the union. Because of Taft-Hartley, each union member must sign a statement authorizing this deduction. Dues checkoff is an important factor for the union. It eliminates much of the expense and time-consuming task of collecting dues from each member.

Compensation and Benefits

This section typically constitutes a large portion of most labor agreements. Virtually any item which can affect compensation and benefits may be included. Some of the items frequently covered are:

- *Wage rate schedule:* The base rates to be paid each year of the contract for each job are included in this section. At times, unions are able to include a cost-of-living allowance or escalator clause in the contract in order

[4]*Collective Bargaining,* p. 286.

to protect the purchasing power of employees' earnings. These clauses are generally related to the Consumer Price Index (CPI) prepared by the Bureau of Labor Statistics and they permit a worker's real wage to remain relatively constant.

- *Overtime and premium pay:* Provisions covering hours of work, overtime, and premium pay are included here. Shift differentials may also be stated.

- *Jury pay:* Some firms pay an employee's entire salary when he or she is serving jury duty. Others pay the difference between jury pay and the compensation that would have been earned. The precise procedure covering jury pay is typically stated in the contract.

- *Layoff or severance pay:* The amount that employees in various jobs and/or seniority levels will be paid if they are laid off or terminated is presented in this section.

- *Holidays:* The holidays to be recognized and the amount of pay that a worker will receive if he or she has to work on a holiday are specified here. In addition, the pay procedure is provided for times when a holiday falls on a worker's normal day off.

- *Vacation:* This section spells out the amount of vacation that a person may take, based on seniority. Any restrictions as to when the vacation may be taken will also be stated.

Grievance Procedure

A major portion of the labor agreement is often devoted to the grievance procedure. It contains the means through which employees can voice dissatisfaction with specific management actions. Also included within this section are the procedures for disciplinary action by management and the termination procedure which must be followed. Chapter 16 will be devoted to disciplinary action and the grievance process.

Employee Security

This section of the labor agreement establishes the procedures which cover the security of individual employees. Seniority and grievance handling procedures are the key topics related to employee security.

Seniority involves the amount of time that an employee has worked in various capacities with the firm. Seniority may be company-wide, by division, by department, or by job. Establishment of a seniority policy in the labor agreement is quite important because the person with the most seniority, as defined by the labor agreement, is typically the last to be laid off and the first to be recalled. The seniority system also provides a basis for promotion decisions. Employees with the greatest seniority will likely be considered first for promotions to higher level jobs.

Many of the rules which govern employee actions while at work are included here. Some of the more important factors are company work rules, work standards, and rules related to safety. This section varies depending upon the nature of the industry and the product which is manufactured.

NEGOTIATING

There is no perfect set of steps to take to ensure speedy and mutually acceptable results from negotiations. At best, the parties can attempt to create an atmosphere that will lend itself to productive results. For example, the two negotiating teams usually meet at an agreed upon neutral site, such as a hotel. It is generally important that a favorable relationship be established early so as to avoid "eleventh hour" bargaining.[5] It is equally important that the union and management negotiators strive to develop and maintain clear and open lines of communication. Collective bargaining is a problem-solving activity, so good communications are essential to its success. It is best that negotiations be conducted in the privacy of the conference room, not in the press. If it is felt necessary, joint releases to the press may avoid unnecessary conflict.

The negotiating phase of collective bargaining begins with each side presenting its initial demands. Because a collective bargaining settlement can be expensive for a firm, it is important that the various proposals be "costed out." An example of how one company evaluated a union proposal is shown in Table 15–2. As you see, there were no changes in some instances, while in others the cost increase was substantial.

As the term implies, negotiating suggests a certain amount of give and take. An example of the negotiating for wage increases is provided in Figure 15–3. In this illustration, labor initially demands a $.40 per hour increase. Management counters with an offer of only $.10 per hour. In this example, both labor and management—as expected—reject the other side's demands. Plan B for labor calls for lowering its demand to a $.30 increase per hour. Management counters with an offer of $.20. In this example, both positions are feasible to the other side. We are now in the bargaining-zone for both labor and management. Wages will be agreed upon somewhere between a $.20 and $.30 per hour increase. The exact amount will be determined by the power of the bargaining unit and the skills of the negotiators.

Negotiations at times are similar to a high-stake poker game. A form of power politics tends to evolve. The party with the greater leverage can expect to extract the most concessions. A certain amount of bluffing and raising of the ante also takes place in many negotiations. The ultimate bluff for the union would be when a negotiator says, "If our demands are not met, we are

[5]Eleventh-hour bargaining refers to last minute settlement attempts just prior to the expiration date of an existing agreement. Failure to reach agreement in this manner frequently results in a strike.

Table 15–2. Costing out changes in contract terms

Changes in Costs	Increased Cost
1. Direct payroll—annual	
Straight time earnings—36¢ per hour general increase	
100 employees × 2,080 hours × 36¢	$74,800
Premium earnings—second shift established differential—10¢ per hour	
30 employees × 2,080 hours × 10¢	6,240
Overtime—overtime cost increased by increased straight time rate—average straight time rate increases 39¢	
39¢ × 12,000 overtime hours × .5 overtime rate	2,340
Bonus	None
Other direct payroll cost increases	None
Total increase in direct payroll costs	83,460
2. Added costs directly resulting from higher payroll costs—annual F.I.C.A.—5.85% times increase in average straight time earnings below $9,000 annual	
100 employees × 36¢ × 5.85% × 2,080 hours	4,380.48
Federal and state unemployment insurance tax	
number of employees × 4,200 × 2.5% tax rate	No change
Workmen's compensation (Total cost or estimate)	No change
Other	No change
Total additional direct payroll costs	4,380.48
3. Nonpayroll costs—annual	
Insurance—company portion	
Health insurance	No change
Dental insurance	None
Eye care	None
Life insurance—added employer contribution $100 per year	
$100 × 100 employees	10,000
Pension costs—fully vested pension reduced from 25 years and age 65 to 20 years and age 62	
Estimated additional cost	52,000
Miscellaneous	
Tuition reimbursements (addition)	600
Service rewards	No change
Suggestion awards (addition)	350
Loss on employee cafeteria	No change
Overtime meals	No change
Cost of parking lots	No change
Company parties	No change
Personal tools	No change
Personal safety equipment (addition)	1,200
Personal wearing apparel	No change
Profit sharing	No change
Other	No change
Total additional nonpayroll costs—annual	64,150

Table 15–2.   (continued)

505

Chapter 15
Collective
Bargaining

Changes in Costs	Increased Cost
4a. Changes in nonwork paid time	
Holidays—2 new holidays added to 6 already in contract	
100 employees × 8 hours × 2 holidays × $3.96 average new wage	6,336
Vacation—new category added—4 weeks (160 hours annual vacation) with 20 or more years service—former top was 3 weeks after 15 years	
Average number of employees affected annually 15 employees × 40 hours × $3.96 average new wage	2,376
Paid lunch time—paid ½ hour lunch time added to contract	
100 employees × ½ hour × 236 days worked yearly × $3.96 average new wage	46,728
Paid wash-up time	None
Coffee breaks	No change
Paid time off for union activity—new 1 hour per week per Shop steward	
10 shop stewards × $4.20 shop steward average new wage × 1 hour × 52 weeks	2,184
Paid sick leave	None
Paid time off over and above worker's compensation paid time	None
Jury service time off—no change	None
Funeral leave time off—no change	None
Paid time off for safety or training—no change	None
Other	None
Total change in hours paid for but not worked—annual	57,624
4b. Financial data derived from costing out (Items 1–4, above)	
Total increase in contract costs	
Item 1 + Item 2 + Item 3	151,990
Average total increase in contract costs per employee payroll hour	
Item 1 + Item 2 + Item 3 ÷ 2,080 hours	.73
Average total increase in direct payroll costs per employee hour	
Item 1 + Item 2 ÷ 2,080 hours ÷ 100 employees	.422
Average total increase in nonpayroll costs per payroll hour per employee	
Item 3 ÷ 2,080 hours ÷ 100 employees	.308
Average total increase in nonwork paid time expense per payroll hour per employee	
Item 4 ÷ 100 employees	576.24
Average total increase in direct payroll costs per productive (worked) hour per employee	
Item 1 + Item 2 ÷ 1,888 hours ÷ 100 employees	.49
Average total increase in nonpayroll costs per productive (worked) hour per employee	
Item 3 ÷ 1,888 hours ÷ 100 employees	.34

Source: Reprinted by permission from "Positive Collective Bargaining," by Reed C. Richardson, Chapter 7.5 of ASPA Handbook of Personnel and Industrial Relations, copyright © 1979 by The Bureau of National Affairs, Inc., Washington, D.C.

prepared to strike." Management's version of this bluff would be to threaten a lockout. Each of these tactics will be discussed later. The realities of negotiation are not for the weak of heart.

Even though one side in the negotiating process may appear to possess the greater power, care is often taken to keep the other side from losing face. Negotiators recognize that the balance of power may switch rapidly. By the time the next round of negotiations occurs, the pendulum may be swinging in a different direction. Even if management appears to have the upper hand, minor concessions may be made which will make the labor leader appear to have gained benefits for the union. Management may demand that workers pay for any grease rags that are lost. (Assume that the loss of these rags had become excessive.) In order to obtain labor's agreement to this demand, management may agree to provide new uniforms for the workers if the cost of these uniforms would be much less than the cost of the lost rags. Thus labor leaders, although forced to concede to management's demands, could show their workers that they have obtained concessions from management.

As was previously mentioned, each side likely does not expect to obtain all the demands presented in its first proposal. However, management must remember that if it concedes to a demand from labor, the concession will be quite difficult to reverse in future negotiations. For instance, if management agrees to provide dental benefits, it will be difficult to withdraw these benefits in the next round of negotiations. Labor, on the other hand, can lose a demand and continue to bring it up in the future. In fact, the union does not even expect to receive all of its demands as they are first made. Demands in this category are known as **"beachhead" demands**.

BREAKDOWNS IN NEGOTIATIONS

At times, negotiations may break down even though both labor and management may sincerely want to arrive at an equitable contract settlement. In order to get negotiations moving again, there are several means that may be used to assist in removing these roadblocks. Breakdowns in negotiations can be overcome through third party intervention, union tactics, and management recourses.

Third Party Intervention

Often a person(s) from outside both the union and the organization can intervene to provide assistance when an agreement cannot be reached and a breakdown occurs. At this point there is an impasse. The reasons behind each party's position may be quite rational. Or, the breakdown may be related to emotional disputes which tend to become distorted during the heat of negotiating. Regardless of the cause, something must be done to continue the ne-

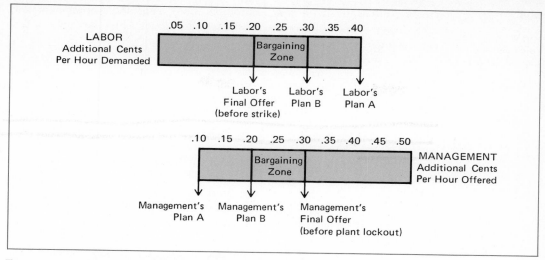

Figure 15–3. **An example of negotiation for a wage increase.**

gotiations. The basic types of third party intervention are mediation and arbitration.

Mediation. **Mediation** is a process whereby a neutral third party enters a labor dispute when a bargaining impasse has occurred. The objective of mediation is to persuade the parties to resume negotiations and reach a private settlement. A mediator has no power to force a settlement, but can help in the search for solutions, make recommendations, and work to open blocked channels of communication. Successful mediation depends to a substantial degree on the tact, diplomacy, patience, and perseverance of the mediator. The mediator's fresh recommendations are often needed to get discussions progressing smoothly again.

Arbitration. **Arbitration** is a process in which a dispute is submitted to an impartial third party to make a binding decision. There are two principal types of union–management disputes: rights cases and interests cases. Those that involve disputes over the interpretation and application of the various provisions of an existing contract are referred to as "rights" arbitration. This type of arbitration is used in settling grievances. Grievance arbitration is common in the United States and will be discussed in Chapter 16. The other type of arbitration, "interest" arbitration, involves disputes over the terms of new or proposed collective bargaining agreements. Interest arbitration has been uncommon in the United States. Unions and employers rarely agree to submit the basic terms of a contract (i.e., wages, hours, and working conditions) to a neutral party for disposition. They prefer to rely on collective bargaining and the threat of economic pressure (i.e., strikes and lockouts) to decide these issues.[6] However, changing circumstances in recent years have generated in-

[6]Raymond A. Smardon, "Arbitration is no Bargain," *Nation's Business* (October 1974): 80–83.

creasing discussion of interest arbitration. Both labor and management may suffer heavy financial losses due to strikes and lockouts which no doubt underlies this increased attention.

Sources of Mediators and Arbitrators

The principal organization involved in mediation efforts, other than the available state and local agencies, is the Federal Mediation and Conciliation Service (FMCS). The FMCS was established as an independent agency by the Taft-Hartley Act in 1947. Either or both parties can seek the assistance of the FMCS, or the agency can offer help should it feel the situation warrants it. Federal law requires that sixty days prior to the expiration of a contract, any party wishing to change the contract must give notice of this intention to the other party. If no agreement has been reached thirty days prior to the expiration date, the FMCS must be notified.

In arbitration, the disputants are free to select any person as their arbitrator so long as they both agree on the selection. Most commonly, however, they make a request for an arbitrator to either the American Arbitration Association (AAA) or the FMCS. The AAA is a non-profit organization with offices in many cities. Both the AAA and the FMCS maintain lists of arbitrators, who are selected on the basis of their own application. Both organizations select only people who can show, through references, experience in labor-management relations and acceptability to both labor and management as neutrals.[7] Because of the complexity of many cases, arbitrators are discovering that a legal background is necessary.

Union Strategies for Overcoming Negotiation Breakdowns

There are times when a union believes that it must revert to extreme measures to exert pressure upon management to agree to its bargaining demands. Strikes and boycotts are the primary means which the union may use to overcome breakdowns in negotiations.

Strikes. When union members refuse to work in order to exert pressure upon management in negotiations, their action is referred to as a **strike**. When a strike is called, the union attempts to exert pressure—resulting in lost customers and lowered revenue—which will force management to submit to labor's terms.

The timing of a strike is important in determining its effectiveness. An excellent time is when business is thriving and the demand for the firm's product or service is expanding. On the other hand, the union might be hard pressed to obtain major concessions from a strike if the firm's sales are down

[7]Donald Austin Woolf, "Arbitration in One Easy Lesson: A Review of Criteria Used in Arbitration Awards," *Personnel 55* (September/October 1978): 76.

and the organization has built up a high inventory. In this instance, the company's welfare would not be severely damaged.

Contrary to many opinions, unions prefer to use the strike only as a last resort. Strikes are extremely expensive not only for the employer, but also for the union and its members. A union's treasury is often depleted when strike benefits are paid to its members during the strike. In addition, members suffer because they are not receiving their normal pay. Strike benefits help, but union members certainly cannot maintain a normal standard of living. Strike benefits, when paid at all, are nominal, perhaps $10 to $30 a week.[8]

Sometimes during negotiations (especially at the beginning) the union may want to strengthen its negotiator's position by taking a strike vote of the membership. The members traditionally give overwhelming approval. This vote does not necessarily mean that there will be a strike, only that the union leaders have the authority to call one if negotiations reach a stalemate. It can put a sense of urgency into efforts to reach an agreement.[9]

Successful passage of a strike vote has additional implications for the union members. Virtually every national union's constitution contains a statement requiring the members to support and participate in a strike if one is called. If a union member fails to comply with this requirement, he or she can be fined. Thus, union members place themselves in jeopardy if they cross a picket line without the consent of the union. Fines may be as high as 100 percent of wages for as long as the union remains outside the company to advise people that the union is on strike and to encourage all people (employees, delivery people, etc.) to support the union.

In a few instances, both sides have agreed to eliminate strikes and send unresolved contract issues to arbitration. The United Steelworkers of America and ten major steel companies agreed in 1973 to negotiate without the threat of strikes. In 1976 National Airlines and the Air Line Employees Association agreed to a no-strike contract when the issues were economically related.

Boycotts. The boycott is another of labor's weapons to encourage management to agree to its demands. A boycott involves an agreement by union members to refuse to use or buy the firm's products. As such, a boycott exerts economic pressure on management. The effect of a boycott is often much longer lasting than a strike. Once shoppers change their buying habits, their behavior will likely continue long after the boycott has been called off. At times, significant pressures can be exerted upon a business when union members, their families, and friends refuse to purchase the firm's products. This is especially true when it is a retail product which is easily identifiable by name. For instance, the boycott against Farrah in the 1970s was effective because the product could easily be associated with the company.

The practice of a union attempting to encourage third parties (i.e., suppliers and customers) to cease doing business with the firm is known as a secondary boycott. This type of boycott was declared illegal by the Taft-Hartley Act.

[8]*Collective Bargaining*, p. 232.
[9]Ibid., pp. 221–222.

Management's Strategies for Overcoming Negotiation Breakdowns

Management also has strategies to encourage unions to reconvene negotiations. One form of action that is somewhat analogous to a strike is called a lockout. In a **lockout,** management temporarily ceases operation of the business. The employees are unable to work and do not get paid. Although the lockout is used rather infrequently, the fear of a lockout may bring labor back to the bargaining table. A lockout is particularly effective when dealing with a weak union, when the union treasury is depleted, or when the business has excessive inventories.

Another tactic that a company has at its disposal, should the union decide to strike, is to keep the firm operating by utilizing management and nonunion personnel in the striking workers' jobs. The type of industry involved has considerable effect on the impact of this maneuver. If the firm is capital intensive, such as a petroleum refinery or a chemical plant, this practice may be quite effective. When the tactic is employed, management will likely attempt to show how production actually increases using nonunion employees. At times, management personnel will actually live in the plant and have food and other necessities delivered to them.

As one might expect, this strategy can also prove expensive and ineffective. In 1978 the United Farm Workers walked out of negotiations with a major food processing firm. The firm decided that it would keep its mushroom farms open by using management personnel to pick the mushrooms. Managers from all levels and from all parts of the United States were sent to the California farms. Every two weeks, another group of managers would replace their counterparts. In addition to their normal salaries, the managers who went to the farms were paid substantial bonuses. Living expenses and transportation costs were also substantial. Costs for this operation became prohibitive. After six weeks, management decided that the tactic was not effective and labor's demands were met.

RATIFYING THE AGREEMENT

Considerable time and effort may be expended before the agreement is ready to be submitted for approval by the rank-and-file members. Even though the labor and management negotiating teams reach an agreement, there is still work to accomplish before it becomes final. The approval process for management is often easier than for labor. The president or chief executive officer is kept up-to-date regarding the progress of negotiations. Any difficulty in obtaining top management's approval will likely be passed rapidly to the negotiators.

However, the approval process can be more difficult for the union. Until receipt of a majority approval of those voting in a ratification election, the proposed agreement is not final. At times, union members reject the proposed agreement and a new round of negotiations must begin. In recent years, approximately ten percent of all tentative settlements have been rejected when presented to the membership. Many of these rejections might not have occurred if union negotiators had been better informed of the desires of the general union membership.

ADMINISTRATION OF
THE AGREEMENT

Negotiating may be likened to the tip of an iceberg as it relates to the total collective bargaining process. It is the visible phase, the part that makes the news. The larger and perhaps more important part of collective bargaining is the administration of the agreement, which is seldom viewed by the public.[10] The agreement establishes the union-management relationship for its effective length. Usually no changes in contract language can be made until the expiration date except by mutual consent. Administering the contract is a day-by-day activity. Ideally, the aim of both management and the union is to make the agreement work to the mutual benefit of all concerned. Often, this is not an easy task. In the daily stress of the work environment, terms of the contract are not always uniformly interpreted as to their application and meaning.

Management is primarily responsible for implementing the agreement which must be communicated to all affected levels. This could include meetings or training sessions not only to point out significant features, but also to provide a clause-by-clause analysis. Supervisors in particular need to know their responsibilities and what to do when disagreements arise. Additionally, managers can be encouraged to notify top management of any contract provisions that are causing problems so that they can be considered when preparing for the next round of negotiations.

In the day-to-day administration of contract provisions, Personnel plays a key role. It gives advice in matters of discipline and works to resolve grievances arising out of the agreement. In addition, it works with line management to establish good working relationships with all employees affected by the terms and conditions of the contract. As a final note, it should be pointed out that when a union is represented in an organization, the role of Personnel tends to change rather significantly. In major corporations in which the large majority of the operative employees are unionized, the personnel department may be organized quite differently. For instance, there may be a vice president of personnel and a vice president of industrial relations. The Bendix Corporation provides an excellent example of this separation of activities by having both a vice president of human resources and a vice president of industrial relations. (See Figures 15–4 and 15–5.) In situations such as this, the vice president of personnel may perform all personnel related tasks with the exception of industrial relations. The vice president of industrial relations would likely

[10]Harold W. Davey, *Contemporary Collective Bargaining*, 3d ed. (Englewood Cliffs, N.J.: Prentice-Hall, Inc., 1972), p. 141.

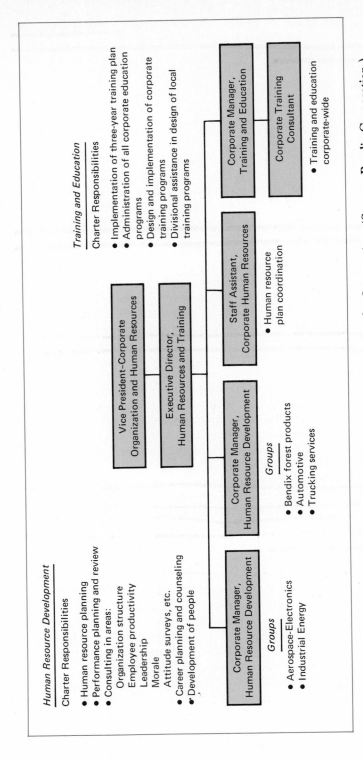

Figure 15–4. The organization of the personnel department at Bendix Corporation. (Source: Bendix Corporation.)

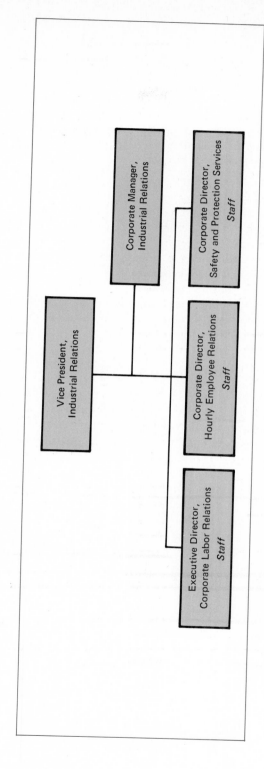

Figure 15–5. The corporate industrial relations department at Bendix Corporation by functional responsibility. (Source: Bendix Corporation.)

deal with union related matter. As one vice president of industrial relations stated:

> My first challenge is, wherever possible, to keep the company union-free and the control of its operations in the hands of corporate management of all levels. Where unions represent our employees, the problem becomes one of negotiating collective bargaining agreements which our company can live with, administering these labor agreements with the company's interests paramount (consistent with good employee relations), and trying to solve all grievances arising under the labor agreement short of their going to arbitration, without giving away the store.

TRENDS IN COLLECTIVE BARGAINING

The future of collective bargaining is, at best, difficult to predict. Many forces will affect the labor-management relationship. Pressures will differ in magnitude and pull at the relationship from diverse directions. The conflicting forces cannot be ignored and both labor and management must be willing to respond in positive and innovative ways to resolve their problems in the decade ahead.

Economic Environment

A factor which pervades all areas of collective bargaining is the changing economic environment. Inflation will probably continue to cause problems for both labor and management. It is difficult for management to forecast costs accurately because wages are often tied to the inflation rate in addition to negotiated flat rate increases. This creates problems for labor, too, because wage gains tend to be eaten away by inflation.

Coupled with the problem of inflation are other problems related to recession and productivity. The 1970–1971 recession was more severe than those of the late 1950s and early 1960s. The recession period of 1974–1976 was the most severe since the depression of the 1930s, and the recession of 1980 was one of the sharpest on record.[11] Recessions cause layoffs, unemployment, bankruptcies, and pressures for economizing. A continuing decline in the rate of productivity growth adversely affects labor's bargaining power. Productivity increased 3.2 percent in 1955 but decreased slightly in 1980.[12] Falling productivity makes it difficult for labor to win increases in purchasing power which, in turn, affects workers' living standards.

 Inflation, recession, and the spectre of productivity declines have shifted labor's interest from income security to job security. Threatened plant closings and the loss of one's job without any expectation of getting it back place tre-

---

[11]Daniel Quinn Mills, *Labor-Management Relations* 2d ed. (New York: McGraw-Hill Book Co., 1982): 577 (hereafter cited as "Mills").
[12]Joseph Krislov and J. Lew Silver, "Current Challenges in Industrial Relations," *Labor Law Journal* (August 1981): 482; and Mills, p. 581.

mendous strains on workers. John L. Lewis once remarked, "bankrupt companies aren't good employers." Recently such terms as "labor concessions," "wage increase moratorium," and "take-back bargaining" have entered negotiation discussions as possible means of preserving jobs.

Labor has fought back. In early 1982 American Motors and the UAW signed a contract which calls for workers to invest certain wage increases and pay for time not worked into a new company product development program. One union official pointed out, "There can be no job security unless AMC can provide consumers with a new line of high quality autos."[13] The workers will also invest all Annual Improvement Factor (AIF) increases, which have been set at 3 percent a year, in the program. In February 1982 Ford Motor Company negotiated an agreement at two of its plants which guarantees lifetime job security to the most senior eighty percent of the hourly employees.[14] A different approach is being taken at General Electric. Thirteen allied unions have squared off against GE in bargaining for a new contract covering 100,000 workers throughout the United States. The unions have staked out job security as their major demand. A union official stated, "At this bargaining table we will be urging protection against job losses from whatever cause — whether the introduction of robots, the transfer of work overseas or to unorganized locations in the U.S., subcontracting of work, the discontinuance of product lines, or other causes."[15]

Union Growth

Although membership in unions and employee associations has increased over the years, the percentage of workers belonging to unions relative to total employment has fallen.[16] Organized labor is going to have to reassess its structure, role, and function if it is going to appeal to the unorganized. To the degree that it is successful, new challenges in collective bargaining will come about.

Occupational and Industrial Change

During the last several decades, major occupational and industrial employment changes have influenced union membership. The heavily unionized industries of earlier years have not grown as fast as the economy in general. Increased employment has occurred, however, in the wholesale and retail trades, finance and insurance, other service industries, and state and local governments. The shift in employment from production of goods to delivery of services has had a significant impact on the occupational structure of the work force. The result

---

[13]*Solidarity* (June 1982): 4–6.
[14]Ibid., p. 6.
[15]Ibid., p. 19.
[16]Sources for discussion in this section and following sections include: Bureau of Labor Statistics, *Directory of National Unions and Employee Associations, 1979* (Washington, D.C.: U.S. Government Printing Office, 1980); U.S. Department of Labor, *Employment and Training Report of the President* (Washington, D.C.: U.S. Government Printing Office, 1980); and Mills.

is a major shift from blue-collar to white-collar occupations, where unionization has been limited in the past. Unions are aggressively working to organize white-collar employees. However, the concerns of this group do not necessarily parallel those of blue-collar workers.

Women

In recent years the participation of women in the nation's labor force has continued to rise. By 1980 more than 45 percent of all adult women were full-time workers and about 42 percent of all full-time workers were women. However, women constituted only 23.5 percent of union membership in 1978. Appeals to women workers must reflect their interests in such areas as equal pay and equal opportunity.

Migration

Recent trends show industry migrating to the South and Southwest sunbelt area. Most of the states in this area have right-to-work laws and the local attitude is historically nonunion. Before collective bargaining can take place, organization must be accomplished and unionization in this area is difficult.

While these are not all of the issues which will influence the future of collective bargaining and the nature of the labor-management relationship, they are at least indicative of what lies ahead. The next decade will challenge the leadership capabilities of both labor and management.

SUMMARY

The process through which union and management negotiators reach a contractual agreement is referred to as collective bargaining. Although there is no precise format, a generalized collective bargaining process may be developed. The external and internal environments impact the process. Depending upon these factors, the process may be relatively simple or it may be a long, tension-filled experience for both parties.

The first step in the collective bargaining process is preparing for negotiations. This is often an extensive and on-going process for both union and management. Issues to be negotiated are determined. Negotiating involves the two sides attempting to decide upon a mutually acceptable contract. But, at times, breakdowns in negotiations occur. Both labor and management have at their disposal tools which can be used to convince the other side to accept their views.

The next step consists of the union membership ratifying the agreement. The labor agreement defines the rules of the game for labor and management to abide by for the duration of the contract. There is also a feedback loop from administration of the agreement to preparing for negotiations. In many instances, preparing for negotiations begins virtually from the time the contract is ratified.

Questions for Review

1. Describe the basic steps involved in the collective bargaining process.

2. Why is it so critical for management to be thoroughly prepared prior to conducting contract negotiations?

3. Why is it said that "at times negotiations are similar to a high-stake poker game"?

4. Define each of the following: (a) management rights, (b) closed shop, (c) union shop, (d) agency shop, (e) maintenance of membership, (f) checkoff dues.

5. What are the primary means through which breakdowns in negotiations may be overcome? Briefly describe each.

6. Describe the role of a personnel manager in a unionized firm.

7. Describe the potential difficulties that might be involved in ratifying the labor agreement?

8. What is involved in the administration of the labor agreement?

Terms for Review

Bargaining issues
Mandatory issues
Permissive issues
Prohibited issues
Management rights
Closed shop
Union shop
Agency shop
Checkoff of dues

Exclusive bargaining shop
Open shop
Seniority
Beachhead demand
Mediation
Arbitration
Strike
Boycott
Lockout

Barbara Washington, the chief union negotiator, was meeting with management on a new contract. The union team had been preparing for this encounter for a long time. Barbara felt that she was on top of the situation. Her only worry was whether the union members would support a strike vote if one were called. Due to the recession there was high unemployment in the area. The members' attitude was one of "We are generally pleased, but get what you can for us." She believed, however, that skillful negotiating could keep the union team from being placed in a position where the threat of a strike would be needed.

In the first session, Barbara's team presented its demands to management. Pay was the main issue, and a 30 percent increase spread over three years was demanded. Management countered with an offer of a 10 percent raise over three years. After some discussion, both sides agreed to reevaluate their positions and meet again in two days.

Barbara met with her negotiating team in private, and it was the consensus that they would decrease the salary demand slightly. They felt that the least they could accept was a 25 percent raise.

At the next meeting, Barbara presented the revised demands to management. They were not well received. Bill Thompson, the director of industrial relations, began by saying: "Our final offer is a 15 percent increase over three years. Business has been down and we have a large backlog of inventory. If you feel that it is in your best interest to strike, go ahead."

Barbara's confidence collapsed. She knew that there was no way that a strike vote could be obtained. Management must have accurately read the mood of the workers. She asked for a recess to review the new proposal.

Questions

1. How important is the threat of a strike to successful union negotiations?

2. What do you recommend that Barbara do when she next confronts management?

Alonzo Alexander, personnel manager for Hyatt Manufacturing, had a problem that he did not know how to handle. His firm was unionized and the relationship between management and the union had generally been good. The firm also had a strong affirmative action program. Hyatt had made major strides in implementing this plan throughout the firm, with the notable exception of the machine department. In this department there were no minority employees.

Alonzo had recommended many blacks and females to the production manager. Some of them had been hired but they never stayed long. In their exit interviews, they often made comments such as the following:

"I just wasn't part of the team. No one would even talk to me."
"They helped one another. But no one would help me."
"I was blamed if I was nearby when something went wrong."

The problem was further complicated by the fact that the union employees were uncooperative. When Alonzo attempted to talk to the workers, he was told, in no uncertain terms, that if he wanted problems, he could keep sending minorities to the department. He knew that if this department shut down because of a strike, the entire company would have to close. Alonzo wanted to maintain the affirmative action program but also knew the impact that a wildcat strike could have on the company.

Questions

1. What is the underlying cause of the problem of Hyatt Manufacturing?

2. How would you suggest that Alonzo deal with this situation? Discuss.

Chapter Objectives

1. Distinguish between discipline and disciplinary action.
2. Identify and describe the steps involved in the disciplinary process.
3. Distinguish between the hot stove rule of discipline and progressive discipline.
4. Name and explain the guidelines that should be used in creating rules.
5. Explain why managers may want to avoid disciplinary action.
6. Explain how grievance handling is typically conducted under a collective bargaining agreement.
7. Describe how grievance handling is conducted for nonunion employees.
8. State how termination conditions may differ when operant employees, executives, managers, or professionals are involved.

Chapter 16 _____

Discipline and the Grievance Process

Bill Morton, a ten-year employee at Ketro Productions, arrived at Personnel to turn in his letter of resignation. He was obviously upset at his supervisor. When personnel manager Robert Noll asked what was wrong, Bill replied: "Yesterday, I made a mistake and set my machine up wrong. It was the first time in years that I've done that. My supervisor chewed me out in front of my friends. I'm not going to take that from anyone."

Bob Halmes, the production supervisor for American Manufacturing, was mad at the world when he arrived for work today. The automobile repairman had not had his car fixed on time the day before so he had had to take a taxi to work this morning. No one was safe around Bob today and it was not the time for Phillip Martin, a member of Local 264, to be caught smoking in an unauthorized area. Without hesitation, Bob said, "You know it's company policy not to smoke in this part of the plant. I don't want to see you around here anymore. You're fired." Just as quickly, Phillip replied, "You can't do that. Our contract calls for three warnings. My steward will hear about this."

The situations described above suggest some of the problems associated with disciplinary action. Bill Morton's supervisor committed an error by disciplining him in front of everyone. Bob Halmes had just been reminded that certain factors can affect his power to fire Phillip Martin. In years past, a supervisor who did not like an employee's behavior often reacted by merely stating, "You're fired." No justification or explanation was required. The worker had little if any recourse other than to pick up his or her final paycheck and leave the company. Today, the manner in which discipline is maintained is often quite different. Workers are better educated and no longer accept the supervisor's disciplinary action as being absolute. Unions also exert considerable influence in the manner in which disciplinary action is administered.

When violations of company policies or rules occur, the firm needs a program to administer disciplinary action. Not only is there a need for a disciplinary program, but a process should also exist to assist employees in appealing disciplinary decisions. Unjustified disciplinary action has contributed to numerous firms losing their nonunion status. It has also resulted in unionized firms having unauthorized wildcat strikes, walkouts, and slowdowns.[1] The effect of these actions can result in unnecessary expense and loss of time.

OBJECTIVES OF DISCIPLINARY ACTION

We all have different impressions of what is meant by the term discipline. As a child, you may have been punished by your parents for something you did wrong. You may have known better, but you did it anyway. Perhaps you thought that your act would go undetected. At other times, you may not have realized that what you did was wrong. On these occasions, disciplinary action may have taught you not to repeat those acts.

Discipline refers to the state of employee self-control and orderly conduct present within an organization. It indicates the development of genuine teamwork. **Disciplinary action** occurs "when standards are maintained by invoking a penalty against an employee who fails to meet them." Effective disciplinary action condemns the employee's wrongful act, not the employee as a person.[2]

In spite of a firm's desire to solve its employee problems in a positive manner, at times it is not possible. A major purpose of disciplinary action is to ensure that employee behavior is consistent with the firm's goals. Rules are established to assist the organization in accomplishing its objectives. When a rule is violated, the effectiveness of the organization is diminished to some degree depending upon the severity of the infraction. For instance, if a worker reports late to work, the loss to the firm may be minimal. However, if a worker

[1]Richard F. Gibson, "Discipline: Search for New Solutions," *Industry Week* 182 (July 15, 1974): 52.
[2]Keith Davis, *Human Behavior at Work* (New York: McGraw-Hill Book Company, 1977), p. 261.

fails to use the safety guard on a machine and becomes severely injured, the loss may be substantial. Supervisors must realize that disciplinary action can be a positive force for the enterprise. The firm benefits from developing and implementing an effective disciplinary action program. Without a healthy state of discipline, or the threat of disciplinary action, the firm's effectiveness may be severely limited.

Disciplinary action can also help the employee become more effective. For example, if a worker is disciplined because of failure to monitor the quality of his or her output, and the quality improves after the disciplinary action, it has been useful in the worker's development. Because of the improved quality, the individual may receive a promotion or pay increase. The individual becomes aware of what is expected and fulfills these requirements. An effective disciplinary program can thus encourage the individual to improve his or her performance.

THE DISCIPLINARY ACTION PROCESS

The disciplinary action process is dynamic and on-going. One person's actions can affect others in the group. For instance, if you were disciplined by one of your teachers in high school, it is likely that this action affected other students when they learned that your mistake would not be tolerated.

The disciplinary action process is shown in Figure 16–1. The external environment affects every area of personnel management. Changes in technology may render a rule inappropriate. At the same time, it may necessitate the establishment of new rules. For instance, a firm may purchase a modern piece of equipment that has new and different maintenance requirements. Laws which affect company policies and rules are also constantly changing. OSHA, for instance, has caused many firms to establish new safety rules. Unions must also be considered as an external factor. Specific punishment for rule violations may be negotiated. For instance, the union may negotiate three written warnings for tardiness instead of the two warnings a present contract might require.

Changes in the internal environment of the firm can also alter the disciplinary process. Through organizational development, the firm may alter its climate. This change may result in first-line supervisors handling disciplinary action in a more positive manner. Organization policies can also impact the disciplinary process. For instance, a firm treating its employees as if they were mature human beings would significantly affect the process.

The disciplinary action process continues within the firm's external and internal environment. Rules—specific guides to action—are created to facilitate the accomplishment of organizational goals. The do's and don'ts associated with accomplishing tasks are highly inflexible. A company rule may prohibit smoking in a given area. Or, it may require that hard hats be worn in hazardous areas.

Once rules have been established, they must be communicated to the affected employees. Individuals cannot obey a rule if they do not know it exists.

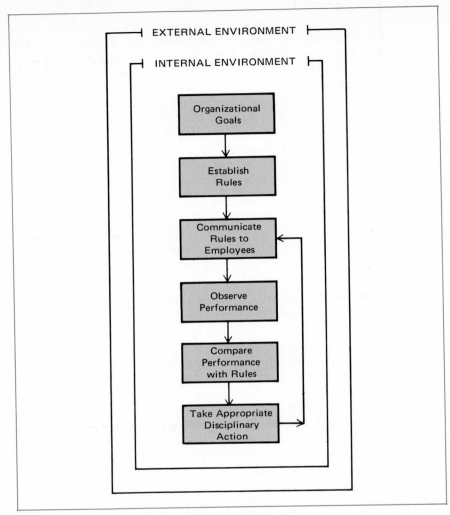

Figure 16–1. **The disciplinary action process.**

As long as employee behavior does not vary from acceptable practices, there will be no need for disciplinary action. But, when an employee's behavior violates a rule, corrective action may be taken. The purpose of this action is to alter behavior which can have a negative impact upon achievement of organizational goals.

Notice that Figure 16–1 shows a feedback loop from "Take Appropriate Disciplinary Action" to "Communicate Rules to Employees." Some of us only find out that a rule is being enforced when one of our peers receives disciplinary action. We may then conform to the rule because we choose not to receive similar disciplinary action.

APPROACHES TO DISCIPLINE

525

Chapter 16
Discipline and
the Grievance
Process

Several concepts regarding the administration of disciplinary action have been developed. Two of these views—the hot stove rule and progressive discipline— will next be discussed. Although they are treated separately, many of the hot stove concepts are incorporated in the use of progressive discipline.

The Hot Stove Rule

One view of administering disciplinary action is referred to as the **"hot stove rule."** According to this approach, disciplinary action should have the following consequences:

1. *Burns immediately:* If disciplinary action is to be taken, it must occur immediately so the individual will understand the reason for it. With the passage of time, people have the tendency to convince themselves that they are not at fault.

2. *Provides warning:* It is also extremely important to provide advance warning that punishment will follow unacceptable behavior. As you move closer to a hot stove, you are warned by its heat that you will be burned if you touch it.

3. *Gives consistent punishment:* Disciplinary action should also be consistent in that everyone who performs the same act will be punished accordingly. As with a hot stove, each person who touches it is burned the same.

4. *Burns impersonally:* Disciplinary action should be impersonal. There are no favorites when this approach is applied.

Although the hot stove approach has some merit, it also has weaknesses. If the circumstances surrounding all disciplinary situations were the same, there would be no problem with this approach. However, they are often quite different. For instance, does the organization penalize a loyal, twenty-year employee the same as an individual who has been with the firm less than six weeks? Many variables could be present in a disciplinary case. Therefore, a supervisor often finds that he or she cannot be completely consistent and impersonal in the action taken. Because situations do vary, the progressive discipline philosophy may be more realistic.

Progressive Discipline Approach

When the **progressive discipline** approach is followed, an attempt is made to make penalties appropriate to the violation (or accumulated violations). The manager must ask a series of questions—in sequence—to determine the proper disciplinary action (see Figure 16–2). After it is determined that disciplinary

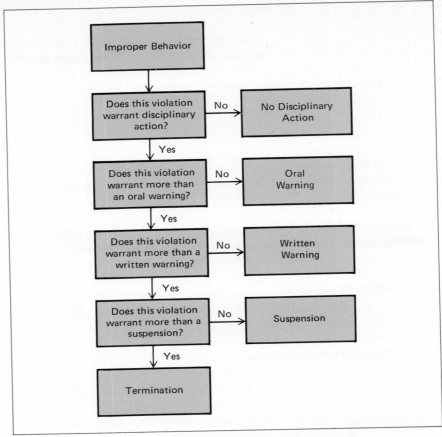

Figure 16–2. The progressive disciplinary action process.

action is appropriate, the question is asked: "Does the violation warrant more than an oral warning?" If the improper behavior is minor and has not previously occurred, perhaps only an oral warning will be sufficient. Also, an individual may receive several written warnings before a "yes" answer might apply to the question, "Does this violation warrant more than a written warning?" The manager does not consider termination until each lower level question is answered "yes." However, major violations, such as striking one's immediate supervisor, may justify the immediate termination of the employee.

In order to assist a manager to recognize the proper level of disciplinary action, some firms have formalized the procedure. One approach in the establishment of progressive disciplinary action may be seen in Table 16–1. In this example, a worker who is tardy will first receive an oral warning; a written warning the second time; and the third time, the employee will be terminated. Fighting on the job is an offense which normally results in immediate termination. However, specific guidelines should be developed to meet the needs of

Table 16–1. Suggested guidelines for disciplinary action

A. Examples of offenses resulting in immediate discharge:

1. Intoxication or use of drugs
2. Fighting
3. Refusal to work
4. Theft
5. Willful destruction of property
6. Gross insubordination
7. Gross misconduct unbecoming an employee
8. Conviction of a felony charged by court of proper jurisdiction, provided the felony is relevant to the position
9. Falsifying time cards
10. Use of undue influence to gain or attempt to gain promotion, leave, favorable assignment, or other individual benefit
11. Falsification, fraud, or omission of information in applying for a position
12. Failure to report to work without notification for a period of three days
13. Failure or inability to complete a required training program that is a part of a job assignment
14. Failure to obtain or maintain a current license or certificate required by law or organizational standards as a condition of employment
15. Any other act which endangers the safety, health, or well-being of another person, or which is of sufficient magnitude that the consequences cause or act to cause disruption of work or gross discredit to the organization

B. Examples of offenses resulting in first, a written warning; and second, an immediate discharge:

1. Gambling
2. Careless, negligent, or improper use of property
3. Unauthorized or improper use of any type of leave
4. Failure to report to work without notification for a period of one or two days
5. Releasing confidential information without proper authority
6. Sleeping on job
7. The violation of, or failure to comply with, an executive order, or published rules and regulations of the organization

C. Examples of offenses resulting in first, an oral warning; second, a written warning; and third, an immediate discharge:

1. Uncivil conduct
2. Tardiness
3. Unauthorized absence from the job
4. Failure to maintain satisfactory and harmonious working relationships with the public or other employees
5. Smoking in an unauthorized area
6. Failure to punch the time clock
7. Foul and abusive language
8. Inefficiency, incompetency, or negligence in the performance of duties

Source: "Administering Disciplinary Actions," by Rodney L. Oberle. Reprinted with permission *Personnel Journal* copyright January 1978.

the industry and the organization. For instance, smoking in an unauthorized area may be grounds for immediate dismissal in an explosives factory. On the other hand, the same violation may be less serious in a plant producing concrete products.

GUIDELINES TO THE CREATION OF RULES

Our industrial system would likely be far less efficient if firms did not establish appropriate rules for their employees. However, excessive rules may contribute to labor-management conflict. In creating rules, certain basic guidelines should be followed.

Need for the Rule

The question must constantly be asked, "Is this rule necessary?" A rule may be appropriate for one segment of the firm but not for another. In addition to creating the potential for conflict, unnecessary rules are costly because of the time and effort required in their administration. Also, workers recognize when a rule is not necessary and resent management creating arbitrary constraints.

Applicable to Everyone

A rule should apply to everyone in the organizational unit and not just a select few. For example, if there is a rule against smoking, everyone in the department should be required to adhere to it. Workers seeing a department head smoking while others cannot may feel considerable resentment.

Clearly Communicated

If employees are to comply with rules, they must be advised of their existence. Rules must be clearly communicated to all affected employees. They must not be ambiguous or difficult to understand. Grievances often result from situations where the rules are not properly communicated.

Reasonable

People have a wide range of personalities, needs, and desires. Rules must be tailored, as much as possible, to accommodate these differences. For instance, it would be unreasonable to state that a person can have only two restroom breaks each day—one in the morning and another in the afternoon.

Enforceable

If a particular rule would be impossible to enforce, it should not be made. For instance, it would be quite difficult to enforce a rule which limited the number of times a person could be absent from work. In this instance, there are simply too many factors beyond the employee's control to enforce the rule effectively.

Establishment of Penalties That Fit the Violation

Workers recognize when the punishment they receive is inappropriate to the situation. To have a rule specifying that a worker can be terminated for reporting late only one time would be unreasonable; a verbal warning for smoking in a highly explosive area would likely not be sufficient.

THE ADMINISTRATION OF DISCIPLINARY ACTION

As might be expected, disciplinary actions are not pleasant supervisory tasks. Many people find it difficult to punish another worker. Reasons why managers may want to avoid disciplinary action include:

1. *Lack of training:* Some supervisors do not have the knowledge and skill necessary to handle disciplinary problems.
2. *Fear:* There may be concern that top management will not support a disciplinary action.
3. *The only one:* The supervisor may feel, "No one else is disciplining employees, so why should I?"
4. *Guilt:* The manager may think, "How can I discipline someone if I've done the same thing?"
5. *Loss of friendship:* The supervisor may believe that disciplinary action will damage friendship with an employee or the employee's associates.
6. *Time loss:* The interview takes valuable time.
7. *Loss of temper:* The supervisor may be afraid of losing his or her temper when talking to an employee about a rule violation.
8. *Rationalization:* The manager may reason, "The employee knows it was the wrong thing to do, so why do we need to talk about it?"[3]

These reasons apply to all forms of disciplinary action—from an oral warning to termination. There are, however, some additional reasons that should be mentioned when termination is required. Managers often avoid this form of disciplinary action even when it is in the company's best interests. This prob-

[3]Wallace Wohlking, "Effective Discipline in Employee Relations," *Personnel Journal* 54 (September 1975): 489.

Executive Profile

Charles E. "Charlie" Brown
Vice President, Executive Personnel
Honeywell, Inc.

Charles Brown says, "My career in employee relations came about quite by accident. After serving as a noncommissioned infantry officer in World War II, I was attached to a personnel unit. It was there that I first encountered the 'personnel business'."

Returning to Indiana, Charlie noted that a number of management schools had a personnel emphasis, which he decided to pursue. Many years later, as head of employee relations for Honeywell, he had personnel responsibilities for 100,000 employees throughout thirty-five countries. Since 1980 Charlie has handled personnel matters for Honeywell's 500 top executives.

Upon leaving Indiana University in 1949 with B.S. and M.S. degrees in personnel management, he joined the Glidden Company's corporate personnel staff. In 1959 he became director of industrial relations for the Cleveland Pneumatic Tool Company, and in 1962 accepted an opportunity to join Honeywell Inc. as Director of Industrial Relations. This decision proved to be a good one as he progressed steadily through the ranks to the two highest personnel positions in Honeywell.

Charlie believes that a business enterprise, or a department of a business enterprise, is very much like a professional athletic team.

lem often stems from breakdowns in other areas of the personnel functions. For instance, if the performance appraisal system is not valid, managers may be in a weak position to terminate a worker. It is embarrassing to decide to fire a worker and then be asked why this individual was rated so high on the previous evaluation.

Another problem related to managers' reluctance to fire employees for cause is lack of record keeping. When no documentation is maintained, it may be difficult to justify to upper management that a person should be terminated. Rather than run the risk of a decision being overturned, the ineffective worker is retained.

Finally, some managers have come to believe that it is useless even to attempt to terminate members of protected groups. Naturally this attitude is inaccurate. Anyone whose performance is consistently below standard can be terminated. However, managers must conduct performance appraisals so that they distinguish between levels of productivity, keep good records, and maintain a careful even-handed treatment of all workers. In order to assist the manager in the disciplinary process, there are various do's and don'ts with regard to the administration of disciplinary action. A supervisor may be justified in

"We are the managers of our teams and we have players in various positions. We compete with other teams, winning some games and losing some, and we are highly interested in finding ways to improve our win-loss ratio." He suggests that team building starts with the basic task of selection and placement. "When we have big wins or losses they are normally traceable to a small group of managers who were well suited to the task, or vice versa."

Mr. Brown believes that managers should devote more time to the selection of new entrants into the department. He says, "We spend a lot of time examining proposals for new buildings and equipment, but we tend to neglect the process of carefully selecting the best qualified candidate for each opening."

When asked about motivation Charlie replies, "What can you and I as managers do to cause people who work for us to apply their very best efforts? You might say, 'Pay them more than they can earn elsewhere', and it is true that pay is an important factor. More important, however, is the working climate which is made up of many ingredients. Among these important ingredients is the attitude employees have toward their job and toward the boss. Is the boss basically fair? Does he or she care about the well-being of employees? Is he or she approachable? Can an employee talk with the boss on issues of real concern, both business and personal matters?"

When asked what he would do differently if he were starting over in his chosen field of personnel management Charlie replied, "I would learn more about my company's business—its products, customers, financial requirements, etc. I would establish priorities more carefully, concentrating on those items which are most critical to the success of the business. Finally, I would spend more time developing strong interpersonal relationships among employees at all levels so that I knew the organization more from personal contact than from studying reports."

administering discipline. However, he or she may create considerable dissention among other employees by the improper handling of the disciplinary action.

The old philosophy of reprimanding in private and praising in public remains as valid today as ever. Disciplining a worker in the presence of others may embarrass the worker and actually defeat the purpose of the discipline. All of us have a desire to save face in front of our peers. Even if we are wrong, we resent the disciplinary action if it is in public. The case at the beginning of the chapter in which Bill Morton quit his job because of being disciplined before his peers provides an excellent illustration.

In addition, many managers may be too lenient early in the disciplinary process and too strict in later stages. This lack of consistency does not permit the worker to gain a true understanding of the precise punishment associated with the action. As Robert F. Garrett, manager, labor relations, Georgia-Pacific Corporation, stated: "A supervisor will often endure an unacceptable situation for an extended period of time. Then, when the supervisor finally does take action, he or she is apt to overreact and come down excessively hard." Consistency does not necessarily mean that the same penalty must be applied to two different workers for the same offense. For instance, employers

Table 16–2. Code on discipline procedure

- All employees should be given a copy of the employer's rules on disciplinary procedures. The procedures should specify which employees they cover and what disciplinary actions may be taken, and should allow matters to be dealt with quickly.
- Employees should be told of complaints against them and given an opportunity to state their case. They should have the right to be accompanied by a trade union representative or fellow employee of their choice.
- Disciplinary action should not be taken until the case has been fully investigated. Immediate superiors should not have the power to dismiss without reference to senior management, and, except for gross misconduct, no employee should be dismissed for a first breach of discipline.
- Employees should be given an explanation for any penalty imposed, and they should have a right of appeal, with specified procedures to be followed.
- When disciplinary action other than summary dismissal is needed, supervisors should give a formal oral warning in the case of minor offenses, or a written warning in more serious cases.

Source: "Code on Discipline Procedure," *Industrial Management 7* (August 1977): 7. Used with permission.

would be consistent if they always considered the worker's past record and length of service. A long-term employee might only receive a suspension. A worker with only a few months' seniority might be terminated for the same act. This type of action could be reasonably viewed as being consistent.[4]

In order to assist management in administering discipline properly, a Code on Discipline Procedure has been prepared by the Advisory, Conciliation and Arbitration Service. The purpose is to give practical guidance on how to draw up disciplinary rules and procedures and how to use them effectively. The code recommends actions as shown in Table 16–2. As you can see, the code stresses communication of rules, telling the employee of the complaint, full investigation, and an opportunity for the employee to tell his or her side of the story.

GRIEVANCE HANDLING UNDER A COLLECTIVE BARGAINING AGREEMENT

If the employees in an organization are represented by a union, workers who feel that they have been disciplined or dealt with unjustly can appeal through the grievance and arbitration procedures of the collective bargaining agreement. The grievance procedure has been described as "one of the truly great accomplishments of American industrial relations. For all its defects . . . it constitutes a social invention of great importance."[5] The grievance system en-

[4]John E. Tobin, "How Arbitrators Decide to Reject or Uphold an Employee Discharge," *Supervisory Management* 21 (June 1976): 21.
[5]Neil W. Chamberlain, *The Labor Sector* (New York: McGraw-Hill Book Company, 1955), p. 240.

courages and facilitates the settlement of disputes between labor and management. A grievance procedure permits employees to express a complaint without jeopardizing their jobs. It also assists management in seeking out the underlying causes and solutions to grievances.

The Grievance Procedure

Virtually all labor agreements include some form of grievance procedure.[6] **A grievance** can be broadly defined as an employee's dissatisfaction or feeling of personal injustice relating to his or her employment relationship. A grievance under a collective bargaining agreement is generally well defined. It is usually restricted to violations of the terms and conditions of the agreement. Other conditions which may give rise to a grievance are:

- A violation of law
- A violation of the intent of the parties as stipulated during contract negotiations
- A violation of company rules
- A change in working conditions or past company practices
- A violation of health and/or safety standards[7]

There are many common features in the procedures through which disputes involving aggrieved employees may be resolved. However, variations may result from such factors as differences in organizational or decision-making structures or the size of a plant or company. Larger organizations tend to have more formal procedures involving a succession of steps. Some general principles which have gained widespread support and which can serve as guidelines in establishing a system of positive grievance administration are:

- Grievances should be adjusted promptly.
- Procedures and forms airing grievances must be easy to utilize and well understood by employees and their supervisors.
- Direct and timely avenues of appeal from rulings of line supervision must exist.[8]

The most common type of grievance procedure may be seen in Figure 16–3. The first step usually involves an informal oral presentation of the employee's grievance to the immediate supervisor in the presence of the union

[6]U.S. Department of Labor, Bureau of Labor Statistics, *Characteristics of Major Collective Bargaining Agreements*, July 1, 1975, Bureau of Labor Statistics Bulletin 1957, 1977 (Washington, D.C.: U.S. Government Printing Office), (hereafter cited as "U.S. Department of Labor").
[7]K.L. Sovereign and Mario Bognanno, "Positive Contract Administration," *ASPA Handbook of Personnel and Industrial Relations: Employee and Labor Relations*, Dale Yoder and Herbert G. Heneman, Jr. eds., Vol. III (Washington, D.C.: The Bureau of National Affairs, Inc., 1976), pp. 7–161 and 7–162.
[8]Ibid., p. 7–164.

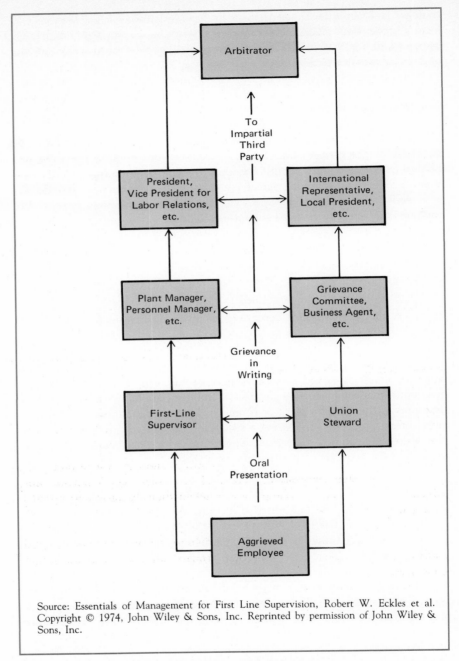

Source: Essentials of Management for First Line Supervision, Robert W. Eckles et al.
Copyright © 1974, John Wiley & Sons, Inc. Reprinted by permission of John Wiley &
Sons, Inc.

Figure 16–3. **A multiple-step grievance procedure.**

steward. This step offers the greatest potential for improved labor relations. A
large majority of grievances are settled here.

The procedure ends if the grievance can be resolved at the first step. If it
remains unresolved, the next step involves the plant manager or personnel

manager meeting with higher level union officials such as the grievance committee or the business agent or manager. Prior to this meeting the grievance is placed in writing, dated, and signed by the employee involved and the union steward. Events are stated as they are perceived, identifying the portion of the contract which allegedly has been violated and the settlement desired. If the grievance is not adjusted at this meeting, it is appealed to the third step. This step typically involves the firm's top labor representative (such as the vice president of industrial relations) and high level union officials. At times, depending on the severity of the grievance, the president may represent the firm. A grievance that still remains unresolved at the conclusion of the third step may go to arbitration if it is provided for in the contract and the union decides to proceed that far.

Labor relations problems become major when the supervisor is not equipped to handle grievances at the first step. Although the first step is usually handled informally by the union steward, the aggrieved party, and the supervisor, the supervisor must be prepared. The supervisor should obtain as many facts as possible before the meeting since the union steward is likely to have done his or her homework also.

The supervisor needs to recognize that the grievance may not reflect the real problem. For instance, the employee might be mad at the company for modifying the pay policies even though the change was approved by the union. In order to voice discontent, the worker may file a grievance for a minor violation of the contract. The idea of hidden causes of grievances has been referred to as the "iceberg theory."[9]

Arbitration

The grievance procedure has been a successful instrument for the peaceful resolution of labor-management problems. However, most grievance procedures provide a final step, arbitration, to resolve any issues which remain unresolved.[10] **Arbitration** allows the parties to submit their dispute to an impartial third party for resolution. Although most agreements restrict the arbitrator's decision to application and interpretation of the agreement, the decision is final and binding upon the parties. While arbitration is at times used to settle conflicts in contract negotiations, its primary use has been in settling grievances.

If the union decides to go to arbitration, it notifies management. At this point, the union and the company must select an arbitrator. Most agreements make provision for the method of selection. The selection is usually made from a list supplied by the Federal Mediation and Conciliation Service (FMCS) or the American Arbitration Association (AAA), discussed in Chapter 15. When considering potential arbitrators, both management and labor will study their previous decisions in an attempt to detect any biases. Neither party wants to select an arbitrator who might be unfavorable to its position.

[9]Ibid., p. 7–159.
[10]Of the 1,514 agreements studied, 1,455 provided for arbitration. (U.S. Department of Labor, Bureau of Labor Statistics Bulletin, 1957).

When arbitration is used to settle a grievance, a variety of factors may be used to evaluate the fairness of the management actions which caused the grievance. Some of these factors include:

- Nature of the offense
- Due process and procedural correctness
- Double jeopardy
- Grievant's past record
- Length of service with the company
- Knowledge of rules
- Warnings
- Lax enforcement of rules
- Discriminatory treatment[11]

The large number of interacting variables makes the arbitration process difficult. High degrees of patience and judgment on the part of the arbitrator are required.

After the arbitrator has been selected and he or she has agreed to serve, a time and place for a hearing will be determined. The issue to be resolved will be presented to the arbitrator in a document that summarizes the question or questions to be decided and any contract restrictions that prohibit the arbitrator from making an award that would change the terms of the existing contract.

At the hearing each side presents its case. Arbitration is an adversary proceeding, so a case may be lost because of poor preparation and presentation. The arbitrator may conduct the hearing much like a courtroom proceeding. Witnesses, cross-examination, transcripts, and legal counsel may all be used. The parties may also submit or be asked by the arbitrator to submit formal written statements (so-called "briefs"). After the hearing, the arbitrator studies the material submitted and testimony given and reaches a decision within thirty to sixty days. The decision is usually accompanied by a written opinion giving the reasons supporting the decision.

The courts will generally enforce an arbitrator's decision unless: (1) the arbitrator's decision is shown to be unreasonable or capricious in that it did not address the issues, (2) the arbitrator exceeded his or her authority, or (3) the award or decision violated a federal or state law.

Proof that Discipline Was Needed

When discipline is administered, it is possible that it will ultimately be taken to arbitration. Employers have learned that they must prepare records that will constitute proof before an arbitrator.[12]

[11]F. Elkouri and E. A. Elkouri, *How Arbitration Works*, 3d ed. (Washington, D.C.: The Bureau of National Affairs, Inc., 1973).
[12]William E. Lissy, "Necessity of Proof to Support Disciplinary Action," *Supervision* 40 (June 1978): 13.

- "Get some real world experience and scar tissue in field operations (e.g., labor relations, grievance handling, benefits, and safety).
- Some supervisory experience is helpful.
- Frequently, graduates cannot get directly into Personnel. They may have to accept some other position in a company and maneuver into Personnel."

Cliff Harrison, Director of Human Resources
Nabisco, Incorporated

The supervisor should document any actions which suggest that disciplinary action may ultimately be required. Since the burden of proof is on the employer, the supervisor should collect information regarding events, circumstances, places, and witnesses. It is not sufficient to allege that the employee is incompetent; the arbitrator will demand clear proof.

Although the format of a written disciplinary warning may vary, the following information should be included:

1. Statement of facts concerning the offense
2. Identification of the rule that was violated
3. Statement of what resulted or could have resulted because of the violation
4. Identification of any previous similar violations by this individual
5. Statement of possible future consequences should the violation occur again
6. Signature and date[13]

An example of a written warning may be seen in Figure 16–4. In this instance, the worker has already received an oral warning. The individual is also warned that continued absences could lead to termination. It is important to document oral warnings since they may be the first step to disciplinary action leading to arbitration.

Weaknesses of Arbitration

Arbitration has achieved a certain degree of success in resolving grievances between labor and management. However, it is not without its weaknesses. There are those who say that arbitration is losing its effectiveness because of the long time lapse between the first step and the settlement of the grievance. Often, 100 to 250 days may pass before a solution is determined.[14] The reason

[13]Adapted from Robert D. Buchanan, "How to Apply Constructive Discipline," *Food Service Marketing* 40 (October 1978): 64.
[14]Lawrence Stessin, "Expedited Arbitration: Less Grief Over Grievances," *Harvard Business Review* 55 (January/February 1977): 129.

Interdepartmental
Correspondence

DATE: July 1, 1984

TO: J. Jones
FROM: J. Doe
SUBJECT: *Written Warning*

On this date, you were thirty minutes late to work with no justification for your tardiness. A similar offense occurred last Friday. At that time you were told that failure to report to work on schedule would not be condoned. I now find it necessary to tell you in writing that you must report to work on time. Failure to do so will result in the termination of your employment. Please sign below that you have read and that you understand this written warning.

_____

NAME

_____

DATE

Source: "Administering Disciplinary Actions" by Rodney L. Oberle. Reprinted with permission *Personnel Journal* copyright January 1978.

Figure 16–4. **An example of a written warning.**

for the initial filing of the grievance may actually be forgotten before it is finally settled.

Another problem is its costs, which have been rising at an alarming rate. Even costs to settle a simple arbitration case can be quite high. These expenditures are typically shared by labor and management. At times this dollar outlay may be used to place an underfinanced union in a difficult situation by forcing every grievance to arbitration.

GRIEVANCE HANDLING FOR NONUNION EMPLOYEES

While the step-by-step procedure for handling union grievances is common practice, the means of resolving complaints in nonunion firms varies.[15] Nonunion companies can set up an organizational appeal system, although it is not typically done. Scott in his study found that only 11 percent of responding organizations (91 out of 793) had any kind of procedure.[16] A consideration of

[15]Ronald L. Miller, "Grievance Procedures for Non-Union Employees," *Public Personnel Management* 7 (September/October 1978): 302.
[16]Wilson G. Scott, *The Management of Conflict: Appeal Systems in Organizations* (Homewood, Ill.: Richard D. Irwin, Inc., 1977), pp. 56–80.

these procedures is important because approximately 80 percent of the work force in the United States is nonunion. In nonunionized firms, employers have more flexibility in designing a grievance procedure which satisfies both management and employee needs.

The grievance procedure must be viewed by employees as being comprehensive and impartial. As such, there are many versions which may prove acceptable. The grievance procedure may consist of an informal dialogue between employee and supervisor or it may, as a last resort, involve calling in an arbitrator to settle disputes. An acceptable grievance procedure must be perceived as fair by both employees and management.

A well-designed nonunion grievance procedure ensures that the worker has ample opportunity to make complaints without fear of reprisal. If the system is to work, employees must be well informed of the program and be convinced that management wants them to use it. "Most employees are hesitant to formalize their complaints and must be constantly urged to avail themselves of the arrangement."[17] The fact that a manager says, "Our workers are happy because I have received no complaints," does not indicate that grievances do not exist. In a closed, threatening organizational climate, workers may be afraid to voice their dissatisfaction to management.

Typically, the employee initiates a complaint with her or his immediate supervisor. However, if the complaint involves the supervisor, the individual is permitted to bypass the immediate supervisor and proceed to the employee relations specialist or the next level manager. The grievance ultimately may be taken to the organization's top executive, who will make the final decision.

An example of one firm's salaried employees' grievance procedure is provided in Table 16–3. As may be seen, the procedure is initiated by the employee first sharing his or her complaint with the immediate supervisor and it culminates with a decision being made by the general manager.

Another possibility is to use the Swedish **ombudsman** concept. The ombudsman is a person outside the normal chain of command who handles complaints and grievances which adversely affect an individual or a small group of individuals. The ombudsman investigates and makes recommendations to the aggrieved employee(s) and the manager involved. Unresolved disputes are then forwarded to the top executive of the organization for a decision. An ombudsman should be able to exercise independent and impartial judgment and be highly skilled in human relations. The Singer Company uses an ombudsman system. In a recent company newsletter, Harry P. Hancock, Jr., senior director, employee relations program, describes their program (Figure 16–5).

TERMINATION

Termination is the most severe penalty that an organization can give to its members. The experience of being terminated is traumatic for employees re-

---

[17]James P. Swann, Jr., "Formal Grievance Procedures in Non-Union Plants," *Personnel Administrator* 26 (August 1981): 67.

Table 16–3. One company's action review of salaried employees' grievances

Policy. It is our policy to provide a pleasant working environment for all employees. This is achieved by developing and maintaining cooperative working relationships among employees based on mutual respect and understanding. We recognize the need for a procedure that will allow employees to call attention to work-related matters that they feel need correction. The following procedure may be used for resolving such work-related problems.

Procedure. A grievance is defined as an alleged violation by the company of its established policies and/or practices with respect to wages, hours, or conditions of work, or where an employee claims that the company has shown discrimination among employees in the application of its policies and/or practices.

It is the employee's right to make his grievances known. Any employee who feels that he has a just grievance is encouraged to make use of the following procedure with the guarantee that in so doing he will in no way place his standing or job in jeopardy. If the basis of his complaint is found valid, immediate steps will be taken to correct the matter.

The Employee Relations Specialist is available upon request by the employee to assist in preparation and presentation of grievances at any step. The employee should be advised of this service.

Step 1. Immediate Supervisor

A. The employee normally is expected to present his grievance to his immediate supervisor either verbally or in writing, but must do so within three working days of the alleged violation.

B. In unusual cases where the grievance is of a personal nature, the employee may discuss it with the Employee Relations Specialist. The Employee Relations Specialist will then arrange a meeting between the employee and his supervisor, and the Employee Relations Specialist will attend if the employee so requests.

C. The immediate supervisor will, within three working days, give the employee an answer (in writing if the employee so requests).

To retain flexibility and to reduce the number of formal steps in this procedure, the immediate supervisor should confer with all appropriate line management below the level of Department Head where it is deemed necessary. The answer given to the em-

continued

gardless of their position in the organization. Senses of failure, fear, disappointment, and anger can all become manifest at the same time. It is also an uneasy time for the person making the termination decision. Knowing that termination may affect not only the employee but an entire family increases the tension. Not knowing how the terminated employee will react also may create considerable anxiety on the part of the manager who must do the firing. Regardless of the similarities in the termination of employees of various levels, distinct differences exist with regard to operative employees, executives, managers, and professionals.

Termination of Operative Employees

The procedure used to terminate operative employees is typically well defined. Specific violations which could lead to termination are normally spelled out in

Table 16–3. (continued)

541

Chapter 16
Discipline and
the Grievance
Process

ployee will then represent the combined opinion of the section head, foreman, assistant foreman, etc.

Step 2. Department Head

A. If the grievance is not resolved in Step 1 above, the employee may, within three working days, state his grievance in writing. Grievance forms may be obtained from the immediate supervisor or the office of the Employee Relations Specialist.

B. The immediate supervisor will add his answer to the written grievance and immediately submit it to the Department Head.

C. The Department Head will, within three working days, meet with the employee.

All levels of supervision involved in the Step 1 answer shall initial the written grievance before it is sent to the Department Head.

The Employee Relations Specialist shall be notified by the immediate supervisor of any grievance reduced to writing for Step 2 consideration.

The Department Head will discuss the grievance with the immediate supervisor and other appropriate supervisors before meeting with the employee and may call the immediate supervisor into the meeting to clear up any conflicting information given by the employee during the meeting.

Step 3. General Management Review

A. If the grievance is not resolved in Step 2 above, it may be referred to the Director of Personnel who will, within five working days, establish a date for a meeting with the General Manager and the employee.

The Department Head shall refer the grievance to the Director of Personnel in all cases requiring Step 3 consideration. The Director of Personnel shall contact the employee to orient him to his Step 3 session with the General Manager.

The General Manager will discuss the grievance with the immediate supervisor and other appropriate supervisors before meeting with the employee and may call the immediate supervisor into the meeting to clear up any conflicting information given by the employee during the meeting.

B. After hearing the facts presented by the parties, the General Manager will, within five working days, render his decision in writing to the employee through the employee's immediate supervisor.

Source: Reprinted, by permission of the publisher, from "Resolving Personnel Problems in Nonunion Plants," Maurice S. Trotta and Harry R. Gudenberg, *Personnel* (May-June 1976) © 1976 by AMACOM, a division of American Management Associations. Pages 60–61. All rights reserved.

the labor agreement. For example, drinking on the job might be identified as a reason for termination. Excessive absences may require three written warnings by the supervisor before termination action is taken. When no union is present, the reasons justifying termination are at times included in the firm's policy manual.

Some organizations direct the personnel function to assist terminated employees in locating new jobs. However, the reason for the termination will likely play an important role in determining the amount of effort that will be devoted. If the individual was terminated because of a reduction in the work force, more effort will likely follow. For instance, when a major meat packing company in the Southwest closed, a massive effort was made to find jobs for the terminated workers. On the other hand, a person who is terminated for theft will likely receive little if any support from management in finding a new job.

See the Ombudsman

An employee is fired for cause, disciplined or preceives himself or herself a victim of discrimination. To reverse the decision or remedy the situation, the employee tries normal channels—but remains dissatisfied with the results.

In many organizations, the story would end here. At Singer, because of the Corporate Ombudsman program started in 1976, the story can have another chapter or two. And, although the story may not necessarily have a happy ending, employees are guaranteed that they won't be subjected to harrassment or retribution for contacting the Ombudsman.

A concept borrowed from Scandinavia, the Ombudsman function entails an impartial investigation of and assistance in equitably settling complaints. At Singer this corporate-wide function is the responsibility of Harry P. Hancock, Jr., senior director, employee relations programs. "Because the program is informal raather than formal and the range of cases is varied," explains Mr. Hancock, "there is really no single modus operandi. I handle each case as it presents itself."

The range of cases include grievances about performance appraisals, involuntary discharge, sexual harrassment, sexual discrimination, denial of promotion, formal reprimand and conflict with or unfair treatment by a supervisor.

For the purpose of illustrating the thoroughness of the Ombudsman proceedings, Mr. Hancock describes how he might deal with a discharge-for-cause case brought to his attention by an employee who had exhausted all normal channels and remained dissatisfied.

"In the investigation and evaluation," he explains, "we rely heavily on the division personnel staff. Our objective is to make sure that:

- The rule or policy allegedly broken by the employee has been published, posted or otherwise made known to employees.

- The employee has been warned about any earlier infractions and given counseling.
- The employee has given a reasonable length of time to improve performance.
- The proposed disciplinary action is appropriate to the infraction.
- Other employees charged with similar infractions have been treated in a similar manner."

If it is determined that the employee has been unfairly discharged, the case is discussed with the immediate supervisor who initiated the action. If the decision is not reversed or amended at this level—which it usually is—then the discussion is brought to successively higher levels. On the other hand, if it is judged that the decision was appropriate, the employee is so advised and the case is closed.

Most problems are resolved, of course, through Singer's normal channels. Resolving a problem via normal channels includes an initial discussion with the immediate supervisor. If the issue is not settled at that level, then the matter is taken to higher levels, in the specific unit. Equal Opportunity coordinators, industrial relations personnel and other employee relations specialists may become involved.

In cases of terminations of employees with more than ten years of continuous service, standard procedure requires that those terminations be approved by members of the Management Committee.

If employees, after having gone through normal channels, still believe that they have received unfair treatment then they can bring the matter to the attention of the Ombudsman.

Source: Used with permission of The Singer Company.

Figure 16–5. **A description of an ombudsman program.**

Termination of Executives

Executive termination must be analyzed from a different perspective. There is likely no formal appeals procedure for executives. The decision to terminate an executive has probably been approved by the top level officer in the organization. In addition, the reasons for termination may not be as clear as with lower level employees. Some of the reasons include:

1. *Economic:* At times, business economic conditions may force a reduction in the number of executives.

2. *Reorganization:* In order to improve efficiency, a firm may reorganize, resulting in the elimination of some executive positions.

3. *Philosophical differences:* A difference in philosophy of conducting business may develop between an executive and other key company officials. In order to maintain consistency in management philosophy, the executive may need to be replaced.

4. *Decline in productivity:* The executive may have been capable of performing satisfactorily in the past, but, for various reasons, he or she can no longer perform the job as required.

The above list does not include factors related to illegal activities or actions taken which are not in the interest of the firm. Under those circumstances, the firm has no moral obligation to the terminated executive.

In recent years, the practice of firing employees has become more acceptable, and there has been a significant increase in the annual number of executives who are terminated. In 1979 it was estimated that approximately 6 percent of all executives from major corporations lost their jobs through terminations.[18] While an organization may derive positive benefits from executive terminations, they also present "a potentially hazardous situation for the organization."[19] Many corporations are concerned about developing a negative public image reflecting insensitivity to the needs of their employees. They fear that such a reputation would impede their efforts to recruit high quality managers. Also, terminated executives have, at times made public statements which were detrimental to the reputation of the firm.

Many organizations have established a systematic means of executive **outplacement** designed to assist terminated employees. In instances where such services exist, an outside consultant is employed to aid the terminated executive in finding appropriate employment elsewhere. In executive termination, the use of outside consultants may be superior to in-house personnel. The fired executive may not trust internal personnel and may be more open with an outsider.

Outplacement consultants provide the executive with a wide variety of services. Some of these typical services may be seen in Table 16–4. Consultants may initially assist the executive in performing a thorough self-assessment to determine his or her future career interests. The consultant will also instruct the worker in proper interviewing techniques. Since it may have been many years since the executive had an interview, the consultant can be helpful in preparing the worker for the job market. The outplacement consultant also may assist the executive in identifying the firms that could best use his or her qualifications. Through outplacement, the firm strives to reduce the trauma

---

[18]Morton Yarmon, "Fired Executives Try a New Tactic," *Parade* (July 22, 1979).
[19]"Outplacement Counseling," pamphlet developed by Drake Bean Morin, Inc., consultants in Human Resources Management, 1979.

Table 16–4. Typical services provided by outplacement consulting firms

- Pretermination counseling for the manager who is doing the termination.
- Travel to the place where the termination will occur. (No extra fee should be charged for this service, but travel expenses for the consultant should be reimbursed by the company or organization.)
- Vocational counseling by a trained psychologist.
- Resume development, printing, and distribution.
- Training on how to be interviewed (preferably using closed circuit TV).
- Consultation for the wife or husband of the terminated individual.
- Feedback to the client corporation or organization on the status of the individual.
- Continuous consultation available to the individual until placement.

Source: William J. Morin, "Outplacement Counseling: What Is It?," *The Personnel and Guidance Journal* 55 (May 1977): 555. Used with permission.

associated with termination of an executive who has been with the firm for a long time.

Termination of Mid- and Lower-Level Managers and Professionals

Effort is sometimes devoted to outplacing executives. However, in the past the most vulnerable and perhaps the most neglected group of employees with regard to termination has been mid- and lower-level managers and professionals, who are generally neither members of a union nor protected by a labor agreement. Nor do they have the political clout that a terminated executive may have. The reasons for their termination may be based solely on the attitude of their immediate superior on a given day.

This practice may be changing. In the past, courts have adopted the doctrine of "employment at will." If a person is hired for an unspecified length of time, the individual serves at the pleasure of the employer. Under this philosophy, management has tended to terminate at will. Recent court decisions in California, Illinois, Kansas, Maryland, Michigan, New Jersey, and Pennsylvania, however, have weakened or set aside the doctrine of employment at will.[20] Members of middle management have often been the most militant of the groups fighting the doctrine.

SUMMARY

Discipline refers to the state of employee self-control and orderly conduct that is present in an organization. Disciplinary action occurs when standards are

[20]David L. Nye, "Firing Managers: You Could End Up In Court," *Administrative Management* 53 (May 1982): 457.

maintained by invoking a penalty against an employee who has failed to meet these standards. Effective disciplinary action condemns the employee's wrongful act, not the employee as a person. A major purpose of disciplinary action is to ensure that employee behavior is consistent with the firm's goals.

The disciplinary action process is dynamic and on-going. The external and internal environments can have a major impact on the process. Within these environments, rules are created to facilitate the accomplishment of organizational goals. Once rules have been established, they must be communicated to the affected employees. Individuals cannot obey a rule if they do not know it exists. As long as employee behavior does not vary from acceptable practices, there will be no need for disciplinary action. But, when an employee's behavior violates a rule, corrective action may be taken. The purpose of this action is to alter behavior which can have a negative impact upon achievement of organizational goals. There is a feedback loop from taking appropriate disciplinary action to communicating rules to employees.

Questions for Review

1. What are the basic objectives of disciplinary action?

2. What steps are typically involved in the disciplinary process? Briefly describe each.

3. Distinguish between the hot stove rule and progressive discipline. What are some weaknesses associated with the hot stove rule?

4. List the basic guidelines for the creation of rules. Why is it important to comply with these guidelines?

5. As a manager, what are some basic rules that should be followed in the administration of discipline? Briefly describe each.

6. Assume that you are the personnel manager in a unionized firm. What are the steps that should typically be followed in grievance handling?

7. Why is arbitration often used in the settlement of grievances in a unionized firm?

8. How would grievances typically be handled in a nonunion firm? Briefly describe.

9. Termination is a traumatic experience for most employees. How does it often differ with regard to operative employees, executives, managers, and professionals?

Terms for Review

Discipline

Disciplinary action

Hot stove rule

Progressive discipline

Grievance

Arbitration

Ombudsman

Outplacement

Barney Cline, the new personnel manager for Ampex Utilities, was just getting settled in his new office. He had recently moved from another firm to take over his new job. Barney had been selected over several in-house candidates and numerous other applicants because of his record of getting things done. He had a good reputation for working through people to get the job accomplished.

Just then his phone rang. The person on the other line said, "Mr. Cline, could I set up an appointment to talk with you?" "Certainly," Barney said, "when do you want to get together?" "How about after work? It might be bad if certain people saw me speaking to anyone in management."

Barney was a bit puzzled, but he set up an appointment for 5:30 P.M., when nearly everyone would be gone. At the designated time, there was a knock on his door. It was Mark Johnson, a senior maintenance worker who had been with the firm for more than ten years.

After the initial welcome, Mark began by saying, "Mr. Cline, several of the workers asked me to talk to you. The grapevine has it that you're a fair person. The company says it has an open-door policy. We're afraid to use it. Roy Edwards, one of the best maintenance men in our section, tried it several months ago. They hassled him so much that he quit only last week. We just don't know what to do to get any problems settled. There have been talks of organizing a union. We really don't want that, but something has to give."

Barney thanked Mark for his honesty and promised not to reveal the conversation. In the weeks following the conversation with Mark, Barney was able to verify that the situation existed as Mark had described it. There was considerable mistrust between managers and the operative employees.

Questions

1. What are the basic causes of the problems confronting Ampex Utilities?

2. How do you feel that Barney should attempt to resolve this problem?

Dora Martinez had recently been promoted to supervisor at Gannon Manufacturing. Dora had been recognized as one of the hardest working machine operators. Thus, when a supervisory vacancy occurred, she was asked if she wanted to move into management. She quickly accepted and after a brief orientation moved into her new position.

The first day on the job, Dora called all of her operators together to tell them her philosophy of management. When the topic of discipline arose, Dora said, "I'm going to be fair, but firm. I'll do my best to treat everyone alike. There will be no special treatment for anyone."

Her disciplinary philosophy did not appear to disturb anyone. It seemed quite logical until the day Dora caught two of her workers sleeping on the job. At Gannon, this was a serious offense. The standard penalty was a five-day suspension without pay for the first offense. Immediately and without question she suspended both workers.

The results of the disciplinary action did not take long to reach the desk of Barry Thomas, Dora's supervisor. Barry called Dora in to discuss the suspensions. Dora said, "I caught them both sleeping on the job. That's all that matters." When Barry asked if she had checked into any extenuating circumstances, Dora looked surprised. She knew that they were both guilty. "Dora," said Barry, "I'm overriding your suspension of Charles and substituting a written reprimand." Barry explained that both men had complained to him about the disciplinary action and he had listened to their stories, then investigated.

Charles Branford, one of the violators, had been with the firm for ten years and had never received any disciplinary action. His wife had recently had a baby who had been keeping him up all night. On the other hand, Tom Roberts, a worker with only six months seniority, already had two violations for the same offense. He had apparently been sleepy because he had stayed out all night at a party.

Questions

1. Why did Barry change the punishment for Charles? Do you agree?

2. Has Dora's authority been weakened? Explain.

Chapter Objectives

1. State why employees choose not to join a union.
2. Identify the reasons why a firm may resist unionization attempts.
3. List and describe the various strategies and tactics a firm might use to maintain its nonunion status.
4. Explain the process by which a union can be removed.
5. Describe the role of Personnel in a nonunion organization.

Chapter 17 _____

Nonunion Organizations

Wayne Smith, a new production worker for Ampax Manufacturing, recently moved from the North to the Southwest. He was carrying on a conversation with several workers on his shift. "I don't see why we don't have a union here. Who's going to represent us when management puts the screws on?" Wayne's conversation was cut off fast by one of the other workers, who replied, "We don't believe in unions in this plant. The plant management has done a good job. If you believe you need a union to represent you, maybe you don't need to work here." Wayne nodded his head to indicate his understanding and did not mention unionization again to his co-workers.

Brad Carpet, production manager for the Thompson Manufacturing Company, was upset. He had just been walking through the plant and accidentally heard one of his supervisors severely reprimanding an employee in front of his co-workers. Brad called the supervisor aside and said, "We're a nonunion organization and hope to remain this way. What you just did was one of the fastest ways to create a feeling among our employees that they need a union."

The above incidents describe some employee and management attitudes in nonunionized firms. Wayne Smith had just discovered that not all employees feel that they need to be represented by a union. On the other hand, Brad Carpet is quite concerned that the action of one of his supervisors may create an atmosphere where employees feel that they need a union. Nonunionized firms comprise an important part of the industrial scene in the United States. Also, many employees who work under collective bargaining agreements are not union members. The overall purpose of the chapter is to acquaint you with some of the characteristics of nonunion firms and the factors related to maintaining this status.

WHY EMPLOYEES AVOID JOINING UNIONS

Most employees in the United States do not belong to unions. Their reasons are many and varied. Some of these may be seen in Figure 17–1. In the first place, it costs money to be a member of a union. There is typically an initiation fee followed by dues that must be paid on a regular basis in order to remain a union member. From time to time, there may also be assessments. Although dues typically do not amount to more than two percent of before-tax pay, many individuals would rather use this money in other ways. A worker who makes $24,000 annually, would pay dues of approximately $40 per month in addition to the initiation fee.

Also, many employees think that unions are unnecessary. It is their belief that they should not have to depend on a third party to help satisfy their needs. These individuals feel that their value to the organization should be judged on an individual basis and that everyone should not be treated equally. If their performance is superior, the reward should be appropriate and direct. They believe that joining a union is an admission that others control their destiny. These individuals feel that joining the union would limit their opportunities for advancement.

In addition, just as there may be peer pressure in some firms to encourage employees to join the union, in other instances there may be as much pressure against union affiliation. Even if an individual might desire to join a union, the informal work group may be so powerful as to preclude the strongest of wills from outwardly supporting a union. As Wayne Smith discovered in the incident at the beginning of the chapter, the prevailing attitude of his co-workers was to maintain a nonunion status.

Reprisals for union activities are illegal in the United States. Even so, some employees would feel insecure about their jobs if they engaged in union activities. Perhaps they have seen workers who supported the union receive what they perceive as unfair treatment from their employers. If a worker has a skill which is easily replaced, the employee may decide not to take a chance of losing his or her job by supporting union activities.

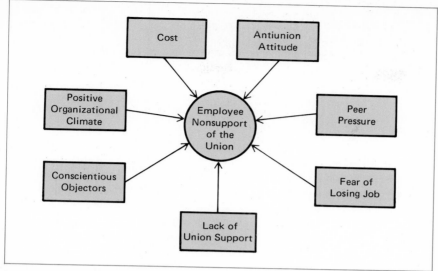

Figure 17–1. **Why employees do not join unions.**

Establishing a union is much like starting a business. The cost to start and maintain a union must be evaluated in relation to the revenue or benefits to be gained. The union may decide to expend minimum or no effort in the establishment of a new bargaining unit. For instance, a union would tend to look more favorably on organizing a section of five hundred skilled workers as opposed to a group of five semiskilled employees. Although the union might like to help the five employees, the cost of organizing and supporting them would likely be excessive.

Unions also recognize that there are certain industries, firms, and locations in the country with a tradition of resisting unions. For instance, even though the Sunbelt states offer unlimited opportunities for unionization, unions have experienced difficulties there. For example, a union may believe that additional attempts to unionize IBM Corporation are a waste of money because previous efforts have proven fruitless.

Certain employee groups have religious or moral beliefs which preclude them from joining organizations. Because unions are organizations, these employees refuse to work for a firm where union membership is required.

Finally, there may be factors within the company that keep employees from joining a union. The organization climate, as discussed in Chapter 2, may be one which encourages open communication and employee participation. Workers may have excellent relationships with their supervisors. Trust may exist to the point that workers may feel that they do not need a third party to represent them in their dealings with the company. Where this attitude is present, the employees identify strongly with the objectives of the company.

COST/BENEFITS ANALYSIS—
UNIONIZATION

Valid reasons exist for management's acceptance or rejection of unionization (see Figure 17–2). Rationales for both philosophies will be described next.

Acceptance of Unionization Attempts

There may be times when resistance to unionization attempts is not advantageous. In these situations, management must set aside personal feelings and make decisions which are in the firm's best interest. As was mentioned in Chapter 15, the maritime and construction unions often provide a ready source of labor from their hiring halls. A firm operating in one of these industries may find it advantageous to accept unionization in order to obtain qualified workers. In other instances, management may realize benefits by utilizing the political influence of unions. For example, a union's effective lobbying efforts may help a firm obtain contracts which will benefit both the union members and the firm.

In addition, there are situations where the relationship between management and the union is quite good and well established. In these instances, it may be prudent to keep that union. A more demanding union may take its place. Management rationalizes that it can work within the present system; the future with a different union may be uncertain.

Management may also desire unionization of competing organizations. If a competitor attempts to enter the industry by paying lower nonunion wages, the larger established firms operating with greater economy of scale will likely desire unionization of the new firm.[1] Through this practice, costs to all firms producing similar products remain relatively constant when all the competing firms are unionized.

Figure 17–2. Should the firm resist unionization?

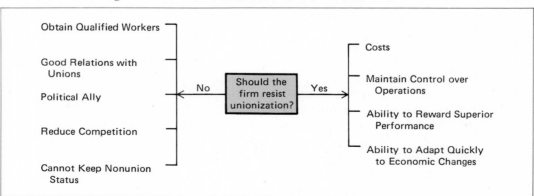

[1]John G. Kilgour, "Before the Union Knocks," *Personnel Journal* 57 (April 1978): 186.

An additional factor determining whether a firm should resist unionization attempts involves a realistic appraisal of whether it can remain nonunionized. There are numerous instances in which the firm would have little hope of staying nonunion. For instance, there would likely be little chance for a maritime company located in New York City to remain nonunion. If there is no reasonable way the firm could remain nonunion, it would likely be in its best interest to begin developing a strategy for working within a unionized environment. The presence of a union will increase the demands made upon the firm's human resources management.

Resistance to Unionization Attempts

Although there may be valid reasons for a firm to accept unionization, it is likely that a large percentage of company executives would prefer to remain nonunion. In fact, a major goal for many organizations is to remain nonunion. Some reasons for desiring to remain nonunion are described next.

Costs. In many instances, the compensation provided union members is considerably higher than for nonunion workers. However, the firm realizes that it must remain competitive in order to survive. For instance, it is likely that Montgomery Ward would want to remain nonunion because its primary competition (Sears, Roebuck) is also nonunion. If Montgomery Ward were unionized, the firm would likely experience higher labor costs. However, because of a highly competitive situation, it could not pass these costs along to the consumer.

At times, however, union wages may actually be lower than nonunion wages. But, the additional cost associated with a unionized firm may quickly overcome this wage differential. In fact, it has been estimated that unionization increases labor costs as much as 20 to 35 percent.[2] Factors that cause this increased labor cost include: "the high cost of complex, payroll-padding work rules; work stoppages, strikes and slowdowns; lengthy negotiations and the grind of arbitration cases; and layoff by seniority."[3] Naturally, the working relationship between labor and management will have considerable impact on cost. However, it is generally conceded that the overall cost of labor is higher in a unionized firm.

Maintaining Control Over Operations. Management typically wants to operate without restrictive union work rules and other provisions which have the potential to reduce management's authority.[4] When a firm is unionized, management relinquishes some of its control over the work environment.

[2]Wiley I. Beavers, "Employee Relations Without a Union," *ASPA Handbook of Personnel and Industrial Relations: Employee and Labor Relations,* Dale Yoder and Herbert G. Heneman, Jr. eds., vol. III (Washington, D.C.: The Bureau of National Affairs, Inc., 1976), p. 7–82 (hereafter cited as "Employee Relations Without a Union").
[3]Ibid.
[4]"What Put Labor on the Defensive," *Business Week* 2563 (December 4, 1978): 56.

John L. Quigley, Jr., AEP
Vice President-Human Resources
Dr Pepper Company

"The impact of the personnel profession on the bottom line of corporations will only begin to be felt in the 1980s," says John Quigley, vice president-human resources for the Dr Pepper Company. John has seen tremendous changes in the personnel field since he joined Dr Pepper in 1967. To those now entering the personnel field, he says, "You will be challenged as none before you, due to the focus on people and productivity. You are entering on the ground floor of the personnel profession with lots of room to grow."

John graduated with a degree in personnel management and has grown with Dr Pepper Company over the years. He has seen the personnel field change considerably during this time. John now manages and coordinates all personnel functions for the company in both domestic and international operations. Those functions include personnel policy development, employment and recruiting, benefit administration, EEO and Affirmative Action planning, labor relations, compensation, and security. As Dr Pepper Company has grown from a $30 million to a $700 million per year operation offering major consumer products such as Dr Pepper, Sugar Free Dr Pepper, Canada Dry Ginger Ale, Sparkling Soda and Tonic Water, Barrelhead Rootbeer, and Welch's Carbonated Grape and other flavors, John's responsibilities have evolved from a centralized, manual personnel system to a decentralized system servicing several wholly-owned domestic and international subsidiaries.

In addition to his work with Dr Pepper Company, Mr. Quigley has been involved in many professional societies including the

Nonunionized firms face less risk of strikes which interfere with their operations. A strike during a critical period can be disastrous to a firm. Its competitors can then step in to take up the slack.

"Be patient. Entry level positions for personnel management are scarce, but the future looks better, particularly for women and other minorities. In my opinion the personnel field is still evolving. The basic problem for people in Personnel is whether to specialize or stay a generalist. Also, personnel people have yet to establish themselves as part of top management."

N. Skelton, Director of Staffing
Motorola, Incorporated

American Society for Training and Development (ASTD) and the American Society for Personnel Administration (ASPA). His dedication to the development of personnel professionals has taken him to the presidency of local chapters in both ASPA and ASTD, as well as the national leadership ranks of ASPA from district director of North Texas to chairman of the board of ASPA in 1982 and a member of the executive committee of that organization. He has also served as a member of the board of the Personnel Accreditation Institute, the ASPA Foundation, and CLEAR—the Council on Legislation, Education and Research.

John believes that the academic community and personnel practitioners must work together in order to solve the complex problems confronting human resources management. In order to remain in touch with the academic community, he teaches seminars sponsored by North Texas State University in his spare time. John specializes in "Labor Relations for Nonunion Companies" and he enjoys the opportunity to share his views with other members of the profession.

John feels that the personnel and human resources field is one of business's most challenging, rewarding, and changing professions. Change has forced the personnel practitioner to learn and grow. John believes that further change is forthcoming as Congress will pass additional laws to change the way we do things and to influence business's bottom line. "The human resources function truly affects the bottom line. Over the last several years we participated in several acquisition team assignments to evaluate and implement changes in benefit coverage, operating procedures, and personnel policies. As a result of these changes we will realize operating expense savings of millions of dollars over several years. This kind of human resource management gives the corporation the best value for dollars invested and the best benefits for employees from the money available." Management demands more of this type professional and sophisticated personnel execution. "We must meet the challenge," says Mr. Quigley. "The future is wide open for the well-rounded professional personnel executive to make a key contribution to any company's success. As contributions are made to corporate objectives, the opportunities for personal compensation will continue to move upward."

Ability to Reward Superior Performance. It is often much easier to reward superior performance in a nonunionized firm. A recent study involving twenty-six nonunion firms revealed that "company executives believe they achieve higher productivity than they would if they were organized."[5] Promotions and salary increases may be based solely on performance as opposed to seniority. In a unionized firm, the compensation that is paid to each worker is specified by the agreement.

Ability to Adapt Quickly. Most organizations experience fluctuations in the demand for their product. Some firms undergo severe business downturns before the cycle is reversed. Nonunion firms are typically able to respond much more rapidly to changing conditions. If wages must be reduced to remain competitive, the nonunion firm can generally adjust more rapidly. The unionized firm

[5]Fred K. Foulkes, "How Top Nonunion Companies Manage Employees," *Harvard Business Review* 59 (September–October 1981): 90 (hereafter cited as "Foulkes").

is bound by the labor agreement and cannot lower wages unless the union agrees to a contract change.

When workers must be laid off as a result of declining demand, management in a nonunion firm is able to terminate employees whose work productivity is marginal. The seniority system determines who will be laid off in a unionized company.

STRATEGIES AND TACTICS FOR MAINTAINING NONUNION STATUS

Some managers believe that "the presence of a union is evidence of management failure to treat employees fairly."[6] Following this reasoning, management insensitivity to the demands of its people often results in unionization. The AFL-CIO lists several factors which, if present in a plant that it is attempting to organize, will significantly reduce chances of unionizing. They are provided in Table 17–1.

If a firm's goal is to remain nonunion, it must establish its battle plan long before an organization attempt begins. The development of long term strategies and effective tactics to remain nonunion is critical because employees' decisions to consider forming a union is usually not made overnight. Negative attitudes regarding the company are typically formed well in advance of any attempt at unionization.[7]

If a firm desires to remain nonunion, it must borrow some of the union's philosophy. In fact, unions have done much to improve the conditions of nonunionized employees. Basically, management must be able to offer workers equal or better conditions than they could expect with the union. Some major strategies and tactics to keep a union out will next be described. A total management system is needed to avoid unionization. Weaknesses in any critical area may develop into an open invitation to the union. As you can see in Figure 17–3, all factors must interrelate if the firm is to maintain its nonunion status.

First-Line Supervisors

A most important factor in a firm's ability to remain nonunion is the overall effectiveness of management, particularly first-line supervisors. The first-line supervisor represents the first line of defense against unionization. The ability or inability of these managers often determines whether unionization will be successful. The supervisor assigns work, evaluates each individual's work, and gives out praise and punishment. The manner in which he or she communicates with the employee in these and other matters can affect the individual's

---

[6]"Employee Relations Without a Union," p. 7–83.
[7]John G. Kilgour, "Responding to the Union Campaign," *Personnel Journal 57* (May 1978): 242.

Table 17–1. Factors that reduce the chances for union organizing

1. A conviction by employees that the boss is not taking advantage of them.
2. Employees who have pride in their work.
3. Good performance records kept by the company. Employees feel more secure on their jobs when they know their efforts are recognized and appreciated.
4. No claims of highhanded treatment. Employees respect firm but fair discipline.
5. No claim of favoritism that's not earned through work performance.
6. Supervisors who have good relationships with subordinates. The AFL-CIO maintains that this relationship of supervisors with people under them—above all—stifles organizing attempts.

Source: "What to Do When the Union Knocks," *Nation's Business* 54 (November 1966): 107. (© 1977 by *Nation's Business*. Reprinted by permission.)

557

Chapter 17
Nonunion
Organizations

attitude toward the firm. To the employee, the supervisor is management. At the workplace, the supervisor is the most influential person to the employees.

The supervisor also must communicate information about the firm to employees. Information regarding profits, sales, how the firm's product compares to competitors', and the like are important. The grapevine may reveal that sales are declining, which would likely disturb many workers. If the supervisor had explained that sales are down across the industry but are expected to return to normal in the next quarter, less anxiety might be experienced.

Figure 17–3. Strategies and tactics for remaining nonunion.

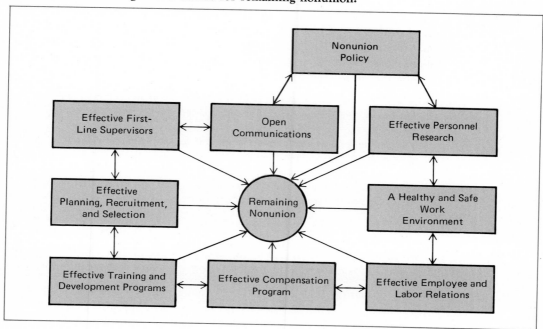

In order for a supervisor to be able to communicate effectively with employees, he or she must possess timely and accurate information. If the employee is aware of company plans before the supervisor, the supervisor's credibility is diminished. For instance, if top management changes a company policy regarding smoking in a particular area and the supervisor is not advised, the manager might be quite embarrassed if the employees are instructed to adhere to the old policy. Because of the speed of the grapevine, it is likely that the workers would know of the change soon after it occurred. If a grievance resulted from such a situation, the supervisor would be quite embarrassed.

The supervisor must also be adept at interpreting nonverbal communication signals. A well-trained supervisor can identify symptoms of unrest among employees. For instance, increasing signs of resentment, where there were none before, may indicate union activity. The recent creation of informal groups may also indicate unrest. The supervisor might notice that workers may stop talking or change the conversation when he or she approaches. A competent supervisor will notice these signs and report them immediately to upper management. There may be patterns of similar activities in other departments, suggesting an attempt at unionization. This knowledge may assist management in developing appropriate strategies and tactics.

One of the fastest ways to convert a nonunion person into a union advocate is to have an environment that promotes favoritism. To the worker, favoritism is equivalent to discrimination. The supervisor must establish an atmosphere in which the worker believes that he or she can receive fair treatment.

Nonunion Policy

As we discussed in Chapter 2, effective communication in an organization extends to all employees. The fact that the organization's goal is to remain nonunion should be clearly and forcefully communicated to all members of the organization. A recommended policy statement might read as follows:

> Our success as a company is founded on the skill and efforts of our employees. Our policy is to deal with employees as effectively as possible, respecting and recognizing each of them as an individual.
>
> In our opinion, unionization would interfere with the individual treatment, respect and recognition the company offers.
>
> Consequently, we believe a union-free environment is in the employees' best interest, the company's best interest and the interest of the people served by the corporation.[8]

This type of policy evolves into a philosophy that impacts everyone in the firm. All employees, from the lowest paid worker to upper management, must understand this goal of the firm. It should be so strong that no personnel related decision is made without asking, "How will this affect our nonunionized status?"

[8]James F. Rand, "Preventive-Maintenance Techniques for Staying Union-Free," *Personnel Journal* 59 (June 1980): 497 (hereafter cited as "Rand").

The nonunionization policy should be continuously transmitted to every worker. Workers must be told why the company advocates the policy and how it affects them. This involves much more than sending a memo each year to all employees stating that the objective is to remain nonunion. All means to ensure effective communication may be needed to convince company employees that the firm intends to remain nonunion.

Open Communication

One of the most important considerations for a firm that wants to remain nonunion is the establishment of credible communication.[9] Effective two-way communication is essential in maintaining nonunion status. Employees must be given the information they need to perform their jobs and provided feedback on their performance. Management should aggressively share information with workers concerning activities taking place within the firm. In addition, management must collect information from subordinates to make them aware of employee needs and their perceptions of the results of management policy and practice.

One approach taken to encourage open communication is the **open-door policy.** This means that employees have the right to take any grievance to the person next in the chain of command if a satisfactory solution cannot be obtained from their immediate supervisor. An effective open-door policy represents an attitude of openness and trust among people within the organization. It is not sufficient to state that an open-door policy exists and then punish the employee for bypassing his or her immediate supervisor. The employee must not fear that talking to the manager next in line will be detrimental to his or her career. Although on the surface one might expect that an open-door policy would result in wasted time for upper and middle level supervisors, in most instances this has not proven to be the case. The mere knowledge that an employee can move up the chain with a complaint without fear of retribution often encourages the immediate supervisor and the employee to work out their differences.

Personnel Planning, Recruitment, and Selection

A firm's ability to remain nonunion relates closely to its personnel planning, recruitment, and selection practices. For instance, if a firm used only word of mouth from current employees as a recruiting source, a very homogeneous work force of friends and relatives could develop. Such a work force would likely have strong interpersonal relationships. Should management take arbitrary action against any worker, the work group might perceive this as a negative action affecting them all. For this reason, Personnel will likely wish to recruit from a wide variety of sources.

[9]Charles L. Hughes, *Making Unions Unnecessary* (New York: Executive Enterprises Publication Company, Inc., 1976), p. 15.

A firm's method of personnel planning can also have a major impact on its susceptibility to unionization. If the firm is constantly hiring and terminating employees in reaction to demand for its products, the firm may face unionization. A firm can often maintain employment stability with adequate planning.

Training and Development Programs

Effective training and development programs are critical if a firm is to remain nonunion. A philosophy that is genuinely supportive of T&D would extend all the way from top management to the lowest level employee. As we discussed in Chapter 7, the success of any company-wide training program depends upon the support and interest shown by top management. Management support is critical because its attitude will filter down and influence the lower levels in the organization.

One important requirement of training and development is for employees to have a genuine desire for self-improvement. Some employees are content in their present positions, while others desire to develop their potential. More employees will wish to improve their skills if they are able to see a relationship between increased training, higher pay, and other rewards. A firm takes a giant step to remain union free when it provides avenues for advancement in skill and status. The seniority system often hinders union employees in these opportunities.

Supervisors also need training to prepare them for union organizing attempts. If the union knows that a firm's supervisors have been thoroughly trained in tactics to deal with the union, it may decide against organizing attempts. This type of training will also assist in preventing costly mistakes that could lead to charges of unfair labor practices. Training is necessary because the supervisor's actions can actually bind the employer. Ignorance on the part of the supervisor is no excuse.

Compensation Programs

The compensation employees receive is the most tangible measure they have of their worth to the firm. If an individual's salary is substantially below that paid by other firms in the area for similar work, dissatisfaction will surely occur. Compensation must remain competitive if the company expects to stay union free. Contrary to the belief of many, however, nonunion firms are not paying excessive wages and benefits.[10]

The compensation program in a nonunion firm should be intelligently planned and communicated to all employees. They must understand what they are being compensated for and how the system works. The firm is a prospect for unionizing activities if employees perceive the system as being unfair.

[10]Rand, p. 498.

The same approach with regard to pay should be followed in the benefits area. A firm need not have the best benefits in a geographic area or an industry to protect its nonunion status. However, the benefit package must be competitive. Employees must know what benefits they are actually receiving. Too often, firms do not inform their employees about their benefits. When such a situation exists, the financial resources of the company are being wasted and its union-free status is jeopardized.

A Safe and Healthy Work Environment

A firm which has gained a reputation for failure to maintain a safe and healthy work environment leaves itself wide open for unionization. For years unions have campaigned successfully by convincing workers that the union will provide them with a safer environment. In fact, labor unions were leading advocates of OSHA and continue to support this type of legislation.

Effective Employee and Labor Relations

A means of resolving employee complaints, whether perceived or actual, should be available. Total commitment to such a policy needs to start with top management and be instilled into each and every manager. Supervisors should develop an attitude of wanting to resolve problems before they become formal complaints.[11] Employees who believe that management is concerned with attempting to resolve their problems lack a major reason for needing a union.

Personnel Research

Personnel research can reveal changes in attitudes within the organization which could ultimately lead to unionization. Ignored problems often lead to attitudes which encourage unionization. One purpose of personnel research is to identify human resources problems at an early date. Corrective action should be taken before workers feel a need for a union to solve their problems.

Research may reveal symptoms of worker unrest. For instance, turnover statistics may reveal an alarming trend in a certain department within the company. When general employee dissatisfaction exists, the turnover rate normally increases. Good exit interviews, as part of the research effort, can assist management in identifying problems before they become critical.[12]

Another indicator of employee dissatisfaction is the number of customer complaints. If research reveals that customer complaints are increasing because of reduced quality, it might mean that the employees have problems on their

[11]Foulkes, p. 95.
[12]Wanda R. Embrey, R. Wayne Mondy, and Robert M. Noe, "Exit Interview: A Tool for Personnel Development," *The Personnel Administrator* 24 (May 1979): 48.

minds which need resolving. Naturally, there are many other factors which could cause complaints to increase. Accident frequency, maintenance costs, and theft are other indicators of employee dissatisfaction.[13]

REMOVAL OF THE UNION

Some managers believe that nothing can be done to remove the union once their firm has been unionized. Of course, this is not true. Employees have two basic means through which they can express their dissatisfaction with the union: decertification and deauthorization, or withdrawal of union shop authority.

Decertification

Until 1947, once a union was certified, it was certified forever.[14] However, the Taft-Hartley Act of 1947 made it possible for employees to decertify a union. When a union loses its right to act as the exclusive bargaining representative of a group of employees, it is referred to as **decertification.** The process is essentially the reverse of what a union must accomplish to be recognized as an official bargaining unit. In recent years, many decertification elections have been held. By 1979, employee groups favoring removal of the union were winning 75 percent of the elections. Of the 777 decertification elections, only 194 resulted in union victories.[15]

The Adolph Coors Company has been one of the most successful firms in decertification elections. In fact, it has been said that, "For years, Adolph Coors Company has been almost as well known for taming unions as it has been for its brewing skills."[16] In 1968, Coors had six thousand union workers. As of July 20, 1978, it had none. On this date, the NLRB held an election that resulted in the decertification of Local 366 of the Brewery, Bottling, Can & Allied Industrial Union, an independent local affiliated with the AFL-CIO. Seventy-one percent of the workers voted to decertify the union. Factors other than wages caused the employees to want to rid themselves of the union. Coors wage rates were much higher than in other nearby industries. Coors simply wanted the freedom to run its organization without union interference.[17]

Decertification elections have also been won in such well-known firms as Holiday Inn, Goodyear, Dow Chemical, Sears, American Airlines, and The Washington Post. However, the smaller firms appear to be achieving the great-

[13]"Employee Relations Without a Union," pp. 7–69, and 70.
[14]93 Daily Congressional Record 3954 (23 April 1947).
[15]William F. Fulmer, "Decertification: Is the Current Trend a Threat to Collective Bargaining?" *California Management Review* 24 (Fall 1981): 16.
[16]"Coors Undercuts Its Last Big Union," *Business Week* 2544 (July 24, 1978): 47.
[17]"Coors Brewery Says Workers Vote to Decertify the Union," *The Wall Street Journal* 52 (December 15, 1978): 23.

Table 17–2. Decertification elections by unit size

Employees	Number of Elections	Number Company Won (% Won)
1– 49	2,209	1,715 (78)
50– 99	391	205 (52)
100–149	129	65 (50)
150–199	77	39 (51)
200–499	96	41 (43)
500 or more	21	8 (38)

Source: Reprinted, by permission of the publisher, from "How to Win a Decertification Election," by Woodruff Imberman, MANAGEMENT REVIEW, September 1977 © 1977 by AMACOM, a division of American Management Associations. Page 27. All rights reserved.

est win–loss record (see Table 17–2). Perhaps this is because it is easier for management to reestablish trust with employees in smaller firms.

Decertification Procedure. As mentioned previously, decertification is essentially the reverse process of union certification. The rules established by the NLRB are specific in stating the prerequisites for filing a decertification petition. In order for the NLRB to conduct a decertification election, at least 30 percent of the bargaining unit members must petition for an election. As might be expected, this task by itself may prove difficult because prounion supporters are likely to oppose the move strongly. Although the petitioners' names are supposed to remain confidential, many union members are fearful that they will be discovered to be parties to the petition.

Timing of the NLRB's receipt of the decertification petition is also critical. It must be submitted between sixty and ninety days prior to the expiration of the current contract. Once the above conditions have been met, the NLRB Regional Director will schedule a decertification election by secret ballot.

The NLRB carefully monitors the events leading up to the election. If it is determined that management initiated the election, it will likely not certify the election. Current union members must initiate the request for the election. After the petition has been accepted, management can support the decertification election attempt. If a majority of the votes cast are against the union, the employees will be free of that union. However, the strong union supporters are all likely to vote. If a substantial number of employees are indifferent to the union and choose not to vote, decertification may not be approved.

Management and Decertification. When management senses employee discontent with the union, it often does not know how to react. Many management officials decide to do nothing, reasoning that it is best not to get involved. Some even believe that it is illegal to participate. But, if management does desire to get involved, there are various tactics which may be used. Basically, if a firm really wants the union decertified, it must learn how to be active rather than passive.

Meetings with union members to discuss the benefits of becoming non-union have proven beneficial. In fact, they are often cited as being the most effective campaign tactic. These meetings may be one-on-one, or consist of small groups or even entire units. Management explains the benefits of being nonunion and answers questions that may arise in these meetings.[18]

Management may also provide the workers with legal assistance concerning how to prepare for decertification. Because the workers have likely never experienced a decertification election, this assistance may prove invaluable. The NLRB may not permit an election if the paperwork has not been properly completed. A major point to remember is that management cannot initiate the decertification action; it is entirely the workers' responsibility.

The most effective means through which decertification can be accomplished is to improve the firm's organizational climate so that workers will no longer feel the need to have a union. This climate cannot be created overnight. Mutual trust and confidence must be developed between worker and employer.

If decertification is to take place, management must eliminate the causes that initially led to unionization. Although many corporate executives believe that pay and benefits are the primary reasons for union sentiments, these factors likely do not represent the real cause.[19] Failure to treat employees as individuals is often the primary reason for unionization. The real problems often stem from practices such as failing to listen to employees' opinions or not treating workers fairly and honestly. It is extremely difficult for employees to remain loyal to a firm with managers who know them only as numbers and not by name. Many factors within an organization do provide employees with an indication of how the firm feels toward them. Some of these indicators are:

- Poor housekeeping
- Poor supervision
- Inadequate wage differentials among the various skill levels
- Inadequate preventive maintenance
- Arbitrary company policies
- Unfair promotional policies
- An ineffective complaint and discipline procedure[20]

Naturally, the above list is far from complete. However, existence of these factors in organizations may initially have led to the firm's unionization. Even if a firm truly desires to become nonunion, it cannot be accomplished immediately. Elimination of the above conditions will take time.

[18]William E. Fulmer, "When Employees Want to Oust Their Unions," *Harvard Business Review* 56 (March/April 1978): 167–168.
[19]"Win a Decertification Election," p. 38.
[20]Ibid.

Decertification is not the only method by which employees may end their membership in the union. The second means is through withdrawal of union shop authority.[21] This procedure, often referred to as **deauthorization,** permits employees to vote to determine if they desire to change their form of union security from a union shop to an exclusive bargaining shop. Thirty percent of the employees must support the petition which goes to the NLRB and 51 percent of the employees must vote to obtain an open shop.

Some believe that the next step after deauthorization is decertification. Once deauthorization occurs, antagonism may grow between the union and company employees. Some employees will drop their union membership and cease paying dues because they are now working in an open shop. The union's reaction to this loss of membership and revenue will likely be negative. The relationship between union and employees may seriously deteriorate. Ultimately, employees may choose to decertify the union rather than permit the bitterness to continue.

THE ROLE OF PERSONNEL IN A NONUNION ORGANIZATION

The personnel manager in a nonunion firm has a slightly different role than his or her counterpart in a unionized company. As previously mentioned, the tasks of the personnel manager in a unionized firm often revolve around contract negotiations and grievance handling. The personnel manager in a nonunionized firm must work toward creating an atmosphere in which the workers will not feel a need for union representation. Personnel managers serve as the catalyst for developing and maintaining nonunion attitudes. The personnel manager, therefore, must ensure that all managers are trained to work with their employees in a positive manner so that workers can maintain their self-esteem.

In nonunion organizations, the personnel professional is often assigned a role with greater responsibility. This executive more often reports directly to the president and is often a member of the board of directors.[22] In addition, the ratio of personnel professionals to employees is often higher—perhaps one per 100 employees as opposed to one per 200 employees.

SUMMARY

Nonunionized firms comprise an important part of the industrial scene in the United States. Many employees who work under collective bargaining agree-

[21]Ibid.
[22]Foulkes, p. 93.

ments are not union members. Some of the reasons that employees do not belong to unions include: (1) cost, (2) antiunion attitude, (3) peer pressure, (4) fear of job loss, (5) lack of union support, (6) conscientious objectors, and (7) positive organizational climate.

If a firm desires to remain nonunion, a total management system is needed. The primary factors in maintaining nonunion status are: (1) effective first-line supervisors, (2) open communication, (3) personnel planning, recruitment, and selection practices, (4) effective personnel research, (5) effective employee and labor relations programs, (6) effective compensation and benefits programs, (7) effective training and development programs, and (8) personnel research.

Employees have two basic means through which they can express their dissatisfaction with the union: decertification and deauthorization (withdrawal of union shop authority). Decertification occurs when a union loses its right to act as the exclusive bargaining representative of a group of employees. The process is essentially the reverse of what a union must accomplish to be recognized as an official bargaining unit. The second means is through withdrawal of union shop authority. This procedure, often referred to as deauthorization, permits employees to vote to determine if they desire to change their form of union security from a union shop to an exclusive bargaining shop.

Questions for Review

1. What do you believe are the most important reasons for employees not joining a union? Discuss.

2. There are reasons both for and against a firm resisting unionization attempts. What are they?

3. If you were developing a battle plan to remain nonunion, what strategies and tactics might be used? Briefly describe each.

4. What role does the first-line supervisor play to help a firm remain nonunion?

5. Distinguish between decertification and deauthorization. When do you believe that deauthorization would prove more effective?

6. How might the role of a personnel manager change if he or she moves from a unionized firm to a nonunionized firm? Discuss.

Terms for Review

Open-door policy
Decertification
Deauthorization

Ed Davis is a supervisor at the Montero, New Mexico, plant of Paxma Manufacturing Company, a manufacturer of a special kind of filler material for packaging. Ed was transferred there from another plant. He accepted the transfer because he felt it would provide better promotional opportunities. Ed's new section includes fifteen workers whose jobs are essentially identical. The workload at Paxma often fluctuates, requiring extensive use of overtime. This overtime is very popular among the workers and Ed's predecessor had distributed it on a simple rotation basis.

When Ed took over he felt that overtime should be a reward for excellent performance. He also felt that there were certain workers who needed the overtime more than others. Ed didn't discuss this with the workers but simply began to assign the overtime as he saw fit.

Everything seemed to be going well until the day Ed was called to the office of Mary Donnelly, the personnel manager. After a brief greeting Mary said, "Ed, I hear through the grapevine that there's a good deal of dissension in your crew. Some of the workers feel they're not being given their fair share of overtime." Ed replied, "I assign everybody their fair share. It's just not always an equal share." "That may be true, Ed," said Ms. Donnelly, "but at least a couple of the workers believe that most of the overtime has been going to the three new people you've hired." "Who told you that?" asked Ed. "I don't think that should be important," Mary answered, "but you need to think about whether there's any substance to the impression your workers have." "You may be right," said Ed. "I suppose I could unconsciously have favored the people I selected."

Questions

1. Do you think the personnel manager was correct in getting involved in the line function of assigning overtime? Explain.

2. What would you do if you were Ed?

———

David Dorries is a supervisor for the Modern Supply Corporation (MSC), a large wholesale distributor of toiletries. All twenty of the warehousers who work for David belong to a union. During the five years that the firm has been unionized, there have often been serious disagreements between the union and management. Management has been working for several years to foster an atmosphere that would lead to improved relations, but some of the longstanding union members have resisted.

As David was walking through the warehouse recently, he heard two of his best workers talking. "Bob," one worker said, "we work our tails off and make the same as those lazy clods." "Yeah Bill, I know," said Bob. "It doesn't seem fair. Seems like something should be done."

At that moment Bob and Bill realized that David had heard them. David casually commented, "I certainly agree that you guys are two of the best workers here. I sure would like to give you both a raise. You really deserve it. Unfortunately, you're unionized and I'm bound to pay precisely what the contract specifies. I'm sorry."

"Well," Bob said, "how do we get rid of the union? I didn't want it in the first place and don't believe the majority of the other guys wanted it either."

Questions

1. How should David respond to this question? Discuss.

2. Describe the procedure, if one exists, for "getting rid of the union."

PARMA CYCLE COMPANY: THE ORGANIZING EFFORT

The Clarksdale, Mississippi plant of Parma Cycle Company had been open for only six months when the first efforts at unionization became apparent. A known union organizer was in town and prounion leaflets began to appear around the factory. As the personnel director at Clarksdale, Edward Deal had been expecting this to occur. He knew that the workers who had been brought down from the main plant in Parma, Ohio had a strong union tradition. He also knew that the wage and benefits package at Clarksdale was far less liberal than that at the Cleveland plant. So far, this had created no major problem. Most of the workers recruited from the Clarksdale area felt that they were well paid in comparison with others in that area.

In the plant that same day, Janice Snively was thinking about whether or not she should talk to the personnel director. Janice had been hired by Parma two weeks prior to start-up time. She had previously worked as a maintenance supervisor at a garment factory about sixty miles from Clarksdale. She had taken a slight pay cut in order to take what she thought would be a better job in the long run and to be nearer her family, who lived in Clarksdale.

Janice's crew of ten machine operators and two parts handlers was among the best in the plant. Janice had made friends with each of them and they obviously respected her. She felt that one reason she was a good leader was her willingness to "get her hands dirty." Because of her experience in maintenance she was able to repair the machines herself when they broke down. When an operator was absent, she would simply take over that machine in order to keep the workflow going.

Lately she had noticed a change. The workers seemed to be shutting her out. In a couple of instances, when several of her crew were congregated at one table in the lunch room, the conversation stopped as she approached and then awkwardly began again. The change of topic was obvious. For the first time, too, she began to hear complaints from the employees. For example, the operator of the cut-off machine, which cuts certain frame members to size, complained of the speed with which the machine operated. "I have less than one second to move the cut off piece before the tubing feeds through to start another cut. I'll be lucky not to lose an arm," he said. There had been a number of similar complaints, many of them related to safety, some to working conditions, and a number of workers had asked about when their next raise was coming.

Janice just thought that handling all of these kinds of problems was part of the supervisor's job and so she wasn't too concerned. Because of something that had happened this

DID YOU KNOW?

• Parma's workers in Ohio do not pay for their dependent's medical insurance. You do!

• Parma's employees in Ohio have dental insurance. You don't!

• Employees in Ohio have ten paid holidays. You have only eight.

• Trainees at the Ohio plant get $6.75 per hour. At Clarksdale, they get minimum wage.

• Senior machine operators in Ohio get $12.60 an hour. Here, they get $8.90 or less.

morning, though, Janice decided it was time to talk to the personnel director.

Janice walked in as Ed was thinking about the advantages and disadvantages of having a union. "Ed," she said, "I want you to look at this. One of the workers gave it to me and asked if it is true. I didn't know how to answer." Janice handed Ed the mimeographed sheet which is reproduced on page 569. After studying the sheet for a moment Ed said, "It's basically true, but I wish it weren't."

Questions

1. What do you think caused the unionizing attempt at Parma Cycle's Clarksdale plant?

2. What sequence of events is likely to occur before the Clarksdale plant becomes unionized?

3. Assuming that Parma Cycle wishes to prevent unionization of the Clarksdale plant, what might the union and management legally do before and after a union representation election is ordered by the NLRB?

____ Experiencing Personnel Management ____

ADVICE FOR THE SUPERVISOR

A major part of the personnel director's job is to advise managers at all levels regarding personnel matters, particularly matters related to dealing with the union. In this exercise you will play the role of a personnel director who has been asked for advice by a supervisor, Larry Bradley.

Role Descriptions

Larry Bradley. You have been with Parma Cycle Company for twelve years, the last four as a supervisor at the Parma, Ohio, plant. You are a very safety-conscious supervisor with a reputation for strictly enforcing the rules. Because of this, you believe, you have not had a lost time accident in your division since you became supervisor. There is a rule in the plant, well known to everyone, that every intersection is a "4-way stop" for fork-lift trucks. According to the labor/management agreement, even minor safety violations justify a three-day suspension and a written warning.

Tuesday you asked for a volunteer to stay late and move some pallets of materials using a small fork-lift truck. Charlie Fox volunteered. While he was moving materials that evening, you worked in your office, getting caught up on some paperwork. You had only about an hour's work to do. When you finished, you started walking back to the area where Charlie was working. You saw the fork-lift truck with Charlie at the wheel round the corner at a high speed and without stopping. You informed Charlie Fox that you were suspending him for three days and placing a written warning in his personnel folder. You told him not to bother reporting for work the next morning. Charlie appeared upset but that did not concern you particularly. You have a job to do and you want it to be done safely. That night, a friend called you and warned you to be ready because the union steward, Eugene Wilson, is upset about your treatment of Charlie. Early the next morning you call the personnel director, Jesse Heard, for advice.

You know you will soon have to confront Charlie and Eugene.

Charlie Fox. You have been with Parma only two years. You are twenty-two years old, married, and have a new child. You want to move into management one day and do not want any bad marks on your record. You also need every dime you can get just to keep up with monthly bills and expenses related to the new child. You realize that in a technical sense, Larry is correct in imposing the penalty. You think it is unreasonable, however, because there was no one else in the plant except the night watchman. Larry had told you he'd be ready to leave in about an hour. So you were hurrying to complete the work before that hour was up just to keep from holding him up. You wanted to explain but he didn't give you a chance, just told you that you that you were suspended. When you spoke to the union steward about it, he actually seemed eager to help, immediately taking your side. You hope that you can convince Larry to change his mind about punishing you.

Eugene Wilson. You were elected union steward for the Wheel Assembly Division last year. There have been few grievances since then and you have had a rather uneventful year as steward. A couple of times workers have brought complaints to you but you thought that management was correct in each case and you told the workers so. You like being the union steward but feel that you might not be elected next time unless you are able to make a "show". The situation involving Charlie Fox gives you your chance. Your believe Larry Bradley was unreasonable in suspending Charlie. The purpose of the traffic rule in the plant is to keep people from getting run over by fork-lift trucks. Because there was practically nobody in the plant, there was really no danger. You hope you can convince Larry to back down.

Questions

1. How might your advice differ depending on whether you have heard Charlie's side of the story?

2. If Larry does not back down, what are the steps that may have to be taken to resolve the disagreement?

3. What is likely to be the impact of Larry's authority over the workers if he backs down?

Part VII

Personnel: Preparation for the Future

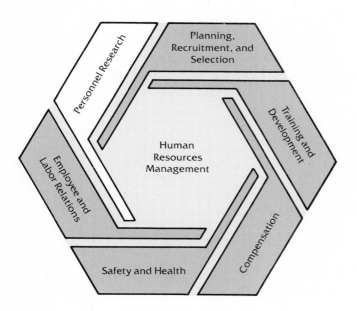

Chapter Objectives

1. Explain the importance of research to human resources management.
2. Identify the basic methods of inquiry for research.
3. Describe the steps that need to be accomplished in the research process.
4. Describe how quantitative methods may be used in human resources research.

Chapter 18 ⎯⎯⎯⎯⎯⎯⎯⎯⎯

Personnel Research

Mary Carter, personnel manager for Ajax, Inc., noted that the turnover rate in the research and development department was approaching 200 percent. She knew that the loss of qualified researchers could have a serious impact upon the success of Ajax, which was known for its leadership in developing new products. Mary decided to propose a confidential questionnaire to be administered to all employees in the department in an attempt to identify reasons for the excessive turnover.

Bob Stephens, president of Queens Manufacturing Company, was concerned as he viewed profit figures for the year. Sales had been good but he had been hearing rumblings of discontent throughout the organization. Somehow, people at Queens just did not appear to be happy. Because the company employed approximately 5000 workers, he wondered how he could uncover the problems facing the organization.

Additional information provided through personnel research could benefit both Bob and Mary. Mary might be able to determine the reason for the high turnover rate. Bob would like to uncover the problems that appear to pervade the entire organization. Personnel research may be able to assist both managers in their endeavors.

The personnel manager's job, as discussed in Chapter 1, is vastly different from only a few years ago. In order to contend with mounting responsibilities, the personnel manager has discovered that information derived from research is constantly required. **Personnel research** involves the systematic study of human resources for the purpose of maximizing personal and organizational goal achievement.

Unless an organization possesses the resources to afford a separate personnel research function, it is likely that each human resources manager or specialist will, at one time or another, be called upon to conduct research. This chapter is designed to provide an overview of the research function as it pertains to human resources management.

COST/BENEFITS ANALYSIS—PERSONNEL RESEARCH

Applications of personnel research are numerous and appear to be increasing rapidly. However, a major difficulty, and therefore a cost, is that personnel professionals are often not qualified in that area. Although this personnel function is not highly developed, it is potentially beneficial to companies. Personnel professionals may need to take the time and effort to upgrade themselves in the area. Firms who desire to conduct personnel research may find it necessary to recruit specialists in statistics and computer science to provide the expertise.

The potential benefits of meaningful personnel research far exceed the costs. Organizations have only recently begun to realize the significance of the human element upon the firm's ability to achieve its goals. This realization has occurred at a time when the competitive nature of business is making it increasingly difficult to obtain and retain individuals. Many of the traditional concepts regarding human resources management have been questioned and new ideas are needed if tasks are to be effectively accomplished.[1] Workers no longer feel compelled to remain with a firm for life. Other options are available, such as beginning a second career or taking a job with a competitor. Naturally, larger firms use personnel research extensively. But the benefits have yet to be realized in many other organizations.

The specific applications for personnel research depend to a large extent upon the firm's needs. As you can see in Table 18–1, although there is considerable overlap in the type of research presently being conducted, differences do exist. These variations are attributable to such factors as size, goals, and particular problems of the individual organization.

[1]Kenneth Knight, "The Role of Personnel Research in the Real World," *Personnel Management* 7 (December 1975): 14.

Table 18–1. Areas where personnel research is used

Company	Areas of Personnel Research
Atlantic Richfield Company	• Selection test validation Assessment center validation Survey research
Fleming Companies, Inc.	• Specific emphasis on turnover, turnover reasons, turnover costs Identification of high potential employees for accelerated development Impact of union contracts on compensation Improving performance appraisal
Control Data Corporation	• Staffing, compensation, interviewing, performance appraisal, management training, surveys of employee attitudes, productivity enhancement, employee development, selection
Ashland Oil, Inc.	• Selection at both the exempt and nonexempt levels and also in the early identification of people with potential to become high-level managers
Ford Motor Company	• Selection, opinion surveys, career progress, performance appraisal, quality motivation, management potential, organization

Effective Management

Many human resources management practices have been questioned because of recent government laws and regulations.[2] For instance, it is no longer acceptable to use job specifications containing arbitrary requirements as a basis for recruiting and selecting employees. Managers are now called upon to prove that their employment decisions are based upon valid requirements. However, as Walter Tornow, executive consultant and director of personnel research for Control Data Corporation, states, "On the whole, government regulations have had a positive effect because they cause organizations to examine and document their practices in ways that heretofore were not deemed necessary for some."

Another reason for the increased need for personnel research relates to the rapid changes that have occurred in our environment. Because of change, management may need to alter its approach in adapting to new conditions. In the last twenty years the nature and composition of the work force has been significantly altered. Protected groups are entering the work force in ever increasing numbers. Research is required to identify how the goals of these new work force members can be integrated with the needs of the firm.

Largely because of increased educational opportunities, both managers and nonmanagers have become more sophisticated in their expectations from employment. Management styles may need modification to achieve optimum results. While a highly autocratic manager may have been successful in the past,

[2]Richard W. Beatly, "Research Needs of PAIR Professions in the Near Future," *The Personnel Administrator* 23 (September 1978): 17 (hereafter cited as "PAIR Professions").

Executive Profile

Paul A. Banas, Ph.D., APD
Manager, Personnel Research Section
Ford Motor Company

Dr. Paul A. Banas, manager of the Personnel Research Section of Ford Motor Company's Personnel and Organization Staff, brings a unique set of experiences to his position, which makes him an invaluable asset to his company. Under his direction, the Personnel Research Section has grown steadily to become a unit which deals with a broad array of human resources management issues, including productivity, quality of work life, and organizational change and development. His major contribution has been in helping the organization focus on accurate identification of problems and selection of appropriate tools to solve them.

Dr. Banas believes that to identify and resolve work related problems requires accurate information and the involvement of management, employees, and—where appropriate—union leadership. He says, "Too often managers act on their perceptions rather than actual data, treating the symptoms rather than the causes of the problem." Also, he feels that too few managers see the employee as a valuable resource in problem identification and resolution. Paul goes on to state, "At Ford, there are indications that the management climate is changing. For example, over the last three years, a process called employee involvement (EI) has been implemented at most Ford plants. EI is underway at sixty-five facilities, with an estimated 10,000 hourly employees actively participating in problem solving groups. This is a joint effort of the United Auto Workers Union and the Ford Motor Company. There are over thirty-five facilities with projects in place, with an estimated 2000 salaried employees participating in team development activities. As a result of the efforts of these groups, there have been significant improvements in product quality, efficiency, and the quality of work life."

Paul acknowledges that the kinds of changes needed in the workplace cannot be legislated from the top of the company. Action planning requires involvement of both

a similar style in today's organizations may lead to resentment and, in the long run, lower productivity. Also, the nature of the organizational structure may need modification. The means of identifying appropriate managerial styles and organizational structure will continue to be a major task of personnel research.

The actual nature of the work has also been changing rapidly. This has caused Personnel to seek solutions to determine how the work force can be continuously updated. One of management's most difficult tasks is to get employees to accept change as a result of technological advancement. It is not easy for a person to be told that his or her skill is no longer needed and that a new skill must be learned. Research may well provide the means by which people may learn to accept change more readily and thereby continue to be productive members of our society.

management and employees at the local level if the actions are to be on target and implement effectively. He says, "The results I've seen from our hourly and salaried EI groups show commitment, creativity, and hard work. The recommendations that are being put into effect represent a significant and meaningful investment in the company's human resources. Over the years, this investment should reenforce the link between satisfying employee needs and attaining company goals."

According to Dr. Banas, "The personnel research consultant of the future is the person with a broad knowledge of human resources management and a thorough understanding of individual differences, group dynamics, and management processes."

Dr. Banas originally intended to pursue a career in the physical sciences, graduating with a bachelor's degree in chemistry. During subsequent service in the U.S. Navy, he was assigned as the safety officer at a rocket and explosive producing plant which employed about 5000 people. As safety officer, he investigated industrial accidents to determine their probable causes. Inevitably, he recalls, they resulted from human action.

As a result of this assignment with the Navy, Dr. Banas determined to learn more about human behavior in industry, so he earned a Ph.D. in industrial psychology from the University of Minnesota. While pursuing the degree, he was head of the undergraduate psychology office and was elected president of the local chapter of Psi Chi, an honorary psychology society.

After receiving his doctorate, Dr. Banas worked as a research psychologist for the U.S. Army Personnel Research Office, where he specialized in selection techniques. Subsequently he became a research scientist and consultant for Human Sciences Research, Inc. While with Human Sciences Research he was asked to join Ford Motor Company's Personnel Research Section.

Dr. Banas has written more than twenty-five publications and participates actively in several professional organizations, including Division Fourteen of the American Psychological Association and the Personnel/Human Resources Division of the Academy of Management, which he has chaired. He is an Accredited Personnel Diplomat, a member of the editorial boards of *Personnel Psychology* and *Human Resource Planning*, an advisor to the Ball Foundation, and a member of the board of trustees of the Michigan Quality of Worklife Council. In addition, he maintains contact with the academic world through his teaching. He has taught courses in organizational behavior, human resources management, industrial psychology, and survey research.

Personnel Planning, Recruitment, and Selection

Plans must be made to recruit, select, and retain the type of employees who are capable of working toward achievement of organizational objectives. An organization possesses a distinct personality as does an individual. Just as each of us has observed personalities with whom we feel uncomfortable, organizations must seek to find the best match between the needs of the firm and its employees. An individual may be considered an excellent worker in one firm and a poor producer in another even though similar tasks are performed.

Recruitment research is directed toward determining means through which individuals with high potential can be encouraged to make application with the firm. For instance, firms need to determine the most likely source of

- "If you need to be perceived as the one in charge—the one who thought up the idea, or was responsible for implementing the entire plan, or otherwise deserves the credit—then you will be taking credit away from the line managers who are ultimately responsible to those who finance the organization.

- The best personnel managers are consultants. Line managers are in charge and the personnel professionals are their in-house consultants. If you enjoy working in the wings, then you will probably enjoy Personnel. But if you need to be center stage, Personnel would be a poor choice."

**Erik H. Rambusch, Manager—Personnel Planning,
Recruitment, and Placement
The Dun & Bradstreet Corporation**

qualified candidates for the sales force. It does little good to know the qualities that prospective employees should possess and not know where and how to recruit these individuals.

The goal of employee selection research is to identify prospective employees with the greatest potential for achieving success. As one might expect, the definition of a successful employee varies by organization. This research often attempts to identify factors such as background and experience, education, hobbies, and test scores associated with differentiating between successful and less successful applicants.[3]

Another major consideration in developing a selection process based upon specific qualities is that the profile of successful workers often varies by geographical location. Research continues in this area as firms attempt to improve the selection process as a viable means of identifying individuals with the greatest potential for success.

Another difficulty is that various groups tend to possess different qualities depicting success. For instance, in one study, a profile of successful men and women was developed for a firm. Although there were as many successful women as men, the profiles based upon biographical data were essentially different.[4]

Training and Development

Personnel research is also quite important in the area of training and development. In the past, there have been numerous instances of improper allocation of training dollars. Studies may identify the firm's employees who can benefit from training. For instance, a high error rate associated with certain

[3]R. Wayne Mondy and Frank N. Edens, "An Empirical Test of the Decision to Participate Model," *Journal of Management* 2, no. 2, (Fall 1977): 11–16.
[4]"Job Longevity Differs by Sex," *Convenience Store News* 11, no. 9 (May 2, 1975): 1.

employees might indicate that they need additional training.

Also, research into the usefulness of the training program may be needed. Are workers better prepared to do their jobs after training, or is the training an exercise in futility? Training and development is expensive and its cost must be justified.

In addition, the type of training and development that is needed may be identified through personnel research. The productivity level of different departments may suggest that certain managers require development in the areas of managerial concepts and practices. Finally, an analysis of employee performance may suggest additional areas of training and development.

Compensation

Both actual and perceived inequities in the firm's compensation systems can create problems. Managers must be able to identify the actual inequalities and make the needed corrections as well as be able to provide information to employees which will solve the problem. In order to maintain a fair compensation policy, it is not uncommon for firms to conduct extensive surveys. In addition, surveys are often conducted in-house to determine employee's attitudes regarding their pay.

Compensation research is widely used to identify potential problems before they get out of hand. In this inflationary era of firms constantly bidding for skilled employees, an organization's compensation program can rapidly become outdated.

Employee and Labor Relations

When research is used in the area of employee and labor relations, its focus is on topics that can affect individual job performance. Some of this research may be needed to identify factors which will permit the firm to remain union free. Factors within the environment, such as working conditions, may be found to have a detrimental effect upon employees' productivity and job satisfaction. This type of information would likely be beneficial in maintaining nonunion status. When problems are left unsolved, the worker may believe that the only remedy to the situation is to join the union.

Safety and Health

The primary task of research in health and safety relates to identification of problem areas before they become critical. For instance, research may be conducted to analyze the locations and causes of accidents.[5] It also can be used to

[5]W. H. Weiss, "Accident Investigation: A Major Responsibility of Supervisors," *Supervision* 40 (July 1978): 1–3.

identify characteristics of workers with higher probabilities of having accidents. Patterns may often be identified and changes recommended to prevent their occurrence.

METHODS OF INQUIRY IN PERSONNEL RESEARCH

The type of problem confronting the personnel manager determines, to a large extent, the method of inquiry that will be used. The use of each method or combination of methods depends upon the particular needs of the organization. Research methods—the case study, the survey, and the experiment—will next be described.

The Case Study

When the personnel manager is called upon to uncover the underlying reason for occurrence, the **case study** is often used. The problem confronting Mary Carter described at the beginning of the chapter may well be solved through use of the case study. Employees in the research and development department likely are experiencing problems entirely different from those of other departments. Mary must work with the department head to determine the underlying cause of the difficulty. Solutions to problems associated with a plant, department, or section are sought through the use of the case study. In using this method, an attempt is made to identify causes of specific problems. Typical problems for which the case study might be used include identifying the reason for:

- An excessively high turnover at a particular plant
- A high absenteeism rate in a specific department
- A high accident rate at a certain building site
- Low morale in a particular department
- The low number of minority members in a certain plant
- The underlying reasons for a wildcat strike at a particular location

Naturally, there are many more situations in which the case study method may be used. No conscious attempt is made to develop new theories or make broad generalizations, although possible new approaches may be suggested from the study.

The Survey

A major function of human resources research is to periodically check the pulse of the organization to determine the attitudes of employees toward such factors as job satisfaction, pay, and supervision. Responses to questions may also reveal ways by which productivity can be improved.[6] The primary tool for the researcher in this endeavor is often the attitude survey, which is also known as the opinion survey. For instance, Ford Motor Company uses the survey to obtain the opinions of its salaried personnel. Every other year, Ford administers the Salaried Personnel Opinion Survey. The results are published in Ford's in-house publication, *The American Road*. With information such as this, management is in a position to correct problems before they become serious.

When surveys are used, they may be either the objective-multiple choice type (see Figure 18–1) or a scaled answer to suggest agreement or disagreement to a particular question (see Figure 18–2). Objective analysis of survey results often requires a more detailed study. Possible bases for comparison of survey results might be by:

1. Section or department
2. Age
3. Sex
4. Seniority
5. Job level or degree of responsibility
6. Changes in attitudes from a previous survey
7. Comparison with other divisions, departments, etc.
8. Comparison with a standardized score if a validated instrument is being used

Figure 18–1. Examples of multiple choice responses to survey questions.

Why did you decide to do what you are now doing?

a. Desire to aid or assist others

b. Influenced by another person or situation

c. Always wanted to be in this vocation

d. Lack of opportunity or interest in other vocational fields

e. Opportunities provided by this vocation

f. Personal satisfaction from doing this work

What do you like least about your job?

a. Nothing

b. Pay

c. Supervisor relations

d. Problems with fellow workers

e. Facilities

f. Paper work and reports

[6]Robert Loffreda, "Employee Attitude Surveys: A Valuable Motivating Tool," *The Personnel Administrator* 24 (July 1979): 42.

Considering all aspects of your job, evaluate your compensation with regard to your contributions to the needs of the organization. Circle the number that best describes how you feel.

Pay Too Low		Pay Low		Pay Average		Pay Above Average		Pay Too High	
1	2	3	4	5	6	7	8	9	10

What are your feelings about overtime work requirements? Circle the number that best indicates how you feel.

Unnecessary			Necessary on Occasion				Necessary		
1	2	3	4	5	6	7	8	9	10

Figure 18–2. **Examples of scaled responses to survey questions.**

The information becomes more meaningful to management when survey data are analyzed by various subgroups. A major point to consider is that survey responses often identify symptoms rather than actual causes. When surveys are administered, the researcher should avoid concentrating upon isolated responses. Instead, the data should be viewed from a broader perspective. A pattern which depicts a general trend may be found. Responses will likely reflect this trend if there are difficulties in the organization. For instance, even if the compensation and benefits program is quite competitive, a low evaluation in this area may reflect—not an inadequate compensation system—but general dissatisfaction.

When surveys are used to identify attitudes and opinions of organizational members, certain cautions must be observed. First, confidentiality of responses must be assured.[7] Employees must believe that their specific responses will not be communicated to management. It is for this reason that outside consultants are often employed to administer the questionnaire. Even if members of the personnel department are quite ethical, employees may still perceive the department as being a tool of management. Rightly or wrongly, the employee may always wonder whether Personnel would succumb to management pressure to reveal responses given by specific employees.

Confidentiality means more than merely omitting a worker's name on the questionnaire. Even in a large firm, there are numerous sections that consist of only a small number of employees. Or, in a large department, a characteristic of a particular worker may make him or her easily identified. For instance, one large department of fifty workers may have only one female. Protection of such a person's confidentiality is critical to obtaining accurate results. The researcher must constantly be alert to these situations and be prepared to consolidate groups when necessary to assure that anonymity is preserved.

The results of the surveys must be communicated to the various affected groups. Employees need to see that their responses are being heard. If surveys

[7]R. Wayne Mondy and Wallace F. Nelson, "Job Satisfaction Among Radiologic Technologists," *Applied Radiology* 7 (July/August 1978): 66.

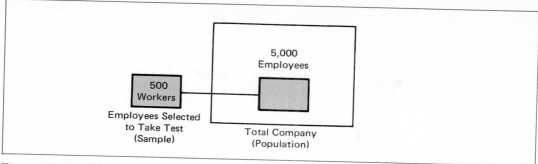

Figure 18–3. **The distinction between population and sample.**

are to be used on a continuous basis, management must take some action on the results.

When survey results are communicated to management, it is often best for each department or section head to be contacted individually.[8] For instance, if the survey suggests that problems exist in the marketing department, the department head will likely be more receptive to criticism if his or her peers are not listening. Just as workers do not like to be disciplined in the presence of their co-workers, survey results should be presented only to the affected parties. Superior results are typically obtained when the data are discussed with each group separately.

At times, surveying each person is infeasible because of time or cost restraints. **Sampling** is the process by which only a portion of the total number of individuals are studied, from which conclusions are drawn for the entire group. Bob Stephens, the president of Queens Manufacturing Company, might ask his personnel manager to administer a questionnaire to a sample of the workers. As you can see in Figure 18–3, the total number of workers in the firm is 5000. The time, effort, and cost necessary to survey the entire 5000 workers may be prohibitive. The researcher may then decide to select at random a smaller number of workers and draw conclusions based upon the smaller number.

The Experiment

A method of inquiry which involves certain variables being manipulated while others are held constant is referred to as the **experiment**. With this method, there is both a control group and an experimental group. The control group remains constant and operates as it did under the old environment whereas selected variables are manipulated within the experimental group. For instance, we may desire to determine the effect a new training program will have upon productivity. The control group would continue to perform tasks in the conventional manner. The experimental group would receive the training. It

[8]"A Productive Way to Vent Employee Gripes," *Business Week* 2556 (October 16, 1978): 169.

is assumed that if a change in productivity occurs in the experimental group, it results from the training.

On the surface, the experiment would appear to be an excellent means of inquiry. In actuality, it is sometimes difficult to isolate the many interrelated variables affecting people. This point was vividly made during the Hawthorne experiments at Western Electric beginning in the late 1920s. In one study a control group and an experimental group were selected to determine the effect of lighting upon productivity. The control group was to have a constant level of illumination whereas the experimental group was to experience different levels of light. Just as the industrial engineers expected, as the level of illumination increased, productivity also increased. But, strangely, productivity also continued to increase as the level of lighting was decreased. Only when lighting became so low that the workers could barely see, did productivity begin to fall. A major conclusion was that the study did not take into consideration the influence of the small, informal work group on productivity. This phenomenon (which is known as the Hawthorne Effect) reminds researchers of how difficult it is to control the many variables when human resources are being studied.

PERSONNEL AND THE RESEARCH PROCESS

In order to accomplish human resources research, the firm needs to develop a systematic approach. You have likely discovered that you make better grades when you follow a systematic procedure for studying. Likewise, the most fruitful research is accomplished by following a logical process. The research process consists of six basic steps subjected to external and internal environmental constraints which you can see in Figure 18–4.

Recognize the Problem

One of the most difficult tasks in the research process is to recognize that a problem exists. For instance, at what point does absenteeism become excessive? When does a turnover problem actually exist? A certain amount of turnover may be healthy for an organization. However, it often becomes convenient to explain away a potential problem. A manager may state, "Even though turnover is high, we really don't have a problem because those people didn't fit in the organization anyway." Such a comment leads one to suspect that this manager may not be open to problem recognition. In actuality, the problem may be caused by an inadequate selection process, insufficient management training, or a multitude of other reasons. Or, as the manager suggests, there may be no problem. Regardless of the situation, openness on the part of the manager is the cornerstone of problem recognition.

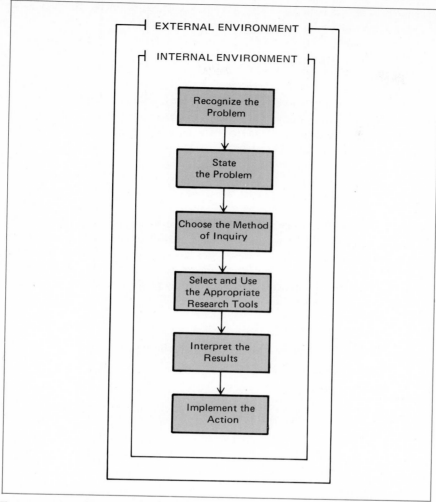

Figure 18–4. **Personnel and the research process.**

State the Problem

The next step in the process is to clearly state the purpose of the research. The major hurdle to overcome is that the problem—not the symptoms—must be identified. Research should not focus upon symptoms but should concentrate instead upon solving problems. As you might expect, this may prove difficult. For instance, a manager might maintain that the cause of decreased production is low employee morale when in actuality this is not the real problem. Research may determine that dictatorial supervisors have been exerting so much pressure upon employees that they could care less about productivity. If the manager attempted to solve the morale problem through means such as increasing benefits, it is unlikely that conditions would improve. A clear definition of the problem is essential for effective research.

Choose the Method of Inquiry

The method of inquiry chosen depends to a large extent upon the nature of the research. The case study, the survey, and the experiment are all viable alternatives as methods of inquiry. However, most personnel research involves either the case method or the survey.

Select and Use the Appropriate Research Tool

Numerous quantitative tools are available for use by the personnel researcher. Specific techniques will be reviewed later in this chapter. These quantitative approaches are merely tools and we do not suggest that all managers must be experts in mathematics and statistical theory in order to take advantage of their use. However, if managers are to adequately perform research, knowledge of the following is needed:

- Available quantitative tools
- Circumstances under which these tools should be used
- Strengths and weaknesses of each method
- Ability to interpret the results

The selection of a tool depends upon the particular purpose for which the research is being conducted.

Interpret the Results

The person closest to the problem should participate in interpreting the results. Strange conclusions have often occurred when outsiders alone have attempted to interpret the results. For instance, the survey may suggest that major dissatisfaction exists in the engineering department. A person not close to the situation might unjustly assign the problem to inadequate supervision. In actuality, the engineers may have voiced their dissatisfaction over the poor facilities in which they work.

Implement the Necessary Action

The most difficult phase of the research process is to implement the necessary action based upon the research conclusions. The research results may have identified areas where changes need to be made. Personnel now becomes the catalyst to convince management that a change is necessary. In many instances, this task is quite difficult. Telling a manager that his or her managerial style is causing excessive turnover can be a tedious undertaking. However, the benefits of the research occur at this stage.

QUANTITATIVE METHODS IN PERSONNEL RESEARCH

When we begin to discuss quantitative methods, some of us throw up our hands in frustration and say, "I can't do it." A mystique has arisen that often tends to place a barrier between those who conduct research and the so-called real world. This need not be the case. Personnel research is needed if many of the problems associated with human resources management are to be solved. And, as previously mentioned, the people closest to the problem should be involved in conducting and interpreting the results. Potential quantitative tools which are available for use by human resources managers will next be briefly discussed.

Correlation Analysis

There are many times when a researcher would like to determine the relative strength of the relationships which exist between two or more variables. The purpose of **correlation analysis** is to measure the degree of association or correlation that exists between two or more variables.[9] For instance, is there a relationship between job satisfaction and employee absenteeism? In the scatter diagram shown in Figure 18–5, a high but negative relationship appears to exist between job satisfaction and employee absenteeism. As job satisfaction goes down, absenteeism goes up. On the other hand, in the firm portrayed in Figure 18–6, there appears to be a high, positive correlation between employees' amount of education and their level of productivity. Apparently, the higher the education level, the greater the productivity.

The benefits of correlation analysis are considerable, but caution must be exercised in its use. There are times when a correlation can prove deceptive because the relationship does not reflect cause and effect. A high correlation may exist, but it might be meaningless. For instance, one study indicated a high positive correlation between the number of grey squirrels in North Louisiana and the political activity in Washington, D.C. Here, a high relationship existed but the two variables were obviously unrelated. Personnel should be alert to this potential problem, and not make decisions based on inappropriate interpretations.

[9]Charles T. Clark and Lawrence L. Schkade, *Statistical Analysis for Administrative Decisions,* 3d ed. (Cincinnati: Southwestern Publishing Company, 1979), pp. 386–387.

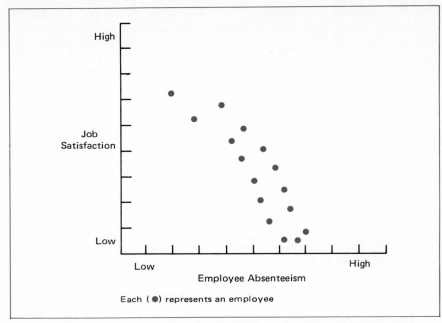

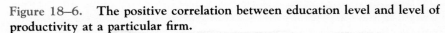

Figure 18–5. The negative correlation between job satisfaction and employee absenteeism at a particular firm.

Figure 18–6. The positive correlation between education level and level of productivity at a particular firm.

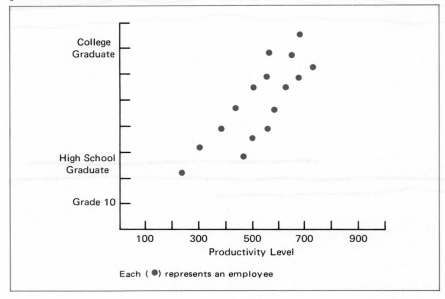

Regression Analysis

Regression analysis was described in Chapter 4 as a technique which has proven useful in personnel planning. It has also proven beneficial in personnel research. As you remember, the purpose of **regression analysis** is to "utilize the relation between two or more quantitative variables so that one variable can be predicted from the other, or others."[10] Suppose, for instance, that you would like to determine if employees' productivity can be estimated through knowledge of their educational attainment (refer to the scatter diagram in Figure 18–6). In regression analysis terminology, the productivity level that we are attempting to estimate is referred to as the dependent variable. The education level used to estimate the level of productivity is called the independent variable. In this example, there is only one independent variable, so the process is referred to as simple linear regression. The use of two or more independent variables is termed multiple regression.

When regression analysis is used in personnel research, some possible dependent variables might be:

- Satisfaction level of employees
- Length of employment of employees
- Productivity level of employees
- Accident rate of employees

Personnel data which might be used as the independent variable include:

- Background and biographical data
- Work history with the firm
- Personal goals and aspirations
- Test scores

The use of biographical data in screening is expected to increase in the future.[11]

The researcher might attempt to determine through regression analysis which of the above factors aid in differentiating between productive and less productive workers. The level of productivity becomes the dependent variable and information such as biographical data, work history, or test scores becomes the independent variable. The regression model that is developed may be capable of assisting the manager in identifying prospective employees who will become successful workers. Therefore, selection decisions are improved. Naturally, the model's accuracy must be validated through other statistical means. But, if the equation proves appropriate, it can be useful in the selection process.

[10]John Netter and William Wasserman, *Applied Linear Statistical Models* (Homewood, Ill.: Richard D. Irwin, Inc., 1974), p. 21.
[11]"PAIR Professions," p. 19.

The purpose of **discriminant analysis** is to identify factors which differentiate between two or more groups in a population.[12] This statistical technique is beginning to be used in personnel research. When two group discriminant analysis is used, an attempt might be made to identify factors which differentiate between some of the following:

- Satisfied versus less satisfied employees
- Long-term versus short-term employees
- Productive versus less productive employees
- Accident-prone versus less accident-prone workers

Only the imagination of the researcher limits the factors which should be used. Some potential factors which the researcher might use to differentiate between the two groups include:

1. Background and biographical data
2. Work history with the firm
3. Personal goals and aspirations
4. Test scores

For instance, suppose the researcher was attempting to determine if there were background or biographical factors which differentiated between satisfied and less satisfied workers. Much as with regression analysis, the level of satisfaction becomes the dependent variable. However, unlike regression, individuals in the two groups are identified as either satisfied or less satisfied. Through the use of discriminant analysis, independent variables are identified which are capable of distinguishing between the two selected groups. The mechanics of discriminant analysis also permit determining the reliability of the equation.

Time Series Analysis

A technique which has proven quite helpful in making projections over time is **time series analysis**. As in regression analysis, both a dependent variable and an independent variable are required. However, the independent variable is now associated with time and the dependent variable is associated with demand.[13] Figure 18–7 provides a scatter diagram in which the dependent variable is the demand for the firm's product. When the number of employees required in a company is closely associated with demand for the firm's product, time series analysis may prove useful in forecasting the organization's human

[12]For an in depth look at discriminant analysis, see Donald F. Morrison, *Multivariate Statistical Methods*, 2d ed. (New York: McGraw-Hill Book Company, 1976), pp. 230–245.
[13]Joseph G. Monks, *Operations Management: Theory and Problems* (New York: McGraw-Hill Book Company, 1977), pp. 277–278.

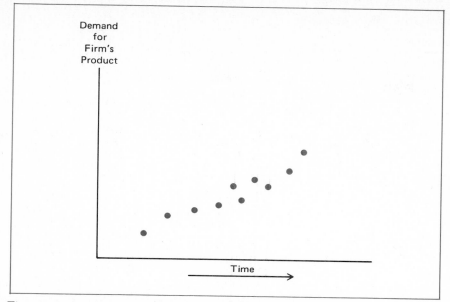

Figure 18–7. **A scatter diagram for time series analysis.**

resources needs. Using the same general mathematical procedure as in regression analysis, a time series equation can be calculated and estimates of future demand may be made.

PERSONNEL RESEARCH: AN ILLUSTRATION

In order to illustrate how personnel research may be used in an organization, an actual example will next be described. At the firm's request, its name will not be identified. The techniques used and the benefits which were achieved are factual. The organization, a regional medical center in the Southwest, had experienced rapid growth and the accompanying growing pains. The personnel director and the hospital administrator recognized that some potential difficulties were developing and called upon an outside consultant. He was to work with them in identifying and solving problems before they became critical.

The consultant first talked with numerous organizational members to get a general feel for the situation. Refusal of the employees to talk about specific subjects and their apparent nervousness during the informal interviews suggested that potential problems did exist.

The next phase of the research project involved developing a survey tailored specifically for the hospital. Sample questions which were developed are shown in Figure 18–8. As you can see, topics ranged from managerial style to compensation. Administration of the questionnaire to all hospital personnel

What do you like most about your job?

a.   Helping or providing service for others
b.   Learning opportunities
c.   Personal satisfaction
d.   Being around people
e.   The work you perform at this hospital at this job
f.   Nothing
g.   Other (Specify)
h.   Other (Specify)

What do you like least about your job?

a.   Nothing
b.   Pay
c.   Supervisor relations
d.   Problems with fellow workers
e.   Facilities
f.   Paper work and reports
g.   Patient related problems
h.   Doctor related problems
i.   Other (Specify)
j.   Other (Specify)

How would you describe your overall working environment? Circle the number that best describes how you feel.

Extremely Frustrating		Frustrating		Acceptable		Above Average		Excellent Work	
1	2	3	4	5	6	7	8	9	10

What do you think of strikes in the health care field? Circle the number which indicates how you feel.

Strongly Favor		Favor		Neutral		Opposed		Strongly Opposed	
1	2	3	4	5	6	7	8	9	10

What do you think about the system of giving pay increases at this hospital? Circle the number that best describes how you feel.

Very Bad		Poor		Satisfied		Good		Excellent	
1	2	3	4	5	6	7	8	9	10

Considering all aspects of your job, evaluate your compensation with regard to your contributions to the needs of the hospital. Circle the number that best describes how you feel.

Pay Too Low		Pay Low		Pay Average		Pay Above Average		Pay Too High	
1	2	3	4	5	6	7	8	9	10

Figure 18–8.   **Sample survey questions.**

was a critical phase. Because potential problems appeared to exist, maintaining each participant's confidentiality was critical. The hospital administrator's role was to notify each employee that the survey was to be taken. From that point on, the employees would have no further contact with any member of the administration regarding the survey.

As groups of employees entered the room where the survey was to be administered, the survey's purpose was first explained and confidentiality assured. Employees were told that summary results only would be returned to the administration. At this phase, it became more obvious than ever that problems actually did exist. Many employees wanted to know in detail the relationship between the consultant and the administration. Continuous assurances of confidentiality had to be made. Because of the nature of hospital work, the researcher had to administer the questionnaire over a forty-eight hour period. To ensure further confidentiality, the respondents were told that they should put their surveys in blank envelopes so no identifications could be made. Some even chose to mail their responses to the consultant rather than risk having the survey get lost at the hospital.

The next phase entailed analyzing the results. Data from each employee were coded on a general purpose computer card and were analyzed according to the entire hospital and for each department in the hospital.

Statistics for the entire hospital proved inconclusive. However, when the survey results were evaluated by departments, some obvious problems began to surface. Employees in certain departments appeared to be much more discontented than other workers. For instance, the levels of satisfaction in radiology and lab departments appeared to be consistently below the satisfaction level of the hospital in general. You can see in Figure 18–9 an overview of the question, "Describe your overall working environment."

At this point, however, only symptoms had been uncovered. The next phase entailed identification of specific problems. The results of the survey were next presented to each department head individually before the results were given to the hospital administrator. It would be useless to provide the administrator with symptoms and not causes.

The analysis of the radiology department provides an excellent illustration of the difference between the identification of symptoms as opposed to problems. The hospital had experienced rapid growth during the past few years, and, while other departments had increased staff to handle the increased workload, the radiology department had not. This caused department members, in addition to the department head, to work overtime. Also, questioning of other supervisors revealed that the salary level of this department had not kept pace with radiology departments in nearby hospitals. The combination of these two factors—understaffing and unrealistic salary level—resulted in considerable job dissatisfaction. The cause of the dissatisfaction had now been determined. To continue with the research, the same procedure was used with other departments where there was low satisfaction.

The consultant was now able to provide the hospital administration with not only the survey results but also some sound recommendations. Suggestions were made to each department, and some which affected the entire hospital were also made. They included:

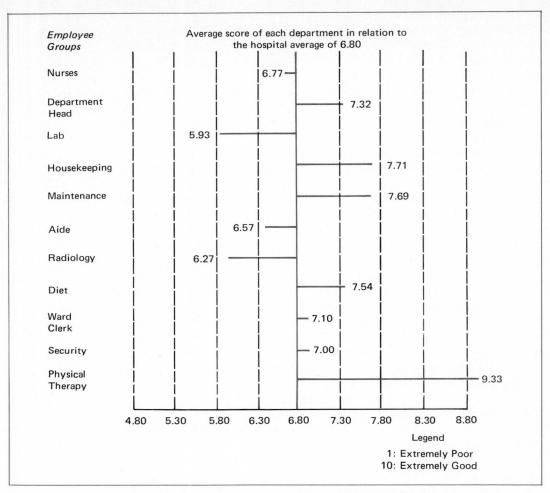

Figure 18–9.   **Descriptions of overall working environments.**

1. Implementation of a management training program which emphasized communication skills, leadership, motivation, and other human relations techniques.

2. Reevaluation of the hospital's compensation program including reacquainting employees with their fringe benefit package, clarifying the method of granting pay increases, and evaluating new fringe benefits methods

The timing of the research and resulting implementation of the recommendations later proved to be critical. Within one year, there was a major attempt at unionizing the hospital that failed. The research study which identified these human resources problems was credited as the major factor in preparing the hospital for its successful efforts in resisting unionization.[14]

SUMMARY

Personnel research involves the systematic study of human resources for the purpose of maximizing personal and organizational goal achievement. The specific applications for personnel research depend to a large extent upon the needs of the particular firm. From time to time, all of the personnel functions have needs for personnel research.

The type of problem confronting the personnel manager determines, to a large extent, the method of inquiry that will be used. When the personnel manager is called upon to uncover the underlying reasons for a particular occurrence, the case method is often used. Surveys are used to determine employees' attitudes. A method of inquiry that involves certain variables being manipulated while others are held constant is referred to as the experiment.

In order to accomplish human resources research, a systematic approach needs to be developed. The six basic steps in the research process are: (1) recognizing the problem, (2) stating the problem, (3) choosing the method of inquiry, (4) selecting and using the appropriate research tool, (5) interpreting the results, and (6) implementing the action.

Numerous quantitative tools are available for use by human resources managers. The purpose of correlation analysis is to measure the degree of association that exists between two or more variables. The purpose of regression analysis is to determine the relationship that exists between two or more variables so that one variable can be predicted from the others. The purpose of discriminant analysis is to identify factors which differentiate between two or more groups in a population. Time series analysis permits projections to be made over time.

Questions for Review

1. Describe the general methods of inquiry which are available for use by the personnel researcher.

2. Why would the experiment as a method of research often not provide an excellent means of inquiry in the area of personnel and human resources?

3. Identify the basic steps that should be accomplished in the research process.

4. Why have firms begun to realize that they can benefit from effective personnel research?

5. Briefly define each of the following quantitative tools as they may be used in personnel research: (a) correlation analysis, (b) regression analysis, (c) discriminant analysis, (d) time series analysis.

[14]R. Wayne Mondy and Wallace F. Nelson, "Job Satisfaction Among Radiologic Technologists," *Applied Radiology 7*, no. 4 (July/August 1978): 65–67. (copyright by Barrington Publications, Inc., 825 S. Barrington Avenue, Los Angeles, California 90049. Reprinted by permission.)

Terms for Review

Personnel research
Case study
Survey
Sampling
Experiment

Correlation analysis
Regression analysis
Discriminant analysis
Time series analysis

Incidents

Mike Manton is president of Lewis Milling Company of Muncie, Indiana. The company has about 100 employees and Mike has owned and managed the company since he founded it in the 1950s. Mike has always felt a good deal of pride in the fact that he knows every employee by name. To him the company is just one big happy family.

Last year, however, Mike sensed a growing level of dissatisfaction. Turnover increased and the workers just didn't seem as happy anymore. When Mike mentioned it to his office manager, Jeffry Wilson, Jeffry agreed that there had been a change. "I don't know what has caused it," said Jeffry, "but I do know that things are getting worse." Jeffry suggested a professionally conducted attitude survey to identify the problem. Mike approved this, and the survey was conducted with the assistance of a professor from State University. Employees were encouraged to give honest answers and were given the usual assurances of anonymity. They were told that the company management would receive only generalized summaries of the survey results.

Mike found the results shocking. It was evident that a large number of his people were dissatisfied with various aspects of their jobs. Some thought the pay was too low. Others felt the supervision was inadequate or arbitrary. Many objected to the harsh working conditions. A few even mentioned the "high and mighty" attitude of the "big boss."

Mike demanded and received the individual questionnaire results from the consultant. As Mike studied the individual questionnaires he became even more disturbed. By noting certain demographic data, he felt he could identify some of the respondents. He simply could not believe that trusted employees could be so unappreciative of the jobs he had provided them over the years.

He called in his department heads and gave them the names of workers whose questionnaire responses showed the most dissatisfaction. He ended the meeting with the following statement: "If they aren't happy with this company they can leave. If you find anyone else who isn't happy here, I want to know about it."

Questions

1. What critical mistakes were made in conducting and using the attitude survey?

2. Do you feel that Mike's attitude toward disgruntled employees was justified? Discuss.

Isabelle Anderson is plant manager for Hall Manufacturing Company in Alexandria, Louisiana, a company that produces a line of relatively inexpensive painted wood furniture. Six months ago, Isabelle became concerned about the turnover rate among workers in the painting department. Manufacturing plant turnover rates in that area of the south generally average about 30 percent and this was true at Hall. The painting department, however, had experienced a turnover of nearly 200 percent for each of the last two years. Because of the limited number of skilled workers in the area, Hall had an extensive training program for new painters and Isabelle knew that the high turnover rate was extremely costly.

Isabelle conducted exit interviews with many of the departing painters. Some of them said they were leaving for more money, others for better benefits, and most cited some kind of "personal reasons" for quitting. Isabelle checked and found that Hall's wages and fringe benefits were competitive with if not better than those of other manufacturers in the area. She then called in Nelson Able, the painting supervisor, to discuss the problem. Nelson's response was, "You know how this younger generation is. They work to get enough money to live on for a few weeks and then quit. I don't worry about it. Our old timers can take up the slack." "But Nelson," Isabelle replied, "we have to worry about the turnover rates. It's really costing the company a lot of money. I'm going to ask Joe Swan to administer a survey to get to the bottom of this." Nelson replied, "Do whatever you think is right. I don't see any problem."

Questions

1. Do you agree that a survey of employees is the best way to identify the problem? Explain.

2. What kind of survey would you conduct and how would you analyze the results?

Chapter Objectives

1. Describe some of the developmental needs that personnel managers of the future will face.
2. Explain some of the future developments that will likely impact Personnel and the personnel manager.

Chapter 19 _____

Personnel: The Future Environment

Many firms are aware that human resources are one of their most valuable assets. As Harry P. Hancock, senior director and personnel administrator for the Singer Company, has stated:

> "People are our most important assets" is becoming more meaningful for many companies. While in the past it may have been said for good public relations, it is now a more meaningful statement said out of conviction. The appreciation of the economic need to develop and retain people, as assets, is becoming more universal in the face of rising personnel costs.

Many of you will have the opportunity to become human resources managers. As your careers progress, you will confront an environment quite different from that facing today's managers. None of us can accurately predict what will happen during the next twenty years. But, because the future will soon become your present, it must be considered.

The past is not always a reliable indicator of coming events. However, a review of the numerous developments which have influenced Personnel since 1960 may provide a point of departure. A partial list of major personnel-related developments is shown in Table 19–1. At that time, personnel managers would have found it difficult to accurately predict their occurrence or their impact on Personnel.

After reviewing these developments, you can better understand Personnel's increased stature and influence. Minorities and females have gained prominence in organizations because of legislation and rapidly changing values. Workers' attitudes have been altered as our society has become better educated, more affluent, and more mobile. Mind-boggling technological developments have required considerable upgrading of the work force's skills. Looking back, you can quickly recognize the difficulties that personnel managers might have had as they attempted to look ahead. Future personnel managers must be prepared to meet still more changes in the coming decades. In this chapter, we will first describe some developmental needs of future per-

Table 19–1. Major developments affecting personnel since 1960.

- The significant impact of government legislation and executive orders:
  Equal Pay Act of 1963—Amended 1972
  Title VII of the Civil Rights Act of 1964—Amended 1972
  Age Discrimination in Employment Act of 1967—Amended 1978
  Occupational Safety and Health Act of 1970
  Vocational Rehabilitation Act of 1973
  Federal Privacy Act of 1974
  Vietnam Veterans Readjustment Act of 1974
  Employee Retirement Income Security Act of 1974
  Pregnancy Discrimination Act of 1978
  Executive Orders 11246 and 11375
- Extensive use of computers and high technology in organizations
- Substantial changes in societal values regarding the family, roles of men and women, and sex
- Rapid increases in the entry and promotion of women and ethnic minorities in the work force
- Significant improvements in the educational level of the work force
- Increasing economic and geographic mobility in our society
- Rapid inflation
- Growth of the sunbelt states
- Rapid technology developments
- Rising affluence of American families
- A change in attitude toward increased government spending
- Increased professionalism of Personnel
- Increase in the number of dual career families

sonnel managers. We will then take the position of "nothing ven-
tured, nothing gained," and attempt to project some of the challenges
which will affect the future practice of personnel management.

DEVELOPMENTAL NEEDS OF FUTURE PERSONNEL MANAGERS

Future personnel managers must be ready to cope with tomorrow's changes and
challenges. To gain an appreciation of their developmental needs, human resources executives were asked, "What type of continuing training and development will a person need in order to progress to a responsible personnel management position within your firm?" Responses consistently stressed a need for
continuous education (see Table 19–2).

Table 19–2. Training needs for progress in personnel

- **American General Life Insurance Company**—Company sponsored professional
  development courses plus in-house management development courses.
- **Bristol–Myers Products**—Continually broadening education to cope with the
  variety of disciplines to be encountered. Studies in psychology are especially important. The development of a broad overview of business operation is particularly useful. The development of good interpersonal skills is also needed.
- **Denny's Incorporated**—In order to maintain a position, as well as grow, it is
  necessary to belong to professional organizations and meet with other members of
  personnel units. In addition, it is necessary to continue to keep up to date on
  various legal matters by attending conferences that deal with current legislation,
  information on pension retirement programs, etc.
- **GAF Corporation**—An individual should pursue an advanced degree (either an
  M.B.A. or L.L.B.). Advanced training is also needed regarding workers' compensation hearings, unemployment hearings, and labor arbitration. In addition,
  training regarding sensitivity to people, language arts, and quantitative methods is
  needed.
- **Grumman Aerospace Corporation**—A person should obtain on-the-job training
  in all phases of personnel work and take company sponsored courses that increase
  awareness of corporate structure. Personnel workers should continue their education by obtaining an M.B.A. with a concentration in human resources management or organizational development.
- **Hart Schaffner & Marx**—The most effective personnel professionals in senior
  positions are those who begin their careers in a line personnel function and spend
  several years rotating through personnel functions of increasing responsibility in
  the field.
- **International Paper Company**—Progressive training and self-development in a
  variety of personnel technical skills. Beyond the technical courses, a seminar on
  general management techniques is highly recommended to facilitate the adapta-
  tion of technical proficiency in a managerial capacity.

continued

Table 19–2. (continued)

- **Kemper Insurance Companies**—A business education and background (combined with a sprinkling of human resources management, liberal arts, and legal coursework) will be required for those individuals who aspire to the top personnel jobs. An appreciation of the economic purpose of an organization is another prerequisite.
- **Motorola Incorporated**—An M.B.A. would be helpful after several years on the job. There are also mini-courses which would be helpful.
- **Nabisco, Inc.**—An M.B.A. or law degree would be most helpful. Graduate courses in the behavioral sciences are also beneficial.
- **Shell Oil Company**—We encourage employees to continue their education either by taking coursework at a local university or by attending Shell-sponsored training seminars.
- **Squibb Corporation**—To develop into a responsible personnel specialist, a person must have a clear understanding of how the personnel function integrates into the entire business operation and how to apply the basic tools of management to the function.
- **Teledyne McKay**—It is important for the individual to have enough initiative and drive to get involved in the overall operations of the company. An individual has to be recognized as a "comer," one who is willing to put forth extra effort. In addition, general management courses and perhaps an M.B.A. would be helpful.
- **Trans World Airlines**—There are two branches of knowledge that personnel managers should develop. First, the body of legislation affecting employees grows more complex each day, making personnel work far more technical than in the past. Second, in order to make appropriate policy decisions in today's business environment, the personnel manager must maintain an up-to-date knowledge of business skills.

Many executives suggest a need for increased education—both formal and self-developmental—with concentration in human relations areas. In addition, legal backgrounds are increasingly important for individuals employed in unionized firms.

Developmental efforts through professional organizations will receive greater attention. Members need to share ideas of common interest through meetings, conferences, and seminars. Active participation in professional groups should preclude the need to continually "reinvent the wheel."

Personnel managers will need to learn as much as possible about the firm's total operations. If a person enters Personnel directly, additional efforts must be made to become familiar with other organizational areas. This requirement becomes increasingly important as the individual progresses. Such knowledge of the organization will greatly facilitate interdepartmental communication. The personnel manager also needs a knowledge of the personnel function. Although you may begin your career in a specialized area, broad personnel experience will be helpful in your career progression.

PERSONNEL: CHALLENGES OF THE FUTURE

"There are no problems, only challenges." Even if this statement is not entirely true, the problems of Personnel must be considered challenges or situations that can and will be met. Personnel has experienced rapid growth as a profession. This is due, in part, to progressive-thinking firms which have recognized the need for effective human resources management.

In Table 19–3, comments from leading personnel executives provide insight into the most challenging areas that they believe will confront human resources managers in the future. These executives' opinions touch every facet of Personnel and provide the bases for the following discussion.

Effective Management Practices

Personnel's responsibilities will continue to expand because human resources will be increasingly recognized as a critical factor in an organization. Personnel managers' tasks will likely impact the entire culture of organizations because of their potential to alter firms' climates.[1] This influence will become even more common as personnel executives gain greater trust and responsibilities.

Personnel policies have been quite defensive in the past. Human resources were often viewed as expense items rather than as assets.[2] Largely because of the personnel executive's enlarged job scope, future corporate human resources policies will become more positive in nature. Some of the more critical areas will now be considered.

Social Responsibility. Business organizations have many different objectives, not the least of which is to make a profit. However, as mentioned in Chapter 2, organizations which plan to survive must establish goals which relate to social responsibility. In the past, the federal government has responded to deficiencies in this area by enacting legislation to fill the gaps. There is reason to believe that this emphasis will continue. A large part of the responsibility of maintaining an organization's social conscience will be borne by the personnel executive.

Preserving Our Free Enterprise System. The free enterprise system has proven to be the most effective in the world. Capable people must be employed and motivated toward increased productivity in order for the system to function properly. The personnel executive must ensure that people with high potential are chosen. Competent human resources are vital not only to an individual firm

---

[1]Kenny Foger, "The Future Top Personnel Executive," *The Personnel Administrator* 23 (December 1978): 17–18.
[2]D. Quinn Mills, "Human Resources in the 1980s," *Harvard Business Review* 57 (July/August 1979): 154 (hereafter cited as "Human Resources in the 1980s").

Table 19–3. The most challenging areas in personnel and human resource management in the future

Personnel Executive	Comments
Arco Oil and Gas Company Drew M. Young, AEP Vice President Employee Relations (Retired)	To provide up-to-date expertise (counsel, services) to enable the organization to maintain a viable position in a changing governmental, sociological, and economic environment and, as much as possible within practical limits, to be on the leading edge of change. The above includes keeping current on government regulations and their application, effective behavioral science techniques, the labor market, compensation and benefits, organizational structures, employee expectations, and social developments.
Cessna Aircraft Company Alan Roskam, Ph.D. Director Human Resources	The most challenging areas in personnel management and human resources management during the next decade will be the training and retraining of employees to fill jobs of a changing nature and the development of compensation and benefits packages which are acceptable to employees while being affordable to the organization. These things must be done while abiding by the increasingly complex and often vague regulatory requirements in the areas of affirmative action, compensation and benefits, occupational safety and health, and so forth.
Crown Central Petroleum Corporation Jerome L. Valentine Employee Relations Manager	To assure that individual needs are maintained in proper perspective to those of the organization. I am concerned that the increasing pace and the competitive nature of free enterprise may tend to place the personal and individual needs of the employee far below those of the organization. This is not a condemnation of our system, for no greater one exists. However, we need to ensure that a proper balance is maintained.
Detroit Edison Company M. Jane Kay, AEP Vice President Employee Relations	• Improving the quality of work life and lessening the adversary relationship of workers and management. • Coping with the frustrations of increasing government regulation and legislation regarding human resources. • Devising personnel policies that will increase productivity. • Developing future managers.
Fairchild Camera and Instrument Corporation W. J. Bowles Vice President of Industrial Relations	• Management education and development. • People planning in every arena from hiring to retiring. • General professionalism.

continued

Table 19–3. (continued)

609

Chapter 19
Personnel:
The Future
Environment

Honeywell, Inc.
Charles E. Brown
Vice President
Employee Relations

- Building greater support for our economic system and greater cooperation among employees and their unions in making the system work.
- Tapping latent potential to increase productivity.

Merck and Company, Inc.
Sam R. Clare, AEP
Personnel Manager

Continued emphasis on the safety and health fields, affirmative action, and federal legislation (mandatory retirement, for example) will focus attention on corporate images as perceived by policies, benefits, and compliance. Our challenge will be to balance the desires of employees, stockholders, and government agencies.

Pacific Gamble Robinson Company
Jerry F. Scroggs, AEP
Personnel Manager

Effective utilization of manpower.

Pennzoil Company
John Kajander
Vice President
Employee Relations

- Prevention of the stifling effect of excessive regulation.
- Improvement of productivity.
- Keeping compensation (direct and indirect) from being completely offset by inflation.
- Motivation of employees.

PPG Industries
Donald E. Van Cleef
Director of Employees
Public and Government
Relations, Chemicals

- Effectively utilizing a changing workforce which will be older, more educated, and composed of a much higher proportion of women and minorities—all of whom will have different expectations of their work than prior generations.
- Keeping high talent employees challenged even if the predicted period of slower economic growth becomes a reality.
- Selecting, training, and motivating employees to achieve greater efficiency and productivity as a partial answer to inflation.

The Singer Company
Harry P. Hancock, Jr., AEP
Senior Director,
Personnel Administration

Communicating the Company's desire for uniformly fair and equitable treatment for each employee and its desire for similar benefit programs while operating on a decentralized basis with many dissimilar types of business.

Southeast Banking Corporation
Robert J. Rowe, Ph.D.,
AEP
Rowe Associates

- Coping with the mass of information needed to effectively run a personnel operation.
- Handling the ever increasing reporting and control function required by the various levels of government.
- Reducing turnover by providing a satisfactory working climate for a vastly mobile society.
- Obtaining, training, and keeping professional, competent people in personnel.

but also to the survival of our entire economy.[3] One personnel director stated, "The survival of business in a free economy will be determined by the influence and use of the human resources, but they must be relevant and productive, and they must pay off in long-range objectives." Personnel "must take the leadership role in providing policies and programs for more fully realizing human potential in the workplace as a means of increasing both productivity and the quality of work life."[4]

Negative feelings about business must be overcome in order for organizations to attract top caliber personnel. In the 1970s, many individuals with high potential were choosing nonbusiness careers. Other untapped resources are females and minority groups. Although women constitute approximately 50 percent of the population, their full capabilities remain underutilized. Black, Mexican–American, and other protected groups have only recently realized some of the benefits of the free enterprise system. If maximum productivity is to be achieved, all people in our society must be fully utilized.

Government Regulation. Throughout the 1960s and 1970s, government regulation of business was greatly expanded. Overseeing implementation of the various laws and regulations has typically been placed in the hands of the personnel executive. More and more government injected into employment relations has required more expertise in the form of qualified personnel executives. Because legislation can have such a major influence, sometimes even affecting the survival of the firm, the importance of the personnel function has greatly increased.

Future personnel managers will have the opportunity to counteract the trend toward increased government intervention. Government regulation of business often results from the public belief that business has not been responsible in areas of social concern. Personnel managers must be aware of societal values. They must be at the leading edge of organizational change. Personnel managers are the experts in this area and must initiate changes which balance the needs of individuals and employers.

Personnel Planning, Recruitment, and Selection

Attracting the best available people to the organization will continue to be an overriding challenge. Employees of the future will seek jobs in organizations that permit them to attain their personal goals. Most employees now consider the entire job and its environment prior to making decisions about joining and remaining with a firm. One of the most crucial organizational problems entails handling employees' growing expectations of a more meaningful work experience. This situation was put another way by Donald E. Van Cleef, director of employee, public, and government relations—chemicals for PPG Industries, when he said the challenge consists of "effectively utilizing a changing work

---

[3]Fred E. Schuster, "Human Resources Management: Key to the Future," *The Personnel Administrator* 23 (December 1978): 33 (hereafter cited as "Key to the Future").
[4]Donald L. Lunda, "Personnel Management: What's Ahead?" *Personnel Administrator* 26 (April 1981): 60.

Executive Profile

Paula M. Stone
Assistant Director of Personnel
Presbyterian Hospital of Dallas

When Paula was in college, math and science were her favorite subjects. Anxious to start her career, she compressed four years of study into three. Paula received a Bachelor of Science degree in mathematics and education from Boston University in 1973, graduating cum laude. Paula said, "I enjoyed working with math, but my student teaching experience quickly convinced me that I should seek another field."

Paula's math background proved valuable during the next three years when she held a job in a systems/computer environment for a health care foundation. Although she was successful and rose to the position of Data Analyst by the age of twenty-three, she continued to search for viable alternatives. Paula said, "During this period I began to read personnel books and journals and became quite interested in the field. Finally, I decided to enter Personnel and I didn't care where I had to start."

The only position that Paula could find in Personnel was as a secretary, but she accepted it and was trained in all facets of Personnel. Paula's talents were quickly recognized and she was promoted to a position which required her to recruit and hire all nurses for a Boston hospital. After six years in health care she decided to move into the business world. She became the corporate personnel director of a large restaurant chain and later joined an executive search firm to get a taste of being "on the other side of the fence." This latter experience led her back into health care and into her present position overseeing the personnel function for approximately 2500 employees.

"There have been several occasions when I questioned my reasons for ever having started a career in this field. Events such as having to fire your best friend, finding out last about a layoff, trying to hire competent individuals without the benefit of a current salary system, have all contributed to the frustrations of my career. But at least I'll never be bored!"

Paula is glad that she worked her way up through the ranks of a personnel function especially with the field changing so rapidly. She states, "I feel that working my way up within the field gave me greater ability to relate to employees and to gain their respect. The varied experiences throughout my career (in both non-profit and profit businesses) have been extremely rewarding and fulfilling. The opportunities are vast in the personnel field. With four essential elements—hard work, determination, flexibility, and adaptability to change—you will create and be an integral part of a successful personnel function."

force which will be older, more educated, and composed of a much higher proportion of women and minorities—all of whom will have different expectations of their work than prior generations."

As people increasingly recognize that companies possess distinct personalities, just as individuals do, they will make a concerted effort to find the

The Personnel Professional of the 1980s Will Be:

- A leader with a consistent style, not just occasional bursts of charisma, who leads rather than points.
- Relentless in the pursuit of personal excellence and a personal discipline that precludes periodic coasting.
- Sensitive to the needs not only of those above but, more importantly, to those around and below.
- Honest enough to do the right thing when smart enough to know what that is; frank enough to admit when the right thing isn't known; and committed enough to search it out.
- Proud of the profession, the work, the contribution.
- Possessed of a sense of humor to take the job seriously enough to contribute, lightly enough to put it in perspective.
- The best—the best at what we do and what we are.

Robert L. Berra, Senior Vice President, Administration, Monsanto Company. (Mr. Berra is a member of the Monsanto Corporate Administrative Committee, the highest internal Monsanto policy-making group and an advisory member of the Board of Directors. He is a past national president of the American Society for Personnel Administration and frequently addresses personnel groups on "Personnel Professionalism.")

most desirable employer. When a firm no longer provides a means for satisfying an individual's needs, the employee will likely quit. This will occur without the trauma that often accompanies changing jobs today. Job changes will become much more socially acceptable. In fact, many employers will place a high value on people who possess varied experiences.

The work force's composition will also be different. Personnel must continuously adapt its policies to meet changing employee needs. Women and minorities will enter the work force in ever increasing numbers and will progress to top management positions. The myth depicting men as the primary breadwinners will diminish. It will be replaced by a philosophy accepting and often encouraging careers for wives. The multiple societal effects of this new "work-wife" are far reaching and complex.[5] The entire family's lifestyle will be affected. Managers must be trained to accept and effectively deal with this social change.

The growing number of single employees will also modify the composition of the work force. Many people are choosing to remain single or to delay marriage. Employers' attitudes toward divorce have also been changing and the trend is expected to continue. It was not long ago that a divorce could virtually shatter an executive's career. Future managers may actually benefit from being single. A person without close family attachments may be viewed as one who will be more devoted to a career and will more readily accept job de-

[5]Suzanne H. McCall, "Meet the 'Workwife,' " *Journal of Marketing* 41 (July 1977): 55.

mands. For example, transferring single people can often be accomplished with fewer problems than transferring those with families. Dual career families may find it more difficult to move because of its disruptive effect. No longer will the faithful wife willingly pack up and leave whenever her husband is offered a transfer. And, the husband may find it necessary to resign from a job when his professional wife has a job opportunity in another location.

The age old task of retaining the best qualified people will also receive additional emphasis. No longer will the "cradle to the grave" philosophy of employment dominate. The gold watch syndrome, where a person receives a token of appreciation for thirty years work, will lose its appeal. The fear of changing jobs or even careers will be reduced. In fact, there is likely to be a trend toward multiple careers. Many individuals may decide that they would like to pursue a different line of work. This trend may already have begun as colleges and universities are experiencing an increased enrollment of middle-aged students.

Increased professionalization of managers and specialists will significantly affect an organization's recruitment, selection, and retention efforts. Employees will become increasingly loyal to their profession as opposed to a particular firm.[6] These individuals will view their jobs as a means of growing and developing professionally. Such employees will likely leave if a company fails to provide them with professional growth. Innovative firms which meet the non-financial needs of their professional employees will be in a better position to select and retain top talent. The factors discussed above will change the nature of the work force with which Personnel must relate.

Training and Development

It is expected that one of the major focuses of Personnel in the 1980s will be in the area of training, education, and development.[7] Henry L. Dahl, manager of employee development and planning for the Upjohn Company, said, "The most demanding challenges confronting training and development specialists are helping our present officers and directors build and maintain a competent management team that will achieve corporate goals, and, at the same time, perpetuate company philosophy of treating people as individuals." In earlier years, management concentrated primarily upon money, machines, materials, and land as its means of accomplishing the firm's objectives. If a defective machine was only 50 percent efficient, a maintenance person would be called in to repair it. Enlightened managers of tomorrow must recognize that people also need revitalization if maximum efficiency is to be achieved. An employee with marketable skills today may need to acquire extensive training and development to perform effectively in tomorrow's business environment.

There is currently a shortage of highly skilled employees, and this situation is expected to become more acute. Low birth rates from 1960 to 1980 will restrict the future supply of qualified applicants. The number of individuals age

---

[6]G. Lowell Martin, "A View of Work Toward the Year 2000," *Personnel Journal* 56 (October 1977): 503 (hereafter cited as "A View of Work").
[7]Lunda, p. 54.

fifty-five or older will decrease substantially as a percentage of the work force until the year 2000.[8] People in this age group often fill critical middle or top management positions. All human resources must be continuously developed and upgraded if firms are to maintain a high level of performance.

It has been estimated that beginning in 1980 there has been 30 percent fewer new workers entering the work force than in the period between 1967 and 1977. This will have serious implications for human resources management. Personnel will need to develop creative and innovative ways to bring the previously unemployed, marginally qualified workers into the work force. Organization will be forced to assume a greater role in the training and development of these individuals.[9]

Skills can become obsolete within a few years because of rapid technological changes. Firms must constantly engage in T&D to prevent worker obsolescence. They must also develop programs to upgrade underqualified personnel. These actions are taken to secure trained employees and also to fulfill the firm's social responsibility.[10] Developing underqualified employees will be expensive. However, the alternative of not having qualified people overrides any objections. Personnel directors will be challenged with the prospect of creating an environment within which all people can grow and develop.

The successful firms of the future will also have ongoing, comprehensive, and innovative organization development programs. Organizational environments will become more open and adaptive. The emphasis will be upon promoting group decision making and the development of interpersonal skills. In the past, the most common way to learn managerial skills was by trial and error. Future managers will have access to more sophisticated managerial techniques. As a result, they will know more about people and be willing to develop interpersonal skills. Executives must be able to adapt their managerial styles to meet the needs of the organization and their subordinates. The trend toward participative management will continue because people are becoming more sophisticated and highly educated. As a result, workers—especially younger employees—are increasingly challenging management's decisions. While this attitude change may threaten some managers, it actually provides them with opportunities because better educated employees are potentially more productive.[11]

Compensation

Tomorrow's reward systems will be designed to recognize that employees have different needs. Emphasis will not only be directed toward what most employees want. Instead, management will recognize that people differ and that in many instances these differences are substantial. The future work force will generally want a reward system that encourages innovation and creativity. A

[8]"Human Resources in the 1980s," p. 154.
[9]Lunda, p. 54.
[10]"Key to the Future," p. 66.
[11]Ibid., p. 34.

person will not have to be a manager to have their contribution recognized.[12] Compensation programs must ensure that rewards are meaningful to each employee.

By the year 2000, a society that is even more affluent and demanding than today's will appear on the scene. Employment will be characterized by a shorter workweek. The average workweek is expected to decline to about twenty-eight hours.[13] Pay is likely to decrease in importance relative to other forms of compensation. Overtime work will increasingly be declined even though it provides additional earnings. Employment will be seen as a means of satisfying human needs and not as an end in itself.

Although the number of employee benefits provided today seems almost endless, the list continues to grow. Benefits which may become a part of future compensation programs include the possibilities listed below. Some are government sponsored while the cost of others would be borne by industry.

- Employer-conducted retraining as a part of severance benefits
- Minimum annual income guaranteed by government
- Jobs guaranteed for everyone, with the government being the employer of last resort
- Credit assistance to all employees through "employer credit cards" or cosigning of credit notes
- Increased access to company facilities, such as computers, for personal use
- Educational leave pay available to employees whenever they choose to take such a leave
- Several shorter workweeks during the year, permitting, say, half a dozen mini-vacation weekends
- Bonuses offered to selected employees for joining the corporation
- Optional retirement at age fifty-five with full benefits
- Pension plans extended to include benefits for retirees other than money, such as: recreation, education, medical services, residential costs, apartments in company-sponsored retirement communities, and legal services
- Life insurance in which cost of living adjustments are routinely applied to both coverage and premiums
- Company taking over the job of educating employees' family members[14]

Whether these benefits and others predicted for the future become a reality remains to be seen. But, as Kathryn D. McKee, vice president of compensation and benefits at First Interstate BanCorp said, "In the future, compensa-

[12]Wendell L. French and Alvar O. Elbing, "Predictions for Personnel and Industrial Relations in 1985," *Personnel Journal* 61 (May 1982): 349 (hereinafter referred to as "French and Elbing").
[13]"A View of Work," p. 526.
[14]Excerpt from T. J. Gordon and R. E. LeBleu, "Employee Benefits, 1970–1985," *Harvard Business Review* 48 (January/February 1970), pp. 93–107. (© 1969 by the President and Fellows of Harvard College; all rights reserved. Reprinted by permission.)

tion executives will have to be even more creative than they are today. Unless our government comes up with equitable rules for taxation, we will have to find ways to keep dollars in employees' pockets—at all levels. We also have to make sure that we are competitive in the marketplace. We have to ask ourselves what kinds of things we can offer that will make our program more attractive than our competitors."[15]

Safety and Health

Public sentiment for a national health care program is growing. This increasing concern for every citizen's well-being will likely carry over to the workplace. Although current legislation and sound management practices have greatly improved working conditions, future gains will be significant. Advancing technology will assist organizations in controlling such health hazards as dust, fumes, and noise. Spearheaded by personnel executives, an enlightened management will take positive steps to protect the health of its employees. These efforts will be preventative rather than curative. Organizations will become much more aware of the costs of failing to provide health assistance to employees.

Periodic physical examinations will be provided at company cost for all employees. The emphasis will be on detecting and providing early health treatment. The stigma of alcoholism and drug addiction will be lessened and a more positive attitude will be taken to deal with these treatable diseases. Management, labor, and government will work together in handling these problems that adversely impact our entire society. Management will also continue to expand its role in the area of physical and mental fitness. Tension and stress reduction will be emphasized to develop healthier and more productive employees. Employers will accelerate their efforts in this area, not only because of humanitarian reasons, but also because of an economic payoff.

Employee and Labor Relations

The personnel executive must strive to narrow the gap that too often exists between the goals of the organization and employees. As M. Jane Kay, vice president for employee relations for Detroit Edison Company, states, "Two major challenges in the area of human resources management are improving the quality of work life and lessening the adversary relationship of workers and management." In the past, and to a large extent today, there was a notion that it was "us" against "them." This attitude is particularly apparent with union–management relationships. As employees and employers begin to recognize that their needs are largely compatible, the barriers to closing the gap will be lowered. William B. Pardue, president of American General Life Insurance Company, supported this view by saying, "A major challenge of the

[15]Karen E. Debats, "The Continuing Personnel Challenge," *Personnel Journal* 61 (May 1982): 333–4.

next decade is to develop policies and programs that facilitate strengthening the relationships between management and employees so that corporate goals of profitability, efficiency, growth, and survival can be attained."

In the years ahead, some organizations will opt to develop closer ties with unions which represent their employees.[16] It seems just as clear that many nonunion employers will continue to battle aggressively to keep the union out. Management has become more aware of the type of environment needed for employees to feel that union representation is unnecessary.[17] Consultants specializing in maintaining nonunion status have practically created a new industry. Additionally, some unionized companies will seek to decertify their unions.

Personnel Research

Efforts in personnel research will become more widespread in the years to come. Today, research is often a luxury for all but the larger firms. In the future, competitive pressures to fully utilize human resources will require that more firms devote greater efforts in the area. One such area which requires further research is human resources accounting. This approach, which is used presently on a very limited basis, requires placing a dollar value upon the firm's employees. Under this concept, recognition is given to the tremendous value of people to an organization.

Personnel research will touch every area of human resources management. Better means will be needed to select those individuals who can best assist the firm in achieving its objectives. Research into training and development may suggest new ways to impart knowledge to employees. Research may suggest additional ways in which management styles may be improved. It is also quite feasible that personnel research will be needed to develop new and innovative compensation programs to meet the needs of the new work force. New means will be achieved through research to ensure that workers have a safe and healthy work environment. And finally, all aspects of research will be needed to help improve the relationship between management and employees. The need for personnel research is growing and will continue to expand as we move into the future of human resources management.

Questions for Review

1. What type of developmental needs do you believe the personnel manager of the future will have? Discuss.

2. Describe why effective utilization of human resources can work to preserve our free enterprise system.

3. Describe the various challenges that you envision will impact human resources of the future.

16"A View of Work," p. 502.
17French and Elbing, p. 350.

PARMA CYCLE COMPANY: LOOKING AHEAD

Edward Deal was jubilant. He had just received notification from the National Labor Relations Board that the union representation election at Parma Cycle's Clarksdale, Mississippi, plant had gone against the union. The margin was small, only 53 percent to 47 percent, but Ed considered it a significant victory. As personnel director at Clarksdale, he had done everything within his power to prevent the plant from becoming unionized. For example, wages and benefits at Clarksdale had started far below those at the Parma, Ohio plant. At Edward's insistence, the package had been made competitive in the labor market. His recommendation for this had not been approved until top management was convinced that a unionizing effort was underway at Clarksdale.

With the new wage and benefits package, Parma Cycle became the highest paying employer in the Clarksdale area. From Ed's vantage point, morale seemed to be quite high in the plant. Jobs with Parma were much sought after. An average day saw twenty or thirty new job applicants. In fact, the rush of job applicants had forced Edward to post a sign reading "No Jobs Available."

There were still a couple of things which concerned Edward, though. First, the representation election had been extremely close. Twenty-five more votes would have swung it in the union's favor. Ed thus felt a certain insecurity about the prospects for future unionization attempts at the plant. He knew that the company would have to live up to workers' expectations in order to keep the union out. He was also concerned about the qualifications of the workers he had hired. During the recruiting process, all that Ed had been able to offer to new trainees was minimum wage. The average wage for beginning workers at Parma's

Clarksdale plant had been only $5.20 an hour. Consequently, only very young, mostly unskilled workers had applied. These had been trained to some degree but were certainly no match for the work force at Parma's Ohio plant.

He decided to call Jesse Heard, his old boss and the personnel director at the Parma Ohio plant. After a friendly greeting, Ed got right to the point. "Jesse," he said, "I thought we were surely going to lose the representation election and I'd have been thrilled to get even a 1 percent victory margin. But, let's not kid ourselves. If we don't do a super job of keeping our workers satisfied, the union will get those extra 25 votes next time." "You're right," replied Jesse, "and even if you do, the result might be the same in the long run." "Why is that?" asked Ed. Jesse answered, "There has been a good deal of pressure by the union up here for us to recognize a bargaining unit at Clarksdale. I don't know how long top management will have the will to resist." "You really know how to let the air out of a fella's balloon," said Ed. "I don't mean to do that," Jesse replied, "but I do think we need to take a realistic view."

"Speaking of being realistic," continued Ed, "let's face it, we started the plant in Clarksdale to reduce labor costs and we hired a full complement of employees here at very low rates compared to those we are paying now. We have raised the wages and we still have the same workers. The only way we can really have lower costs now is for the workers here to produce more than those at Parma." "I see what you mean," said Jesse, "I'll be down for a visit in a couple of months. I don't know if I can help in any way but we can sure talk about it."

A few weeks later Ed decided that it was time to find out a little more about his work force. He called Jules Cagney, a professor of personnel administration at Mississippi State University in Starksville, and asked him to recommend a research design. "Dr. Cagney," said Edward, "I am not as concerned about keeping the union out as I am about treating our people fairly and maintaining a level of motivation. I mainly want to know what their attitudes and concerns are so that we can design the personnel program around that." "I'll do some thinking about that," said Dr. Cagney, "and be back in touch with you within a day or two."

Questions

1. What kind of study do you think that Dr. Cagney will recommend? Explain.
2. What are the trends in personnel administration that Edward should consider in designing or redesigning the personnel program at Clarksdale?

—— Experiencing Personnel Management ——

LOOKING AHEAD

Personnel research is conducted to determine what has happened in the past as well as to determine certain things about the present, such as personal attitudes of employees. This has been done at Parma Cycle Company's Clarksdale, Mississippi plant by Dr. Jules Cagney. Information developed from such studies as that conducted by Dr. Cagney form the foundations of personnel strategic planning.

Implied in making plans is some assumption about what the future holds. Consequently, it is worthwhile for personnel managers to try to judge the human resources management environment at least a year or two ahead of time. Based on what you have learned about Parma Cycle Company and the trends in personnel management, consider the questions below and write or discuss your answers.

Questions

1. Will the Clarksdale plant be unionized two years from now? Why or why not?
2. How will worker productivity at Clarksdale compare to that of Parma, Ohio? Explain.
3. What national or regional trends will affect personnel management at the Ohio plant? The Mississippi plant?

References

Chapter 1—Personnel: An Overview

"Accreditation Counts Among Personnel Pros." *Industry Week* 210 (August 24, 1981): 34.

Bamforth, Mike. "What Future for the Personnel Function?" *Personnel Management* 9 (December 1977): 75–78.

Bell, Chip. "The HRD Manager's 'Rules for Living'." *Training and Development Journal* 30 (December 1976): 38–39.

Belt, John, and Richardson, James. "Academic Preparation for Personnel Management." *Personnel Journal* 52 (May 1973): 373–380.

Burdick, Walter. "A Look at Corporate and Personnel Philosophy." *The Personnel Administrator* 21 (July 1976): 21–26.

Clewis, John E. "People Management in the 80s." *Journal of the College and University Personnel Association* 32 (Winter 1981): 14–21.

Cooper, Lloyd. "HRD—Stepping Forward Toward Professionalism." *Training and Development Journal* 33 (February 1978): 30–31.

Edgren, Robert J. "Goal Setting: Get Everyone Involved." *Infosystem* 23 (July 1976): 57–78.

Franke, Arnold G., Harrick, Edward J. and Klein, Andrew J. "The Role of Personnel in Improving Productivity." *Personnel Administrator* 27 (March 1982): 83–88.

Goodwin, Susan A. "The Personnel Director as High-Status Friend." *Supervisory Management* 22 (August 1977): 2–10.

Knicely, H. V. "Employee Relations: It's a Whole New Ball Game." *Dun's Business Month* 119 (April 1982): 121–122.

LaBau, Marilyn L. "Human Resource Accounting: Is Quality of Worklife Profitable?" *Management World* 11 (January 1982): 45–46.

McKendrick, Joseph. "The Office of 1990: Human Resources." *Management World* 11 (January 1982): 14–17.

Miles, R. E. and Rosenberg, H. R. "Human Resources Approach to Management: Second-Generation Issues." *Organizational Dynamics* 10 (Winter 1982): 26–41.

Miner, John and Miner, Mary. "Managerial Characteristics of Personnel Managers." *Industrial Relations* 15 (May 1976): 225–234.

Nardoni, R. "Personnel Office of the Future is Available Today." *Personnel Journal* 61 (February 1982): 132–134.

Odiorne, George S. *Personnel Administration by Objectives.* Homewood, IL: Richard D. Irwin, Inc., 1971.

Paperman, Jacob and Martin, Desmond. "Human Resource Accounting: A Managerial Tool?" *Personnel* 54 (March/April 1977): 41–50.

Patten, R. H., Jr. "Human Resource Management and the Energy Crisis—An Ostrich Posture?" *Human Resource Management* 20 (Fall 1981): 2–8.

The Personnel Executive's Job. Englewood Cliffs, NJ: Prentice-Hall/American Society for Personnel Administration, 1977.

Prock, Dan and Henson, Bob. "The Educational Needs of and the Future Labor Market Demand for Human Resource Managers." *Personnel Journal* 56 (December 1977): 602–607.

Pursell, D. E. "Planning for Tomorrow's Personnel Problems," *Personnel Journal* 60 (July 1981): 559–561.

Salman, Sandra. "Personnel: A New Route to the Top." *International Management* 32 (May 1977): 24–26.

Skinner, W. "Big Hat, No Cattle: Managing Human Resources." *Harvard Business Review* 59 (September/October 1981): 106–114.

Tichy, Noel M., Fombrun, Charles J. and Devanna, Mary A. "Strategic Human Resource Management." *Sloan Management Review* 23 (Winter 1982): 47–61.

Wangler, Lawrence A. "The Intensification of the Personnel Role." *Personnel Journal* 58 (February 1979): 111–119.

White, H. and Boynton, R. "The Role of Personnel: A Management View." *Arizona Business* 21 (1974): 17–21.

White, Harold C. and Wolfe, Michael N. "The Role Desired for Personnel Administration." *Personnel Administrator* 25 (June 1980): 87–97.

Chapter 2—The Environment of Human Resources Management

Arvey, Richard D. *Fairness In Selecting Employees.* Reading, MA: Addison-Wesley Publishing Company, 1979.

Atherton, Roger M., Jr. and Scanion, Burt K. "Participation and the Effective Use of Authority." *Personnel Journal* 60 (September 1981): 697–703.

Baroni, Barry J. "Age Discrimination in Employment: Some Guidelines for Employers." *Personnel Administrator* 26 (May 1981): 97–101.

Bairol, Lloyd. "Managing Dissatisfaction." *Personnel* 58 (May–June 1981): 12–21.

Beerbower, Albert. "Junk the Jargon." *Supervision* XLIII (May 1981): 7–8.

Belohlav, James A. and Ayton, Eugene. "Equal Opportunity Laws: Some Common Problems." *Personnel Journal* 61 (April 1982): 282–285.

Bergmann, B. R. and Darity, W., Jr. "Social Relations, Productivity, and Employer Discrimination." *Monthly Labor Review* 104 (April 1981): 47–49.

Brewer, Richard. "Personnel's Role in Participation." *Personnel Management* 4 (September 1978): 27–29 + .

Brunner, Nancy R. "Blue-Collar Women." *Personnel Journal* 60 (April 1981): 273–282.

Copperman, Lois Farrer and Keast, Fred D. "Older Workers: A Challenge for Today and Tomorrow." *Human Resource Management* 20 (Summer, 1981): 13–18.

Copperman, Lois F., Keast, Fred D. and Montgomery, Douglas G. "Older Workers and Part-Time Work Schedules." *Personnel Administrator* 26 (October 1981): 35–65.

Denova, Charles C. "Develop a Self-Motivating Attitude." *Supervision* 43 (June 1981): 7.

"Dilemma of Management Leadership." *Training and Development Journal* 35 (August 1981): 6–7.

Driscol, Jeanne Bosson. "Sexual Attraction and Harassment: Management's New Problems." *Personnel Journal* 60 (January 1981): 33 + .

Driver, Russell W. "Opening the Channels of Upward Communication." *Supervisory Management* 25 (March 1980): 24–29.

Ellig, Bruce R. "The Impact of Legislation on the Personnel Function." *Personnel* 57 (September–October 1980): 49–53.

Equal Employment Opportunity Commission. 29 CFR Part 1604, Discrimination Because of Sex Under Title VII of the Civil Rights Act of 1964, as Amended; Adoption of Final Interpretive Guidelines. *Federal Register* 45, no. 219 (Monday, November 10, 1980): 74676–74677.

Fitz-enz, Jac. "Measuring Human Resources Effectiveness." *Personnel Administrator* (July 1980): 33–36.

Foltz, Roy G. "Labor Relations Communication." *Personnel Administrator* 26 (March 1981): 12.

Foltz, Roy G. "Productivity and Communications." *Personnel Administrator* 26 (August 1981): 12.

Greene, Jeanne Polston. "People Management: New Directions for the 80s." *Administrative Management* 42 (January 1981): 22.

Greenlaw, Paul S. and Kohl, John P. "Age Discrimination in Employment Guidelines." *Personnel Journal* 61 (March 1982): 224–228.

Hay, Christine D. "Women in Management: The Obstacles and Opportunities They Face." *Personnel Administrator* 25 (April 1980): 31–39.

Hoyman, Michele and Robinson, Ronda. "Interpreting the New Sexual Harassment Guidelines." *Personnel Journal* 59 (December 1980): 996–1000.

Ledvinka, James. *Federal Regulation of Personnel and Human Management.* Boston: Kent Publishing Company, 1982.

Lee, Nancy. "The Dual Career Couple: Benefits and Pitfalls." *Management Review* 70 (January 1981): 46–52.

Lesly, Philip. "Functioning in the New Human Climate." *Management Review* 70 (December 1981): 24–28 + .

Lewin, David. "Collective Bargaining and the Quality of Work Life." *Organizational Dynamics* (August 1981): 37 + .

Lester, Richard I. "Leadership: Some _____ and Concepts." *Personnel Journal* 60, no. 11 (November 1981): 868–871.

Likert, Rensis. *The Human Organization: Its Management and Value.* New York: McGraw-Hill Book Company, 1976.

Linenberger Patricia and Keaveny, Timothy J. "Performance Appraisal Standards Used by the Courts." *Personnel Administrator* 26 (May 1981): 89–94.

Loban, Lawrence. "The Handicapped—Sometimes Your Best Employee." *Supervision* 42 (February 1980): 3–7.

Lundborg, Louis. "The Art of Being an Executive." *Industry Week* 210 (August 24, 1981): 51.

Magnus, Margaret. "Employee Recognition: A Key to Motivation." *Personnel Journal* 60 (February 1981): 103–104.

March, James G. and Simon, Herbert A. *Organizations.* New York: John Wiley & Sons, Inc., 1963.

McCulloch, Kenneth J. *Selecting Employees Safely Under the Law.* Englewood Cliffs, NJ: Prentice-Hall, Inc., 1981.

McDaniel, Reuben R. and Donde, P. Ashmas. "Participatory Management: An Executive Alternative for Human Service Organizations." *Human Resource Management* 19 (Spring 1980): 14–18.

McGregor, Douglas. *The Human Side of Enterprise.* New York: McGraw-Hill Book Company, 1960.

Miller, William B. "Motivation Techniques: Does One Work Best?" *Management Review* 70 (February 1981): 47–52.

Myers, Donald W. "The Impact of a Selected Provision in the Federal Guidelines on Job Analysis and Training." *Personnel Administrator* 26 (July 1981): 41–45.

Nathanson, Robert B. and Lambert, Jeffrey. "Integrating Disabled Employees Into the Workforce." *Personnel Journal* 60 (February 1981): 103–113.

Owens, James. "A Reappraisal of Leadership Theory and Training." *Personnel Administrator* 26 (November 1981): 75–84.

Rhodes, Susan R., Schuster, Michael and Doering, Mildred. "The Implication of an Aging Workforce." *Personnel Administrator* 26 (October 1981): 19–22.

Robertson, David E. "Quotas and the Courts." *Business Law Review* 13 (Winter 1980–81): 1–6.

Robertson, David E and Johnson, Ron. "Reverse Discrimination: Did Weber Decide the Issue?" *Labor Law Journal* 31 (November 1980): 693–699.

Rogers, Carl R. and Roethlisberger, J. J. "Barriers and Gateways to Communication." *Harvard Business Review* 30 (July/August 1952): 46–52.

Ruck, Frank J., Jr. "A Participative Management Concept Shares Successes, Responsibility, at ETC." *Personnel Administrator* 27 (June 1982): 65–71.

Sheahan, Robert E. "Labor Relations: Age Discrimination

is a Growing Concern for Employers." *Personnel Journal* 61 (January 1982): 14–16.

Sheppard, I. Thomas. "Rite of Passage . . . Women for the Inner Circle." *Management Review* 70 (July 1981): 8–14.

Sinetar, Marsha. "Developing Leadership Potential." *Personnel Journal* 60 (March 1981): 193–196.

Somers, Patricia, Poulton-Callahan, Charles and Bartlett, Robin. "Women in the Workforce: A Structural Approach to Equality." *Personnel Adminstrator* 26 (October 1981): 61–64.

Tavernier, Gerard. "Improving Managerial Productivity: The Key Ingredient Is Better Communication." *Management Review* 70 (February 1981): 12–16.

Thurston, Kathryn A. "Sexual Harassment: An Organizational Perceptive." *Personnel Administrator* 25 (December 1980): 59–64.

Trotter, Richard, Zacur, Susan Rawson and Greenwood, Wallace. "The Pregnancy Disability Amendment: What the Law Provides, Part II." *Personnel Administrator* 27 (March 1982): 55–58.

Weidenbaum, Murray L. "The True Obligation of the Business Firm to Society." *Management Review* 70 (September 1981): 21–22.

Chapter 3—Job Analysis

Arvey, Richard D. *Fairness In Selecting Employees.* Reading, MA: Addison-Wesley Publishing Company, 1979.

De Cotiis, Thomas A., and Morano, Richard A. "Applying Job Analysis to Training." *Training and Development Journal* 31 (July 1977): 20–24.

Ellig, Bruce R. "The Impact of Legislation on the Personnel Function." *Personnel* 57 (September–October 1980): 49–53.

Henderson, Richard I. "Job Descriptions—Critical Documents, Versatile Tools." *Supervisory Management* 20 (November 1975): 2–10.

Myers, Donald W. "The Impact of a Selected Provision in the Federal Guidelines on Job Analysis and Training." *Personnel Administrator* 26 (July 1981): 41–45.

Wendt, George R. "Should Courts Write Your Job Descriptions?" *Personnel Journal* 55 (September 1976): 442–450.

Yoder, Dale, and Heneman, Herbert G., Jr., eds. *ASPA Handbook of Personnel and Industrial Relations and Auditing PAIR, Vol. 4.* Washington, DC: The Bureau of National Affairs, Inc., 1976.

Chapter 4—Human Resources Planning

Allen, Louis A. "Managerial Planning: Back to Basics." *Management Review* 70 (April 1981): 15–20.

Alpander, Guvenc G. and Boher, Constant H. "An Integrated Model of Strategic Human Resource Planning and Utilization." *Human Resource Planning* 4 (1981): 189–207.

Awad, E. M. "Using Computers as an EEO Compliance Tool." *Data Management* 20 (February 1982): 25–28.

Brunner, Nancy R. "Blue-Collar Women." *Personnel Journal* 60 (April 1981): 279–282.

"Computerized Personnel Systems." *Personnel Journal* 60 (November 1981): 826 +.

Ein-Dor, Phillip and Segev, Eli. "MIS Development Practices." *Data Management* 19 (July 1981): 25–28.

Frantzreb, Richard B. "Human Resource Planning: Forecasting Manpower Needs." *Personnel Journal* 60 (November 1981): 850–857.

"Human Resources Has Its Own Computer." *Personnel* 53 (January/February 1978): 81–93.

Jennings, Eugene E. "How to Develop Your Management Talent Internally." *Personnel Administrator* 26 (July 1981): 20–23.

Lopez, Felix M. "Toward a Better System of Human Resource Planning." *S.A.M. Advanced Management Journal* 46 (Spring 1981): 4–14.

Mackey, Craig, B. "Human Resource Planning: A Four-Phased Approach." *Management Review* 70 (May 1981): 17–22.

Moore, John M. "Employee Relocation: Expanded Responsibilities for the Personnel Department." *Personnel* 58 (September/October 1981): 62–69.

Muller, David G. "A Model for Human Resources Development." *Personnel Journal* 55 (May 1976): 238–243.

"A New Target: Reducing Staff and Levels." *Business Week* (December 21, 1981): 69–70 +.

Odiorne, George S. "Developing a Human Resource Strategy." *Personnel Journal* 60 (July 1981): 534 +.

Olivas, Louis. "Adding a Different Dimension to Goal-Setting Processes." *Personnel Administration* 26 (October 1981): 75–78.

Piron, Stephen F. "Data vs. Information: The Difference." *Management Accounting* 62 (March 1981): 57.

Porter, Grover. "The Development of a MIS: A Pyramid." *Management Accounting* 62 (February 1981): 53.

Pursell, Donald E. "Planning for Tomorrow's Personnel Problems." *Personnel Journal* 60 (July 1981): 559–562.

Rowland, Kendrith M. and Summers, Scott L. "Human Resources Planning: A Second Look." *Personnel Administration* 26 (December 1981): 73–80.

Russ, Charles F., Jr. "Manpower Planning Systems: Part 1." *Personnel Journal* 61 (January 1982): 40–45.

Scarborough, Norman and Zimmerer, Thomas W. "Human Resources Forecasting: Why and Where to Begin." *Personnel Administrator* 27 (May 1982): 55–61.

Taguiri, Renato. "Planning: Desirable and Undesirable." *Human Resource Management* 19 (Spring, 1980): 11–14.

Walker, A. J. "The 10 Most Common Mistakes in Developing Computer-Based Personnel Systems." *Personnel Administrator* 25 (July 1980): 39–42.

Walker, A. J. "Management Selection Systems that Meet the Challenges of the 80s." *Personnel Journal* 60 (October 1981): 775–780.

Walker, Alfred J., Jr. "Personnel Uses the Computer." *Personnel Journal* 51 (March 1982): 204–207.

Walker, James W. *Human Resource Planning.* New York: McGraw-Hill Book Company, 1980.

Zippo, M. "Human Resources Data: Out of the Filming Cabinet, Into the Computer." *Personnel* 58 (November/December 1981): 51–53.

Chapter 5—Personnel Recruitment

Arvey, Richard D. *Fairness In Selecting Employees* (Reading, Mass.: Addison-Wesley Publishing Company, 1979).

"Attracting Graduates in 1982." *Personnel Executive* 9 (March 1982): 22–25.

Bjerregaard, Wayne J. and Gold, Mark E. "Employment Agencies and Executive Recruiters: A Practical Approach." *Personnel Administrator* 26 (May 1981): 127–135.

Bredwell, Jo. "The Use of Broadcast Advertising for Recruitment." *Personnel Administrator* 26 (February 1981): 45–49.

"Bright Prospects in the Executive Job Market." *Nation's Business* 65 (February 1977): 30–34.

Burton, G. E. "How to Prevent Dry Rot in College Recruiting." *The Personnel Administrator* 20 (September 1975): 56–58.

Cronin, Richard J. "Executive Recruiters: Are They Necessary?" *Personnel Administrator* 26 (February 1981): 31–34.

Durrill, David C. "Imagination in Personnel Management." *United States Banker* 88 (November 7, 1977): 30–33.

Garcia, J. Robert. "Job Posting for Professional Staff." *Personnel Journal* (March 1981): 189.

Heneman, Herbert G., III, and Schwab, Donald P. *Perspectives on Personnel/Human Resource Management.* Homewood, IL: Richard D. Irwin, Inc., 1978.

Huxtable, Fulton L. "Executive Hiring Deserves More than Spare-Time Treatment." *Personnel Administrator* 27 (March 1982): 35–38.

Kenney, Robert M. "The Open House Complements Recruitment Strategies." *Personnel Administrator* 27 (March 1982): 27–32.

Kenny, Roger M. "Executive Search Today." *California Management Review* 20 (Summer 1978): 79–82.

Ledvinka, James. *Federal Regulation of Personnel and Human Resource Management.* Boston, Mass.: Kent Publishing Company, 1982.

Lubliner, Murray J. "Developing Recruiting Literature

That Pays Off." *Personnel Administrator* 26 (February 1981): 51–54.

Mangum, Stephen L. "Recruitment and Job Search: The Recruitment Tactics of Employers." *Personnel Administrator* 27 (June 1982): 96–102.

Marr, Richard and Schneider, Joseph. "Self-Assessment Test for the 1978 Uniform Guidelines on Employee Selection Procedures." *Personnel Administrator* 26 (May 1981): 103–108.

McCulloch, Kenneth J. *Selecting Employees Safely Under the Law.* Englewood Cliffs, NJ: Prentice-Hall, Inc., 1981.

Nemei, Margaret McClure, "Recruitment Advertising—It's More Than Just 'Help Wanted'." *Personnel Administrator* 26 (February 1981): 57–60.

A Professional and Legal Analysis of the Uniform Guidelines on Employee Selection Procedures ed. by Virgil B. Day, Frank Erwin, and Alan M. Koral. Berea, OH: The American Society for Personnel Administration, 1981.

Robertson, David E. "New Direction in EEO Guidelines." *Personnel Journal* 57 (July 1978): 360–363.

Ross, Richard. "One Way to Get Good Workers." *Nation's Business* (September 1977): 39–40.

Schweitzer, Nancy J. and Deely, John. "Interviewing the Disabled Job Applicant." *Personnel Journal* (March 1982): 205–209.

Soothill, Keith. "The Extent of Risk in Employing Ex-Prisoners." *Personnel Management* 13 (April 1981): 35–37+.

Stoops, Rick. "Recruitment." *Personnel Journal* 60, no. 10 (October 1981): 768–769.

Wallrapp, Gary G. "Job Posting for Nonexempt Employees: A Sample Program." *Personnel Journal* (October 1981): 796–798.

"What Recruiters Watch for in College Graduates." *Nation's Business* 64 (March 1976): 34–36.

White, Reba. "Headhunting in Wall Street." *Institutional Investor* II (February 1977): 31–36.

Chapter 6—Personnel Selection

Acuff, Hall A. "Quality Control in Employee Selection." *Personnel Journal* 60 (July 1981): 562–565.

Arvey, Richard D. *Fairness In Selecting Employees.* Reading, Mass.: Addison-Wesley Publishing Company, 1979.

Bekiroglu, H. and Gonen, H. "Labor Turnover: Roots, Costs, and Some Potential Solutions." *Personnel Administrator* 26 (July 1981): 67–72.

Bucalo, Jack. "The Balanced Approach to Successful Screening Interviews." *Personnel Journal* 57 (August 1978): 420–426.

Chastin, Sherry. "On the Job." *Working Woman* (October 1981): 30–36.

Cronin, Richard J., APD. "Executive Recruiters: Are They Necessary?" *Personnel Administrator* (February 1981): 31–34.

Decker, Robert L. "The Employment Interview." *Personnel Administrator* 26 (November 1981): 71–73.

Frew, David R. "Diagnosing and Dealing With Task Complexity." *Personnel Administrator* 26 (November 1981): 87–92.

Gatewood, Robert D. and Schoenfeldt, Lyle F. "Content Validity and EEOC: A Useful Alternative for Selection." *Personnel Journal* 56 (October 1977): 520–523.

Goodale, James G. "The Neglected Art of Interviewing." *Supervisory Management* 26 (July 1981): 2–10.

Huxtable, Fulton L. "Executive Hiring Deserves More Than Spare-Time Treatment." *Personnel Administrator* 27 (March 1982): 35–38.

Jablin, Fredric M. "Use of Discriminatory Questions in Screening Interviews." *Personnel Administrator* 27 (March 1982): 41–43.

Jeffrey, Ray. "Taking the Guesswork Out of Selection." *Personnel Management* 9 (October 1977): 40–42.

Kanouse, Daniel N. and Warihay, Philomena I. "A New Look at Employee Orientation." *Training and Development Journal* 34 (July 1980): 34–36.

Kleiman, Lawrence S. and Faley, Robert H. "Assessing Content Validity: Standards Set by the Court." *Personnel Psychology* 31 (Winter 1978): 701–711.

Kravetz, Dennis J. "Selection Systems for Clerical Positions." *Personnel Administrator* 26 (February 1981): 39–42.

Langer, Steven. "Budgets and Staffing: A Survey." *Personnel Journal* 60 (June 1981): 464–468.

Lawrence, Daniel G.; Salsburg, Barbara L.; Dawson, John G.; and Fasman, Zachary D. "Design and Use of Weighted Application Blanks." *Personnel Administrator* 27 (March 1982): 47–53.

Ledvinka, James. *Federal Regulation of Personnel and Human Resource Management.* Boston: Kent Publishing Company, 1982.

Mahoney, Thomas A., Milovich, George T. and Weiner, Nan. "A Stock and Flow Model for Improved Human Resources Measurement." *Personnel* 54 (May/June 1977): 56–66.

Malinowski, Frank A. "Job Selection Using Task Analysis." *Personnel Journal* (April 1981): 288.

Marr, Richard and Schneider, Joseph. "Self-Assessment Test for the 1978 Uniform Guidelines on Employee Selection Procedures." *Personnel Administrator* 26 (May 1981): 103–108.

McCulloch, Kenneth J. *Selecting Employees Safely Under the Law.* Englewood Cliffs, NJ: Prentice-Hall, Inc. 1981.

Meyers, Donald W. "The Impact of a Selected Provision in the Federal Guidelines on Job Analysis and Training." *Personnel Administrator* 26 (July 1981): 41–45.

Moro, James L. "Oral Interviews for Screening Social Working Applicants." *Public Personnel Management* 6 (November 1977): 437–441.

Mullins, Terry W. and Davis, Ronald H. "A Strategy for Managing the Selection Interview Process." *Personnel Administrator* 26 (March 1981): 65–67 + .

Pace, Larry A. and Schoenfeldt, Lyle F. "Legal Concerns in the Use of Weighted Application Blanks." *Personnel Psychology* 30 (1977): 159–166.

Pursell, Elliott D., Campion, Michael A. and Gaylord, Sarah R. "Structured Interviewing: Avoiding Selection Problems." *Personnel Journal* 59 (November 1980): 907–912.

Reed-Mendenhall, Diana and Millard, C. W. "Orientation: A Training and Development Tool." *Personnel Administrator* 25 (August 1980): 40–44.

Rehfuso, John. "Management Development and the Selection of Overseas Executives." *Personnel Administrator* 27 (July 1982): 35–43.

Rickard, Scott T. "Effective Staff Selection." *Personnel Journal* 60 (June 1981): 475–478.

"Saying 'HELLO' to New Employees." *Industry Week* 205 (May 26, 1980): 81–82.

Sewell, Carole, "Pre-Employment Investigations: The Key to Security in Hiring." *Personnel Journal* 60 (May 1981): 376–379.

Shea, Gordon F. "That Critical First Day." *Supervision* 43 (April 1981): 3–5.

Short, Lawrence O. and Taber, Lynville E. "The Selection Interview: An Interim Approach." *Public Personnel Management* 7 (March 1978): 143–147.

Sleveking, Nicholas, Anchor, Kenneth and Marston, Ronald C. "Selecting and Preparing Expatriate Employees." *Personnel Journal* (March 1981): 197.

Standards for Educational and Psychological Tests and Manuals. American Psychological Association. Washington, DC, 1976.

Sterrett, John H. "The Job Interview: Body Language and Perceptions of Potential." *Journal of Applied Psychology* 63 (June 1978): 388–390.

Tauber, Mark S. "New Employee Orientation: A Comprehensive Systems Approach." *Personnel Administrator* 26 (January 1981): 65–69.

"Why It Pays to Put New Employees at Ease." *Management Review* 70 (January 1981): 5–6.

Chapter 7—Training and Development: Macro-Level Approaches

Alber, Antone F. "Making Job Enrichment Pay Off." *Supervisory Management* 27 (January 1982): 30–33.

Allen, Robert F. and Silverzweig, Stanley. "Changing Community and Organizational Cultures." *Training and Development Journal* 31 (July 1977): 28–34.

Argyris, Chris. *Management and Organizational Development.* New York: McGraw-Hill Book Company, 1971.

Baker, H. Kent and Holmberg, Stevan R. "Stepping Up to Supervision: Coping with Change." *Supervisory Management* 27 (March 1982): 21–27.

Bennis, Warren G. *Changing Organizations.* New York: McGraw-Hill Book Company, 1966.

Blanchard, Kenneth H. and Hersey, Paul. "The Management of Change." *Training and Development Journal* 34 (June 1980): 80–98.

Brook, Alexis. "Coping with the Stress of Change." *Management International Review* 18 (1978): 9–15.

Cohen, Michael H. and Ross, Mary E. "Team Building: A Strategy for Unit Cohesiveness." *The Journal of Nursing Administration* XII (January 1982): 29–34.

Cohen, Michael L. "Job Redesign: An Organization Development Approach." *Personnel Journal* 55 (December 1976): 608–610.

Cox, Martha Glenn and Brown, Jane Covey. "Quality of Worklife: Another Fad or Real Benefit?" *Personnel Administrator* 27 (May 1982): 99–153.

Craig, Robert L., ed. *Training and Development Handbook: A Guide to Human Resource Development.* New York: McGraw-Hill Book Company, 1976.

Davis, Philip A. "Building a Workable Participative Management System." *Management Review* 70 (March 1981): 26–28 +.

"Developing HRD and OD: The Profession and the Professional." *Training and Development Journal* 36 (January 1982): 18–30.

Donegan, Priscilla. "Quality Circles—New Productivity Power Source." *Progressive Grocer* 61 (January 1982): 105–110.

Fannin, William R. "Making MBO Work: Matching Management Style to MBO Program." *Supervisory Management* 26 (September 1981): 20–27.

Frank, Frederic; Struth, Michael and Donovan, Jim. "Practitioner Certification: The Time Has Come." *Training and Development Journal* 34 (October 1980): 80–83.

Franke, Arnold G.; Harrick, Edward J. and Klein, Andrew J. "The Role of Personnel in Improving Productivity." *Personnel Administrator* 27 (March 1982): 83–88.

Franklin, Jerome L. "Improving the Effectiveness of Survey Feedback." *Personnel* 55 (May/June 1978): 11–17.

George, William W. "Task Teams for Rapid Growth." *Harvard Business Review* 55 (March/April 1977): 71–80.

Gery, Gloria. "Equal Opportunity—Planning and Managing the Process of Change." *Personnel Journal* 56 (April 1977): 184–203.

Grahn, John L. "White Collar Productivity: Misunderstandings and Some Progress." *Personnel Administrator* 26 (August 1981): 27–31.

Greenwood, Ronald G. "Management by Objectives: As Developed by Peter Drucker, Assisted by Harold Smiddy." *Academy of Management Review* 6 (April 1981): 225–230.

Herzberg, Frederick and Zautra, Alex. "Orthodox Job Enrichment: Measuring True Quality in Job Satisfaction." *Personnel* 53 (September/October 1976): 54–68.

Huseman, Richard C. and others. "Managing Change Through Communication." *Personnel Journal* 57 (January 1978): 20–25.

Jackson, John H. "Using Management By Objectives: Case Studies of Four Attempts." *Personnel Administrator* 26 (February 1981): 78–81.

Johnston, Robert W. "Seven Steps to Whole Organization Development." *Training and Development Journal* 33 (January 1979): 12–22.

Kanarick, Arnold. "The Far Side of Quality Circles." *Management Review* 70 (October 1981): 16–17.

Kanter, Rosabeth Moss and Stein, Barry A. "Ungluing the Stuck Motivation Performance and Productivity Through Expanding Opportunity." *Management Review* 70 (July 1981): 45–49.

"Lessons from the Volvo Experience." *International Management* 33 (February 1978): 42–46.

Littlejohn, Robert F. "Team Management: A How-to Approach to Improved Productivity, Higher Morale, and Lasting Job Satisfaction." *Management Review* 71 (January 1982): 23–28.

Mahoney, Francis X. "Team Development, Part 2: How to Select the Appropriate TD Approach." *Personnel* 58 (November–December 1981): 21–38.

Marchington, Mick. "Employee Participation—Consensus or Confusion?" *Personnel Management* 13 (April 1981): 38–41.

McManus, George J. "Team Concept Stressed in Productivity Confab." *Iron Age* (December 7, 1981): 45–47.

Michalak, Donald F. and Yager, Edwin G. *Making the Training Process Work.* New York: Harper & Row, Publishers, 1979.

Miller, Ernest C. "Organization Development: A Dynamic New Force?" *Personnel* 54 (November/December 1977): 4–9.

Myers, Donald W. "The Impact of a Selected Provision in the Federal Guidelines on Job Analysis and Training." *Personnel Administrator* 26 (July 1981): 41–5.

Niehoff, Marilee and Romans, M. Jay. "Needs Assessment as One Step Toward Enhancing Productivity." *Personnel Administrator* 27 (May 1982): 35–39.

O'Toole, James. "How Management Hinders Productivity." *Industry Week* 210 (August 10, 1981): 55–58.

Ozley, Lee M. and Ball, Judith S. "Quality of Work Life: Initiating Successful Efforts in Labor-Management Organizations." *Personnel Administrator* 27 (May 1982): 27–33.

Patten, Thomas M., Jr. "The Productivity of Human Resources in Government: Making Human Effort and Energy Count for More." *Human Resource Management* 19 (Spring 1980): 2–10.

"Quality Circle Boom Part of Growing American Trend."

Supervision XLIII (September 1981): 8–11.

Quigley, John. "Consider 'People Value' in Gaining More Productivity." *The Office* 95 (January 1982): 168.

Rohrer, Robert. "Low Productivity is Everybody's Fault." *Supervision* XLIII (August 1981): 12–13.

Scott, Walter B. "Participative Management at Motorola—The Results." *Management Review* 70 (July 1981): 26–28.

Shea, Gordon. "What to do with Those Dull, Routine, Repetitive Dead-End Jobs." *Supervision* XLIII (November 1981): 3–5.

Snyder, Robert A. "A Model for the Systematic Evaluation of Human Resource Development Programs." *Academy of Management Review* 5 (July 1980): 431–443.

Stanton, Erwin S. "The Problems of Productivity." *Supervisory Management* 27 (March 1982): 34–36.

Strauss, Nan and Castino, Anthony. "Human Resource Development: Promise or Platitude?" *Personnel Administrator* (November 1981): 25–27.

Chapter 8—Training and Development: Micro-Level Approaches

Aplin, John C. and Gerster, Darlene K. "Career Development: An Integration of Individual and Organizational Needs." *Personnel* 55 (March/April 1978): 23–29.

Baird, John E., Jr. "Supervisor and Managerial Training Through Communication by Objectives." *Personnel Administrator* 26 (July 1981): 28–32.

Bowen, Donald D. and Hall, Douglas T. "Career Planning for Employee Development: A Primer for Managers." *California Management Review* 20 (Winter 1977): 23–35.

Braun, Alexander. "Assessing Supervisory Training Needs and Evaluating Effectiveness." *Training and Development Journal* 33 (February 1979): 3–10.

Connelly, Sharon L. "Career Development: Are We Asking the Right Questions?" *Training and Development Journal* 33 (March 1979): 8–11.

Craig, Robert L., ed. *Training and Development Handbook: A Guide to Human Resource Development*. New York: McGraw-Hill Book Company, 1976.

Decker, Phillip J. and Moore, Rusti C. "More Hints on Successful Modeling." *Training: The Magazine of Human Resources Development* 19 (January 1982): 26–27.

Decotiis, Thomas A. and Morano, Richard A. "Applying Job Analysis to Training." *Training and Development Journal* 31 (July 1977): 20–24.

Dethlefs, Dennis and Sellentin, Jerry L. "How to Be a 'Houdini' in Training." *Personnel Administrator* 24 (January 1979): 66–67.

Dickey, John D. "Training With a Focus on the Individual." *Personnel Administrator* 27 (June 1982): 35–38.

Elsbree, Asia Rial and Howe, Christine. "An Evaluation of Training in Three Acts." *Training and Development Journal* 31 (July 1977): 10–14.

Eng, Jo Ellen E. and Gottsdanker, Josephine S. "Positive Changes from a Career Development Program." *Training and Development Journal* 33 (January 1979): 3–7.

Ezzell, William W. "Orientation: Tell Them What They Need to Know!" *Training and Development Journal* 33 (January 1979): 54–56.

Frank, Frederic D. and Preston, James R. "The Validity of the Assessment Center Approach and Related Issues." *Personnel Administrator* 27 (June 1982): 87–95.

Gottheimer, Debra. "A Manager's Training Film Festival." *Administrative Management* 38 (July 1977): 24–27+.

Guyot, James F. "Management Training and Post-Industrial Apologetics." *California Management Review* 20 (Summer 1978): 84–93.

"Harry Shoemarker: AT&T's 'Mr. Training'." *Training: The Magazine of Human Resources Development* 19 (June 1982): 60–61.

"Highlights from AMA's Human Resources Conference." *Personnel* 58 (July–August 1981): 53–55.

"Incentives in Training: How You can Raise the Reward for Learning." *Training: The Magazine of Human Resources Development* 19 (February 1982): 43+.

Jamieson, David W. "Developing the Profession and the Professional." *Training and Development Journal* 36 (May 1982): 118–121.

Jobe, Ernest D.; Boxx, W. Randy and Howell, D. L. "A Customized Approach to Management Development." *Personnel Journal* 58 (March 1979): 150–153.

Kempfer, Homer. "Getting Your Money's Worth from Outside Training?" *Training and Development Journal* 34 (May 1980): 116–118.

Kirkpatrick, Donald L. "Determining Training Needs: Four Simple and Effective Approaches." *Training and Development Journal* 31 (February 1977): 22–25.

Kirkpatrick, Donald L. "Evaluating Training Programs: Evidence vs. Proof." *Training and Development Journal* 31 (November 1977): 9–12.

Kronenberger, George K. and Banker, David L. "Effective Training and the Elimination of Sexual Harassment." *Personnel Journal* 60 (November 1981): 879–933.

Langford, Harry. "Needs Analysis in the Training Directors." *Training and Development Journal* 23 (August 1978): 18–25.

Levine, Hermine Zagat. "Consensus: Employee Training Programs." *Personnel* 58 (July–August 1981): 4–11.

Malone, Robert L. and Petersen, Donald J. "Personnel Effectiveness: Its Dimensions and Development." *Personnel Journal* 56 (October 1977): 498–501.

McLagan, Patricia A. "The ASTD Training & Development Competency Study: A Model Building Challenge." *Training and Development Journal* 36 (May 1982): 18–24.

Michalak, Donald F. and Yager, Edwin G. *Making the*

Training Process Work. New York: Harper & Row, Publishers, 1979.

Milbrath, Mona A. "Professional Accreditation Training Programs: An Overlooked Resource?" *Training: The Magazine of Human Resources Development* 19 (June 1982): 52–53.

Miles, Wilford G. and Briggs, William D. "Common, Recurring and Avoidable Errors in Management Development." *Training and Development Journal* 33 (February 1979): 32–35.

Monat, Jonathan S. "A Perspective on the Evaluation of Training and Development Programs." *Personnel Administrator* 26 (July 1981): 47–52.

Neff, Leslie A. "A Training Program with a Small Town Touch." *Management World* 7 (January 1978): 13–14.

Newstrom, John W. "Catch-22: The Problems of Incomplete Evaluation of Training." *Training and Development Journal* 32 (November 1978): 22–24.

Newstrom, John W. "Evaluating the Effectiveness of Training Methods." *Personnel Administrator* 25 (January 1980): 55–60.

Niehoff, Marilee S. and Romans, M. Jay. "Needs Assessment as Step One Toward Enhancing Productivity." *Personnel Administrator* 27 (May 1982): 35–39.

O'Toole, James. "Integrating Work and Learning." *Training and Development Journal* 31 (June 1977): 36–48.

Ponthieu, J. F. "Gaining Mutual Independence Through Training." *Supervisory Management* 27 (April 1982): 16–19.

Post, Charles T. "Ball Corp. Makes Certain Its Workers Understand." *Iron Age* 221 (June 12, 1978): 28–29.

Reed, Warren H. "ASTD/NYU Professional Certification Program." *Training and Development Journal* 32 (September 1978): 44–45.

Smith, Judson. "A Trainer's Guide to Successful Productivity Improvement Planning." *Training: The Magazine of Human Resources Development* 19 (March 1982): 41–44.

Smith, Peter. "Coming to Terms with Job Crises." *Personnel Management* 10 (January 1978): 32–35.

Truskie, Stanley D. "Getting the Most from Management Development Programs." *Personnel Journal* 61 (January 1982): 66–68.

Truskie, Stanley D. "Guidelines for Conducting In-House Management Development." *Personnel Administrator* 26 (July 1981): 25–27.

"Who is Responsible for Employee Career Planning? . . . A Personnel Symposium." *Personnel* 55 (March/April 1978): 10–22.

Yeomans, William N. "How to Get Top Management Support." *Training and Development Journal* 36 (June 1982): 38–40.

Zemke, Ron. "Job Competencies: Can They Help You Design Better Training?" *Training: The Magazine of Human Resources Development* 19 (May 1982): 28–31.

Zenger, John H. and Hargis, Kenneth. "Assessing Training Results: It's Time to Take the Plunge." *Training and Development Journal* (January 1982): 11–16.

Chapter 9—Career Planning and Development

Amico, Anthony M. "Computerized Career Information." *Personnel Journal* 60 (August 1981): 632–633.

Beam, H. H. "Framework for Personal Development." *Human Resource Management* 19 (Summer 1980): 2–8.

Berardo, Don. "Increasing Upward Mobility—The Stuff Achievement is Made of." *Data Management* 19 (March 1981): 40–43.

Bolles, Richard Nelson. *What Color Is Your Parachute?* Berkeley, CA: Ten Speed Press, 1972.

Camden, Thomas M. "Use Outplacement as a Career Development Tool." *Personnel Administrator* 27 (January 1982): 35–37.

Carter, M. N. "Ins and Outs of Switching Jobs." *Money* 10 (October 1981): 124–126+.

Crites, John O. "Testing for Career Adjustment and Development." *Training and Development Journal* 36 (February 1982): 20–28.

Dauw, Dean C. *Up Your Career.* Prospect Heights, IL: Waveland Press, 1975.

Douglass, Merrill E. and Baker, Larry. "Success in Your Own Good Time." *Supervisory Management* 26 (April 1981): 30–35.

Fear, Richard A. *The Evaluation Interview.* New York: McGraw-Hill Book Company, 1973.

Ferratt, T. W. and Starke, A. "How to Know When It's Time to Change Jobs." *Journal of Systems Management* 32 (July 1981): 6–11.

Flynn, W. R. and Litzsinger, J. U. "Careers Without Conflict." *Personnel Administration* 26 (July 1981): 81–85.

German, Donald R. and German, Joan W. *Successful Job Hunting for Executives.* Chicago: Henry Regnery Company, 1974.

Granovetter, Mark. *Getting a Job.* Cambridge, Mass.: Harvard University Press, 1974.

Greco, Benedetto. *How to Get the Job That's Right for You.* Homewood, IL: Dow Jones-Irwin, 1975.

Halatin, Theodore J. "Becoming a Mentor: Are the Risks Worth the Rewards?" *Supervisory Management* 27 (February 1982): 27–29.

Hall, Douglas T. *Careers in Organizations.* Pacific Palisades, CA: Goodyear Publishing Company, 1976.

Hastings, Robert E. "No-Fault Career Counseling Can Boost Middle- and Upper-Middle Management." *Personnel Administrator* 27 (January 1982): 22–27.

Hickerson, Karl A. and Anderson, Richard C. "Career Development: Whose Responsibility?" *Personnel Administrator* 27 (June 1982): 41–49.

Holland, J. L. *Making Vocational Choices: A Theory of Careers.* Englewood Cliffs NJ: Prentice-Hall, Inc., 1973.

Hutcheson, Peggy and Chalofsky, Neal. *Training and Development Journal* (July 1981): 13–15.

Jameson, Robert H. *The Professional Job Hunting System: World's Fastest Way to Get a Better Job.* Verona, NJ: Performance Dynamics, 1972.

Jennings, Eugene. *The Mobile Manager.* New York: McGraw-Hill Book Company, 1967.

Kaye, Beverly L. "Career Development: The Integrating Force." *Training and Development Journal* 35 (May 1981): 36–40.

Kelly, Nancy, "Zale Corporation's Career Development Program." *Training and Development Journal* 36 (June 1982): 70–75.

Kent, William E. and Otte, Fred L. "Career Development: The Ultimate Incentive." *S.A.M. Advanced Management Journal* 47 (Spring 1982): 8–17.

Keyser, Marshall. "How to Apply for a Job." *Journal of College Placement* 35 (Fall 1974): 63–65.

Kotter, John P.; Faux, Victor A. and McArthur, Charles C. *Self-Assessment of Career Development.* Englewood Cliffs, NJ: Prentice-Hall, Inc., 1978.

Lattimer, Robert L. "Developing Career Awareness Among Minority Youths: A Case Example." *Personnel Journal* 60 (January, 1981): 17.

Leach, J. J. "Career Planning Process." *Personnel Journal* 60 (April 1981): 283–287.

Mangum, Stephen L. "Recruitment and Job Search: The Recruitment Tactics of Employers." *Personnel Administrator* 27 (June 1982): 96–102.

McCaffrey, William T. "Career Growth Versus Upward Mobility." *Personnel Administrator* 26 (May 1981): 81–87.

Meckel, Nelson T. "The Manager as Career Counselor." *Training and Development Journal* 35 (July 1981): 65–69.

Moravec, Milan. "A Cost Effective Career Planning Program Requires a Strategy." *Personnel Administrator* 27 (January 1982): 28–32.

Morgan, Marilyn A. *Managing Career Development.* New York: D. Van Nostrand Company, 1980.

Muniz, Peter and Chasnoff, Robert. "Counseling the Marginal Performer." *Supervisory Management* 27 (May 1982): 2–14.

Osipow, S. H. *Theories of Career Development.* New York: Appleton-Century-Crofts, 1973.

Otte, Fred L. "Creating Successful Career Development Programs." *Training and Development Journal* 36 (February 1982): 30–37.

Randolph, A. Benton. "Managerial Career Coaching." *Training and Development Journal* 35 (July 1981): 54–55.

Schaeffer, Dorothy. "Counseling—No Easy Task." *Supervision* 43 (February 1981): 7–8.

Schwartz, Eleanor B. and MacKenzie, R. Alec. "Time Management Strategy for Dual-Career Women." *The Business Quarterly* 42 (Autumn 1977): 32–41.

Taylor, Harold. "Personal Goal Setting." *Supervision* XLII (September 1981): 3.

Veiga, J. F. "Do Managers on the Move Get Anywhere?" *Harvard Business Review* 59 (March–April 1981): 20–22 + .

Walker, James W. *Human Resource Planning.* New York: McGraw-Hill Book Company, 1980.

Wolf, James F. and Bacher, Robert N. "Career Negotiation: Trading Off Employee and Organizational Needs." *Personnel* 58 (March–April 1981): 53–59.

Zenger, John H. "Career Planning: Coming in From the Cold." *Training and Development Journal* 35 (July 1981): 47–52.

Chapter 10—Performance Appraisal

Baird, Lloyd S. "Self and Superior Ratings of Performance: As Related to Self-Esteem and Satisfaction With Supervision." *Academy of Management Journal* 20 (1977): 291–300.

Baird, Lloyd S, Beatty, Richard W. and Schneier, Craig Eric. *The Performance Appraisal Sourcebook.* Amherst, Mass.: Human Resource Development Press, 1982.

Baroni, Barry J. "The Legal Ramifications of Appraisal Systems." *Supervisory Management* 27 (January 1982): 40–43.

Berg, Gary J. *Managing Compensation.* New York: AMA-COM, A Division of American Management Association, 1976.

Birch, William J. "Performance Appraisal: One Company's Experience." *Personnel Journal* 60 (June 1981): 456–460.

Brett, Randall and Fredian, Alan J. "Performance Appraisal: The System is Not the Solution." *Personnel Administrator* 26 (December 1981): 61–68.

Bucalo, Jack. "Personnel Directors . . . What You Should Know Before Recommending MBO." *Personnel Journal* 56 (April 1977): 176–178.

Cangemi, Joseph P. and Claypool, Jeffrey C. "Complimentary Interviews: A System for Rewarding Outstanding Employees." *Personnel Journal* 57 (February 1978): 87–90.

Carey, James F. "Participative Job Evaluation." *Compensation Review* 9 (4th quarter 1977): 29–38.

Carroll, Stephen J. and Schneier, Craig E. *Performance Appraisal and Review Systems.* Glenview, IL: Scott, Foresman and Company, 1982.

Catalanello, Ralph E. and Hooper, John A. "Managerial Appraisal." *Personnel Administrator* 26 (September 1981): 75–81.

Cummings, L. L. and Schwab, Donald P. "Designing Appraisal Systems for Information Yield." *California Management Review* 20 (Summer 1978): 18–25.

Ford, Robert C. and Jennings, Kenneth M. "How to Make Performance Appraisals More Effective." *Personnel* 54 (March/April 1977): 51–56.

Grant, Philip C. "How to Manage Employee Job Performance." *Personnel Administrator* 26 (August 1981): 59–65.

Haynes, Marion G. "Developing an Appraisal Program." *Personnel Journal* 57 (January 1978): 14–19.

Henderson, Richard. *Performance Appraisal: Theory and Practice.* Reston, VA: Reston Publishing Company, Inc., 1980.

Holley, William H. and Field, Hubert S. "Will Your Performance Appraisal System Hold Up in Court?" *Personnel* (January–February 1982): 59–64.

Holley, William H.; Field, Hubert S. and Barnett, Nona J. "Analyzing Performance Appraisal Systems: An Empirical Study." *Personnel Journal* 55 (September 1976): 457–463.

Johnson, Michael L. and McClosky, Kenneth R. "Ask Me—A Merit Promotion System." *Personnel Journal* 57 (August 1978): 430–433.

Kothari, Vanay. "Promotional Criteria: Three Views." *Personnel Journal* 55 (August 1976): 402–405.

Lee, M. Blaine and Zwerman, William L. "Designing a Motivating and Team Building Employee Appraisal System." *Personnel Journal* 55 (July 1976): 354–357.

Locker, Alan H. and Teel, Kenneth S. "Performance Appraisal—A Survey of Current Practices." *Personnel Journal* 56 (May 1977): 245–247.

Lotham, Gary P. and Wexley, Kenneth N. *Increasing Productivity Through Performance Appraisal.* Reading, Mass.: Addison-Wesley Publishing Company, 1981.

Maravec, Milan. "Performance Appraisal: A Human Resource Management System With Productivity Payoffs." *Management Review* 70 (June 1981): 51–54.

McAjee, R. Bruce. "Performance Appraisal: When Function?" *Personnel Journal* 60 (April 1981): 238–239.

Nix, Dan H. "Getting Ready for the Appraisal Interview." *Supervisory Management* 25 (July 1980): 2–9.

Presnick, Walter J. "Measuring Managerial Productivity." *Administrative Management* XLI (May 1980): 26–28.

Schnake, M. E. "Apples and Oranges: Salary Review and Performance Review." *Supervisory Management* 25 (November 1980): 32–36.

Winstanley, N. B. "Legal and Ethical Issues in Performance Appraisals." *Harvard Business Review* 58 (November–December 1980): 186.

Yager, Ed. "A Critique of Performance Appraisal Systems." *Personnel Journal* 60 (February 1981): 129–133.

Yoder, Dale and Heneman, Herbert G., Jr., eds. *ASPA Handbook of Personnel and Industrial Relations: Staffing Policies and Strategies* Vol 1. Washington, DC: The Bureau of National Affairs, Inc., 1974.

Chapter 11—Financial Compensation

Ash, Ronald A. "Job Elements for Task Clusters: Arguments for Using Multi-methodological Approaches to Job Analysis and a Demonstration of Their Utility." *Public Personnel Management* 11 (Spring 1982): 80–90.

Belcher, David W. *Compensation Administration.* Englewood Cliffs, NJ: Prentice-Hall, Inc., 1974.

Berg, Gary J. *Managing Compensation.* New York: AMACOM, A Division of American Management Association, 1976.

Chruden, Herbert J. and Sherman, Arthur W., Jr. *Readings in Personnel Management.* Cincinnati: South-Western Publishing Co., 1976.

"Companies Let the Sunshine in on Salaries." *Industry Week* 19 (November 15, 1976): 70–72.

Dunn, J. D. and Rachel, Frank M. *Wage and Salary Administration: Total Compensation Systems.* New York: McGraw-Hill Book Company, 1971.

Dunn, N. "How to Give Raises and Get Your Money's Worth." *Black Enterprise* 8 (December 1977): 67+.

Ellig, B. R. "Compensation Management: Its Past and Its Future." *Personnel* 54 (May 1977): 30–40.

Farrell, R. J. "Compensation and Benefits." *Personnel Journal* 55 (November 1976): 557–563.

Feeney, Edward J. "Developing the High Performance Edge," *S.A.M. Advanced Management Journal* 46 (Autumn 1981): 29–30+.

Ferebee, J. S. "Wage and Salary Administration." *Supervisory Management* 21 (October 1976): 26–35.

Ferratt, Thomas W. and Starke, Frederick A. "How to Know When It's Time to Change Jobs." *Journal of Systems Management* 32 (July 1981): 6–11.

Finegan, T. A. "Discouraged Workers and Economic Fluctuations." *Industrial and Labor Relations Review* 35 (October 1981): 88–102.

Foster, K. and Kanin-Covers, S. "Determinants of Organizational Pay Policy." *Compensation Review* 9 (3d quarter 1977): 35–41.

Frew, D. R. "Diagnosing and Dealing with Task Complexity." *Personnel Administrator* 26 (November 1981): 87–88+.

Heller, George L. "Demystifying Job Evaluation." *Supervisory Management* 27 (January 1982): 20–25.

Henderson, R. I. "Changing Role of Wage and Salary Administrator." *Personnel* 53 (November 1976): 53–63.

Henderson, Richard I. *Compensation Management: Rewarding Performance in the Modern Organization.* Reston, VA: Reston Publishing Co., 1976.

Heneman, Herbert G., III and Schwab, Donald P. *Perspectives on Personnel/Human Resource Management.* Homewood, IL: Richard D. Irwin, Inc., 1978.

Langer, S. "Personnel Salaries: A Survey." *Personnel Journal* 59 (December 1980): 983–987.

Lawler, Edward E., III. "New Approaches to Pay: Innovations That Work." *Personnel* 53 (September–October 1976): 11–23.

Lawler, Edward E., III. *Pay and Organizational Effectiveness: A Psychological View.* New York: McGraw-Hill Book Company, 1971.

Lee, J. A. and Mendoza, J. L. "Comparison of Techniques Which Test for Job Differences." *Personnel Psychology* 34 (Winter 1981): 731–748.

Lindroth, Joan. "How to Beat the Coming Labor Shortage." *Personnel Journal* 61 (April 1982): 268–272.

Moss, R. W. "Challenge to the System." *Personnel Journal* 55 (September 1976): 454–456.

Mruk, E. S. and Giblen, E. J. "Compensation as a Management Tool." *Management Review* 66 (May 1977): 50–58.

Nielson, N. H. "Strategic Use of Compensation and Benefits in a Changing Environment." *Risk Management* 24 (August 1977): 22–24+.

Olsen, R. N. and Lawler, E. E. "Designing Reward Systems for New Organizations." *Personnel* 54 (September 1977): 48–60.

Patten, Thomas H., Jr. *Pay: Employee Compensation and Incentive Plans.* New York: The Free Press, 1977.

Patton, John A.; Littlefield, C. L. and Self, Stanley N. *Job Evaluation: Text and Cases,* 3d ed. Homewood, IL: Richard D. Irwin, Inc., 1964.

Perham, J. "Changing Compensation Package." *Compensation Review* 10 (2d quarter 1978): 46–48.

Pierce, Jon L. "Job Design in Perspective." *Personnel Administrator* 25 (December 1980): 67–74.

Piso, E. "Task Analysis for Process-Control Tasks: The Method of Annett et al. Applied," *Journal of Occupational Psychology* 54 (1981): 247–254.

Rock, Milton L. *Handbook of Wage and Salary Administration.* New York: McGraw-Hill Book Company, 1977.

Sibson, Robert E. *Compensation.* New York: AMACOM, A Division of American Management Association, 1974.

Spelfogel, Evan J. "Equal Pay for Work of Comparable Value: A New Concept." *Labor Law Journal* 32 (January 1981): 30–39.

Thomsen, D. J. "Unmentioned Problems of Salary Administration." *Compensation Review* 9 (4th quarter 1977): 11–21.

VanAdelsberg, H. "Relating Performance Evaluation to Compensation of Public Sector Employees." *Public Personnel Management* 7 (March 1978): 72–79.

Zollitsch, Herbert G. and Langsner, A. *Wage and Salary Administration.* Cincinnati: South-Western Publishing Company, 1970.

Chapter 12—Additional Compensation Considerations

Applebaum, Stephen H. and Millard, John B. "Engineering a Compensation Program to Fit the Individual Not the Job." *Personnel Journal* 55 (March 1976): 121–124.

Belcher, David W. *Compensation Administration.* Englewood Cliffs, NJ: Prentice-Hall, Inc., 1974.

Breakwell, Barbara. "Profit-Sharing Schemes Under the New Rules." *Accountancy* 91 (July 1980): 107–109.

Brinks, J. T. "Executive Compensation: Crossroads of the '80s." *Personnel Administrator* 26 (December 1981): 23–26+.

Brooks, L. D. and others. "How Profitable are Employee Stock Ownership Plans?" *Financial Executive* 50 (May 1982): 32–34.

Burt, Tim. "Making the Most of Time with Flexible Working Hours." *Personnel Executive* (March 1982): 37–43.

Bushardt, S. C. and Fowler, A. R. "Compensation and Benefits: Today's Dilemma in Motivation." *Personnel Administrator* 27 (April 1982): 23–26.

Chen, Yung-Ping. "The Growth of Fringe Benefits: Implications for Social Security." *Monthly Labor Review* (November 1981): 3–8.

Cockrum, Robert B. "Has the Time Come for Employee Cafeteria Plans?" *Personnel Administrator* 28 (July 1982): 66–72.

Collins, S. R. "Incentive Programs: Pros and Cons." *Personnel Journal* 60 (July 1981): 571–5.

Coltrin, S. A. and Barendse, B. D. "Is Your Organization a Good Candidate for Flextime?" *Personnel Journal* 60 (September 1981): 712–15.

Compflash: News Developments in Employee Compensation and Benefits. New York: AMACOM-F, a division of American Management Association, 1981.

Cook, Frederic W. "Long-Term Incentives for Management, Part 1: An Overview." *Compensation Review* 12 (Second Quarter 1980): 15+.

Crowder, Robert H., Jr. "The Four-day, Ten-hour Workweek." *Personnel Journal* 61 (January 1981): 26+.

Cumming, Charles M. "Executive Pay and Its New Wrinkles." *Best's Review* 82 (November 1981): 22+.

Curry, Talmer E., Jr. and Haerer, Deane N. "The Positive Impact of Flextime on Employee Relations." *Personnel Administrator* 26 (February 1981): 62–66.

Ellig, Bruce R. "Perquisites, The Intrinsic Form of Pay." *Personnel* 58 (January-February 1981): 23–31.

"Employee Stock Plans: Far Short of Ideal." *Office,* 92 (September 1980): 72.

Fannin, Rebecca A. "American Can Employees Test New Flexible Benefits Programs." *Business Insurance* 12 (March 6, 1978): 1.

Foegen, J. H. "Basing Benefits on Employee Performance." *Administrative Management* 42 (November 1981): 60–63.

Freedmand, S. M. and others. "Compensation Program: Balancing Organizational and Employee Needs." *Compensation Review* 14 (1982): 47–53.

"GAO Study Reveals ESOPs May Adversely Affect Participants." *The Journal of Taxation* 53 (October 1980): 222.

Genin, Roland. "Annual System of Executive Compensation; No Sign of Recession." *Business Week* (May 10, 1982): 76+.

Hamilton, E. K. "How to Set Up Flexible Benefits." *Compensation Review* 14 (1981): 68–74.

Hammer, Edwon G.; Ahmadi, Mohammad and Ettkin, Laurence P. "Long-term Forecasting of Employee Benefits: An Impossible Task?" *Personnel Administrator* 26 (December 1981): 30–34+.

Haneberg, Ron. "Cash-Deferred Profit Sharing Plans." *Financial Executive* 48 (July 1980): 36–38.

Jay, Wendy. "Long-Term Incentives for Management, Part 2: What's New in Stock Option and Appreciation Right Plans." *Compensation Review* 12 (1980): 21–33.

Kenny, John B. "Competency Analysis for Trainers: A Model for Professionalization." *Training and Development Journal* 36 (May 1982): 142–148.

Lawler, Edward E., III. "New Approaches to Pay: Innovations That Work." *Personnel* 53 (September–October 1976): 11–23.

Lawyer, M. S. and Gourlay, J. G., Jr. "Having Capital Problems? ESOPs May be the Answer." *ABA Banking Journal* 74 (March 1982): 117+.

"Letting Employees Choose Their Own Fringe Benefits." *International Management* 35 (September 1980): 36–38+.

Lindsey, Fred D. "Employee Benefits' Bigger Bite." *Nation's Business* 69 (December 1981): 75–76.

Littrell, Earl K. "Designing a Profit-Sharing Plan for a Service Company." *Management Accounting* 62 (October 1980): 47+.

McLaughlin, D. J. "Reinforcing Corporate Strategy Through Executive Compensation." *Management Review* 70 (October 1981): 8–15.

Miller, Ernest C. and Wagel, William H. "Roundup: Flextime at GM of Canada." *Personnel* 55 (January–February 1978): 41–43.

Milligan, J. W. "ESOP's: Stock Ownership Plans Grant Companies Pension Flexibility." *Business Insurance* 15 (July 1981): 29+.

Morehart, Thomas B. and O'Connell, John J. "The Risk Manager's Role in Employee Benefits Administration." *Risk Management* 24 (October 1977): 42–46.

"Sales Incentives Get the Job Done." *Sales and Marketing Management* 127 (September 1981): 67–120.

"Scanlon Plan Puts Everyone On the Team." *Iron Age* 218 (August 9, 1976): 17–20.

Schuster, M. and Flortowski, G. "Wage Incentive Plans and the Fair Labor Standards Act." *Compensation Review* 14 (1982): 34–46.

Schwartz, Jeffrey D. "Maintaining Merit Compensation in a High Inflation Economy." *Personnel Journal* 61 (February 1982): 147–152.

"Social Change Spurs Flexible Benefit Plan Growth." *The National Underwriter* 27 (July 3, 1981): 85–88.

"A Spectacular Debunking of Social Security Critics." *Business Week* (September 22, 1980): 25–26.

Thomas, Edward G. "Update on Alternative Work Methods." *Management World* 11 (January 1982): 30–32.

Tinsley, LaVerne C. "Workers' Compensation: Key Legislation in 1981." *Monthly Labor Review* 105 (February 1982): 24–30.

"Travel as an Incentive." *Dun's Business Month* 119 (April 1982): 26–7.

Weitzul, J. B. "Money Talks Sometimes." *Best's Review Life Edition* 82 (January 1982): 86+.

Yoder, Dale and Heneman, Herbert G., Jr., eds. *ASPA Handbook of Personnel and Industrial Relations: Motivation and Commitment*, Vol 2. Washington, DC: The Bureau of National Affairs, Inc., 1975.

Chapter 13—Health and Safety

Brief, Arthur P. "How to Manage Managerial Stress." *Personnel* 57 (September–October 1980): 25–30.

Briscoe, D. R. "Learning to Handle Stress—A Matter of Time and Training." *Supervisory Management* 25 (February 1980): 35–38.

Camisa, Kenneth P. "How Alcoholism Treatment Pays for Itself." *SAM Advanced Management Journal* 47 (Winter 1982): 53–57.

Cordtz, Dan. "Safety on the Job Becomes a Major Job for Management." *Fortune* 86 (November 1972): 112–117+.

Crumpacker, Martha. "A Study of Organizational Stressors as Perceived by Middle Management and Supervisory Management." Dissertation from Louisiana Tech University, May 1980.

"Executive Fitness: Shape Up." *Sales and Marketing Management* 126 (May 18, 1981): 53–86.

Foulkes, Fred K. "Learning to Live with OSHA." *Harvard Business Review* 51 (November–December 1973): 57–67.

Freudenberger, Herbert J. "Burnout—An Unnecessary Tax on the Successful." *Administrative Management* XLIII (April 1982): 99.

Friedman, Dick. "Job Burnout." *Working Woman* 5 (July 1980): 34–35+.

Grimaldi, Joseph and Schnapper, Bette P. "Managing Employees Stress: Reducing the Costs, Increasing the Benefits." *Management Review* 70 (August 1981): 23–28+.

Herzberg, Frederick. "Putting People Back Together." *Industry Week* 198 (July 24, 1978): 48–50+.

Interview with J. Lightbody, "Safety Valve for Employee Stress." *International Management* 36 (February 1981): 17–18.

"Investing in a Safety Program Can Pay Off in the Development of Better Work Attitudes." *Inland Printer/American Lithographer* 181 (May 1978): 80.

Ivancevich, J. M. and Matteson, M. T. "Optimizing Human Resources: A Case for Preventive Health and Stress Management." *Organizational Dynamics* 9 (Autumn 1980): 5–25.

Ivancevich, John M. and Matteson, Michael T. *Stress and*

Work: A Managerial Perspective. Glenwood, IL. Scott, Foresman and Company, 1980.

Ivancevich, John M.; Matteson, Michael T. and Preston, Cynthia. "Occupational Stress, Type A Behavior, and Physical Well Being." *Academy of Management* 25 (June 1982): 373–389.

Jennings, Ken. "The Problem of Employee Drug Use and Remedial Alternatives." *Personnel Journal* 56 (November 1977): 554–560.

Kahn, R. L. "Work, Stress and Individual Well Being." *Monthly Labor Review* 104 (May 1981): 28–30.

Kutchins, Albert. "The Most Exclusive Remedy Is No Remedy at All: Workers' Compensation Coverage for Occupational Diseases." *Labor Law Journal* 32 (April 1981): 212–228.

Ledvinka, James. *Federal Regulation of Personnel and Human Resource Management.* Boston: Kent Publishing Company, 1982.

Levinson, Harry. "When Executives Burn Out." *Harvard Business Review* 59 (May–June 1981): 73–81.

Lourie, Roger H. "Executive Stress: Pressure In a Grey Flannel Suit." *Direct Marketing* 44 (December 1981): 46–49.

Martin, Jack. "The New Business Boom—Employee Fitness." *Nation's Business* 66 (February 1978): 68–73.

Medman, Alan R. "Self-Health—A Survivor's Guide to Taking Charge and Combatting Stress." *Data Management* 19 (December 1981): 25–26.

Milbourn, Gene, Jr. "Alcohol and Drugs: Poor Remedies for Stress." *Supervisory Management* 26 (March 1981): 35–42.

Miller, Marc E. "What the Doctors Say About Stress." *Supervisory Management* 26 (November 1981): 35–39.

Musacchio, Carl. "Close-Up on a High-Powered Security System." *Management Review* 65 (May 1976): 57–59.

Nelson, John G. "Burn Out—Businesses Most Costly Expense." *Personnel Administrator* 25 (August 1980): 81–87.

Norman, Beverly. "Career Burnout." *Black Enterprise* 11 (July 1981): 45–48.

Organ, D. W. "Meanings of Stress." *Business Horizons* 22 (June 1979): 32–40.

"Persuading Employees to Stop Smoking." *International Management* 36 (April 1981): 26–29.

Pesci, Michael. "Stress Management: Separating Myth From Reality." *Personnel Administrator* 27 (January 1982): 57–67.

Price, Bill. "Mental Illness: A Case for Company Concern." *Personnel Management* 10 (December 1978): 39–43.

"Putting a Lid on Corporate Health Costs." *Dun's Review* 116 (September 1980): 96–99.

Raudsepp, Eugene. "Coping With Job-Related Stress." *Supervision* XLIII (March 1981): 10–14.

Reddig, William. "Industry's Preemptive Strike Against Cancer." *Fortune* 97 (February 13, 1978): 116–119.

Renwick, Patricia A. and Lawler, Edward E. "What You Really Want from Your Job." *Psychology Today* 11 (May 1978): 53–122.

Rummel, Rose Mary and Rader, John W. "Coping With Executive Stress." *Personnel Journal* 57 (June 1978): 305–307+.

Rutherford, Derek. "Alcoholic Solution." *The Accountant* (August 21, 1980): 309–310.

Schaeffer, Dorothy. "Burnout—The Headache of the 1980s." *Supervision* XLIV (February 1982): 11–12+.

Schuler, Randall S. "Managing Stress Means Managing Time." *Personnel Journal* 58 (December 1979): 851–854.

Schuler, Randall S. "Occupational Health in Organizations: Strategies for Personnel Effectiveness." *Personnel Administrator* 27 (January 1982): 47–55.

Steiner, Robert E. "Labor Relations: The Labor Management Cooperation Act." *Personnel Journal* 60 (May 1981): 344–346.

Tardy, Walter. "Ways to Cope with Stress in Your Working Environment." *Black Enterprise* 8 (November 1977): 39–44.

"They're Bringing Problem Drinkers Out of the Closet." *Chemical Week* 123 (November 15, 1978): 85–91.

Weigel, Randy and Pinsky, Sheldon. "Managing Stress: A Model for the Human Resource Staff." *Personnel Administrator* 27 (February 1982): 56–60.

Weiss, W. H. "Accident Investigation." *Supervision* 40 (July 1978): 1–3.

Wilkerson, Roderick. "Keep That Safety Committee Moving." *Supervision* 40 (March 1978): 24.

Yankelovich, Daniel. "Managing in an Age of Anxiety." *Industry Week* 195 (October 24, 1977): 52–58.

Chapter 14—The Labor Union

Balke, W. M.; Hammond, K. R. and Meyer, G. D. "An Alternate Approach to Labor-Management Relations." *Administrative Science Quarterly* 18 (1973): 311–327.

Batt, William L., Jr. and Weinberg, Edgar. "Labor-Management Cooperation Today." *Harvard Business Review* 56 (January–February 1978): 96–104.

Bethell, Tom. "Working Man's Fate Ignored by Unions." *Data Management* 16 (July 1978): 28–29.

Bureau of National Affairs, Inc. *Basic Patterns in Union Contracts*, 8th ed. Washington, DC: The Bureau of National Affairs, Inc., 1975.

Derek, Bob and Dunlop, John. "How Trade Union Policy Is Made." *Monthly Labor Review* 93 (February 1970): 17–20.

Fanning, John. "We Are Forty: Where Do We Go?" *Labor Law Journal* 27 (January 1976): 3–10.

Franklin, James R. "The 'Cause' That Kills Jobs." *Business and Society Review* 24 (Winter 1977–1978): 47–50.

Gray, Robert T. "Where the Public Stands on Union Power Grab." *Nation's Business* 66 (February 1978): 74–79.

Hanson, John A. "How to Bargain in the Public Sector." *Public Management* 57 (February 1975): 15–18.

Hendricks, Wallace. "Labor Market Structure and Union Wage Levels." *Economic Inquiry* 13 (September 1975): 401–416.

Hickman, Charles W. "Labor Organizations' Fees and Dues." *Monthly Labor Review* 100 (May 1970): 19–24.

Imundo, Louis. "Attitudes of Non-Union White Collar Federal Government Employees Toward Unions." *Public Personnel Management* 3 (January–February 1974): 87–92.

Kilgour, John G. "Responding to the Union Campaign." *Personnel Journal* 57 (May 1978): 238–242.

Kroger, William. "The Coal Strike—An Expensive Lesson." *Nation's Business* 66 (April 1978): 50–53.

Levenson, Mark. "Big Labor's First Big Defeat: The Taft-Hartley Act." *Dun's Review* 112 (October 1978): 35–36.

Lowenberg, J. Joseph. "Some Aspects of Bargaining in Government Enterprise." *Monthly Labor Review* 101 (April 1978): 32–34.

McCullough, George B. "Transaction Bargaining—Problems and Prospects." *Monthly Labor Review* 101 (March 1978): 33–34.

Messick, D. M. "To Join to Not to Join: An Approach to the Unionization Decision." *Organizational Behavior and Human Performance* 10 (August 1973): 145–156.

Moore, William J. and Pearce, Douglas K. "Union Growth: A Test of the Ashenfelter-Pencavel Model." *Industrial Relations* 15 (May 1976): 244–247.

"The New Strategies Unions Are Trying." *Business Week* 2563 (December 4, 1978): 63–64.

Pestillo, Peter J. "Can Unions Meet the Needs of a 'New' Work Force?" *Monthly Labor Review* 102 (February 1979): 33–36.

Reilly, Ann M. "Big Labor's Crumbling Clout." *Dun's Review* 112 (October 1978): 52–61.

Sebris, Robert. "Formal or Informal: What Are the Union's Rights?" *Public Personnel Journal* 6 (May–June 1970): 156–165.

Siegal, Allen C. "The Union's Demand to Bargain." *Food Service Marketing* 39 (November 1977): 16.

Standohar, Paul D. "The Steel Industry's Agreement to Eliminate Strikes." *Training and Development Journal* 30 (December 1978): 40–42.

Strauss, George and Warner, Malcolm. "Research on Union Government; Introduction." *Industrial Relations* 16 (May 1977): 115–125.

"Unions Try to Brighten Their Public Image." *U.S. News & World Report* 84 (March 1978): 73–75.

Chapter 15—Collective Bargaining

"Arbitration: A Contract Clause That May Keep You Out of Court." *Engineering News-Record* 200 (May 25, 1980): 25.

Baer, Walter E. "Preserving Management's Upper Hand in Negotiations." *Administrative Management* 39 (June 1978): 80–82.

Bonn, Robert L. "Arbitration: An Alternative System for Handling Contract Related Disputes." *Administrative Science Quarterly* 17 (1972): 254–264.

Cohen, Abraham. "Coordinated Bargaining and Structures of Collective Bargaining." *Labor Law Journal* 26 (June 1975): 375–385.

Cook, Daniel D. "Boycott! Labor's Last Resort." *Industry Week* 189 (June 28, 1976): 23–27.

Cook, Daniel D. "Is Federal Mediation Hurting Labor-Management Relations?" *Industry Week* 190 (September 20, 1976): 17–19.

Freedman, Audrey and Fulmer, William E. "Last Rites for Pattern Bargaining." *Harvard Business Review* 60 (March/April 1982): 39–42 +.

Granof, Michael. *How to Cost Your Labor Contract.* Washington, DC.: The Bureau of National Affairs, Inc., 1973.

Greenberg, Murray and Harris, Philip. "The Arbitrator's Employment Status as a Factor in the Decision-making Process." *Human Resource Management* 20 (Winter 1981): 26–29.

Hammerman, Herbert. "The Resolution of Job Bias Cases Through Mediation and Arbitration." *Monthly Labor Review* 101 (April 1978): 43–45.

Hay, Greg. "The Whys and Wherefores of Private Arbitration." *Personnel Management* 10 (September 1978): 35–38.

Hoover, John J. "Union Organization Attempts: Management's Response." *Personnel Journal* 61 (March 1982): 214–219.

Jones, Benjamin. "Public Employee Labor Arbitration and the Delegation of Governmental Powers." *State Government* 51 (Spring 1978): 109–114.

Kilgour, John G. "'Wrapping the Package' of Labor Agreement Costs." *Personnel Journal* 56 (June 1977); 298–299.

Klein, Stuart M. and Rose, Kenneth W. "Formal Policies and Procedures can Forestall Unionization." *Personnel Journal* 61 (April 1982): 275–281.

Kochan, Thomas. "Municipal Collective Bargaining: A Model and Analysis of Bargaining Outcomes." *Industrial and Labor Relations Review* 29 (October 1975): 46–66.

Krinke, Keith B. "Five Steps For Handling Contract Grievances." *Supervisory Management* 22 (September 1977): 14–20.

Krislov, J. and Silver, J. L. "Current Challenges in Industrial Relations: Union Bargaining Power in the 1980s." *Labor Law Journal* 32 (August 1981); 480–484.

Kruger, Daniel H. and Jones, Harry E. "Compulsory Interest Arbitration in the Public Sector: An Overview." *Journal of Collective Negotiations in the Public Sector* 10 (1981): 355–380.

Lewin, David. "Collective Bargaining and the Quality of

Work Life." *Organizational Dynamics* 10 (Autumn 1981): 37–53.

Long, Gary and Feuille, Peter. "Final Offer Arbitration: Sudden Death in Eugene." *Industrial and Labor Relations Review* 27 (January 1974): 186–203.

"Management Rights: Key to Ford Strike." *Industry Week* 191 (October 1976): 27.

Meyer, Ryder, et al. *Management Preparation for Collective Bargaining.* Homewood, IL: Dow Jones-Irwin, 1976.

Miller, Ronald. "Preparations for Negotiations." *Personnel Journal* 57 (January 1978): 36–39.

Murphy, Betty Southard. "Interest Arbitration." *Public Personnel Management* 6 (September–October 1977): 295–299.

Murray, T. J. "New Union Bargaining Issue (Quality Circles)." *Dun's Business Month* 118 (September 1981): 119.

Myers, Charles A. "Voluntary Arbitration of Disputes Over New Labor Contracts." *Sloan Management Review* 18 (Fall 1976): 73–79.

Ogden, S. G. "The Reform of Collective Bargaining: A Managerial Revolution?" *Industrial Relations Journal* 12 (September/October 1981): 30–42.

Primeaux, William and Brannen, Dalton. "Why Few Arbitrators are Deemed Acceptable." *Monthly Labor Review* 98 (September 1975): 27–30.

Richardson, Reed. *Collective Bargaining by Objectives.* Englewood Cliffs, NJ: Prentice-Hall, Inc., 1977.

Rohrer, Robert. "Not the Union . . . the People!" *Supervision* 44 (March 1982): 13.

Sloane, Arthur and Whitney, Fred. *Labor Relations*, 3d ed. Englewood Cliffs, NJ: Prentice-Hall, Inc., 1977.

Stessin, Lawrence. "Expedited Arbitration: Less Grief Over Grievances." *Harvard Business Review* 55 (January–February 1977): 128–134.

"Unions Move Into the Office." *Business Week* (January 25, 1982): 90+.

Vanderback, H. W. "Where to Next? Strike Planning." *Personnel Journal* 56 (November 1977): 573–574.

Wilson, M. "Big Labor Faces Reality." *Dun's Business Month* 119 (February 1982): 37–38.

Woolf, Donald Austin. "Arbitration in One Easy Lesson: A Review of Criteria Used in Arbitration Awards." *Personnel* 55 (September–October 1978): 70–78.

Wynne, John M., Jr. "Unions and Bargaining Among Employees of State Prisons." *Monthly Labor Review* 101 (March 1978): 10–16.

Chapter 16—Discipline and the Grievance Process

Barkhaus, Robert S. and Meek, Carol L. "A Practical View of Outplacement Counseling." *Personnel Administrator* 27 (March 1982): 77–81.

Bearak, Joel A. "Termination Made Easier: Is Outplace-ment Really the Answer?" *Personnel Administrator* 27 (April 1982): 63–71.

Camden, Thomas M. "Use Outplacement as a Career Planning Tool." *Personnel Administrator* 27 (January 1982): 35–37.

"Code on Discipline Procedure." *Industrial Management* 7 (August 1977): 7.

Dalton, Dan R. and Todar, William D. "Win, Lose, Draw: The Grievance Process in Practice." *Personnel Administrator* 26 (March 1981): 25–29.

"Discipline: Laying Down the Law Productively." *Industry Week* 189 (May 17, 1976): 51–52.

Dreyer, R. S. "The Slightly Breakable Rule." *Supervision* XLIII (May 1981): 11–13.

"Fair and Effective Discipline." *Personnel Management* 9 (February 1977): 25.

Galambos, Aniko. "There Is an Alternative to 'Shape Up or Ship Out'." *Supervisory Management* 22 (November 1977): 16–21.

Gibson, Richard F. "Discipline: Search for New Solutions." *Industry Week* 182 (July 15, 1974): 52–61.

Himes, Gary K. "Handling Gripes and Grievances." *Supervision* XLIII (February 1981): 3–6.

Huberman, John. "Discipline Without Punishment Lives." *Harvard Business Review* 53 (July–August 1975): 6–8.

Lissy, William E. "Necessity of Proof to Support Disciplinary Action." *Supervision* 40 (June 1978): 13.

Mathis, Robert L. and Jenkins, William M., Jr. "Rules for Rule-Makers." *Supervisory Management* 19 (January 1974): 19–24.

Murphy, Betty Southard. "Interest Arbitration." *Public Personnel Management* 6 (September–October 1977): 295–299.

Myers, Charles A. "Voluntary Arbitration of Disputes Over New Labor Contracts." *Sloan Management Review* 18 (Fall 1976): 73–79.

Notz, William W. and Starke, Frederick A. "Final-Offer Versus Conventional Arbitration as Means of Conflict Management." *Administrative Science Quarterly* 23 (June 1978): 189–203.

Oberle, Rodney L. "Administering Disciplinary Action." *Personnel Journal* 57 (January 1978): 29–31.

Pingpank, Jeffrey C. and Mooney, Thomas B. "Wrongful Discharge: A New Danger for Employers." *Personnel Administration* 26 (March 1981): 31–35.

Powell, Jon T. "Listening to Help the Hostile Employee." *Supervisory Management* 26 (November 1981): 2–5.

Scott, Dow and Markham, Steve. "Absenteeism Control Methods: A Survey of Practices and Results." *Personnel Administrator* (June 1982): 73–84.

Shane, Joseph. "Due Process and Probationary Employees." *Public Personnel Management* 2 (May–June 1973): 171–178.

Shershin, Michael J., Jr. and Boxx, W. Randy. "Due Process in Discipline and Dismissal." *Supervisory Management* 21 (November 1976): 2–9.

Stessin, Lawrence. "Expedited Arbitration: Less Grief

Over Grievances." *Harvard Business Review* 55 (January–February 1977): 128–134.

Stoeberl, Philipp A. and Schneiderjans, Marc J. "The Ineffective Subordinate: A Management Survey." *Personnel Administrator* 26 (February 1981): 72–76.

Tobin, John E. "How Arbitrators Decide to Reject or Uphold an Employee Discharge." *Supervisory Management* 21 (June 1976): 20–23.

Veglahn, Peter A. "Making the Grievance Procedure Work." *Personnel Journal* 56 (March 1977): 122–123.

Weiss, Bernard. "Constructing Your Criticism." *Supervisory Management* 26 (May 1981): 12–18.

Welch, Barry. "Keeping the Discipliners in Line." *Personnel Management* 10 (August 1978): 21–24.

Wheeler, Hoyt N. "Punishment Theory and Industrial Discipline." *Industrial Relations* 15 (May 1976): 235–243.

Wohlking, Wallace. "Effective Discipline in Employee Relations." *Personnel Journal* 54 (September 1975): 489–493.

"The Wrongful Dismissal." *Personnel Management* 8 (January 1976): 40.

Chapter 17—Nonunion Organizations

Anderson, John C.; O Reilly, Charles A., III and Busman, Gloria. "Union Decertification in the U.S.: 1947–1977." *Industrial Relations* 19 (Winter 1980): 100–107.

Anthony, Richard J. "When There is a Union at the Gate." *Personnel* 53 (November–December 1976): 51–52.

Bethell, Tom. "Working Man's Fate Ignored by Unions." *Data Management* 16 (July 1978): 28–29.

Bohlander, George W. "Employee Protected Concerted Activity: The Nonunion Setting." *Labor Law Journal* (June 1982): 344–351.

Carney, Christopher F. "What Supervisors Can do About Union Organizing." *Supervisory Management* 26 (January 1981): 10–15.

Foulkes, Fred K. "How Top Nonunion Companies Manage Employees." *Harvard Business Review* 59 (September–October 1981): 90–96.

Fulmer, William E. "When Employees Want to Oust Their Union." *Harvard Business Review* 56 (March–April 1978): 163–170.

Fulmer, William E. "Decertification: Is the Current Trend a Threat to Collective Bargaining?" *California Management Review* 24 (Fall 1981): 14–22.

Harrison, Edward L.; Johnson, Douglas and Rachel, Frank M. "The Role of The Supervisor in Representation Elections." *Personnel Administrator* 26 (September 1981): 67–71.

Hoover, John J. "Union Organization Attempts: Management's Response." *Personnel Journal* 61 (March 1982); 214–219.

Hughes, Charles L. *Making Unions Unnecessary*. New York: Executive Enterprises Publication Company, Inc., 1976.

Imberman, Woodruff. "How to Win a Decertification Election." *Management Review* 66 (September 1977): 26–39.

Kovach, K. A. "Do We Still Need Labor Unions?" *Personnel Journal* 58 (December 1979): 849–850.

Kovach, K. A. "Fear of Unions." *Data Management* 16 (July 1978): 10.

"Labor's Changing Profile." *Nation's Business* 67 (April 1978): 31–35.

Lewis, R. "Treat Employees Fairly to Keep the Unions Away (Chain Store Operators)." *American Druggist* 184 (August 1981): 48+.

Miller, Ronald L. "Grievance Procedures for Nonunion Employees." *Public Personnel Management* 7 (September–October 1978): 302–311.

Murray, L. "Why Employees Join Unions." *Management World* 7 (July 1978): 8–10.

Myers, M. Scott. *Managing Without Unions*. Reading, Mass.: Addison-Wesley Publishing Company, 1976.

Pestillo, Peter J. "Can Unions Meet the Needs of a 'New' Work Force?" *Monthly Labor Review* 102 (February 1979): 33.

Pfeffer, Jeffrey and Ross, Jerry. "Union-Nonunion Effects on Wage and Status Attainment." *Industrial Relations* 19 (Spring 1980): 140–150.

Rand, James F. "Preventive-Maintenance Techniques for Staying Union-Free." *Personnel Journal* 59 (June 1980): 497–499.

Sappir, Mark Z. "The Employer's Obligation Not to Bargain When the Issue of Decertification is Present." *Personnel Administrator* 27 (February 1982): 41–45.

Stokes, A. "What to Do When the Union First Appears." *Food Service Marketing* 43 (April 1981): 18.

Swann, James P., Jr. "Formal Grievance Procedures in Nonunion Plants." *Personnel Administrator* 26 (August 1981): 66–70.

Trotta, Maurice S. and Gudenberg, Harry R. "Resolving Personnel Problems in Nonunion Plants." *Personnel* 53 (May–June 1976): 55–63.

Westin, A. F. "Dealing Fairly with Nonunion Employees." *National Underwriter* (Prop. ed.) 85 (June 26, 1981): 19+.

"What Put Labor on the Defensive?" *Business Week* 2563 (December 4, 1978): 56–58.

"What to Do When the Union Knocks." *Nation's Business* 54 (November 1966): 42–45.

Chapter 18—Personnel Research

Bass, B. M. and Barrett, G. V. *People, Work and Organizations: An Introduction to Industrial and Organizational Psychology*, 2nd edition. Boston: Allyn and Bacon, Inc., 1981.

Bennis, Warren G. *Changing Organizations.* New York: McGraw-Hill Book Company, 1966.

Byham, William C. "The Uses of Personnel Research." *AMA Research Study,* American Management Association, Inc., 1968.

Gordon, Michael E. and Kleiman, Lawrence M. "The Prediction of Trainability Using a Work Sample Test and an Aptitude Test: A Direct Comparison." *Personnel Psychology* 29 (Summer 1976): 243–253.

Harkman, J. Richard and Oldham, Greg R. "Motivation Through the Design of Work: Test of a Theory." *Organizational Behavior and Human Performance* 16 (August 1976): 250–279.

Herzberg, Frederick. *Work and the Nature of Man.* Cleveland: The World Publishing Company 1966.

Knight, Kenneth. "The Role of Personnel Research in the Real World." *Personnel Management* 7 (December 1975): 14–17.

Likert, Rensis. *The Human Organization.* New York: McGraw-Hill Book Company, 1967.

Mondy, R. Wayne and Mills, Harry N. "Choice Not Chance in Nurse Selection." *Supervisor Nurse* 9 (November 1978): 35–39.

Pajer, Robert G. "Finding Selection Research Data: Federal Agencies as a Source." *Public Personnel Management* 6 (November–December 1977): 442–446.

Peters, William S. and Chanpous, Joseph E. "The Use of Moderated Regression in Job Redesign Decisions." *Decision Sciences* 10 (January 1979): 85–95.

Sharplin, A. D. "Coercive Power: Indispensable or Inconsequential." *Northeast Louisiana Business Review* (Spring–Summer 1982): 10–14.

Strauss, George and Warner, Malcolm. "Research on Union Government." *Industrial Relations* 16 (May 1977): 115–125.

Thurstone, L. L. "What is Personnel Research? (Part II)." *Personnel Journal* 61 (May 1982): 371.

Wehrenberg, Stephen B. "The Exit Interview: Why Bother?" *Supervisory Management* 25 (May 1980): 20–25.

White, William F. and Hamilton, E. *Action Research for Management.* Homewood, IL: Richard D. Irwin, Inc., 1965.

Yerkes, Robert M. "What is Personnel Research? (Part 1)." *Personnel Journal* 61 (May 1982): 370.

Chapter 19—Personnel: The Future Environment

Bradley, A. V. "Management and Labor in the Next Decade." *Personnel Journal* 59 (December 1980): 981–982.

Brinks, James T. "Executive Compensation: Crossroads of the '80s." *Personnel Administrator* 26 (December 1981): 23–28.

Copperman, Lois Farrer and Keast, Fred D. "Older Workers: A Challenge for Today and Tomorrow." *Human Resource Management* 20 (Summer 1981): 13–18.

Debats, Karen E. "The Continuing Personnel Challenge." *Personnel Journal* 61 (May 1982): 332–336.

French, Wendell L. and Elbing, Alvar O. "Predictions for Personnel and Industrial Relations in 1985." *Personnel Journal* 61 (May 1982): 347–352.

Greene, Jeanne Polston. "People Management: New Directions for the '80s." *Administrative Management* 42 (January 1981): 22.

Hennigar, Ross A. "People Management in the 1980s: A CEO's View." *Personnel Journal* 59 (November 1980): 898–903.

Interview with J. Sellentin, "Commitment to the Future." *Personnel Administrator* 26 (January 1981): 19–21.

Kenny, Roger M. "Executive Search Today." *California Management Review* 20 (Summer 1978): 79–82.

Kuraitis, Vytenis P. "The Personnel Audit." *Personnel Administrator* 26 (November 1981): 29–34.

Lunda, Donald L. "Personnel Management: What's Ahead?" *Personnel Administrator* 26 (April 1981): 51–60.

Martin, Lowell G. "A View of Work Toward the Year 2000." *Personnel Journal* 56 (October 1977): 502–504+.

Mills, D. Quinn. "Human Resources in the 1980s." *Harvard Business Review* 57 (July–August 1979): 154–162.

Moore, James M. "Relocation Policy Update: Innovations and Changes for the '80s." *Personnel Administrator* 26 (December 1981): 39–42.

"The New Corporate Revolutionaries?" *Personnel* 55 (January–February 1978): 46–47.

Pursell, Donald E. "Planning for Tomorrow's Personnel Problems." *Personnel Journal* 60 (July 1981): 559–562.

Robinson, David. "AT&T Women Employees Making Faster Strides Into Middle Management." *World of Work Report* 3 (January 1978): 1.

Rockefeller, David. "The Chief Executive in the Year 2000." *Vital Speeches* 46 (January 1980): 162.

Talpaert, Roger. "Looking into the Future Management in the Twenty-first Century." *Management Review* 70 (March 1981): 21–25.

Tomkiewicz, Joseph and Brenner, O. C. "Organizational Dilemma: Sex Differences in Attitudes Toward Women Held by Future Managers." *Personnel Administrator* 27 (July 1982): 62–65.

Tomkiewicz, J. and Brenner, O. "Union Attitudes and the Manager of the Future." *Personnel Administrator* 24 (October 1979): 67–70+.

Touretzky, Simeon J. "Changing Attitudes: A Question of Loyalty." *The Personnel Administrator* 24 (1979): 35–36.

Wangler, Lawrence A. "The Intensification of the Personnel Role." *Personnel Journal* 58 (February 1979): 111–119.

Woodworth, Margaret and Woodworth, Warner. "The

Female Takeover: Threat or Opportunity." *The Personnel Administrator* 24 (January 1979): 19–29.

Yoder, Dale and Heneman, Herbert G., Jr., eds. *ASPA Handbook of Personnel and Industrial Relations, Volume VII, PAIR Policy and Program Management.* Washington, DC: The Bureau of National Affairs, Inc., 1978.

Yoder, Dale and Heneman, Herbert G., Jr., eds. *ASPA Handbook of Personnel and Industrial Relations, Volume VIII, Professional PAIR.* Washington, DC: The Bureau of National Affairs, Inc., 1979.

Glossary

ability test: An instrument used to determine how well an individual can perform job related tasks.

adverse impact: occurs when members of protected groups receive unequal consideration for employment.

Affirmative Action Programs (AAP): Programs designed to ensure that a firm hires members of protected groups in proportion to their representation in the relevant area of recruitment.

Age Discrimination Act of 1967: Amended in 1978, it prohibits employers from discriminating against individuals who are at least forty but less than seventy.

agency shop: A type of union security in which employees are not required to join the union. However, the labor agreement requires that as a condition of employment each nonunion member of the bargaining unit must pay the union the equivalent of monthly dues for its services as bargaining agent.

alcoholism: A treatable disease that involves excessive consumption of liquor and affects every stratum within our society.

American Federation of Labor (AFL): A labor group comprised of craft unions that was founded in 1886. It merged with the Congress of Industrial Organizations (CIO) in 1955 to form the AFL-CIO.

Anti-Injunction Act of 1932: Also referred to as the Norris-LaGuardia Act. A federal law severely restricting the use of injunctions in labor disputes and making the yellow dog contract legally unenforceable.

appraisal interview: An interview which should be scheduled soon after the end of an employee's appraisal period to discuss performance rating.

apprenticeship training: A combination of classroom and on-the-job training traditionally used in craft jobs.

aptitude tests: An instrument designed to determine a person's potential to learn in a given area.

arbitration: A process in which a dispute between labor and management is submitted to an impartial third party to make a binding decision.

assessment center: An organizational approach used to identify employees who have higher level management potential, to select supervisors, and to determine employees' developmental needs.

authorization card: A card which employees can sign to show an interest in a union.

background investigation: A procedure to determine if an applicant's past work experience is related to the qualifications needed for the job.

bargaining issues: All subjects to be bargained over during contract negotiations between labor and management.

bargaining unit: A group of employees recognized by an employer or certified by an administrative agency as appropriate for representation by a labor organization for purposes of collective bargaining.

beachhead demands: A demand which the union makes in current negotiations which it does not expect to receive at this time, but hopes to receive in future negotiations.

behaviorally anchored rating scale: A rating method in which various performance levels are shown along a scale and described in terms of an employee's specific job behavior.

benefit: Any financial compensation cost (other than pay) that is borne by the employer and that can be attributed to individual employees.

BFOQ: Bonafide occupational qualification.

biofeedback: A method of learning to control involuntary bodily processes.

board interview: An interview where one candidate is quizzed by several company representatives.

body language: A nonverbal method of communication in which physical actions such as motions, gestures, and facial expressions convey thoughts and emotions.

boycott: An agreement by union members to refuse to use or buy a firm's products.

burnout: A state of fatigue or frustration that stems from devotion to a cause, way of life, or relationship that did not provide the expected reward.

business game: A simulation which represents an actual business situation. It attempts to duplicate selected parts of a particular situation which are then manipulated by the participants.

cafeteria compensation: A plan which permits employees to decide from among many alternatives how their financial compensation will be allocated.

career: A general course of action a person chooses to pursue throughout life.

career anchors: Motives which account for the way people select and prepare for a career.

career development: A formalized approach taken by the organization to ensure that people with the proper qualifications and experience are available when needed.

career paths: Flexible lines of progression through which employees typically move.

case study: The use of simulated business problems as an instructional method. Individuals are expected to study the information given in the case and make decisions based upon the situation.

central tendency: A common error in performance appraisal rating that occurs when employees are incorrectly rated near the average or middle of the scale.

change agent: The person(s) responsible for ensuring that the planned change in organization development is properly implemented.

checkoff of dues: A condition where the company withholds union dues from members' checks and forwards the money directly to the union.

Civil Rights Act of 1866: Based on the Thirteenth Amendment. It prohibits race discrimination in hiring, placement, and continuation of employment.

Civil Rights Act of 1871: Based on the Fourteenth Amendment. It prohibits deprivation of equal employment rights under coverage of state law.

Civil Rights Act of 1964: As amended by the Equal Opportunity Act of 1972, a federal law prohibiting employment discrimination based on race, color, sex, religion, and national origin.

Civil Service Reform Act of 1978: The act, and two related agency reorganization plans, resulted in the abolition of the U.S. Civil Service Commission, the creation of the Office of Personnel Management and the Merit Systems Protection Board, and an expanded action mission for the EEOC.

classification method: A job evaluation method in which jobs are grouped in a number of classes or grades.

closed shop: A type of union security in which union membership is a prerequisite for employ-

ment. Prohibited by the Taft-Hartley Act.

coaching: A form of management development which is similar to OJT.

collective bargaining: A process where the employer and the representative of its employees meet to confer in good faith about certain matters, and to put into writing any agreement reached if requested by either party.

comparable worth: A broader interpretation than the Equal Pay Act requiring equal pay for comparable work.

Committee on Political Education (COPE): The political arm of the AFL-CIO.

company mission: A company's overall purpose for existing. It is a major internal factor which affects the task of the personnel manager.

compensation: Every type of reward that individuals receive in return for performing organizational tasks.

compressed work week: An arrangement of work hours which permits employees to fulfill their work obligation in less than the typical five-day work week by working, for example, four ten-hour shifts.

computer assisted instruction: An extension of programmed instruction by use of computers.

concurrent validity: With this form of validity the test scores and the criterion data are obtained at essentially the same time.

conference method: An instructional approach which brings together individuals with common interests to discuss and attempt to solve problems.

Congress of Industrial Organizations (CIO): Labor federation of unions formed in 1938 to promote the organization of workers in mass production and unorganized industries. Merged with the American Federation of Labor in 1955 to form the AFL-CIO.

conspiracy: A condition that exists when two or more persons band together to prejudice the rights of others.

construct validity: A form of validity used to determine whether or not a test measures certain traits or qualities identified as important in performing the job.

content validity: When this form of validity is used, a person performs certain tasks (tests) which are actual samples of the kind of work required of the job.

correlation analysis: A means of measuring the degree of association or correlation between two or more variables.

correlation coefficient: Provides a summary of the strength of the relationship between two variables.

cost of living allowance (COLA): A clause in the labor agreement which is designed to protect the purchasing power of employee earnings against inflation.

craft union: A type of local union composed of members of a particular trade or skill in an area or locality.

criterion-related validity: When this form of validation is used, the scores on the tests are compared to some aspect of job performance as determined by performance appraisal.

critical incidents: A method of performance appraisal which requires a written record of highly favorable and highly unfavorable actions occurring in an employee's work.

cyclical demand: Variations in demand for a product due to such factors as war, political elections, economic conditions, and sociological pressures. Typically greater than one year and less than five years.

Davis-Bacon Act of 1931: A federal law requiring that federal construction contractors pay the prevailing wage in a particular geographic area.

deauthorization: A procedure which permits employees to vote to determine if they desire to change their form of union security from a union shop to an exclusive bargaining shop.

decertification: a procedure through which a group of unionized employees vote to take away the union's right to act as their exclusive bargaining representative.

deferred compensation: Pay which is held in trust for a manager until retirement.

Delphi Technique: A nonquantitative technique for demand forecasting developed by the Rand Corporation.

development: Activities which strive to prepare individuals so they can keep pace with the organization as it changes and grows.

Dictionary of Occupational Titles: Listing of standardized and comprehensive descriptions of job duties and related information for over 20,000 occupations.

direct financial compensation: The pay a person receives in the form of wages, salaries, bonuses, and commissions.

disciplinary action: An action to maintain standards by invoking a penalty against an employee who fails to meet them.

discipline: The state of employee self-control and orderly conduct that is present in an organization.

discriminant analysis: A quantitative tool used to identify factors which differentiate between two or more groups in a population.

education: Activities which are conducted to improve the employee's competence in a specific direction and beyond the current job.

empathy: The ability to identify with another person's feelings and thoughts.

Employee Assistance Programs (EAP): Programs designed to provide emotionally troubled employees with the consideration and assistance given employees suffering from physical illnesses.

employee orientation: A program to provide needed job and company related information to new employees.

Employee Retirement Income Security Act of 1974 (ERISA): A federal law passed to protect the interests of participants in employee benefit plans.

employee stock ownership plan: A plan through which a firm provides its employees with company stock allocated on the basis of their base pay.

employment agency: An organization which assists firms in recruiting employees and aids individuals in their attempts to locate jobs.

Equal Pay Act of 1963: An amendment to the Fair Labor Standards Act that made it illegal to discriminate in pay on the basis of sex where the jobs require equal skills, effort, and responsibility and are performed under similar working conditions. As a result of the 1972 Education Amendment, the Act was expanded to cover employees in executive, administrative, professional, and outside sales force categories as well as employees in most state and local government agencies, hospitals, and schools.

essay method: A method of evaluation in which the rater simply writes a brief narrative describing the employee's performance.

exclusive bargaining shop: With this form of recognition, the company is legally obligated to deal with the union which has achieved recognition.

executive: A top level manager who reports directly to a corporation's chief executive officer or the head of a major division.

Executive Order 10988: Greatly expanded unionism in the federal government. Designed to permit collective bargaining in the public sector.

Executive Order 11246: Prohibited discrimination on the basis of race, color, creed, or national origin by contractors doing business with the federal government. It was later amended by EO 11375 which changed the word "creed" to "religion" and added sex discrimination to the other prohibited items.

Executive Order 11375: *See* Executive Order 11246.

executive search firm: A company used by organizations to locate experienced professionals and top level executives when other sources prove inadequate.

exempt employees: Employees (categorized as executive, administrative, or professional) who are exempt from overtime provisions of the FLSA.

experiment: A method of inquiry which involves certain variables being manipulated while others are held constant.

external environment: Factors which affect a firm's human resources from outside the organizational boundaries.

factor comparison method: A complex method of job evaluation which assumes the existence of five universal job factors: mental requirements, skill, physical requirements, responsibilities, and working conditions.

Fair Labor Standards Act of 1938 (FLSA): A federal law establishing the forty-hour workweek as the legal standard for most American workers. It also set minimum wages, overtime pay, and child labor standards. Known as the Wage and Hour Law.

Federal Privacy Act of 1974: An act applying primarily to government agencies and designed to protect the privacy of individuals by restricting access to files containing personal information.

flextime: A process that permits employees to choose, within certain limitations, their own working hours. For example, any eight-hour period between 6:30 A.M. and 9 P.M.

forced choice performance report: A rating method featuring a series of statements about an employee, arranged in blocks of two or more, from which the rater must choose which is most or least descriptive of the person.

forced distribution: A rating system similar to a normal frequency distribution because the rater is required to assign individuals in the work group to a limited number of categories.

four-fifths rule: A guideline used to indicate adverse impact. Adverse impact occurs when members of protected groups are not hired at the rate of at least 80 percent of the best achieving group.

frequency rate: A statistical formula which, for example, computes the number of lost-time accidents per million people-hours worked.

functional job analysis: A form of job analysis which focuses upon what gets done and what workers do to get things done.

generalist: A person who performs tasks in a wide variety of Personnel related activities.

going rate: The average wage that most employers pay for a specific job in a particular labor market.

grievance: An employee's dissatisfaction or feeling of personal injustice relating to his or her employment relationship.

group appraisal: The appraising of an employee by several managers who know the employee.

group interview: A type of interview consisting of several applicants interacting in the presence of one or more company representatives.

halo error: A rating error occurring when the evaluator perceives one factor as being of paramount importance and gives an employee who scores high on this factor a better overall rating than he or she deserves.

hazard pay: Additional pay provided to employees who work under extremely dangerous conditions.

health: Refers to employees' freedom from illness as well as their general physical and mental well-being.

hot stove rule: A view of administering disciplinary action which stresses that disciplinary action should be immediate, provide warning, give consistent punishment, and burn impersonally.

human resources information system: A collection of data organized in a logical, reliable, and valid manner and used to make Personnel decisions.

human resources management: *See* Personnel management.

hypnosis: An altered state of consciousness which

is artificially induced and characterized by increased receptiveness to suggestion.

in-basket training: A training method in which the participant is given a number of business papers that would typically come across a manager's desk. The participant is required to prioritize and act on the information contained in these papers.

incentive compensation: Compensation based upon relating pay to productivity.

incident rate: A frequency rate developed by OSHA which includes both injuries and illnesses.

indirect financial compensation: All financial rewards such as insurance plans which are not included as direct pay.

individual career planning: A process whereby goals are set and the means to achieve them are established.

industrial union: A type of local union generally consisting of all workers in a particular plant or group of plants.

injunction: A legal procedure in which a party is forbidden to take a certain action. It may be used by employers to prevent certain union activities or by employees to prevent certain antiunion activities.

internship: A program which gives students the opportunity to integrate theory learned in the classroom with the practice of management by working for an organization while attending classes.

job: A group of tasks that must be performed if the organization is to achieve its goal.

job analysis: The process of determining the duties and skills required for performing jobs in the organization.

job bidding: A system which permits individuals in an organization to apply for a specific job within the organization.

job cluster: A group of similar jobs in a company.

job description: A document containing information regarding the duties and responsibilities of a particular job.

job enrichment: The deliberate restructuring of a job to make it more challenging, meaningful, and interesting.

job evaluation: A systematic approach in determining the relative value or worth of the jobs in an organization.

job overload: Occurs when employees are given more work than they can possibly handle.

job posting: A method of internal recruitment that is used to communicate the fact that job openings exist.

job pricing: The placement of a dollar value on the worth of a job.

job rotation: The movement of employees from one job to another for the purpose of providing them with broader experiences.

job sharing: Two part-time people who split the duties of one job in some manner and are paid according to their contribution.

job specification: The minimum acceptable qualifications that a person should possess to perform a particular job.

key job: A job which is well known in the company and industry and one that can be easily defined.

Labor-Management Relations Act of 1947: Also referred to as the Taft-Hartley Act. A major amendment to the Wagner Act, it gave employees the right to refrain from union activity. Supervisors were denied protection of the law in obtaining union recognition. The law also enumerated six unfair labor practices by unions. The closed shop was outlawed and state right-to-work laws were authorized.

Labor-Management Reporting and Disclosure Act of 1959: Also referred to as the Landrum-Griffin Act. A major labor reform act aimed at regulating the internal affairs of unions (including their relationships with their members) and regulating certain managerial activities. It also contains important amendments to the Taft-Hartley Act.

labor market: The geographical area from which employees are recruited for a particular job.

labor supply analysis: A means by which a firm determines the availability of needed employees.

leadership: The directing and influencing of other individuals' activities.

leniency: In performance evaluation, this involves the giving of undeserved high ratings.

likes and dislikes analysis: A listing of one's personal likes and dislikes that could have an impact upon successful accomplishment of a job.

local union: The basic element in the structure of the American labor movement which acts as the exclusive bargaining agent for the rank and file members during negotiations and represents the workers in handling grievances.

lockout: Management's ceasing operating of the business in order to exert pressure upon the union.

long-run trend: A projection of the demand for a firm's products, typically five years or more into the future.

macro-level approach: A means of change that affects the entire organization. (The opposite of micro-level approach, which affects only some individuals or groups within the organization.)

maintenance of membership: A requirement that employees who are union members at the time the labor agreement is signed, or who later voluntarily join, must continue their membership until the termination of the agreement, as a condition of employment.

management: The process of planning, organizing, staffing, directing, and controlling to accomplish organizational goals through the coordinated use of the firm's resources.

management by objectives: A systematic approach which facilitates achievement of results by directing efforts toward attainable goals.

management development: Consists of all learning experiences provided by an organization for the purpose of providing and upgrading skills and knowledge required in current and future positions.

management inventory: A file which contains detailed data regarding each manager and which is used to identify individuals with the potential to move into higher level positions.

management position description questionnaire: A form of job analysis designed for management positions which uses a checklist method to analyze jobs.

management rights: A section in the labor agreement which spells out the rights of management.

mandatory issues: Bargaining issues which usually have an immediate and direct effect on workers' jobs.

media: Special methods of communicating ideas and concepts (i.e., videotapes, films, slide projectors, etc.).

mediation: A process whereby a neutral third party enters a labor dispute when a bargaining impasse has occurred.

micro-level approach: A method used to respond to change of small magnitude, such as for individuals or groups. (The opposite of a macro-level approach, which involves change for an entire organization.)

motivation: Refers to the goal directed behavior of individuals which results in needs satisfaction.

National Labor Relations Act of 1935: Also referred to as the Wagner Act, a federal law which guaranteed employees the rights to self-organization and to collective bargaining with their employers. It specifically prohibited five unfair labor practices by management.

National Labor Relations Board (NLRB): A board that was created in 1935 with the passage of the National Labor Relations Act (Wagner Act). Its major purposes include overseeing bargaining, unit elections and investigating complaints involving unfair labor practices.

national union: The parent organization which charters local unions.

nondirective interview: A comprehensive interview which uses probing, open-ended questions. (The opposite of the patterned interview.)

nonfinancial compensation: A form of compensation—other than pay and benefits—that includes the satisfaction a person receives by performing meaningful job related tasks.

objective: The end result or goal that an organization or person is striving to achieve.

objectivity: A quality of a test whereby two or more people can interpret the results of that test and derive the same conclusions.

Occupational Safety and Health Act of 1970 (OSHA): A federal law designed to ensure that, so far as possible, every man and woman in the nation has a safe, healthful work environment.

ombudsman: A person outside the normal chain of command who handles complaints and grievances of an individual or a small group of individuals.

on-the-job training (OJT): A form of training in which a person learns job tasks by actually performing them.

open door policy: A policy giving an employee the right to take any grievance to the person next to the immediate supervisor in the chain of command if a satisfactory solution cannot be obtained from the supervisor.

open shop: Strictly defined, work in the organization is open on equal terms to members and non-members of unions.

organization climate: The psychological environment that exists in a firm.

organization development: A type of change effort which involves the entire organization. Macro-level approaches are used here.

orientation: Involves introducing new employees to their company, jobs, and members of the work group.

outplacement: A service to assist terminated employees find appropriate employment elsewhere.

paired comparison: An extension of the ranking method which involves rating the performance of each employee against every other employee in the group.

patterned interview: A type of interview consisting of standardized questions which are asked of all applicants for a specific group of jobs. (The opposite of non-directive interview.)

pay compression: Problem which occurs when pay differences between jobs of different levels of importance grow small.

pay equity: Refers to the relationship between what employees believe they should receive and what they believe they are actually receiving.

pay grade: A number of similar jobs grouped together to simplify the job pricing process.

pay range: A range which includes minimum and maximum rates with enough variance between the two to allow some significant pay difference and to reflect such concerns as seniority and/or productivity.

performance appraisal: The process of evaluating an individual's work performance. Also referred to as performance rating, employee performance review, personnel appraisal, performance evaluation, employee evaluation, and merit rating.

perquisites: Benefits designed exclusively for top level executives. They provide a form of rewards that either are not considered earned income or are taxed at a low level.

personality test: A test to determine a prospective employee's ability to function in a particular work environment.

Personnel: A major activity performed within organizations which includes such functions as personnel planning, recruitment, selection, training and development, compensation, health and safety, employee and labor relations, and personnel research.

personnel demand analysis: A method of determining the number and type of employees required to achieve a firm's objectives.

personnel management: The process by which management attempts to obtain the firm's objectives through employees' efforts.

personnel manager: A manager who normally acts in an advisory or staff capacity and who is primarily responsible for coordinating a firm's human resources management activities.

personnel planning: The analysis of future personnel requirements which will be needed to accomplish a firm's objectives.

personnel research: The systematic study of human resources for the purpose of maximizing personal and organizational goal achievement.

point method: A method of job evaluation which uses job factors as standards for evaluating jobs.

policy: A general statement or guide which directs the actions of people within a firm.

position: A group of job tasks requiring the services of one employee.

position analysis questionnaire (PAQ): A form of a structural analysis questionnaire which provides for the analysis of jobs in terms of 194 job descriptors.

predictive validity: Involves administering a test and then obtaining the criterion information at a later date.

Pregnancy Discrimination Act of 1978: An amendment to the 1964 Civil Rights Act prohibiting discrimination in employment based on pregnancy, childbirth, or complications arising from either.

premium pay: Additional compensation given employees for working long periods of time or working under dangerous or undesirable conditions.

probationary period: A period of time when a new employee may be terminated with little or no explanation.

profession: The occupation of a group of individuals who possess a common body of knowledge specifically applicable to their positions. A procedure for certifying members of the group may exist.

profit sharing: A compensation plan which results in the distribution of a predetermined percentage of a firm's profits to employees.

programmed instruction: A teaching method which provides instruction without the intervention of an instructor.

progressive discipline: A system of management stressing that disciplinary action should make penalties appropriate to the violation (or accumulated violations).

prohibited issue: An issue which cannot be bargained over in management-labor discussions.

promotion from within: A policy in which the firm emphasizes promotion from within the ranks of current employees.

quality circles: Groups of employees who meet regularly with supervisors to identify production problems and recommend actions for solution.

quality of work life: Any activity that takes place at every level of an organization and that seeks greater organizational effectiveness through the enhancement of human dignity and growth.

Railway Labor Act of 1926: A federal law which provided the procedures for collective bargaining and settling disputes between labor and management.

random demand: Variations in demand which follow no pattern.

ranking method (job evaluation): The simplest form of job evaluation in which the rater evaluates the job descriptions and arranges jobs in order according to their difficulty.

ranking method (performance appraisal): A method of performance appraisal in which the rater ranks employees in a given group on the basis of each one's overall performance.

rating scale: Probably the most common method of appraising employees. It involves evaluating employees according to defined job and personal factors.

realistic job preview: Conveying important job information to the applicant in an unbiased manner.

recruitment: The process of encouraging people to make application for employment with a firm.

reference check: A procedure used to verify the accuracy of information contained in an applica-

tion blank and/or increase knowledge about the applicant.

regression analysis: A quantitative forecasting technique which is used to predict one item (known as the dependent variable) through knowledge of other item(s) (known as the independent variable).

The Relaxation Response: A technique for dealing with the stressful consequences of living.

reliability: The extent to which the selection tool provides consistent results.

requisition: A specification of details such as job title, department, and the date an employee is needed for work.

right-to-work: Legislation stemming from the Taft-Hartley Act, which prohibited management and unions from developing agreements requiring union membership as a condition of employment.

role ambiguity: Exists when employees lack clear information about the content of their jobs.

role conflict: Occurs when an individual is placed in the position of seeking opposing goals.

role playing: A technique in which problems (real or imaginary) involving human interaction are presented and then spontaneously acted out.

safety: Protection of employees from injuries due to work related accidents.

sampling: The process by which only a portion of the total population is studied, following which conclusions are drawn for the entire group.

Scanlon Plan: A cost savings plan which features participation by most of a firm's employees.

seasonal demand: Fluctuations in demand for a product over a twelve-month period. Varies around the cyclical demand and may fluctuate drastically.

selection: The process of identifying those recruited individuals who will best be able to assist a firm in achieving organizational goals.

selection ratio: A ratio expressed as the number of individuals hired to fill a particular job divided by the number of applicants.

self-appraisal: An appraisal method which allows employees to become actively involved in thinking about work contributions and appraising themselves.

self-assessment: An evaluation which can help one gain a realistic understanding of oneself in terms of likes and dislikes and/or strengths and weaknesses.

seniority: The length of time an employee has worked in various capacities with the firm. Seniority may be company wide, by division, by department, or by job.

sensitivity training: An organization technique that is designed to make us more aware of ourselves and our impact on other people.

severity rate: A formula used to compute the number of days lost because of accidents per million people-hours worked.

simulation: Uses the computer to assist in performing experiments on a model of a real system.

simulator: Equipment which is similar to actual equipment used on the job, and which is used to train employees.

skills inventory: A file which contains data regarding nonmanagerial employees' abilities.

social responsibility: An organization's basic obligation to ensure that its decisions and operations meet the needs and interests of society.

Social Security Act of 1935: Legislation providing for a federal tax to be placed on payrolls in order to finance unemployment and retirement benefits.

special events recruiting: An effort on the part of a single employer, or a group of employers, to attract a large number of applicants for interviews by use of job fairs, open houses, etc.

specialist: A person who is typically concerned with one of the six functional areas of Personnel.

standard hour plan: A method of incentive compensation which uses time allowances rather than piece rate.

standardized test: An examination administered under fixed conditions to a large group of persons who are representative of the individuals for whom the test was intended.

steward: A union representative who ensures that the employer lives up to provisions of the labor agreement. The steward may also perform other miscellaneous duties for the union.

stock option plan: A form of management compensation which is designed to integrate an individual's interests with those of the organization. It permits the manager to buy a specified amount of stock in the future at or below the current market price.

straight piecework plan: A method of compensation whereby a predetermined amount of money is paid for each unit produced. An alternative to the hourly rate.

strategic plan: A plan designed to help a firm achieve its primary objectives.

strengths/weaknesses balance sheet: An individual's listing of all his or her perceived strengths and weaknesses that could have an impact upon successful accomplishment of a job.

stress: Our body's reaction to any demand made upon it.

stress interview: A type of interview that intentionally creates stress on the candidate.

strike: Employees' refusal to work in order to exert pressure upon management.

suggestion system: A means by which employees can make recommendations and express dissatisfaction in confidence.

survey: A questionnaire administered to selected individuals in order to check the pulse of the organization.

systemic discrimination: Perpetuation of the effect of past discrimination even after the original practices are discontinued.

team building: A conscious effort to develop effective work groups throughout the organization.

telecommuting: An approach to work which permits employees to perform their jobs at home.

time series analysis: A technique used to accomplish projections over time. Similar to regression analysis.

training: Activities which serve to improve an employee's performance on a currently held job or one related to it.

training and development (T&D): The process of designing programs to assist individuals, groups, and the entire organization to become more effective.

transactional analysis: A macro-level technique for training and development programs. Three separate ego states are identified: the Parent, the Adult, and the Child. The manner in which individual ego states interact can have a significant impact upon interpersonal relations and an organization's effectiveness.

Transcendental Meditation (TM): Using a secret word or phrase to induce an altered state of consciousness.

unemployment compensation: Government-funded temporary compensation to individuals who have been laid off from employment.

Uniform Guidelines on Employee Selection Procedures: Adopted in 1978, these Guidelines cover the major federal equal employment opportunity statutes.

union: An organization of employees who have joined together to present a united front in dealing with management.

union shop: A type of union security in which all employees are required to become union members within a specified time after being hired (usually thirty days).

validity: The extent to which a test measures what it is designed to measure.

vestibule training: Training of employees away from the production area through use of equipment which closely resembles the actual equipment used on the job.

Vietnam Era Veterans Readjustment Act of 1974: Relates only to government contractors or subcontractors who have contracts with the federal government in the amount of $10,000 or more. Covers honorably discharged persons who have served more than 180 days on active duty between August 5, 1964 and May 7, 1975.

Vocational Rehabilitation Act of 1973: A federal law prohibiting discrimination against physically and mentally handicapped workers who are employed by organizations with government contracts of $2,500 or more.

voluntary issue: An issue which may be raised in collective bargaining, though neither side may insist that it be bargained over.

wage curve: A line used to create a smooth progression between pay grades.

Walsh-Healey Act of 1936: A law requiring firms doing business with the federal government to pay at least the equivalent of the prevailing wages in the area where the firm is located.

weighted application blank: A technique used to differentiate between successful and less successful employees through the use of application blank factors.

weighted checklist: A method of appraisal in which the rater completes a form similar to the forced-choice performance reporting, but the various responses have been assigned different weights.

workers' compensation: A government program providing a degree of financial protection for employees who incur expenses resulting from job related accidents or illnesses.

yellow dog contract: A written agreement between employee and employer prohibiting a worker from joining a union or engaging in union activities. Such contracts are unenforceable under the Anti-Injunction Act of 1932 (also called the Norris-LaGuardia Act).

Index